Microprocessors
and Programmed Logic

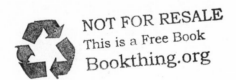

Microprocessors
and Programmed Logic

Kenneth L. Short

STATE UNIVERSITY OF NY
STONY BROOK, NY 11790

PRENTICE-HALL, INC.,   Englewood Cliffs,   NJ 07632

Library of Congress Cataloging in Publication Data

Short, Kenneth L
  Microprocessors and programmed logic.

  Bibliography: p.
  Includes index.
  1. Microprocessors. I. Title.
QA76.5.S496   001.6′4   79-23167
ISBN 0-13-581173-2

Editorial/production supervision and interior design by Steven Bobker
Cover design by Edsal Enterprises
Manufacturing buyers: Gordon Osbourne and Anthony Caruso

Printed in the United States of America

10 9 8 7 6 5 4 3

Prentice-Hall International, Inc.; *London*
Prentice-Hall of Australia Pty. Limited, *Sydney*
Prentice-Hall of Canada, Ltd., *Toronto*
Prentice-Hall of India Private Limited, *New Delhi*
Prentice-Hall of Japan, Inc., *Tokyo*
Prentice-Hall of Southeast Asia Pte. Ltd., *Singapore*
Whitehall Books Limited, *Wellington, New Zealand*

To my parents
Robert F. and Floretta H. Short
and in memory of my brother
Robert M. Short

Contents

Preface

The single most significant development in digital systems design in recent years has been the advent of the microprocessor, a central processing unit integrated on a single chip of silicon. The processing power and economics of the microprocessor have had a tremendous impact on the way digital systems are designed and on their scope of application.

This book is about the microprocessor. It is also about its related integrated circuits and the hardware and software design of microprocessor based systems. Its purpose is to first provide the reader with a thorough understanding of the basic hardware and software concepts necessary for the design of microprocessor based systems, and, further, to provide the reader with an in-depth knowledge of specific actual devices and the attendant practical considerations and design techniques necessary to effectively design systems using them.

A unique feature of this book is its utilization of a single microprocessor, the 8085A, as the example used to illustrate fundamental concepts. Use of a single microprocessor as the instructional example allows an increased depth of coverage of the operation, features, and limitations of a real device.

In addition, it allows use of a single consistent set of signals and signal names for interfacing the many logical devices which constitute a microprocessor system. Use of a single set of signal names simplifies the reader's task in understanding hardware interfacing concepts and the functional operation of various LSI devices.

The 8085A is a general purpose 8-bit microprocessor. This microprocessor was chosen because of its widespread use in industrial applications and its widespread support. This support manifests itself in the form of documentation, application notes, and software and hardware development aids for the 8085A. In addition, there exists a large family of peripheral LSI devices which are designed to be compatible with the 8085A. Because of its wide applicability, the reader will find that the knowledge gained about the 8085A and its support devices is immediately applicable to many actual designs in industry.

A further advantage of studying a single microprocessor in depth is that the reader not only learns of the features of the device but also learns that with these features come attendant limitations which must be dealt with in any practical application. It should be noted that a reader following a device specific instructional approach will find that once a specific microprocessor and its application in digital system design has been mastered, it is relatively easy to understand the operation and application of other microprocessors from a study of the manufacturers' user's manuals and application notes. This has been the experience of university and industry students who have followed this approach in the author's microprocessor courses over the past several years.

The design of microprocessor systems requires a knowledge of both hardware and software. It is assumed that the reader has a basic knowledge of digital hardware at the gate and flip-flop levels. This material can be found in any introductory book on digital systems design. The software concepts in this book are illustrated using assembly language for the 8085A. However, prior knowledge of assembly language programming is not necessary. Some general knowledge of computer programming in a high level language is desirable.

The goal has been to introduce the necessary hardware and software concepts in an elementary, systematic, and integrated fashion and to logically build upon these concepts. While the study of no single text can provide mastery in a subject area, it is believed that this text will provide the reader with a solid foundation for the development of proficiency in the design of microprocessor systems.

This book covers the topics recommended for inclusion in the course DL-3 Microprocessor Systems as part of a computer science and engineering curriculum as proposed by the Model Curriculum Subcommittee of the IEEE Computer Society.[1]

Acknowledgments

A number of people have contributed to this book being written. While I cannot thank them all, I would like to express my appreciation to Mr. Paul

---

[1] "A Curriculum in Computer Science and Engineering Committee Report." IEEE Service Center, 445 Hoes Lane, Piscataway, NJ 08854, January, 1977.

Becker, Mr. Don Buchout, Dr. Velio Marsocci, Mr. Casey Powell, Mr. Rich Reeder, and Dr. David Smith.

I would also like to thank the many students who, in using rough drafts of this text as class notes, have provided comments and suggestions which have led to the improvement of the text.

A very special thanks to Lee Cushman whose editing, organizational, and typing skills were critical to the writing of this book.

Kenneth L. Short

1

Introduction

A technological advance which is affecting the practice of logic design is the existence of the LSI microprocessor; a data flow and control on one to several LSI chips. In this case the logic designer's building blocks are data flows, control stores, and read/write memory chips. He arranges the chips and programs the control store.

Glen G. Langdon, Jr.*

*Logic Design: A Review of Theory and Practice. New York: Academic Press, Inc., 1974.

1.1 THE IMPACT OF LSI ON LOGIC DESIGN

The basic goal of logic design is a system that functions as required and is reliable, easy to maintain, and cost effective. As a rule, simplicity of design is the key to the attainment of this goal. Whereas an overly complex design might meet the first requirement, it undoubtedly would fall short in the other areas.

In practical design, of course, cost effectiveness is of great importance. Generally speaking, the most cost effective design is usually the simplest and, because of its simplicity, more reliable and easier to maintain.

The total cost of a design at the system level includes expenditures for development, components, tooling, assembly, testing, system repair and maintenance, as well as a spare parts inventory. [1,2] This total cost is directly proportional to the number of components in a system, and the number of components has, in the past, been directly proportional to the number of gates and flip-flops. Conventional switching theoretic techniques of digital systems design are geared toward minimizing the number of gates and flip-flops, thereby minimizing the number of components in order to minimize system cost. See Figs. 1.1-1(a) and 1.1-1(b). These minimization techniques were developed originally for systems which used relays to implement gates and flip-flops. As technology advanced, vacuum tubes, then discrete component solid state devices replaced relays. Since the number of components was still proportional to the number of gates and flip-flops, even in designs constructed from vacuum tubes or discrete component solid state devices, the switching theoretic design techniques were still effective in minimizing system cost.

However, in the early 1960's, *Small Scale Integration, SSI*, provided small scale integrated circuits with as many as 12 gates integrated on a single silicon chip and packaged as a single multilead component. With integrated circuits, ICs, the number of components in a system was no longer proportional to the number of gates and flip-flops but was simply equivalent to the number of IC packages in the system. Thus, the reduction of system cost was dependent on the reduction of the total number of IC packages required. Although system designers could still apply the same switching theoretic techniques, simplification of a circuit which reduced the required number of gates or flip-flops resulted in a savings only if it also reduced the number of IC packages.

As IC technology advanced further, *Medium Scale Integration, MSI,* provided circuits with a logic complexity of 13 to 99 equivalent gates per package, and *Large Scale Integration, LSI*, provided circuits with a logic complexity of 100 or more equivalent gates per package, seriously compromising the effectiveness of conventional switching theoretic design techniques in reducing system cost. Fabrication techniques for MSI and LSI circuits, which make it as inexpensive to put 100 or more gates on a chip as 10 destroyed the gate-flip-flop/component-count relationship, and now, for systems implemented with

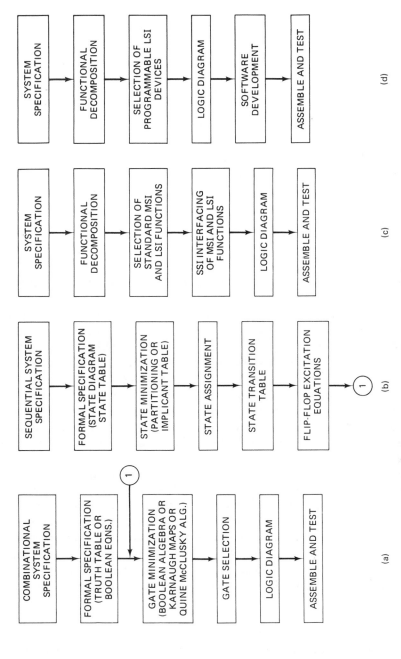

Figure 1.1-1. Steps in digital system design: (a) combinational and (b) sequential design using gates and flip-flops (c) design using standard MSI and LSI circuits (d) design using programmable LSI circuits.

3

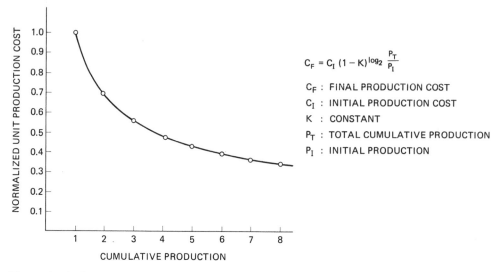

$$C_F = C_I (1 - K)^{\log_2 \frac{P_T}{P_I}}$$

C_F : FINAL PRODUCTION COST

C_I : INITIAL PRODUCTION COST

K : CONSTANT

P_T : TOTAL CUMULATIVE PRODUCTION

P_I : INITIAL PRODUCTION

Figure 1.1-2. Semiconductor learning curve.

integrated circuits, total cost is directly proportional to the number of IC packages.[1]

Maximum utilization of LSI results in decreased system costs because LSI circuits provide more logic per package and require less power consumption. And reducing the number of lead connections by replacing many SSI and MSI packages with fewer LSI packages provides greater reliability, since a common source of failure for an IC is at a lead connection to the chip.

The economics of IC manufacture demand that entire functions requiring large numbers of gates be fabricated on a single chip. [3] The complexity of the functions is limited primarily by the chip area required for their fabrication. This area must not exceed that compatible with a high manufacturing yield. *Yield* is the percentage of acceptable ICs resulting from the manufacturing process. To limit the chip area, the number of external connections to the chip, which provide input and output data and control signals, must also be limited.

When medium and large scale integrated functions are produced in large quantities, the production cost can be amortized so that the price of these functions is far less than that of the equivalent functions implemented with SSI circuits. Utilization of standard MSI and LSI functions, although they might include gates which are unused in a particular application, is usually more economical than designing minimized logic implemented at the gate level. See Fig. 1.1-1(c).

---

[1]Exceptions to this relationship occur in LSI systems which use microprocessors. In some applications, software development costs may have a greater impact on total system cost than the hardware component count.

Production quantity is, therefore, a major consideration in the implementation of LSI devices because it affects their production cost. The empirical relationship between quantity and cost is plotted in the learning curve (see Fig. 1.1-2)[2]. The *learning curve* relationship states that *each time the cumulative production doubles, the unit production cost decreases by a constant percentage.* The concept is based on the principle that as a manufacturer becomes more familiar with a device through actual production experience, manufacturing skills improve; i.e., as production efficiency increases, production cost decreases. Eventually a point is reached beyond which additional manufacturing experience produces only a minimal reduction in production cost. The constant for integrated circuits, including LSI, is approximately 30 percent. [4] The learning curve is important to system designers because for standard ICs the selling price follows a similar curve.

1.2 APPROACHES TO THE UTILIZATION OF LSI

Because of the availability of complex functions in IC form and the lack of formal synthesis methods applicable to designs using LSI and MSI circuits, system design has largely replaced logic design. The lack of formal synthesis methods is accounted for by the fact that the LSI structures implemented are not typically amenable to mathematical description. [5] Thus, design procedures when using MSI and LSI circuits are largely heuristic in nature, requiring specification of the logical interconnection of subsystems rather than gates and flip-flops.

1.2.1 Custom LSI

One approach to the utilization of LSI is the manufacture of one or more custom circuits to provide the functions required in a particular system. The use of custom LSI circuits, however, entails increased development costs which must be amortized over the number of devices required. For systems which are not manufactured in very large quantities, the development cost for the design of custom LSI circuits is usually prohibitive. On the other hand, for systems which are produced in large quantities, this approach is often viable. Because of the lack of competition, the decrease in production cost due to large quantity production, predicted by the learning curve, is not typically passed along as a reduction in selling price to the system designer by the manufacturer custom LSI.

A major problem inherent in custom LSI is the cost of modifying a design. For example, changes may require that the entire LSI circuit design process be repeated for the modified system. Another problem is that the expertise and special facilities needed for the design and manufacture of custom LSI circuits generally require that the actual design and manufacture be contracted to a semiconductor manufacturer; this can lead to a considerable increase in development time. And finally, it is usually difficult, if not impossible, to obtain second sources for custom LSI circuits. A *second source* is a different manufacturer for the same device.

1.2.2 Catalog LSI

An approach to the utilization of LSI that obviates the problems of custom LSI employs the selection and interconnection of *off-the-shelf* or *catalog* LSI subsystems. (The interconnection of catalog LSI circuits may, in addition, require SSI and MSI circuits.) The use of catalog LSI circuits in design is analogous to the use of MSI circuits capable of providing medium complexity functions. MSI functions such as adders, comparators, counters, shift registers, and code converters are used as subsystems and interconnected in a heuristic manner.

With catalog devices, competition and second sourcing cause IC manufacturers to pass along to the designer the cost reductions associated with the learning curve. But to provide low cost devices, the IC manufacturer must have a large production base, which requires wide acceptance by system designers of the function the IC manufacturer has chosen to produce. IC manufacturers had little difficulty in deciding what functions to implement as SSI and MSI ICs because of the demand apparent from existing systems designed with gates and flip-flops. On the other hand, the selection of appropriate complex functions for integration as catalog LSI devices is more difficult. Since the development costs are greater for LSI than for SSI or MSI, the risk the LSI manufacturer takes is much greater. The need for certain complex functions, however, is clear, and LSI subsystems such as the *Universal Asynchronous Receiver Transmitter, UAR/T,* have become de facto industry standards. [6]

A brief examination of the UAR/T provides an idea of the degree of logic complexity available even in a low complexity LSI subsystem. The UAR/T, a digital communications subsystem, is capable of receiving serial data and providing a parallel output and/or of receiving parallel data and providing a serial output. Furthermore, this operation is *full duplex*; that is, both the receiving and transmitting can occur simultaneously. The *character* sent or received serially contains a start bit, five to eight data bits, one or two stop bits, and either an odd, even, or no parity bit. To provide versatility, the bit rate, the number of data bits, the parity mode, and the number of stop bits are externally selectable. The entire UAR/T is integrated on a single monolithic chip housed in a 40-pin *Dual In-Line Package, DIP.* UAR/Ts are widely used in interfacing peripheral devices, such as Teletypes® to digital systems, and their status as catalog LSI is reflected in their being second sourced by several manufacturers.

1.2.3 Programmable LSI

LSI subsystems that the designer, not the semiconductor manufacturer, can tailor to suit a variety of applications are advantageous because the greater the

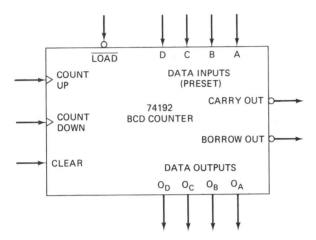

Figure 1.2-1. 74192 BCD counter.

degree of flexibility, the wider the usage the device will find. Such flexibility is achievable through hardware programming.

The concept of *hardware programming* of an IC is nothing new. Although not thought of as such, many MSI circuits are routinely programmed in their normal usage; for example, a presettable counter such as the 74192 has control inputs for presetting (programming) the initial count and for controlling the count direction—up or down (see Fig. 1.2-1). For a particular application, the values of these inputs can be programmed using the output of a bank of switches or a latch, thus dynamically modifying the counter's function.

UAR/Ts are also programmable. Here, programming inputs set parameters which determine the number of bits in a word; even, odd, or no parity; and the number of stop bits.

The term *programmable LSI*, however, is usually reserved for LSI devices which have a much greater degree of programmability. The function of these LSI devices—Read Only Memories (ROMs), Programmable Logic Arrays (PLAs), and Microprocessors (μPs)—is totally defined by programming. See Fig. 1.1-1(d).

1.2.3.1 Read Only Memories

One of the early successful applications of LSI was the implementation of semiconductor memories. The regular structure of the logic required in memories facilitates the achievement of high circuit density and yield. Semiconductor memories configured to have wide application have become high-production catalog devices; two are common: *Read/Write Memory* or *R/W Memory*, *RWM*, and *Read Only Memory, ROM*.

ROMs are LSI components with a high degree of programmability and are useful in the design of combinational and sequential digital systems. The contents of a ROM may be specified at the time of manufacture or may be

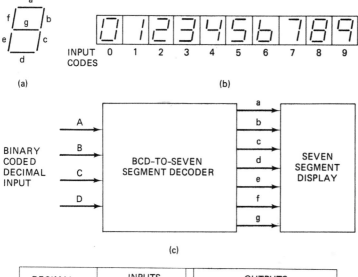

(a)

(b)

(c)

Figure 1.2-2. BCD-to-seven segment decoder: (a) Segment identification; (b) seven segment representation of the decimal digits; (c) combinational decoder; and (d) decoder truth table.

DECIMAL DISPLAYED	INPUTS				OUTPUTS						
	A	B	C	D	a	b	c	d	e	f	g
0	0	0	0	0	1	1	1	1	1	1	0
1	0	0	0	1	0	1	1	0	0	0	0
2	0	0	1	0	1	1	0	1	1	0	1
3	0	0	1	1	1	1	1	1	0	0	1
4	0	1	0	0	0	1	1	0	0	1	1
5	0	1	0	1	1	0	1	1	0	1	1
6	0	1	1	0	0	0	1	1	1	1	1
7	0	1	1	1	1	1	1	0	0	0	0
8	1	0	0	0	1	1	1	1	1	1	1
9	1	0	0	1	1	1	1	0	0	1	1

(d)

programmed by the user. A ROM which can be programmed by the user is called a ***Programmable Read Only Memory, PROM***. To permit modification of the contents of the memory, PROMs are also available which can be erased and reprogrammed after removal from the system; they are referred to as ***Erasable Programmable Read Only Memories, EPROMs***.

The following example indicates the way in which a ROM is used to implement a combinational design and compares it with other implementation methods. The truth table required for the implementation of a BCD-to-seven segment decoder is shown in Fig. 1.2-2(d). The BCD-to-seven segment decoder takes a 4-bit binary code, representing a decimal digit, as its input and generates a 7-bit code which can control a seven segment display to provide a visual representation of the decimal digit. If the circuit is implemented using gates, ***Karnaugh maps*** for each of the seven outputs can be drawn. If the input conditions 1010 to 1111 are considered **don't cares**, the following simplified **sum-of-products** equations for the segments result:

$$a = A + \bar{B} \cdot \bar{D} + B \cdot D + \bar{B} \cdot C$$
$$b = \bar{B} + C \cdot D + \bar{C} \cdot \bar{D}$$
$$c = B + \bar{C} + D$$
$$d = \bar{B} \cdot \bar{D} + \bar{B} \cdot C + C \cdot \bar{D} + B \cdot \bar{C} \cdot D$$
$$e = \bar{B} \cdot \bar{D} + C \cdot \bar{D}$$
$$f = A + B \cdot \bar{C} + \bar{C} \cdot \bar{D} + B \cdot \bar{D}$$
$$g = A + B \cdot \bar{C} + B \cdot \bar{D} + \bar{B} \cdot C$$

If only the **normal form** of the input variables A, B, C, and D is available, the circuit can be implemented with three inverters, nine AND gates, and seven OR gates. Using standard SSI integrated circuits, this would require six 14-pin packages.

This function, BCD-to-seven segment decoding, is so common that it has been integrated as a 16-pin MSI circuit, e.g., the 7448. This circuit contains additional features such as a lamp test input (LT), which makes all outputs logic 1 when LT = 0, and a ripple blanking input (RBI), which makes all outputs logic 0 when inputs $A = B = C = D = 1$ and when LT $= \overline{RBI} = 1$.

If the BCD-to-seven segment decoder were implemented with a ROM, the input variables A, B, C, and D would be assigned to the address inputs of the ROM, A_3, A_2, A_1, A_0, and the contents of each of the first 10 ROM addresses would be programmed as indicated by the truth table (see Fig. 1.2-3). The ROM would consist of words of at least 7 bits, and the number of words required would be 2^n, where n was the number of input variables. In the case of the seven segment decoder, $n = 4$, and 16 words of memory are required. The total number of bits of memory required when directly implementing a combinational circuit with a ROM is $2^n * m$, where m is the number of output variables. The seven segment decoder would require 112 bits. If the lamp test capability were included, another input, LT, would be required; thus n would increase to five, and the number of words required would double to 32 for a total of 224 bits. Addition of a ripple blanking input would again double the number of words and correspondingly the number of bits required. This illustrates one of the major drawbacks in using a ROM for directly implementing combinational circuitry: The size of the ROM doubles with each additional input.

In fact, the BCD-to-seven segment decoder is too small a function to be implemented economically using a ROM. However, as an example it illustrates several points: Implementation of a combinational circuit with a ROM does not require the application of logic minimization techniques, simply the definition of functions with a truth table; the size of a ROM doubles with each additional input; and cognizance of what is available in catalog MSI and LSI is important before any design is started.

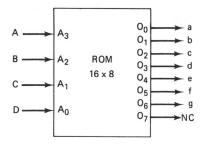

Figure 1.2-3. ROM implementation of BCD-to-seven segment decoder.

An example of a clocked sequential circuit, a 2-bit, binary, up-down counter implemented with a ROM and a data latch is shown in Fig. 1.2-4. The inputs to the ROM are the external control input and the present state. The ROM provides the external outputs and next-state inputs. Using D-type flip-flops and a ROM, sequential circuit design requires only the generation of the state transition table. Since the state assignment in a ROM implementation of a

STATE TRANSITION TABLE

PRESENT STATE		CONTROL INPUT	NEXT STATE		FLIP-FLOP INPUTS	
A	B	U	A	B	D_A	D_B
0	0	0	0	1	0	1
0	1	0	1	0	1	0
1	0	0	1	1	1	1
1	1	0	0	0	0	0
0	0	1	1	1	1	1
0	1	1	0	0	0	0
1	0	1	0	1	0	1
1	1	1	1	0	1	0

ROM

ADDRESS			CONTENTS	
A_2	A_1	A_0	Y_1	Y_0
0	0	0	0	1
0	0	1	1	0
0	1	0	1	1
0	1	1	0	0
1	0	0	1	1
1	0	1	0	0
1	1	0	0	1
1	1	1	1	0

Figure 1.2-4. ROM implementation of a 2-bit up-down counter.

sequential circuit has little or no effect on design complexity, it can be made arbitrarily.

1.2.3.2 Programmable Logic Arrays

LSI *Programmable Logic Arrays, PLAs*, also can be used for the implementation of combinational logic. These devices contain a two-level, AND-OR circuit on a single chip (see Fig. 1.2-5). The number of AND gates and OR gates and their inputs is fixed for a given PLA. For example, the National DM7575 has 14 inputs, 96 product terms, and eight outputs. The AND gates provide the product terms, and the OR gates logically sum these product terms to generate a sum-of-products expression. Some inputs to the AND gates are connected to a logic 1, making the corresponding inputs don't cares. An AND gate so connected provides a logic 1 output for more than one input combination. This *nonexhaustive decoding* allows a PLA to implement more complex functions than a comparably sized ROM.

The programming of a PLA consists of specifying, for each output, all the product terms to be logically summed. Formal minimization techniques are useful in reducing the number of product terms. [7] The configuration of a PLA occurs during the manufacturing process. *Field Programmable Logic Arrays,*

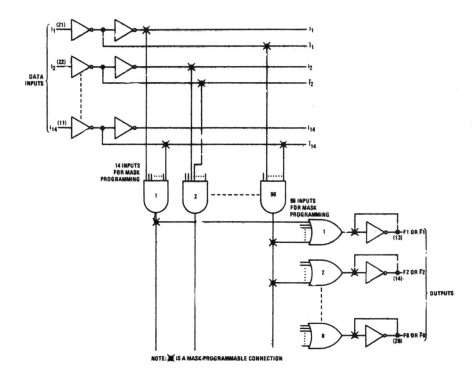

Figure 1.2-5. Logic diagram representation of a PLA (Courtesy of National Semiconductor Corp.).

FPLAs, on the other hand, are PLAs which can be programmed by the system designer using special programming equipment.

Implementation of a BCD-to-seven segment decoder driver requires a PLA with four inputs, nine product terms, and seven outputs. The extra inputs, product terms, and outputs in a catalog PLA can be used to implement other functions required in the system.

1.2.3.3 Microprocessors

As greater flexibility (programmability) is sought in an LSI circuit, the need for a *universal logic element* is encountered. Were it economically and physically feasible to consider a general purpose computer as a component for use in logic design, the goal of a universal logic element would be attained. A general purpose computer contains the following functional subsystems:

1. *Central Processor Unit, CPU*, containing arithmetic and logic unit and registers.
2. Control unit.
3. Memory.
4. Input-output, I/O.
5. Clock.

LSI technology has made available LSI devices which, when interconnected as a system, provide on a smaller scale and at a reasonable cost, the capabilities of a general purpose computer. Such systems are called *microcomputers* (μC, MC) and have as a key system component an LSI device called a *microprocessor* (μP, MP). A microprocessor performs the function of the central processor unit and the control unit. Therefore, the microprocessor, in combination with memory, I/O, and a clock, is essentially a microcomputer (see Fig. 1.2-6).

The first commercially available microprocessor was a PMOS (P-Channel Metal Oxide Semiconductor) device manufactured in 1971 by the Intel Corporation: the 4004. [8] This single chip, 117×159 mil, 4-bit microprocessor is

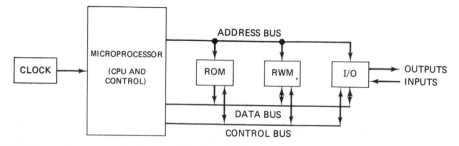

Figure 1.2-6. Block diagram of a microcomputer.

housed in a 16-pin DIP and contains approximately 2,250 transistors. Integrated on the silicon microprocessor chip are read/write memory structures for temporary data storage, PLA structures for decoding and control, and random logic structures.

1.3 MICROPROCESSOR SYSTEMS

A *microprocessor based digital system* or *microprocessor system* has a microprocessor as its key system component. Depending upon the architecture of the particular microprocessor, its functions—those of the CPU and the control—may be contained on a single IC chip, as in a single chip microprocessor, or distributed across several chips. One method of distribution results in a multichip microprocessor—one chip containing the control section and several identical chips containing 2-bit or 4-bit "slices" of the arithmetic and logic unit and registers. The slices are connected in parallel, allowing the construction of microprocessors of different word lengths. Another approach, which in fact results in a single-chip microcomputer rather than a microprocessor, places the μP, ROM, RWM, and I/O on one chip.

Under *program* control, a microprocessor performs arithmetic and logic operations and generates control signals for the memory and I/O. The instructions which constitute the program are stored in memory. When the system is operated, instructions are read from memory and executed by the microprocessor. Thus, a microprocessor is a *hardware* structure driven by a *software* program.

Since a microprocessor is controlled by a program, its operation is sequential in nature, regardless of the functions implemented. In most applications this sequential nature of operation is no problem; however, in some high speed, *real-time* applications, instruction execution time results in a system which is too slow to meet critical time constraints.

A microprocessor program consists of a sequence of binary words stored in memory. The number of words in a program is contingent upon the particular application, the system structure, and the ability of the designer to efficiently program the system. A program can be written directly in *machine language*—the form in which it is stored in memory—that is, as patterns of 1s and 0s. While this method of programming may be adequate for very small programs, it becomes very time consuming and error prone as the program size and complexity increase.

Program writing and interpretation is simplified by an *assembly language* which uses mnemonics such as ADD, SUB, or JMP instead of machine language instructions. However, since the microprocessor can only execute the bit patterns of machine language instructions, the assembly language program must ultimately be converted to machine code. This conversion can be carried out by hand, but this procedure, also, is error prone, time consuming, and generally impractical. Special programs are available for each type of microprocessor, which convert their assembly language programs to the equivalent machine code. These programs are called *assemblers* and are run either on the microcomputer itself (*resident* or *self-assemblers*) or on a minicomputer or main frame computer (*cross assemblers*).

A number of microprocessors have available programs called *compilers*, which allow the systems designer to write a program in a *high level language* such as FORTRAN, BASIC, PASCAL, or PL/M (similar to PL1). The compiler, using the high level language program as data, then generates machine language code for the microprocessor. Compilers require a considerable amount of memory for execution, and are frequently written to run on a large computer, not a microcomputer. Typically they generate machine code that is less efficient than code generated from an assembly language program by an assembler, efficiency here being measured in terms of the number of machine language instructions required to perform a particular task. Less efficient programs require more memory and longer execution times.

Without an actual comparison of the machine code resulting from each approach, it is impossible to determine the relative efficiency of programs written in assembly language as opposed to a high level language. High level language programs have been known to generate code anywhere from 10 to 200 percent less efficient than assembly level language programs. In applications where program size or speed of execution is critical, assembly language programming has the advantage of a one-to-one correspondence between each assembly language instruction and each machine language instruction, whereas a single high level language instruction, when compiled, may produce several machine language instructions. Thus, assembly language allows the programmer a greater degree of control over microprocessor operations.

When a microprocessor system is used in a dedicated application, the *control* or *application program* is fixed and stored in ROM. Because changes in the control program are only necessary when the functions implemented by the system are to be altered, the control program in ROM is referred to as *firmware* rather than software. Computations and logical operations performed by the microprocessor under program control produce intermediate results which are stored in registers internal to the microprocessor or in RWM external to the microprocessor. The arithmetic and logical capabilities of a microprocessor allow alternative portions of the control program to be executed based on the results of previous computations or on data from external devices which has been input through I/O circuitry.

The BCD-to-seven segment decoding function introduced in Section 1.2.3.1 can be implemented by a microprocessor system. A microprocessor implements this combinational function in a sequential manner by inputting the BCD digit and using it as an index to a table of values stored in memory. This table specifies those segments of the seven segment display which should be ON and those which should be OFF for each BCD digit. The microprocessor outputs the appropriate value from the table to a latch—the outputs of which drive the

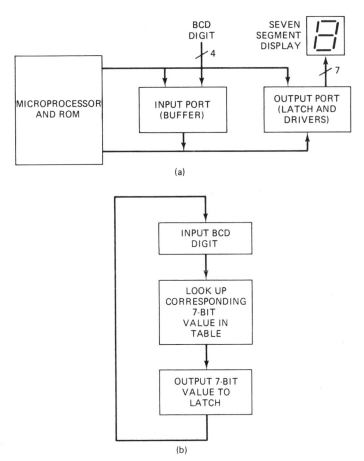

0000	210F00	START:	LXI H, TABLE	;	SET POINTER TO BEGINNING OF TABLE
0003	DB00		IN 0	;	INPUT BCD DIGIT
0005	5F		MOV E, A	;	USE BCD DIGIT AS OFFSET INTO TABLE
0006	1600		MVI D, OOH		
0008	19		DAD D	;	ADD OFFSET TO BEGINNING ADDRESS OF TABLE
0009	7E		MOV A, M	;	TRANSFER 7-SEGMENT CODE FROM TABLE TO A
000A	D300		OUT 0	;	OUTPUT 7-SEGMENT CODE
000C	C30000		JMP START	;	JUMP BACK TO START OF PROGRAM
000F	7E306D79	TABLE:	DB 7EH, 30H, 6DH, 79H, 33H, 58H, 1FH, 70H, 7FH, 73H
0013	335B1F70		
0017	7F73		END	(c)

Figure 1.3-1. Microprocessor implementation of seven segment display: (a) system block diagram (b) program flowchart (c) assembly language program.

various segments in the display. The structure of the microprocessor system, the system operation *flowchart,* the assembly language program, and the machine language code for implementing a seven segment display are shown in Fig. 1.3-1. This method of implementing a BCD-to-seven segment decoder is obviously not economically justifiable on its own. However, if this were only one of a large number of functions that the microprocessor system implemented, such as keyboard scanning, arithmetic operations, receipt printing, etc., then the resulting system, for example, a point-of-sale terminal, could be easily justified economically.

1.4 AREAS OF APPLICATION

The major areas of microprocessor application are in:

1. The replacement of random logic.
2. The replacement of custom LSI.
3. The replacement of minicomputers.
4. New applications not economically feasible with previous technology.

Table 1.4-1 lists a few specific areas of application where microprocessors have been utilized. Within these areas, the majority of microprocessor applications have been in the replacement of random logic. [9] ***Random logic*** systems are implemented with gates and flip-flops interconnected in a manner such that the resulting structure is not regular or repetitive. Randomness here obviously refers to system structure as typified by a logic diagram and not to the methods used to determine the logical interconnections!

For those systems where microprocessors are suitable for the replacement of random logic, certain advantages exist in their utilization: Substantial hardware design effort is replaced by programming effort, with an increase in system capability and versatility, and logic gates are replaced by memory. Development time is reduced through a programmed approach, and the ability to make

TABLE 1.4-1

Microprocessor Applications

Analytical scientific instruments	Computer aided instruction
Smart terminals	On line control of laboratory instrumentation
Stacker crane controls	Desk top computers
Conveyor controls	Check processors
Word processors	Payroll systems
Point of sale systems	Inventory control
Stand alone electronic cash registers	Automatic typesetting
Electronic games	Compact business machines
Vending and dispensing machines	Medical instrumentation
Market scales	Automobile diagnostics
Traffic light controls	Data communication processing
Home heating and lighting controls	Optical character recognition
Security and fire alarm systems	I/O terminals for computers
Home appliances	

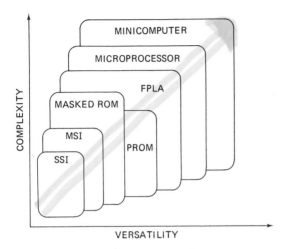

Figure 1.4-1. Applicability of various approaches to logic design as a function of system complexity and versatility. (Copyright © 1976 by the Institute of Electrical and Electronics Engineers, Inc. Reprinted by permission, from IEEE SPRECTRUM, Vol. 13, no. 1, January 1976, pp. 50–56.)

changes in the control program greatly enhances the ease with which a design can be modified. For extremely small random logic systems, microprocessors are not an appropriate replacement. A microprocessor system always requires a certain minimum amount of hardware (microprocessor, memory, and I/O circuitry), and thus there is a minimum cost associated with its use independent of the simplicity of the function implemented. With random logic, for all practical purposes, no such base cost exists; i.e., a random logic circuit can consist of as little as a single, small scale integrated circuit. On the other hand, for relatively small digital systems, an implementation structured around ROMs or PLAs can be the most cost effective. Figure 1.4-1 shows how various approaches to system implementation compare in terms of versatility and complexity.

How large should a random logic system be before considering its replacement with a microprocessor? Designers have postulated various rules of thumb in terms of the number of IC packages in the random logic system. Thresholds of 30 to 40 SSI or MSI packages have been proposed. Such guides are, however, very rough estimates and probably inappropriate. As the costs of microprocessors and associated memory circuits decrease, this threshold decreases. And the availability of microcomputers which contain ROM, RWM, and I/O on a single chip—providing a complete system on a single chip—are producing a significant lowering of the aforementioned thresholds.

Very high-speed random logic systems are another category where microprocessors may be an inappropriate replacement. Although progress in LSI technology has provided microprocessors with faster instruction-execution times, the sequential operation of a microprocessor system is a fundamental speed limitation. Assuming that the same technology is used, for instance, T^2L, a random logic system can be designed which will operate faster than a microprocessor based system. A random logic system can be designed to operate in parallel, whereas a microcomputer must execute its program sequentially. Given the same clock rate, a random logic system can do more in a single clock period. For example, a microprocessor can change at most a number of bits equal to its word length. A random logic circuit, on the other hand, can change all its memory elements during a single clock pulse.

Custom LSI can be replaced by a microprocessor programmed to implement the same functions. This not only alleviates the relatively long development time associated with custom LSI but also, if a second sourced microprocessor is employed, minimizes the problem of availability.

Microprocessors often are used to replace minicomputers that are under utilized. However, as more powerful microcomputers are developed, those using 12- and 16-bit microprocessors, their performance capabilities approach and often exceed those of the less powerful minicomputers. Soon microcomputers will replace less powerful minicomputers—even in applications where the minicomputer is fully utilized.

The differentiation, however, between minicomputers and microcomputers has become less clear as more powerful microprocessors have been developed. The former criteria for delineation—word length, speed, architecture, instruction set, and cost—can no longer be rigidly applied. For instance, there are microprocessors which are designed to execute the instruction sets of minicomputers and microprocessors with architectural advances and features which supersede those of some minicomputers. Microprocessors fabricated with Schottky T^2L, I^2L, and even ECL have fast execution times. Several minicomputers have been designed which contain either catalog or custom microprocessors yet are called minicomputers. The only suitable distinction between minicomputers and microcomputers is the degree of LSI utilization, the distribution of logic on these circuits, and the resulting smaller cost and size.

Many new products and products with significantly extended capabilities are available because of the small size, low power consumption, and low cost of microprocessors (see Table 1.4-1). Products with extended capabilities are typified by intelligent instrumentation: instrumentation which carries out a significant amount of arithmetic and/or logical processing. Microprocessor based intelligent instrumentation is available which displays computed functions of various measured signals, formats data for the instrument's input/output interface, conducts self-diagnosis, linearizes inputs from nonlinear transducers, and controls the overall system operation. A generalized intelligent instrument is shown in the block diagram of Fig. 1.4-2. New products employing microprocessors include a significant number of applications where digital processing is used for tasks previously handled by nonelectronic means. And applications previously implemented with analog electronic circuits are susceptible to digital implementation as the cost of microprocessors, RWM, ROM, and integrated analog-to-digital and digital-to-analog converters rapidly decreases.

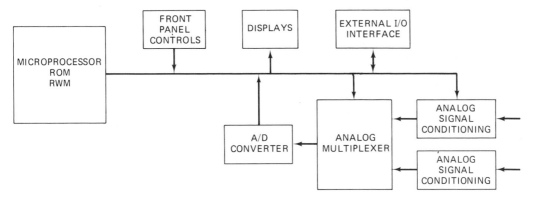

Figure 1.4-2. Generalized microprocessor based instrument.

1.5 DESIGNING MICROPROCESSOR SYSTEMS

The effective design of a microprocessor system requires expertise in three areas: hardware design, software design, and system synthesis. The purpose of this text is to present the fundamental concepts required to develop expertise in these areas. [10, 11]

It is the nature of microprocessor systems that knowledge in any one of these areas cannot be pursued in isolation of the others. Thus, each of the following chapters involves varying amounts of hardware design, software design, and system synthesis. Early chapters deal primarily with one area, while later chapters essentially are balanced among two or all three.

Before attempting the hardware design of a microprocessor system, the designer must be familiar with the hardware available for use as system components. Hardware components used in the design of microprocessor based systems range from gates and flip-flops to programmable LSI devices to completely packaged subsystems such as floppy disks. Familiarity with these components includes a knowledge and understanding of their function, logical organization, operation, performance characteristics, and limitations.

Depending on the level at which the design is begun, the designer may be determining the interconnection of individual ICs or the interconnection of premanufactured subsystems. In any event, to be really effective, the designer's knowledge of hardware must extend down to the level of individual ICs.

It is assumed that the reader has a basic knowledge of digital system design using gates and flip-flops. In Chapter 2 the organization and operation of integrated circuit memory devices, including flip-flops, latches, and various types of random access memories are discussed, as is the use of random access memory devices to form a memory system.

In Chapter 3 microprocessor organization and operation are presented using Intel's 8085A microprocessor as an instructional example. The 8085A is a general purpose 8-bit microprocessor which is an enhancement of the popular 8080A. Once a thorough understanding of the operation and application of a specific microprocessor is developed, it is relatively easy to understand other microprocessors from a study of their manufacturer's data sheets and application notes. Interconnection of a microprocessor to memory and simple I/O structures is also covered in this chapter.

To accomplish software design at the assembly language level, the designer must first have a knowledge of the microprocessor's instruction set and the function of each instruction. The designer must also know how to combine instructions to form a program which carries out a desired function using a particular hardware configuration. Once the program is written, procedures for translating it into machine language for loading into memory and techniques for testing and correcting any errors in the program must be understood.

The instruction set of the 8085A is introduced in Chapter 4. In particular, the instructions which implement data transfer, logical operations, and branching are presented in detail. These instructions are used in simple sequences and programs. The process of translating an assembly language program to machine code and subsequently testing that program is presented in Chapter 5.

A special memory structure common to microprocessors is the **stack**. The operation of the stack and the instructions which control it are introduced in Chapter 6. Among its other uses, the stack provides the hardware mechanism to support subroutines. Subroutines and their associated instructions are covered, which leads to a discussion of the use of subroutines in modular program development and some initial considerations of software design.

Carrying out arithmetic functions in a microprocessor based system is considered in detail in Chapter 7. Software approaches, which implement arithmetic computations in the microprocessor itself using its arithmetic instructions are considered. Binary, two's complement, decimal, and floating point arithmetic are covered.

The next two chapters deal with various methods of implementing data transfers between a microprocessor and its memory and between a microprocessor and the system's input and output devices. In Chapter 8, the hardware and software to implement I/O transfers which are initiated and completely controlled by the application program are discussed. Both serial and parallel I/O are covered, as is the use of special programmable peripheral LSI devices for implementing I/O interfaces. The important concept of hardware/software tradeoff in microprocessor systems as it relates to I/O is illustrated here. In the remainder of the text, hardware/software tradeoffs are considered as they relate to different aspects of system design.

In Chapter 9 interrupt and DMA techniques for carrying out I/O are considered. These techniques require additional hardware but have the advantage of providing higher I/O data rates and in some cases allowing the microprocessor to carry out other functions concurrently with the I/O transfers.

Because of the diversity of applications for microprocessor systems, they are commonly interfaced to peripheral devices covering a wide range from integrated circuits to complex electromechanical subsystems. These devices are essentially analog or digital in nature. Common digital peripherals and methods for interfacing them to a microprocessor are discussed in Chapter 10. Interfacing analog devices to microprocessors is extensively covered in Chapter 11.

The previous chapters having presented the basic concepts of hardware and software design and the integration of hardware and software to implement the synthesis of common subsystems, Chapter 12 ties these concepts together and presents techniques for designing complete systems. The basic steps in the design of a microprocessor based system are shown in Fig. 1.5-1.

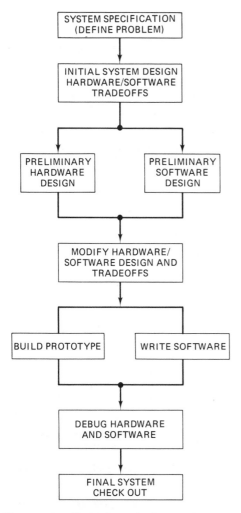

Figure 1.5-1. Steps in designing a microprocessor based system.

REFERENCES

1. BLAKESLEE, T.R., *Digital Design With Standard MSI and LSI*. New York: John Wiley & Sons, Inc., 1975.

2. CARR, W.N., and J.P. MIZE, *MOS/LSI Design and Application*. New York: McGraw-Hill Book Company, 1972.

3. OLDHAM, W.G., "The Fabrication of Microelectronic Circuits," *Scientific American*, Vol. 237, No. 3, September 1977, pp. 111–128.

4. NOYCE, R.N., "Microelectronics," *Scientific American*, Vol. 237, No. 3, September 1977, pp. 63–69.

5. LEWIN, D., "Outstanding Problems in Logic Design," *The Radio and Electronic Engineer*, Vol. 44, No. 1, January 1974, pp. 9–17.

6. *UAR/T Universal Asynchronous Receiver/Transmitter* (AY-5-1013 Data Sheet). Hicksville, New York: General Instruments Corporation, 1974.

7. AREVALO, Z., and J.G. BREDESON, "A Method to Simplify a Boolean Function into a Near Minimal Sum-of-Products for Programmable Logic Arrays," *IEEE Transactions on Computers*, Vol. C-27, No. 11, November 1978, pp. 1028–1039.

8. FAGGIN, F., and M.E. HOFF, JR., "Standard Parts and Custom Design Merge in Four-Chip Processor Kit," *Electronics*, Vol. 45, No. 9, April 1972, pp. 112–116.

9. LEWIS, D.R., and W.R. SIENA, "Microprocessor or Random Logic?" *Electronic Design*, Vol. 21, No. 18, September 1973, pp. 106–110.

10. CUSHMAN, R.H., "Microprocessors are Changing Your Future. Are You Prepared?" *EDN*, Vol. 18, No. 21, November 1975, pp. 26–32.

11. GLADSTONE, B., "Designing with Microprocessors Instead of Wired Logic Asks More of Designers," *Electronics*, Vol. 46, No. 21, October 1973, pp. 91–104.

BIBLIOGRAPHY

ALTMAN, L. (Ed.). *Microprocessors*, Electronics Book Series. New York: McGraw-Hill Book Company, 1975.

"Collection of Articles on Microelectronics," *Scientific American*, Vol. 237, No. 3, September 1977.

"EDN Microprocessor Design Series II," (Collection of Articles), *EDN*. Boston, Massachusetts: Cahners Publishing Company, 1975.

HILBURN, J.L., and P.M. JULICH, *Microcomputers/Microprocessors: Hardware, Software, and Applications*. Englewood Cliffs, New Jersey: Prentice-Hall, Inc., 1976.

KLINGMAN, E.E., *Microprocessor Systems Design*. Englewood Cliffs, New Jersey: Prentice-Hall, Inc., 1977.

LANGDON, G.G., JR., *Logic Design: A Review of Theory and Practice*. New York: Academic Press, Inc., 1974.

LEVENTHAL, L.A., *Introduction to Microprocessors: Software, Hardware, Programming*. Englewood Cliffs, New Jersey: Prentice-Hall, Inc., 1978.

McGlynn, D.R., *Microprocessors: Technology, Architecture and Applications*. New York: Wiley-Interscience, 1976.

Meisel, W.S., "New Components for Digital Design: Fad or Revolution?" in W.C. Liles, W.S. Meisel, and M.D. Teener (Eds.), *New Components and Subsystems for Digital Design: A Report*. Santa Monica, California: Technology Service Corporation, 1975, pp. 3–6.

"Microprocessor Design Series," (Collection of Articles), *EDN*. Denver, Colorado: Cahners Publishing Company, 1974.

Neth, J., and R. Forsberg, "Microprocessors and Microcomputers: What Will the Future Bring?" *EDN*, Vol. 29, No. 22, November 1974, pp. 24–29.

Noyce, R.N., "From Relays to MPUs," *Computer*, Vol. 9, No. 12, December 1976, pp. 26–29.

Ogdin, C.A., *Microcomputer Design*. Englewood Cliffs, New Jersey: Prentice-Hall, Inc., 1978.

Osborne, A., *An Introduction to Microcomputers*. Berkeley, California: Adam Osborne and Associates, Inc., 1974.

Peatman, J.B., *Microcomputer-Based Design*. New York: McGraw-Hill Book Company, 1977.

"Special Report: Climbing Aboard the Microprocessor Bandwagon," *Electronics*, Vol. 47, No. 14, July 1974, pp. 81–108.

Torrero, E.A. (Ed.), "Microprocessors: New Directions for Designers," (Collection of Articles), *Electronic Design*. Rochelle Park, New Jersey: Hayden Book Company, Inc., 1975.

Vacroux, A.G., "Microcomputers," *Scientific American*, Vol. 232, No. 5, May 1974, pp. 32–40.

Wester, J.G., and W.D. Simpson. *Software Design for Microprocessors*. Dallas, Texas: Texas Instruments, Inc., 1976.

PROBLEMS

1-1. Many IC chips are fabricated on a single wafer of silicon. Assume that the manufacturing defects are evenly distributed, and explain how and why the yield varies inversely with the area of the individual chips.

1-2. At the end of the first year of production, a single LSI circuit is selling for $200. Assume that the price of the IC follows the learning curve with a constant of 30 percent. Assume also that production increases 50 percent each year for four years thereafter. What will be the price of the IC at the end of the fifth year of production?

1-3. Repeat problem 1-2, assuming that production increases 175 percent each year.

1-4. In 1974 a microprocessor was introduced and sold for $360 in single quantities. In 1976 the single quantity cost of this device was $75. Assume that the price of this IC followed the learning curve with a constant of 0.3. What conclusions can be drawn concerning the cumulative production of these microprocessors in the two-year period between 1974 and 1976?

1-5. List the factors which could cause the price of an IC to increase after reaching the bottom of the learning curve. Give a short explanation of the reason for each factor.

1-6. Examine a data sheet for the 7495 shift register. Which inputs are control inputs? Which can be used for programming the IC? What is the function of each of these control or programming inputs?

1-7. Using the truth table for the BCD-to-seven segment decoder in Fig. 1.2-2(d), verify the equations for the decoder outputs using Karnaugh maps.

1-8. Determine the minimum size (number of words and number of bits per word) and the contents of a single ROM programmed to implement all of the following functions:

$$F_1(A, B, C, D) = A'D + BD + B'D$$
$$F_2(A, B, C, D) = (A + B' + C)(A + B')$$
$$(A + C' + D')(A' + B + C + D')$$
$$F_3(A, B, C) = (A' + B)(B' + C)$$
$$F_4(B, C) = A' + B + AB'$$

1-9. Determine the size and contents of a ROM programmed to output the product in binary coded decimal (BCD) of two decimal input digits represented in BCD.

1-10. Determine the size and contents of a ROM which implements a 4-bit comparator (i.e., a comparator that compares two 4-bit words: $A_3A_2A_1A_0$ and $B_3B_2B_1B_0$) that provides three outputs which indicate, by a logic 1 at the appropriate output, one of the following conditions: $A > B$, $A = B$, or $A < B$.

1-11. Design a 4-bit binary up counter using a ROM and D-type flip-flops. Make a provision to clear (set all the outputs to zero) the counter.

1-12. A BCD up-down counter is implemented using programmed logic techniques with a ROM and data latch. The up-down control is represented by the variable U, where $U = 1$ to count up. The output of the counter is $DCBA$, where D is the most significant bit. Draw a block diagram of the system, and show the contents of the ROM required to implement the counter.

1-13. Using a ROM and D-type flip-flops, design a 4-bit counter which counts up in binary if its control input equals 0 and counts up in BCD if its control input equals 1. What is the total number of bits required? How many D-type flip-flops are required?

1-14. Modify the design in problem 1-13 to allow the presetting of the initial value of the count. When this provision is added, what problems may arise and how can they be solved?

1-15. Implement the following state diagram using ROMs and D-type flip-flops. Indicate the state assignment chosen.

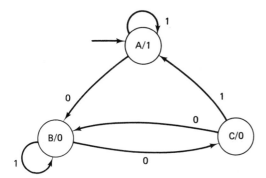

Figure P1.15

1-16. A standard ROM implements combinational functions. It has eight inputs and four outputs (256 words, each containing 4 bits). Six of the inputs implement functions $F_1(A, B, C, D, E, G)$ and $F_2(A, B, C, D, E, G)$. Can NAND and EX-OR functions be implemented on inputs X and Y using the same ROM? If so, how?

1-17. For each of the following microprocessor system applications, give a brief functional description of the system and list the system features you deem important. What input and output devices are required for each application?
   a. Taxi meter
   b. Microwave oven controller
   c. Automobile trip computer
   d. Home fire and intrusion alarm system

1-18. For an electronic consumer device of your choosing, explain how the device's capability could be enhanced by implementation as a microprocessor system.

2

Random Access Semiconductor Memories

But the microcomputer itself is not the complete source of new ideas and perspectives. Other developments in LSI technology—the LSI ROM, PROM and RAM—form integral parts of the success of microcomputer applications. Without low-cost, low-power and physically small memories, the microcomputer CPU would have a greatly reduced impact. Progress in memory technology is inextricably intertwined into every microcomputer application.

Douglas A. Cassell*

*"Only Small, Clever Programs Need Apply," *Digital Design,* Vol. 5, No. 3, March 1975, pp. 24–26, 30, and 32.

Memory is a major consideration in all microprocessor system designs. Control programs are usually stored in one type of memory and intermediate results in another. And, while this is the major use of memory in terms of the number of bits of storage involved, memory in various forms pervades all the major subsystems of a microprocessor system.[1]

For reasons of compatibility with regard to physical size, speed, power consumption, and logic levels, semiconductor memories are used with microprocessors. These memories are manufactured either as separately packaged IC devices or as a portion of the same IC on which the microprocessor is integrated.

2.1 BASIC MEMORY CONCEPTS

2.1.1 Flip-Flops/1-Bit Registers

The smallest unit of information a digital system can store is a binary digit, a *bit*, which has a logic value of 0 or 1. A bit of data is stored in an electronic device called a *flip-flop* or a *1-bit register*. [1] A flip-flop is a type of general *memory cell* and, as such, has two stable *states* in which it can remain indefinitely—as long as its operating power is not interrupted—and inputs which allow its state to be changed by external signals. A very simple type of flip-flop is the *D-type flip-flop* illustrated in Fig. 2.1-1. It has a single data input, D, and two outputs, Q and $\bar{Q}$. Output Q represents the state of the flip-flop, and $\bar{Q}$ represents the complement of the flip-flop's state. The logic value at a flip-flop's D input when a clock signal, CK, occurs is stored in the flip-flop. If the stored value is equal to 1, ($Q = 1$), the flip-flop is *set*. If the stored value is equal to 0, ($Q = 0$), the flip-flop is *cleared*.

The logical operation of a D-type flip-flop is expressed by the characteristic equation, $Q_{n+1} = D_n$. This equation indicates that after the occurrence of a clock pulse, the output of a D-type flip-flop, Q_{n+1}, is equal to the logic value of the D input before the occurrence of the clock pulse, D_n. But D-type flip-flops differ with regard to the precise time at which the clock pulse causes the input data to be accepted, the output to change in accordance with the input, and the output to be held or latched.

Two clock pulses are shown in Fig. 2.1-2. The clock pulse shown in Fig. 2.1-2(a) is a *positive clock pulse*. This signal is logic 0 in its quiescent state, makes a transition to logic 1, remains at logic 1 momentarily, and then returns to logic 0. The *leading edge* of the pulse is a 0 to 1 or *positive transition*, and the *trailing edge* is a 1 to 0 or *negative transition*. The clock pulse in Fig. 2.1-2(b) is a *negative clock pulse*; its quiescent value is logic 1, and it makes a momentary negative transition to logic 0 followed by a positive transition back to logic 1.

---

[1]Memory inside microprocessors and I/O devices—registers and flags—is discussed in Chapters 3, 8, and 9. Some peripheral devices are mass memories, and these are covered in Chapter 10.

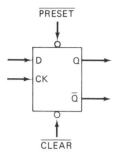

Figure 2.1-1. D-type flip-flop.

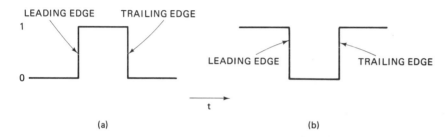

Figure 2.1-2. Single clock pulse: (a) positive clock pulse; (b) negative clock pulse.

An *edge triggered* D-type flip-flop latches the logic value at the *D* input during the clock pulse's transition from one logic value to the other. The sensitivity of the flip-flop to the transition (edge) of the clock is indicated on the flip-flop's logic symbol by a triangle, $>$, at the clock input. Positive edge triggered flip-flops latch on the positive transition of the clock. See Fig. 2.1-3(a). Negative edge triggered flip-flops latch on the negative transition of the clock. To indicate negative edge sensitivity, an inversion circle is used together with a triangle at the clock input, as shown in Fig. 2.1-3(b).

If the clock pulse of Fig. 2.1-2(a) is applied to a positive edge triggered D flip-flop, the data is latched at the leading edge of the pulse. If the clock pulse of Fig. 2.1-2(b) is applied to a positive edge triggered flip-flop, the data is latched at the trailing edge of the pulse. Note that with an edge triggered flip-flop, the input is accepted, and the output changes and is latched during a single clock transition.

A *level triggered* flip-flop, usually referred to simply as a *latch*, has a clock input which is sensitive to the level of the clock signal. The output of a positive level triggered D flip-flop follows the D input when the clock is logic 1. When the clock makes a transition from 1 to 0, the data present at the D input is latched. The output of a negative level triggered D flip-flop follows the input when the clock is logic 0 and latches the input on a 0 to 1 clock transition. Figures 2.1-3(c) and (d) show how positive and negative level triggering is

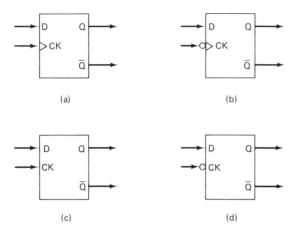

(a)   (b)

(c)   (d)

Figure 2.1-3. Symbols for various types of flip-flop triggering: (a) positive edge triggered; (b) negative edge triggered; (c) positive level triggered; (d) negative level triggered.

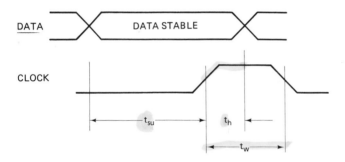

Figure 2.1-4. Timing diagram for a positive edge triggered flip-flop, showing clocking requirements.

indicated at the flip-flop's clock input. Thus, for a level triggered flip-flop, the output follows the input when the clock is at the trigger level, and the input data is latched on the transition from the trigger level to the quiescent level.

The D flip-flop symbol (Fig. 2.1-1) shows two additional inputs common to most IC flip-flops: *preset* and *clear*. The inversion circles on the flip-flop symbol indicate that both these inputs are active low. Preset and clear are asynchronous inputs; they affect the state of the flip-flop independent of the clock's level or transition. Thus, preset and clear override the clocked, or synchronous, input D. A logic 0 at the preset input sets the flip-flop; a logic 0 at the clear input clears it. For proper operation, the preset and clear inputs are not strobed simultaneously.

In order for a flip-flop to operate correctly, certain timing constraints on the input data and clock signals must be adhered to. Figure 2.1-4 is a timing diagram of the clock and data input signals to a positive edge triggered D

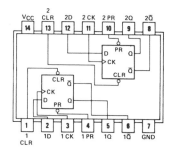

Figure 2.1-5. Logic symbol for a 74LS74A dual D-type positive edge triggered flip-flop. (Courtesy of Texas Instruments Inc.)

flip-flop. The minimum acceptable clock pulse width for proper operation is t_w. The input data must be stable for a minimum time period, t_{su}, before the positive transition of the clock and must remain stable for a minimum time period, t_h, after this transition. The time period, t_{su}, is called the *setup time*, and the time period, t_h, the *hold time* for the flip-flop.

A 74LS74A IC which contains two D-type positive edge triggered flip-flops is shown in Fig. 2.1-5. The minimum clock pulse, t_w, for this device is 25 nS. The setup time, t_{su}, is 25 nS, and the hold time, t_h, is 5 nS. A variety of other types of IC flip-flops, in addition to the D type, are available. [1] However, the D-type flip-flop is generally used in microprocessor systems.

2.1.2 M-Bit Registers

To store several bits of data simultaneously, the clock inputs of several D flip-flops are connected in parallel to form an *m-bit register*. MSI circuits containing 4-, 6-, or 8-bit registers are readily available. (See Fig. 2.1-6.) Such registers store m bits of data (D_0 to D_{m-1}) under control of the clock and provide m data outputs (O_0 to O_{m-1}). These circuits may be either edge

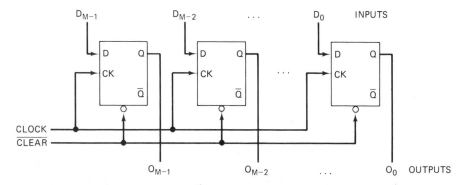

Figure 2.1-6. m-bit register consisting of m D-type flip-flops.

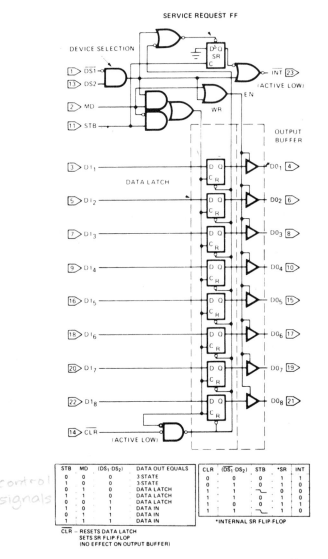

control
signals

STB	MD	$(DS_1 \cdot DS_2)$	DATA OUT EQUALS
0	0	0	3 STATE
1	0	0	3 STATE
0	1	0	DATA LATCH
1	1	0	DATA LATCH
0	0	1	DATA LATCH
1	0	1	DATA IN
0	1	1	DATA IN
1	1	1	DATA IN

CLR	$(\overline{DS_1} \cdot DS_2)$	STB	*SR	INT
0	0	0	1	1
0	1	0	1	0
1	1	⎍	0	0
1	1	1	0	0
1	0	0	1	1
1	1	⎍	0	1
1	1	1	1	0

*INTERNAL SR FLIP-FLOP

CLR – RESETS DATA LATCH
      SETS SR FLIP-FLOP
      (NO EFFECT ON OUTPUT BUFFER)

Figure 2.1-7. Logic diagram of an 8212 latch. (Courtesy of Intel Corp.)

triggered or level triggered. The clock input to a level triggered register is frequently referred to as an *enable* or *device select signal*.

Intel's 8212 [2] latch, for example, is a 24-pin MSI device often used in microprocessor systems. The logic diagram of an 8212 is shown in Fig. 2.1-7. It contains an 8-bit latch which can be clocked in several ways. The eight flip-flops that make up the latch are positive level triggered devices. As can be seen from the logic diagram, the clock signal to the D flip-flops is derived from four inputs —MD, $\overline{DS1}$, DS2, and STB—through a combinational circuit.

$\overline{DS1}$, DS2, or STB can be used as the clock input. If the mode input, MD, is logic 1, the latch is clocked when $\overline{DS1} = 0$ and DS2 = 1. Thus, MD and DS2 can be fixed at logic 1 and $\overline{DS1}$ used as the clock input to provide negative level triggering. For positive level triggering, MD can be fixed at logic 1, $\overline{DS1}$ at logic 0, and DS2 used as the clock input.

At the output of each D flip-flop in the 8212 is a ***three-state*** buffer. Three-state buffers are buffers with three output states. Two of the output states are the common logic states 0 and 1. When the buffer is enabled by a control input, its output is either logic 0 or 1. The output impedance is low when the buffer is enabled, allowing the output to source or sink current to the circuits it drives. The third state which exists when the buffer is disabled does not provide a conventional logic level output but, rather, causes the output to be a very high impedance. This high impedance state prevents the output from driving or loading any circuit connected to it. Thus, when disabled, three-state outputs are electrically disconnected from any logic circuits to which they are physically connected and are said to be *floating*. The electrical characteristics of three-state outputs are discussed in Appendix A.

Three-state outputs allow the outputs of several devices to be multiplexed onto the same bus. In Fig. 2.1-8, two 8212s have their outputs connected to a single 8-bit output data bus. An address input is required to select one of the two 8212s for reading or writing. To read the contents of an 8212, its output buffers are enabled. With MD = 0, this requires that $\overline{DS1} = 0$ and DS2 = 1. An address input, A_0, is connected to DS2 of one 8212, and its complement $\overline{A_0}$, is connected to the other. The $\overline{DS1}$ input of each 8212 is connected to a read control pulse, $\overline{RD}$. When $\overline{RD}$ is logic 0, the contents of the addressed 8212 appear on the output data bus.

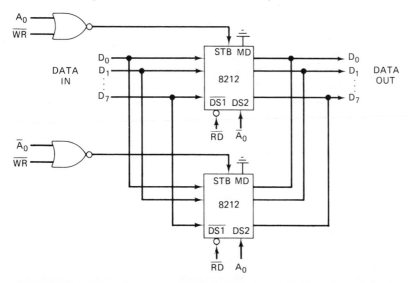

Figure 2.1-8. Connection of two 8212s to a common input and common output data bus.

It is important when using three-state outputs for multiplexing that only one of the devices with common outputs is enabled at a given time. If two or more devices with common outputs are enabled simultaneously, they may be damaged.

The inputs of the two 8212s are also connected to a common input data bus. Data to be written into either latch is placed on the common data bus, and the address input gates the write pulse, $\overline{\text{WR}}$, to the addressed 8212.

The act of storing data in a register is called a ***write*** operation. Determining the value of the contents of a register is called a ***read*** operation.

The m bits of data stored in a register comprise a word. A ***word*** is simply a number of contiguous bits operated upon or considered by the hardware as a group. The number of bits in the word, m, is the ***word length***. Frequently, the word length in a digital system is 8 bits. Eight bits of information considered as a unit are referred to as a ***byte***. This practice has led to the use of the term ***nibble*** to refer to smaller, 4-bit units of information.

The m inputs to the register are provided by an m-bit input data bus, and the m outputs by an m-bit output data bus. A ***bus*** is a parallel group of signal lines, grouped together because of similarity of function, which connect two or more systems or subsystems.

2.1.3 Memories

Several equal length registers can be incorporated in a single IC and share a common set of inputs, a common set of outputs, and a single clock line (see Fig. 2.1-9). Such a circuit is simply referred to as a ***memory***. It is necessary, of course, to distinguish among the various registers.

Each register occupies a distinct ***location*** which has a unique numerical ***address***. Thus, memory can be thought of as a collection of ***addressable registers***. Logic is necessary in the IC to decode address inputs to ensure that only a single register outputs its contents when data is being read from the memory, and only a single register has data stored in it when data is being written into the memory. This address decoding logic is considered in Section 2.3.

A conceptual representation of the memory of Fig. 2.1-9 for $n = 3$ and $m = 4$ is shown in Fig. 2.1-10(a). In this representation, the addresses of locations are represented by the integers from 0 to $2^n - 1$, and the content of each location is the binary word stored at that address. Memories typically have word lengths which are multiples of 4 bits. This has led to the convenient practice of specifying memory contents and addresses as hexadecimal quantities. (See Appendix B for a discussion of hexadecimal numbers.) Figure 2.1-10(b) shows this convention applied to the addresses and memory contents of Fig. 2.1-10(a). The letter H is used as a suffix to indicate that the number is expressed in hexadecimal notation.

The ***capacity*** of a memory is specified in terms of the maximum number of bits or the maximum number of words the memory can store. Assuming that the memory has an n-bit address and each word is of length m, the memory has a

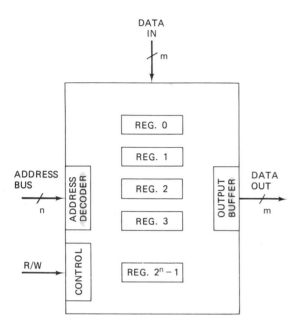

Figure 2.1-9. Register representation of a memory.

MEMORY LOCATION	n-BIT ADDRESS	MEMORY CONTENTS				HEX ADDRESS	HEX CONTENTS
0	000	0	1	1	0	0H	6H
1	001	0	0	1	0	1H	2H
2	010	1	1	0	0	2H	CH
3	011	0	0	0	1	3H	1H
4	100	1	1	1	0	4H	EH
5	101	1	1	1	0	5H	EH
6	110	0	0	0	0	6H	0H
7	111	0	1	1	0	7H	6H

←— m BITS —→

(a) (b)

Figure 2.1-10. Conceptual representation of $2^n \times m$-bit memory: (a) binary notation; (b) hexadecimal notation.

capacity of $2^n * m$ bits, organized as 2^n words each of m bits. Such an organization is referred to an $2^n \times m$ memory. For example, if $n = m = 8$, the memory is called a "two hundred fifty six by eight memory," and is written "256 × 8." The letter K, when used as a suffix in specifying the capacity of a large memory, is equal to 1,024 (2^{10}). Therefore, 1 K words represents 1,024 words; 2 K words represents 2,048 words, etc.

The n address bits are the address inputs to the memory. With n address bits, one of 2^n unique locations (L) can be specified: $L = 2^n$. Thus, the number of locations in a memory is always a power of two. Given L, the number of address bits required to distinguish between L locations is $n = \log_2 L$. The number of address bits required for memories with capacities up to 1,024 words is easily memorized. To quickly determine the number of address bits required for memories containing more than 1,024 locations, remember first that 10 bits are required to specify 1,024 locations, $(2^{10} = 1{,}024 = 1 \text{ K})$; then $L = P*K$ locations require $\log_2 L = \log_2 P + \log_2 K = \log_2 P + 10$ address bits. Thus, 4 K locations require $\log_2 4 + 10 = 2 + 10$, or 12 address bits, and 64 K locations require $\log_2 64 + 10 = 6 + 10$, or 16 address bits.

All memories provide a method for reading the contents of a memory location in response to the application of an address and appropriate control signals. The representation of the memory in Fig. 2.1-9 shows a control input, R/W, which, when logic 1, causes a copy of the contents of the location specified by the address inputs to appear at the memory's output. There is a time lag between the application of an address and the appearance at the output of the contents of the addressed location; this time lag is known as the memory's *access time* and is dependent both on the technology and on the structure used to implement the memory. For the memory structure of Fig. 2.1-9, the access time for each read operation is essentially independent of the order in which addresses are applied. Such a memory is called a ***Random Access Memory, RAM***; thus, with a RAM, the contents of any one location can be accessed in essentially the same time as can the contents of any other location chosen at random.

Writing data into a memory also involves a time delay—following the application of an address, input data, and a write control signal—before the new data is reliably written into the memory. This time period is known as the memory's ***write time***. For the memory shown in Fig. 2.1-9, the R/W control input is momentarily brought to logic 0 for a write operation. This logic 0 pulse is the clock signal which latches the input data.

The notational convention used with the R/W input warrants further explanation. In general, slashes are used to separate symbols for positive and negative true functions which share the same signal line. The symbol in front of the slash represents the function which is true when the signal is high or logic 1, and the symbol behind the slash represents the function which is true when the signal is low or logic 0. Thus, when the R/W input is 1, R is true, and a read operation occurs; when R/W is 0, W is true and a write operation occurs. The indication that W is true when the input is logic 0 is written more explicitly as R/$\overline{\text{W}}$.

2.2 MEMORY CLASSES

Memories, in general, are classified on the basis of several attributes. Figure 2.2-1 provides an organizational structure for the classification of semiconductor memories. Access time divides memories into two classes: random access

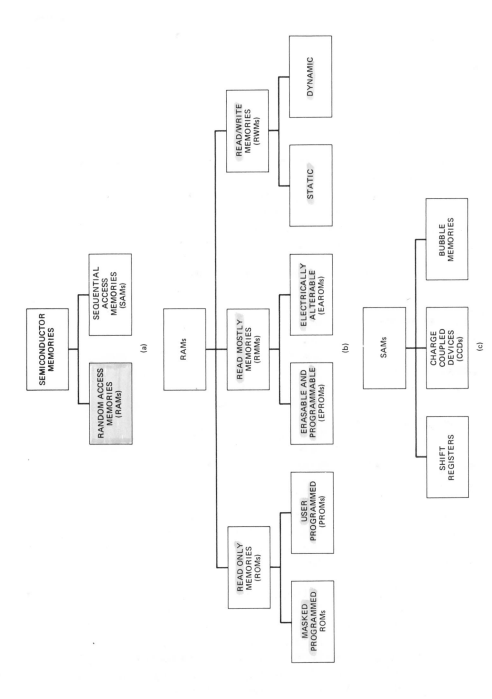

Figure 2.2-1. Organizational structure for the classification of semiconductor memories: (a) subdivision of semiconductor memories into RAMs and SAMs; (b) subdivision of RAMs; (c) subdivision of SAMs.

memory, introduced in Section 2.1, and sequential access memory. If the access time varies significantly depending upon the order in which addresses are applied, the memory is a *sequential access memory*. Memories composed of shift registers are an example of sequential access semiconductor memories. In the remainder of this chapter, only random access semiconductor memories are discussed. Sequential access memories are discussed in Chapter 10.

Based on their write times and on the ease with which they can be written, random access memories are further classified as read only memories, read mostly memories, or read write memories. Memories whose contents are specified only once, during manufacture, are Read Only Memories, ROMs. After being written (mask programmed) during manufacture, a ROM's write time is considered infinite, since it cannot be written again. The memory cell used in a ROM is significantly different and simpler than the flip-flop used as a memory cell in a read/write memory, since the state of the memory cell is fixed. The control program in most dedicated microprocessor systems is stored in ROM.

A variation of the ROM is the *Programmable Read Only Memory, PROM*. Like the ROM, a PROM can be written only once. However, when a PROM is obtained from the manufacturer, all of its bits are fixed at either 1s or 0s, depending on the device. Opposite bit values are programmed into it where desired by the designer, using a special piece of equipment—the PROM programmer. Bit values, once programmed, cannot be subsequently altered.

Memories which can be written into more than once and which have short write times, typically on the order of hundreds of nanoseconds, are called *Read/Write Memories* or *R/W Memories, RWMs*. In dedicated microprocessor based systems, RWMs are used primarily for storing intermediate results of computations. The memory shown in Fig. 2.1-9 is a RWM. RWMs are either static or dynamic in operation. *Static Memories* have memory cells which are similar to a common flip-flop. *Dynamic Memories* have memory cells which must be *refreshed*, read and rewritten periodically or the memory cells' contents are lost.

The term "RAM" is often used to signify read/write memory to the exclusion of read only memory. However, read only memories are also random access. This exclusive labeling of read/write memory as RAM, though not strictly correct, has found widespread usage. RAM is used here in its strict interpretation, i.e., a random access memory, and includes both ROMs and RWMs.

A class of memories exists which lies between ROMs and RWMs in terms of the ease and the speed of writing. Memories in this class are sometimes referred to as *Read Mostly Memories, RMMs*, and include *Erasable Programmable Read Only Memories, EPROMs*, and *Electrically Alterable Read Only Memories, EAROMs*. These memories can be written into more than once. They are distinguishable from RWMs by requiring significantly longer write times; many by requiring that all locations be erased simultaneously; and, in the case of EPROMs, by requiring that the memory be removed from the microprocessor system in order to erase it. The desirability of RMMs stems from the fact that they are, like ROMs, nonvolatile, but are also, in effect, reusable ROMs. A *nonvolatile* memory is one whose contents are not lost when the power supplied to the memory is interrupted or removed; the contents of a *volatile* memory are lost with a loss of power. The term ROM is frequently used in this text to refer to any of the various types of ROMs and RMMs when the distinction is not important.

The ideal general purpose memory is a low-cost, high-speed, nonvolatile read/write memory. The fact that this ideal is still to be met is clearly illustrated by the numerous types of memory just discussed. Each of those memory types is noted for certain advantages in terms of economics and performance in particular applications.

2.3 SEMICONDUCTOR RAM DEVICE ORGANIZATION

Semiconductor RAM devices (single IC packages) are available with a limited number of bits of storage. In some applications a single memory device may not only meet the bit capacity requirements but also be organized into the required number of words and bits per word. In general, however, the requirements of an application for word length and total number of words necessitates the interconnection of several memory devices and additional logic circuits to form a *memory system*.

Semiconductor memory devices are designed so that a single device meets all the functional requirements of a memory system. To do so a device contains:

1. An array of memory cells each of which can store a single bit.
2. Logic to address any location in the memory.
3. Circuitry to allow the reading of the contents of any memory location.
4. For writable memories, circuitry to allow any memory location to be written.

For easy interconnection of a memory device with other memory devices or logic circuits, memory devices contain input drivers, output buffers, and circuitry for address expansion.

Semiconductor memories are internally organized several ways in an effort to obtain a memory with high speed, a large bit capacity, and low peripheral circuit and memory array costs. [3] Conceptually, the simplest organization is a *word organized* array with *linear selection*. The memory array in such an organization has a column length equal to the number of words, W, and a row length equal to the number of bits per word, B (see Fig. 2.3-1). Word selection requires a 1-out-of-W decoder; i.e., a decoder with a mutually exclusive output for each word in the memory. The address inputs to the decoder select one, and

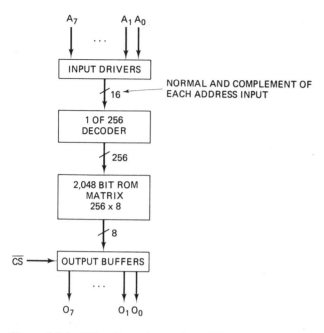

Figure 2.3-1. 256 × 8 word organized ROM using linear selection.

only one, of the decoder's outputs—thus selecting one word in the memory array. Clearly, although conceptually simple, the linear selection method requires a large decoder for a large number of words, which is very costly in chip area. For memories with a small number of words, this organization is acceptable and has the advantage of a short access time.

Address decoder size is substantially reduced by organizing the memory array and the word selection logic to allow *coincident selection* or *two-level decoding.* In a memory array utilizing two-level decoding, one level corresponds to a physical word and one to a logical word. A *physical word* consists of the number of bits in a row of the memory array. A *logical word* consists of the number of bits of a physical word which are sensed and gated to the output at one time. Two-level decoding requires two decoders: a row decoder which selects a physical word and a column decoder, actually several multiplexers, which then selects one logical word from the selected physical word. A physical word is divided into S segments (logical words); the row decoder is a 1-out-of-P decoder, where P is equal to W/S; and the column decoder consists of B, 1-out-of-S multiplexers.

The block diagram of a ROM with 2,048, 8-bit words (2,048 × 8) organized for two-level decoding is shown in Fig. 2.3-2. The memory array is 128 × 128 bits; thus, it contains 128 physical words. A physical word is selected by decoding the seven address bits A_0 through A_6. Thus, the row decoder is a 1-out-of-128 decoder. Segmentation is accomplished by dividing the physical

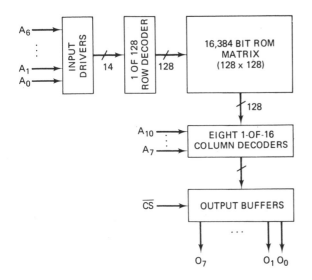

Figure 2.3-2. 2048 × 8 ROM with 128 × 128 memory array using two-level decoding.

word into eight groups of 16 bits. The first group contains the most significant bits of each of the 16 logical words; the next group contains the next most significant bits of each of the 16 logical words, etc., until the eighth group, which contains the least significant bits of each of the 16 logical words. Thus, each physical word is segmented into 16 logical words, and therefore S equals 16. Column decoding, then, requires eight 1-out-of-16 multiplexers to provide an 8-bit output logical word. In this example, address bits A_7 through A_{10} control the column decoders.

When the number of segments in a physical word is equal to the number of bits in a physical word, the result is a ***bit organized*** memory; i.e., each logical word is a single bit in length. The bit organized memory has a single output, a square memory array, and row and column decoders of equal complexity. The row and column decoders each decode $n/2$ address bits, resulting in a simplification of the decoders required. A 1,024 × 1-bit organized memory, for example, consists of a 32 × 32 memory array, a 1-out-of-32 row decoder, and a 1-out-of-32 column decoder.

In addition to the memory array and decoding logic which comprise the memory device structure, output buffers are used to buffer data from a memory array before it is output to the pins of the memory package. These buffers not only provide the desired output voltage levels and drive current but also provide three-state or open collector outputs which allow easy multiplexing of the outputs of several packages. (See Section 2.5.) The output buffers are controlled by one or more ***chip select, chip enable*** or ***output enable*** inputs. Depending on the logic levels applied to these inputs, output of data from the device, through the buffers, is either permitted or prevented.

functional block diagram

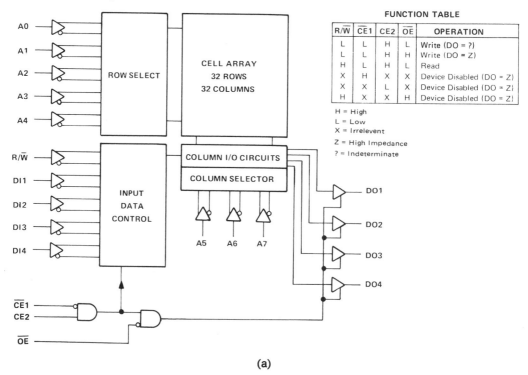

FUNCTION TABLE

R/W	CE1	CE2	OE	OPERATION
L	L	H	L	Write (DO = ?)
L	L	H	H	Write (DO = Z)
H	L	H	L	Read
X	H	X	X	Device Disabled (DO = Z)
X	X	L	X	Device Disabled (DO = Z)
H	X	X	H	Device Disabled (DO = Z)

H = High
L = Low
X = Irrelevent
Z = High Impedance
? = Indeterminate

(a)

Figure 2.3-3. (a) 256 × 4 memory with separate I/O; (b) 256 × 4 memory with common I/O. (Courtesy of Texas Instruments Inc.)

Depending on the logic level applied to a chip select or chip enable input, the entire operation of the device, including writing into the device, can be enabled or disabled. A chip select or chip enable input differs in function from an output enable input in that it prevents writing into the device when it disables the output, whereas an output enable does not. The terms chip enable and chip select are used interchangeably.

Read/write memories also require input data control or write logic, as shown in Figs. 2.3-3(a) and (b). The chip must be enabled for data to be written into it. For the particular control logic configuration shown in Fig. 2.3-3(a), a write operation first requires $\overline{CE1} = 0$ and CE2 = 1. A low level on the read/write control input (R/$\overline{W}$) then writes the data at the data inputs into the addressed memory location. Note that the write operation is independent of the level on the output enable input ($\overline{OE}$).

The 256 × 4 memory of Fig. 2.3-3(a) has *separate I/O*; that is, separate sets of pins on the package are used for data inputs and data outputs. The memory in Fig. 2.3-3(b), on the other hand, has *common I/O*; the same pins are used for data input and output. To write into or read from this memory requires $\overline{CE1} = \overline{CE2} = 0$. In addition, the data outputs from the memory array are

functional block diagram

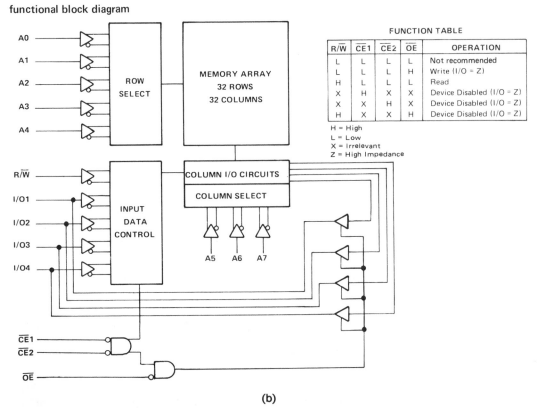

R/$\overline{\text{W}}$	$\overline{\text{CE1}}$	CE2	$\overline{\text{OE}}$	OPERATION
L	L	L	L	Not recommended
L	L	L	H	Write (I/O = Z)
H	L	L	L	Read
X	H	X	X	Device Disabled (I/O = Z)
X	X	H	X	Device Disabled (I/O = Z)
H	X	X	H	Device Disabled (I/O = Z)

H = High
L = Low
X = Irrelevant
Z = High Impedance

(b)

Figure 2.3-3. Continued

internally connected, through the output buffers, to the data inputs. This requires that the data output buffers be disabled, $\overline{\text{OE}} = 1$, when writing into the memory.

2.4 MEMORY DEVICE TIMING AND OPERATION

To ensure proper operation, there are timing constraints on the sequencing of address, data, and control signals to a random access semiconductor memory device. These constraints are specified on the manufacturer's data sheet in the form of AC characteristics and timing diagrams.

The simplest type of memory, in terms of its operation, is the ROM. In the basic operation of a ROM:

1. An address is applied to the address inputs of the ROM.
2. The ROM is selected by application of the proper logic level(s) at its chip select input(s).
3. The contents of the selected memory location appear at the data outputs of the ROM after a period of time equal to its access time.

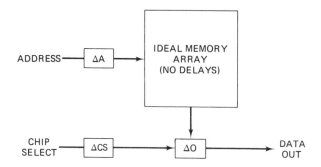

Figure 2.4-1. Lumped delay model of a ROM.

A simplified model of a ROM is shown in Fig. 2.4-1. In terms of timing constraints the memory array in this model is ideal, having no signal propagation delays associated with it. The device delays which exist in any real device are shown as lumped delays associated with the device's inputs and outputs. [4] Two input delays are shown in Fig. 2.4-1: ΔA associated with the address inputs and ΔCS associated with the chip select inputs. The delay ΔA includes all propagation delays associated with address input buffers, row and column decoders, and the memory array. The delay ΔCS includes all the propagation delays associated with the chip select logic. Delays associated with the output buffers are represented by ΔO.

Assume that a memory device is selected by proper logic levels at its chip select input. The time elapsed from the subsequent application of an address at the address inputs to the appearance at the memory's output of a stable copy of the addressed data is the address access time, t_A.[2] This time is simply the address to output delay, $\Delta A + \Delta O$.

If a stable address exists at the address inputs of a ROM, and the chip select inputs are changed to select the ROM, the delay between the application of proper chip select signals and stable output data is $\Delta CS + \Delta O$, the chip select to output delay, t_{CO}, or chip select access time. These two parameters, t_A and t_{CO}, are shown in the timing diagram in Fig. 2.4-2. The diagram shows the application of the address and chip select signals at the proper times for their effects on the output to occur simultaneously. The reference point is the occurrence of valid output data. As shown in the diagram, t_{CO} is usually significantly smaller than t_A. This is due to the fact that the chip select logic is connected directly to the output buffers (see Fig. 2.3-1). This timing diagram uses the 10 and 90 percent points of signal transitions for reference; other timing diagrams use the 50 percent point.

The various access times of a memory indicate its speed. In a microprocessor system, the microprocessor supplies the address and chip select signals

---

[2]Although parameter names and symbols vary from manufacturer to manufacturer and among different devices from the same manufacturer, the parameters themselves are common.

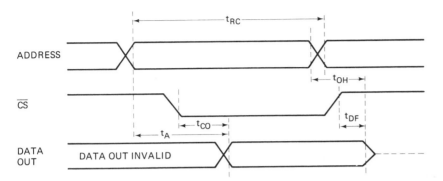

Figure 2.4-2. Timing diagram of a read operation for a ROM.

to a memory and then must wait a period of time equal to the access time before it can use the output from the memory. Slow memories limit a microprocessor's speed.

Three other parameters are shown in the timing diagram, two of these are the output hold time, t_{OH}, and the chip deselect to output float time, t_{DF}. These parameters are referenced to the time when the valid output data changes to invalid data or to a floating condition. Output hold time, t_{OH}, indicates how long the previous output data is valid after the address is changed. The chip deselect to output float time indicates how long the output data remains valid when the memory device is no longer selected. The third parameter, read cycle time, t_{RC}, specifies the maximum rate at which different memory locations can be successively read.

As previously indicated, R/W memories are of two types: static and dynamic. Static RWMs have the simplest operational requirements. In addition to the address, chip enable, and data-out lines necessary for ROMs, RWMs require a set of data-in lines and a control line which determines whether the operation is to be a read or write. The R/W control line is held high for a read operation and taken low for a write operation. The address, chip enable, output disable, and read/write inputs must be sequenced properly for correct operation of the memory. The sequence of operations and timing requirements for reading a static RWM are similar to those for reading a ROM.

The basic sequence of operations for writing into a static read/write memory is as follows:

1. An address is applied to the address inputs of the RWM.
2. The RWM is enabled by application of the proper logic levels at the chip enable inputs.
3. Data to be written into the memory is applied at the data-in inputs.
4. The R/W line is pulsed low.
5. The address and chip enable signals can then be changed to select another memory location for reading or writing.

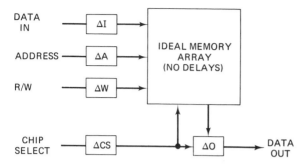

Figure 2.4-3. Lumped delay model of a RWM.

The RWM model shown in Fig. 2.4-3 includes two more delays than the ROM model of Fig. 2.4-1: the input delay, ΔI; and the write enable delay, ΔW.

A *write pulse*, usually a logic 0, must occur at the R/W input for a minimum length of time, t_{WP}, to guarantee writing into the slowest memory devices. The write pulse begins and ends the write operation and is a convenient reference for specifying other parameters associated with the write operation. It begins when the R/W line undergoes a 1 to 0 transition. However, in most memories, the levels on the data lines are not important until the R/W line makes a 0 to 1 transition because most memories accept input data at this transition. This is similar to the situation that exists with a positive edge triggered flip-flop.

When the 0 to 1 transition of the R/W line occurs, the data present at the memory array represents the data to be stored. The R/W line affects the memory array, ΔW, seconds after the signal is changed at the package pin. Changes in input data values at the package pins reach the memory array, ΔI, seconds later. Thus, data must be stable at the package pins at least $\Delta I - \Delta W$ seconds earlier. This corresponds to a period of time, $\Delta I - \Delta W$, before the 0 to 1 transition of the external R/W line. This time, $\Delta I - \Delta W$, is referred to as the data setup time, t_{DW}. Data at the data inputs must be stable for a time equal to or greater than t_{DW} to guarantee proper storage. Figure 2.4-4 shows t_{DW} referenced to the 0 to 1 transition of the R/W line. Note that the timing diagrams represent signals at the package pins.

It is also necessary to hold the input data stable for a period of time after the 0 to 1 transition of the R/W line; this time period is the data hold time, t_{DH}.

Whenever address inputs are changed, a finite amount of time elapses before the outputs of the address decoders have settled to their final value. During these transients, other memory locations are inadvertently addressed. If the write strobe is applied before these transients end, the data to be written into the memory may be written into several memory locations in addition to that intended. To preclude this, the address lines must be stable for a period of time preceding and following the occurrence of the write pulse. The write delay, t_{AW}, indicates how long the address must be stable before the 1 to 0 transition of the write pulse, and the write recovery time, t_{WR}, indicates how long the address must be held stable after the 0 to 1 transition of R/W.

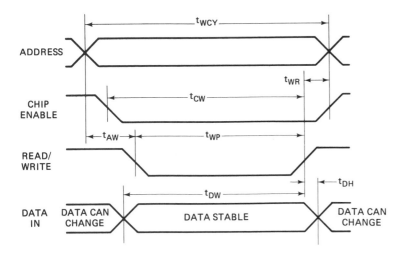

Figure 2.4-4. Write timing diagram for a R/W memory.

Similar to the address inputs, the chip enables must be stable for a period of time referred to as the chip enable to write time, t_{CW}, before the 0 to 1 transition of the R/W line. A final parameter, t_{WCY}, the write cycle time, specifies the minimum time between write operations. On most static semiconductor memory devices, the read and write cycle times are equal.

The memory cell of a dynamic R/W memory loses its stored information if it is not rewritten, refreshed, periodically. Dynamic memories require additional control signals for refreshing. In some cases these control signals are generated by logic on the memory chip itself, and only a clock signal must be connected to the memory package. In other cases, microprocessors contain logic for carrying out the refresh operation on the microprocessor chip, and, in still other cases, manufacturers provide a separate LSI controller specifically for generating the necessary refresh control signals. The timing requirements for dynamic RWMs are very stringent and differ considerably among different devices. The motivation for using dynamic RWMs, in spite of the drawbacks of refreshing and strict timing requirements, is their cost effectiveness in large memory systems.

2.5 MEMORY SYSTEM ORGANIZATION

The memory requirements of a typical microprocessor system frequently cannot be met with a single memory device. Several memory devices must then be interconnected to form a memory system. In a memory system, capacity is expanded by increasing the number of words and/or by increasing the word length above that attainable from a single memory device. Word length is increased by placing the outputs of two or more memory devices in parallel. For example, m, 1,024 × 1-bit memories can be arranged in parallel to make a 1,024 × m-bit memory system (Fig. 2.5-1).

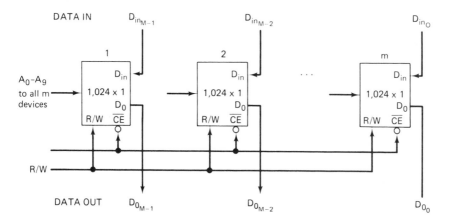

Figure 2.5-1. 1,024 × *m*-bit memory from 1,024 × 1 memory components.

The number of words in a memory system is increased by multiplexing outputs from two or more memory devices. Semiconductor memory devices have features that facilitate this. For example, chip select or chip enable inputs are provided on individual memory devices for this purpose. The chip select inputs provide on-chip gating to minimize the external gating required to select or enable a particular memory device.

A memory system with an increased number of words requires a provision for address expansion: expanding the number of memory address bits to which the memory system responds. The number of address bits that a microprocessor provides dictates its *memory address space* or the range of memory locations it can directly address. A memory system can be designed to fill the entire memory address space of the microprocessor with which it is used, although most applications do not require that much memory.

Depending on the size of the memory system, external address decoding logic, in addition to the memory's chip select inputs, may also be required for address expansion. This external logic decodes the additional address bits required to select a memory device. MSI decoders, which decode two, three, or four inputs are used for this purpose. A decoder with two inputs and four mutually exclusive outputs, for example, is referred to as a 2-line-to-4-line (two input lines, four output lines) or a 1-out-of-4 (only one output of the four is selected) decoder. A decoder with three inputs has eight mutually exclusive outputs and is called a 3-line-to-8-line decoder or a 1-out-of-8 decoder. Typically, the selected output is active low.

The additional address lines required for memory expansion are connected to the decoder's inputs, and the decoder's outputs provide the signals for the chip select inputs of the memory devices. Decoders, themselves, may also have one or more enable inputs for the purpose of interconnecting decoders to create

LOGIC SYMBOL

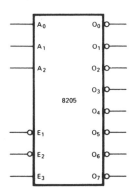

ADDRESS			ENABLE			OUTPUTS							
A_0	A_1	A_2	E_1	E_2	E_3	0	1	2	3	4	5	6	7
L	L	L	L	L	H	L	H	H	H	H	H	H	H
H	L	L	L	L	H	H	L	H	H	H	H	H	H
L	H	L	L	L	H	H	H	L	H	H	H	H	H
H	H	L	L	L	H	H	H	H	L	H	H	H	H
L	L	H	L	L	H	H	H	H	H	L	H	H	H
H	L	H	L	L	H	H	H	H	H	H	L	H	H
L	H	H	L	L	H	H	H	H	H	H	H	L	H
H	H	H	L	L	H	H	H	H	H	H	H	H	L
X	X	X	L	L	L	H	H	H	H	H	H	H	H
X	X	X	H	L	L	H	H	H	H	H	H	H	H
X	X	X	L	H	L	H	H	H	H	H	H	H	H
X	X	X	H	H	L	H	H	H	H	H	H	H	H
X	X	X	H	L	H	H	H	H	H	H	H	H	H
X	X	X	L	H	H	H	H	H	H	H	H	H	H
X	X	X	H	H	H	H	H	H	H	H	H	H	H

Figure 2.5-2. 8205 1-out-of-8 decoder. (Courtesy of Intel Corp.)

a larger decoder. If the decoder is not enabled, all of its outputs are high. The logic symbol of an Intel 8205, 1-out-of-8 decoder is shown in Fig. 2.5-2 together with its function table. [2] The inversion circles on two of the enable inputs (E_1, E_2) indicate that they must be low for the decoder to be enabled. The third enable input (E_3) must be high in order to enable the decoder. Inversion circles on the outputs indicate that the selected output is low. Figure 2.5-3 shows an 8205 decoder used to generate chip select signals to eight, 1 K $\times$ 8 memory devices connected to form 8 K $\times$ 8 of ROM. When decoders are used in this fashion, the memory devices are linearly selected, similar to the way a word is linearly selected by the address decoder within a memory device.

When memory devices are combined to form a memory system, with an expanded number of words, the corresponding data outputs of the memory devices must be multiplexed to form a single set of data outputs for the entire memory system. The output buffers on each memory device are either three state or *open collector* to allow the multiplexing of output data, without using external multiplexer devices. Open collector outputs from several devices can be directly connected, without damage, to provide a usable output, as can three-state outputs. This, of course, is not the case for standard logic outputs. The

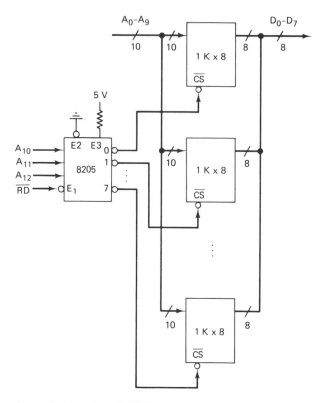

Figure 2.5-3. 8 K × 8 ROM memory system using 1 K × 8 memory devices.

address decoding logic decodes the higher order address bits and enables the three-state outputs of only one memory device. The electrical characteristics of three-state and open collector outputs are discussed in greater detail in Appendix A.

2.6 INTERFACING MEMORY

Microprocessors communicate with external memory via buses: address, data, and control buses. Address buses are unidirectional, providing information to devices external to the microprocessor only. Data buses, on the other hand, are bidirectional, transmitting information from the microprocessor to memory and from memory to the microprocessor. The direction of transfer on the microprocessor's data bus (to or from) is indicated by control signals from the microprocessor. These signals are detailed in Chapter 3. Each of the signals on a control bus is unidirectional. Some of these are outputs from the microprocessor; others are inputs to the microprocessor.

The data inputs and outputs of some RWMs are tied together internally, providing a single pair of data lines for input and output, and are thus directly compatible with bidirectional data buses. See Fig. 2.3-3(b). Others have separate output lines which can be externally connected to the input lines without requiring external logic. See Fig. 2.3-3(a). In either case, RWMs have output disable controls which place the three-state output buffers in their high impedance state when disabled; this action is independent of the chip select or chip enable and is used when data is being written into the memory via a bidirectional data bus. A memory device must be selected in order to be written into, and its outputs must be in their high impedance state to preclude both the microprocessor and the selected memory device from trying to drive the data bus simultaneously; thus, the need for both a chip select and output disable control in memories with common inputs and outputs. The data outputs are connected to the data inputs of the chip, and the chip is used with a common input-output (bidirectional) data bus. And, when a selected device is written into, the data output buffers are disabled by activating its output disable control. A signal indicating a memory read or write operation generated by the microprocessor controls the output disable.

In some memories with separate data inputs and outputs, the outputs are automatically enabled whenever the chip is selected. To interface such a memory to a bidirectional bus, external three-state buffers connect the memory's outputs back to its inputs, making them common. The signal that enables these buffers is analogous to the output enable. Devices such as the Texas Instruments 74LS244 and National INS8202 are octal buffer/drivers which contain eight, three-state buffers with a common enable input. Such devices are particularly appropriate for systems with an 8-bit data bus.

One or more memory devices can be combined with decoders, bidirectional bus drivers, and other logic to form one of two memory systems: a read only memory system or a R/W memory system. A read only memory system is constructed from one or more of the various types of ROMs and a decoder. See Fig. 2.6-1(a). Such a system has inputs from the address bus, data bus, and $\overline{\text{MEMR}}$ control signal. The $\overline{\text{MEMR}}$ control signal is used along with the address to select a particular device and address a single memory location within the selected device. The memory device which contains the addressed location only drives the data bus when $\overline{\text{MEMR}}$ is low.

An R/W memory system can be constructed using R/W memory devices, decoders, and three-state buffers—if a bidirectional data bus is required and memory devices with separate I/O are used. See Fig. 2.6-1(b). A read/write memory system has four basic inputs: the address, data, and $\overline{\text{MEMR}}$ and $\overline{\text{MEMW}}$ control signals. The address selects a memory location which is written if $\overline{\text{MEMW}}$ goes low or read if $\overline{\text{MEMR}}$ goes low. As long as $\overline{\text{MEMR}}$ is high, the data bus is not driven by the memory system.

Memory systems of any word length or number of words can be constructed with memory devices having chip select inputs and either three-state or open

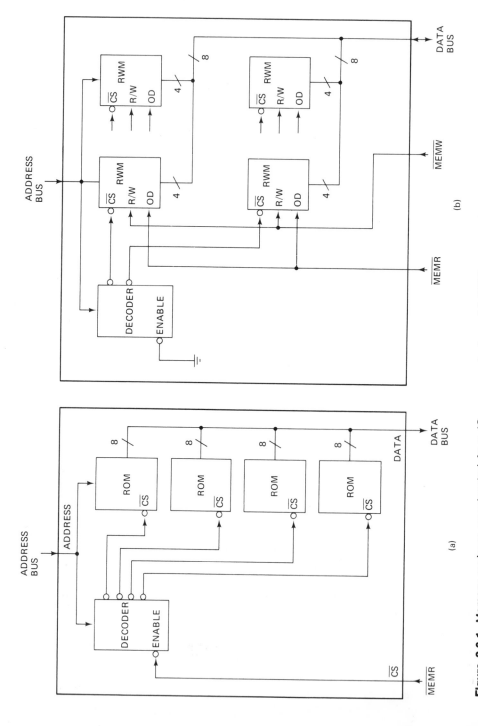

Figure 2.6-1. Memory systems constructed from IC memory devices: (a) ROM system; (b) RWM system.

collector outputs. Various types of memory can be used (RWM, ROM, PROM) and interspersed in the microprocessor system's memory address space. For example, the first 1 K words of memory can be ROM followed by 1 K words of RWM. An additional 512 words of ROM followed by 512 words of RWM could complete the memory system. In an actual system, memory does not always fill the address space consecutively or completely; some areas may be left empty.

The basic concepts of memory expansion demonstrate that memories of any required size can be constructed from memory packages with limited bit capacities. However, the access, write, and cycle times for the constructed memory system may be greater than the corresponding times for a single memory device due to several factors, including the need for additional decoding to generate chip select signals and the capacitive loading of outputs of one package by the outputs of other packages tied to the same data bus.

2.7 MEMORY TECHNOLOGY

Both bipolar and MOS IC technologies are used in the manufacture of semiconductor memories and microprocessors. The active components in MOS ICs are *Field Effect Transistors, FETs*. These transistors are unipolar, involving a single charge carrier in the conduction process. Bipolar ICs, on the other hand, use bipolar transistors as the active components.

MOS ICs are classified according to the conduction type of the field effect transistors: P-channel MOS (PMOS), N-channel MOS (NMOS) or P and N channel—complementary MOS (CMOS). Table 2.7-1 lists some of the key parameters for comparing these technologies. [5] PMOS devices are easier to fabricate because of a smaller number of masking steps and diffusions. And, although most early MOS memories and microprocessors are PMOS, PMOS devices are slow and consume more power than the other MOS technologies. NMOS is faster and denser (less area per gate) than PMOS and is widely used in low- and medium-speed applications and applications where high density is important. NMOS is and is expected to continue to be the dominant technology for implementing semiconductor memories and microprocessors. The primary advantages of CMOS technology are its low power dissipation and high speed. However, with CMOS the achievable density is lower and the fabrication process is more complex than with either P or NMOS technologies.

Bipolar ICs are primarily classified by circuit type. The main classifications include *Transistor-Transistor Logic, T^2L, Emitter Coupled Logic, ECL*, and *Integrated Injection Logic, I^2L*. Important parameters of the primary bipolar technologies are also listed in Table 2.7-1.

T^2L devices are generally faster than MOS devices but much less dense. Because T^2L is used so widely for SSI and MSI circuits, T^2L compatibility is frequently desirable in LSI devices. T^2L LSI is excellent for easy interfacing. The fastest technology is ECL, but the price paid for this high-speed performance is low density, high power consumption, and complexity of fabrication. I^2L is a

TABLE 2.7-1

Key Parameters for Leading LSI Technologies

Technology	PMOS	NMOS	CMOS	T²L	ECL	I²L
Area/gate (mil²)	8–12	6–8	10–30	20–60	20–50	4–6
Prop. delay/gate (nS)	>100	40–100	15–50	3–10	0.5–2	>5
Static power/gate (mW)	2–3	0.2–0.5	<0.001	1–3	5–15	<0.2
"Representative" speed-power product (pJ)	200	10–50	3	10	10	<1
Number of masking steps	5	6	7	7	8–9	5–7
Number of diffusions or implants	2	3	4	4	4–5	3–4
Ease of interface	Poor	Reasonable	Reasonable	Excellent	Excellent	Good

potentially very dense technology with good speed characteristics and low power consumption. In very general terms MOS provides high density with lower speed, and bipolar provides high speed with lower density.

On-chip peripheral circuitry, i.e., decoders, control logic, and drivers, is fabricated using the same process employed for the memory array. However, since circuits external to the memory may utilize a different technology, the compatibility of memory inputs and outputs with external circuitry is important. Frequently, external circuitry is T²L, and many memories are designed to be T²L compatible.

The term "compatibility" refers to two different conditions: (1) logic level compatibility in the sense that the output can directly interface with and drive at least a single low-power T²L load, and (2) power supply compatibility in the sense that the memory operates from a single 5 V supply. The inherent compatability of the different technologies is listed in Table 2.7-1. NMOS memories are usually designed to be T²L compatible.

2.8 ROMS

Read only memories store permanent information; the contents of the memory are fixed during fabrication of the integrated circuit and cannot be altered after manufacture. Both bipolar and MOS technology are used for manufacturing ROMs. The primary difference between bipolar and MOS ROMs is access time:

Bipolar access times are as low as 50–90 nS; MOS access times are about ten times higher. Bipolar ROMs are faster and have higher drive capability, while MOS devices are smaller for a given number of bits and consume less power.

Integrated circuits are fabricated on a wafer of silicon. The fabrication involves a number of processing steps, including photo masking, etching, and diffusion, to produce a pattern of junctions and interconnections across the wafer which creates the semiconductor devices. In manufacturing *mask programmed* ROMs, the connection of the coupling cell between the word and the bit lines is determined by a single step in the fabrication. The system designer specifies the desired programming of the ROMs, and this information is used to control a computerized operation which produces the mask used to custom program the ROM. The nonrecurring cost of developing the customized mask makes mask programmed ROMs economical only in high quantity applications. If an error is made by the system designer in determining or specifying the ROM contents, then the manufactured ROMs are useless.

2.8.1 MOS ROMs

MOS is an ideal technology for the fabrication of ROMs because the very dense geometrical layouts that are possible in MOS permit the design of matrix structures containing many thousands of MOS devices. The basic storage

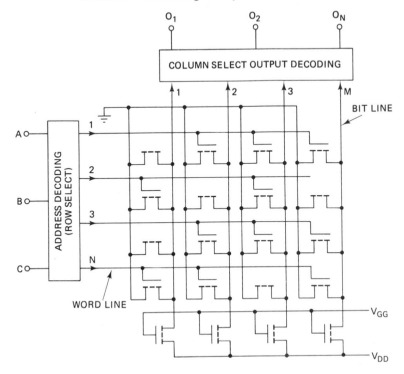

Figure 2.8-1. PMOS ROM.

PROGRAMMABLE EMITTER CONTRACTS

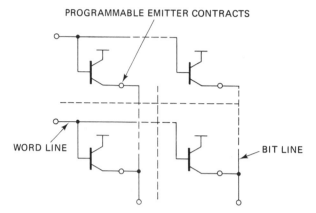

WORD LINE

BIT LINE

Figure 2.8-2. Bipolar ROM array.

element in a MOS ROM is a MOS transistor. A MOS ROM using P-channel enhancement mode transistors is shown in Fig. 2.8-1. The existence of a MOS transistor coupling the word and bit lines is determined in this particular MOS ROM by the oxide thickness at each transistor location. During fabrication, if the oxide is left thick, no transistor action occurs; where the oxide is thin, a MOS transistor exists between the particular word and bit lines. The existence of a transistor between the word and bit lines corresponds to a logic 1 for that bit position. This insertion or deletion of transistors from the matrix is accomplished by a single photo mask used in the fabrication process.

2.8.2 Bipolar ROMs

In bipolar ROMs, the coupling element between word and bit lines is a bipolar transistor. A typical bipolar memory element array is shown in Fig. 2.8-2. A transistor is connected between a word and bit line by making a connection to the emitter of the transistor. Such connections are controlled by a single step in the fabrication process. Sense amplifiers detect the current in a selected column to determine the existence of a logic 1 or logic 0.

2.9 PROMS, EPROMS, AND EAROMS

PROMs, EPROMs, and EAROMs are all *field programmable* read only memories; i.e., they are programmed after manufacture.

PROMs can be programmed, written into, only once. PROM programming requires circuits which provide the high currents necessary to burn in the desired bit patterns. These circuits can be constructed by the user, or one of the many commercial PROM programmers can be used. Some PROM vendors provide programming services for their customers. Because of this programming cost, PROMs are generally more expensive than ROMs and are advantageous only in low volume applications.

EPROMs and EAROMs, although more expensive than PROMs, can be written into more than once and are thus reprogrammable and reusable. EPROMs are advantageous in the early development of control programs when many changes are likely to be made, although erasure and reprogramming must be carried out with the memory package removed from the circuit. EAROMs have the further advantage of being erasable by electrical means while still in the circuit; however, EAROMs are more costly.

2.9.1 Fusible Link PROMs

A common type of programmable read only memory uses, as a connecting element between the word and bit lines, a transistor in an emitter-follower configuration with a fuse in series with the emitter. A bipolar element with a fusible link is shown in Fig. 2.9-1. The fuse is typically nichrome or polycrystalline silicon. When the word line is selected, the transistor is turned on. If the fuse is intact, the bit line is pulled toward 5 V (V_{CC}); if the fuse is blown or open, the bit line is left floating.

Fusible link PROMs are programmed by selectively blowing the fuses in connecting elements. For example, with the polycrystalline fuse, pulse trains of 20–30 mA amplitude and successively wider duration are applied until the fuse is blown.

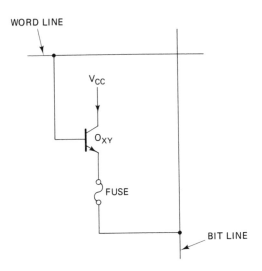

Figure 2.9-1. Typical fuse cell.

2.9.2 Floating Gate EPROMs

Floating gate EPROMs, extremely useful in the development of microprocessor systems, were introduced in 1971 by Intel. Intel's original device, the 1702, is a 256×8 memory using PMOS technology in a 24-pin package. EPROMs are designed with a unique memory cell which allows the memory contents to be erased and then reprogrammed. ROMs are available with identical pin assignments as EPROMs, and, therefore, when the control program in an EPROM is completely debugged, its contents can be used to specify a mask programmed ROM for final production runs. Thus, advantage can be taken of the low cost of mask programmed ROMs for high volume products without risking the quantity production of incorrectly programmed ROMs.

The storage element in the 1702 EPROM is a floating gate, avalanche, injection, charge storage device. The device is essentially a silicon gate, MOS field effect transistor with no connection to the silicon gate. [6, 7, 8] The structure and electrical symbol for this floating gate device are shown in Fig. 2.9-2(a). To store a logic 1 in the cell, a voltage pulse of -35 V is applied between the source and the drain and results in the injection of high energy electrons from the p-n junction surface avalanche region into the floating silicon

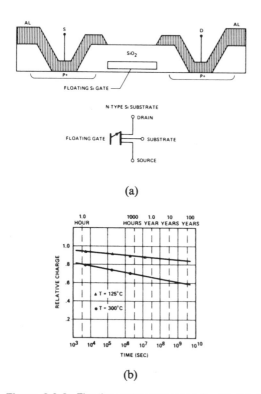

(a)

(b)

Figure 2.9-2. Floating gate memory: (a) cell; (b) decay curves. (Courtesy of Intel Corp.)

gate. The amount of charge stored is a function of the amplitude and duration of the applied voltage. When the applied voltage is removed, there is no conduction path for the accumulated charge; therefore, it remains on the gate. Extrapolation of charge decay data indicates that 80 percent of the initially induced charge is retained for as long as 100 years at a temperature of 125°C. A plot of charge decay versus time for Intel's 1702 EPROM is shown in Fig. 2.9-2(b).

During programming the address and data inputs required for the 1702 are 0 and −48 V. This requirement and the requirement of a −35 V programming pulse complicate the circuitry required for programming. A later, stacked gate version of the floating gate device, used in the 2716—a 2,048 × 8 EPROM—results in a much simpler device in terms of programming. Address, data, and control inputs are all T²L levels, and a high voltage programming pulse is not used. To program the 2716, the address of the location to be programmed is applied to the address inputs, the data to be programmed is applied to the outputs of the 2716, and the program input is pulsed high for a 50 mS period. This process is repeated for each memory location. All 16,384 bits can be programmed in 100 seconds. Figure 2.9-3 shows the pin configuration, names, mode selection, and block diagram of the 2716.

Because the gate electrode is not electrically accessible in EPROM devices, the charge cannot be removed by an electrical pulse. However, the initial uncharged state of the cell can be restored by the application of ultraviolet light at wavelength 2,537 Å, which results in a photocurrent from the floating gate to

PIN CONFIGURATION

```
A7  [ 1       24 ]  VCC
A6  [ 2       23 ]  A8
A5  [ 3       22 ]  A9
A4  [ 4       21 ]  VPP
A3  [ 5       20 ]  CS
A2  [ 6       19 ]  A10
A1  [ 7       18 ]  PD/PGM
A0  [ 8       17 ]  O7
O0  [ 9       16 ]  O6
O1  [ 10      15 ]  O5
O2  [ 11      14 ]  O4
GND [ 12      13 ]  O3
```

PIN NAMES

A0−A10	ADDRESSES
PD/PGM	POWER DOWN/PROGRAM
C̄S̄	CHIP SELECT
O0−O7	OUTPUTS

MODE SELECTION

MODE \ PINS	PD/PGM (18)	C̄S̄ (20)	VPP (21)	VCC (24)	OUTPUTS (9-11, 13-17)
Read	V_{IL}	V_{IL}	+5	+5	D_{OUT}
Deselect	Don't Care	V_{IH}	+5	+5	High Z
Power Down	V_{IH}	Don't Care	+5	+5	High Z
Program	Pulsed V_{IL} to V_{IH}	V_{IH}	+25	+5	D_{IN}
Program Verify	V_{IL}	V_{IL}	+25	+5	D_{OUT}
Program Inhibit	V_{IL}	V_{IH}	+25	+5	High Z

BLOCK DIAGRAM

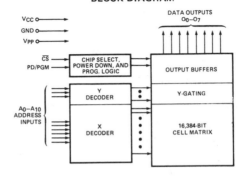

Figure 2.9-3. 2716 2 K × 8 UV erasable PROM. (Courtesy of Intel Corp.)

Figure 2.9-4. 2716 EPROM with transparent quartz lid. (Courtesy of Intel Corp.)

the silicon substrate. In the packaged memory device, the memory array is covered by a transparent quartz lid which seals the package but allows the device to be erased (see Fig. 2.9-4). With typical ultraviolet light sources, erasing Intel's 2716 requires approximately 20 minutes. The entire content of the memory is erased at once so that changes in a single word or bit are not possible. Some EPROMs, such as the 2716, when erased, have all bit positions equal to 1; during programming, 0s are programmed in.

2.9.3 PROM Programmers

A PROM programmer is an instrument which generates the address, data, and programming pulses required to program a PROM. Dedicated instruments program one type or generic family of PROMs. Universal PROM programmers, on the other hand, program any PROM by using an appropriate personality module (see Fig. 2.9-5). The personality module adapts the programmer to the unique programming voltages, currents, and pin configuration for a particular PROM.

PROM programmers are frequently microprocessor systems themselves. Figure 2.9-6 is a block diagram of the major subsystems in a typical universal programmer. The data to be programmed into the PROM is temporarily stored in R/W memory under the control of the microprocessor. Several modes of input are provided. For manual input a keyboard is used. The display indicates the entered data and the PROM address into which it is to be programmed. For machine input, interfaces are available which allow data entry from a paper tape reader, remote equipment, or a master ROM or PROM—a device already programmed with the desired data.

The PROM programmer's software can verify that a PROM is unprogrammed and allows editing of the data loaded into R/W memory before programming. It also generates the address, provides the data to be programmed, and controls the timing of the program pulses. The personality card for a particular ROM provides the higher voltage levels and pulses specifically required for that PROM and the pulse timing specified by the manufacturer. After programming, the PROM programmer ascertains whether the data was correctly written.

Figure 2.9-5. M900 universal PROM programmer with PM9052 personality module for programming 2716 EPROMs. (Courtesy of PRO-LOG Corp.)

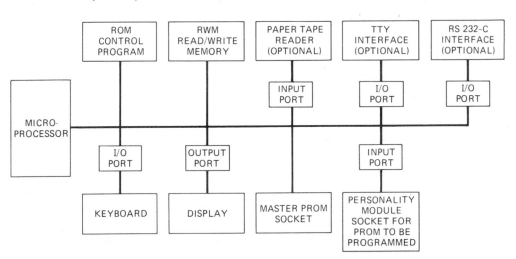

Figure 2.9-6. Block diagram of a typical universal PROM programmer.

Because fusible link PROMs cannot be completely tested before being programmed, parametric tests are particularly important. These tests, which check the PROM's output leakage current, worst-case supply voltage operation, and simulated high temperature operation, often are features of a PROM programmer.

2.9.4 EAROMs

Electrically alterable read only memories are technically RWMs with long write times and separate erase operations. For example, General Instrument's ER3400 is a 1,024 × 4 EAROM with a 1 mS write time, a 10 mS erase time, and a 900 nS read access time. [9]

In EAROMs, memory locations must be erased before they are written. Erasing is accomplished without removing the memory device from the circuit in which it operates by using a word erase mode or block erase mode. In the word erase mode, data at a single addressed location is erased. In the block erase mode, the erase operation is performed on all locations simultaneously.

EAROMs are used in applications which require not only nonvolatile memory but also require that the contents of the memory be altered occasionally in circuit. The ER3400, for example, can maintain its memory contents for 10 years without operating power.

One drawback of using EAROMs in designs is that a number of different voltage levels must be supplied to the device to accomplish erasing, writing, and reading. The generation and control of these voltages adds to the complexity of the circuitry required to support the memory's operation. The ER3400 requires three supply voltages: $+12$, -5, and -30 V.

An alternative to EAROMs for providing nonvolatile read/write memory is a volatile read/write memory with a battery backup. The battery provides power to the memory when the regular power supply is not operating. Under normal operation, such a memory is written at the typical R/W memory speeds rather than the much slower speeds of an EAROM. In addition, the numerous power supply voltages and their associated control circuitry required for the operation of an EAROM are eliminated. CMOS R/W memories are used with battery backup because of their extremely low power consumption.

2.10 READ/WRITE MEMORY

RWMs are used most often in microprocessor systems for storage of intermediate or temporary results during execution of the control program. The internal structure of a RWM is similar to that of a ROM, with some notable exceptions. In the memory array of the RWM, instead of connecting cells there are memory cells. Each memory cell is essentially a flip-flop (bistable multivibrator) which is capable of two stable states corresponding to the storage of either logic 0 or logic 1. Provision is made for quickly changing the state of each memory cell, i.e., writing in a 0 or a 1, and control signals determine whether data is read from or written into the addressed location. Since some type of flip-flop is used for the memory cell, the memory is volatile.

2.10.1 Bipolar RWM

The bistable flip-flop used as the memory cell in bipolar memories typically consists of a pair of cross-coupled multiemitter transistors (see Fig. 2.10-1). One transistor is always conducting, and the other is always cut off—except when the state of the flip-flop is being intentionally changed.

In the basic operation of this flip-flop, the bit lines are held at a higher voltage than is the unselected word line; in this condition, the emitters connected to the bit lines are reverse biased and do not conduct. However, one transistor still conducts through the emitter connected to the word line, while the other transistor is cut off. To read the state of the flip-flop, the word line voltage is raised, and the conducting transistor passes a current through the associated bit line which, in turn, is sensed to determine the state of the flip-flop. To write data, the word line voltage is again raised, and the voltage on one of the bit lines is lowered, causing the transistor associated with that bit line to conduct.

In the memory array all the cells in a column share the same bit line, and all the cells in a row have the same word line. Variations of this bipolar flip-flop exist, some using Schottky diodes in the structure and alternate gating means. Typical of these devices is the fact that one of the transistors is always conducting, causing power to be dissipated even when the memory cell is not selected.

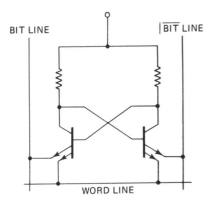

Figure 2.10-1. Bipolar flip-flop.

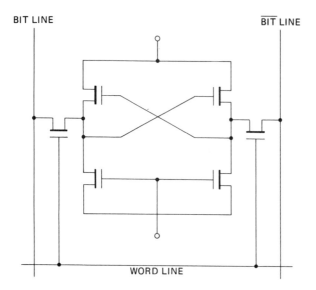

BIT LINE $\overline{\text{BIT}}$ LINE

WORD LINE

Figure 2.10-2. Static MOS flip-flop.

2.10.2 Static MOS RWM

A static MOS memory uses a MOS rather than bipolar flip-flop for the memory cell. The term "static" refers to the fact that as long as operating power is applied to the cell, it retains stored information indefinitely. Complex MOS static memory cells using six transistors are common. The circuit diagram of a typical memory cell is shown in Fig. 2.10-2.

2.10.3 Dynamic MOS RWM

The virtually infinite input resistance of a MOS field effect transistor provides the basis for another type of memory cell which uses the presence or absence of charge on the gate of a MOS transistor to store information for a finite length of time. The simplest such application of this concept uses a single transistor in series with a MOS storage capacitor (see Fig. 2.10-3). The transistor acts as a switch and allows charge to flow either into or out of the capacitor when read or write select is activated. The voltage stored on the capacitor is rather small, requiring the use of sense amplifiers in this circuit. Due to junction leakage in the transistor, the cell has to be recharged before the voltage stored on the capacitor drops below the threshold level of the sense amplifier used. This requires the periodic occurrence of a refresh cycle, where the voltage on the capacitor is sensed (the state 1 or 0 determined) and that logic level rewritten into the cell.

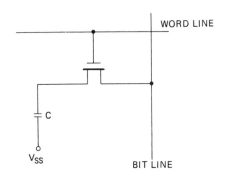

Figure 2.10-3. Single transistor MOS storage cell.

Where a refresh operation is required, the operation of the memory cell is dynamic. Additional circuitry is necessary to carry out the refresh operation. This overhead circuitry, which may be external to the memory device, adds to the cost of this type of memory. The advantage of using a dynamic memory cell is the small number of components required and, concomitantly, the small area required for the cell itself. Some variations of this type of memory cell use three or four transistors.

The preceding sections have given an overview of several types of semiconductor devices which implement memories. The bit capacity of these memory components continues to increase with advances in LSI technology: 64 K ROMs and 16 K RWMs on a single chip are readily available at present, and even larger devices are expected in the future. Memory speeds can be expected to increase and power dissipation to decrease.

REFERENCES

1. MANO, M.M., *Computer Logic Design*. Englewood Cliffs, New Jersey: Prentice Hall, Inc., 1972.

2. *MCS-85 User's Manual*. Santa Clara, California: Intel Corporation, 1978.

3. MATICK, R.E., "Memory and Storage," in H.S. STONE (Ed.), *Introduction to Computer Architecture*. Chicago, Illinois: Science Research Associates, Inc., 1975, Chapter 5.

4. ALFKE, P., and I. LARSEN (Eds.), *The T^2L Applications Handbook*. Mountain View, California: Fairchild Semiconductor, 1973.

5. VERHOFSTADT, P.W.J., "Evaluation of Technology Options for LSI Processing Elements," *Proceedings of the IEEE*, Vol. 64, No.6, June 1976, pp. 842–851.

6. FROHMAN-BENTCHKOWSKY, D., "A Fully Decoded 2048-Bit Electrically Programmable FAMOS Read-Only Memory," *IEEE Journal of Solid State Circuits*, Vol. SC-6, No. 5, October 1971, pp. 301–306.

7. GREENE, B., and D. HOUSE, *Designing With Intel PROMs and ROMs.* Santa Clara, California: Intel Corporation, 1975.

8. *PRO-LOG PROM Users Guide.* Monterey, California: PRO-LOG Corporation, 1975.

9. *General Instruments Microelectronics Data Catalog.* Hicksville, New York: General Instruments Corporation, 1978.

BIBLIOGRAPHY

ALTMAN, L., "Semiconductor Random Access Memories," *Electronics,* Vol. 47, No. 12, June 1974, pp. 108–110.

ALTMAN, L. (Ed.), *Large Scale Integration,* Electronics Book Series. New York: McGraw-Hill Book Company, 1976.

BOND, J., "Designing Memories with 4 K RAMs Will be Easier than with 1 K Chips," *EDN,* Vol. 19, No. 13, July 1974, pp. 26–30.

DAVIS, S., "Selection and Application of Semiconductor Memories," *Computer Design,* Vol. 13, No. 1, January 1974, pp. 65–77.

"Designing Memory Systems Using the MM5267," (Application Note AN-144), *Memory Data Book.* Santa Clara, California: National Semiconductor, 1976.

FRANKENBERG, R.J., *Designers' Guide to Semiconductor Memories.* Boston: Cahners Publishing Company, 1975.

HODGES, D.A. (Ed.), *Semiconductor Memories.* New York: IEEE Press, 1972.

HOFF, M., "Designing with Semiconductor RAMs," Part I, *EDN,* Vol. 18, No. 15, August 1973, pp. 30–35.

HOFF, M., "Designing with Semiconductor RAMs," Part II, *EDN,* Vol. 18, No. 16, August 1973, pp. 50–60.

Intel Memory Design Handbook. Santa Clara, California: Intel Corporation, 1974.

KOEHLER, H.F., "Advances in Memory Technology," *Computer Design,* Vol. 13, No. 5, June 1974, pp. 71–77.

LUECKE, G., J.P. MIZE, and W.N. CARR, *Semiconductor Memory Design and Application.* New York: McGraw-Hill Book Company, 1973.

McDOWELL, J.J., "Improve ROM Systems with PROMs," *Electronic Design,* Vol. 22, No. 14, July 1974, pp. 92–96.

McDOWELL, J.J., "Large Bipolar ROMs and PROMs Revolutionize Logic and System Design," *Computer Design,* Vol. 13, No. 6, June 1974, pp. 100–104.

Semiconductor Memory Data Book. Dallas, Texas: Texas Instruments Incorporated, 1975.

SHANKS, R.R., "Amorphous Semiconductors for Electrically Alterable Memory Applications," *Computer Design,* Vol. 13, No. 5, May 1974, pp. 95–100.

SPRINGER, J., "Designers' Guide to Semiconductor Memory Systems," *EDN,* Vol. 19, No. 17, September 1974, pp. 49–56.

PROBLEMS

2-1. For the clock and data waveforms below draw the output waveform, Q, for a D-type flip-flop for each of the following types of triggering:
   a. positive edge triggered
   b. negative edge triggered
   c. positive level triggered. Assume $Q = 0$ initially.

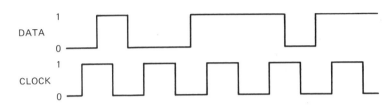

2-2. Give the number of address bits required to address any word in a memory which contains the following number of words.
   a. 1,024
   b. 4,096
   c. 512
   d. 8,192
   e. 64,536

2-3. List the hexadecimal equivalents of the following memory addresses specified in decimal:
   a. 123
   b. 750
   c. 2,048
   d. 6,743

2-4. A 256 × 4 ROM can be organized using linear selection or two-level decoding.
   a. Draw a block diagram of the logical organization of the ROM if linear selection is used.
   b. If two level decoding is used and the memory array consists of 32 physical words, draw a block diagram of the logical organization of the ROM; specify all appropriate parameters and the method of segmentation.

2-5. A 1,024 × 8 electrically reprogrammable read only memory uses a 64 × 128 memory array and two-level decoding. Determine the size and number of the row and column decoders necessary for this decoding, and draw a block diagram of the internal organization of this memory device.

2-6. Draw a block diagram of the internal structure of a 1,024 × 1 RWM which uses a square memory array and two-level decoding. List the size and number of all required decoders and the address inputs associated with each.

2-7. A 256×4 RWM has separate data input and output lines. The memory has three-state outputs controlled by the chip select. Whenever the memory is selected, the three-state outputs are enabled. Draw a logic diagram to show how this memory can be interfaced to a 4-bit bidirectional data bus using external three-state buffers. Assume the buffers are enabled with an active low control signal.

2-8. The 2114 is a $1,024 \times 4$ RWM with common I/O. Give the size of the memory array, and the number of row and column decoders required by this device. Also indicate an assignment of address lines to the row and column decoders.

2-9. Given any number of 256×4 ROMs, each having two chip select inputs—$\overline{CS1}$ and $\overline{CS2}$, sketch the logic diagram of a $1,024 \times 8$ ROM memory constructed with the 256×4 ROMs and a BCD-to-decimal (4-to-10) decoder with active low outputs.

2-10. A 256×8 RWM is implemented with semiconductor memory devices which are each 256×4, have common I/O, three-state outputs, and a single chip select input. This memory is interfaced to a bidirectional data bus. It is allocated to the memory space from 0000H to 00FFH and does not respond to any other addresses. The system address bus is 16 bits. Draw a block diagram of the memory system showing how the memory devices are interconnected. Show all other logic and control signals required.

2-11. The 2114, as indicated in problem 2-8, is externally organized as a $1,024 \times 4$ memory with common I/O. It has only two control inputs, $\overline{CS}$ and $\overline{WE}$. To read the device, $\overline{CS} = 0$ and $\overline{WE} = 1$. To write the device, $\overline{CS} = 0$ and $\overline{WE} = 0$. Design a $2\ K \times 8$ memory system using the 2114. This memory system should respond only to addresses 0400H to 0BFFH, and its inputs from the microprocessor are address lines A_0–A_{15}, bidirectional data lines D_0–D_7, and control lines $\overline{MEMR}$ and $\overline{MEMW}$. Draw a logic diagram of the memory system and label all connections. For address decoding use an 8205 or similar type of decoder. Implement all other logic with standard gates.

2-12. Draw the block diagram of the internal structure of a $2\ K \times 8$ ROM which uses two-level decoding. Use the optimal memory array size. Indicate the size of all decoders and the address inputs associated with each. How many physical and logical words exist in this memory organization? What is the segmentation value?

2-13. Construct a memory system which provides $1\ K \times 8$ of EPROM and 512×8 of RWM, using EPROM memory devices which are each 512×8 and RWM devices which are each 256×4. Each EPROM has one and each RWM two active low chip select inputs. The RWM devices also have an active high output disable input, OD, and a read/write control line $R/\overline{W}$. The inputs to the memory system consist of 16 address lines (A_0–A_{15}) and a memory read, $\overline{MEMR}$, and memory write, $\overline{MEMW}$, strobe. Draw the logic diagram showing the interconnection of the memory devices so that address 0000H to 03FFH corresponds to the EPROM and 0400H to 05FFH to the RWM. Use an 8205 decoder and any common gates to accomplish any necessary decoding.

2-14. The 2141 is a 4096 × 1 RWM. Determine the size of the memory array, and row and column decoders required inside this device. Also indicate the assigment of address lines to the row and column decoders that you would expect.

3

Microprocessor Architecture and Operation

'With circuits, which once would have filled many equipment cabinets, now reduced to a handful of ICs, the formerly awesome computer (in the form of a microprocessor) is today being looked upon simply as a system component, taking its place with power supplies, instruments, transducers, etc. Of course, the similarity exists only in size and possibly cost, not necessarily in complexity or importance.

Gerald Lapidus*

Copyright © 1974 by The Institute of Electrical and Electronics Engineers, Inc. Reprinted, by permission, from IEEE SPECTRUM, vol. 11, no. 3, March 1974, pp. 80–82.

The microprocessor is, of course, the central component in any microprocessor system. It controls the functions performed by the other system devices and provides the system's arithmetic and logic capability. The microprocessor fetches instructions from memory and decodes and executes them. It references memory and I/O devices for data and responds to control signals from external devices.

Control signals generated by external devices may cause the microprocessor to do any of the following:

1. Reset, so that program execution begins at some initial location.

2. Wait a sufficient amount of time to access a specified memory location.

3. Interrupt the current program execution and branch to a memory location where a subroutine, which services the external device causing the interrupt, begins.

4. Suspend its operation and float its address and data pins, allowing other devices to read or write memory directly.

In this chapter the basic concepts of the structure and operation of microprocessors are presented, and detailed examinations of Intel's 8085A and 8080A microprocessors illustrate the practical implementation of these concepts. The 8080A is studied because of its wide popularity, which is evidenced by the fact that it is second sourced by many manufacturers.[1] The 8085A is an enhanced version of the 8080A, which integrates on a single chip many of the required functions that are auxiliary to the 8080A. The 8085A is also widely second sourced[2] and finds widespread application in new designs.

3.1 BASIC MICROPROCESSOR CONCEPTS

The microprocessor system shown in Fig. 1.2-6 is redrawn in Fig. 3.1-1 to emphasize the most fundamental purpose of a microprocessor system: to process digital data which is input from the outside world and to provide as outputs digital data which is a desired function of the input data. Where data in analog form is to be processed or generated by the microprocessor system, suitable analog-to-digital and digital-to-analog conversion subsystems are employed to convert analog input data to the required digital form and vice versa. See Chapter 11.

While this purpose may seem so obvious that it need not be stated, it is for its effective, efficient, and economic accomplishment in different application

---

[1]The original manufacturer of the 8080A is Intel Corp.; second sources: Advanced Micro Devices, National Semiconductor, NEC Microcomputers, Texas Instruments, Hitachi, and Siemens.

[2]The original manufacturer of the 8085A is Intel Corp.; second sources: Advanced Micro Devices, NEC Microcomputers, and Siemens.

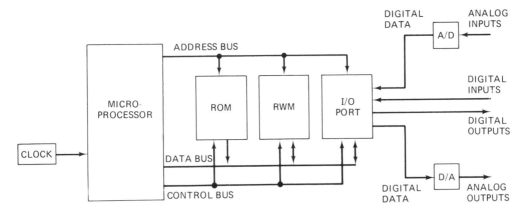

Figure 3.1-1. Microprocessor-based system with digital and analog inputs.

areas that all the various microprocessors and all the various system design techniques for using them have been developed.

To understand microprocessor systems, it is advantageous to view the entire system—microprocessor, ROM, RWM, and I/O ports—as a collection of addressable registers. Those registers which reside within the microprocessor are *internal registers*, and those which exist in the ROM, RWM, and I/O ports are *external registers*.

The collection of registers which constitutes a particular system and the data transfers which are possible among them comprise the *system architecture*. The types of registers in the microprocessor and the possible data transfers among them determine the *microprocessor's architecture*.

A microprocessor system implements its functions by *transferring* and *transforming* data in registers of the system. Typically, transformations on data occur in internal registers, many of which are operational registers. *Operational registers* differ from storage registers in that they and their associated circuitry implement arithmetic or logic operations on the data contained in the register, thus transforming the data.

The microprocessor controls and synchronizes the data transfers and transformations according to instructions read into it from the application program in the system's ROM.

The registers in the various subsystems of the microprocessor system are externally interconnected by the *system bus*, which includes the address bus, data bus, and control bus. A typical set of system bus signals is listed in Table 3.1-1. In this case, the system has a 16-bit address bus and an 8-bit data bus. The remaining signals are part of the control bus. Generally, the control bus contains additional signals which are considered in later chapters.

Two equivalent sets of control signals for reading and writing external registers are listed. A particular system uses one or the other or both sets. One

TABLE 3.1-1

A Typical Partial Set of System Bus Signals

Name	Function	Number	Direction*
A_0–A_{15}	Address bus	16	Output
D_0–D_7	Data bus	8	Bidirectional
$\overline{RD}$	Generalized read strobe	1	Output
$\overline{WR}$	Generalized write strobe	1	Output
IO/$\overline{M}$	Status (I/O or memory reference)	1	Output
$\overline{MEMR}$	Memory read strobe	1	Output
$\overline{MEMW}$	Memory write strobe	1	Output
$\overline{I/OR}$	Input device read strobe	1	Output
$\overline{I/OW}$	Output device write strobe	1	Output
Reset	System reset out	1	Output

*The direction is specified with respect to the microprocessor.

set consists of the signals $\overline{RD}$, $\overline{WR}$, and IO/$\overline{M}$. $\overline{RD}$ and $\overline{WR}$ are generalized, active low read and write strobes.

The microprocessor provides an address on the address bus and timing signals on the control bus to synchronize the reading and writing of external devices. A read strobe, $\overline{RD}$, is generated by the microprocessor when it is ready to read data from memory or an input port. A write strobe, $\overline{WR}$, is generated by the microprocessor after the data it has placed on the data bus is stable and can be transferred to memory or an I/O port. The additional status signal, IO/$\overline{M}$, specifies whether an I/O device or memory is being addressed by the microprocessor for reading or writing.

Instead of a microprocessor directly generating $\overline{RD}$, $\overline{WR}$, and IO/$\overline{M}$, an equivalent but more specific set of strobes—memory read, $\overline{MEMR}$; memory write, $\overline{MEMW}$; I/O read, $\overline{I/OR}$; and I/O write, $\overline{I/OW}$—can be generated. These strobes are all active low.

In some system architectures, the second set of control signals is preferable to the first. This second set—$\overline{MEMR}$, $\overline{MEMW}$, $\overline{I/OR}$, and $\overline{I/OW}$—is easily derived from $\overline{RD}$, $\overline{WR}$, and IO/$\overline{M}$ signals. If advantageous, all seven control signals can be used in a single system.

External or peripheral devices which generate data for input to a microprocessor system are called *input devices*. Input devices include a large variety of electronic and electromechanical devices. These devices range in complexity from simple switches to other microprocessor systems which preprocess data before inputting it to the main microprocessor. Data generated by an input device is stored temporarily in a register until it can be read by the microprocessor (see Fig. 3.1-2). The loading of the input register with data is carried out by the input device. Once loaded with data, the input register can be read by the microprocessor.

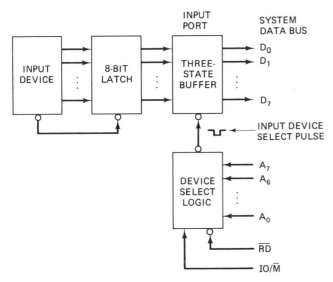

Figure 3.1-2. Simple input port for a microprocessor-based system.

In order to place the contents of an input register on the microprocessor system data bus, its outputs are connected to the data bus through a three-state buffer. This buffer is enabled by an ***input device select pulse***, obtained by gating the read strobe and the $IO/\overline{M}$ signal generated by the microprocessor on the control bus with a device address generated by the microprocessor on the address bus. The address is decoded by a decoder that passes the read strobe to the three-state buffer only if that buffer's unique address is present on the address bus. The resulting active low device select pulse for address XXH is denoted by $\overline{IDSPXXH}$. A read strobe is generated by the microprocessor when it executes an instruction inputting data from an input device. The strobe occurs during the instant of time that the microprocessor is ready to input the data on the bus. The input instruction also specifies the address placed on the address bus which selects a single input register from among many in the system.

The three-state buffer alone or the three-state buffer and its associated input register are referred to as an ***input port***. A single physical input device may contain more than one input port. In such cases, each input port still has a unique address. As discussed in Chapter 2, unique addresses are required to prevent bus conflicts which occur when two or more three-state buffers with common outputs are enabled simultaneously.

Output devices, of which there are a large variety, accept data from the microprocessor system. The data to be output from the system is placed in a register connected to the data bus. This register is called an ***output port*** and is clocked by an output device select pulse (see Fig. 3.1-3). The ***output device select pulse*** is obtained by gating the write pulse, $\overline{WR}$, with $IO/\overline{M}$ and the address on the address bus. The address of the output port for which the data is intended is

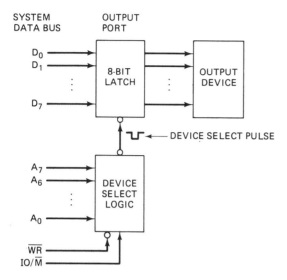

SYSTEM DATA BUS
OUTPUT PORT

D_0
D_1

8-BIT LATCH

D_7

OUTPUT DEVICE

DEVICE SELECT PULSE

A_7
A_6

DEVICE SELECT LOGIC

A_0

$\overline{WR}$
$IO/\overline{M}$

Figure 3.1-3. Simple output port for a microprocessor-based system.

part of the instruction which places data on the bus and creates the write pulse. The convention for representing an active low output device select pulse for output port XXH is $\overline{ODSPXXH}$.

In addition to its registers, the microprocessor contains two other major functional units—the control unit and the arithmetic/logic unit, ALU.

3.1.1 Control Unit

The microprocessor's control unit controls and synchronizes all data transfers and transformations in the microprocessor system and is the key sequential subsystem in the microprocessor itself. All actions attributable to the microprocessor are actions implemented by the control unit.

The control unit uses inputs from the master clock to derive timing and control signals which regulate the transfers and transformations in the system associated with each instruction. The control unit also accepts, as input, control signals generated by other devices in the microprocessor system, which alter the state of the microprocessor (see Fig. 3.1-4).

The basic operation of a microprocessor is regulated by the control unit, is cyclical, and consists of the sequential fetching and execution of instructions. Each instruction execution cycle has two primary states:[3] the fetch state and the execute state. The fetch state transfers an instruction from memory into the microprocessor, and the execute state executes the instruction. The microprocessor normally cycles between the fetch and execute states unless and until it executes a halt instruction, in which case it enters a halt state and stops (see Fig. 3.1-5).

[3]Each of these states actually consists of a number of substates.

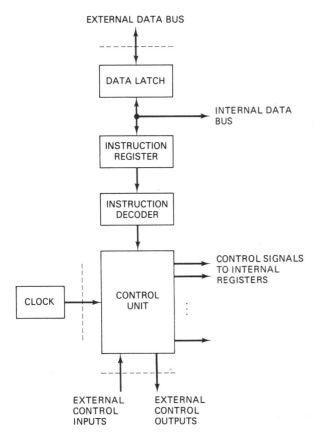

Figure 3.1-4. Microprocessor control unit, instruction register, and instruction decoder.

3.1.2 Internal Registers

To keep track of which instruction is to be executed next, the control unit maintains a special purpose or dedicated register, the *Program Counter, PC*, (see Fig. 3.1-6). The program counter is an operational register which always holds the address of either the next instruction to be executed or the address of the next word of a multiword instruction which has not been completely fetched. In either case, at the completion of the execution of any instruction, the program counter contains the address of the first word of the next instruction to be executed. The operational nature of the program counter allows its contents to be incremented by the control unit.

One of the control inputs to the microprocessor's control unit is the reset input. When the microprocessor is reset, the control unit sets the program counter to zero. This initial value establishes the memory address from which the first instruction is to be obtained.

To actually obtain the first word of the instruction, the address contained in the program counter is placed on the address bus. To do this, the control unit

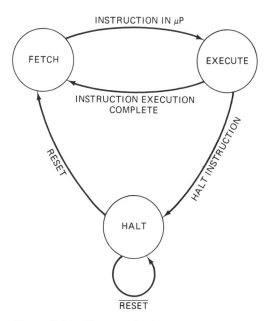

Figure 3.1-5. Alternate fetch and execute cycles of a microprocessor.

transfers the contents of the program counter to the **address register**. The program counter is then incremented to point to the next memory location. The outputs of the address register are the address pins of the microprocessor. The control unit then generates a memory read strobe which transfers the data from the addressed memory location to the microprocessor. The data is transferred into the microprocessor through the data bus buffer latch and then into

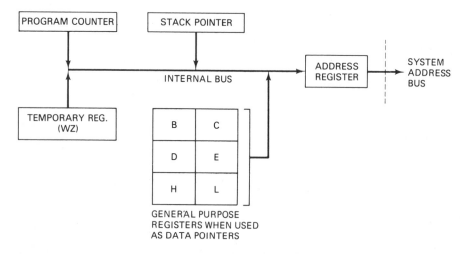

Figure 3.1-6. Various sources of addresses for the address register.

the *Instruction Register, IR*, (Fig. 3.1-4). Registers within the microprocessor are interconnected by an internal data bus.

The first word of an instruction is the operation code for that instruction. The *operation code* indicates to the control unit those operations required to execute the instruction. The output of the IR is decoded and used by the control unit to develop a sequence of operations and register transfers that execute the instruction.

The operation code in the IR addresses a starting location in a control ROM or PLA within the microprocessor where a sequence of very elementary instructions—microinstructions—is located. Each instruction in the fixed instruction set of a microprocessor is implemented by the control unit sequencing through the set of microoperations associated with a particular instruction. For single chip microprocessors, the microinstruction and thus the microprocessor's instruction set is fixed at manufacture.

Microprocessor instructions often require more information than can be provided in a single word of memory, which tends to be the case with 8-bit microprocessors. Therefore, it is common for instructions to consist of two or three words. The first word is always the operation code (OP code). The second and third bytes are data which represent either an address or a data constant. After the OP code is fetched and placed in the instruction register, its decoding indicates whether the instruction requires additional bytes of data. The bytes of multibyte instructions are contained in successive locations of memory.

To complete the instruction fetch, the additional bytes of the instruction remaining in memory must be copied into the microprocessor. Each memory read or write operation by the microprocessor is called a *memory reference*. If the instruction in question has 2 bytes, a second memory reference is required to input the second byte of the instruction to the microprocessor. The destination of this second byte of data depends on the particular instruction in question. Frequently, it is placed in a temporary register.

Temporary registers are used by the control unit to hold operands or addresses which are part of an instruction, until they are transferred to another register in the microprocessor or used as operands in a computation. For example, two temporary registers shown in Fig. 3.1-6 are labeled W and Z. Each of these is an 8-bit register. When a 3-byte instruction containing a 2-byte address is to be fetched into the microprocessor, the first byte, the operation code, is placed in the IR by the first memory reference. Two additional memory references obtain the two address bytes, which are placed in the temporary registers W and Z. Registers W and Z are used together as a register pair. During instruction execution, the address in W and Z is transferred to the address latch to address memory or I/O for a data transfer.

If additional general purpose storage registers are provided in the microprocessor, temporary results from computations can be stored internally, as opposed to storing them in external read/write memory. Instructions which transfer data between these general purpose registers require only a few bits to address the internal registers, since the number of internal registers is limited.

This results in a shorter instruction execution time because the instruction requires fewer bytes and fewer memory references are required to fetch it. In addition, the actual transfer of data between the accumulator and general purpose register does not require a memory reference, since the transfer takes place within the microprocessor.

To allow greater flexibility, instructions can carry out transfers between general purpose registers. The microprocessor in Fig. 3.1-6 has six 8-bit general purpose registers labeled B, C, D, E, H, and L. These registers constitute a register array. Registers in this array are used and operated upon either singly or in pairs.

The address of data to be transferred to or from the microprocessor can be kept in a pair of general purpose registers. Because these registers have a limited operational capability, instructions can increment or decrement their contents, but these instructions do not contain the source or destination address. Another instruction loads the register pair with the source or destination address, and subsequent instructions transfer data to or from the memory location corresponding to that address. The contents of the register pair are then incremented so the next data transfer involves the next consecutive memory location. When an instruction uses the address in a register pair as the source or destination address in a data transfer, that address is copied into the address latch during the memory reference in which the data transfer occurs. When used in this manner, the register pair is frequently called a ***data pointer***.

3.1.3 Arithmetic and Logic Unit

Arithmetic or logic operations on one or two operands constitute the basic data transformations implemented in a microprocessor. The microprocessor contains an ***Arithmetic and Logic Unit, ALU***, for this purpose. One of the two ALU registers, the ***accumulator***, holds one operand; the other, a temporary register, holds the second (see Fig. 3.1-7). The result of an arithmetic or logic operation is

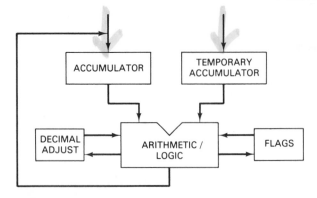

Figure 3.1-7. Arithmetic logic unit (ALU) consisting of the accumulator, temporary accumulator, flags, and logic for the arithmetic and logical operations.

placed in the accumulator at the completion of the operation, replacing one of the original operands.

The ALU is capable of performing the following operations on binary data:

1. Binary addition and subtraction.
2. Logical AND, OR, EX-OR.
3. Complement.
4. Rotate left or right.

The ALU also contains a number of flip-flops called *flags*, which store information related to the result of an arithmetic or logic operation. Taken together, these flags constitute a *flag register*. For example, a flag indicates whether a carry occurred out of the most significant bit after an addition operation; another flag indicates that the result left in the accumulator after some arithmetic or logic operation is zero. Most microprocessors contain several flags.

In many applications it is appropriate to represent data in binary coded decimal, BCD, form. The ALU shown contains additional logic to adjust the results of addition operations when the operands are interpreted as BCD data.

3.1.4 The Microprocessor's State

The body of information that completely describes the condition of the microprocessor at any point in the execution of a program is the *status* or *state* of the microprocessor. The state of a microprocessor becomes important when the execution of a program is interrupted and is later resumed. Consider the case of a microprocessor which has two separate programs in memory: task A and task B. At some point during the execution of task A, it is necessary to execute immediately task B. This transfer of control to task B requires that the PC be loaded with the starting address of task B. If, after the execution of task B is complete, task A had to be restarted from the beginning, the results of the processing before the interrupt would be lost. However, if the state of the microprocessor at the time of the interrupt is saved and later restored, processing is switched back to task A with no loss of the results of previous processing.

The information that constitutes the state of the microprocessor includes the contents of the PC, the accumulator, the flag register, and the general purpose registers. Saving and restoring the value of the program counter allows task A to be restarted with the next instruction after the one executed before the interrupt. Because the processing of program task B requires the accumulator, the flag register, and the general purpose registers, their task A contents are saved and later restored.

The interruption of sequential processing is initiated by the execution of a subroutine call instruction or by a signal from an external device. The subroutine call instruction causes a branch from one task to another—the subroutine. The address of the beginning of the subroutine is part of the call instruction. An external device may initiate a hardware interrupt, a branch, to a predetermined memory location when the external device requires servicing. The memory location branched to is the starting location for the interrupting device's service subroutine.

A *stack* is a storage structure in which a microprocessor saves its register contents during subroutine calls and interrupts. The stack consists of a group of specifically allocated locations in external read/write memory. A *stack pointer* is required to address a register or location in the stack. Depending on the convention used with a given microprocessor, the stack location is either the last location written into or the next location available to be written into. The stack pointer is designed in such a way that items are read from the stack in the reverse order from which they are written into it. This storage structure is referred to as a *Last-In, First-Out, LIFO*, stack. Access to data stored in the stack is, therefore, sequential, not random.

Writing data into a stack is called a *push* operation, and reading data from a stack is called a *pop* operation. To retrieve a data item pushed onto the stack, all subsequent data items on the stack must be retrieved first.

3.2 LSI IMPLEMENTATION OF MICROPROCESSORS

Various MOS technologies are used in the fabrication of microprocessors on a single IC chip. The first such microprocessors used PMOS technology and are referred to as "first generation devices." NMOS was used to fabricate second generation microprocessors and is presently the most prevalent technology. CMOS microprocessors are also available for applications requiring low power consumption.

Table 3.2-1 presents an overview of the evolution of MOS microprocessor development by presenting the characteristics of a few closely related microprocessors from among the many devices available.

The Intel 4004, introduced in 1971, was the first commercially available microprocessor. Its IC chip uses PMOS technology and measures 117×159 mils. The *instruction set* consists of 45 instructions, and the device is capable of carrying out a register to register addition in 10.8 μS. In order to have a complete microcomputer system, however, two other ICs are required: a 4001 ROM and a 4002 RWM. These special memory chips also contain I/O ports. This *family of devices* makes implementation of small systems possible with only three ICs.

Also in 1971, Intel introduced the first 8-bit microprocessor, the 8008. The 8008 also uses PMOS technology but a larger, 125×170 mil, IC chip. In addition to its larger word size, the 8008 is designed to be used with standard semiconductor ROM and RWM, allowing systems with large amounts of memory to be implemented more economically than with the 4004. The disadvantage of the 8008 is that it requires several additional external T^2L circuits,

TABLE 3.2-1

Microprocessor Hardware Evolution: Some Related Devices

	4004	8008	8080	Z80	8085A
Date	71	71	73	76	77
Class	4 bit	8 bit	8 bit	8 bit	8 bit
Technology	PMOS	PMOS	NMOS	NMOS	NMOS
Word size data/Instr.	4/8	8/8	8/8	8/8	8/8
Address capacity	4 K	16 K	64 K	64 K	64 K
Clock kHz/Phases	740/2	800/2	2,083/2	2,500/1	3,125/1
Add time	10.8 μS	20 μS	2 μS	1.6 μS	1.3 μS
Internal regs. ALU/GP	1/16	1/6	1/6	2/12/2	1/6
Stack size words/Bits	3 × 12	7 × 14	RWM	RWM	RWM
Voltages	15 or − 10, 5*	− 9, 5	− 5, + 5, 12	+ 5	+ 5
Package size	16 pin	18 pin	40 pin	40 pin	40 pin
Instructions	45	48	72 (includes 8008 instructions)**	158 (includes 8080 instructions)	74 (includes 8080 instructions)**
Chip size	117 × 159 mil	125 × 170 mil	164 × 191 mil	—	164 × 222 mil
# Chips/System (exclusive of memory and I/O)	1	12–20	3	2	1
Manufacturer (original)	Intel	Intel	Intel	Zilog	Intel

*The 4004 can be used with a + 15V supply or a − 10V, + 5 V supply.

**The number of basic instructions for the 8080 and 8085A is often given as 78 and 80 respectively. The numbers 72 and 74 are consistent with the instruction set listing in Appendix C.

for latching and interfacing, to provide a complete microprocessor. Depending on the degree of capability of the 8008 utilized, anywhere from 12 to 30 additional ICs are required, over and above those necessary for main memory.

Further advances in IC technology led to the introduction, in 1973, of the Intel 8080 microprocessor. The 8080 includes all 48 instructions of the 8008 plus 24 additional instructions, each of which implements an operation previously requiring several 8008 instructions. Thus, the 8080 is upward software compatible with the 8008. Upward compatibility of software allows savings in software development cost, which, in many designs, is the major system cost.

The technology used in the 8080 is the faster NMOS technology, and much of the external logic required with the 8008 is included on the 8080 chip. ICs were later introduced which included the remaining logic in two devices: a clock generator (8224) and a system controller (8228), resulting in a family of devices designed to be used together.

In 1976, Zilog introduced the Z80, an NMOS microprocessor which uses a single +5 V supply and has 158 instructions which include those of the 8080. In 1977 Intel introduced the 8085A, which combined the 8080 and its clock and system controller into a single package. The 8085A also requires only a single +5 V supply and has 74 instructions, including the 72 of the 8080. Table 3.2-1 indicates that as IC technology advances, microprocessors are produced that have greater capability and are easier to design into a system.

3.3 THE 8085A MICROPROCESSOR

The 8085A is an 8-bit microprocessor suitable for a wide range of applications. It is a single-chip, NMOS device implemented with approximately 6,200 transistors on a 164×222 mil chip contained in a 40-pin dual-in-line package. The package pins and their configuration are shown in Fig. 3.3-1.[1] The instruction set of the 8085A consists of 74 instructions.

The 8085A operates on a single 5 V power supply connected at V_{CC}; power supply ground is connected to V_{SS}. The frequency of the internal clock generator, which synchronizes the operation of the 8085A, is determined by a crystal or RC network connected at pins X_1 and X_2. The internal clock generator oscillates at twice the basic microprocessor frequency. A 50 percent duty cycle, two phase, nonoverlapping clock is derived from the oscillator. A 6.25 MHz crystal provides a 3.125 MHz internal clock frequency. A T^2L level clock output, CLK (OUT), derived from one phase of the internal clock, provides a clock signal which can be used for synchronizing external devices. Instead of a crystal or RC network, an external clock can be connected to X_1. The remaining package pins provide the address, data, and control signals.

An 8085A microcomputer system can be constructed with standard ROM and RWM or with specially designed ICs which contain memory and I/O ports.

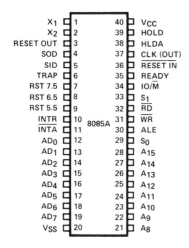

Figure 3.3-1. 8085A microprocessor pin configuration. (Courtesy of Intel Corp.)

Figure 3.3-2 shows a microcomputer system using standard ROM and R/W memory. The 8085A is capable of directly addressing up to 64 K memory locations with its 16-bit address. Eight of the 16 bits, A_8–A_{15}, are provided directly on the three-state address pins, A_8–A_{15}. The other eight bits, A_0–A_7, are provided on the bidirectional, three-state address/data pins, AD_0–AD_7. The address/data pins are time multiplexed: at times carrying addresses, at other times carrying data. Address information is provided on the address/data pins by the 8085A at the beginning of each memory reference, and is latched and held during the remainder of the memory reference to provide address bits A_0 to A_7. The 8-bit latch in Fig. 3.3-2 latches the address information from the address/data pins when clocked by the address latch enable signal, ALE. The 8085A generates this signal at the appropriate time when providing address information on its address/data pins. Time multiplexing of the address/data pins reduces the number of pins on the microprocessor package. At other times during a memory reference, a byte of data is transferred to or from the memory on the address/data pins. The 8085A generates two control pulses to indicate whether it is reading, $\overline{RD}$, or writing, $\overline{WR}$, an external register.

I/O ports are basically external registers. They can be treated as memory and written to and read from by any instruction that references memory. Alternatively, special instructions can read or write an I/O port. The 8085A directly addresses up to 256 input and 256 output ports, using special I/O instructions with an 8-bit address. This 8-bit address is repeated on pins AD_0–AD_7 and A_8–A_{15} when an I/O device is addressed, and, therefore, the I/O device need only decode one set of these identical address bits. Another control signal, $IO/\overline{M}$, generated by the 8085A indicates whether the microprocessor wants to read or write memory or I/O. When this signal is logic 0, memory is being referenced; when it is logic 1, I/O is being referenced. The

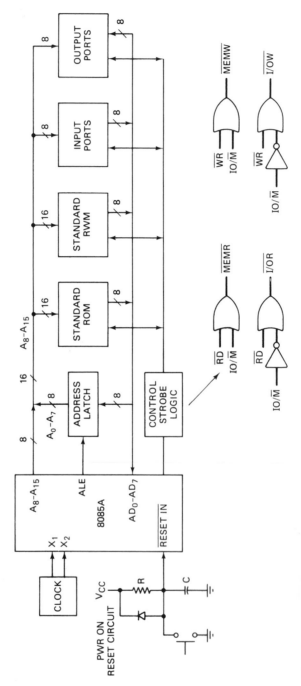

Figure 3.3-2. 8085A microprocessor system using standard ROM and R/WM.

signals $\overline{\text{RD}}$, $\overline{\text{WR}}$, and IO/$\overline{\text{M}}$ are used together in the system design to control the reading and writing of external memory and I/O ports. I/O ports and their design and operation are covered extensively in Chapter 8.

In Fig. 3.3-2, four active low control signals—memory read, $\overline{\text{MEMR}}$; memory write, $\overline{\text{MEMW}}$; I/O read, $\overline{\text{I/OR}}$; and I/O write, $\overline{\text{I/OW}}$—are derived from the $\overline{\text{RD}}$, $\overline{\text{WR}}$, and IO/$\overline{\text{M}}$ control signals provided by the 8085A, using OR gates and inverters. These particular signals are useful for control when using standard memory and I/O. For example the $\overline{\text{MEMR}}$ signal is logic 0 only when a read operation ($\overline{\text{RD}}$ = 0) from the memory (IO/$\overline{\text{M}}$ = 0) is taking place. The $\overline{\text{MEMR}}$ and $\overline{\text{MEMW}}$ signals are used to control the standard ROM and RWM, as shown in Fig. 3.3-2.

The functions of the other 8085A control signals are discussed later in this chapter and in later chapters when the topics to which they relate are presented.

3.3-1 Architecture of the 8085A

A block diagram of the internal architecture of the 8085A is shown in Fig. 3.3-3. The 8085A contains a register array with both dedicated and general purpose registers:

1. A 16-bit program counter (PC).
2. A 16-bit stack pointer (SP).
3. Six 8-bit general purpose registers arranged in pairs: BC; DE; HL.
4. A temporary register pair: WZ.

The 16-bit program counter fetches instructions from any one of 65,536 possible memory locations. When the $\overline{\text{RESET IN}}$ pin of the 8085A is made logic 0, the program counter is reset to zero; when the $\overline{\text{RESET IN}}$ pin is returned to logic 1, the control unit transfers the contents of the PC to the address latch, providing the address of the first instruction to be executed. Thus, program execution in the 8085A begins with the instruction in memory location zero.

8085A instructions are 1 to 3 bytes in length. The first byte always contains the operation code (OP code). During the instruction fetch, the first byte is transferred from the memory by way of the external data bus through the data bus buffer latch into the instruction register. The PC is automatically incremented so it contains the address of the next instruction if the instruction contains only 1 byte, or the address of the next byte of the present instruction if the instruction consists of 2 or 3 bytes.

In the case of a multibyte instruction, the timing and control section provides additional operations to read in the additional bytes. The timing and control section uses the instruction decoder output and external control signals to generate the state and cycle timing signals and signals for the control of external devices. After all the bytes of an instruction have been fetched into the microprocessor, the instruction is executed. Execution may require transfer of data between the microprocessor and memory or an I/O device. For these transfers, the memory or I/O device address placed in the address latch comes from the instruction which was fetched or from one of the register pairs used as a data pointer: HL, BC, or DE. The timing and sequencing of the 8085A are discussed in detail in the next section.

The six general purpose registers in the register array can be used as single 8-bit registers or as 16-bit register pairs. The temporary register pair, WZ, is not program addressable and is only used by the control unit for the internal execution of instructions. For example, to address an external register for a data transfer, WZ is used to hold temporarily the address of an instruction read into the microprocessor until the address is transferred to the address and address/data latch.

The 16-bit stack pointer, SP, maintains a pointer to the top of the stack allocated in external memory. The stack, as previously indicated, primarily supports interrupt and subroutine programming.

The 8085A's arithmetic logic unit, ALU, performs arithmetic and logic operations on data. The operands for these operations are stored in two registers associated with the ALU: the 8-bit *accumulator* and the 8-bit *temporary register*. The accumulator is loaded from the internal bus and can transfer data to the internal bus. Thus, it serves both as a *destination* and *source* register for data. The temporary register temporarily holds one of the operands during a binary operation. For example, if the contents of register B are to be added to the contents of the accumulator and the result left in the accumulator, the temporary register holds a copy of the contents of register B while the arithmetic operation is taking place.

Associated with the ALU is the 5-bit flag register, F, which indicates conditions associated with the results of arithmetic or logic operations. The flags indicate zero, a carry out of the high order bit, the sign (most significant bit), parity, and auxiliary carry (carry out of the fourth bit).

The 8085A's internal data bus is 8 bits wide and transfers instructions and data among various internal registers or to external devices through the multiplexed address/data bus buffer latch. The bidirectional, three-state *address/data bus buffer latch* isolates the microprocesssor's internal data bus from the external system address/data bus. In the output mode, the information on the internal bus is loaded into the 8-bit data latch which drives the address/data bus output buffer. The output buffers are floated during input or nontransfer operations. During the input mode, data from the external data bus is transferred to the internal data bus.

A serial I/O register and an interrupt control register are also shown in Fig. 3.3-3. These registers and their functions will be discussed in Chapters 8 and 9, respectively.

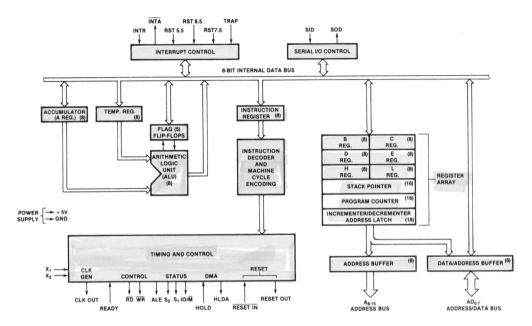

Figure 3.3-3. 8085A architecture. (Courtesy of Intel Corp.)

3.3.2 TIMING AND SEQUENCING

During normal operation, the microprocessor sequentially fetches and executes one instruction after another until a *halt* instruction (HLT) is processed. The fetching and execution of a single instruction constitutes an ***instruction cycle***, which consists of one or more read or write operations (references) to memory or an I/O device. Each memory or I/O reference requires a ***machine cycle***.

There are seven different types of machine cycles in the 8085A:

1. OPCODE FETCH
2. MEMORY READ
3. MEMORY WRITE
4. I/O READ
5. I/O WRITE
6. INTERRUPT ACKNOWLEDGE
7. BUS IDLE

Three status signals, IO/$\overline{\text{M}}$, S1, and S0, generated at the beginning of each machine cycle, identify each type and remain valid for the duration of the cycle. Figure 3.3-4 shows how the machine cycles are coded with these three bits.

MACHINE CYCLE			STATUS			CONTROL		
			IO/$\overline{\text{M}}$	S1	S0	$\overline{\text{RD}}$	$\overline{\text{WR}}$	$\overline{\text{INTA}}$
OPCODE FETCH	(OF)		0	1	1	0	1	1
MEMORY READ	(MR)		0	1	0	0	1	1
MEMORY WRITE	(MW)		0	0	1	1	0	1
I/O READ	(IOR)		1	1	0	0	1	1
I/O WRITE	(IOW)		1	0	1	1	0	1
ACKNOWLEDGE OF INTR	(INA)		1	1	1	1	1	0
BUS IDLE	(BI):	DAD	0	1	0	1	1	1
		ACK. OF RST, TRAP	1	1	1	1	1	1
		HALT	TS	0	0	TS	TS	1

Figure 3.3-4. Machine cycle and state information for the 8085A.

The instruction fetch portion of an instruction cycle requires a machine cycle for each byte of the instruction to be fetched. Since instructions consist of 1 to 3 bytes, the instruction fetch is one to three machine cycles in duration.

The first machine cycle in an instruction cycle is always an OPCODE FETCH, and the 8 bits obtained during an OPCODE FETCH are always interpreted as the OP code of an instruction. Note that to fetch an instruction, i.e., to transfer an entire instruction from memory to the microprocessor, always necessitates an OPCODE FETCH machine cycle. However, one or two MEMORY READ machine cycles are also needed to complete the fetch for 2- and 3-byte instructions, respectively.

The number of machine cycles required to execute the instruction depends on the particular instruction. Some instructions require no additional machine cycles after the instruction fetch is complete; others require additional machine cycles to write or read data to or from memory or I/O devices. The total number of required machine cycles varies from one to five, with no one instruction cycle containing more than five machine cycles. Machine cycles like the MEMORY READ or MEMORY WRITE may occur more than once in a single instruction cycle.

For example, the *store accumulator direct*, STA, instruction transfers the contents of the accumulator to an external register, whose address is part of the instruction. Since this register is located anywhere in the 64 K memory space that the 8085A can directly address, 16 bits are required for the address. Thus, the STA instruction contains 3 bytes: a 1-byte OP code and a 2-byte address. The instruction is stored in memory as follows:

OPCODE
LO ADDR
HI ADDR

Three machine cycles are required to fetch this instruction: OPCODE FETCH, transfers the OP code from memory to the instruction register. The

2-byte address is then transferred, 1 byte at a time, from memory to the
temporary register WZ; this calls for two MEMORY READ machine cycles.
When the entire instruction is in the microprocessor, it is executed. Execution
entails a data transfer from the microprocessor to memory. The contents of the
accumulator are transferred to the external register, corresponding to the
address previously transferred to the microprocessor by the preceding two
MEMORY READ machine cycles. The address of the memory location to be
written into is generated as follows: The high order address byte in temporary
register W is transferred to the address latch, and the low order address byte in
Z is transferred to the address/data latch. This data transfer is effected by a
MEMORY WRITE machine cycle. Thus, the 3-byte STA instruction has four
machine cycles in its instruction cycle:

Mnemonic	Instruction byte	Machine cycle
STA	OPCODE	OPCODE FETCH
	LO ADDR	MEMORY READ
	HI ADDR	MEMORY READ
		MEMORY WRITE

The timing and control section of the microprocessor automatically generates
the proper machine cycles required for an instruction cycle from information
provided by the OP code. Figure 3.3-5 shows the timing diagram of an STA
instruction.

Each machine cycle is divided by the system clock into a number of state
transitions, or T states, which correspond to the period between two negative
going transitions of that clock. Thus, one complete transition from state T_1
through the state diagram and back to T_1 constitutes a complete machine cycle.
A simplified state transition diagram for a machine cycle of the 8085A is given
in Fig. 3.3-6. Each machine cycle consists of three to six T states. Each T state,

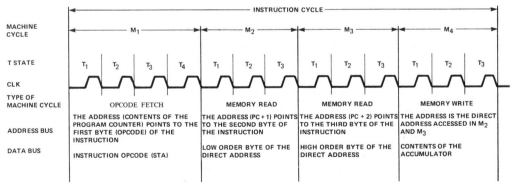

Figure 3.3-5. CPU timing for the Store Accumulator Direct (STA) instruction. (Courtesy of
Intel Corp.)

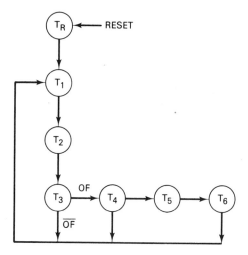

Figure 3.3-6. Simplified state transition diagram for the 8085A.

T_1–T_6, is one clock period (state time) in duration. Instruction cycles for various 8085A instructions require from 4 to 18 states. If a 3.125 MHz clock rate is used — a 320 nS state time—instruction execution ranges from 1.3 μS to 5.8 μS. This is the fastest speed at which the 8085A can be operated.[4] The slowest the 8085A can be operated is with a 2,000 nS state time.

The activities associated with each T state are listed in Table 3.3-1. Although the actual states traversed in a single machine cycle depend on the particular instruction and machine cycle within the instruction, the 8085A passes through at least three states in each machine cycle (T_1, T_2, and T_3). All OPCODE FETCH machine cycles consist of either four or six states. All other machine cycles consist of three states. As shown in the state diagram (Fig. 3.3-6), each machine cycle starts in state T_1.

During state T_1, the microprocessor loads the address lines (AD_0–AD_7 and A_8–A_{15}) with a memory address or I/O device address. During state T_2 of any machine cycle fetching a multibyte instruction, the program counter is incremented by one. And, during T_3 a data transfer from the microprocessor to the external data bus occurs, or vice versa, depending on the type of machine cycle.

> OPCODE FETCH: The OP code is transferred from memory to the instruction register of the microprocessor.
> MEMORY READ, I/O READ, or INTERRUPT ACKNOWLEDGE[5]: A data byte is transferred from the external data bus to the microprocessor.
> MEMORY WRITE, I/O WRITE: A data byte is transferred from the microprocessor to the external data bus.
> BUS IDLE:[5] No data is transferred on the external data bus.

---

[4]A faster version of the 8085A, the 8085A-2, can be operated at a 200 nS state time.
[5]The INTERRUPT ACKNOWLEDGE and BUS IDLE machine cycles are special cases and are detailed in Chapter 9.

TABLE 3.3-1

Activities Associated with the T States of the 8085A Microprocessor

---

T_1: A memory or I/O device address is placed on the address/data bus (AD_0–AD_7) and address bus (A_8–A_{15}). An Address Latch Enable, ALE, pulse is generated to facilitate latching the low order address bits on AD_0–AD_7. Status information is placed on $IO/\overline{M}$, S1, and S0 to define the type of machine cycle. The halt flag is checked.

T_2: Ready and hold inputs are sampled. PC is incremented if machine cycle is part of an instruction fetch.

T_W (optional): This state is entered if the ready line is low.

T_3: An instruction byte or data byte is transferred to/from the microprocessor.

T_4: The contents of the instruction register are decoded.

T_5–T_6: These states are used to complete the execution of some instructions.

At the end of a pass through the state diagram, a machine cycle is complete, and state T_1 is entered to start the next machine cycle. In the simplified diagram of Fig. 3.3-6, this process continues indefinitely, since no provision to stop instruction execution is shown.

For the STA instruction, the number of states required for each machine cycle is:

Instruction	Machine cycle	States
STA	OPCODE FETCH	4
	MEMORY READ	3
	MEMORY READ	3
	MEMORY WRITE	3
		13

STA has a total of 13 states. If the 8085A is operating at a 320 nS state time, the STA instruction cycle is executed in 4.16 μS. This time period is the instruction's execution time, although it actually includes both the instruction fetch and the execution times (see Fig. 3.3-5).

The timing diagram of an OPCODE FETCH machine cycle containing six states is shown in Fig. 3.3-7. The timing diagram for a four-state OPCODE FETCH is identical except that states T_5 and T_6 are omitted, and state T_4 is followed by state T_1 of the next machine cycle.

As Fig. 3.3-7 shows, at the beginning of state T_1 the $IO/\overline{M}$, S1, and S0 status signals indicate the type of machine cycle which has been initiated. For the OPCODE FETCH, $IO/\overline{M} = 0$, S1 = 1, and S0 = 1. This status information remains constant for the duration of the machine cycle. The 16-bit address, A_0–A_{15}, of the memory location containing the OP code is obtained from the PC and placed in the address and address/data latches. The high order byte of

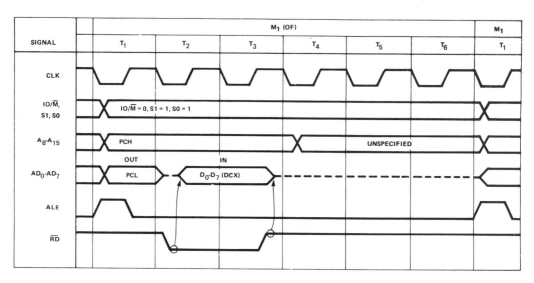

Figure 3.3-7. OPCODE FETCH machine cycle. (Courtesy of Intel Corp.)

the address appears on the address bus, A_8–A_{15}, and remains constant until the end of state T_3. During states T_4 through T_6, the data on the address bus is unspecified. The low order byte of the address is placed on the address/data bus at the beginning of T_1. This data, however, remains valid only until the beginning of state T_2, at which time the address/data bus is floated. The address latch enable, ALE, clocks an external register which latches the low order address byte on its falling edge.

During state T_2, the $\overline{RD}$ control signal goes low, and the OP code to be fetched is placed on the data bus by the addressed memory location. On the rising edge of the $\overline{RD}$ control signal in T_3, the OP code obtained from memory is transferred to the microprocessor's instruction register. During T_4 the 8085A decodes the instruction and determines whether to enter state T_5 or to enter state T_1 of the next machine cycle. From the operation code the microprocessor determines what other machine cycles must be executed to complete the instruction cycle. States T_5 and T_6, when entered, are used for internal microprocessor operations necessitated by the instruction.

MEMORY READ and I/O READ are similar to the OPCODE FETCH machine cycle. However, they use only states T_1 to T_3, and the status signal values appropriate for the particular machine cycle are issued at the beginning of T_1. For MEMORY READ and I/O READ, the source of the address issued during T_1 is not always the program counter but may be one of several other possible register pairs in the microprocessor, depending on the particular instruction of which the machine cycle is a part.

The MEMORY WRITE and I/O WRITE timing diagrams are similar to the corresponding read operations, except that the $\overline{WR}$ control, instead of $\overline{RD}$, goes low during T_2.

3.3.3 Memory and I/O Synchronization—The WAIT State

According to timing specifications for the 8085A, during a read operation the device providing data to the microprocessor must have valid data on the data bus within $((\frac{5}{2})T - 225)$ nS after the microprocessor provides a valid address at its address pins. For $T = 320$ nS, the memory or input device must have an access time of 575 nS or less.

Sometimes microprocessors are used with memories or I/O devices which have longer access times. In the case of memories, the lower the cost, generally the longer the access time. To accommodate longer access times, the 8085A has a state called the WAIT state, T_{WAIT}, shown in the state diagram of Fig. 3.3-8. When the microprocessor sends an address to memory or I/O in state T_1, external control logic can request that the microprocessor wait for a period of time equal to an integral number of clock periods. The external control logic does this by making the READY input to the microprocessor logic 0 during state T_2. When this input is logic 0, the microprocessor enters state T_{WAIT} instead of T_3. When the READY line becomes logic 1, the microprocessor's machine cycle continues.

The effect of entering a WAIT state is to hold all external signals from the microprocessor in the same state they were in at the end of state T_2. This stretches the duration of the address and the $\overline{\text{RD}}$ pulse, so devices with access times greater than 575 nS can be read. If N WAIT states are introduced into the machine cycle, the required access time is $((\frac{5}{2} + N)T - 225)$ nS. That is, for each clock period that the microprocessor is in the WAIT state, the instruction cycle time is increased by 320 nS. A single transition into the WAIT state increases the shortest instruction cycle time of the 8085A to 1.6 μS. The timing diagram of Fig. 3.3-9 shows a single WAIT state transition in a machine cycle. Sampling of the READY line in state T_2 and the transition into the WAIT state

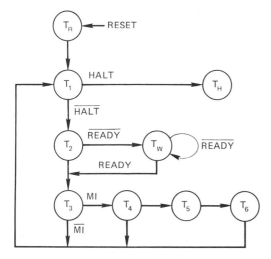

Figure 3.3-8. Simplified 8085A state transition diagram including T_{wait} and T_{halt}.

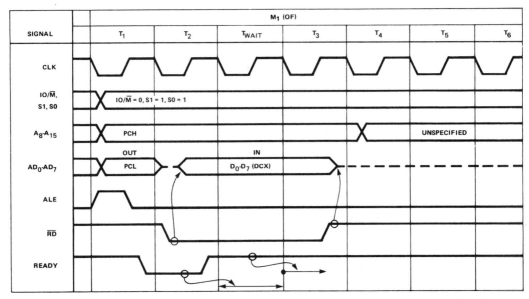

Figure 3.3-9. OPCODE FETCH machine cycle with one WAIT state. (Courtesy of Intel Corp.)

allow the microprocessor to synchronize to memories or I/O devices with slow access times. Concomitant, of course, is the associated cost of increased instruction cycle time and additional logic to control the READY input to effectively time out the necessary WAIT period.

For a write operation, the device receiving data from the microprocessor must be able to accept the data from the data bus within $((\frac{5}{2})T - 130)$ nS after the microprocessor provides a valid address at its address pins. Introduction of WAIT states during a write operation also extends the duration of the signals from the microprocessor, including the $\overline{\text{WR}}$ strobe.

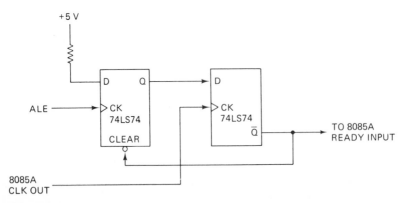

Figure 3.3-10. Logic for creating one wait state in each machine cycle of an 8085A microprocessor.

External logic controlling the READY line can be designed so that none, a variable number, or a fixed number of WAIT state transitions occur during each machine cycle. In Fig. 3.3-10, a simple logic circuit is shown which creates one WAIT state in each machine cycle. When the number of WAIT states varies, the address of the external register involved in the transfer is used by external logic to determine the number. This technique enables the use of both slow and fast memories and I/O devices in a single system. WAIT states can be introduced into any of the machine cycles except the BUS IDLE machine cycle.

External READY line control logic ascertains from IO/$\overline{\text{M}}$, S1, and S0 whether the present machine cycle is a MEMORY READ, MEMORY WRITE, I/O READ, or I/O WRITE. With this information, the logic which controls the READY line creates WAIT states for memory read operations, only, or for I/O write, only, etc.

3.3.4 The HALT State

The state transition diagram of Fig. 3.3-8 includes a provision to stop the microprocessor: the HALT state, T_{HALT}. Assume that an OPCODE FETCH machine cycle is initiated, and the OP code transferred to the instruction register during state T_3 is that of the halt instruction, HLT. During state T_4, the control unit decodes the instruction OP code and sets a halt flip-flop inside the 8085A. Upon exiting state T_4, the microprocessor enters state T_1 of the next machine cycle. As Fig. 3.3-8 indicates, the halt flip-flop is checked in state T_1 of the next machine cycle; if it is set, instead of entering state T_2, the HALT state, T_{HALT}, is entered. Thus, five states are required to reach the HALT state. In the HALT state, the address and address/data buses, along with ALE, $\overline{\text{RD}}$, $\overline{\text{WR}}$, and IO/$\overline{\text{M}}$ are placed in their high impedance states (floated). In this simplified diagram (Fig. 3.3-8), the HALT state can only be exited by resetting the microprocessor, causing the halt flip-flop to be reset and state T_1 to be entered.[6]

3.3.5 Power-ON Reset and Manual Reset

When power is first applied to a microprocessor, the various registers and flip-flops assume random states, and the operation of the microprocessor system is unpredictable. Therefore, the microprocessor must be reset when it is first powered up in order to fetch the first instruction.

The 8085A is not guaranteed to work until 500 μS after V_{CC} reaches its minimum operating voltage of 4.75 V. The microprocessor is automatically reset at power on by an *RC* circuit connected to the $\overline{\text{RESET IN}}$ input of the 8085A, as shown in Fig. 3.3-2. When power is first applied to the circuit, the voltage across the capacitor is 0 V. The capacitor charges, at a rate determined by *RC*,

---

[6]Two other ways of temporarily exiting the HALT state, not shown in this figure, are discussed in Chapter 9.

to a final voltage of V_{CC}. Values of R and C are selected to maintain RESET IN at the logic 0 level for the required amount of time.

Once the system is operating, it can be reset manually by the push button switch. Pressing this switch shorts the capacitor and discharges it. For proper resetting, the $\overline{\text{RESET IN}}$ input must remain at logic 0 for three clock pulses. Releasing this switch causes the capacitor to charge, bringing the $\overline{\text{RESET IN}}$ input back to logic 1.

Resetting the 8085A places it in the reset state, T_R, and clears the PC and IR registers and several flip-flops in the microprocessor, including the halt flip-flop. However, the A, F, B, C, D, E, H, and L registers are not cleared by resetting.

When $\overline{\text{RESET IN}}$ is logic 0, RESET OUT is logic 1. RESET OUT resets external devices in the microprocessor system. In the reset state, the same pins of the microprocessor which are floated in the halt state are again floated. When $\overline{\text{RESET IN}}$ becomes logic 1, the 8085A enters state T_1 of an OPCODE FETCH machine cycle and fetches the first instruction from memory location 0.

3.4 A MINIMUM CONFIGURATION 8085A MICROCOMPUTER

Three special peripheral components designed to be used with the 8085A allow small microprocessor systems to be configured around the 8085A using a minimum number of IC packages. One of these is the 8155, which contains 256 words of R/W memory, two 8-bit and one 6-bit I/O ports, and a 14-bit programmable timer, and is, itself, contained in a 40-pin DIP. The direction of the ports (in or out) is determined by a command word output to the 8155 by the application program.

The other two devices are pin compatible ROMs. One, the 8355, contains 2 K bytes of mask programmed ROM; the other, the 8755, contains 2 K bytes of EPROM. The EPROM device can be used during system development and in low-production quantity systems. For high-production quantity systems, once the software is debugged, the masked ROM can be used. Each of these devices also contains two 8-bit ports whose directions are programmable. All three of these devices have internal latches which use the ALE strobe to latch the low order byte of the address.

The 3-chip microcomputer system shown in Fig. 3.4-1 attests to the fact that design of the microcomputer portion of a system using this chip set is simple. Merely connect the corresponding signals! More than one 8355/8755 and 8155 can be used in a system by using address lines A_{11} through A_{15} to select the different devices. As the amount of memory required by a system increases, a point is reached beyond which the number of bits of I/O required does not increase proportionally. At this point, it is more cost effective to use standard ROM and R/W memory (see Fig. 3.3-2).

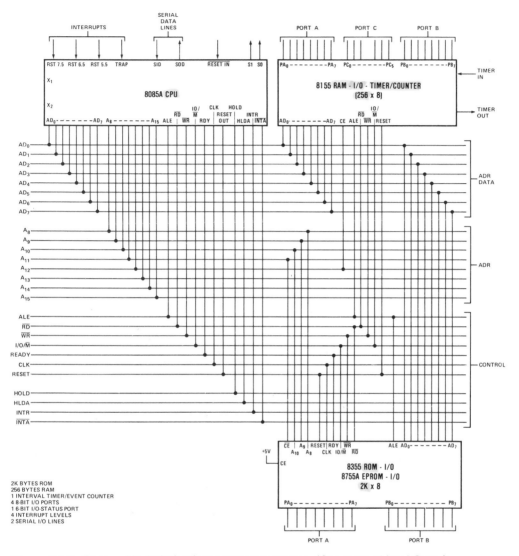

Figure 3.4-1. Three-chip 8085A microcomputer system. (Courtesy of Intel Corp.)

3.5 THE 8080A MICROPROCESSOR AND CPU GROUP

The 8080A is an 8-bit microprocessor and is the predecessor of the 8085A. It is a single-chip, NMOS device implemented with approximately 4,000 transistors on a 165×191 mil chip. [2, 3, 4] The chip is contained in a 40-pin dual in-line package. Sixteen pins of the 40-pin package provide three-state outputs (A_0–A_{15}) for addressing memory and I/O (see Fig. 3.5-1). Eight pins provide bidirectional three-state data (D_0–D_7) for data transfer and internal state information, and 10

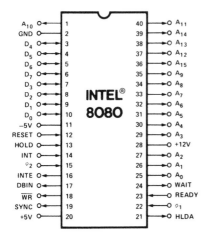

Figure 3.5-1. 8080 pin configuration. (Courtesy of Intel Corp.)

pins provide timing and control signals. These address, data, and control signals are all T^2L compatible. Voltages required for power are $+12$ V, $+5$ V, and -5 V.

The instruction set of the 8080A consists of 72 instructions, all of which are contained in the instruction set of the 8085A. Instruction execution times range from a minimum of 2 μS to a maximum of 9 μS when the microprocessor is driven at a 2 MHz clock rate. A block diagram indicating the architecture of the 8080A is shown in Fig. 3.5-2. Examination of this figure indicates that the registers of the 8080A are identical to those of the 8085A, with the exception of the interrupt control and serial I/O control, which are not contained in the 8080A. The function of each register in the 8080A is the same as the corresponding register in the 8085A.

The 8080A utilizes an external, two-phase clock to provide clock inputs ϕ_1 and ϕ_2 which, in turn, need pulses of 12 V amplitude. The ϕ_1 clock divides the processing cycle into states, a state being defined as the period between two positive going transitions of the ϕ_1 clock.

The 8080A requires additional ICs to support its operation, exclusive of the memory and I/O required in a system.

Two special ICs reduce the requisite number of IC packages. One is the 8224 clock generator and driver, shown in Fig. 3.5-3. Primarily this device provides the ϕ_1 and ϕ_2 clock signals for the 8080A. The 8224 needs a crystal with a frequency nine times greater than that of the desired clock signal.[7] The clock generator can accept an active low reset signal with a slow fall time, and, using Schmitt trigger circuitry, provide a fast rise time, active high reset to the 8080A. The 8224 also contains circuitry to synchronize wait requests from memory or I/O. This synchronization guarantees the setup and hold times needed at the READY input to the 8080A.

---

[7]The 8080A is nominally run at 2 MHz and, thus, the 8224 requires an 18 MHz crystal. Faster versions of the 8080A are available.

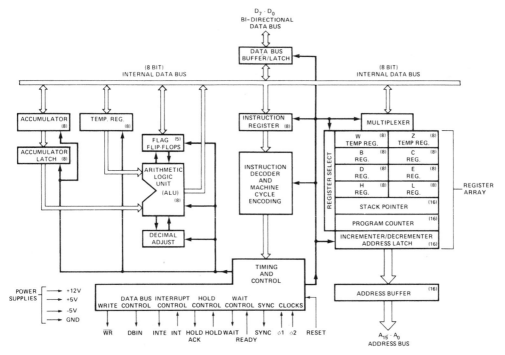

Figure 3.5-2. 8080A Functional block diagram. (Courtesy of Intel Corp.)

The 8080A provides signals which control the various memory and I/O devices connected to it. The 8080A does this in two ways: (1) by directly generating control signals (INTE, HLDA, DBIN, $\overline{WR}$, and WAIT) and (2) by providing status information on the data bus at the beginning of each machine cycle. The other support IC in Fig. 3.5-3 is the 8228 system controller and bus driver. Its primary purpose is generating control signals for external devices from the status and timing signals provided by the 8080A. For a complete microprocessor system, all that need be added to Fig. 3.5-3 is the memory and I/O. And, depending on the amount of memory required, drivers may be necessary on the address lines.

The state transition diagram of the 8080A differs from that of the 8085A. See Fig. 3.5-4. During T_1 of each machine cycle, the 8080A places on the data bus 8 bits of status information which identify that machine cycle. The 8080A has 10 different types of machine cycles:

1. OPCODE FETCH
2. MEMORY READ
3. MEMORY WRITE
4. STACK READ
5. STACK WRITE
6. INPUT READ

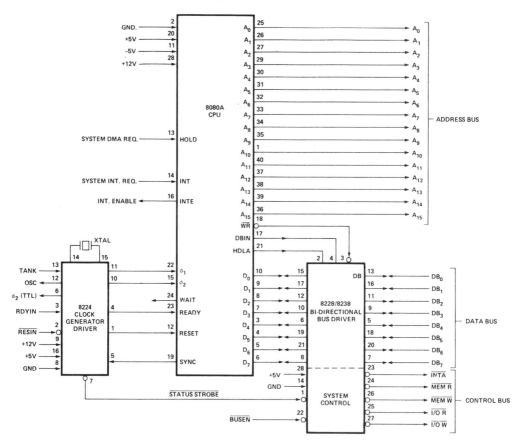

Figure 3.5-3. 8080A CPU group. (Courtesy of Intel Corp.)

7. OUTPUT WRITE
8. INTERRUPT ACKNOWLEDGE
9. HALT KNOWLEDGE
10. INTERRUPT ACKNOWLEDGE WHILE HALT

The eight status bits which identify these cycles, their symbols, and their definitions appear in Table 3.5-1. The relationship between these bits and the type of machine cycle is provided by the status word chart of Table 3.5-2. The status information appears on the external data bus at the beginning of each machine cycle and is available during the SYNC pulse. SYNC occurs during T_1 of each machine cycle following the rising edge of ϕ_2, as shown in Fig. 3.5-5, and is terminated by the rising edge of ϕ_2 during the second state. The SYNC pulse and the ϕ_1 clock pulse are used by the 8228 to latch the status information and hold it for the duration of the machine cycle. The 8228 gates bits D_0–D_7 and control strobe signals such as SYNC, DBIN, and $\overline{WR}$ to control memory and I/O devices.

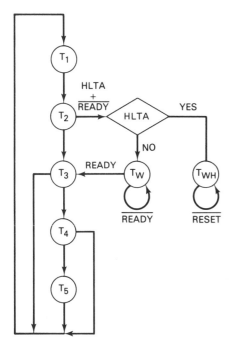

Figure 3.5-4. Simplified 8080A state transition diagram.

The data bus in, DBIN, signal from the microprocessor is an active high strobe which occurs during state T_3 of all machine cycles transferring data to the microprocessor. The pulse duration of this strobe is equal to one state time, 500 nS at 2 MHz. It indicates the time at which the bidirectional data bus is in the input direction and when input data should be placed on it.

The write signal, $\overline{WR}$, is an active low strobe which occurs during T_3 of all machine cycles where the bidirectional data bus is in the out direction and data output from the microprocessor is latched. This pulse is also one state time in duration. The durations of DBIN and $\overline{WR}$ are, of course, extended if the WAIT state is entered.

Five active low strobes generated by the 8228 synchronize and control all devices external to the microprocessor. These five strobes are:

1. Memory Read ($\overline{MEMR}$).
2. Memory Write ($\overline{MEMW}$).
3. I/O Read ($\overline{I/OR}$).
4. I/O Write ($\overline{I/OW}$).
5. Interrupt Acknowledge ($\overline{INTA}$).

These same strobes are obtainable from the 8085A by logically combining the IO/$\overline{M}$, $\overline{RD}$, and $\overline{WR}$ signals.

TABLE 3.5-1

Status Word Machine Cycle Relationship

Data Bus Bit	Status Information	Instruction Fetch (1)	Memory Read (2)	Memory Write (3)	Stack Read (4)	Stack Write (5)	Input Read (6)	Output Write (7)	Interrupt Acknowledge (8)	Halt Acknowledge (9)	Interrupt Acknowledge While Halt (10)
D_0	INTA	0	0	0	0	0	0	0	1	0	1
D_1	$\overline{WO}$	1	1	0	1	0	1	0	1	1	1
D_2	STACK	0	0	0	1	1	0	0	0	0	0
D_3	HLTA	0	0	0	0	0	0	0	0	1	1
D_4	OUT	0	0	0	0	0	0	1	0	0	0
D_5	M_1	1	0	0	0	0	0	0	1	0	1
D_6	INP	0	0	0	0	0	1	0	0	0	0
D_7	MEMR	1	1	0	1	0	0	0	0	1	0

(N) STATUS WORD

TABLE 3.5-2

Status Word Chart

STATUS INFORMATION

Symbols	Data Bus Bit	Definition
INTA*	D_0	Acknowledge signal for INTERRUPT request. Signal should be used to gate a restart instruction onto the data bus when DBIN is active.
$\overline{WO}$	D_1	Indicates that the operation in the current machine cycle will be a WRITE memory or OUTPUT function ($\overline{WO}$ = 0). Otherwise, a READ memory or INPUT operation will be executed.
STACK	D_2	Indicates that the address bus holds the pushdown stack address from the Stack Pointer.
HLTA	D_3	Acknowledge signal for HALT instruction.
OUT	D_4	Indicates that the address bus contains the address of an output device and the data bus will contain the output data when $\overline{WR}$ is active.
M_1	D_5	Provides a signal to indicate that the CPU is in the fetch cycle for the first byte of an instruction.
INP*	D_6	Indicates that the address bus contains the address of an input device and the input data should be placed on the data bus when DBIN is active.
MEMR*	D_7	Designates that the data bus will be used for memory read data.

*These three status bits can be used to control the flow of data onto the 8080 data bus.

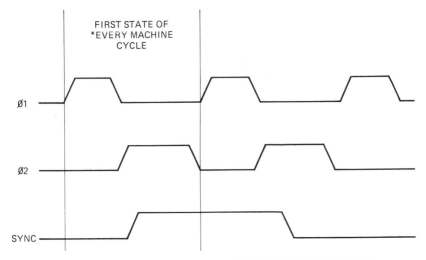

FIRST STATE OF
*EVERY MACHINE
CYCLE

Ø1

Ø2

SYNC

*SYNC DOES NOT OCCUR IN THE SECOND AND THIRD MACHINE
CYCLES OF A DAD INSTRUCTION SINCE THESE MACHINE CYCLES
ARE USED FOR AN INTERNAL REGISTER-PAID ADD.

Figure 3.5-5. ϕ_1, ϕ_2 and SYNC timing for the 8080A. (Courtesy of Intel Corp.)

A bidirectional bus driver is also contained on the 8228 which buffers the 8080A data bus from memory and I/O devices. The 8080A data bus has an input requirement of 3.3 V (minimum) for logic 1 and can only drive (sink) 1.9 mA. A typical T^2L device, on the other hand, has an output value of 2.4 V for logic 1. Thus, the direct connection of a T^2L device to the 8080A data bus requires pull up resistors. The output drive capability of 1.9 mA is just above the 1.6 mA of a single T^2L load. The data bus driver accepts T^2L levels on the system side of the data bus and provides the proper logic levels to the 8080A on the processor side. The data bus driver can sink 10 mA, so that a number of memory and I/O devices can be directly connected to the data bus.

3.6 SIMILARITY OF THE 8085A AND THE 8080A

Since the 8085A is an enhanced, upward compatible version of the 8080A, the two microprocessors are nearly functionally equivalent. Basically, the 8085A is a single-chip version of the three-chip combination of the 8080A microprocessor and its companion 8224 clock driver and 8228 system controller.

When the address data bus of the 8085A is demultiplexed with a latch, for use with standard memory and I/O, the resulting address and data buses are comparable to those of the 8080A. Additionally, the primary control signals—$\overline{\text{MEMR}}$, $\overline{\text{MEMW}}$, $\overline{\text{I/OR}}$, $\overline{\text{I/OW}}$, and $\overline{\text{INTA}}$—generated by the 8228 system controller can be derived from the IO/$\overline{\text{M}}$, $\overline{\text{RD}}$, and $\overline{\text{WR}}$ signals of the 8085A with a few gates. This results in a set of compatible control signals.

Since the 74 instructions in the 8085A instruction set include those of the 8080A, programs written for the 8080A can be run on the 8085A. In general, the execution times of such programs are different, even when clock frequencies are chosen which provide identical state times for the two microprocessors. This disparity is a result of differences in the number of states in the instruction cycles of identical instructions on the two machines. Because of this, software timing loops in a program written to run on one machine have to be adjusted to run on the other machine.

The two additional instructions in the 8085A instruction set support additional interrupt features available in the 8085A as well as its serial input and output. The instruction sets are essentially the same, with the exception of these two instructions and are called the "8085A instruction set" in this text. When the other two instructions are being used, the distinction is made clear.

REFERENCES

1. *MCS-85 Users Manual.* Santa Clara, California: Intel Corporation, 1978.

2. SHIME, M. and F. FAGGIN, "In Switching to n-MOS Microprocessor Gets a 2-Microseconds Cycle Time," *Electronics*, Vol. 47, No. 8, April 1974, pp. 95–100.

3. CUSHMAN, R.H. "Intel 8080: The First of the Second-Generation Microprocessors," *EDN*, Vol. 19, No. 9, May 1974, pp. 30–36.

4. *Intel 8080 Microcomputer Systems User's Manual.* Santa Clara, California: Intel Corporation, 1975.

BIBLIOGRAPHY

Intellec 8/Mod 80 Microcomputer Development System: Reference Manual. Santa Clara, California: Intel Corporation, 1974.

MANO, M.M., *Computer System Architecture.* Englewood Cliffs, New Jersey: Prentice-Hall, Inc., 1976.

NOYCE, R.N., "From Relays to MPUs," *Computer*, Vol. 9, No. 12, December 1976, pp. 26–29.

STONE, H.S. *Introduction to Computer Architecture.* Chicago: Science Research Associates, Inc., 1975.

TANENBAUM, A.S., *Structured Computer Organization.* Englewood Cliffs, New Jersey: Prentice-Hall, Inc., 1976.

PROBLEMS

3-1. Using NAND gates, draw the logic diagram of a circuit that generates the control strobes $\overline{\text{MEMR}}$, $\overline{\text{MEMW}}$, $\overline{\text{I/OR}}$, and $\overline{\text{I/OW}}$ from $\overline{\text{RD}}$, $\overline{\text{WR}}$, and $\text{IO}/\overline{\text{M}}$. See Table 3.1-1.

3-2. Using a single quad, 2-line-to-1-line multiplexer (e.g., 74LS257), draw the connections necessary to generate the control strobes $\overline{\text{MEMR}}$, $\overline{\text{MEMW}}$, $\overline{\text{I/OR}}$, and $\overline{\text{I/OW}}$ from $\overline{\text{RD}}$, $\overline{\text{WR}}$, and $\text{IO}/\overline{\text{M}}$. See Table 3.1-1.

3-3. Repeat problem 3-2 using an 8205 decoder.

3-4. Draw the logic diagram showing how an 8212 latch can be configured to function as an input port providing both the 8-bit latch and three-state buffer of Fig. 3.1-2. Assume that an active low device select pulse is provided.

3-5. Draw the logic diagram showing how an 8212 latch can be configured as an output port, as in Fig. 3.1-3. Assume that an active low device select pulse is provided.

3-6. An input device which has its own 8-bit latch is to be interfaced to an 8-bit bidirectional data bus. Draw the logic diagram illustrating how this can be accomplished with an octal three-state buffer (e.g., 74LS244).

3-7. Using an 8205 1-out-of-8 decoder and a minimal amount of additional logic, design a circuit to generate eight active low input device select pulses, $\overline{\text{IDSP(00H)}}$ to $\overline{\text{IDSP(07H)}}$. These eight pulses should correspond to the input port addresses 00H to 07H.

3-8. Using the same logic as in problem 3-7, generate and list eight active low output device select pulses, $\overline{\text{ODSP(00H)}}$ to $\overline{\text{ODSP(07H)}}$.

3-9. List the internal registers in an 8085A, their abbreviations and lengths. Describe the primary function of each register.

3-10. Give the clock out frequency and state time, T, of an 8085A operating with each of the following frequency crystals: 6.25 MHz, 6.144 MHz, 5 MHz, and 4 MHz.

3-11. From the written description of each of the following instructions (see Appendix C), list in their order of occurrence the machine cycles which constitute the following instruction cycles:
  a. MOV r_1, r_2 **1**
  b. LXI rp, data 16   **3**
  c. INR M   **3**
  d. LHLD addr   **5**
  e. XRA r   **1**

3-12. The instruction descriptions in Appendix C list the number of states in each instruction's instruction cycle. Give the instruction cycle time for each of the following instructions if the 8085A is used with a 6.144 MHz crystal.
  a. MOV r, M   **2,7**   *cycle, state*
  b. LDAX rp   **2,7**
  c. XCHG   **1,4**
  d. ADD r   **1,4**

3-13. An 8085A is operated with a 6.25 MHz crystal. If three instructions which normally consist of 4, 7, and 10 states are executed and external logic requests a single wait state for each machine cycle, what is the instruction cycle time for each instruction.

3-14. If external logic controls the READY line so that one additional state is introduced for each machine cycle, what is the instruction cycle time for each instruction in problem 3-12?

4

Data Transfer, Logic Operations, and Branching

The use of microprocessors, or MOS/LSI "computers-on-a-chip," requires programming skills. And that may seem to be a disadvantage. Hardware designers once concerned with such matters as latch selection, clock phases and propagation delay must now consider less familiar software-oriented factors like subroutine nesting, indirect addressing and computational algorithms.

Dennis C. Weiss*

*"Software for MOS/LSI Microprocessors," Electronic Design, Vol. 22, No. 7, April 1974, pp. 50–57.

Each subsystem in a microprocessor system—the main memory, the microprocessor, and the input/output devices—can be thought of in terms of the registers it contains. Random access semiconductor memory, of which the main memory is composed, is a collection of registers. A microprocessor itself consists of general purpose and dedicated registers. Input and output devices contain registers which hold their data.

The function of a microprocessor system is implemented by a sequence of data transfers between registers in the main memory, the microprocessor, and I/O devices and data transformations which occur primarily in registers within the microprocessor. Each register which can be manipulated under program control is addressable in some manner—allowing it to be singled out for use in a data transfer or transformation.

The kinds of individual transfers and transformations which are possible are specified by the microprocessor's *instruction set*. Each instruction in the set causes one or more data transfers and/or transformations. A sequence of instructions constitutes a software program. The control section of a microprocessor decodes the program instructions in turn, and, using timing signals derived from the system clock, controls what register transfers or transformations take place and when.

4.1 INSTRUCTION SETS

Each microprocessor is designed to execute a particular instruction set. The 8080A, for example, has an instruction set consisting of 72 basic instructions. Many, however, have variations increasing the actual number of distinct operations to 244. The 8085A contains 74 basic instructions: the 72 of the 8080A plus two additional ones, providing 246 distinct operations.

For the 8085A, instructions are 1 to 3 bytes in length. The bit pattern of the first byte is the OP code. This bit pattern is decoded in the instruction register and provides information used by the timing and control section to generate a sequence of elementary operations—microoperations—which implement the instruction. The second and third bytes, the instruction operands, are either addresses or constants.

It is common to divide an instruction set into groups of functionally similar instructions for ease in learning or evaluation. For the 8085A, one such grouping is as follows:

1. Data transfer group: instructions which move data between registers.
2. Logic group: instructions which carry out logic operations, such as AND, OR, or EX-OR, between data in the accumulator and a register, or rotate or complement data in the accumulator.
3. Branch group: instructions which change the execution sequence of a program, such as conditional and unconditional jump instructions and subroutine call and return instructions.

4. Stack and machine control group: instructions for maintaining the stack and internal control flags.

5. Arithmetic group: instructions which add, subtract, increment, or decrement data in the registers.

The actions which are the result of the execution of each instruction in an instruction set must be precisely specified. A commonly used method is *register transfer expressions*, which concisely represent the transfer of data among registers and the arithmetic and logic operations on data. They do not, however, include those register transfers required to fetch an instruction from memory to the microprocessor prior to its execution. Register transfer expressions are written in a *register transfer language*. There are many of these, and all have relatively similar forms. [1] Symbols used by Intel in their register transfer expressions are defined in Table 4.1-1.[2]

TABLE 4.1-1

Symbols and Abbreviations (Courtesy of Intel Corp.)

The following symbols and abbreviations are used in the description of the 8085A instructions:	RP — The bit pattern designating one of the register pairs B,D,H,SP:

SYMBOLS	MEANING
accumulator	Register A
addr	16-bit address quantity
data	8-bit data quantity
data 16	16-bit data quantity
byte 2	The second byte of the instruction
byte 3	The third byte of the instruction
port	8-bit address of an I/O device
r,r1,r2	One of the registers A,B,C,D,E,H,L
DDD,SSS	The bit pattern designating one of the registers A,B,C,D,E,H,L (DDD = destination, SSS = source):

RP	Register Pair
00	BC
01	DE
10	HL
11	SP

DDD or SSS	Register Name
111	A
000	B
001	C
010	D
011	E
100	H
101	L

rh	The first (high order) register of a designated register pair.
rl	The second (low order) register of a designated register pair.
PC	16-bit program counter register (PCH and PCL are used to refer to the high order and low order 8 bits, respectively).
SP	16-bit stack pointer register (SPH and SPL are used to refer to the high order and low order 8 bits, respectively).
r_m	Bit m of the register r (bits are number 7 through 0 from left to right).
Z,S,P,CY,AC	The condition flags: Zero, Sign, Parity, Carry, Auxiliary Carry.
( )	The contents of the memory location or registers enclosed in the parentheses.
←	"Is transferred to"
∧	Logical AND

rp — One of the register pairs:
B represents the BC pair with B as the high order register and C as the low order register;
D represents the DE pair with D as the high order register and E as the low order register;
H represents the HL pair with H as the high order register and L as the low order register;
SP represents the 16-bit stack pointer register.

∀	Exclusive OR	—	The one's complement, e.g., (A̅)
∨	Inclusive OR	n	The restart number 0 through 7
+	Addition	NNN	The binary representation 000
−	Two's complement subtraction		through 111 for restart number 0
*	Multiplication		through 7, respectively.
↔	"Is exchanged with"		

4.2 DATA TRANSFER INSTRUCTIONS

In instruction sets, many instructions are devoted to the transfer of data between two registers of a microprocessor system. One of the registers is always located in the microprocessor itself; the other may be located in:

1. An I/O device.
2. Main memory.
3. The microprocessor.

The various registers which make up an 8085A microprocessor system are shown in Fig. 4.2-1. Registers located in the microprocessor are referred to as internal registers, and those in I/O, RWM, or ROM are referred to as external registers. The register from which data is transferred is the source register, and the register to which data is transferred is the destination register. A transfer involves copying the contents of the source register into the destination register;

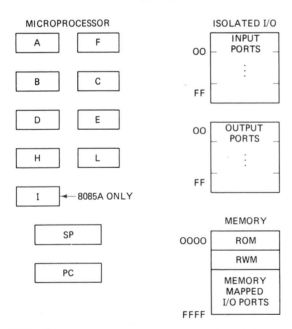

Figure 4.2-1. Register representation of an 8085A/8080A microprocessor system.

the contents of the source register are not altered. Each data transfer instruction identifies the source register and the destination register. Identification of one or both of these registers may be implied by the instruction mnemonics or may be explicit. Internal registers, for example, are frequently implied, whereas external registers are usually identified by an explicit address which is part of the instruction.

4.2.1 Data Transfers to and from I/O Devices

Data is transferred from the microprocessor to an output device in an output transfer and from an input device to the microprocessor in an input transfer. Output devices contain one or more registers, each of which is addressable and strobed by the microprocessor to latch the data on the data bus at the appropriate time during an output transfer. Input devices usually contain a register which holds the data to be transferred to the microprocessor and an addressable three-state buffer which is enabled by a strobe from the microprocessor at the appropriate time to place data on the data bus.

I/O structures fall into two categories—*isolated I/O* and ***memory mapped I/O***—and each is associated with a specific type of data transfer instruction. An isolated I/O structure uses special input and output instructions, and usually the number of devices addressable by these instructions is limited to a few hundred or less. Memory mapped I/O structures treat I/O registers as memory locations and use memory reference instructions to transfer data to them. All microprocessors are capable of memory mapped I/O. The 8085A, for instance, uses either or both isolated and memory mapped structures in a single system.

Two 8085A instructions are used for isolated I/O: IN for input to the microprocessor and OUT for output from the microprocessor. IN and OUT are the mnemonics for the OP codes. During execution, the *input* instruction places an 8-bit device address on the address bus, where it is repeated as both the low and high order address bytes. An external decoder decodes the device address, the IO/$\overline{\text{M}}$, and the $\overline{\text{RD}}$ strobe in order to generate an input device select pulse to enable the addressed input port's three-state buffer, thus placing the input port's data on the data bus. The register transfer expression for this operation is:

$$(A) \leftarrow (\text{port})$$

The parentheses mean "contents of a register," and the left arrow means "is transferred to." Thus, the register transfer expression indicates that the contents of the addressed input port are transferred to the accumulator. In assembly language, the instruction is written as follows, where port is the 8-bit address of the input port[1]:

IN port

---

[1] Instructions in this text are written in assembly language, and the bit patterns for the OP codes are represented by mnemonics. Addresses and constants are written symbolically or as decimal, octal, or hexadecimal numbers.

IN is a 2-byte instruction; the first byte is the OP code, and the second byte is the 8-bit input device (port) address:

OP CODE
PORT ADDRESS

With eight address bits, any one of 256 possible input devices is addressable with this instruction. If data is input from input port number 12, for example, the IN instruction is written:

IN 12

The destination register, the accumulator, is implied in the IN instruction, whereas the source register is identified by an explicit address which constitutes the second byte of this instruction. If the input device is a switch bank and three-state buffer, the address is used with $IO/\overline{M}$ and $\overline{RD}$ to generate an input device select pulse which enables the three-state buffer (see Fig. 4.2-2).

Data in the accumulator can be output to an I/O device using the 2-byte *output* instruction, OUT. Again, the first byte is the OP code, and the second byte is the 8-bit output port address:

OUT port
(port) ← (A)

In the OUT instruction the source register—the accumulator— is implied, and the destination register is explicitly identified by the port address, the second byte of the instruction. The output device decodes the address on the address bus in order to latch the output. For example, if the output device is a data latch and display, the decoded address is used with $IO/\overline{M}$ and $\overline{WR}$ to generate an output device select pulse for strobing the latch (see Fig. 4.2-3).

With only IN, OUT, and HLT, a simple data routing task can be carried out which inputs data from a switch bank and outputs it to two latches; reads data from a second switch bank and outputs it to two other latches; then halts.

IN	1
OUT	1
OUT	2
IN	2
OUT	4
OUT	5
HLT	

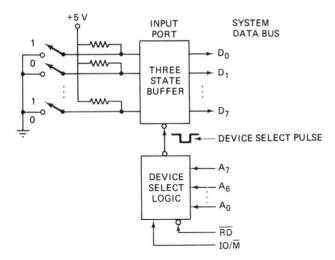

Figure 4.2-2. Simple input switch bank.

Numbers in the IN and OUT instructions are decimal, although numbers used in the assembly language representation of instructions can be decimal, binary, octal, hexadecimal, or symbolic. Binary numbers are written with a B suffix; octal numbers are written with an O or Q suffix; and hexadecimal numbers are written with an H suffix. Decimal numbers are represented with a D suffix or no suffix at all. This particular notation is compatible with Intel assemblers which are used in this text for examples. Symbolic names also represent numbers; for example, the previous program can be written

```
IN    ONE[2]
OUT   ONE
OUT   TWO
IN    TWO
OUT   FOUR
OUT   FIVE
HLT
```

Note that there are input and output devices with the same numbers. Both device address decoders respond to the same address; however, the input device's address decoder also requires the $\overline{RD}$ strobe to produce an output strobe, which limits response to the IN instruction. The output device's address decoder requires the $\overline{WR}$ strobe, which limits response to the OUT instruction. Thus, because of distinct strobes for reading and writing, the 8-bit device address can address 256 unique input devices and 256 unique output devices.

---

[2]The way in which the values associated with these names are assigned is discussed in Chapter 5.

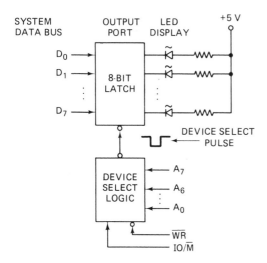

Figure 4.2-3. Output data latch and display.

The last instruction in the sample program is a *halt*, HLT. This single-byte control instruction, when executed, simply stops the microprocessor. If this instruction is not included in the program, the microprocessor fetches the contents of the memory location following OUT FIVE for decoding and execution.

Memory mapped I/O structures use memory reference instructions to transfer data to or from an I/O device. Although the term memory reference instruction applies to the group of instructions which transfer data to or from memory, these instructions, in fact, do not distinguish between an addressable register located in memory and one located in an I/O device. Thus, the same instructions which reference memory can be used for I/O if appropriate decoding logic is provided (see Chapter 8). These memory reference instructions use various **addressing modes** to identify the registers involved in the transfer of data. **Direct addressing** is conceptually one of the simplest methods of addressing because the instruction contains the address of the external register involved in the transfer. The 8085A provides a 16-bit memory address, requiring that the address contained in the instruction be 16 bits long. Thus, it must be a 3-byte instruction:

OP CODE
LOW ADDRESS
HIGH ADDRESS

For example, the *load accumulator direct* instruction, LDA, has the following assembly language representation:

LDA addr
(A) ← ((byte 3)(byte 2))

Here the address (addr) is 16 bits long. The effect of the instruction, as indicated by the register transfer expression, is to transfer 8 bits of data from the external register—identified by the 16-bit address contained in bytes 2 and 3 of the instruction—to the accumulator. The register transfer expression reads: "The contents of the register specified by the contents of bytes 2 and 3 of the instruction are transferred to the accumulator." The second byte of the instruction is the low order 8 bits of the address, and the third byte is the high order 8 bits. This reverse ordering of the address bytes is typical of all 8085A instructions that contain 16-bit addresses.

To transfer data from the microprocessor to a memory or output register, the *store accumulator direct* instruction is used.

$$\text{STA addr}$$
$$((\text{byte 3})(\text{byte 2})) \leftarrow (A)$$

These two instructions, LDA and STA, when used for I/O, function like IN and OUT instructions. A program equivalent to the previous examples, but using memory mapped I/O, can be written with the LDA and STA instructions:

```
LDA FIRST
STA FIRST
STA SECND
LDA SECND
STA FORTH
STA FIFTH
HLT
```

LDA and STA, however, have 16-bit addresses; thus, the number of addressable I/O registers is increased, at the expense of an additional byte required to specify the additional eight address bits.

Transfers to and from external registers using memory mapped I/O are not limited to the accumulator nor do they necessarily involve only a single byte of data. Two instructions which utilize direct addressing involve the H and L register pair and allow the transfer of 2 bytes of data during a single instruction cycle. Two bytes of data in consecutively numbered external registers are transferred to H and L with the *load H and L direct* instruction, LHLD.

$$\text{LHLD addr}$$
$$(L) \leftarrow ((\text{byte 3})(\text{byte 2}))$$
$$(H) \leftarrow ((\text{byte 3})(\text{byte 2}) + 1)$$

The 16-bit address contained in the instruction specifies the address of the source register for the transfer to register L. The source register for the transfer to H is simply the register with an address one higher than the address contained in the instruction.

To transfer data from H and L to two external registers with consecutively numbered addresses, the *store H and L direct* instruction, SHLD, is used.

SHLD addr
((byte 3)(byte 2)) ← (L)
((byte 3)(byte 2) + 1) ← (H)

Register indirect addressing is another addressing mode used by the 8085A. Here the address contained in the instruction specifies a register which contains another address, instead of the data itself. This second address is the actual or *effective address* of the external register involved in the transfer. In minicomputers and large computers, both of the registers involved in indirect addressing are usually external registers in RWM. With microprocessors, however, the register which contains the actual address of the operand is usually an internal register; this form of indirect addressing is called *register indirect, pointer*, or *implied addressing*. Since it contains the address of the external register, the internal register points to the external register. The internal register used as a pointer is implied by the instruction. Thus, a particular internal register is the pointer register for a particular instruction which uses register indirect addressing.

The H and L register pair is used as a pointer in many 8085A register indirect instructions (see Fig. 4.2-4). The H register holds the high and the L register holds the low byte of the effective address. The *move from memory* instruction, MOV r, M, transfers a single byte from any external register, M, to any one of the seven internal working registers, r. The specification of M as a register in the instruction actually means the external register pointed to by H and L.

MOV r, M
(r)←((H)(L))

The register transfer expression for this instruction indicates that the content of the external register whose address is in H and L is transferred to register r. The corresponding instruction for transfer in the opposite direction is the *move to memory* instruction.

MOV M, r
((H)(L)) ← (r)

Note that in MOV instructions, the destination register is written first, followed by the source register. Before these register indirect instructions are

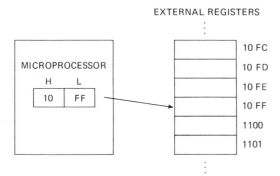

Figure 4.2-4. Function of the pointer register in register-indirect addressing.

used in a program, a previous instruction must load register pair HL with the appropriate address.

The register pairs BC and DE are also used as pointer registers in two 8085A instructions. The internal register involved in the transfer for these instructions is, however, always the accumulator. These instructions are *load accumulator indirect*,

$$\text{LDAX rp}$$
$$(A) \leftarrow ((rp))$$

and *store accumulator indirect*,

$$\text{STAX rp}$$
$$((rp)) \leftarrow (A)$$

Here rp stands for the register pair. Only rp = B (register pair BC) and rp = D (register pair DE) are allowable values in these instructions.

4.2.2 Additional Data Transfers to and from Memory

The direct and register indirect instructions, which transfer data to and from I/O registers when using memory mapped I/O, also transfer data to or from main memory. The operation of the instruction is the same, the only difference being that the 16-bit address is that of a location in main memory.

Another addressing mode, which transfers data from memory, is *immediate addressing*. With immediate addressing, the data transferred is part of the instruction. After the instruction's OP code is fetched, the program counter contains the effective address of the data. The simplest immediate addressing instruction is the *move immediate*. The second byte of this instruction is the data to be transferred to any general purpose register or to the accumulator.

MVI r, data
(r) ← (byte 2)

This instruction is used for loading a single register with a constant. To load a register pair with a constant, the *load register pair immediate* instruction is used:

LXI rp, data 16
(rl) ← (byte 2)
(rh) ← (byte 3)

The second byte of the instruction is the data to be placed in the low order register, and the third byte is the data for the high order register.

The *move to memory immediate* instruction, a combination of immediate and register indirect addressing, moves data in an instruction to a memory location pointed to by the H and L register pair.

MVI M, data
((H)(L)) ← (byte 2)

4.2.3 Creation of Additional Addressing Modes

Some microprocessors use other addressing modes that are not available via single instructions in the 8085A. However, these addressing modes can be synthesized by combining two or more 8085A instructions. In large computers and minicomputers the term *indirect addressing* traditionally refers to the use of a main memory location to contain the address of data, as opposed to having this address in an internal register—as in the register indirect addressing previously described. Conventional indirect addressing is implemented with two instructions, for example, for an indirect load:

LHLD addr
MOV r, M

The address of the data is contained in the memory location corresponding to the address (addr) in the LHLD instruction. LHLD loads the address of the data into the HL register pair, and the MOV instruction transfers the data from the memory location pointed to by HL to the internal register, r. To store data indirectly, only the MOV instruction is modified:

LHLD addr
MOV M, r

Another mode, ***indexed addressing***, is characterized by the effective address being the sum of a base address plus a displacement provided by an index register. The index register is usually incremented or decremented during the execution of a program to access a number of consecutive memory locations.

```
LXI B, BASE    ;  load BC with an initial base value
LHLD INDEX     ;  load HL from INDEX and INDEX + 1
DAD B          ;  add index contained in HL to BC
MOV r, M       ;  transfer data
```

The DAD B instruction adds the 16-bit register pairs HL and BC; the result is left in HL. The DAD instruction is described in detail in Chapter 7.

Indirect addressing and indexed addressing can be combined to provide indirect addressing with indexing. For example, to obtain a data value from a table, the indirect address provides the pointer to the beginning of the table, and the index register, an offset into the table.

4.2.4 Transfer of Data within the Microprocessor

Once data has been input to one of a microprocessor's registers, it is often necessary to move it to another register in the microprocessor. The *move register* instruction effects this transfer.

$$MOV \ r1, \ r2$$
$$(r1) \leftarrow (r2)$$

In this instruction, the variables r1 and r2 represent any of the six general purpose registers or the accumulator.

For example, some logic instructions (see Section 4.3) have two operands, each in a different internal register. One of the operands is always in the accumulator, and the other is always in one of the other internal general purpose registers. If the IN instruction inputs both operands from external registers, the first operand input must be transferred from the accumulator to another register before the second operand is input. Here r2 can be A, and r1 can be any of the registers but A. If register B is used for temporary storage of the first operand, the following instruction sequence can be used:

```
IN 1
MOV B, A
IN 2
```

If the same register is specified for both r1 and r2, execution of the *move register* instruction does not change the contents of any of the working registers but becomes a null operation. The only use for such an instruction is the generation of delays to allow a certain amount of time to elapse before the next instruction is fetched and executed.

Another data transfer instruction, *exchange H and L with D and E*, allows the contents of these two register pairs to replace each other. This instruction is very useful in alternately pointing to locations in different blocks of memory.

$$\text{XCHG}$$
$$(H) \leftrightarrow (D)$$
$$(L) \leftrightarrow (E)$$

Note that a double arrow in a register transfer expression indicates that the contents of the two registers are exchanged.

4.3 LOGIC OPERATIONS

In all of the logic instructions in the 8085A instruction set, except those operating exclusively on the carry flag, one operand is in the accumulator. In operations requiring two operands, the second operand may be contained in the instruction (as immediate data), in an internal general purpose register, or in an external register.

Information concerning the results of a logic or arithmetic operation, which is often needed by subsequent instructions for decision purposes, is indicated by the bits in a special register in the microprocessor called the flag register, F. The flag register operates as a 5-bit register: Only five of the bits can be set or reset; the other 3 bits have undefined values. The bits of the F register and their condition codes are:

BIT #	7	6	5	4	3	2	1	0	
	S	Z		AC		P		C	bits 5, 3, and 1 have undefined values.

Bits in the microprocessor's registers are labeled from right to left in ascending order. For 8-bit registers, the *most significant bit, msb*, is bit 7; the *least significant bit, lsb*, is bit 0.

S: Sign (bit 7): If the msb of the result is 1, this flag is set; otherwise it is reset.

Z: Zero (bit 6): If the result of an instruction is 0, this flag is set; otherwise it is reset.

AC: Auxiliary Carry (bit 4): If the instruction results in a carry out of bit 3 and into bit 4, this flag is set; otherwise it is reset.

P: Parity (bit 2): If the modulo 2 sum of the bits is 0 (even parity), the flag is set; otherwise it is reset.

CY: Carry (bit 0): If the instruction results in a carry (from addition) or a borrow (from subtraction or comparison) out of the high order bit, this flag is set; otherwise it is reset.

Certain instructions have no effect on some or any of the flags. For instance, the data transfer instructions affect no flags, whereas the *decrement register* instruction, DCR r, affects four—Z, S, P, and AC. Appendix C describes all 8085A instructions and lists the flags they affect.

Most microprocessor instruction sets, like that of the 8085A, include instructions for carrying out the logic operations NOT, AND, OR, and EX-OR. These operations are equivalent to those commonly used in logic design at the gate level, with one important exception: They are carried out on corresponding bits of 2 entire bytes of data for binary operations and on all the bits of a single byte for a unary operation.

The instruction which corresponds to the NOT operation is the *complement accumulator*:

CMA

$(A) \leftarrow (\overline{A})$ *Flags:* None

The 0 bits of the byte in the accumulator become 1, and the 1 bits become 0. Thus, every bit in the accumulator is complemented simultaneously. Another instruction complements a single bit of the flag register, the carry bit. This instruction is the *complement carry* instruction.

CMC

$(CY) \leftarrow (\overline{CY})$ *Flags:* CY

Another sets the carry: *set carry*,

STC

$(CY) \leftarrow 1$ *Flags:* CY

Execution of the *complement accumulator* instruction, CMA, affects none of the flags, and the *complement carry* instruction, CMC, and *set carry* instruction, STC, affect only the carry flag.

The contents of the accumulator can be ANDed bit by bit with a data byte, using any one of several forms of the AND instruction. The forms differ in terms of the source of the data byte. For instance, with the *AND immediate* instruction, ANI, the second byte of the 2-byte instruction contains the data to be ANDed with the accumulator. The *AND register* version, ANA, ANDs the contents of an internal register with the accumulator, and the *AND memory* ANDs the contents of an external register with the accumulator. The various versions are:

AND immediate	AND register	AND memory
ANI data	ANA r	ANA M
$(A) \leftarrow (A) \wedge (byte\ 2)$	$(A) \leftarrow (A) \wedge (r)$	$(A) \leftarrow (A) \wedge ((H)(L))$

Flags: All; CY is cleared[3]

The three AND instructions affect all of the flags. The carry flag is always cleared, and the sign, zero, and parity flags are set or cleared, depending on the result left in the accumulator.

The AND function is often used for **masking**. In masking, certain bits of a word are set to 0 or, in effect, removed. The bits of the mask byte corresponding to the accumulator bits to be removed (cleared) are set to 0; bits corresponding to those to remain are set to 1. To set to 0 the most significant 4 bits of a byte in the accumulator, the mask byte, 00001111 = 0FH, is used.

Consider as an example a situation in which ASCII data, representing a decimal digit, is input from the data output register of a UAR/T connected to a Teletype. The last 4 bits of the ASCII code for decimal digits are the binary equivalent of the decimal digit (see Appendix D). To store only this binary equivalent in a register, the most significant bits of the ASCII code must be removed. The following program segment accomplishes this, and the mask, is the second byte of the ANI instruction, 0FH.

IN 1
ANI 0FH

In some applications a logic instruction is used solely to set flags. For example, since data transfer instructions do not affect the flags, the instruction ANA A can be used after the transfer to set all the flags of the F register, except the carry. The flags are set based on the data in the accumulator without changing the value of that data, and the carry is set to 0.

Analogous to the AND are three versions of the OR instruction:

OR immediate	OR register	OR memory
ORI data	ORA r	ORA M
$(A) \leftarrow (A) \vee (byte\ 2)$	$(A) \leftarrow (A) \vee (r)$	$(A) \leftarrow (A) \vee ((H)(L))$

Flags: All; CY and AC are cleared

---

[3]The auxiliary carry flag is handled differently in the 8085A and 8080A microprocessors. The 8085A AND instructions always set the AC. In the 8080A, the AC flag takes the value of the logic OR of bit 3 of the two operands. The AND instructions are the one exception where flags are treated differently by the same instruction in the 8085A and 8080A.

The OR instructions are used to merge the bits of two operands; i.e., to set specific bits of the accumulator to 1. The accumulator is left with 1s corresponding to 1s in either of the operands. For example, the following program segment outputs as an ASCII character the binary equivalent of a decimal digit in register B:

```
MOV A, B
ORI 30H
OUT 0
```

To change a single bit of an output port without changing any other bits—a necessity when several bits of an output latch are controlling separate devices—a copy of the last control word output to the port, its image, is kept in memory, in location CWORD. To set the bit, bit 4 in this case, the following program segment is used:

```
LXI H, CWORD    ;   load address of control word into HL
MOV A, M        ;   transfer copy of present control word
                ;   to accumulator
ORI 10H         ;   set bit 4
MOV M, A        ;   update copy of control word
OUT PORT0       ;   output new control word to external latch
```

To reset bit 4:

```
LXI H, CWORD    ;   load address of control word into HL
MOV A, M        ;   transfer copy of present control word
                ;   to accumulator
ANI 0EFH        ;   reset bit 4
MOV M, A        ;   update copy of control word
OUT PORT0       ;   output new control word
```

The ORA A instruction is also frequently used to set the flags following a data transfer to the accumulator without altering the contents of the accumulator.

The EX-OR operation sets the bits of the accumulator for the bit positions where the two operands differ; the bit positions corresponding to those where the operands are the same are cleared. In other words, the bits of the accumulator which correspond to 1 bits in the data EX-ORed with the accumulator are complemented. The other bits in the accumulator are not altered. The three versions of EX-OR are:

EX-OR immediate	*EX-OR register*	*EX-OR memory*
XRI data	XRA r	XRA M
$(A) \leftarrow (A) \; \forall \; (\text{byte 2})$	$(A) \leftarrow (A) \; \forall \; (r)$	$(A) \leftarrow (A) \; \forall \; ((H)(L))$

Flags: All; the CY and AC are cleared

When data is EX-ORed with itself, the result is zero. XRA A EX-ORs the accumulator with itself, thus clearing the accumulator and the carry flag.

Frequently, an input port transmits status information to the microprocessor concerning one or more external devices or processes. To ascertain whether any change has occurred in the status of the external process, a copy of the previous status is kept in a memory location and compared with the present status:

```
LXI H, STATUS    ;   load HL with address of copy of past status
MOV B, M         ;   transfer copy of past status to register B
IN PORT1         ;   input present status
MOV M, A         ;   update status copy
XRA B            ;   test for status change
```

At the end of this sequence, the zero flag is set to 1 to indicate no change in the status or reset to 0 to indicate a change.

The comparison of 2 bytes to determine which is greater in terms of binary magnitude can be carried out in hardware by using MSI comparator circuits. The software equivalent of the hardware comparator is the compare instruction. This instruction compares 2 bytes, one of which is in the accumulator, by subtracting the second byte from it. This instruction is unusual in that neither of the bytes compared is altered. The compare instruction has three forms:

Compare immediate	*Compare register*	*Compare memory*
CPI data	CMP r	CMP M
(A) - (byte 2)	(A) - (r)	(A) - ((H)(L))

Flags: All; Z = 1 if (A) = (r); CY = 1 if (A) < (r)

After execution, the flag register is tested to determine whether the bytes are equal or, if unequal, which is greater. Assuming that the bytes of data being compared are interpreted as unsigned binary numbers, the zero flag is set if they are equal. If the content of the accumulator is greater than the byte with which it is compared, the carry flag is reset. Since the compare instruction is used exclusively for setting flags on which branch decisions are made, examples of its application are deferred until after branch instructions are introduced later in this chapter.

The remaining logic instructions in the instruction set are those which rotate the contents of the accumulator. The action of the *rotate accumulator left*, RLC, instruction is indicated by the following register transfer expressions and diagram:

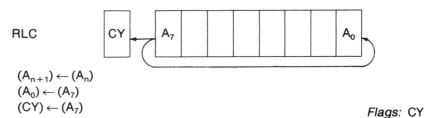

RLC

$(A_{n+1}) \leftarrow (A_n)$
$(A_0) \leftarrow (A_7)$
$(CY) \leftarrow (A_7)$

Flags: CY

When the RLC instruction is executed, each bit of the accumulator is shifted left, $(A_{n+1}) \leftarrow (A_n)$, and the most significant bit, A_7, is copied into the least significant bit, A_0, and into the carry, CY.

The corresponding rotate instruction in the opposite direction is the *rotate accumulator right*, RRC, instruction.

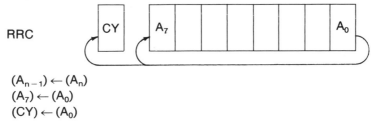

RRC

$(A_{n-1}) \leftarrow (A_n)$
$(A_7) \leftarrow (A_0)$
$(CY) \leftarrow (A_0)$

Flags: CY

Two other rotate instructions treat the accumulator and carry together, as if they constitute a 9-bit register. The *rotate accumulator left through carry*, RAL, instruction has the following form:

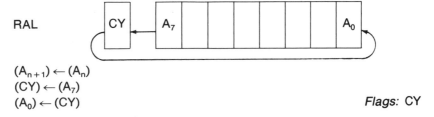

RAL

$(A_{n+1}) \leftarrow (A_n)$
$(CY) \leftarrow (A_7)$
$(A_0) \leftarrow (CY)$

Flags: CY

A 9-bit rotation in the opposite direction is implemented with the *rotate accumulator right through carry* instruction.

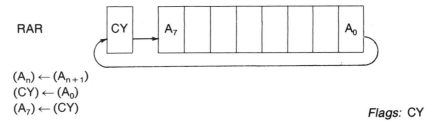

RAR

$(A_n) \leftarrow (A_{n+1})$
$(CY) \leftarrow (A_0)$
$(A_7) \leftarrow (CY)$

Flags: CY

Consider a situation where input port 7 inputs sequentially generated BCD digits, as the least significant 4 bits of a byte. After being input, the BCD digits are packed, two digits to a byte, and stored in main memory. The following program segment carries out part of this task: It inputs and packs two digits, leaving the result in the accumulator.

```
IN PORT7    ;   input most significant of the two digits
ANI 0FH     ;   clear most significant 4 bits of byte input
RLC         ;   shift BCD digit four places to the left
RLC
RLC
RLC
MOV B, A    ;   store shifted digit in B
IN PORT7    ;   input next digit
ANI 0FH     ;   clear most significant 4 bits of byte input
ORA B
```

4.4 FLOWCHARTING

Once the functions to be implemented in software have been defined, the designer selects or develops appropriate algorithms to affect their implementation. An *algorithm* is a computational or logical method of producing a desired result. The development and representation of an algorithm is facilitated by a *flowchart*, a graphic method of representing the order in which operations are carried out and the decisions which determine that order.

The flowchart is the software counterpart of the block diagram used in hardware design. In hardware design, the least detailed block diagram indicates the major hardware subsystems required to implement the overall system function and the information transfer among these subsystems. In software design, the least detailed flowchart indicates the major software subsystems required to implement the overall system function and their order of execution.

Just as the hardware designer must know the function and characteristics of MSI circuits in detail, the software designer must know the functions and characteristics of available instructions in similar detail. For an instruction, its function is represented by its register transfer expressions and a statement of the flags affected by its execution. The characteristics of an instruction are the number of bytes, machine cycles, and states associated with it.

In flowcharts a rectangle represents an operation or process, and a diamond represents a decision (see Fig. 4.4-1). An oval represents the beginning and/or the end of the instruction sequence. Abbreviated statements indicating the operations or decisions associated with each symbol appear inside it. The symbols are interconnected by directed line segments which indicate program

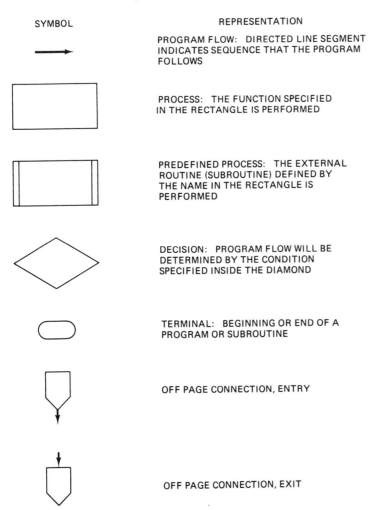

SYMBOL   REPRESENTATION

PROGRAM FLOW: DIRECTED LINE SEGMENT
INDICATES SEQUENCE THAT THE PROGRAM
FOLLOWS

PROCESS: THE FUNCTION SPECIFIED
IN THE RECTANGLE IS PERFORMED

PREDEFINED PROCESS: THE EXTERNAL
ROUTINE (SUBROUTINE) DEFINED BY
THE NAME IN THE RECTANGLE IS
PERFORMED

DECISION: PROGRAM FLOW WILL BE
DETERMINED BY THE CONDITION
SPECIFIED INSIDE THE DIAMOND

TERMINAL: BEGINNING OR END OF A
PROGRAM OR SUBROUTINE

OFF PAGE CONNECTION, ENTRY

OFF PAGE CONNECTION, EXIT

Figure 4.4-1. Flowcharting symbols.

flow, just as directed line segments in a hardware block diagram indicate information flow. In an overall system flowchart, rectangles and diamonds can represent small programs or subroutines. At the most detailed level, each symbol corresponds to a single instruction.

In the process of creating a program, a flowchart is first developed to represent the overall algorithm. This flowchart is progressively partitioned into more and more detail until each symbol can be converted into an instruction or group of instructions.

Knowledge of a set of basic program logic structures which can be combined to implement any algorithm or program facilitates the development of a

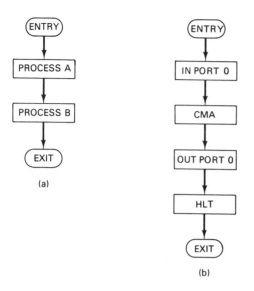

Figure 4.4-2. SEQUENCE structure. (a) Basic structure. (b) Example with four processes each consisting of a single instruction.

flowchart. Although these structures and their terminology derive from concepts typically applied to high level language programming, they are useful in studying assembly language program design. See Chapter 12.

The basis of structured programming is a set of logical structures, each of which has only a single entry and a single exit point. By combining these basic structures, more complex logical structures are formed which also possess a single entry/single exit point. The advantage of this technique is the development of programs which are more reliable and easier to understand, document, and modify.

The syntax of some high level languages directly supports the implementation of the basic logic structures in structured programming. When programming in assembly language, however, it is more difficult to adhere strictly to the structured programming concepts because implementation of the basic logic structures necessitates programs which themselves require many more instructions than their unstructured counterparts. However, it is helpful to study these basic structures and how they can be implemented in assembly language. In practice these logic structures and their variations are the foundation of program design.

The basic logic structures are:

1. The SEQUENCE structure.
2. The IF-THEN/ELSE structure.

3. The SELECT structure.

4. The DO-WHILE structure.

5. The DO-UNTIL structure.

These structures are themselves constructed from two elements: the process element and the decision element of Fig. 4.4-1. In a process element, control is transferred into the element, a process is performed, and control is transferred out of the element. In a decision element, control is transferred into the element, a condition is tested, and control is transferred out through one of two possible paths according to the condition.

The simplest basic logic structure consists of one or more process elements in sequence with a single entry and single exit (see Fig. 4.4-2). Each process can be as simple as a single instruction or as complex as an entire algorithm or program.

4.5 BRANCH INSTRUCTIONS

The program segments considered thus far are SEQUENCE structures involving the execution of instructions stored in consecutive memory locations. There are, however, instructions which change program control and fetch the next instruction from a memory location other than the next consecutive one. *Branch instructions* transfer program control by changing the value of the program counter to the address of a nonconsecutive instruction. The next OPCODE FETCH machine cycle uses this new address in the program counter to obtain the next instruction.

Some branch instructions are conditioned on a flag being set or reset by the execution of a previous instruction. These conditional branch instructions give the microprocessor its capacity for making decisions; i.e., its ability to execute one or another instruction or program segment, depending on previous results.

There are two types of branch instructions: jump instructions and call instructions. Jump instructions are considered in this section, and call instructions are considered in Chapter 6. The execution of an unconditional jump instruction alters the normal sequential program flow by replacing the contents of the program counter with the address contained in the jump instruction. This address is the location of the first byte of the next instruction to be executed, and thus control is transferred to the instruction whose address is specified in bytes 2 and 3 of the jump instruction. The *jump* instruction, JMP, has the form:

JMP addr

(PC) ← (byte 3)(byte 2)   *Flags:* None

In a conditional jump, transfer to the address contained in the jump instruction occurs only if a specified condition is satisfied. If the condition is not

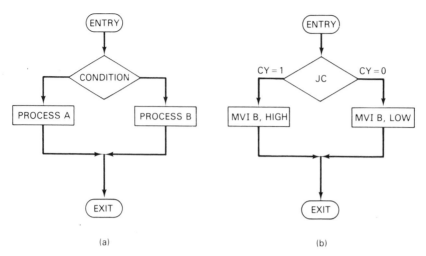

Figure 4.5-1. IF-THEN/ELSE structure. (a) Basic structure. (b) Example with the decision based on the carry value.

satisfied, program execution continues with the instruction following the jump. The conditional jump instruction allows the microprocessor to decide between alternative actions based on the results of previous computations.

Eight conditional jumps are included in the instruction set. The conditions are indicated by the flags of the F register. The *conditional jump* instructions have the general form:

J⟨condition⟩ addr

If ⟨condition⟩ = true, then

(PC) ← (byte 3)(byte 2)   *Flags:* None

Conditions:

NZ: not zero (Z = 0)
Z: zero (Z = 1)
NC: no carry (CY = 0)
C: carry (CY = 1)
PO: parity odd (P = 0)
PE: parity even (P = 1)
P: plus (S = 0)
M: minus (S = 1)

Conditional branch instructions are often used as decision elements in constructing basic logic structures. However, unlike the sequence element, a decision element cannot by itself be a basic logic structure because of the single entry/single exit requirement. A decision element has two exits.

A sequence element can be combined with one or two process elements to create an IF-THEN/ELSE structure, as shown in Fig. 4.5-1. Based on the condition tested, one of two possible processes occurs. One of the processes in Fig. 4.5-1 is a null process, which results in a simpler form of the IF-THEN/ELSE, the IF-THEN structure.

The following program segment, which incorporates an IF-THEN/ELSE structure, inputs a byte of data and determines whether it is less than, greater than, or equal to a previously determined threshold value stored in register B. The result is indicated by lighting one of two light-emitting diodes, LEDs, driven by output port 0. If the input is less than the threshold, bit 0 is set. If the input is greater than or equal to the threshold, bit 1 is set.

```
TEST:    IN PORT0
         CMP B
         JC LESS
         MVI A, 02H
         JMP DSPLY
LESS:    MVI A, 01H
DSPLY:   OUT PORT0
```

The selection of one process from among many possible processes is facilitated by nesting several IF-THEN/ELSE structures or simply by placing several IF-THEN/ELSE structures in sequence. Or, even more appropriate is the SELECT structure shown in Fig. 4.5-2. This structure tests data for multiple cases and selects the appropriate process for the given case. As the flowchart shows, SELECT has only a single entry and a single exit.

An instruction useful in creating a SELECT structure is the *move H and L to PC*, PCHL, instruction.

$$PCHL$$
$$(PCH) \leftarrow (H)$$
$$(PCL) \leftarrow (L) \qquad \qquad \textit{Flags: None}$$

This is actually a register indirect jump instruction. H and L contain the address to be branched to before the PCHL is executed. With the execution of PCHL, the program counter is set to the value of H and L.

The PCHL instruction can be used to create a *jump table*, which is another type of select structure. The jump table contains starting addresses of alternative processes. Each address has two bytes: The low order address byte is in the first location associated with that entry, and the high order byte is in the second. The

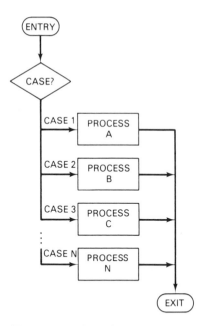

Figure 4.5-2. SELECT structure.

determination of which routine to branch to is based on a number which provides an index to the table. To maintain the single exit of a SEQUENCE structure, the last instruction of each routine is an unconditional jump to the same location.

For example, a small keypad on a controller contains eight keys. Each key is associated with a function that the controller carries out when the key is pressed. The input port associated with the keypad contains logic to encode the key pressed to a binary number in the range from 0 to 7. The following program segment implements the required branch:

```
LXI H, TBL   ;  load pointer to start of table
IN 0         ;  input encoded binary number
RLC          ;  multiply input value by two
MOV C, A     ;  create low order byte of offset
MVI B, 0     ;  set high order byte of offset to 0
DAD B        ;  add offset to H and L
MOV E, M     ;  place low order byte of jump address in E
INX H        ;  increment pointer to high order jump address
MOV D, M     ;  place high order jump address in D
XCHG         ;  exchange HL and DE
PCHL         ;  jump
```

4.6 PROGRAM LOOPING

A program loop is a sequence of instructions which is executed repeatedly. A jump instruction at the end of the loop transfers program control back to the beginning of the sequence. Conditional jump instructions provide a means for executing a loop a desired number of times and then exiting.

There are two basic loop structures: the DO-WHILE and the DO-UNTIL, both shown in Fig. 4.6-1. In the DO-WHILE structure, the condition which governs loop termination is first tested, and, depending on the results of this test, either the process is executed or the loop is exited. With this structure, it is possible to enter and exit the loop without ever executing the process. In the DO-UNTIL structure, when the loop is entered, the process is executed and the condition tested. Therefore, the process is always executed at least once when the loop is entered.

There are two methods for controlling the number of times a loop is executed. The first counts the number of passes through the loop. The second tests for some specific event and, when this event occurs, exits the loop. Because counting the number of passes through a loop also requires testing for an event —the occurrence of the required count—the methods may at first appear to be equivalent. However, in the first method, the number of loop executions that occurs is known before the loop is entered; in the second method, it is not.

The first method is simply referred to as *counting*. Counting requires that a register be loaded with some initial value and incremented or decremented for each pass through the loop. A conditional branch instruction determines when the counter register overflows or underflows and exits the loop.

The following arithmetic instructions increment or decrement a single register. The register can be one of the internal working registers or an external register:

Increment register	*Increment memory*
INR r	INR M
$(r) \leftarrow (r) + 1$	$((H)(L)) \leftarrow ((H)(L)) + 1$

Flags: Z, S, P, and AC

To decrement a register, the following instructions are used:

Decrement register	*Decrement memory*
DCR r	DCR M
$(r) \leftarrow (r) - 1$	$((H)(L)) \leftarrow ((H)(L)) - 1$

Flags: Z, S, P, and AC

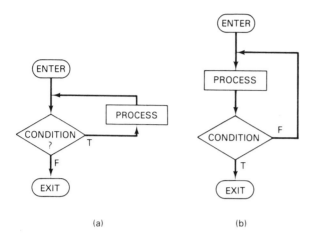

Figure 4.6-1. Loop structures: (a) DO-WHILE structure; (b) DO-UNTIL structure.

The increment and decrement instructions affect all flags except the carry, CY. Note that the flags are set to indicate the conditions associated with the register or memory location operated upon by the instruction. And for these instructions, the register operated upon is not necessarily the accumulator. It is reasonable to expect that if an 8-bit register containing FFH is incremented, the carry is set—analogous to incrementing an MSI counter and obtaining a carry out; however, this is not the case with the increment instruction. After incrementing the register, its contents are 00H, but the carry flag is unaffected. Thus, when incrementing a register, overflow is determined by testing for the register being zero.

Internal register pairs are incremented or decremented with a single instruction:

Increment register pair	Decrement register pair
INX rp	DCX rp
$(rh)(rl) \leftarrow (rh)(rl) + 1$	$(rh)(rl) \leftarrow (rh)(rl) - 1$

Flags: **None**

These two instructions have no effect on the condition flags. In general, no assumptions concerning the actions or effects of any instructions on the flags can be made; the instruction summary must be referred to for the effect of each instruction.

Either the DO-WHILE or DO-UNTIL structure can be used when counting. The DO-WHILE structure, when used for counting, is frequently called the **count-then-execute** method, and the DO-UNTIL is called **execute-then-count**. The choice determines the value used in presetting the registers to be counted. The two methods are flowcharted in Fig. 4.6-1.

The following DO-UNTIL structure inputs 10 bytes of data from input port DATA and stores them in a buffer area in memory.

```
INDU:   LXI H, BUFF   ; load HL pair with starting address of data buffer
                      ; in memory
        MVI C, 10     ; initialize the count
LOOP:   IN DATA       ; input data
        MOV M, A      ; store data in memory buffer location
                      ; pointed to by HL
        INX H         ; increment pointer to buffer
        DCR C         ; decrement counter
        JNZ LOOP      ; test for last data item
```

The same routine written as a DO-WHILE structure requires an initial value of 11 to input 10 data items:

```
INDW:   LXI H, BUFF
        MVI C, 11
LOOP:   DCR C
        JZ FINI
        IN DATA
        MOV M, A
        INX H
        JMP LOOP
FINI:
```

In other words, to loop N times using a DO-UNTIL structure requires an initial value of N. To loop N times in a DO-WHILE structure requires an initial value of $N + 1$.

If counting is not used, a special character must terminate the loop. In the following example the character used for this purpose is 0DH.

```
INXX:   LXI H, BUFF
LOOP:   IN DATA
        MOV M, A
        INX H
        CPI 0DH
        JNZ LOOP
```

The following routine incorporates SEQUENCE structures, an IF-THEN/ELSE, and a DO-UNTIL structure. In this particular program segment, the result is not a properly structured program, as is typically the case in practical assembly language programs.

This routine ascertains whether a 1 K EPROM is completely erased so it can be programmed. As such, this routine can be utilized in a microprocessor based EPROM programmer. The 1 K EPROM is plugged into a socket with 1,024 (400 H) locations starting at address EPRM0. When erased, the contents of the EPROM are logic 1. If the EPROM is completely erased, bit 0 of output port DSPLY is set; if not, bit 1 is set. These bits turn LEDs on or off to give a visual display of the result.

```
ERSD?:    XRA A          ;   clear accumulator
          OUT DSPLY      ;   clear LED display
          LXI H, EPRM0   ;   set up pointer to first EPROM location
          LXI B, 400H    ;   set up counter for number of EPROM
                         ;   words
NEXT:     MVI A, 0FFH    ;   set up constant for comparison
          CMP M          ;   compare constant with a word from
                         ;   EPROM
          JNZ NO         ;   if not equal, test is complete
          INX H          ;   increment pointer to next word
          DCX B          ;   decrement counter (does not set flag)
          MOV A, C       ;   move low byte of counter to A
          ORA B          ;   OR with high byte of counter—flags set
          JNZ NEXT       ;   if test not complete, loop
          MVI A, 01H     ;   test complete; set display to passed
          JMP DONE
NO:       MVI A, 02H     ;   set display to indicate not erased
DONE:     OUT DSPLY
```

4.7 SOFTWARE DELAYS

Counting can create time delays. Since the execution times of the instructions used in a counting routine are known, the initial value of the counter register required to obtain a specific time delay can be determined. The following example illustrates how the initial value for the counter register is ascertained.

Consider an output device which consists of a single flip-flop and a device address decoder. The address decoder uses the IO/$\overline{\text{M}}$ and $\overline{\text{WR}}$ signals so that the set-reset flip-flop is cleared by an OUT 0 instruction and set on an OUT 1 instruction (see Fig. 4.7-1). The output of the flip-flop is programmed to be logic 1 for a desired period of time, thus, implementing the hardware function of a single shot.

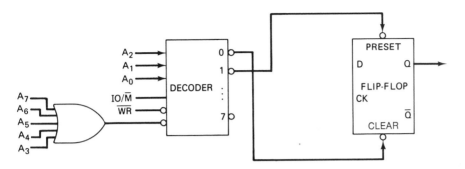

Figure 4.7-1. Setting and resetting an external flip-flop under microprocessor control.

The pulse duration of this single shot is controlled by the counting loop:

		Number of States	
		8085A	8080A
	MVI B, N	7	7
	OUT 1	10	10
LOOP:	DCR B	4	5
JZ FIN	7/10	10	
JMP LOOP	10	10	
FIN:	OUT 0	10	10

$N-1$ passes

The columns to the right of the instructions indicate the number of states in the execution cycle. Note that the same instruction executed on the 8085A and on the 8080A may involve a different number of states.

Consider first this program executed on an 8085A. There are $N - 1$ passes through the loop where the zero condition is not met, and each pass requires 21 states. Two state values are given for the conditional jump instruction's execution on the 8085A. When the condition is not met, 7 states are required for the instruction's execution, and when the condition is met, 10 states are required. The pass through the loop where the condition is satisfied and the flip-flop reset requires 24 states. Thus,

$$T = ((N - 1) * 21 + 24)t_s \quad \text{for } 0 < N \le 255$$
$$= (N - 1) * 21 * 320 \text{ nS} + 7.7 \text{ } \mu\text{S}$$
$$= (N - 1) * 6.7 \text{ } \mu\text{S} + 7.7 \text{ } \mu\text{S}$$

where

$$t_s = \text{duration of a single state} = 320 \text{ nS at } 3.125 \text{ MHz}$$

and

$$T = 255 * 6.7 \text{ } \mu\text{S} + 7.7 \text{ } \mu\text{S} = 1.72 \text{ mS} \quad \text{for } N = 0$$

The resolution for delays implemented with this program is 6.7 μS. The range of this delay is from 7.7 μS to 1.72 mS. Note that the longest delay occurs when N has the value zero because register B is decremented before testing it for zero. When $N = 0$, the loop is traversed 256 times.

If this same program is executed on an 8080A, there are $N - 1$ complete passes through the loop where the zero condition is not met; each pass requires 25 states. The pass through the loop where the condition is satisfied and where the flip-flop is reset also requires 25 states. This programmed delay is balanced when executed on the 8080A; i.e., cycles through the loop require the same number of clock periods whether the termination condition is met or not. This simplifies the calculation of the delay. The time interval during which the flip-flop is set is:

$$T = (N * 25)t_s \qquad \text{for } 0 < N \leq 255,$$
$$= N * 25 * 500 \text{ nS}$$
$$= N * 12.5 \ \mu\text{S}$$

where

$$t_s = \text{duration of a single state} = 500 \text{ nS at 2 MHz}$$

and

$$T = 256 * 12.5 \ \mu\text{S} = 3.2 \text{ mS} \quad \text{for } N = 0$$

A comparison of these two examples illustrates a problem in software compatibility between the 8085A and 8080A that occurs when precise time intervals are generated by software. If a program written to generate a precise time delay on the 8080A is transferred to the 8085A, the duration of the time delay is different. There are two reasons for this: differences in the nominal state times for the two machines and differences in the number of states in the instruction cycles of identical instructions. For $N = 0$ in the previous examples, the same routine gives a delay of 3.2 mS in the 8080A and 1.72 mS in the 8085A. The difference in state times can be resolved by running the 8085A at the slower 500 nS state time of the 8080A. However, instruction cycles with different numbers of states, if used in a delay, still prevent delay times from being the same. The solution is to calculate a new initial count value which provides the necessary delay on the 8085A.

The previous delays involved the use of an 8-bit register to hold the loop count. Longer delays can be implemented when a register pair is used to hold the count. For example, the DCX rp, *decrement register pair*, instruction controls a 16-bit counter consisting of a register pair such as BC. However, DCX rp does not affect any of the flags. The following routine uses the register pair BC as the counter and checks it for zero.

```
DELAY:   LXI B, COUNT   ;   initialize register pair BC with
                        ;   a 16-bit value
         OUT 1
LOOP:    DCX B          ;   decrement register pair BC
         MOV A, B       ;   check for (B) = (C) = 00H
         ORA C          ;   logically OR B and C, set flags
         JZ FIN
         JMP LOOP
FIN:     OUT 0
```

Longer delays can be implemented by counting down a second register pair each time the first register is counted through. Thus, the second register counts multiples of the delay of the first register. In effect, this is a programmed analogy of cascaded presettable hardware counters.

When a very precise delay is required, a loop is written and initialized with a count value which comes as close to the required delay as possible. The delay is then "tuned" by adding instructions outside the loop to bring it to the required time. One instruction which is particularly appropriate for this purpose is the *no operation*, NOP. This instruction carries out no operation and does not affect any of the registers or flags; its only effect is to cause a delay of four clock periods.

NOP   *Flags:* None

Other instructions can be used for this purpose as long as they don't affect registers that must be preserved.

REFERENCES

1. BARBACCI, M.R., "A Comparison of Register Transfer Languages for Describing Computers and Digital Systems," *IEEE Transactions on Computers*, Vol. 24, No. 2, February 1975, pp. 137–150.

2. *Intel 8080/8085 Assembly Language Programming Manual.* Santa Clara, California: Intel Corporation, 1975.

BIBLIOGRAPHY

8080 Programming for Logic Design. Berkeley, California: Adam Osborne and Associates, 1976.

Introduction to Programming, PDP-8 Handbook Series. Maynard, Massachusetts: Digital Equipment Corporation, 1973.

WELLER, W.J., *Assembly Level Programming for Small Computers*. Lexington, Massachusetts: D.C. Heath and Company, 1975.

WELLER, W.J., A.V. SHATZEL, and H.Y. NICE, *Practical Microcomputer Programming: The INTEL 8080*. Evanston, Illinois: Northern Technology Books, 1976.

WESTER, J.G., and W.D. SIMPSON. *Software Design for Microprocessors*. Dallas, Texas: Texas Instruments, Inc. 1976.

PROBLEMS

4-1. List the data transfer instructions which transfer one byte of data in a single instruction cycle, and list those which transfer two.

4-2. Write a routine which tests an RWM by first writing a block of memory with a checkerboard pattern consisting of alternate bytes of AAH and 55H. The routine next reads back the data written into the block to see whether it is properly stored. If so, the program writes a reversed checkerboard pattern and reads it back to verify its proper storage. If both checkerboard patterns are correctly stored, bit 0 of port 01H is set; if not, bit 1 of port 01H is set. Assume that the block of memory tested starts at location 400H and is 256 bytes long.

4-3. Based on the instructions presented in this chapter, rank the general purpose registers A, B, C, D, E, H, and L and all register pairs in terms of computational power or usefulness. In other words, order the registers in terms of usefulness and capability.

4-4. For the program ERSD? of section 4.6, compute and give the length of time it takes to determine if a PROM is completely erased. Assume a state time of 320 nS.

4-5. The following algorithm converts an n-bit Gray code number, g_{n-1} $g_{n-2} \cdots g_0$, to an n-bit binary number, $b_{n-1}b_{n-2} \cdots b_0$:

$$b_{n-1} = g_{n-1} \text{ for the most significant bit}$$
$$b_i = g_i \forall b_{i+1} \qquad 0 \leq i < n-1$$

Write a program which inputs an 8-bit Gray code number, computes the binary equivalent of this number using the above algorithm, and outputs the binary equivalent. Compare the advantages and disadvantages of this approach with that of a table lookup approach in terms of execution speed and memory requirements.

4-6. The following algorithm converts an n-bit binary number, $b_{n-1}b_{n-2} \cdots b_0$, to an n-bit Gray code number, $g_{n-1}g_{n-2} \cdots g_0$.

$$g_{n-1} = b_{n-1} \text{ for the most significant bit}$$
$$g_i = b_{i+1} \forall b_i \qquad 0 \leq i < n-1$$

Write a program which inputs an 8-bit binary number, computes its Gray code equivalent using the above algorithm, and outputs this equivalent.

4-7. Write a program which generates a single logic 1 pulse with a duration of 0.1 to 25.0 S in 0.1 S steps. Have this program input the desired length of the pulse as a binary number from input port 20H. Also, have it generate the pulse as bit 0 of output port 08H.

4-8. Four status signals, S_0, S_1, S_2, and S_3, are connected to bits 0, 1, 2, and 3 of input port 05H. C_2, bit 2 of output port 34H, is to be controlled as specified by the following Boolean equation:

$$C_2 = S_2\bar{S}_1 S_0 + \bar{S}_2 S_1 \bar{S}_0 + S_3 S_2 S_1 S_0$$

Write a program which controls C_2 as specified. Write the program to loop so that C_2 is continually controlled.

4-9. Write a program that measures the duration of a pulse generated by an external source; samples the pulse as bit 7 of input port 03H; and outputs to output port 06H a binary number equal to the measured pulse duration in mS. Assume that the maximum pulse duration is < 256 mS.

4-10. Write a program that implements a SELECT structure using a jump table. Take into account the following 3 characteristics: The SELECT structure has four possible processes; the particular process to be executed is indicated by a binary number between 0 and 3 which can be input from port 0; and the starting addresses of the four processes are contained in a table called TABLE.

4-11. For the delay routine below, write an expression that gives the total delay time of the routine as a function of N and the state time t. Determine the value of N required for a 1 mS delay assuming an 8085A processor with a 6.25 MHz crystal.

```
DELAY:   LXI B, N
LOOP:    DCX B
         MOV A, B
         ORA C
         JNZ LOOP
```

4-12. Assume that before each of the following instructions is executed, register A contains 4AH, register B contains 8CH, and register F contains 00X0X0X1. Specify in binary the contents of registers A, B, and F immediately after each instruction is executed. Use Xs to represent the unspecified bits of F.
(a) MVI B, 24H
(b) ANA B
(c) RLC
(d) INR A

4-13. Write a program to find the smallest element in a block of data, the length of which is in memory location 2001H, and which itself begins in memory location 2002H. The numbers in the block are 8-bit unsigned binary numbers. Store the smallest element in memory location 2000H.

5

Program Assembly and Simulation

*Software for the microprocessor can be generated using
a time-share service, dedicated minicomputer, large
computer system, manual methods, or a microcomputer built
around a specific microprocessor. Each has advantages
and disadvantages.*

Eli S. Nauful*

*"Software Support for Microprocessors Poses New Design Choices," *Computer Design*, Vol. 15,
No. 10, October 1976, pp. 93–98.

After an application program is written in assembly language, it must be translated—assembled—into machine code. Machine or binary code consists of 0s and 1s and is, of course, the only language which can be stored in the microprocessor's memory and interpreted by its instruction decoder. With the exception of very short programs which can be assembled by hand, a special program called an *assembler* is necessary for efficient translation.

Once the machine code is obtained, the program is tested to determine whether it functions as logically intended. The test may be conducted by loading the machine code into the microprocessor and executing it under the control of a *monitor*. Alternatively, another special program, a *simulator*, can be run on a different computer to simulate execution of the machine code by the microprocessor in order to locate logical errors in the program. In either case, an editor program is then used to correct any errors in the application program, which is subsequently reassembled and tested again. Once all apparent errors are corrected, the assembled program is loaded into a hardware prototype of the microprocessor system for final testing.

5.1 PROGRAMMING LANGUAGES

Programs can be written in any one of three languages: machine language, assembly language, or high level language. Machine language alone is directly executable by a microprocessor. Programs written in assembly language or a high level language must be translated to machine language for execution.

The instruction set for the 8085A microprocessor in Appendix C gives the binary code for each instruction. Consider the following program written in machine language:

Binary
00111010
00001100
00000000
01000111
00111010
00001101
00000000
10000000
10000000
00110010
00000000
01110110

Although it is probably not apparent from scanning, this machine language program adds two numbers obtained from memory, stores the result in memory, and then halts. One disadvantage of a machine language program is obvious: It is difficult to read; it is equally difficult and tedious to write.

The machine language program listing can be simplified somewhat by converting the binary code to octal or hexadecimal:

Binary	Octal	Hexadecimal
00111010	072	3A
00001100	014	0C
00000000	000	00
01000111	107	47
00111010	072	3A
00001101	015	0D
00000000	000	00
10000000	200	80
00110010	062	32
00001110	016	0E
00000000	000	00
01110110	166	76

And, although such a shorthand notation alleviates some of the difficulty of writing the codes, it does not improve the understandability of the program's function. Machine code is usually represented in hexadecimal for conciseness. However, it must be converted back to binary to be loaded into memory. Programs of any appreciable length are not written directly in machine language.

Assembly language uses mnemonic representations for operation codes, data, and addresses. These mnemonics are abbreviations of the names or descriptions of the instructions, addresses, or data and are used to aid the designer's memory. The program given in the previous example is written using 8085A assembly language mnemonics as follows [1]:

Assembly Language	Binary
LDA AUGND	00111010
	00001100
	00000000
MOV B, A	01000111
LDA ADDND	00111010
	00001101
	00000000
ADD B	10000000
STA SUM	00110010
	00001110
	00000000
HLT	01110110

This assembly language program is much more understandable than the corresponding machine language program, which makes the writing and modification of the program easier. The memory reference instructions are represented by the mnemonics introduced in Chapter 4; the addition instruction is represented by ADD; and AUGND, ADDND, and SUM are symbolic names for the memory locations 0CH, 0DH, and 0EH in the hexadecimal version of the program. If an assembler program is available, the translation of the assembly language program to machine code is automatic.

When writing a program in machine language, all addresses used in memory references for data transfers or transfers of control must be specified as absolute addresses. That is, the actual address of the memory location must be specified. The use of symbolic names for addresses in assembly language programs not only makes it easier to write a program but also facilitates the insertion or deletion of instructions. If instructions must be inserted or deleted in a machine language program, the absolute addresses in memory reference and branch instructions are checked to see whether their values must be changed because of the shifting of the actual location of instructions in memory caused by this insertion or deletion. When a program is written in assembly language using symbolic addresses, insertion or deletion causes no problems because, as the modified program is assembled, the correct addresses of all memory references and branch instructions are automatically computed and substituted for their symbolic representations.

Programming ease is further enhanced by a high level language[1], where a single instruction is equivalent to several machine language instructions. For example,

High Level Language	Binary
I = J + K	00111010
	00001100
	00000000
	01000111
	00111010
	00001101
	00000000
	10000000
	00110010
	00001110
	00000000
	01110110

High level language programs must also be translated to machine code for microprocessor execution.

[1]High level languages are discussed in Chapter 12.

5.2 SOFTWARE DEVELOPMENT

Software development is a process which culminates with the creation and verification of a pattern of 0s and 1s which, when placed in the appropriate memory locations of a specific microprocessor system and executed, cause the system to implement its intended function. In general, software development consists of five steps:

1. Design: The determination from the functional specification of the overall structure of the program and the data required as well as a determination of the algorithms to implement the necessary functions.
2. Coding: The actual writing of instructions in a specific programming language to implement the algorithms of the previous step.
3. Translation: The creation of the patterns of 0s and 1s (the object code) from the program (source program) created in step 2.
4. Testing: The determination of whether the object code, when executed, actually causes the system to implement its intended function.
5. Debugging: The process of determining the source of any failures found during testing in order to eliminate them. Correction of a failure requires a repetition of these steps, starting with the first or second one.

Although software can be developed by hand, practical development for any but the smallest programs requires computer assistance. Software development costs often constitute the major portion of system development cost, and the use of computer aids reduces development cost and time and improves software and system reliability.

There are two fundamental approaches to computer assisted software development. One uses a large computer or minicomputer with a number of software development support programs. The other uses a microprocessor based software development system and a functionally similar software development support package. The microprocessor based software development system is a microcomputer which contains a microprocessor of the type for which the software is being developed.

Computer assisted software development typically includes the use of several software development programs: monitor, text editor, translator, loader, simulator, and debugger.

The *monitor* is a program which supervises or controls, at an elementary level, the overall operation of the computer system: the inputting and outputting of programs to and from the computer system and their execution. It also contains software to control the system peripheral devices: the Teletype, CRT, and printer. In microcomputer development systems, the monitor is contained in ROM and is immediately available when the system is turned on. On computer systems with sophisticated peripherals, an enhanced monitor, referred to as an operating system, is also used. This is true for advanced microcomputer development systems and for minicomputers and large computers.

The *text editor* facilitates the creation and modification of a source program file. Editor commands create, modify, or reposition lines of text and add them to or delete them from the program file. This file is usually saved on the computer auxiliary memory (disk or magnetic tape) and can be recalled for processing whenever necessary.

The *translator* takes the program file—the source program—and translates its instructions into machine code. Since this code is the object of the translation process, it is referred to as *object code*. The translator produces a listing of the source program and indicates violations of the grammatical rules of the language.

There are several different types of translators: assemblers, cross assemblers, self assemblers, and compilers. Assemblers accept source programs written in a specific assembly language and generate object code for the corresponding microprocessor. Cross assemblers run on large computers or minicomputers but assemble programs written for a microprocessor. An assembler which runs on a microprocessor and creates object code for that same microprocessor is called a self assembler.

Cross assemblers are usually written in a high level language, like FORTRAN, and are more powerful than self assemblers because of the additional features which can be supported by a minicomputer or a large computer.

If the source program is written in a high level language, a compiler is used for translation. High level languages are essentially independent of a particular microprocessor; thus, the details of the microprocessor's architecture on which the object code is executed are not important during the writing of the high level language program.

The compiler determines the sequence of assembly language instructions necessary for a particular microprocessor to implement the operation indicated by each instruction in the high level language program. The compiler creates, as well, the actual object code which, when executed, carries out the function specified by the high level language program.

A *loader* transfers the object code from some external medium, such as paper tape, into the microprocessor memory. Loaders vary, depending on the configuration of the microprocessor system on which the object code is executed. In the case of a software development system, for example, the loader is a program which runs on the microprocessor and loads the object code into R/W memory for execution. Or, if the object code is loaded into ROM for execution on the system prototype, the PROM programmer functions as the loader.

A *simulator* is a program which runs on large computers or minicomputers and emulates a microprocessor's operation. It uses memory locations in the computer on which it runs to simulate the registers and memory of the microprocessor system. The simulator reads each instruction in the object code and simulates its execution, modifying the simulated microprocessor registers and memory as appropriate.

The simulator executes one or more instructions for each instruction in the object code, and therefore its execution speed differs from that of the actual microprocessor. Real-time operation differences notwithstanding, a simulator can effectively carry out substantial testing of the object program without requiring the presence of the microprocessor.

A *debugger* is a program which facilitates testing the execution of the object program on the microprocessor. It stops execution at the occurrence of specified events and thus allows the examination and modification of the contents of registers and memory locations and/or allows the execution of one instruction at a time for analysis.

When a simulator is used in computer assisted software development, the debugger is part of the simulator. And, in a microcomputer development system, debugging capabilities are often included in the monitor.

There are pros and cons to the use of large computers as opposed to microcomputer development systems for software development. A large computer or minicomputer eliminates the cost of a software development system; however, the cross software—particularly the assembler and simulator—must be available for the particular microprocessor for which the software is being developed. If cross software is available for several different microprocessors, their software developments can be compared for a particular application.

The use of a large computer system becomes costly if many iterations through the software design steps are required. Since simulators are usually appropriate only for initial testing of the software, due to limitations in simulating the real-time nature of external operations such as input/output and interrupts, a final testing of the software on the actual prototype is a necessity.

If access to a large computer is not available, then a dedicated microprocessor based software development system involves the smallest initial investment. Here problems associated with inadequate simulation are eliminated, since initial tests are carried out on the actual microprocessor. Many sophisticated microprocessor development systems provide features for translation and testing which are far superior to those possible using cross software.

Coding, translation, testing, and debugging are basically the same whether software is developed with cross software on a large computer or minicomputer or with a microcomputer development system. The only major difference occurs in the initial testing and debugging stage: In the first case the object program's execution is only simulated; in the second case the program is executed on the actual microprocessor.

The steps in software development using a cross assembler and simulator on a large computer, with the final program testing on a hardware prototype, are outlined in Fig. 5.2-1. First, the assembly language program file, the *source program*, is developed, generally from an interactive device such as a Teletype. Development and any corrections or changes are facilitated by the editor program.

The source program is input to the assembler program, which produces the equivalent machine code along with a listing of the original source program. In the process of assembling the source program, the assembler checks for syntactic

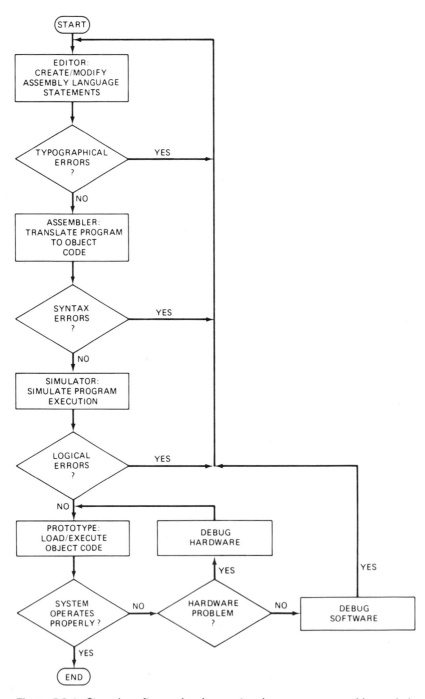

Figure 5.2-1. Steps in software development, using a cross assembler and simulator.

152

errors—violations of the rules governing the structure of instructions—and for consistency and completeness of the program. Syntax errors are indicated by symbols to the left of each incorrect program statement. The editor is then used to make any required corrections in the source program statements; the program is then reassembled. It may take several iterations of assembly followed by use of the editor to locate and correct all the syntax errors in a program.

Logical errors are mistakes in the use of instructions to implement the required algorithm. They are detected by using a simulator program, which executes the object code resulting from the assembly on a computer other than the one for which the assembly language program was written. In addition, the simulator provides the user with a number of execution monitoring commands. After logical errors are detected using the simulator, the original source program is corrected using the editor and reassembled.

When all detectable errors are corrected, the object code is loaded into the memory of the microprocessor system hardware prototype, and hardware and software are tested together for proper system operation.

5.3 ASSEMBLER SOURCE PROGRAMS

Three types of statements are common in an assembly language source program:

1. Symbolic microprocessor instructions which are to be translated into machine language instructions in the object code.
2. Directive statements or pseudo instructions to the assembler program directing the translation of the symbolic microprocessor instructions.
3. Comment statements which are reproduced in the program listing for documentation purposes but have no effect on the translation of the program.

Symbolic microprocessor instructions and pseudo instructions usually are separate lines of the source program. A comment statement can also be a separate line, but may be included as part of a microprocessor instruction or assembler directive.

Whether it is to be assembled on a self assembler or on a cross assembler, the assembly language program must be written to conform to a strict syntax in order to be assembled automatically. Most assemblers require that instructions consist of four separate fields, one or more of which may be blank.

1. The label field: containing the name to be assigned to an instruction's location.
2. The operation code field: specifying the operation to be performed.
3. The operand field: providing address or data information when required by an operation code.

4. The comment field: describing the way in which the instruction relates to the purpose of the program.

To facilitate use with terminals, assemblers have a *free-field format* which allows any number of blanks between separate fields on a line of code. The fields are, however, separated by some type of delimiter. The delimiters used with Intel assemblers and their placements are:

Delimiter	Placement
: (colon)	After each label
(space)	Between an operation code and operand
, (comma)	Between operands in an operand field
; (semicolon)	Preceeding comments

A label on an instruction is optional but, if used, is one to five characters long. The label begins with a letter of the alphabet or with the special characters @ or ? and is terminated with a colon. Operation codes, assembler directive names, and register names are *reserved words* and cannot be used as labels.

The operation field contains the instruction mnemonic and is delimited by a space. If the operand field for an instruction requires two operands, they are separated by commas. Operand field data specifies a register or register pair, immediate data, or an 8- or 16-bit address. There are many ways of expressing operands: as binary, octal, decimal, or hexadecimal numbers; as symbolic names with assigned values; as labels of instructions or data; as ASCII constants; and as arithmetic and logic expressions. For example, to specify the bit pattern of an ASCII code character, the character is placed in quotes, and the assembler substitutes for it the actual bit pattern. To load the accumulator with the ASCII code for a period (.), the single instruction

MVI A, '.'

suffices. The assembler makes the second byte of the resulting object code 2EH, the ASCII code for period.

Assemblers which allow operands to be specified as expressions containing arithmetic or logic operations evaluate the expression during assembly and replace it with its binary equivalent in the object code representation of the instruction. The specific arithmetic and logic operators allowed in expressions and their method of evaluation are determined by the particular assembler used.

Some of the arithmetic and logic operations allowed in expressions include addition, subtraction, multiplication, division, modulo division, NOT, AND, OR, EX-OR, shift right, and shift left. Note that these are operations carried out by the assembler program during translation and have nothing to do with the arithmetic and logic operations available as instructions in the microprocessor's instruction set.

5.4 MANUAL ASSEMBLY OF PROGRAMS

The procedure for manual assembly is simple and parallels that performed by an assembler program. A knowledge of manual assembly facilitates understanding of the operation of two-pass assemblers and the need for assembler directives. Hand assembly is important in its own right when obtaining object code for small programs or when making quick patches to larger programs which have been previously assembled.

For hand assembly, two blank columns are allocated to the left of the label field: After assembly the address column contains the address of the first byte of each instruction, and the object code column contains the hexadecimal representation of the one, two, or three bytes of code which comprise the instruction. See Fig. 5.4-1(a).

Manual assembly is carried out in two steps, each requiring a complete scan or *pass* through the program. The first pass determines the memory location into which the first byte of each instruction is assembled and creates a table for the values of all symbolic names in the program. A starting address in memory, or *origin*, is assigned to the first byte of the first instruction and is recorded in the address column. This is the initial value for a count which is incremented by the number of bytes in each instruction. This count corresponds to the location in memory for which the first byte of each instruction is being assembled. A counter, referred to as the *Location Counter, LC*, keeps track of the count.

The count, or location of the first byte of each instruction, is recorded in the address column. The label, for each instruction which has one, is recorded in a *symbol table* together with the address of the first byte of the instruction. See Fig. 5.4-1(b). These labels are symbolic names used as addresses in various program instructions. For example, if the operand in a jump instruction is represented symbolically, then it appears as a label somewhere in the program. Operands other than addresses are written symbolically, but values must be explicitly assigned to these. These symbolic names and their assigned values are also entered in the symbol table.

At the completion of the first pass through the assembly language program, all the symbolic labels and operands appear in the symbol table along with their assigned values. Thus, at the end of the first pass, the address column and symbol table are complete.

The second pass of the assembly process fills in the object code column. During this pass, each instruction is examined, and the instruction mnemonic is replaced by its machine code written in hexadecimal notation. If the instruction consists of more than a single byte, and the address or constant constituting the additional bytes is written symbolically, the symbol table is consulted to determine the hexadecimal code for the symbolic operand. At the end of the second pass, the assembly process is complete. See Fig. 5.4-1(c). The operation code is found in the listing of machine codes for the various mnemonic instructions (see Appendix C). The resulting object code can be loaded into the microprocessor's memory and executed.[2]

(a) SOURCE

ADDRESS	OBJECT CODE	LABEL	OPERATION	OPERAND(S)	COMMENT
		DELAY:	LXI	B, COUNT	; INITIALIZE REGISTER PAIR BC
			OUT	1	; WITH A 16-BIT VALUE
		LOOP:	DCX	B	; DECREMENT REGISTER PAIR BC
			MOV	A, B	
			ORA	C	; SET FLAGS
			JZ	FIN	; COUNT = 0?
			JMP	LOOP	
		FIN:	OUT	0	

(b) PASS 1

ADDRESS	OBJECT CODE	LABEL	OPERATION	OPERAND(S)	COMMENT
0000H		DELAY:	LXI	B, COUNT	
0003H			OUT	1	
0005H		LOOP:	DCX	B	
0006H			MOV	A, B	
0007H			ORA	C	
0008H			JZ	FIN	
000BH			JMP	LOOP	
000EH		FIN:	OUT	0	

Symbol Table

DELAY	0000H
LOOP	0005H
FIN	000EH
COUNT	0100H

(c) PASS 2

ADDRESS	OBJECT CODE	LABEL	OPERATION	OPERAND(S)	COMMENT
0000H	010001H	DELAY:	LXI	B, COUNT	
0003H	D301H		OUT	1	
0005H	0BH	LOOP:	DCX	B	
0006H	78H		MOV	A, B	
0007H	B1H		ORA	C	
0008H	CA0E00H		JZ	FIN	
000BH	C30500H		JMP	LOOP	
000EH	D300H	FIN:	OUT	0	

Figure 5.4-1. Steps in assembly of a program: (a) source; (b) first pass; (c) second pass.

To complete the manual assembly process, all instruction mnemonics and symbolic addresses and constants are replaced with their absolute values. Insertion or deletion of instructions requires program reassembly. Some modifications, such as changing the value of a constant, can be made in the object code without involving another assembly.

5.5 ASSEMBLER DIRECTIVES—PSEUDO INSTRUCTIONS

To assemble a program automatically, the assembler needs information in the form of *assembler directives* or *pseudo instructions* which control the assembly. Pseudo instructions are commands placed in the program by the designer which provide information to the assembler. They are not part of the instruction set of the microprocessor nor are they translated into executable code. Each assembler has its own unique pseudo instructions and corresponding mnemonics.

Although the mnemonics and details vary, most assemblers contain an essentially equivalent set of pseudo instructions, written in assembly language format. For example, the *origin*, ORG, pseudo instruction tells the assembler the location in memory for which the next instruction or data byte should be assembled. When different parts of a program are to be placed in different areas of memory, an ORG pseudo instruction is used before each part of the program to specify the starting location for assembly of that part of the program. The *origin* pseudo instruction has the following form, where expression evaluates to a 16-bit address:

ORG expression

If no origin pseudo instruction appears before the first instruction in the program, assembly will begin, by default, at memory location 0.

When an assembler scans the program to be assembled, it must know where the program ends. It cannot depend on a *halt* instruction for this because some programs don't contain a *halt* as the last instruction, and others don't contain a *halt* at all. An application program used, for example, in process monitoring or control might run continuously and therefore not contain a *halt* instruction. Thus, an *end assembly*, END, directive must be the last instruction to explicitly indicate the end of the program. This directive has the form:

END

---

[2]Instruction mnemonics used in this book are those recognized by the Intel assembler. Assemblers are available which use different mnemonics for the same instructions but generate identical object code.

The ORG and END assembler directives, in effect, frame the program to be assembled.

ORG 0000H

[Assembly Language Instructions

END

When there is more than one *origin* assembler directive, the assembly of each group of instructions starts at the location specified by the *origin* assembler directive which precedes it. For example,

ORG 0000H

This block of instruc-
tions is assembled start-   Assembly Language Instructions
ing at location 0000H

ORG 0100H

This block of instruc-
tions is assembled start-   Assembly Language Instructions
ing at location 0100H

END

Symbolic names, which appear in assembly language programs as labels, instruction mnemonics, and operands, are translated to binary values by the assembler. As illustrated by the hand assembly of a program in Section 5.4, labels are assigned the current value of the assembler's location counter when encountered in the first pass of the assembly. Instruction mnemonics have predefined values which the assembler obtains from a table which is part of the assembler.

A symbolic operand can be a register name, an address, or a data constant. Register names have predefined values. All addresses correspond to labels in the program, and thus, their values are defined. Data constants, on the other hand, are defined by the designer using an *equate* or *set* assembler directive. *Equate* assembler directives usually appear as a group at the beginning of a program and have the form:

name   EQU   expression

"Name" stands for the symbolic name. The assembler evaluates the expression and equates the symbolic name to it by placing the name in its symbol table along with the value of the expression. From that point on, wherever the name appears in the program, it is replaced by the value of the expression in the *equate* pseudo instructions. Note that the symbolic name is not followed by a colon and is not a label, even though it appears in the label field. The symbolic name in one equate assembler directive cannot be used in another, nor can it be used as the label of another instruction. That is, the name in an equate assembler directive cannot be redefined. If its value is changed, the equate assembler directive must be changed and the program reassembled.

There are a number of advantages in using symbolic data constants when writing a program. Obviously, just as with symbolic addresses, it makes reading the program easier; the designer choses symbolic names which are meaningful to the application and thus more easily recognizable than their binary equivalents. The equate assembler directives which define the values of all symbolic data constants are typically grouped together at the beginning of the program. Thus, if it is necessary to change the value of a data constant, it can be done by simply changing the expression in a single equate assembler directive and reassembling the program. If, instead, the actual value of the data constant is used in the operand field, any change necessitates locating and correcting it throughout the entire program. A final advantage of using a symbolic data constant is that its value need not be known before assembly. It can be specified as an expression in the operand field of the equate directive and evaluated by the assembler.

A variation of the *equate* assembler directive is the *set* assembler directive, SET. This directive also assigns a value to the name associated with it; however, the same symbol can be redefined at various points in the program using SET. Thus, more than one SET instruction can have the same name. The SET assembler directive has the form:

name   SET   expression

Another pseudo instruction, the *define storage*, reserves or allocates read/write memory locations for storage of temporary data. The first of the locations allocated can be referred to by an optional symbolic label. The *define storage* instruction has the form:

opt. label: DS   expression

A number of bytes of memory equal to the value of the expression are reserved. However, no assumption can be made about the initial values of the data in these reserved locations. If a symbolic name is used with the DS pseudo instruction, it has the value of the address of the first reserved memory location. For example, to establish two 1-byte storage registers in R/W memory with the names TEMP1 and TEMP2, the instruction is written:

TEMP1:   DS   1

TEMP2:   DS   1

During the first pass, the assembler assigns the values of its location counter to TEMP1 and TEMP2, respectively, and thus, an address is associated with each label. Instructions in the program can read or write these locations, using memory reference instructions such as STA TEMP1 or LDA TEMP2. TEMP2.

A memory buffer is a collection of consecutive memory locations also used to store data temporarily. When a buffer is established using a DS pseudo instruction, the contents of the memory locations are undefined. For example, the following establishes a buffer consisting of 80 memory locations:

BUFF: DS   80

The address of the first location is BUFF. Such a buffer is usually written and read sequentially using register indirect addressing.

When a table of fixed data values is required, memory must also be allocated. However, unlike the *define storage* assembler directive, each memory location must have a defined data value which is assembled into it. The pseudo instruction for this is the *define byte*, DB, pseudo instruction:

opt. name: DB   list

"List" refers either to one or more arithmetic or logic expressions which evaluate to 8-bit data quantities or to strings of characters enclosed in quotes which the assembler replaces with their equivalent ASCII representations. Assembled bytes of data are stored in successive memory locations until the list is exhausted. The operands of the DS and DB pseudo instructions are defined before the instruction is encountered in the assembly process; forward references cannot be made for these operands.

A pseudo instruction similar to *define byte* is the *define word* instruction:

opt. name: DW   list

The difference between *define byte* and *define word* is that each expression in the *define word* list is evaluated to a 16-bit quantity and stored as 2 bytes. It is stored with the low order byte in the lower of the two memory locations, and the high order byte in the next higher one. This is consistent with the convention for storing 16-bit quantities in 8085A systems.

The *conditional assembly* pseudo instruction allows certain assembly language instructions to be assembled, depending on the value of an expression. The instruction has the following form:

IF expression
[Assembly Language Statements
ENDIF

The assembler evaluates the expression: If it is 0, the assembly language statements between IF and ENDIF are ignored; if it is 1, these statements are assembled.

The *conditional assembly* pseudo instruction facilitates configuring a microprocessor system with optional features. Microprocessor hardware is structured in a modular manner so that the hardware for an optional feature is contained on a separate PC card and can simply be plugged into the basic system. To preclude main memory containing code to handle all optional features, whether included or not, a single program is written which handles all options. Software associated with the optional features is also modular; the conditional assembly pseudo instruction is used so certain subroutines are assembled only if required.

For the pseudo instructions presented, except EQU and SET, labels are optional. EQU and SET require names.

5.6 TWO-PASS ASSEMBLERS

Most assemblers are two-pass assemblers. On pass one, a symbol table is generated which defines the value of all symbols, labels, and symbols assigned values by pseudo instructions. Figure 5.6-1 is a simplified flowchart of the first pass of a two-pass assembler.

The assembler contains an *operation code table* which has an entry for each operation code in the instruction set. Each table entry contains an assembly language instruction mnemonic, its machine code equivalent, and a descriptor word. The descriptor word indicates the number of bytes in the instruction and the format of the data in the operand.

The assembler maintains a location counter, LC, in memory which is initially set to 0. Each line of the program is scanned in turn. If the line has a label, that label is added to the symbol table along with the value of the location counter, which defines its value. The operation code is extracted from the operation code table, and the location counter is incremented by the value specified for it in its descriptor word. In this way the location counter keeps track of the memory locations assigned to each instruction. If a program contains an *origin* pseudo instruction, the location counter is set to the value specified by the operand of the *origin* pseudo instruction. If an attempt is made to set the location counter to a value less than its present value, an error occurs. When the last line of the program is scanned, the *end of assembly* pseudo instruction is detected, and the first pass of the assembly is complete.

The second pass of a two-pass assembler scans the program again. Using the operation code table and the symbol table created in the first pass, it replaces all the symbols with their machine code equivalents and thus generates the binary object code. Figure 5.6-2 is a simplified flowchart for the second pass of an

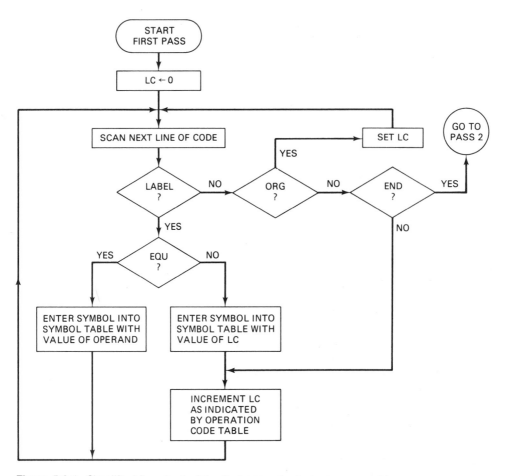

Figure 5.6-1. Simplified flowchart of the first pass of a two-pass assembler.

assembler. In addition to the object code, the assembler provides a program listing of both the source and binary object code and a listing of all errors found in the source program.

Cross assemblers for most microprocessors are available from the manufacturer or from independent software houses. They can be run on a local computer or accessed via local or national timesharing networks. Intel provides a cross assembler, MAC 80 [2], written to generate object code for the 8080A microprocessor. This cross assembler can also be used for the 8085A.[3] It is written in ANSI Standard FORTRAN IV and can be run on any computer having a word

---

[3]The MAC 80 cross assembler does not translate the SIM and RIM instructions of the 8085A. These instructions are covered in Chapters 8 and 9.

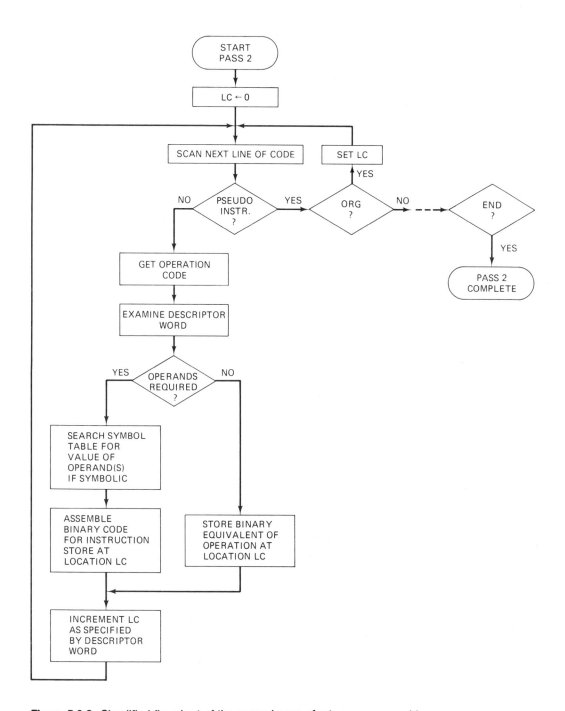

Figure 5.6-2. Simplified flowchart of the second pass of a two-pass assembler.

length of at least 30 bits and a FORTRAN IV compiler. The input to this cross assembler is a previously created and edited, variable length Hollerith code file containing assembly langauge source statements. MAC 80 provides two files as output: (1) a list file containing images of the source statements and a listing of the generated object code plus error messages, and (2) an object code file containing assembled object code.

An assembler error recovery procedure replaces all erroneous expressions with a value of zero. Invalid operation codes are replaced with 2 bytes of zeros to allow for corrections. Excess operands are truncated, and missing operands are replaced with zeros. The symbol table size is set to 1,000 words, and since each symbol stored in the table requires two words, a program can contain as many as 500 symbols. Control options allow modification of the input and output specifications and the type and extent of output information provided by the assembler.

An example assembler output is shown in Fig. 5.6-3 for the program from Chapter 4 which checks to see whether an EPROM is erased. Each line of the assembler listing that corresponds to an instruction in the source program consists of the address of the memory location in which the first byte of the instruction is to be placed, followed by the object code for the instruction and the assembly language instruction from the source program. The addresses and object codes are given in hexadecimal.

There is a one-to-one correspondence between each assembly language instruction and the resulting object code. In this example the first instruction, XRA A, is translated into 1 byte of object code, AFH. This byte is to be loaded into the beginning address of this program segment, address 0100H, as specified by the *origin* assembler directive. The second instruction, OUT DSPLY, is translated into 2 bytes of object code, D3H and 00H. The second byte of this 2-byte instruction, 00H, is the address of the output port, DSPLY. The value 00H is assigned to the symbol DSPLY by the *equate* assembler directive at the beginning of the program. The third instruction, LXI H, EPRM0, is a 3-byte instruction. The second 2 bytes are the address of the first location of the EPROM to be tested. The address is given with the low order byte first, followed by the high order byte. This address is 800H, as established by the *origin* and *define storage* assembler directives at the end of the program. The *define storage* instruction allocates 1 K (400H) locations for the EPROM.

The symbol table is also part of the assembler output. Included in it are symbols for the internal registers and their corresponding numerical values. The labels in this program are listed with the addresses of the memory locations with which they are associated. For example, the label NEXT has been assigned the value 0109H. In a symbol table, an asterisk next to a symbol indicates that it is not referenced in the program. Such is the case for the label ERSD?.

8080 MACRO ASSEMBLER, VER 2.3   ERRORS = 0   PAGE 2

```
0000                    DSPLY   EQU     00H
0100                            ORG     100H
0100        AF          ERSD?:  XRA     A           ; CLEAR ACCUMULATOR
0101        D300                OUT     DSPLY       ; CLEAR DISPLAY
0103        210008              LXI     H, EPRM0    ; SET UP POINTER TO FIRST EPROM LOCATION
0106        010004              LXI     B, 400H     ; SET UP COUNTER FOR # EPROM WORDS
0109        3EFF        NEXT:   MVI     A, 0FFH     ; CONSTANT FOR COMPARISON
010B        BE                  CMP     M           ; COMPARE CONSTANT WITH WORD FROM EPROM
010C        C21B01              JNZ     NO          ; IF N.E. TEST IS COMPLETE
010F        23                  INX     H           ; INCREMENT POINTER TO NEXT WORD
0110        0B                  DCX     B           ; DECREMENT COUNTER
0111        79                  MOV     A, C        ; TEST COUNTER
0112        B0                  ORA     B
0113        C20901              JNZ     NEXT        ; IF TEST NOT COMPLETE LOOP
0116        3E01                MVI     A, 01H      ; TEST COMPLETE SET DISPLAY TO INDICATE ERASED
0118        C31D01              JMP     DONE
011B        3E02        NO:     MVI     A, 02H      ; SET DISPLAY TO INDICATE NOT ERASED
011D        D300        DONE:   OUT     DSPLY
011F        76                  HLT
0800                            ORG     800H
0400                    EPRM0:  DS      400H
                                END
```

NO PROGRAM ERRORS

SYMBOL TABLE

A	0007	B	0000	C	0001	D	0002
DONE	011D	DSPLY	0000	E	0003	EPRM0	0800
ERSD?	0100 *	H	0004	L	0005	M	0006
NEXT	0109	NO	011B	PSW	0006	SP	0006

Figure 5.6-3. Cross assembler output.

5.7 MACROS

The MAC 80 cross assembler introduced in the previous section is a *macro assembler*; it has the capability to process macro instructions. A *macro instruction* is a single instruction which the macro assembler replaces with a group of instructions wherever it appears in an assembly language program. The macro instruction and the instructions which replace it are defined by the system designer only once in the program. Macros are useful when a small group of instructions must be repeated several times in a program, with only minor changes in each repetition.

The use of a macro in assembly language programming entails three steps:

1. The macro definition.
2. The macro reference.

3. The macro expansion.

The first two steps are carried out by the system designer, and the third by the macro assembler. The macro definition has the following format:

Label	*Code*	*Operand*
name	MACRO	list
	[macro body	
	ENDM	

"Name" stands for the name of the macro which appears in the label field of the macro definition. A list of dummy parameters may be specified, and, if so, appears in the macro body. The macro body is the sequence of assembly language instructions which replace the macro reference in the program when assembled. The macro definition produces no object code; it simply indicates to the assembler what instructions are represented by the macro name.

Consider the use of a macro in a program involving a large amount of indirect addressing. An indirect addressing input capability (see Section 4.2.3) is provided by the two instructions:

> LHLD addr
> MOV r, M

This sequence can also be written as a macro named LDIND, with a macro definition of:

> LDIND   MACRO REG,ADDR
>   LHLD ADDR
>   MOV REG,M
>   ENDM

Note that the contents of the HL register pair are lost when this macro is referenced. To have the macro body appear at any given point in the program requires a macro reference. Its format is identical to that of an assembly language instruction:

Label	*Code*	*Operand*
optional label	name	parameter list

"Name" is the label by which the macro is referenced.

The following macro instructions load register C indirectly through the address PTR,

> LDIND C, PTR

and load register E indirectly through the address ENTRY.

LDIND E, ENTRY

When a program containing macros is input to a macro assembler, the assembler carries out a text substitution, the macro expansion; substituting for each macro reference the macro body specified in the macro definition. And, for each dummy parameter in the macro body, the appropriate parameter from the parameter list of the macro reference is substituted. Therefore, when the macro assembler encounters the macro instruction

LDIND C, PTR

it replaces it with the instructions:

LHLD PTR
MOV C, M

The following macro rotates the contents of the accumulator to the left through the carry, N times. This is done with a loop which is terminated when a register is counted down to zero. The number of rotations, N, and the register to be used as the counter are parameters in the macro definition:

```
RALN    MACRO N, REG
        MVI REG, N
LOOP:   RAL
        DCR REG
        JNZ LOOP
        ENDM
```

In Fig. 5.7-1(a), this macro appears in a program which references it twice. Thus, when it is expanded, the label, LOOP, appears in the program listing twice. See Fig. 5.7-1(b). Instructions which are the result of the macro expansion are indicated by a plus sign in the label field of the assembler's program listing. However, this does not cause a multiply-defined symbol error—as is normally the case when a symbol is used as a label at two points in the program—because the MAC 80 associates symbols with a block number. All symbols defined in the main program are in block number one. When the assembler encounters a macro reference, it increments the block number. Thus, symbols defined in the first macro referenced are assigned to block number two; symbols defined in the second macro reference, to block number three, etc. In this way the assembler distinguishes between symbols with identical names associated with different macro references. Such symbols are said to be *locally defined*. The symbol table in Fig. 5.7-1(c) indicates that the program in Fig. 5.7-1(a) has three blocks. Each block is identified by an asterisk and a two-digit number. Blocks two and three

```
        RALN:   MACRO N, REG
                MVI REG, N
        LOOP:   RAL
                DCR REG
                JNZ LOOP
                ENDM
                IN 0
                RALN  2, C
                OUT 0
                IN  1
                RALN  3, C
                OUT  1
                HLT
                END
```

(a)

8080 MACRO ASSEMBLER, VER 2.3   ERRORS = 0   PAGE 1

```
                1                      RALN      MACRO N, REG
                1                                MVI REG, N
                1                      LOOP:     RAL
                1                                DCR REG
                1                                JNZ LOOP
                                                 ENDM
    0000            DB00                +         IN 0
                1                       +        RALN 2, C
    0002        1   0E02                +        MVI C, 00002H
    0004        1   17            +LOOP:         RAL
    0005        1   0D                  +        DCR C
    0006        1   C20400              +        JNZ LOOP
    0009            D300                         OUT  0
    000B            D801                         IN  1
                1                       +        RALN  3, C
    000D        1   0E03                +        MVI  C, 00003H
    000F        1   17            + LOOP:        RAL
    0010        1   0D                  +        DCR  C
    0011        1   C20F00              +        JNZ LOOP
    0014            D301                         OUT  1
    0016            76                           HLT
                                                 END
```

NO PROGRAM ERRORS

(b)

8080 MACRO ASSEMBLER, VER 2.3   ERRORS = 0   PAGE 2

SYMBOL TABLE

* 0

* 01

A	0007	B	0000	C	0001	D	0002
E	0003	H	0004	L	0005	M	0006
PSW	0006	RALN	03DA	SP	0006		

* 02

LOOP   0004

* 03

LOOP   000F

(c)

Figure 5.7-1. Assembly language program using macros: (a) source program; (b) and (c) assembler output.

each contain a locally defined symbol called LOOP. A different address is assigned to this symbol in each block.

The value of a locally defined symbol is valid only for a portion of the program; it can be assigned different values in different local areas. Thus, the block mechanism in the MAC 80 assembler causes labels in a macro to be locally defined to each macro expansion.

Globally defined symbols, on the other hand, have a single value for all instructions in a program. Symbols in all the programs preceding Fig. 5.7-1 are global symbols. Nonmacro assemblers treat all symbols as global. The MAC 80 globally defines a macro label by following it with two colons, as opposed to one for locally defined labels. Other macro assemblers use a macro pseudo instruction to list locally defined labels. Any label not so specified is assumed to be global. Because of this, a macro label can be used as an address in a main program branch instruction. However, if the macro is referenced more than once or the same label also appears in the main program, an error results.

The macro pseudo instruction cannot itself appear in a macro body. In other words, macro definitions cannot be nested. Most macro assemblers do, however, allow macro references to be nested. The level of nesting is limited and is a function of the particular assembler.

In effect, a macro assembler allows the definition of new assembly language instructions. Therefore, a program written for one microprocessor can be run on another if a macro assembler is available for the second and a macro is defined for each instruction in the instruction set of the first. It is also possible with macros to develop a problem-oriented or application language which allows users with limited experience to program the microprocessor efficiently. Thus, macros provide a programming capability between that of assembly language and high level languages.

5.8 SIMULATION

When object code obtained from an assembler is loaded into a prototype microprocessor system and executed, any logical errors in the code prevent the system from operating correctly. Obtaining an assembler output with no program errors simply means that the assembler has detected no errors in syntax. It has no bearing, whatever, on whether the program does what is intended to do.

To debug a program of logical errors requires ascertaining their sources. But the source of a logical error is virtually impossible to determine unless the particular prototype system has a *single step* capability and hardware to monitor activity on the address and data buses. Single step capability allows the execution of one machine or instruction cycle each time a switch is pressed.

A simulator can be used to debug logical errors in a program if a large computer is available. A simulator is a program run on a large computer which accepts the object code produced by a cross assembler and under the direction

```
INTERP/80 VERS 1·5

> $F
> LOAD 7 7.
  32 LOAD OK
> OUTPUT 0.
  OUTPUT OK
> SET MEMORY EPRM0 TO EPRM0 + 400H = 0FFH.
  SET OK
> SET CPU.
  SET OK
> SET PC = 100H.
  SET OK
> BASE HEX.
  ┤HEX BASE OK
> GO 100000.
  GO OK
  PORT 0H = 0H
  PORT 0H = 1H
  HLT CYCLE 54340
> SET MEMORY EPRM0 + 4H = 0FEH.
  SET OK
> SET CPU.
  SET OK
> SET PC = 100H.
  SET OK
> GO 100000.
  GO OK
  PORT 0H = 0H
  PORT 0H = 2H
  HLT CYCLE 294
> D CPU.
  CYZSP  A    B    C    D    E    H    L    HL     SP     PC
  *0000*02H*03H*FCH*00H*00H*08H*04H*0804H*0000H*0120H
> END.
```

Figure 5.8-1. A simulation of the program of Figure 5.6-3.

of user-supplied commands provides a software simulation of the micro-processor's execution of that code (see Fig. 5.8-1). It uses memory locations in the large computer to simulate the microprocessor's internal registers and the microprocessor system's memory and I/O ports. It simulates execution of the object code, modifying the simulated microprocessor's internal registers, memory, and I/O exactly as the actual microprocessor's registers would be modified if the microprocessor itself were executing the code. The simulation is, of course, not real-time. For example, a simulator written in FORTRAN typically requires the execution of more than one FORTRAN instruction on the large computer to simulate the execution of one microprocessor instruction.

The INTERP/80 [3], a FORTRAN IV program, provides a software simulation of the INTEL 8080A.[4] INTERP/80 accepts the machine code of the

---

[4]As written, INTERP/80 can simulate 8085A programs except it cannot simulate execution of the SIM and RIM instructions, nor can it simulate the enhanced interrupt structure of the 8085A. The TIME command is also set up to provide execution times for the 8080A.

TABLE 5.8-1 [3]

Commands Used to Control a Simulation Run

Command	Purpose
LOAD	Causes symbol tables and code to be loaded into the simulated MCS-80 memory.
GO	Starts execution of the loaded 8080 code.
INTER	Simulates an 8080 interrupt.
TIME	Sets and displays the simulated 8080 cycle counter.
CYCLE	Allows the simulated CPU to be stopped after a given number of cycles.
TRACE	Enables tracing feature when particular portions of the program are executed.
REFER	Causes the CPU simulation to stop when a particular storage location is referenced.
ALTER	Causes the CPU simulation to stop when the content of a particular memory location is altered.
CONV	Displays the values of numbers converted to the various number bases.
DISPLAY	Displays memory locations, CPU registers, symbolic locations, and I/O ports.
SET	Allows the values of memory locations, CPU registers, and I/O ports to be altered.
BASE	Allows the default number base used for output to be changed.
INPUT	Controls simulated 8080 input ports.
OUTPUT	Controls simulated 8080 output ports.
PUNCH	Causes output of machine code in BPNF or hexadecimal format.
END	Terminates execution of an 8080 program.

The commands NOINTER, NOTRACE, NOREFER, NOALTER, NOINPUT, and NOOUTPUT are also defined. These commands negate the effects of INTER, TRACE, REFER, ALTER, INPUT and OUTPUT, respectively. In all cases, the commands may be abbreviated.

MAC 80 assembler or PL/M compiler and execution commands for controlling the simulation. The commands appear in Table 5.8-1. Although INTERP/80 runs in either batch or time-sharing modes, for debugging, the time-sharing mode is much more efficient.

Figure 5.8-1 is a simulation of the program assembled in Section 5.6. In the initial simulation run, the program is tested to determine whether the EPROM is properly erased. If it is, the program outputs the value 01H to the DSPLY port. The OUTPUT command indicates to the simulator that any data output to port DSPLY during simulation is to be printed. The BASE command specifies that all numeric output be in hexadecimal.

To simulate an erased EPROM, all memory locations corresponding to the EPROM contain 1s. The SET MEMORY command sets all EPROM locations to 0FFH, and the SET CPU command initializes all simulated microprocessor registers to 00H. Program execution starts with the first instruction which is at location 100H. The SET PC command sets the program counter to 100H, and the GO command starts the actual simulation. The parameter 100000 sets an upper limit on the number of instruction cycles to be executed before control is returned to the user. As a result of program simulation, 2 bytes of data are output to the port DSPLY. The first byte, 00H, is output at the beginning of the program and clears the display. The second, 01H, is output after each location of the EPROM is checked by the simulated program, to indicate that the EPROM is erased. The simulated program then executes a *halt* instruction, and control is returned to the user.

Another simulation run is then made to determine whether the program can detect a single, unerased bit in the EPROM. First, the least significant bit of the fifth byte of the EPROM is set to 0 by the command SET MEMORY EPROM + 4H = 0FEH. The simulated microprocessor is then initialized, and actual simulation begins. This time, after clearing the display, the simulated program outputs 02H to it, indicating that the EPROM is not properly erased.

Other cases can be simulated to test the program and other simulator commands can be used to examine the simulated program's execution in greater detail. Simulator commands allow errors in a program's logic to be detected and traced to their sources to facilitate correction.

When a system is being developed that requires considerable interaction between the microprocessor, its I/O, and real-time data inputs from the operating environment, timing errors can occur. This is especially true for high speed systems. Most peripheral logic is timed and controlled by the microprocessor via its application program, and many errors can be corrected by modifying this program. These errors are not detectable during software simulation and must, therefore, be detected after the assembled and simulated program is loaded into a hardware prototype of the system. Instruments such as logic analyzers are used for this purpose. More sophisticated microcomputer development systems provide a solution to this problem.

5.9 MICROCOMPUTER DEVELOPMENT SYSTEMS

An alternative to the use of a cross assembler and simulator for software development is a stand-alone microcomputer development system. These systems range from minimally configured microcomputers on a single PC board to sophisticated multi-microcomputer systems. Microcomputer development systems can be placed in one of three broad categories:

1. Single board minimal microcomputer systems.
2. Minicomputer-like single microprocessor development systems.
3. Minicomputer-like multiple microprocessor development systems.

The first category includes low cost microcomputer systems which allow the evaluation of a particular microcomputer and the development of programs in machine language only. These systems provide the minimal hardware for an operational microcomputer and are mounted on a single printed circuit board. In the simplest systems, the program and data are entered via switches to read/write memory and then executed. Hardware is usually provided so pro-

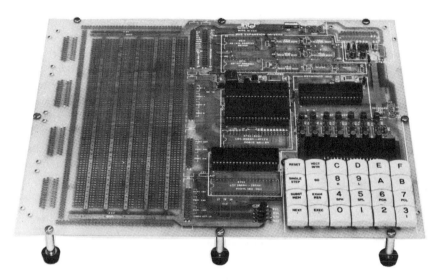

Figure 5.9-1. SDK-85 single-board microcomputer system. (Courtesy of Intel Corp.)

gram execution can be single stepped, and the contents of any memory location can be displayed on LEDs.

Slightly more complex systems provide a small keyboard and display. See Fig. 5.9-1. A monitor program in ROM controls the system through the keyboard. Instructions and data are entered into memory directly in octal or hexadecimal, and the contents of memory or internal registers are displayed in octal or hexadecimal on a seven segment or dot matrix display. The monitor makes it possible to modify internal register and memory contents. And it allows execution of the program under development to start at any location. *Breakpoints* can be set that transfer control to the monitor when the program under development fetches an instruction from a specified memory location, and the microprocessor's internal registers and memory locations can then be examined and/or modified. The debugging commands executable by a comprehensive monitor are similar to those of a simulator.

Generally, in the more complex single board systems, a Teletype interface is available so the Teletype can provide commands to the monitor and print its response. An interface for a low cost audio cassette may also be provided for nonvolatile storage of programs. Often monitors have loaders and routines which read machine code from paper tape and punch the developed program onto paper tape. Many PROM programmers have paper tape readers to simplify transferring the program to PROM.

These low cost development systems do not have a resident assembler and only accept programs in machine code. However, if a cross assembler is available and the object code it produces is punched on paper tape, the loader in the monitor can load the program into memory from a Teletype paper tape reader. The development system then serves the same purpose as a simulator.

The amount of read/write memory in these systems is typically limited to a minimum of 256 words and a maximum of 1,024. Thus, they are practical only for familiarizing a designer with the operation of a particular microprocessor and for developing small applications programs. Address, data, and control bus signals are frequently brought out to edge connectors on the circuit board to allow the interfacing of I/O devices to the system and for memory expansion.

Minicomputer-like single microprocessor development systems are usually structured on a modular basis, allowing expansion of the system capabilities through plug-in printed circuit boards. These systems are enclosed in a cabinet with an operator's console. There is a monitor in ROM, and communication is carried out through a Teletype or CRT terminal. The simplest configuration is a Teletype with a paper tape reader and a punch. The system has enough read/write memory to support an editor and resident assembler, although usually both cannot be resident in memory at the same time.

Minicomputer-like systems operate as follows: The monitor loads the editor, which is on paper tape, into read/write memory. An assembly language program is then entered through the Teletype keyboard and edited. After editing is complete, the assembly language program is punched onto paper tape and becomes the source program. The self-assembler, also on paper tape, is then loaded into read/write memory in place of the editor, and the source program is read into the development system's memory by the assembler program. If the assembler is a two-pass assembler, the source program tape is read into the system twice, once for each pass.

When the assembler has completed both passes, the generated object code is punched onto paper tape, and the monitor loads it for execution and debugging. During debugging, logical errors are usually found whose corrections require that the entire process be repeated, starting with the loading of the editor and source program. This process is repeated until all syntactical errors and logical errors are removed. Using a Teletype paper tape reader and punch operating at 10 cps, repetitive loading results in extremely long development cycles. It may take as long as 30 minutes just to load the assembler!

A high speed paper tape reader and punch can alleviate the loading time problem somewhat, but it is preferable to use magnetic tape or floppy disk peripherals for storage of the editor, assembler, and program files (see Chapter 10). These essentially eliminate the problems associated with loading time.

A part of most microprocessor development systems is an EPROM programmer. A socket on the front panel of the development system or on a separate PROM programmer peripheral holds an erased EPROM. A monitor command then programs the EPROM with the contents of memory, beginning at a specified starting location. An additional command verifies correct EPROM programming.

Use of minicomputer-like single microprocessor systems is restricted primarily to software development. Hardware prototype development is carried out separately, although to a certain extent portions of the hardware prototype can be connected to the software development's system for testing. A limiting

Figure 5.9-2. Intellec Model 220 development system with in-circuit emulation. (Courtesy of Intel Corp.)

consideration is that the bus architecture of the development system may differ considerably from that of the prototype. When the software preliminary testing on the development system is complete and the prototype hardware has been separately tested, the two are integrated. The application program is loaded into EPROMs, which are placed in the prototype, and final system testing is carried out using hardware test instruments only.

More sophisticated development systems use multiple microprocessors, usually two [4,5]. The two processors share a common system bus and system I/O devices (see Figs. 5.9-2 and 5.9-3). One microprocessor, the master, handles system services which are not prototype dependent: file management, text editor, system I/O, system utilities, and debug functions. The slave processor, the microprocessor for which the software is being developed, executes a self-assembler, object code in the debugging phase, and any special I/O required in the prototype. The slave does not have to be the same type of microprocessor as the master. Thus, the development system can be universal: With minor modifications, such as the substitution of a printed circuit card, it can be used with different slave processors.

Multiple microprocessors make possible *in-circuit emulation* whereby the prototype hardware of the system being designed is used with the development system. [6] The microprocessor is removed from the prototype, and a plug, connected to the development system by an umbilical cable, is inserted into the empty socket. In addition to replacing the prototype microprocessor, this con-

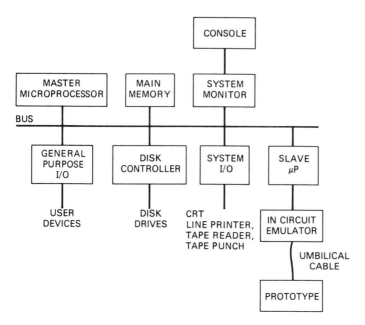

Figure 5.9-3. General structure of a multi-microprocessor development system.

nection interfaces the development system to the prototype's bus structure. The slave processor functions as the prototype's microprocessor.

With in-circuit emulation, prototype hardware and software are developed and debugged together during all phases of the design cycle, rather than being developed separately and integrated for final debugging. In the initial development states, no prototype hardware is required because the development system emulates it. However, as portions of the hardware prototype are completed, they replace their emulations. For example, the read/write memory of the development system initially replaces the read/write and read only memory of the prototype. When the design and construction of the prototype's read/write memory is complete, it replaces its simulation in the development system. And, as portions of the application program are placed in ROM, they replace the equivalent program portions in the development system's read/write memory. At each phase in the prototype development, all of the development system's resources and debug capabilities can be applied to testing the prototype hardware and software.

Eventually the entire hardware prototype is complete. The development system then emulates only the microprocessor itself through the umbilical cable while applying sophisticated debugging techniques to the completed hardware prototype operating in real time. This facilitates the debugging of timing problems involving the prototype's interaction with its specialized I/O. This type of debugging is impossible with simulators and is critical for many real-time applications.

REFERENCES

1. *Intel 8085/8080 Assembly Language Programming Manual.* Santa Clara, California: Intel Corporation, 1977.
2. *External Reference Specification 8080 Macro Assembler MAC80,* Version 2. Santa Clara, California: Intel Corporation, 1974.
3. *Interp/80 User's Manual.* Santa Clara, California: Intel Corporation, 1974.
4. GARROW, R., S. HOU, J. LALLY, and H. WALKER, "Microcomputer-Development System Achieves Hardware-Software Harmony," *Electronics,* May 1975, pp. 95–102.
5. CATTERTON, R.D., and G.S. CASILLI, " 'Universal' Development System Is Aim of Master-Slave Processors," *Electronics,* September 1976, pp. 91–96.
6. KLINE, B., M. MAERZ, and P. ROSENFELD, "The In-Circuit Approach to the Development of Microcomputer-Based Products," *Proceedings of the IEEE,* Vol. 64, June 1976, pp. 937–942.

BIBLIOGRAPHY

BARRON, D.W., *Assemblers and Loaders.* (Computer Monograph Series No. 6). New York: American Elsevier, Inc., 2nd Ed., 1972.

DUSAN, R., "Debug that Microcomputer System with a Mini," *Electronic Design,* Vol. 12, June 1975, pp. 74–77.

MARTINEZ, R., "A Look at Trends in Microprocessor/Microcomputer Software Systems," *Computer Design,* Vol. 14, No. 6, June 1975, pp. 51–57.

NAUFUL, E.S., "Software Support for Microprocessors Poses New Design Choices," *Computer Design*, Vol. 15, No. 10, October 1976, pp. 93–98.

WATSON, I.M., "Comparison of Commercially Available Software Tools for Microprocessor Programming," *Proceedings of IEEE,* Vol. 64, June 1976, pp. 910–920.

PROBLEMS

5-1. Describe the effect or purpose of each of the following assembler directives. For each corresponding example, list the entries generated in the symbol table and the code generated in the object code. Write all code in hexadecimal.

		Assume value of assembler location counter is
a.	TTY EQU 27Q	LC = 0H
b.	BLOCK: DS 16D	LC = 0200H
c.	CON: DB 11B, 10Q, 8, 'A'	LC = 02FFH
d.	ADDR: DW 1024, 0FA4H	LC = 4000H

5-2. Assemble the following program by hand, and create a symbol table for it similar to one created by an assembler. (Do not include symbols for the 8085A

CPU registers). Represent the generated object code in hexadecimal.

```
TTY      EQU   10Q
         ORG   1024D
LINE:    LXI   H, BUFF
LOOP:    IN    TTY
         MOV   M,A
         INX   H
         CPI   0DH
         JNZ   LOOP
         HLT
         ORG   600H
BUFF:    DS    01010000B
         END
```

5-3.   Assemble the following program by hand. Give the object code and addresses in hexadecimal. List the entries in the symbol table and the values associated with this assembly, which are

```
         ORG 100H
SLEN:    LXI H, STRNG −1   ;   set pointer to byte before string
         MVI C, 0FFH        ;   set byte counter = −1
         MVI A, 0DH         ;   load A with CR
SRCH:    INX H              ;   scan string
         INR C
         CMP M
         JNZ   SRCH
         MOV A, C           ;   store string length
         STA LNGTH
         HLT

         ORG 400H
LNGTH:   DS   1
STRNG:   DS   80
         END
```

5-4.   Using as few instructions as possible, write a macro, SWAP, which exchanges the most significant and least significant four bits of the accumulator. If other registers in the microprocessor are required to implement the macro, specify them as parameters in the macro definition. Show the complete macro definition, an example of a reference to the macro, and the macro's expansion.

5-5.   Using as few instructions as possible, write a macro definition and a sample expansion for each of the following macros.
       a. Macro CLC clears the carry flag;
          No other registers or flags are affected.

b. Macro ANIP computes the logic AND of the data from an input port and a mask. The address of the input port and the mask pattern are specified in the macro instruction. The result is left in the accumulator; no other registers are altered except the flag register.

c. Macro DJNZ decrements a register specified in the instruction and jumps to an address, also specified in the instruction, if the register is not zero after being decremented.

5-6. Write a macro, SWAP Q,R, which exchanges (Q ↔ R), the contents of any two of the six general purpose registers B, C, D, E, H, and L. Macro execution should not alter any of the general purpose registers other than the two being swapped. In addition, write the macro expansion for the following two references:

a. SWAP B, C

b. SWAP E, L

5-7. Write a macro JGE, which transfers program control to a specified address, ADDR, if the contents of the accumulator are greater than or equal to the contents of register R. Interpret register contents as unsigned binary numbers. Write the macro in such a way that if the contents of the accumulator are less than R, the instruction which follows the macro reference is executed. Thus the macro implements a conditional jump. The macro should leave all internal registers unaltered with the possible exception of the flag register and PC. In addition to the macro definition, give an example of a reference to it, and give the macro expansion which causes a jump to location STOP if the contents of the accumulator are greater than or equal to the contents of register L.

5-8. The program in problem 5-3 determines the length of a string of ASCII characters, terminated by the ASCII character for a carriage return (0DH). The length of the string does not include the carriage return. Write a set of commands for the Interp 80 Simulator which simulate a single execution of this program.

6

The Stack and Subroutines

"The best place to start is at the top—with the entire software requirement. Working from the top down, just as in many hardware designs, the engineer breaks up the overall requirement into major system blocks and further subdivides these into functional modules—in other words, software subroutines. The next step is to define exactly how these modules interface with one another (in terms of parameter passing) and with system hardware (in the input/output driver routines). Subsequently, the debugging process works back upwards through the design, from the lowest-level elements up through the major blocks to the complete, integrated system."

William F. Dalton*

*"Design Microcomputer Software Like Other Systems—Systematically," *Electronics*, Vol. 51, No. 2, January 19, 1978, p. 97–102. Copyright © McGraw-Hill, Inc., 1978.

6.1 THE STACK AND STACK OPERATIONS

The use of subroutines is a very important technique in designing software for microprocessor systems. And central to their use is a storage structure called a *stack*, which is a collection of registers organized in such a manner that the last data item written is the first item available to be read. In other words a stack is a last-in/first-out memory buffer, or LIFO buffer. The single register accessible for writing or reading at a particular time is the *top* of the stack. When information is written into the top of the stack, the operation is called a *push*. When information is read from the top of the stack, the operation is called a *pop*.

A direct stack implementation is the cascade stack contained in a microprocessor. A cascade stack is a collection of cascaded parallel-in/parallel-out registers (see Fig. 6.1-1). When data is pushed onto a cascade stack, the contents of each register are shifted to the next lower register. And, since the stack is of finite length, (a finite number of registers), data in the bottom register is lost after each push. A pop operation reads the contents of the top register of the stack, and the contents of each register are shifted up to the next higher register. As a matter of convention, the bottom register is cleared after each pop operation. The stack shown in Fig. 6.1-1 has a fixed set of registers within which data is shifted down or up, depending on the type of operation. A stack located in a microprocessor is of fixed and limited depth, typically between four and 16 words.

An alternative and more flexible implementation of a stack is to have a portion of external RWM allocated as the stack. In this approach, which is used in the 8085A, the data placed on the stack can be thought of as remaining in a fixed position while the stack "moves"—expands or contracts—as a function of

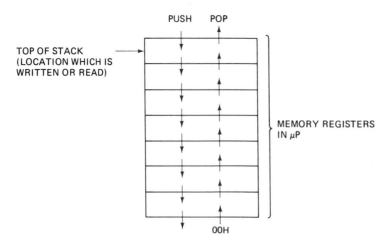

Figure 6.1-1. Representation of a cascade stack storage structure.

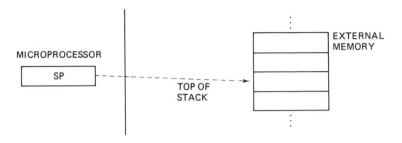

Figure 6.1-2. Stack pointer indicating "top of stack," the last written and not subsequently read memory location.

the execution of push and pop instructions. The top of the stack, at any given time, is pointed to by an internal register, the **Stack Pointer** (SP). See Fig. 6.1-2. This implementation allows the stack length to grow as needed, provided it does not exceed the limits of the RWM.

The beginning of the memory area allocated for the stack is specified by loading the stack pointer with an initial value. This specification is necessary because different systems use different memory configurations. The stack pointer is initialized by the *load register pair immediate* instruction, with the register pair SP specified:

LXI SP, data16

The stack pointer must be initialized before any instructions that use the stack are executed. Therefore, stack initialization is one of the first instructions in a program. Instructions in the 8085A which place data onto the stack, decrement the stack pointer, and, as more data is pushed on the stack, the stack expands into memory locations with lower address values. Therefore, the stack pointer is commonly initialized to the highest RWM location available.

When a designer wishes to set the stack pointer to a value which has been computed by the program, this value is placed in H and L and then moved to the stack, using the *move HL to SP* instruction:

SPHL
(SP) ← (H)(L)   *Flags:* None

With push and pop operations, the stack can be used as a temporary data storage area. For example, the contents of internal register pairs (BC, DE, or HL) are saved by the 1-byte *push* instruction.

PUSH rp
((SP) − 1) ← (rh)
((SP) − 2) ← (rl)
(SP) ← (SP) − 2   *Flags:* None

Register pair rp = SP cannot be specified in a *push* because it creates an invalid instruction. PUSH transfers the contents of the high order register of the pair, rp, to the memory location whose address is one less than the initial value of the stack pointer, and the contents of the low order register to the memory location whose address is two less than its initial value. The stack pointer is left with a value two less than its initial value. The *push* instruction is another example of register-indirect addressing, with SP as the pointer register. All stack instructions in the 8085A involve the transfer of 2 bytes of data. Thus, with this implementation, the top of the stack actually consists of two registers.

Data is transferred from the stack to a microprocessor register pair by the 1-byte *pop* instruction:

POP rp
(rl) ← ((SP))
(rh) ← ((SP) + 1)
(SP) ← (SP) + 2   *Flags:* None

POP is the reverse of PUSH. However, unlike the cascade stack, popping a stack implemented in external memory does not actually remove data from the stack; it simply copies it into an internal register pair. But, the memory locations from which the data is copied are considered empty, and, when a subsequent push operation occurs, these locations are written over. It is clear from the register transfer expressions that the stack pointer in the 8085A points to the last filled (written and not subsequently read) location in the stack.

There are special push and pop instructions which place on or remove from the stack the contents of register A and the flag register, F. These instructions treat A and F as a register pair, with A as the high order register. This pair is referred to as the processor status word, so the *push processor status word* instruction places the contents of registers A and F on the stack:

PUSH PSW
((SP) − 1) ← (A)
((SP) − 2) ← (F)
(SP) ← (SP) − 2   *Flags:* None

The *pop processor status word* transfers the contents of the top of the stack to registers A and F:

POP PSW
F ← ((SP))
A ← ((SP)) + 1
(SP) ← (SP) + 2   *Flags:* All

Instructions that push data onto the stack or pop data from it automatically increment or decrement the stack pointer. Thus, once the stack is initialized, the

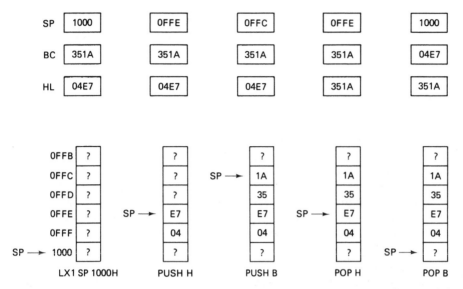

Figure 6.1-3. Use of the stack as temporary storage to implement an exchange of the contents of register pairs BC and HL.

designer does not have to keep track of the address at which data is stored in the stack.

External stacks of microprocessors other than the 8085A may grow in the opposite direction: successive push operations causing data to be written in successively higher memory locations and successive pop operations reading from successively lower ones. Regardless of the direction in which the stack grows, the basic concepts and uses of all stacks are the same.

As an example of *push* and *pop* instructions and their effects on internal registers and the stack, a routine which exchanges the contents of register pairs BC and HL, using the stack for temporary storage, is illustrated in Fig. 6.1-3. Here the contents of the various registers are shown after the instruction listed beneath them is executed. The routine assumes that the stack pointer has been initialized (i.e., LXI SP 1000H), after which four, single byte instructions are required for the exchange:

> PUSH H
> PUSH B
> POP H
> POP B

Another instruction, the *exchange top of stack with H and L*, interchanges the data on the top of the stack with the contents of the registers H and L:

> XTHL
> (L) ↔ ((SP))
> (H) ↔ ((SP) + 1)   *Flags:* None

It does not change the value of the stack pointer and, therefore, allows access to the contents of the stack without changing the position of the stack pointer or losing the contents of H and L.

6.2 SUBROUTINES

It is frequently necessary, at several points in a program, to carry out a task which requires the execution of the same group of instructions or, in several different programs, to carry out the same task. Programming such a task, if it is sufficiently short, can be simplified by writing the group of instructions as a macro (see Chapter 5). However, each macro reference is expanded by the assembler into the group of instructions it represents, thus generating a large amount of object code if many references are made. It is more cost effective in terms of memory usage if the needed group of instructions appears only once in the object code but can be executed from several points in a program. Sub-routines provide this capability.

A subroutine is written like any other group of assembly language state-ments, and it is referred to by name—the label associated with its first instruc-tion. The subroutine is referenced by a *subroutine call* instruction in the main program. CALL saves the address of the instruction following it and then transfers control to the first instruction in the subroutine. Essentially a CALL is a push of the program counter followed by a jump. When subroutine execution is complete, the last instruction, a subroutine return, transfers control back to the instruction following the CALL.

The exact manner in which the transfer of control to a subroutine is made in the 8085A is indicated by the register transfer definition of the *CALL* instruc-tion:

CALL addr
$((SP) - 1) \leftarrow (PCH)$
$((SP) - 2) \leftarrow (PCL)$
$(SP) \leftarrow (SP) - 2$
$(PC) \leftarrow (byte\ 3)(byte\ 2)$ *Flags:* None

The address contained in the CALL (bytes 2 and 3) is the label of the first instruction of the subroutine. Recall that during execution of an instruction, the program counter contains the address of the next instruction. Thus, pushing the program counter onto the stack saves the address of the instruction following the CALL, the return address. The stack pointer is decremented by 2 so that it points to the new top of the stack. The actual transfer to the subroutine, a jump, is implemented by replacing the contents of the program counter with the address of the first instruction of the subroutine.

The execution of the CALL instruction is now complete. The next machine cycle is an OPCODE FETCH which uses the contents of the program counter (the address of the subroutine) as the location from which to fetch the OP code of the next instruction. The transfer of control to the subroutine is now complete.

The last instruction executed in a subroutine is always a *return* which transfers control back to the instruction following the CALL. One type of return instruction is the unconditional *return*, RET:

$$RET$$
$$(PCL) \leftarrow ((SP))$$
$$(PCH) \leftarrow ((SP) + 1)$$
$$(SP) \leftarrow (SP) + 2$$

Execution of the RET instruction transfers the address of the instruction following the CALL from the stack to the program counter. When the OPCODE FETCH of the next instruction cycle is executed, it fetches the operation code of the instruction following the CALL.

In Fig. 6.2-1(a), the transfer of control to two subroutines, SUB A and SUB B, is illustrated. The first subroutine is exited (returned from) before the second subroutine is called. Figure 6.2-1(b) shows the contents of the program counter (PC) and the stack pointer (SP) before and after CALL and RET are executed.

When one subroutine calls another subroutine to complete its processing task, the operation is called **nesting**. The second subroutine may in turn call a third subroutine, etc. Each successive CALL without an intervening return creates an additional **level of nesting**. The effect of each *call* instruction is to store the appropriate return address on the stack. The *return* instructions and their effects on the stack ensure that program control eventually returns to the instruction following the original CALL.

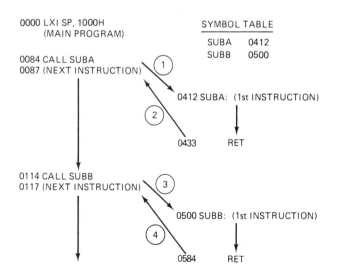

0000 LXI SP, 1000H
    (MAIN PROGRAM)

0084 CALL SUBA
0087 (NEXT INSTRUCTION)

0114 CALL SUBB
0117 (NEXT INSTRUCTION)

SYMBOL TABLE

SUBA 0412
SUBB 0500

0412 SUBA: (1st INSTRUCTION)
0433   RET

0500 SUBB: (1st INSTRUCTION)
0584   RET

Figure 6.2-1. (a) Transfer of control in a program segment containing two subroutine calls.

INSTRUCTION: CALL SUBA

RET

CALL SUBB

RET

	BEFORE	AFTER
*PC	0087	0412
SP	1000	OFFE

BEFORE	AFTER
0434	0087
OFFE	1000

BEFORE	AFTER
0117	0500
1000	OFFE

BEFORE	AFTER
0585	0117
OFFE	1000

STACK (AFTER)

	BEFORE	AFTER
OFFC	?	
OFFD	?	
OFFE	87 (SP →)	
OFFF	00	
1000	? (SP →)	

OFFC	?
OFFD	?
OFFE	87
OFFF	00
1000	? (SP →)

OFFC	?
OFFD	?
OFFE	17 (SP →)
OFFF	01
1000	?

OFFC	?
OFFD	?
OFFE	17
OFFF	01
1000	? (SP →)

*NOTE: PC CONTENTS ARE THOSE BEFORE THE EXECUTION OF THE INSTRUCTION, NOT BEFORE ITS FETCH.

Figure 6.2-1. Continued. (b) Program counter, stack pointer, and stack contents before and after execution of call and return instructions of Fig. 6.2-1 (a).

The level of subroutine nesting cannot exceed that supported by the available stack memory in the system. Since the stack pointer is usually initialized to the highest available RWM location, and the stack grows toward lower addresses, it is possible that too many PUSH or CALL operations without a sufficient number of intervening POP or RET operations result in the overwriting of nonstack data in lower addresses. Care must be taken in memory allocation and program design to prevent this.

Figure 6.2-2(a) illustrates the transfer of control in a program containing one level of nesting. The contents of the program counter, stack pointer, and stack are shown before and after the execution of each CALL and RET instruction in Fig. 6.2-2(b).

In these examples, it is assumed that only return addresses are placed on the stack and that each subroutine is properly exited via a *return* instruction. In fact, however, after a subroutine is called, it can place other data on the stack: for example, if push instructions are part of the subroutine. If it does place other data on the stack, such data must be popped from the stack before the RET instruction is executed, or control is transferred to a location in memory other than that of the instruction following the CALL, causing a logical error. The program logic must ensure that when a RET instruction is executed, the proper return address is left at the top of the stack. This is easily ensured if PUSH and POP instructions are properly paired.

When a subroutine is called, it uses some of the microprocessor's registers to implement its intended function. If data which is in a microprocessor's registers before a subroutine call is needed by the calling program after execution of the subroutine, it must be saved. Register contents are saved by either the calling program or by the subroutine itself. If the subroutine is called from several different places in the main program, less program memory is required if the subroutine saves the register contents. To save all of the microprocessor's

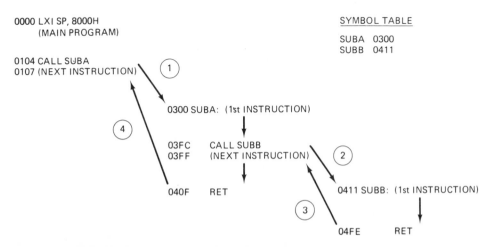

Figure 6.2-2. (a) Transfer on control with nested subroutines.

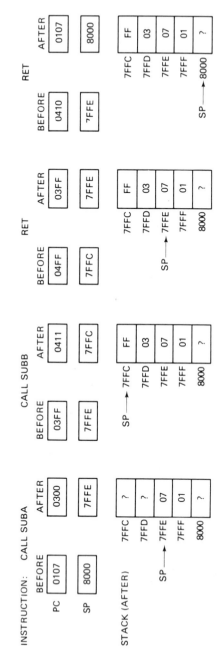

Figure 6.2-2. Continued. (b) Program counter, stack pointer, and stack contents for Fig. 6.2-2 (a).

registers at the beginning and restore them at the end, the following instruction sequence can be used:

```
SUBX:   PUSH H                    ; save all internal registers
        PUSH D
        PUSH B
        PUSH PSW
        : (other instructions of subroutine)
        .
        POP PSW                   ; restore register values
        POP B
        POP D
        POP H
        RET                       ; return (i.e., restore) PC
```

6.3 CONDITIONAL CALLS AND RETURNS

Similar to *conditional jump* instructions—in which transfers are predicated on the result of a previous operation—are conditional forms of call and return. In the 8085A these conditions are the same as for conditional jumps:

```
NZ    : not zero
Z     : zero
NC    : no carry
C     : carry
PO    : parity odd
PE    : parity even
P     : plus
M     : minus
```

The *conditional call* instruction has the form:

```
C ⟨condition⟩ addr
If ⟨condition⟩ = true then
((SP) − 1) ← (PCH)
((SP) − 2) ← (PCL)
(SP) ← (SP) − 2
(PC) ← (byte 3)(byte 2)
```

If the condition associated with the conditional CALL is not met, the instruction following the CALL is executed. If the condition is met, the program counter is saved on the stack, and the address contained in the *call* instruction is transferred to the program counter. The number of machine cycles and states required by a *conditional call* depends on whether the condition is satisfied or not. When the condition is not satisfied, two machine cycles and a total of 9 states are required to fetch and execute the instruction. When the condition is satisfied, five machine cycles and 18 states are required.

Conditional return instructions have the form:

$$R \langle condition \rangle$$
$$If \langle condition \rangle = true \ then$$
$$(PCL) \leftarrow ((SP))$$
$$(PCH) \leftarrow ((SP) + 1)$$
$$(SP) \leftarrow (SP) + 2$$

These conditions are the same as those for *conditional jumps* and *conditional calls*. When *conditional returns* are used in a subroutine, the last instruction in the subroutine listing is not necessarily a *return* instruction. This presents no problem as long as subroutine execution is terminated at some point by satisfying the condition associated with a *conditional return* instruction. Conditional returns also require a varying number of machine cycles and states, depending on whether the associated condition is or is not satisfied. When the condition is not satisfied, the instruction cycle requires one machine cycle and 6 states; when the condition is satisfied, three machine cycles and 12 states are required.

6.4 PASSING PARAMETERS

Many subroutines accept data inputs and provide, as output, results which are a function of the input data. Subroutines with greater applicability, i.e., greater general usefulness, can be written if the subroutine is parameterized. The data, also called the subroutine **parameters** or **arguments**, must be transferred or passed to the subroutine by that portion of the program that calls the subroutine. In addition, results generated by the subroutine must be passed back to the calling program. There are a number of ways of passing data between the calling program and subroutine. The method is often determined by the quantity of data involved. Data can be passed via:

1. Internal registers.
2. Reserved memory locations.
3. Pointers to parameter lists in memory.
4. The stack.

When the number of data items to be passed is fewer than the number of internal general purpose registers, it is convenient to transfer data via internal registers. In this case, when transferring parameters to a subroutine, instructions that load the data into specific internal registers precede the actual CALL instruction. These instructions and the subroutine CALL itself are together referred to as the *subroutine linkage* or *calling sequence*.

The subroutine obtains its parameters from predetermined registers when called. The results generated by a subroutine are placed in predetermined registers before the return instruction is executed. For example, the 8085A microprocessor's instruction set does not contain a multiply instruction, but a subroutine can be written for this purpose (see Chapter 7). If a subroutine, MULT, computes the 16-bit product of two 8-bit operands, one operand, the multiplicand, is in register B, and the other, the multiplier, in register C when the subroutine is called. The subroutine leaves the computed product in registers DE before it returns to the main program. Subsequent instructions in the main program can then use the computed result as desired.

Parameters and results are also passed between the main program and a subroutine or between subroutines by reserved memory locations. A *reserved memory* location is one in RWM set aside to hold the value of a specific variable or parameter. These locations are established by the *define storage*, DS, assembler directive. Instructions in the calling sequence and in the subroutine refer to the parameter by its symbolic name, the label on the assembler directive which reserves its storage.

When a subroutine requires a large number of arguments, they can be placed in RWM, and pointers to the data can be provided in internal registers—or in reserved memory locations—before the subroutine is called. For example, a subroutine which computes the mean of N data items requires that HL and DE be loaded with data to be used as pointers to a parameter list in memory. Thus, HL points to a location containing the value of N and the subsequent N locations contain the data to be averaged. The pointer in DE indicates where the computed mean is to be placed before the subroutine returns.

The stack can be used to pass parameters. The parameters required by a subroutine are placed on the stack by the calling sequence, using push instructions. These parameters, together with the return address, which is automatically pushed onto the stack by the CALL instruction, comprise a *stack frame*. See Fig. 6.4-1(a). When a subroutine is called, the stack pointer points to its return address, which is followed by the required parameters. The subroutine obtains the parameters from the stack, leaving the return address on the top as shown in Fig. 6.4-1(b). The number of parameters passed on the stack when calling a particular subroutine can be fixed, or the last parameter placed on the stack can be a count of the parameters.

A straightforward approach to implement this method of parameter passing is to have the subroutine pop the return address from the stack and save it in an internal register or reserved memory location. The subroutine then pops the parameters from the stack as needed. When all the parameters are removed and processed, the subroutine pushes the return address back onto the stack and

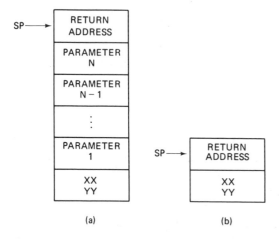

Figure 6.4-1. Stack frame: (a) before subroutine call; (b) after subroutine call.

executes a return instruction. For example, the following instructions use a reserve memory location to save the return address:

```
POP H           ; pop return address into H and L
SHLD RADDR      ; save return address, remove and use
                  parameters
      .
      .
      .
LHLD RADDR      ; obtain return address
PUSH H          ; place it on top of stack
RET
```

If, after executing the PUSH H instruction, all of the parameters pushed onto the stack are popped off, the stack looks like the example shown in Fig. 6.4-1(b). If, on the other hand, they are not all popped off, the stack is left with one or more unused parameters under the return address, which causes a permanent shift of the base of the stack to a memory location numerically lower than its initial value. This condition, referred to as *stack creep*, is cumulative; if each time the subroutine is called, one or more unused parameters is left on the stack, eventually the stack will move into ROM or into RWM locations not allocated for it. In either case, the program will fail.

The XTHL instruction provides a means of obtaining parameters from the stack one at a time while leaving the return address on the top of the stack:

```
POP H       ; pop return address from stack
XTHL        ; place parameter in H and L and place return
              address back on top of stack
```

After control has been transferred to the subroutine, this sequence pops the return address from the stack and places it in H and L, then exchanges the return address in H and L with the parameter on top of the stack. As a result, the top 2 bytes of the parameter are in H and L, and the return address is on the top of the stack. This instruction sequence can be repeatedly executed until all parameters placed on the stack have been removed.

Results of a subroutine execution can also be returned by the same technique. Before the subroutine returns, it pushes the results onto the stack, leaving the return address on the top. Execution of the return instruction pops the return address from the stack. The calling program then pops all the results from the stack.

A parameter stack exclusively for subroutine parameter passing can be established. This stack is in addition to the primary one established when the stack pointer is first initialized by the program. The pointer value for the parameter stack is kept in reserved memory until the stack is manipulated, at which point it is transferred from reserved memory to the stack pointer. The following subroutine saves the primary stack address in SPTR and loads the stack pointer with the parameter stack address. At the beginning of the main program, the reserved memory location, PARAM, is initialized with the base address for the parameter stack.

```
LXI H, 0        ; save primary stack pointer value
DAD SP
SHLD SPTR
LHLD PARAM      ; load SP with parameter stack pointer value
SPHL
```

The subroutine then pops the parameters from the parameter stack. Before it executes the return instruction or calls another subroutine, it reinstates the primary stack pointer value:

```
LXI H, 0
DAD SP
SHLD PARAM
LHLD SPTR
SPHL
RET
```

Of the various methods discussed for passing parameters, the easiest is the use of reserved memory locations. Each value passed is referred to by its symbolic name in both the calling program and the subroutine. This is also true of a parameter list when the pointer is kept in a reserved memory location. However, there are disadvantages: For some applications, this type of parameter passing necessitates the allocation of a large number of RWM locations. And since a memory reference is required to pass each parameter in a reserved memory location, this method is slower than using internal registers.

Subroutines can be written in such a manner that they can be called again before executing a return from the first call. These ***reentrant*** subroutines are required when recursive algorithms are implemented or when a subroutine can be called by both the main program and interrupt routines (see Chapter 9).

6.5 SUBROUTINE DOCUMENTATION

Careful documentation ensures that subroutine functions are clear, as are their responses to error conditions. It also obviates the necessity for closely examining the actual instruction listing when using an established subroutine in a new program or when studying the overall structure of a large program containing many subroutines. Subroutine documentation specifies the parameters and the methods by which they are passed to the subroutine, what results are generated and how, and the method by which results are returned to the calling program. Documentation also indicates what registers, if any—other than those used to pass back the results—are modified by the subroutine.

Adequate subroutine documentation also facilitates subroutine testing and debugging, independent of the program which calls it. And, it allows the designer to accumulate a library of useful subroutines which can be used in later work.

Because subroutines can be nested, any particular subroutine may be called by other subroutines and/or make calls to others. Consequently, documentation for a subroutine in a particular application requires a list of subroutines which it calls and a list of subroutines which call it. The list of subroutines that a particular subroutine calls is fixed and indicates that these subroutines must be included in any program using the subroutine that calls them. On the other hand, the list of subroutines that call a particular subroutine changes from application to application. This procedure helps in determining the effects of any changes made to any subroutine on the overall program.

A *subroutine header* concisely documents the subroutine in a program listing, for example:

```
              ; SUB1: Function accomplished by subroutine SUB1
              ; ASSUMES: Parameters passed to
              ; RETURNS: Results passed back
              ; REGS. MODIFIED: List of internal registers and reserved
              ;    memory locations modified by subroutine
              ; CALLS: List of all subroutines that this subroutine
              ;    calls to carry out its function
              ; CALLED BY: List of all subroutines that call
              ;    this subroutine
              ; STACK LEVEL: Maximum depth of stack required to
              ;    support this subroutine
        SUB 1:
              :      Actual Instructions of subroutine
              .
        RET
```

The total number of bytes of stack storage required to support the subroutine is indicated by the stack level. The minimum stack level is two—the 2 bytes which hold the return address. The maximum value includes the return address plus the amount of stack used for parameter passing and the amount used by nested subroutines. A worst case approximation of the required stack level is established by adding the maximum value for nested subroutines to the value computed for the subroutine itself. The largest stack level value is then checked against allocated RWM to determine whether the space is sufficient.

6.6 MODULAR PROGRAM STRUCTURE

Using subroutines, programs can be structured in a modular fashion: as a main program containing numerous calls to subroutines (modules). A modular program structure reduces the complexity of the software development effect because:

1. The overall program function is implemented by the execution of a number of subfunctions—subroutines—in the proper order.
2. The order in which subroutines are executed is controlled by the order in which they are called by the main program.
3. The programming effort is reduced by writing and debugging smaller programs—subroutines.
4. Previously written subroutines are often used in implementing required subfunctions.
5. Changes in the program are easier to implement.

A typical modular program layout follows:

ROM:

1. *Program Header*: A comment field provides a summary of the program's function and operation and describes the hardware environment on which the software runs.
2. *Symbolic Constant Definitions*: Symbols representing constants in the program are assigned values using EQU and SET assembler directives.
3. *System Hardware Initialization*: Instructions that write appropriate control words into system hardware to initialize or configure that hardware under software control (see Chapter 8).
4. *Macro Definitions*: The definition of all macros.
5. *Branch Tables*: If branch tables are used to structure the program, the jump instructions which comprise the table appear here.
6. *Main Program*: Instructions control the overall program and also control the calling of subroutines.

7. *Subroutines*: All the subroutines required by the main program are collected together in this area.

8. *Data Tables*: Tables of data constants, lookup tables, are used in conversion, linearization, etc., and storage of ASCII for printable messages. The tables are constructed with the use of the DB and DW assembler directives.

RWM:

9. *Reserved Storage*: Reserved memory locations referred to by symbolic names, which store particular temporary data are established by using a DS assembler directive with labels.

10. *Scratch Storage*: Memory locations which are used for temporary storage in an unrestricted manner by the main program or subroutines.

11. *Stack*: A section of RWM is allocated for the stack.

6.7 SIMULATION OF SUBROUTINES

A modular program structure simplifies program development, testing, and debugging. Subroutines can be written and simulated separately, allowing a program to be tested in stages from the bottom up. In bottom-up testing, *elemental subroutines*—those that don't call other subroutines—are written and tested first.

Input data for test cases must not only test the subroutine's performance with typical parameter values but also with values at the extremes of the range of data for which the subroutine is designed. In some applications, the subroutine will have to take appropriate action for invalid input data values or results which exceed representable ranges of values. These cases must also be tested.

After an appropriate set of test cases is determined, the actual simulation is conducted. The subroutine is loaded into the simulator or into a microcomputer development system. Breakpoints are established at the return instructions and at any desired intermediate points. Appropriate commands set the registers (microprocessor, memory, or stack) which pass parameters to the values corresponding to those of each test case. For the simulator described in Chapter 5, the SET command is used for this purpose. After the parameter values are initialized, the PC is set to the starting address of the subroutine, and the subroutine is executed. When the breakpoint associated with the subroutine's return instruction is reached, those registers which return the results are displayed and compared with the expected result.

After all elemental subroutines are tested, the next level of subroutines is tested in combination with the subroutines they call. When all nested subroutines are tested, they are combined with the main program, and the entire software system is tested.

BIBLIOGRAPHY

DALTON, W.F., "Design Microcomputer Software Like Other Systems—Systematically," *Electronics*, Vol. 51, No. 2, January 1978, pp. 97–102.

HETZEL, W., *Program Test Methods*. Englewood Cliffs, New Jersey: Prentice-Hall, Inc., 1973.

MAZOR, S., and C. PITCHFORD, "Develop Cooperative μP Subroutines," *Electronic Design*, June 1978, pp. 116–118.

ROSENFELD, P., and S.J. HANNA, "Developing Modular Hardware for the 8080A," *Electronics*, September 1976, pp. 83–87.

YOURDON, E., *Techniques of Program Structure and Design*. Englewood Cliffs, New Jersey: Prentice-Hall, Inc., 1976.

PROBLEMS

6-1. Write a macro, RDEL, which rotates DE left through the carry. In other words, this macro implements the following register transfers:

$$(CY) \leftarrow (D_7)$$
$$(D_{n+1}) \leftarrow (D_n)$$
$$(D_0) \leftarrow (E_7)$$
$$(E_{n+1}) \leftarrow (E_n)$$
$$(E_0) \leftarrow (CY)$$

Leave only registers DE and F altered by the macro.

6-2. Rewrite the test program of problem 4-2 as a subroutine. Assume that the starting memory location to be tested is in START and the ending location is in STOP. Write your program such that if the test is passed, the subroutine returns with location START containing the value STOP + 1; and if the test is failed, the subroutine returns with START containing the first memory location which failed.

6-3. Write a subroutine which compares two equal length blocks of memory to see whether they are identical. Write your subroutine such that the starting address of block 1 is in HL and of block 2 in DE, and the block length is in register C when the subroutine is called. If the blocks are identical, have the subroutine return with the carry set. If the blocks differ, have it return with the carry cleared and the address of the first location of block 2 that differs from that of block 1 in HL and the contents of that location in register B.

6-4. Modify the subroutine of problem 6-3 so that the starting addresses are obtained from reserved memory locations BLOC1 and BLOC2 and the block length from reserved memory location BLEN. If the blocks are identical, have the subroutine set reserved memory location DIFF to FFFFH; otherwise it should be set to the address of the first location in block 2 that differs.

6-5. Write two macros, SAVE and RSTOR, which use the stack to save and restore the contents of the microprocessor's registers. These macros would be used at the beginning and end of subroutines that save and restore the microprocessor register contents.

6-6. Subroutine, STATE, is part of a monitor program which, among other things, saves, in reserved memory locations, the values of registers A, B, C, D, E, H, L, F, and SP, which exist when the subroutine is called. The PC value pushed on the stack by the calling instruction is also saved in reserved memory. Using as few instructions as possible, write that part of the subroutine which saves the register contents. Provide adequate comments so that your program can be understood. The assembler directives which provide the storage for the register contents are as follows:

VDE:	DS 2	; Storage for E and D registers
VBC:	DS 2	; Storage for C and B registers
VFA:	DS 2	; Storage for F and A registers
VHL:	DS 2	; Storage for L and H registers
VPC:	DS 2	; Storage for PC
VSP:	DS 2	; Storage for SP

6-7. Write a programmable subroutine, DELAY, which counts down register pair HL to zero and then returns. The initial value of HL is passed to the subroutine via reserved memory locations called INIT. Indicate how the reserved memory locations are established in assembly language. Write the subroutine and give an example of a calling sequence which gives HL an initial value of 0123H. Explain how the total elapsed time of the delay is determined so that a given value for INIT could be obtained for a desired delay.

6-8. Write a macro, LHLX (load H and L indirect through DE), which loads L with the contents of the memory location pointed to by the contents of DE and which loads H with the contents of the succeeding memory location. In other words, write the macro to implement the following register transfer expressions:

$$(L) \leftarrow ((D)(E))$$
$$(H) \leftarrow ((D)(E) + 1)$$

The macro should leave all the microprocessor registers except H and L unaltered, including the flag register.

6-9. Write a macro, SHLX (store H and L indirect through D and E), which stores the contents of HL in the memory location specified by the contents of DE. In other words, write the macro to implement the following register transfer expressions:

$$((D)(E)) \leftarrow (L)$$
$$((D)(E) + 1) \leftarrow (H)$$

The macro should leave all the microprocessor registers unaltered, including the flag register.

7

Arithmetic Operations

Digital arithmetic refers to the algorithms which implement the arithmetic operations of a digital machine. These algorithms have been developed to take into account many factors, such as binary circuit operation, method of representing a negative number, the finite range of numbers representable in the computer, the limited (and usually fixed) number of digits in a computer word, and location of the digit point (such as the binary point of a binary number).

Yaohan Chu*

*Digital Computer Design Fundamentals. New York: McGraw-Hill Book Company, 1962.

The operation of most microprocessor systems requires both simple (addition and subtraction) and more complex (multiplication, division, etc.) arithmetic computations. One or more instructions for binary addition are always provided in a microprocessor's instruction set, and instructions for subtraction are usually, but not always, provided. Multiplication and division instructions are not typically included in the instruction sets of 8-bit microprocessors but are usually included in those of 16-bit microprocessors. When specific arithmetic functions are not provided as individual instructions in an instruction set, they can be implemented in software or hardware:[1] in software as macros or subroutines; in hardware with arithmetic processing units implemented as MSI and LSI circuits.

Prior to developing macros or subroutines, the range of the values to be represented numerically and their required degree of precision is determined. After this, a method for representing these numbers is selected. The length of a macro or subroutine varies significantly with the choice of number representation. If an inadequate representation is selected, calculations are in error. If too powerful a representation is chosen, the additional memory required for the longer subroutine and data representation is wasted.

Methods of numerical representation include unsigned binary numbers, two's complement numbers, BCD numbers, fractional numbers, and floating point numbers.

7.1 UNSIGNED BINARY INTEGER NUMBERS

Unsigned binary integer numbers represent positive integer quantities only, because all bits represent the number's magnitude. Unsigned binary is also the simplest of the number representations. With n-bit binary numbers, interpreted as unsigned integers, representable values range between 0 and $2^n - 1$ (see Fig. 7.1-1). When a single byte represents a number, it is called a *single precision number*. Single precision unsigned binary numbers range in value from 0 to 255 (0 to $2^8 - 1$). A single precision unsigned binary number is interpreted as a positive number.

For the general case of an n-bit integer, the number is written in positional notation:

$$X = x_{n-1}x_{n-2} \cdots x_0$$

and has the value:

$$V(X) = \sum_{i=0}^{n-1} x_i 2^i$$

---

[1]This chapter concentrates on the software implementation of arithmetic operations. Hardware approaches are presented in Chapter 10.

n	$2^n - 1$
1	1
2	3
3	7
4	15
8	255
12	4,095
16	65,535
24	16,769,025
32	4,294,967,295

Figure 7.1-1. Largest value representable by an n-bit binary number.

Thus, the value of the n-bit integer equals the sum of the products of each bit, x_i, and the weight associated with its position, 2^i. For example, the 8-bit number

$$N_2 = 10110110$$
$$\text{with bit positions } 76543210$$

is equal to

$$N_{10} = 1(2^7) + 0(2^6) + 1(2^5) + 1(2^4) + 0(2^3) + 1(2^2) + 1(2^1) + 0(2^0)$$
$$= 128 + 0 + 32 + 16 + 0 + 4 + 2 + 0$$
$$= 182_{10}$$

The subscripts 2 and 10 on N indicate that the number is represented in base 2 (binary) and base 10 (decimal). This subscript notation is used only when the base of a number is not clear from the context in which it is used.

7.1.1 Addition

The addition of two 1-bit numbers is defined as follows:

Augend		*Addend*		*Carry*	*Sum*
0	+	0	=	0	0
0	+	1	=	0	1
1	+	0	=	0	1
1	+	1	=	1	0

For an n-bit number, addition starts with the least significant bits of the augend and addend and continues with the addition of successively higher order bits and the carry from the previous lower order bit's addition. As long as the sum of two unsigned integers is less than 256, it can be represented by a single byte. For example;

Carries		00100001	
Augend	X	10110001	177
Addend	Y	00100101	+37
Sum	$X + Y$	0] 11010110	214

In general, for n-bit unsigned numbers, the sum ranges from 0 to $2^{n+1} - 2$.

$$(2^n - 1) + (2^n - 1) = 2(2^n - 1) = 2^{n+1} - 2$$

However, for single byte operands specifically, sums range from 0 to 510. The maximum sum results from the following case:

Carries	11111111	
X	11111111	255
Y	11111111	255
$X + Y$	1] 11111110	510

When the sum of two n-bit unsigned binary integers exceeds $2^n - 1$, it produces an *arithmetic overflow*: The sum cannot be represented with n bits, and a carry bit is required. When adding binary numbers with pencil and paper, this carry represents no problem. The sum is simply represented by $n + 1$ bits. However, in a microprocessor with n-bit registers, the sum cannot be stored in a single register.

For example, when single byte addition is carried out in the 8085A, the sum is left in the accumulator, and, if greater than 255, the carry flip-flop is set. In such a case, two memory locations are required to store the sum properly.

Two 8085A instructions add single byte binary numbers: one (add), which merely adds the two bytes, and another (add with carry), which not only adds the two bytes but also adds the value of the carry from a previous operation. In both cases, the second operand can be immediate data or data contained in an internal or external register. The instructions for add are:

Add immediate	*Add register*	*Add memory*
ADI data	ADD r	ADD M
(A) ← (A) + byte 2	(A) ← (A) + (r)	(A) ← (A) + ((H)(L))

Flags: Z, S, P, CY, AC

See Fig. 7.1-2, for a subroutine, SBADD, which adds the contents of two memory locations—AUGND and ADDND—and stores the result in the location SUM.

```
SBADD:    LXI  B, AUGND    ;    LOAD BC WITH ADDRESS OF AUGND
          LXI  H, ADDND    ;    LOAD HL WITH ADDRESS OF ADDND
          LXI  D, SUM      ;    LOAD DE WITH ADDRESS OF SUM
          LDAX B           ;    MOVE AUGND TO A
          ADD  M           ;    ADD ADDND
          STAX D           ;    STORE IN SUM
          RET
          . . .
AUGND:    DS 1H            ;    RESERVED MEMORY FOR OPERANDS
ADDND:    DS 1H
SUM:      DS 1H            ;    RESERVED MEMORY FOR RESULT
```

Figure 7.1-2. Single byte addition subroutine.

If a system requires greater range or precision, several bytes of data can represent a single number. To add multibyte numbers, the carry which results from the lower order byte addition is included in the next higher order byte addition. The add with carry instructions are used for this purpose:

Add immediate with carry	*Add register with carry*	*Add memory with carry*
ACI data	ADC r	ADC M
$(A) \leftarrow (A) + \text{byte 2} + (CY)$	$(A) \leftarrow (A) + (r) + (CY)$	$(A) \leftarrow (A) + ((H)(L)) + (CY)$

Flags: Z, S, P, CY, AC

See Fig. 7.1-3 for a subroutine, MBADD, which adds two *N*-byte numbers. The value of *N* has been previously defined with an EQU instruction. The numbers are stored low order byte first in memory buffers, beginning at AUGND and ADDND. The computed sum is stored in the memory buffer, ADDND, low order byte first, replacing the original addend. The routine is written so that when control is returned to the calling program, the carry flag indicates whether an arithmetic overflow has occurred. Note that the only instruction within the loop that affects the carry flag is the ADC M instruction.

As Fig. 7.1-3 shows, single byte addition instructions and looping implement multibyte additions. However, a very useful double precision (16-bit) addition instruction in the 8085A instruction set also implements multibyte addition:

Add register pair to H and L

DAD rp

$(H)(L) \leftarrow (H)(L) + (rh)(rl)$ *Flags:* CY

The contents of the register pair, rp, are added to the contents of the register pair H and L. The sum is left in H and L. The carry is the only flag affected.

```
;  N ASSUMED PREVIOUSLY DEFINED
MBADD:    MVI  D, N          ;    INITIALIZE BYTE COUNTER
          LXI  B, AUGND      ;    LOAD BC WITH ADDRESS OF AUGND
          LXI  H, ADDND      ;    LOAD HL WITH ADDRESS OF ADDND
          XRA  A             ;    CLEAR CARRY
LOOP:     LDAX B             ;    ADD TWO BYTES
          ADC  M
          MOV  M, A          ;    STORE SUM
          DCR  D             ;    DECREMENT BYTE COUNTER
          RZ                 ;    RETURN AFTER LAST BYTES ARE ADDED
          INX  B             ;    INCREMENT POINTERS
          INX  H             ;
          JMP  LOOP
          . . .
AUGND:    DS N
ADDND:    DS N
```

Figure 7.1-3. Multibyte addition subroutine.

7.1.2 Subtraction

The following rules define the subtraction operation for two, 1-bit numbers:

Minuend		Subtrahend		Borrow	Difference
0	−	0	=	0	0
0	−	1	=	1	1
1	−	0	=	0	1
1	−	1	=	0	0

For an n-bit number, subtraction starts with the least significant bits of the minuend and subtrahend and continues with the subtraction of successively higher order bits including a borrow from the previous lower order bit. If the subtrahend is greater than the minuend, an ***arithmetic underflow*** condition exists and results in a borrow out of the higher order bit; for example:

$$
\begin{array}{llr}
\text{Borrows} & 10011000 & \\
X & 00110101 & 53 \\
Y & \underline{10011101} & -157 \\
X - Y & 1] \ 10011000 & -104
\end{array}
$$

```
SBSUB:    LXI  B, MINU     ;  LOAD BC WITH ADDRESS OF MINUEND
          LXI  H, SUBTR    ;  LOAD HL WITH ADDRESS OF SUBTRAHEND
          LXI  D, DIFF     ;  LOAD DE WITH ADDRESS OF DIFFERENCE
          LDAX B           ;  MOVE MINU TO A
          SUB  M           ;  SUBTRACT SUBTR
          STAX D           ;  STORE DIFFERENCE IN DIFF
          RET

          . . .
MINU:     DS  1H           ;  RESERVED MEMORY FOR OPERANDS
SUBTR:    DS  1H
DIFF:     DS  1H           ;  RESERVED MEMORY FOR RESULT
```

Figure 7.1-4. Subroutine for single byte subtraction.

There is a single byte subtraction operation analogous to each of the single byte addition operations.

Subtract immediate	*Subtract register*	*Subtract memory*
SUI data	SUB r	SUB M
$(A) \leftarrow (A) - \text{byte 2}$	$(A) \leftarrow (A) - (r)$	$(A) \leftarrow (A) - ((H)(L))$

Flags: Z, S, P, CY, AC

However, in unsigned binary representations, although a borrow flag indicates a negative difference, this difference cannot be represented for subsequent storage. Therefore, unsigned binary is inappropriate and cannot be used as a method for handling subtraction requiring a borrow. This holds true in 1-bit, n-bit, single byte, and multibyte subtraction of unsigned binary numbers.

The subroutine for single byte subtraction shown in Fig. 7.1-4 parallels that for single byte addition. The calling program checks the carry flag for arithmetic underflow after the subroutine is executed.

For multibyte subtraction, the 8085A has instructions that subtract the carry flag, which represents a borrow from the previous lower order byte. These instructions are:

Subtract immediate with borrow	*Subtract register with borrow*	*Subtract memory with borrow*
SBI data	SBB r	SBB M
$(A) \leftarrow (A) - \text{byte 2} - (CY)$	$(A) \leftarrow (A) - (r) - (CY)$	$(A) \leftarrow (A) - ((H)(L)) - (CY)$

Flags: Z, S, P, CY, AC

N ASSUMED PREVIOUSLY DEFINED

```
MBSUB:    MVI  D, N       ;   INITIALIZE BYTE COUNTER
          LXI  B, MINU    ;   LOAD BC WITH ADDRESS OF MINU
          LXI  H, SUBTR   ;   LOAD HL WITH ADDRESS OF SUBTR
          XRA  A          ;   CLEAR BORROW (CARRY)
LOOP:     LDAX B          ;   SUBTRACT TWO BYTES
          SBB  M
          MOV  M, A       ;   STORE DIFFERENCE
          DCR  D          ;   DECREMENT BYTE COUNTER
          RZ              ;   RETURN AFTER LAST BYTES ARE SUBTRACTED
          INX  B          ;   INCREMENT MEMORY POINTERS
          INX  H
          JMP  LOOP
          . . .
MINU:     DS N
SUBTR:    DS N
```

Figure 7.1-5. Multibyte subtraction subroutine.

The SBB instruction implements multibyte subtraction in the subroutine represented in Fig. 7.1-5. The subroutine is similar to the program for multibyte addition and is written so that when control is returned to the calling program, the carry flag is examined for arithmetic underflow.

7.1.3 Logical Shifts

An arithmetic operation which is not implemented in the 8085A instruction set and which therefore must be implemented by a macro or subroutine is the logical shift. Logical shifts multiply and divide unsigned binary integer numbers.

A logical left shift moves each bit of data in a register one position to the left. The bit shifted out of the left end of the register is lost, and a 0 bit is shifted into the right end.

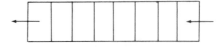

If the data in the register is an unsigned binary integer, if the bit shifted in is a 0, and if the bit shifted out is a 0, the number is multiplied by two. A left shift does not multiply a number by two if the bit shifted out is a 1. For example, shifting the number

$$00011011 = 27$$

three places to the left, results in

$$11011000 = 216$$

```
SUBROUTINE ENTERED WITH N IN REGISTER B
SRN:    ORA  A    ;   CLEAR THE CARRY IN ORDER TO SHIFT IN 0'S
        RAR       ;   SHIFT RIGHT
        DCR  B    ;   DECREMENT COUNTER
        JNZ SRN   ;   IF COUNTER IS NOT ZERO, SHIFT AGAIN
        RET
```

Figure 7.1-6. Subroutine for *n*-bit logical right shift.

or

$$27*2^3 = 27*8 = 216$$

An additional shift to the left, however, gives

$$10110000 = 176$$

which is not equal to $27*2^4$ because a 1 bit was shifted out and lost.

Each logical shift to the right divides a number by two, assuming the bit shifted in is a 0. Since the resulting number is always an integer, any fractional part is lost. Shifting the number 27 three places to the right results in

$$00000011 = 3$$

which is the integer quotient of

$$\frac{27}{2^3} = \frac{27}{8} = 3.38$$

The subroutine in Fig. 7.1-6 implements a logical right shift of *n* places. The subroutine is entered with the data to be shifted in the accumulator and the desired number of shifts in B.

The analogous left shift is implemented similarly, with RAR replaced by RAL. A 16-bit logical left shift of the contents of register pair H and L is carried out by the DAD H instruction. DAD H adds the contents of register pair H and L to itself, thus doubling its original value, or, in effect, shifting the contents one place to the left.

In general, multipliers and divisors are rarely powers of two, thus, limiting the applicability of logical left and right shifts for multiplying and dividing unsigned binary integers. Other methods, however, are available.

7.1.4 Multiplication

Since many microprocessors do not contain multiplication instructions, multiplication is implemented by subroutines or external hardware. A simple subroutine for unsigned binary numbers carries out multiplication by repeated addition. The multiplier is loaded into an internal register as an initial count, the accumulator is cleared, and the multiplicand is added to the accumulator. The multiplier register is then decremented; if it is not zero, the multiplicand is again added to the accumulator, and the process is repeated. When the multiplier register is finally decremented to zero, the multiplication is complete.

If the multiplier is large, the subroutine for multiplying unsigned binary numbers requires the execution of a large number of instructions, and therefore this method is only appropriate in applications where execution speed is not critical.

The multiplication rules for single-bit arithmetic provide the basis for faster algorithms which multiply *n*-bit numbers:

Multiplicand	Multiplier	Product
0 *	0 =	0
0 *	1 =	0
1 *	0 =	0
1 *	1 =	1

An *m*-bit unsigned number multiplied by an *n*-bit unsigned number, produces an $m + n$-bit result. Multiplication of binary numbers on paper is carried out by examining each bit of the multiplier in turn: The bit is multiplied by the multiplicand, producing a partial product which is written in a position that reflects the weight of the multiplier bit. After each multiplier bit has been examined, the partial products are summed to provide the final product.

$$
\begin{array}{lrll}
\text{Multiplicand:} & X & 1011 & \\
\text{Multiplier:} & *\,Y & \underline{1001} & \\
& & 1011 & \\
& & 0000 & \\
& & 0000 & \text{Partial} \\
& & \underline{1011} & \text{products} \\
\text{Product:} & Z = Y*X = & 1100011 &
\end{array}
$$

The subroutine shown in Fig. 7.1-7 implements multiplication in a manner similar to manual multiplication. The essential difference is that partial products are not summed simultaneously but are added to an accumulated partial product in registers H and L as they are generated, except when a multiplier bit is 0, in which case addition of the partial product is not necessary. The

```
MULT:    MVI  D, 0      ;   CLEAR REGISTER D
         MOV  H, D      ;   CLEAR HIGH AND LOW BYTES OF
         MOV  L, D      ;   PRODUCT
MULT0:   MOV  A, C      ;   CHECK FOR ZERO MULTIPLIER
         ORA  A
         RZ
         RAR            ;   PLACE (NEXT) 1SB OF MULTIPLIER IN CARRY
         MOV  C, A
         JNC  MULT1     ;   IF BIT IS ZERO DO NOT ADD
         DAD  D         ;   ADD MULTIPLICAND TO PARTIAL PRODUCT (DE + HL)
MULT1:   XCHG           ;   SHIFT MULTIPLICAND LEFT
         DAD  H
         XCHG
         JMP  MULT0
```

Figure 7.1-7. Multiplication subroutine for 8-bit positive integers.

subroutine is entered with the multiplicand in register E and the multiplier in register C. The product is returned in registers H and L. The multiplier is shifted right to check the value of each multiplier bit by moving the bit into the carry. During the right shift, a zero is moved into the most significant bit of the multiplier. Before each iteration, the multiplier is checked for a value of zero; if zero, the subroutine is exited. The time required for this multiplication varies, depending on the value of the multiplier.

7.1.5 Division

As in the case for multiplication, many microprocessors do not contain division instructions. And, in the same manner in which multiplication is implemented in software as repeated addition, division is implemented as repeated subtraction of the divisor from the dividend. The number of times the divisor is subtracted from the dividend without a borrow occurring is the quotient, Q, and the difference after the last successful subtraction is the remainder, R. This method of division is appropriate when execution time is not critical.

Algorithms can, however, be developed which implement division faster than the repeated subtraction method. The division rules for two 1-bit numbers are as follows:

Dividend	Divisor		Remainder	Quotient
0	÷	0	= Undefined	Undefined
0	÷	1	= 1	0
1	÷	0	= Undefined	Undefined
1	÷	1	= 0	1

In general, if Y is the dividend and X is the divisor, Q the quotient and R the remainder, their relationship is expressed as:[2]

$$\frac{Y}{X} = Q + \frac{R}{X} \quad \text{and} \quad R < X$$

or

$$Y = QX + R$$

For n-bit unsigned binary integers, the equation is written:

$$Y = \left(Q_{n-1}2^{n-1} + Q_{n-2}2^{n-2} + \ldots + Q_0 2^0\right)X + R$$

$$= Q_{n-1}2^{n-1}X + Q_{n-2}2^{n-2}X + \ldots + Q_0 2^0 X + R$$

This equation indicates that division is accomplished by repeatedly subtracting the highest power of the divisor from the dividend and then from the resulting partial remainders. First, Q_{n-1} is determined by subtracting $2^{n-1}X$ from Y. If the difference is positive; i.e., there is no borrow, then $Q_{n-1} = 1$, and the first partial remainder is the difference between Y and $2^{n-1}X$. If a borrow occurs, then $Q_{n-1} = 0$, meaning that $2^{n-1}X$ is larger than Y, and the first partial remainder is equal to Y itself. The next highest power of the divisor is then subtracted from the previous partial remainder to obtain the next bit of the quotient. This process is repeated until all the remaining bits of the quotient are determined. R is the final partial remainder.

[2]To preclude Q being extremely large, some restriction must be placed on the value of X. Since this section deals only with unsigned integers, the restriction is $X \geq 1$.

Division of binary numbers by hand is simply a shorthand version of this algorithm, as shown in the following example:

$$
\begin{array}{r}
0100 \quad \text{Quotient} \\
\text{Divisor:} \quad 0011\,\overline{)1110} \quad \text{Dividend} \\
\underline{11} \\
001 \quad \text{Partial remainder} \\
\underline{000} \\
0010 \quad \text{Partial remainder} \\
\underline{0000} \\
0010 \quad \text{Remainder}
\end{array}
$$

It can, however, be rewritten to resemble a machine implementation:

$$
\begin{array}{r}
0100 \\
0011\,\overline{)0001110} \\
\underline{0000} \\
0011 \\
\underline{0011} \\
0001 \\
\underline{0000} \\
0010 \\
\underline{0000} \\
0010
\end{array}
$$

In this form the divisor is first tested against the dividend divided by 2^{n-1}, which is equivalent to testing 2^{n-1} times the divisor against the dividend. If it is equal to or smaller than the dividend divided by 2^{n-1}, the divisor is subtracted from the dividend; if not, zero is subtracted from the dividend. The divisor is shifted right after each test. In the division routine which appears in Fig. 7.1-8, this final step is accomplished by shifting the dividend to the left, relative to the divisor.

The subroutine in Fig. 7.1-8 divides two 8-bit numbers and generates an 8-bit quotient and an 8-bit remainder. Register B is initially zero and at the completion of the subroutine contains the remainder. Register C initially contains the dividend and at the completion of the subroutine contains the quotient. Register D contains the divisor, and register E contains the count.

The subroutine, as written, has no check for a 0 divisor, instead, the calling routine checks the divisor and only calls the subroutine if it is not zero. Alternatively, the division subroutine can be written to make this check itself.

If a routine divides a 16-bit dividend by an 8-bit divisor, a restriction has to be set on their relative sizes, if the quotient and remainder are to be single byte quantities: The value of the most significant byte of the dividend must be less

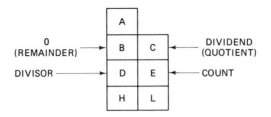

```
DIV:    MVI  B, 0
        MVI  E, 8    ;   SET UP COUNTER
        MOV  A, C    ;   SET UP DIVIDEND DIVIDED BY 2⁷ (RELATIVE TO BC)
        RAL
        MOV  C, A
        MOV  A, B
        RAL
DIV0:   SUB  D       ;   SUBTRACT DIVISOR FROM PARTIAL REMAINDER
        JNC  DIV1
        ADD  D       ;   IF DIFFERENCE IS NEGATIVE, RESTORE PARTIAL REMAINDER
        STC          ;   SET CARRY SO THAT WHEN LATER COMPLEMENTED IT WILL DICTATE
DIV1:   MOV  B, A    ;   QUOTIENT BIT
        CMC          ;   COMPLEMENT CARRY TO INDICATE DIVISOR BIT
        MOV  A, C    ;   MULTIPLY LOW ORDER DIVIDEND BY TWO
        RAL
        MOV  C, A
        DCR  E       ;   CHECK FOR END OF DIVISION
        RZ
        MOV  A, B    ;   MULTIPLY HIGH ORDER DIVIDEND BY TWO
        RAL
        JMP  DIV0
```

Figure 7.1-8. Division subroutine.

than the divisor. If this condition is not met, the quotient requires more than 8 bits.

Errors occur when operands are outside of the range of allowed values or when results are too large or small to be expressed in the number representation. In systems which involve sufficient operator intervention, error messages can be provided to the operator. In other applications, operands or results which are out of range are replaced with either the largest or smallest value expressable in the representation. However, in many systems it is critical for proper operation that no such error conditions ever be allowed to occur. In these systems, the only possible response to an error condition is to shut the system down. Since the range of inputs in most dedicated systems is known, these errors can be avoided by the proper choice of number representation and the correct development of algorithms.

7.2 TWO'S COMPLEMENT NUMBERS

Two's complement numbers provide a binary representation of both positive and negative values, and facilitate subtraction by the same logic circuits in the microprocessor that are used for addition. In an n-bit two's complement number, the most significant bit is the sign. The sign bit of a positive number is $X_{n-1} = 0$. The remaining $n - 1$ bits represent its magnitude. Thus, n-bit positive numbers range from 0 to $+(2^{n-1} - 1)$. The value of the n-bit positive number $x_{n-1}x_{n-2} \ldots x_0$ is:

$$V(X) = + \sum_{i=0}^{n-2} x_i 2^i$$

Two's complement negative numbers have a sign bit, x_{n-1}, equal to 1. In two's complement, n-bit negative numbers range from -1 to -2^{n-1} and have the value:

$$V(X) = -2^{n-1} + \sum_{i=0}^{n-2} x_i 2^i$$

For the general case of positive and negative two's complement numbers, the value of the number is given by:

$$V(X) = \left(-x_{n-1}2^{n-1}\right) + \sum_{i=0}^{n-2} x_i 2^i$$

As an example, several 8-bit numbers are listed below in two's complement form with their decimal equivalents. As this listing shows, with 8-bits, numbers from $-128\ (-2^{n-1})$ to $+127\ (+2^{n-1} - 1)$ can be represented. This range of values is not symmetrical since there is one more negative integer than there is positive.

Weight	Sign Bit -2^7 -128	2^6 64	2^5 32	2^4 16	2^3 8	2^2 4	2^1 2	2^0 1	Decimal Equivalent
	0	1	1	1	1	1	1	1	+127
	0	1	1	1	1	1	1	0	+126
				⋮					
	0	0	0	0	0	0	0	1	+1
	0	0	0	0	0	0	0	0	0
	1	1	1	1	1	1	1	1	−1
	1	1	1	1	1	1	1	0	−2
				⋮					
	1	0	0	0	0	0	0	1	−127
	1	0	0	0	0	0	0	0	−128

Given a two's complement number, X, represented with n bits (a sign bit, x_{n-1}, and $n-1$ magnitude bits), its negative equivalent, $-X$, is equal to $2^n - X$. The computation of $2^n - X$, given X, is referred to as "taking the two's complement of X." [3]

The determination of $2^n - X$ is as follows:

$$X = x_{n-1}x_{n-2}x_{n-3} \ldots x_0$$

The two's complement of X is:

$$2^n - X$$

$$\underbrace{100 \ldots 0}_{n \ \ 0s} - (x_{n-1}x_{n-2}x_{n-3} \ldots x_0)$$

or

$$\underbrace{11 \ldots 1}_{n \ \ 1s} + 1 - (x_{n-1}x_{n-2}x_{n-3} \ldots x_0)$$

or

$$(1 - x_{n-1})(1 - x_{n-2})(1 - x_{n-3}) \ldots (1 - x_0) + 1$$

However, $1 - x_i$ equals $\bar{x}_i$, the logical complement of x_i.

In simpler terms, the two's complement of X is obtained by complementing each bit of X and adding 1 to the result. Any carry out of the high order bit position resulting from the addition is ignored. The resulting n bits represent the two's complement of X.

Consider the following encoding of negative numbers originating as 7-bit unsigned magnitudes. The two's complement representation requires 8 bits:

	Sign	*Magnitude*	*Decimal*
	–	1001101	–77
Concatenate 0 sign bit:		01001101	
Complement:		10110010	
Add 1:		1	
Two's complement representation:		10110011	

[3] A careful distinction must be drawn between the two's complement representation of a number, positive or negative, and the action of "taking the two's complement of a number." The latter refers to the computation of the negative of a number which is already encoded in two's complement form, regardless of whether the number is originally negative or positive.

	Sign	Magnitude	Decimal
	−	1111111	−127
Concatenate 0 sign bit:		01111111	
Complement:		10000000	
Add 1:		1	
Two's complement representation:		10000001	

When the two's complement procedure is applied to a number (positive or negative) initially represented in two's complement form, the negative of that number is obtained:

	Magnitude	Decimal
	11100110	−26
Complement:	00011001	
Add 1:	1	
Two's complement representation	00011010	+26

There is one exception to the above rule: For a given n, the two's complement of the most negative number generates a positive number not representable with n bits. For example, $n = 8$.

	10000000	−128
Complement:	01111111	
Add 1:	1	
	10000000	This is not +128, as desired but −128

7.2.1 Addition of Two's Complement Numbers

Two's complement numbers are added without considering the sign bit. The sum is correct if it is within the allowed range; however, errors arise if the result exceeds this range, producing arithmetic overflow. Consider the addition of two 8-bit two's complement numbers. It is possible to add two positive two's complement numbers and obtain an incorrect negative two's complement number or to add two negative two's complement numbers and obtain an incorrect positive two's complement number. When a positive two's complement and a negative two's complement number are added, the result is always correct. Consider the following addition:

00010101		21
+01110111		+119
10001100	=	140	when interpreted as unsigned integers

When these two numbers are unsigned positive integers, an accurate sum expressable with 8 bits results from the addition. However, when these same numbers are two's complement, the sum is -116, not $+140$, because of arithmetic overflow.

$$
\begin{array}{rr}
00010101 & 21 \\
+01110111 & +119 \\
\hline
10001100 & -116
\end{array}
$$ when interpreted as a two's complement number (overflow!)

Similarly, the addition of two negative two's complement numbers can produce an erroneous positive result:

	unsigned positive integers	*two's complement*
11001010	202	-54
$+10100011$	$+163$	$+(-93)$
1] 01101101	$+109$ (8 bit result)	$+$ 109

carry
lost

Here, however, neither addition is correct. If adding two unsigned positive numbers, the 8-bit result is incorrect unless a carry is included and it is represented with nine bits. And, if the bit patterns are interpreted as two's complement numbers, then the result is a positive number and is obviously incorrect.

Thus, it is the responsibility of the designer to include instructions that not only detect overflow conditions but also take whatever steps are necessary to handle these conditions. The subroutine shown in Fig. 7.2-1 adds two 8-bit numbers in two's complement and checks for overflow.

The subroutine is called with the augend in register B and the addend in register C. The sum is left in register A when the subroutine is exited. If arithmetic overflow occurs, register D contains all 1s; if not, it contains all 0s. To ascertain an arithmetic overflow condition, the sign of the result is checked to determine whether it is appropriate, given the signs of the operands. The signs of the operands are determined by adding the addend to the accumulator, which contains only the sign bit of the augend with the remaining augend bits set to 0. The carry and sign bit from this addition indicate the operand sign bits as follows:

Sign of Augend	Sign of Addend	Carry	Sign Bit
Negative	Negative	1	0
Negative	Positive	0	1
Positive	Negative	0	1
Positive	Positive	0	0

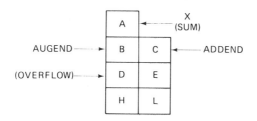

```
TCADD:    MVI  D, 0
          MOV  A, B
          ANI  80H       ;   MASK OUT ALL BUT SIGN BIT OF AUGEND
          ADD  C         ;   ADD ADDEND TO SIGN BIT OF AUGEND
          JC BNEG        ;   IF A CARRY OCCURS BOTH ARE NEGATIVE
          JP BPOS        ;   BOTH POSITIVE
          MOV  A, B      ;   HERE IF SIGNS ARE OPPOSITE AND THERE IS NO CHANCE OF OVERFLOW!
          ADD  C
          RET
BNEG:     MOV  A, B      ;   BOTH AUGEND AND ADDEND ARE NEGATIVE
          ADD  C
          JP ERROR       ;   IF RESULT IS POSITIVE—ARITHMETIC OVERFLOW
          RET
BPOS:     MOV  A, B      ;   BOTH NUMBERS ARE POSITIVE
          ADD  C
          JM ERROR       ;   IF RESULT IS NEGATIVE—ARITHMETIC OVERFLOW
          RET
ERROR:    MVI  D, 0FFH
          RET
```

Figure 7.2-1. Two's complement addition subroutine.

Multibyte two's complement addition is a direct extension of single byte addition. The most significant bit of the most significant byte is the sign of the number. Once the multibyte numbers are in two's complement form, the same subroutine used for unsigned multibyte addition is used. However, no check for arithmetic overflow is provided by this subroutine.

7.2.2 Subtraction of Two's Complement Numbers

As previously stated, taking the two's complement of a number produces the negative of that number. Thus, taking the two's complement of Y produces $-Y$. This allows two's complement numbers to be subtracted by addition; i.e., the two's complement of the subtrahend is *added* to the minuend. The sum is the correct two's complement representation of the difference—if it is within the range of values expressable by the *n*-bit two's complement number. For example:

Minuend:	01110100	(+116)
Subtrahend:	00011101	− (+29)
		(+87)

Take the two's	00011101	
complement of	11100010	Complement
the subtrahend:	1	Add 1
	11100011	

Minuend + two's	01110100	(+116)
complement of	11100011	+ (−29)
the subtrahend:	1] 01010111	(87)

As another example, consider the subtraction of a negative number from a positive one:

Minuend:	00000111	(+7)
Subtrahend:	11000011	− (−61)
		(+68)

Take the two's	11000011	
complement of	00111100	Complement
the subtrahend:	1	Add 1
	00111101	

Minuend and two's	00000111	(+7)
complement of the	00111101	+ (+61)
subtrahend:	0] 01000100	(+68)

Or, consider a subtraction which creates a negative difference:

Minuend:	00011000	(+24)
Subtrahend:	00100000	− (+32)
		(−8)

Take the two's	00100000	
complement of	11011111	Complement
the subtrahend:	1	Add 1
	0] 11100000	

Minuend and two's	00011000	(+24)
complement of the	11100000	+ (−32)
subtrahend:	0] 11111000	(−8)

```
TWOSC:   MVI  C, N        ;   SET COUNTER FOR NUMBER OF BYTES
         LXI  H, SUBTR
         STC              ;   SET CARRY FOR ADDITION OF 1 TO 1SB
LOOP:    MOV  A, M
         CMA              ;   COMPLEMENT BYTE
         ACI  00H         ;   ADD PREVIOUS CARRY
         MOV  M, A        ;   STORE TWO'S COMPLEMENT
         DCR  C           ;   DECREMENT COUNTER
         RZ               ;   RETURN IF 0
         INX  H
         JMP  LOOP
```

Figure 7.2-2. Subroutine to compute the two's complement of an N-byte number.

The 1 in the most significant bit of this result indicates that it is the two's complement representation of a negative number.

In microprocessors that do not have subtraction instructions, subtraction is carried out by the previous technique. Assume that the subtrahend is in register A, and the minuend in register B,

```
CMA        ; complement the subtrahend
ADI 01H    ; add one, obtaining the two's complement
ADD B      ; add minuend, leaving the difference in A
```

Instructions in the 8085A implement an equivalent of the above subroutine as microoperations initiated by a single subtract instruction. There is, however, one difference between the results: In the 8085A, the carry bit is set to indicate the occurrence of a borrow. For instance, in the last example of subtraction by two's complement, $(+24) - (+32)$, the carry bit was zero. If instead, the 8085A SUB instruction is used to subtract $+32$ from $+24$, the carry bit is set to 1 to indicate a borrow.

Multibyte subtraction using two's complement is the same as multibyte addition once the complement of the subtrahend has been obtained. The subroutine in Fig. 7.2-2 obtains the two's complement of an N-byte number stored least significant byte first, starting at location SUBTR.

Subtraction of multibyte two's complement numbers using a subtract instruction can be accomplished using the previous multibyte unsigned integer subtraction subroutine; however, it provides no check for arithmetic overflow.

7.2.3 Arithmetic Shifts

The shifting of a two's complement number, left or right, to multiply or divide the number by two is referred to as an *arithmetic shift*. In arithmetic shifts, unlike the logical shifts of Section 7.1.3, the sign bit is treated in a special manner. In a left shift, the sign bit is never changed. For a left shift of an 8-bit number, bits shifted out of bit 6 never enter bit 7 (the sign bit). For example, if the two's complement number

$$11100101 = -27$$

is shifted left two positions, the result is:

$$10010100 = -108$$

or

$$-27*2^2 = -27*4 = -108$$

An additional left shift of this result gives:

$$10101000 = -88$$

which is not equal to $-27*2^3$. An n-bit left shift of a negative two's complement number results in an arithmetic overflow if the most significant $n + 1$ bits are not equal to 1. For positive two's complement numbers, the conditions for arithmetic overflow are the same as for unsigned numbers.

In an arithmetic right shift, the sign bit is also left unchanged. In addition, the bit shifted into the vacated position is the same as the sign bit. For positive numbers, this is equivalent to the logical shift for unsigned numbers. For negative numbers, some rather interesting results occur. If the two's complement number

$$11100101 = -27$$

is shifted three places to the right, the result is:

$$11111100 = -4$$

but

$$\frac{-27}{2^3} = -3.38$$

An additional right shift by two gives

$$11111111 = -1$$

but

$$\frac{-27}{2^5} = -0.84$$

Finally, one more right shift gives

$$11111111 = -1$$

```
ARN:   RLC         ;   SAMPLE THE SIGN (MSB) BIT
       RAR         ;   RESTORE A
       RAR         ;   SHIFT A RIGHT
       DCR  B      ;   DECREMENT COUNTER
       RZ          ;   DONE WHEN ZERO
       JMP  ARN
```

Figure 7.2-3. Subroutine for *n*-bit right arithmetic shift.

Additional shifting to the right always gives a result of -1. It is clear from these examples that shifting a signed two's complement number (positive or negative) one place to the right results in division by two, with the result rounded to the next most negative integer.

The subroutine shown in Fig. 7.2-3 implements an *n*-bit right arithmetic shift. The subroutine is entered with the number to be shifted in A and the number of positions it is to be shifted in B.

7.2.4 Multiplication and Division of Two's Complement Numbers

Two's complement numbers cannot be multiplied with the algorithm for unsigned binary numbers because if either or both of the operands is negative, the result is incorrect. One method for multiplying two's complement numbers first determines and saves the signs of the operands. Negative operands are made positive, and the operands are multiplied using the add and shift algorithm of Section 7.1.4. If the operand signs are different, the two's complement of the product is taken.

Booth's algorithm is a more direct method of multiplying two's complement numbers. [1, 2] In the previously considered add-and-shift algorithm for unsigned binary integers, each multiplier bit was examined in turn; when the multiplier bit was 1, the multiplicand was added to the accumulated partial product. For each multiplier bit there was a relative 1-bit shift between the multiplicand and partial product, whether an addition was required or not. In Booth's algorithm, however, more than one shift can be made at a time, depending on the grouping of 0s and 1s in the multiplier.

Booth's algorithm is based on the fact that a string of 0s in the multiplier requires no addition, just shifting, and a string of 1s running from bit 2^p to 2^q is treated as $2^{q+1} - 2^p$. Consider the multiplier

$$X = 00011110$$
$$p = 1$$
$$q = 4$$

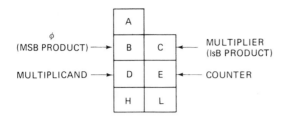

```
SMULT:   MVI  B, 0      ;   CLEAR MSB OF RESULT
         MVI  E, 8      ;   SET COUNTER
         XRA  A         ;   CLEAR CARRY (SET x₋₁ = 0)
         MOV  A, C      ;   PLACE MULTIPLIER IN A
LLA:     JC LLB         ;   CHECK x_{i-1}
         RRC            ;   x_{i-1} = 0, PLACE xᵢ IN CY
         MOV  A, B      ;   MOVE PARTIAL PRODUCT TO A
         JNC LLC        ;   CHECK xᵢ
         SUB  D         ;   xᵢ = 1 AND x_{i-1} = 0, SUBTRACT MULTIPLICAND
         JMP LLC
LLB:     RRC            ;   x_{i-1} = 1, PLACE xᵢ IN CY
         MOV  A, B      ;   MOVE PARTIAL PRODUCT TO A
         JC LLC         ;   CHECK xᵢ
         ADD  D         ;   xᵢ = 0, AND x_{i-1} = 1, ADD MULTIPLICAND
LLC:     MOV  B, A      ;   SAVE MSB OF PARTIAL PRODUCT
         RAL            ;   SET CY TO MSB
         MOV  A, B      ;   LOAD MSB OF PARTIAL PRODUCT
         RAR            ;   ARITHMETIC RIGHT SHIFT
         MOV  B, A      ;   SAVE SHIFTED MSB
         MOV  A, C      ;   LOAD 1SB OF PARTIAL PRODUCT
         RAR            ;   RIGHT SHIFT 1SB, NEW x_{i-1} IN CY
         MOV  C, A      ;   SAVE
         DCR  E         ;   CHECK FOR COMPLETION
         JNZ LLA
         RET
```

Figure 7.2-4. Subroutine to implement multiplication, using Booth's algorithm.

Then $2^{q+1} - 2^p = 2^5 - 2^1 = 32 - 2 = 30$, is the value of X. With Booth's algorithm, multiplication requires only two operations in addition to the shifts: one subtraction and one addition; whereas the add and shift method requires four additions plus the shifts. Booth's algorithm thus results in a faster multiplication because fewer operations are needed.

Booth's algorithm is as follows: Let x_i be the ith bit of an n-bit multiplier. Bit x_{n-1} is the most significant bit, and x_0 is the least significant bit. A bit, $x_{-1} = 0$, is assumed. The multiplicand is Y. Starting with $i = 0$, x_i and x_{i-1} are compared. Depending on the comparison, one of the following actions occurs:

x_i	x_{i-1}	
0	0	Shift Y (left with respect to partial product)
0	1	Add Y to partial product, and shift Y
1	0	Subtract Y from partial product, and shift Y
1	1	Shift Y

The process is repeated until n comparisons are made, completing the multiplication. The procedure is valid for the two's complement numbers Y and X. It is valid for Y because the logic for addition and subtraction of unsigned and two's complement numbers is identical. For X it is valid because if X ends in a string of 1s, the last operation is a subtraction of 2^{n-1}.

The subroutine shown in Fig. 7.2-4 implements Booth's algorithm for an 8-bit multiplicand and an 8-bit multiplier. The subroutine is entered with the multiplicand in register D and the multiplier in register C; the 16-bit product is returned in register pair BC. Booth's algorithm is also used with multibyte operands.

Several different algorithms are used in the software division of two's complement numbers. The simplest one examines the signs of the dividend and divisor to determine the signs of the quotient and remainder. The magnitude of the quotient and remainder are determined by making both the dividend and divisor positive and then dividing. This divides the magnitudes of the numbers, and the magnitudes of the quotient and remainder are then converted to the appropriate signed two's complement representation.

Other algorithms directly divide two's complement numbers [3, 4, 5]. Most of these, developed to carry out division more quickly by manipulating the operands as signed quantities, are designed for implementation with hardware. Therefore, if programmed on a microprocessor, the improvement in execution time may be negligible or nonexistant.

7.3 BCD NUMBERS

Each of the decimal digits, 0 through 9, can be coded in binary by using four bits. The resulting numerical representation is called *Binary Coded Decimal*, or *BCD*. The BCD code for decimal digits is shown in Table 7.3-1.

TABLE 7.3-1

BCD Code for Decimal Digits

Decimal Number	BCD Code
0	0000
1	0001
2	0010
3	0011
4	0100
5	0101
6	0110
7	0111
8	1000
9	1001

Many data input devices represent numbers as decimal digits, and encode them in BCD. For example, a thumbwheel switch is basically a 10 position switch labeled in decimal, whose output is the BCD code corresponding to the selected decimal digit (see Chapter 10). Output displays, as well, for numerical data frequently require BCD inputs. The seven segment display in Chapter 1, for example, is driven by a BCD-to-seven segment decoder driver IC. Some dot matrix decimal displays have an internal display decoder which accepts BCD inputs. And, in systems which require the frequent input and output of decimal data but not a substantial amount of calculation to produce outputs, it is advantageous to have the microprocessor carry out computations in decimal arithmetic rather than binary. In cases of substantial or complex calculation, on the other hand, it is advantageous to convert the BCD input to binary—such as two's complement—carry out the required computations, and then convert the results from binary to BCD for outputting.

7.3.1 Addition of Unsigned BCD Numbers

Special instructions for decimal addition are not available in the 8085A instruction set, and those addition instructions which are available implement only straight binary addition. For BCD, operands are added in binary, and the result is changed to a valid BCD representation. A single data byte can store or pack two BCD digits, but when 2 bytes of data, each representing two decimal digits, are added, the result is generally incorrect if interpreted as two BCD digits. Consider the following addition:

$$
\begin{array}{rrr}
 & 0000 \quad 0111 & 07 \\
 & 0000 \quad 0110 & +06 \\
\hline
AC = 0 \qquad 0] & 0000 \quad 1101 & 13 \\
\end{array}
$$

It is incorrect because 1101 is not a valid code for a BCD digit (see Table 7.3.1). As another example, consider the following:

$$
\begin{array}{rccc}
 & 0000 & 1001 & 09 \\
 & 0000 & 1000 & +08 \\
AC = 1 \quad 0] & \overline{0001} & \overline{0001} & \overline{17}
\end{array}
$$

The BCD result is 11 and not 17 as it should be. Note that the auxiliary carry flag is set, indicating a carry out of bit 3 into bit 4 as a result of the addition.

It is clear that when the sum of two BCD numbers, added using binary arithmetic, is greater than 9 or when a carry out of the most significant of the 4 bits occurs, the result is not valid in BCD. This is true for the least and most significant BCD digit in the byte. If the two previous examples are examined closely, it also becomes apparent that whenever the sum is erroneous, it can be corrected by adding 6 (0110).

$$
\begin{array}{rcclc}
 & 0000 & 0111 & & 07 \\
 & +0000 & 0110 & & +06 \\
AC = 0 \quad 0] & \overline{0000} & \overline{1101} & \text{sum} > 9,\ \text{add } 6 & \overline{13} \\
 & +0000 & 0110 & & \\
AC = 1 \quad 0] & \overline{0001} & \overline{0011} & \text{Adjusted BCD sum} & \\
\end{array}
$$

$$
\begin{array}{rcclc}
 & 0000 & 1001 & & 09 \\
 & 0000 & 1000 & & +08 \\
AC = 1 \quad 0] & \overline{0001} & \overline{0001} & \begin{array}{l}AC = 1,\ \text{sum} > 9, \\ \text{add } 6\end{array} & \overline{17} \\
 & +0000 & 0110 & & \\
AC = 0 \quad 0] & \overline{0001} & \overline{0111} & \text{Adjusted BCD sum} & \\
\end{array}
$$

The 8085A obviates this problem with an instruction which adjusts the results of an addition when the numbers added are interpreted as BCD. This instruction is the *decimal adjust accumulator*, or DAA. It uses two steps to adjust the contents of the accumulator after an addition in order to represent a two-digit BCD result:

1. If the least significant 4 bits of the accumulator represent a number greater than 9, or if the auxiliary carry (AC) is equal to 1, then 6 is added to the accumulator. Otherwise no addition occurs.

2. After step 1 is completed, if the most significant 4 bits of the accumulator represent a number greater than 9 or if the normal carry

(CY) is 1, then 6 is added to the most significant 4 bits of the accumulator. Otherwise no addition occurs. The following example shows the effect of executing a DAA instruction after an addition:

				0110	0111	67
Addition:				0011	0100	34
		AC = 0	0]	1001	1011	101
	DAA step 1			0000	0110	
Decimal		AC = 1	0]	1010	0001	
Adjust						
accumulator:	DAA step 2			0110	0000	
		AC = 1	1]	0000	0001	

The previous multibyte addition routine for unsigned binary numbers is easily modified to handle unsigned BCD numbers by inserting DAA after the addition instruction.

7.3.2 Ten's Complement and Subtraction of BCD Numbers

Because the DAA instruction only works after an addition operation, BCD subtraction is implemented with complementary arithmetic. Signed decimal numbers are represented in *ten's complement* in a manner analogous to two's complement for signed binary numbers. An n-digit positive ten's complement number, $d_{n-1}d_{n-2} \ldots d_0$, has a sign digit of 0, and $n - 1$ decimal digits represent its magnitude. Each of these digits is encoded in BCD when stored in the microprocessor's memory. The representation of a negative decimal number, $-D$, is determined from the ten's complement representation of the positive number of the same magnitude, $+D$, by the process of taking its ten's complement.

The ten's complement of an n-digit decimal number, d, is defined as:

$$10^n - D$$

$$\underbrace{100 \ldots 0}_{n \; 0s} - (d_{n-1}d_{n-2} \ldots d_0)$$

or

$$\underbrace{99 \ldots 9}_{n \; 9s} + 1 - (d_{n-1}d_{n-2} \ldots d_0)$$

or

$$(9 - d_{n-1})(9 - d_{n-2}) \ldots (9 - d_0) + 1$$
$$(9 - d_{n-1})(9 - d_{n-2}) \ldots (10 - d_0)$$

The latter equation shows the way in which the ten's complement of a decimal number is computed by subtracting the least significant digit of the number from 10 and each of the remaining digits from 9. For a negative ten's complement number, the sign bit is $9 - d_{n-1}$, or 9.

In subtracting ten's complement numbers, the ten's complement of the subtrahend is added to the minuend. Assuming that the decimal digits are encoded in BCD, the subroutine shown in Fig. 7.3-1 computes the ten's complement of a multidigit decimal number of $2*N$ digits stored two digits to the byte, least significant two digits first, starting at location SUBTR. The subroutine is entered with N in register C and the address of the least significant byte of the subtrahend in H and L. The ADI 00H and DAA instructions following SUB M convert the difference to BCD before storing it in memory. This sequence correctly adjusts the accumulator contents after subtraction only because in this particular application each minuend digit is either 9 or A. Thus no borrow occurs between BCD digits and, therefore, adjustment of the result is based only on whether digit values are greater than 9. The ADI 00H instruction sets the auxiliary carry to 0. The only case requiring correction occurs when the least significant digit of the number to be complemented is 0. Then 0 is subtracted from A, leaving a result of A. The ACI 00H instruction propagates any carry resulting from this case.

The ten's complement subroutine can be used with a BCD addition subroutine to implement subtraction. Alternatively, as is illustrated in Fig. 7.3-2, a single subroutine can be written which implements BCD subtraction of two $2*N$-digit BCD numbers directly. Here the ten's complement of the subtrahend is taken and added to the minuend. The computed difference replaces the subtrahend. The subroutine is entered with N in register C, a pointer to the subtrahend in registers H and L, and a pointer to the minuend in registers D and E.

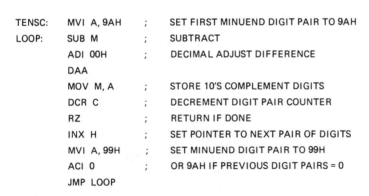

```
TENSC:    MVI  A, 9AH    ;    SET FIRST MINUEND DIGIT PAIR TO 9AH
LOOP:     SUB  M         ;    SUBTRACT
          ADI  00H       ;    DECIMAL ADJUST DIFFERENCE
          DAA
          MOV  M, A      ;    STORE 10'S COMPLEMENT DIGITS
          DCR  C         ;    DECREMENT DIGIT PAIR COUNTER
          RZ             ;    RETURN IF DONE
          INX  H         ;    SET POINTER TO NEXT PAIR OF DIGITS
          MVI  A, 99H    ;    SET MINUEND DIGIT PAIR TO 99H
          ACI  0         ;    OR 9AH IF PREVIOUS DIGIT PAIRS = 0
          JMP  LOOP
```

Figure 7.3-1. Subroutine to compute the ten's complement of a multidigit BCD number.

```
BCDSB:    STC          ;    INITIALIZE CARRY
LOOP:     MVI A,99H    ;    OBTAIN 10'S COMPLEMENT OF SUBTRAHEND
          ACI 0
          SUB M
          XCHG         ;    SWITCH SUBTRAHEND AND MINUEND POINTERS
          ADD M        ;    ADD MINUEND TO SUBTRAHEND COMPLEMENT
          DAA          ;    DECIMAL ADJUST DIFFERENCE
          XCHG         ;    SWITCH POINTERS AGAIN
          MOV M, A     ;    STORE DIFFERENCE
          DCR C        ;    DECREMENT DIGIT PAIR COUNTER
          RZ           ;    RETURN IF DONE
          INX H        ;    INCREMENT POINTERS
          INX D
          JMP LOOP
```

Figure 7.3-2. Subroutine for subtraction of multidigit BCD numbers.

In this routine the ten's complement is formed by initially setting the carry, placing 99 in the accumulator, and adding 0 with carry to form 9A. The first byte of the subtrahend is then subtracted from 9A, forming its ten's complement, and the minuend is added to the result, providing the difference for that byte. Additional bytes of the subtrahend are subtracted from 99 or 9A to form the ten's complement of each byte. Subtraction from 9A occurs if all previous bytes of the subtrahend are zero, and the DAA instruction propagates the carry into the next loop.

7.3.3 Multiplication and Division of BCD Numbers

Multiplication and division of unsigned BCD numbers are carried out by algorithms which implement repeated addition or subtraction, respectively. The execution times of these routines tend to be long, but more sophisticated algorithms are not only slow but also require inordinate amounts of memory. In all but the simplest cases, therefore, it is more efficient to convert BCD data into binary, carry out complex calculations, and then convert the results back to BCD.

7.3-4 BCD-to-Binary Conversion

There are many ways to convert BCD digits to binary. The slowest and simplest method is to count the BCD number down to zero using decimal arithmetic and, for each count, to increment in binary another register which is initially zeroed. The register containing the BCD number is counted down by adding -1 in ten's complement to the BCD value and then decimal adjusting the result. When this register is counted to zero, the other register contains the binary equivalent of the decimal number.

Faster methods utilize the fact that a decimal number, $d_{n-1}d_{n-2} \ldots d_0$, can be written as:

$$D = (\ldots ((d_{n-1})*10 + d_{n-2})*10 + \ldots)*10 + d_1)*10 + d_0$$

An algorithm based on this expression starts with the most significant decimal digit, d_{n-1}, multiplies it by 10, and adds the next most significant decimal digit. This result is then multiplied by 10, and so on, until the least significant digit is added. Subroutine BCDTB, shown in Fig. 7.3-3, converts a four-digit decimal number to a 16-bit binary result. The BCD digits are stored in 4 bytes—one digit per byte—with the most significant byte first (lowest address). The routine is entered with DE containing a pointer to the most significant digit of the BCD number to be converted.

Subroutine BCDTB calls subroutine TEN, which multiplies the contents of register pair HL by 10. The multiplication is carried out by generating 2*HL and 8*HL—through repeated doubling of HL (DAD H)—and then adding these results to obtain 10*HL.

Frequently, binary data is converted to BCD before being output because many display devices accept data in BCD. Binary numbers are easily converted to BCD through repeated division by binary ten (1010). The remainder after each division is a BCD digit. The remainder from the first division provides the

```
BCDTB:    LXI  H, 0H    ;   CLEAR H AND L
          MVI  C, 4H    ;   SET DIGIT COUNTER
LOOP:     LDAX  D       ;   LOAD POINTER TO DECIMAL NUMBER BUFFER
          ADD  L        ;   ADD DECIMAL DIGIT TO H AND L
          MOV  L, A
          MVI  A, 0H
          ADC  H
          MOV  H, A
          DCR  C        ;   CHECK FOR LAST DIGIT
          RZ
          CALL TEN      ;   MULTIPLY H AND L BY TEN
          INX  D        ;   POINT TO NEXT DECIMAL DIGIT
          JMP  LOOP
TEN:      PUSH B        ;   SAVE COUNTER
          DAD  H        ;   HL*2
          PUSH H        ;   SAVE
          DAD  H        ;   HL*4
          DAD  H        ;   HL*8
          POP  B        ;   LOAD BC WITH HL*2
          DAD  B        ;   HL*10
          POP  B        ;   RESTORE COUNTER
          RET
```

Figure 7.3-3. Subroutine for BCD to binary conversion.

low order BCD digit of the number, and each subsequent division provides the next higher order digit. This technique is particularly appropriate if the microprocessor being used has a divide instruction, although a divide subroutine can also be used.

A binary to decimal conversion method which is useful when a divide instruction is not available is repeated subtraction of powers of ten in binary. The highest power of ten possible in the binary number is repeatedly subtracted from the number until the difference becomes negative. The number of times the subtraction can be accomplished without a negative difference provides the digit associated with the power of ten being subtracted. The next highest power of ten is then subtracted from the positive binary difference resulting from the determination of the previous digit. When the digit associated with 10^1 is obtained, the positive remainder is the units digit. The subroutine shown in Fig.7.3-4 converts a 16-bit unsigned binary number to a 4-digit decimal number. The

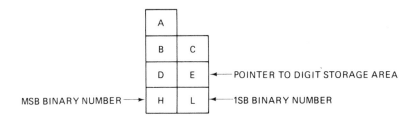

```
BINTD:  MVI  B, 3      ;   INITIALIZE DIGIT COUNTER B, N-1
        XCHG
        SHLD  DEC      ;   SAVE POINTER TO DIGIT STORAGE AREA
        XCHG
        LXI  D, 10     ;   PLACE POWERS OF TEN CONSTANT ON STACK
        PUSH  D
        LXI  D, 100
        PUSH  D
        LXI  D, 1000
        PUSH  D
LOOP:   POP  D         ;   GET POWER OF TEN OF DIGIT TO BE COMPUTED
        CALL  DIGIT    ;   SUBROUTINE RETURNS DIGIT IN C
        PUSH  H        ;   SAVE BINARY DIFFERENCE
        LHLD  DEC      ;   GET POINTER TO DIGIT STORAGE AREA
        MOV  M, C      ;   STORE DIGIT
        INX  H         ;   INCREMENT POINTER
        SHLD  DEC      ;   STORE POINTER
```

Figure 7.3-4. Subroutine for binary to decimal conversion.

```
POP  H          ;    GET BINARY DIFFERENCE
DCR  B
JNZ  LOOP       ;    MORE THAN ONE DIGIT MUST STILL BE DETERMINED
MOV  C, L
LHLD  DEC       ;    GET POINTER TO DIGIT STORAGE AREA
MOV  M, C       ;    STORE D
RET
```

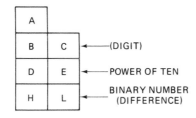

```
DIGIT:  MVI  C, OFFH    ;    INITIALIZE C TO –1
AGAIN:  INR  C
        MOV  A, L       ;    SUBTRACT LOW ORDER POWER
        SUB  E          ;    OF TEN FROM BINARY NUMBER
        MOV  L, A       ;    SUBTRACT HIGH ORDER POWER OF TEN FROM BINARY NUMBER
        MOV  A, H
        SBB  D
        MOV  H, A
        JNC  AGAIN      ;    IF DIFFERENCE IS POSITIVE GO BACK TO SUBTRACT AGAIN
        DAD  D          ;    IF DIFFERENCE IS NEGATIVE, RESTORE
        RET
DEC:    DS  2
```

Figure 7.3-4. Continued.

subroutine is entered with the 16-bit binary number to be converted in HL and
the address of the first digit of the result buffer in DE.

The conversion routines discussed above deal with unsigned numbers. For
signed conversions, the sign is determined and saved. The magnitude of the
number to be converted is determined, and the conversion is carried out on the
unsigned magnitude. After the magnitude conversion is complete, the number is
complemented if it is negative.

7.4 FRACTIONAL NUMBERS

To represent unsigned fractions, simply imagine a binary point in front of the most significant bit of the number. This corresponds to shifting the binary point —imagined in an 8-bit integer to follow x_0—eight places to the left, which is equivalent to dividing the number by 2^8, or 256. The value of an unsigned 8-bit number is:

$$X = {}_{\uparrow} x_7 x_6 \ldots x_0$$
$$\text{Imagined Binary Point}$$

$$V(X) = x_7 2^{-1} + x_6 2^{-2} + \ldots + x_0 2^{-8}$$

And the range of representable unsigned fractions is:

$$.00000000 = \frac{0}{256} = 0$$

to

$$.11111111 = \frac{255}{256} = 0.99609375$$

To represent signed fractions, imagine a binary point after the first bit of the representation; the first bit indicates the sign.

$$X = x_{n-1} . x_{n-2} \ldots x_0$$
$$\text{Imagined binary point}$$

For the two's complement representation of signed fractions:

$$V(X) = (-x_{n-1}) + \sum_{i=0}^{n-2} x_i 2^{-(n-(i+1))}$$

with $n = 8$, $X = x_7 . x_6 \ldots x_0$. Values of X range from $-1.$ to $+0.99218750$. And, as with the integer two's complement case, the range of values is not symmetrical. There is one additional representable negative "fraction": -1 ($+1$ is not representable).

An integer decimal number can be exactly represented by a binary number as long as the range of the binary number is not exceeded. Fractional representation of decimal numbers is only exact in unusual cases where the decimal fraction to be represented has an exact binary representation in n or fewer bits. When there is no exact representation, the binary equivalent is approximate. The approximation is obtained by retaining only the first n bits of the binary equivalent of the decimal fraction and dropping any others. The error which results from **truncating** the binary approximation at n bits is less than 2^{-n}.

Another approach, which provides a more accurate approximation, involves **rounding** the binary approximation to the nearest representable value. With rounding, the error is less than $2^{-(n+1)}$.

Arithmetic operations on fractions, even if the original fractions are exactly representable, includes error because, generally, the result must be truncated or rounded. The designer must ensure, in a particular application, that truncation or roundoff error does not produce unacceptable inaccuracy in the result. These errors are reduced by using more bits to represent the operands.

Arithmetic operations on unsigned and two's complement fractions are carried out in a manner analogous to those operations on integers and two's complement integers.

7.5 FLOATING POINT NUMBERS

In some applications, the required range of numbers is very large. While it is possible to represent such numbers as multibyte integers or multibyte fractions, the memory required for storage is excessive. And, when the number of significant bits required is small, the use of a multibyte representation is wasteful of memory. In addition, most very large or very small numbers do not require the precision of a multibyte representation.

On paper, a more efficient representation of very large or very small decimal numbers is **scientific notation**, which minimizes the number of necessary digits. This notation consists of a **mantissa** multiplied by the decimal base that has been raised to a power represented by an exponent, E:

$$N = M*10^E$$

For example, the number 65,535 is represented by all of the following:

$$65,535*10^0$$
$$6,553.5*10^1$$
$$655.35*10^2$$
$$65.535*10^3$$
$$6.5535*10^4$$
$$0.65535*10^5$$
$$0.065535*10^6$$

Of course, an unlimited number of representations is possible by using different exponents.

Scientific notation delineates the precision and the range of a number. Precision is determined by the number of digits in the mantissa, and range is determined primarily by the base and the number of digits in the exponent.

7.5.1 Floating Point Formats

In digital systems, the counterpart of scientific notation is *floating point notation*. A binary floating point number usually has a base of 2; although others are used in some representations, 10 and 16 being fairly common. In all cases, however, the base is implied, and representation requires only the mantissa (also called *coefficient* or *fraction*) and the exponent (also called *characteristic* or *power*). Similar to scientific notation, the number of bits used in representing the mantissa and exponent determines the precision and range of representable numbers.

The choice of base and format varies widely. It is application-dependent and involves considerations such as precision and range, memory size, computation speed, ease of implementation with a given microprocessor architecture, and ease of interface to other software. For this dicussion, a base of 2 is used. The mantissa and exponent are signed quantities and therefore require a signed number representation. The exponent is represented by seven bits of a single byte in excess-64 (XS-64) form. This is equivalent to a 7-bit two's complement representation with 64 added to it. Or, it is the same as a 7-bit two's complement representation with the sign bit inverted (see Fig. 7.5-1). Thus, exponents range from -64 to $+63$. Using the excess-64 representation with the msb (most significant bit) of the exponent word, makes it easy to distinguish between exponent overflow and underflow.

In this example the mantissa is represented as a 2-byte two's complement fraction. The msb of the 16 bits is the sign bit. An implied binary point is assumed immediately to the right of the sign bit, leaving 15 bits available to represent the magnitude.

To avoid multiple representations of the same number and to maintain as many significant bits as possible in the mantissa, a floating point number is normalized. A normalized nonzero number has a fractional mantissa such that $0.1 \leq |M| < 1$. Zero is a special case because $0 = 0*2^E$ for all E, and therefore cannot be represented in the same manner as nonzero numbers. The convention used for zero is a 0 mantissa and the most negative possible exponent (-64 in the XS-64 representation). Floating point numbers are generally stored in their normalized form, and routines that process them require normalized operands. The normalized range of the mantissa is $\pm(0.5$ to $1.0 - 2^{-15})$.

Combining these representations of the exponent and mantissa, the range of representable numbers in the format of Fig. 7.5-1 is

$$\pm (0.5*2^{-64} \text{ to } (1 - 2^{-15})*2^{63}) \quad \text{or}$$
$$\pm (2.7105*10^{-19} \text{ to } 0.9223*10^{19})$$

EXPONENT:

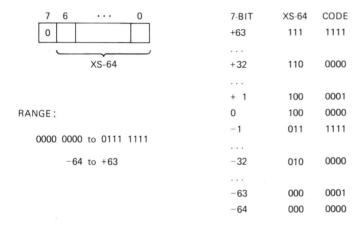

RANGE:

    0000 0000 to 0111 1111

        −64 to +63

7-BIT	XS-64	CODE
+63	111	1111
. . .		
+32	110	0000
. . .		
+ 1	100	0001
0	100	0000
−1	011	1111
. . .		
−32	010	0000
. . .		
−63	000	0001
−64	000	0000

MANTISSA:

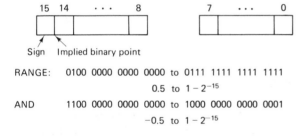

RANGE: 0100 0000 0000 0000 to 0111 1111 1111 1111
                    0.5 to $1 - 2^{-15}$

AND   1100 0000 0000 0000 to 1000 0000 0000 0001
                  −0.5 to $1 - 2^{-15}$

COMBINED FORMAT

Range $\pm(0.5$ to $1.0 - 2^{-15})$

Figure 7.5-1. A 3-byte format for representing floating point numbers.

    This range of values is illustrated in Fig. 7.5-2.

    There are four ranges of numbers which correspond to arithmetic overflow and underflow in Fig. 7.5-2. If a result exceeds the largest positive or negative value representable, the overflow condition means that the result is incorrect. When overflow occurs, it may be possible in subsequent computations to use the largest expressible positive value where positive overflow has occurred and the largest possible negative value where negative overflow has occurred. And, in cases where the value of a result is too small to be expressed, positive or negative underflow, the result is also incorrect. Underflow may not be a serious problem because in most applications zero is a satisfactory approximation.

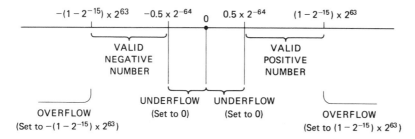

Figure 7.5-2. Range of representable numbers for the floating point format of Fig. 7.5-1.

There are only a finite number of representable values in the four ranges. If the result of a calculation cannot be expressed exactly in the given representation, it must be truncated or rounded off to the nearest expressable number. Roundoff error in floating point numbers is dependent on the exponent. The error in the mantissa can be limited to half the spacing between fractions: For an m-bit mantissa, excluding sign, the error is less than $2^{-(m+1)}$. The actual error is less than $2^{-(m+1)}*2^E$. The error is the smallest when E is the smallest, which is the case with floating point numbers in normalized form. The problem of truncation or roundoff errors in complex floating point calculations can be extreme and must be considered carefully. This problem falls in the domain of numerical analysis.

7.5.2 Floating Point Arithmetic Routines

A typical floating point arithmetic software package contains routines for handling overflow and underflow, negation, addition, subtraction, multiplication, and division. In the floating point routines used here,[4] the following register allocation is used: The first operand at the beginning of a calculation and the result at completion of the calculation are placed in registers B and DE, respectively. The second operand, if any, is placed in registers A and HL. In both cases the exponent is in the first register, the msB (most significant byte) of the mantissa in the second, and the lsB (least significant byte) of the mantissa in the third. Register C stores a count of the negations performed and a copy of the carry bit from the exponent calculation for determining overflow or underflow. Floating point quantities are stored in ascending memory by using 3 bytes of memory: the exponent first, followed by the lsB and msB of the mantissa. This particular register allocation allows optimal use of 8085A instructions in the floating point routines.

---

[4]The routines discussed here follow those developed at Oxford [6]. These routines were selected as a basis of illustration because of their conciseness but have been modified somewhat for instructional purposes.

Both overflow and underflow conditions are handled by the subroutine OUFLW (see Fig. 7.5-3), which has several entry points. OUFLW checks the msb of register C—a copy of the carry produced during an exponent calculation before OUFLW is called. If this bit is 0, an overflow condition exists, and a call is made to a user subroutine, EOFLW, which takes whatever actions are appropriate in the particular application. Upon return from this subroutine, the result registers are loaded with either the largest possible positive or largest possible negative value.

If the msb of C is 1 when the subroutine OUFLW is entered, a call is made to the user subroutine, EUFLW, which takes whatever actions are appropriate to the application in the case of underflow. Upon return from this subroutine, the result registers are all set to zero, giving a value of $0*2^{-64}$ and making zero less significant than the smallest nonzero number. The entry point UFLWE sets

```
OUFLW:   XRA  A          ;   TEST CARRY STORED IN MSB OF C
         ADD  C
         JM  UFLW

OFLW:    CALL EOFLW      ;   CALL ERROR ROUTINE FOR OVERFLOW
         LXI  H, 7FFFH   ;   SET TO LARGEST POSITIVE VALUE
         MVI  B, 7FH

STSGN:   MOV  A, C       ;   CHECK IF VALUE SHOULD BE NEGATIVE
         RAR
         XCHG            ;   PLACE MANTISSA IN DE
         CC  NGDE1       ;   NEGATE
         RET

UFLW:    CALL EUFLW      ;   CALL ERROR ROUTINE FOR UNDERFLOW
         LXI  D, 0H      ;   SET MANTISSA TO ZERO

UFLWE:   MVI  B, 0H      ;   SET EXPONENT TO ZERO (2⁻⁶⁴)
         RET
```

Figure 7.5-3. Subroutine for handling overflow and underflow conditions for floating point operations.

```
NGDE:    INR  C          ;   INCREMENT NEGATION COUNT
NGDE1:   XRA  A          ;   SUBTRACT DE FROM 0
         SUB  E
         MOV  E, A       ;   LEAVE RESULT IN DE
         MVI  A, 0
         SBB  D
         MOV  D, A
         RET
```

Figure 7.5-4. Subroutine to negate a floating point number.

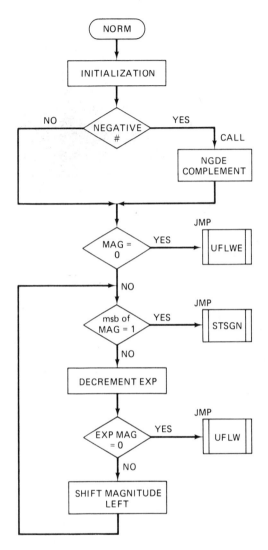

Figure 7.5-5. Flowchart for normalization subroutine.

the result exponent to zero if the result of a calculation is zero. No call is made to EUFLW when the entry point UFLWE is used.

The subroutine OUFLW and the subroutine NORM, which normalize a floating point number, require an additional subroutine which negates a floating point number. This subroutine, NGDE, has two entry points: one which increments the negation count in C and another which does not (see Fig. 7.5-4).

A floating point number is normalized by making the number positive and then shifting it left until its magnitude msb is 1. Each time the number is shifted left, the exponent is decremented, thus maintaining the original value of the number. If the original number is negative, the normalized floating point number must be negated. A flowchart for a normalization routine, NORM, is shown in Fig. 7.5-5 and the subroutine listing in Fig. 7.5-6.

To add two floating point numbers, they must be aligned. Alignment refers to equal exponents and is accomplished by shifting the smaller number to the right and incrementing its exponent until the values of the two exponents are equal. If the shift requires more than 16 places, the addition is unnecessary because the larger number, when added to the smaller number, does not change. Therefore, the sum is simply the larger of the two numbers. A flowchart for the floating point addition routine, FADD, is shown in Fig. 7.5-7.

When aligned numbers are added, their signs and the sign of the result and the carry bit are checked for magnitude overflow. If the modulo-2 sum of the carry and three sign bits is 1, there is overflow. The overflowed bit is the same as the sign bits of the operands. The overflowed bit must be shifted into the result, and the exponent of the result must be incremented. After incrementing the exponent, it is also checked for overflow. In all computations, whether or not they involve overflow, the result may need normalizing—in which case the subroutine NORM is called. The floating point addition subroutine is shown in Fig. 7.5-8.

In floating point subtraction, the subtrahend is negated and added to the minuend. Algorithms for floating point multiplication and division can be developed by using the rules of scientific notation.

```
NORM:    XRA  A
         MOV  C, A    ;   CLEAR C FOR NORMALIZATION
         ORA  D       ;   CHECK FOR NEGATIVE NUMBER
         CM  NGDE     ;   MAKE POSITIVE
         ORA  E       ;   CHECK FOR ZERO MAGNITUDE
         JZ  UFLWE    ;   IF MAGNITUDE IS ZERO, SET EXPONENT TO 0
         XCHG         ;   NORMALIZE IN HL


NORM1:   MOV  A, H    ;   ENTRY FOR POSITIVE NONZERO NUMBERS
         ADD  H
         JM  STSGN    ;   NORMALIZATION COMPLETE; SET SIGN
         DCR  B       ;   DECREMENT EXPONENT
         JM  UFLW     ;   UNDERFLOW
         DAD  H       ;   SHIFT LEFT
         JMP  NORM1
```

Figure 7.5-6. Subroutine to normalize a floating point number; (a) assume number is in B and DE—can be positive or negative; (b) C must be initialized, C = 0.

Additional routines are required to convert decimal numbers input to the system to floating point numbers in the desired format, and vice versa.

When greater precision or range is required, formats that require more than 3 bytes of data represent each floating point number. In such a case, operands, partial results, and the final result are maintained in memory locations.

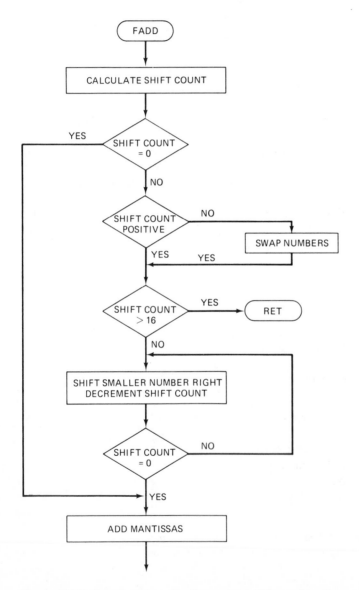

Figure 7.5-7. Flowchart for a floating point addition subroutine.

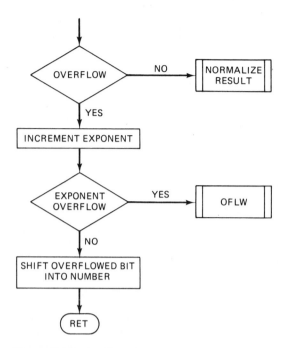

Figure 7.5-7. Continued.

```
FADD:    MOV C, A      ;   SAVE EXPONENT
         MOV A, B
         SUB C
         JZ FADD3      ;   NO SHIFT REQUIRED
         JP FADD1      ;   OPERANDS IN RIGHT ORDER
         CMA           ;   MAKE SHIFT COUNT POSITIVE
         ADI 01H
         XCHG          ;   SWAP OPERANDS
         MOV B, C
FADD1:   CPI 16
         RP            ;   SHIFT > 16 ADDITION UNNECESSARY
         MOV C, A      ;   SAVE SHIFT COUNT
FADD2:   MOV A, H      ;   LOOP TO SHIFT SMALLER NUMBER RIGHT
         RAL               GET SIGN
         MOV A, H
         RAR
         MOV H, A
         MOV A, L
         RAR           ;   LEAVES 1SB IN CARRY
         MOV L, A
         DCR C
         JNZ FADD2
```

Figure 7.5-8. Subroutine for floating point addition.

```
FADD3:   MOV  C, H      ;   SAVE SIGN OF H, L
         DAD  D         ;   ADD MANTISSAS
         XCH G          ;
         SBB  A         ;   SAVE CARRY/OVERFLOW A = 0 OR FF
         XRA  A
         XRA  D
         XRA  H
         JP NORM
FADD4:   MOV A, H       ;   SUPER NORMAL OR NEGATIVE MAX
         RLC
         MOV C, A
         INR  B         ;   ADJUST EXPONENT FOR CARRY
         JM OFLW        ;   REAL OVERFLOW
         MOV  A, D      ;   SHIFT OVERFLOW BIT INTO RESULT
         RAR
         MOV  D, A
         MOV  A, E
         RAR
         MOV  E, A
         RET
```

Figure 7.5-8 Continued.

REFERENCES

1. BOOTH, A.D., "A Signed Binary Multiplication Algorithm," *Quarterly Journal of Mechanics and Applied Mathematics*, Vol. 4, Pt. 2, 1951, pp. 236–240.

2. MICK, J.R., *Understanding Booth's Algorithm in 2's Complement Digital Multiplication.* Sunnyvale, California: Advanced Micro Devices, Inc.

3. LOOMIS, H.H., JR., "Data Representation," in H. Stone (Ed.), *Introduction to Computer Architecture.* Chicago: Science Research Associates Inc., 1975, pp. 23–73.

4. CHU, Y., *Digital Computer Design Fundamentals.* New York: McGraw-Hill Book Company, 1962.

5. MACSORLEY, O.L., "High-Speed Arithmetic in Binary Computers," *Proceedings of the IRE*, Vol. 49, 1961, pp. 67–91.

6. COPE, S.N., *Floating-Point Arithmetic Routines and Macros for an Intel 8080 Microprocessor*, O.U.E.L. Report No. 1123/75. Springfield, Virginia: National Technical Information Service, 1975.

BIBLIOGRAPHY

BURKS, A.W., H.H. GOLDSTINE, and J. VON NEUMANN, "Preliminary Discussion of the Logical Design of an Electronic Computing Instrument," in C. G. Bell and A. Newell

(Eds.), *Computer Structures*: *Readings and Examples*. New York: McGraw-Hill Book Company, 1971. pp. 92–119.

FLORES, I., *The Logic of Computer Arithmetic*. Englewood Cliffs, New Jersey: Prentice-Hall, Inc., 1963.

RICHARDS, R.K., *Arithmetic Operations in Digital Computers*. New York: Van Nostrand Reinhold Co., 1955.

PROBLEMS

7-1. Add the following unsigned binary integers. If the result is to be stored as a single byte, indicate those sums which involve arithmetic overflow. Give the decimal equivalents of the unsigned binary sums.

a.	10110011		b.	01011101	
	+ 01100001			+ 01100010	
c.	10010101		d.	10010011	
	+ 01101011			+ 10101100	

7-2. Subtract the following unsigned binary integers. If the result is to be stored as a single byte, indicate those differences which involve arithmetic underflow.

a.	01100101		b.	11010111	
	− 10010011			− 01101100	
c.	00110010		d.	00101111	
	− 00010110			− 01011101	

7-3. Write a macro, LDHI DATA, which loads DE with the sum of the contents of HL and DATA. In other words, a macro which implements the register transfer expression:

$$(D)(E) \leftarrow (H)(L) + DATA$$

Assume that DATA is an 8-bit constant. This macro should leave all the registers except DE and HL unaltered.

7-4. Write a subroutine, DSUB (double subtraction), which subtracts the contents of register pair BC from the contents of register pair HL, leaving the difference in HL. Indicate those flags which are valid for the result after returning from the subroutine. Use available subtraction instructions.

7-5. Using the DAD instruction write a subroutine which carries out an n-bit logical left shift of a 16-bit quantity in register HL. Include a provision for the calling program to detect whenever an overflow occurs.

7-6. Write a subroutine which multiplies two 8-bit unsigned integers using repeated addition. Give the maximum execution time if the state time is 320 nS.

7-7. Write a subroutine which divides a 16-bit unsigned integer by an 8-bit unsigned integer. Give the maximum execution time if the state time is 320 nS.

7-8. Write a subroutine, ARHL, which implements a 1-bit arithmetic right shift of the contents of HL.

7-9. Compute the sum of the following two's complement numbers using binary arithmetic. Indicate those cases, if any, which involve arithmetic overflow or underflow. Convert all operands to decimal and add them again to check for accuracy.

a.   10110011   b.   00100100
     + 01101011   + 11110101

c.   11101110   d.   01110010
     + 11110100   + 00101101

7-10. Determine the bit pattern of all the following decimal numbers when represented as 8-bit two's complement numbers. Write the bit patterns in hexadecimal.
a. − 1
b. + 126
c. − 13
d. − 74

7-11. A register initially contains the bit pattern 34H. Give the contents of the register (in hexadecimal) after each of the following operations takes place.
a. left logical shift two places
b. left arithmetic shift two places
c. right logical shift two places
d. right arithmetic shift two places
Repeat this problem with an initial register value of E8H.

7-12. List the steps in the operation of the decimal adjust accumulator instruction, DAA. Also list each step of the operation of DAA when executed following the execution of an ADD B instruction with (A) = 87H and (B) = 96H.

7-13. Write a subroutine which subtracts two 16-bit unsigned integers. Enter the subroutine with the minuend in HL and the subtrahend in BC. At its completion have the subroutine leave the difference in HL. What restrictions must be placed on the operands for the result to be valid? Describe what, if any, modification would have to be made in the subroutine to subtract 16-bit two's complement numbers. Also what restrictions must be placed on the two's complement operands for a valid result?

7-14. Repeat problem 7-10 representing each decimal number as a 16-bit two's complement number.

7-15. Write the bit patterns which represent each of the following decimal numbers as 16-bit ten's complement numbers. Write these bit patterns in hexadecimal.
a. + 49
b. − 312
c. − 1
d. − 67

7-16. Without using subtraction instructions write a subroutine, DIFF, which subtracts the content of register pair DE from the content of register pair HL and leaves the difference in HL. Assume that the operands are 16-bit numbers represented in two's complement form.

7-17. Write a subroutine which adds two 4-digit BCD numbers. Assume that the operands are in register pairs BC and DE before the subroutine is called. The subroutine should leave the least significant four digits of the BCD result in register pair DE, and the value of the carry in the least significant four bits of register C.

8

Program Controlled I/O

Since the processor usually talks to all its peripherals over only one or two main interconnecting busses, the interface must insure that processor outputs reach only the intended peripheral. In the reverse direction, the interface must provide a means for information from each peripheral to reach the processor without interfering with other units hanging on the system busses. In addition, the interface must reconcile any differences between microprocessor and peripheral timing. The microprocessor runs on its own internal clock. Peripherals may, or may not, have internal clocks of their own.

Howard Falk*

8.1 INTRODUCTION

Any application of a microprocessor system requires the transfer of data between circuitry external to the microprocessor and the microprocessor itself. This transfer of data is in addition to transfers between the microprocessor and main memory and is referred to as *input/output*, or *I/O*.

There are many ways that the transfer of information is initiated and controlled; however, these can be placed in one of three primary catagories:

1. Program controlled I/O
2. Interrupt-program controlled I/O
3. Hardware controlled I/O[1]

These three methods differ in the degree to which the microprocessor initiates and controls the transfer of data. With program controlled I/O operations, the transfer of data is completely under the control of the microprocessor program; i.e., an I/O operation takes place only when an I/O transfer instruction is encountered in the execution of the program. In many cases it is necessary to determine the "readiness" of the device before the data transfer occurs. This involves testing one or more external flags or status bits associated with the I/O device, which, of course, requires a transfer of status information to the microprocessor—an additional I/O operation.

In contrast, with an interrupt-program controlled approach, an external device indicates directly to the microprocessor its readiness to transfer data by driving an interrupt input of the microprocessor high. Most microprocessor interrupt inputs can be disabled under program control. Other interrupts which occur between the time the interrupt input is disabled and the time it is reenabled are ignored.

When a microprocessor is interrupted, the program being executed is suspended, and control is transferred to an interrupt service subroutine. This subroutine performs the data transfer then returns control to the program at the point it was interrupted, and processing continues. Thus, with an interrupt-program controlled I/O operation, the transfer is initiated by external hardware and then controlled by an interrupt service subroutine.

Hardware controlled transfers, commonly referred to as *Direct Memory Access, DMA*, are direct transfers between an I/O device and memory: Data is not routed from an I/O device to one of the microprocessor's registers and then to main memory, or vice versa, but is routed directly between the external device and memory. The microprocessor still sets up the transfer in the sense that it sends initialization information—the starting address in main memory and the number of words to be transferred—to the DMA device. However, subsequent to this, hardware associated with the DMA device initiates and controls the

---

[1]This chapter considers program controlled I/O only. Interrupt-program controlled I/O and DMA are presented in Chapter 9.

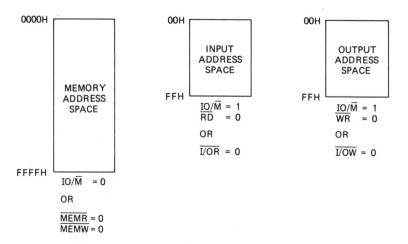

Figure 8.1-1. Control signals and strobes determine to which address space an address refers.

actual data transfer. DMA is used primarily to transfer a number of words or a block of data at high speed. Interfacing some peripheral devices to a microprocessor includes the use of a combination of these primary data transfer methods.

As discussed in Chapter 3, input ports and output ports are basically external registers. Some microprocessors provide control signals which allow external registers associated wtih I/O devices to occupy a separate address space—distinct from the address space of the external registers which comprise main memory. When I/O ports are assigned to a separate address space, they are referred to as *isolated* or *standard I/O*. When assigned to the same address space as memory, they are referred to as *memory mapped I/O*.

The $IO/\overline{M}$ control signal of the 8085A determines whether the address generated during a data transfer refers to memory ($IO/\overline{M} = 0$) or to the separate I/O address space ($IO/\overline{M} = 1$). I/O address space is further divided by control strobes into an input address space ($\overline{RD} = 0$) and an output address space ($\overline{WR} = 0$). Figure 8.1-1 shows how the total address space of the 8085A is divided by these control signals.

8.2 ISOLATED I/O

Only the IN and OUT instructions provide data transfer for isolated I/O. IN and OUT each require three machine cycles for execution. The first is, of course, an OPCODE FETCH. The second is a MEMORY READ, during which the 8-bit port address is transferred from memory to the microprocessor and placed in both the W and Z temporary registers. And the third is either an INPUT or OUTPUT machine cycle, during which the actual data transfer from or to the I/O device occurs.

During the INPUT and OUTPUT machine cycles, the 8-bit port address, in W and Z, is output from the 8085A on address data bus lines AD_0–AD_7 and on address lines A_8–A_{15}. See the IN and OUT instruction cycle timing diagrams for the 8085A in Fig. 8.2-1.[2] The read ($\overline{RD}$) and write ($\overline{WR}$) control strobes from the 8085A specify the exact time at which an input port's three-state buffer is enabled to drive the data bus or the exact time at which an output port latches the data placed on the data bus by the microprocessor, respectively. Figure 8.2-1(a) shows the timing relationship for the 8085A between the availability of the port address and the $\overline{RD}$ during an INPUT machine cycle, and Fig. 8.2-1(b) shows the timing relationship between the port address and $\overline{WR}$ control strobes.

For input ports, external decoding logic combines $\overline{RD}$, IO/$\overline{M}$, and the port address and generates a unique *input device select pulse* for each input port. See Fig. 3.1-2. This pulse occurs only during the INPUT machine cycle of an IN instruction which addresses the decoded port. The input device select pulse enables the input port's three-state buffer. If, through design or programming error, the three-state buffers of two or more ports or a port and a memory device are simultaneously enabled, both drive the data bus and can be physically damaged.

For output operations, external decoding logic combines $\overline{WR}$, IO/$\overline{M}$, and the port address and generates a unique *output device select pulse* for each output port. See Fig. 3.1-3. This pulse occurs only during the OUTPUT machine cycle of an OUT instruction which addresses the port and clocks the decoded output port's register. Typically, each output device select pulse clocks a single output port; however, it is possible and often useful to have two or more output ports selected simultaneously.

The design of device selection logic varies depending on how many I/O devices are required in a system and the logic provided by the ICs that comprise the input and output ports. If only a single input port and a single output port are required, address decoding is unnecessary. The IO/$\overline{M}$ control signal is simply combined with $\overline{RD}$ to generate an input read strobe ($\overline{I/OR}$) and with $\overline{WR}$ to generate an output read strobe ($\overline{I/OW}$). These strobes directly control the input buffer and the output latch, respectively. The port address byte of the I/O instruction is, in cases requiring only a single port, a don't care, but cannot be omitted from the instruction or its object code. IN and OUT are 2-byte instructions, and both bytes must appear in the program wherever the instruction is used.

When more than one input or output port is required in a system, which is usually the case, the port address is decoded to generate device select pulses for specific input or output ports. The simplest form of decoding is the *linear selection method*. This requires the smallest amount of logic but can only be used

---

[2]Timing relationships for the 8080A differ from those of the 8085A; see reference [1] at end of this chapter.

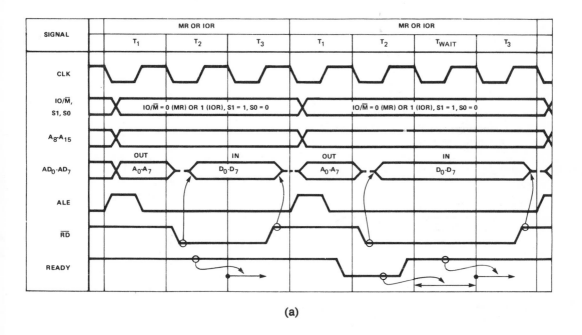

(a)

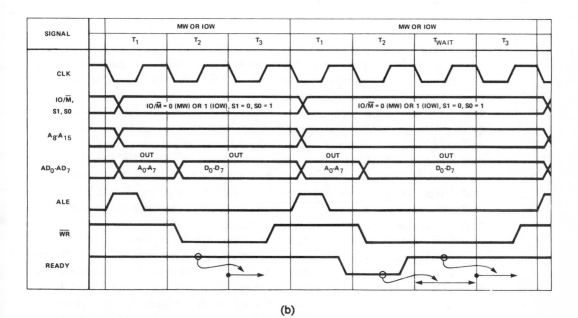

(b)

Figure 8.2-1. Timing diagrams for the 8085A: (a) read timing diagram; (b) write timing diagram.

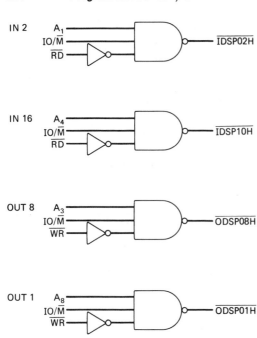

Figure 8.2-2. Input and output device select pulse
generation using linear selection.

for eight or fewer input and eight or fewer output ports. Here, one address bit is
associated exclusively with each I/O port and is logically combined with IO/$\overline{\text{M}}$
and $\overline{\text{RD}}$ or $\overline{\text{WR}}$ to generate an input or output device select pulse (see Fig.
8.2-2). Note that the device select pulse occurs during the machine cycle at
essentially the same time as the $\overline{\text{RD}}$ or $\overline{\text{WR}}$ strobe, delayed only by the
propagation time of the device selection logic. For example, in Fig. 8.2-2,
address bit $A_4 = 1$ selects port 16. If the $\overline{\text{RD}}$ strobe is inverted and NANDed
with A_4 and IO/$\overline{\text{M}}$, an active low input device select pulse, $\overline{\text{IDSP10H}}$[3], is
generated. $\overline{\text{IDSP10H}}$ is connected to the active low enable of a three-state buffer
and determines when the buffer drives the bus. If the IC three-state buffer has
multiple enable inputs, the internal decoding logic of the three-state buffer itself
may be sufficient, requiring no external gates.

A disadvantage of linear selection is the possibility that a programming
error will damage the hardware. If the port address is not exhaustively decoded,
two or more input ports can drive the data bus simultaneously. Suppose, for
example, a particular design using linear selection contains an input port 4 and
an input port 8, selected by address bits A_2 and A_3, respectively. If a programming error results in the use of an IN 12 instruction instead of, for instance, an
IN 8, execution causes input ports 4 and 8 to be selected simultaneously,

[3]Note that port address is specified here in hexadecimal.

possibly damaging the three-state buffers. *When linear selection is used, care must be taken to ensure that two ports are not selected simultaneously!*

Since there are only eight unique address bits in the port address, only eight input and eight output ports can be selected with the linear select method. However, the elimination of the decoders required to decode combinations of address bits is an important savings in small systems. To select from a larger number of I/O devices requires decoding port addresses. With exhaustive decoding, the maximum number of device select pulses which can be generated is 512: 256 associated with IN instructions; 256 with OUT instructions.

When decoding address bits to generate more than one device select pulse, decoders with enable inputs are particularly useful because they reduce the package count. If an application requires four or fewer input and four or fewer output device select pulses, a 74LS139 Dual 1-of-4 Decoder can be used. The active low enable of one of the decoders is connected to the $\overline{I/OR}$ strobe, and the select inputs to address bits A_0 and A_1, providing four input device select pulses (see Fig. 8.2-3). All four remain high until the $\overline{I/OR}$ strobe occurs. The active low strobe enables the decoder, and an active low device select pulse occurs at the output selected by A_0 and A_1. The unselected outputs remain high. The active low enable of the other 1-of-4 decoder is connected to the $\overline{I/OW}$ strobe, and the select inputs to address bits A_0 and A_1, thus providing four output device select pulses.

Because only the least significant two address bits are connected to the decoder, the most significant six port address bits in the second byte of the instruction are don't cares. The effect of these don't cares is the generation of the same device select pulses by a number of IN or OUT instructions with different port addresses. For example, the $\overline{IDSP00H}$ device select pulse is generated by executing an IN 0 instruction or any of the following: IN 4, IN 8, IN 12, IN 16, IN 20, etc.

Decoders with both active low and active high enable inputs provide even greater flexibility. The 8205 and 74LS138, for instance, are 1-out-of-8 binary decoders with two active low and one active high enable inputs. See Fig. 2.5-2. When the required input combination is not applied to the enables, all outputs of the decoder are high, regardless of the select or address input values. When an 8205 or 74LS138 generates device select pulses for the 8085A, the $\overline{RD}$ or $\overline{WR}$ strobe is connected to one of the active low enables, the second active low

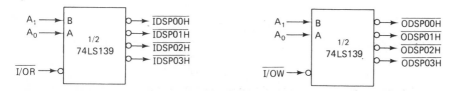

Figure 8.2-3. Four input and four output device select pulses generated with a single 74LS139 1-of-4 decoder.

enable is grounded, and the $IO/\overline{M}$ signal is connected to the active high enable (see Fig. 8.2-4). This arrangement requires no additional logic to generate an $\overline{I/OR}$ or $\overline{I/OW}$ because generation is, in effect, accomplished by the internal enable gating of the 8205 or 74LS138.

Decoders with enable inputs can be cascaded to generate larger numbers of device select pulses. As shown in Fig. 8.2-5, 17 74L154, 1-out-of-16 decoders provide 256 device select pulses.

The isolated I/O address space can be expanded to provide more than 256 input and 256 output ports by using an extended address register. An *extended address register* is simply an output register which holds additional bits for port addressing (see Fig. 8.2-6). It is loaded by an output instruction. The remaining output ports decode the output of this register along with the usual port address. Using an 8-bit extended address register, 65,281 (256*255 + 1—this 1 is the extended address register) unique ports can be addressed. The extended address register can be loaded with any one of 256 unique codes to provide the most significant 8 bits of the port address. The least significant port address can be one of only 255 unique values; one value must be reserved as the extended address register's port address. Programs for this type of I/O structure group together output transfers to I/O ports with a common high order port address so that the extended address register is loaded infrequently.

Device select pulses are also useful as control pulses when controlling external devices where no actual data transfer is intended. The OUT instruction is preferable for generating such pulses because IN causes whatever is on the data bus when the instruction is executed to replace the contents of the accumulator. In Fig. 8.2-7, software generated device select pulses control an external device by setting or clearing a flip-flop. Execution of OUT 1 sets the flip-flop and makes the output of the open collector inverter logic 0, turning ON the solid state relay, which acts like a closed switch. Current flows from the 120V A.C. source through the solid state relay and motor. Execution of an OUT 0 instruction clears the flip-flop, turning OFF the motor. Note that the data placed on the data bus during the execution of the OUT instruction is not latched and has no effect on the system.

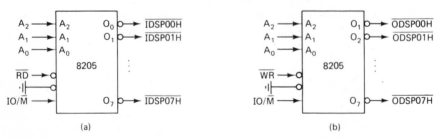

Figure 8.2-4. Generation of (a) input device select strobes and (b) output device select strobes for an 8085A system.

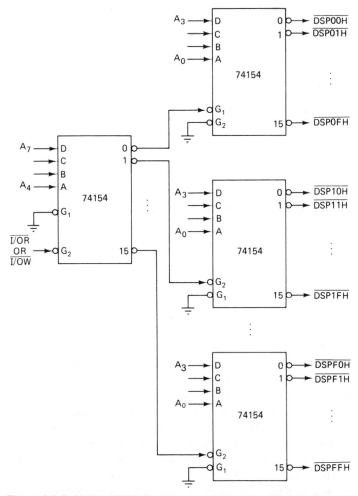

Figure 8.2-5. Using 17 74154 decoders to provide full decoding of 8-bit port addresses.

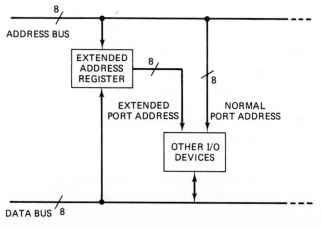

Figure 8.2-6. Extended address register.

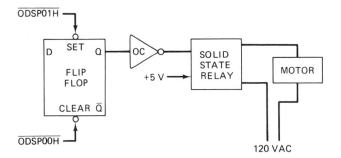

Figure 8.2-7. Use of program generated device select pulses to control an external device.

8.3 MEMORY MAPPED I/O

Any instruction which references memory can also transfer data between an I/O device and the microprocessor, as long as the I/O port is assigned to the memory address space rather than to the I/O address space. The register associated with the I/O port is simply treated as a memory location.

Consider an example in which address bit A_{15} designates whether instructions reference memory or an I/O device. If $A_{15} = 0$, a memory register is addressed; if $A_{15} = 1$, then a memory mapped I/O device is addressed. This assignment devotes the first 32 K of memory address space to memory and the second 32 K to memory mapped I/O, and address decoder logic enables either main memory or memory mapped I/O devices. External logic generates device select pulses for memory mapped I/O only when $IO/\overline{M} = 0$, the appropriate address is on the address bus, and a $\overline{RD}$ or $\overline{WR}$ strobe occurs.

Input and output transfers using memory mapped I/O are not limited to the accumulator. For example, some of the 8085A instructions which can be used for input from memory mapped ports are:

Instruction	Interpretation for memory mapped I/O
MOV r,M	input from a port to any register
LDA	input from a port to accumulator
LHLD	input from two ports to H and L
ADD M	input from a port with arithmetic operation to accumulator
ANA M	input from a port with logical operation to accumulator

ADD M and ANA M provide input data transfer and computation in a single instruction. Some instructions which output data from memory mapped ports are:

Instruction	Interpretation for memory mapped I/O
MOV M,r	output any register to a port
STA	output accumulator to a port
SHLD	output H and L to two ports
MVI M, data	output immediate data to a port

LHLD and SHLD carry out 16-bit I/O transfers with a single instruction, which reduces program execution time considerably. The price paid for this added capability is a reduction in directly addressable main memory and the necessity of decoding a 16-bit rather than an 8-bit port address.

When a microprocessor puts out an address and a control strobe for a memory read, it has no way of determining whether the device that responds with data is a memory device or an I/O device, nor does it care. It only requires that the device which responds does so within the allowable access time or uses the READY line to request a sufficient number of WAIT states. The same is true when a microprocessor executes a write to memory. It supplies an address, data, and a write strobe, and continues its operation. External logic determines whether memory, I/O, or anything at all receives the data transferred.

Many commercially available digital and analog I/O devices (see Chapters 10 and 11) are equipped with interfaces which respond like memory locations, so they are directly compatible with microprocessors.

8.4 MSI I/O PORTS

I/O ports can be implemented with SSI, MSI, or LSI circuits. However, to minimize parts count, MSI or LSI circuits are generally used. Certain MSI circuits provide input and output ports in a single package. An output port in its most basic form is a simple register or latch. An 8-bit output port can be implemented with a single 8-bit latch. Two 8-bit latches, the 74LS373 and the 74LS374, are shown in Fig. 8.4-1.

The 74LS373 contains eight D-type positive level triggered latches, with a single enable (clock). To drive the enable inputs, an active high output device select pulse is required. This pulse is obtained by inverting an active low output device select pulse or by generating an active high strobe directly.

The 74LS374 contains eight D-type positive edge triggered latches with a common clock. Thus, the clock input is driven by either an active low or active high output port select pulse, provided the setup time requirements (20 nS) of the 74LS374 are met. Examination of the I/O write machine cycle shown in Fig. 8.2-1(b) indicates that the 8085A provides a stable data setup only to the trailing edge of $\overline{WR}$.

Both the 74LS373 and 74LS374 have three-state outputs. The three-state output buffers have an active low enable (output control). When used as an

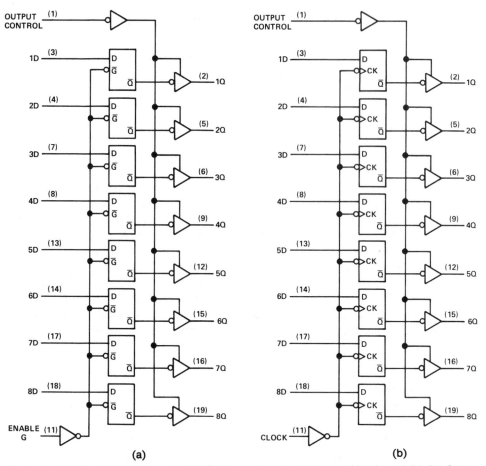

Figure 8.4-1. Two 8-bit latches: (a) 74LS373 positive level triggered latch and (b) 74LS374 positive edge triggered latch. (Courtesy of Texas Instruments, Inc.)

output port, the output buffers are either enabled or are controlled by the output device.

Eight-bit, individually addressable D latches, such as the National 9334 provide output ports without additional decoding. The 9334 functions like a 1-out-of-8 demultiplexer with a D latch on each output (see Fig. 8.4-2). Eight of these latches provide eight output ports, and each package provides 1 bit of each port (Fig. 8.4-3). The address inputs of the 9334 are connected to A_0–A_2 of the address bus, $IO/\overline{M}$ is connected to the enable, and $\overline{WR}$ to the clock. If more output ports are needed, they are added in groups of eight. Additional address bits are logically combined with $\overline{WR}$, as required, to generate the enable signals for each group of eight ports.

A single 9334 addressable latch is used to provide eight single-bit output ports for control purposes. The inputs can be connected in common, for

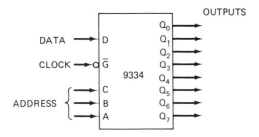

Figure 8.4-2. Eight-bit addressable latch, 9334.

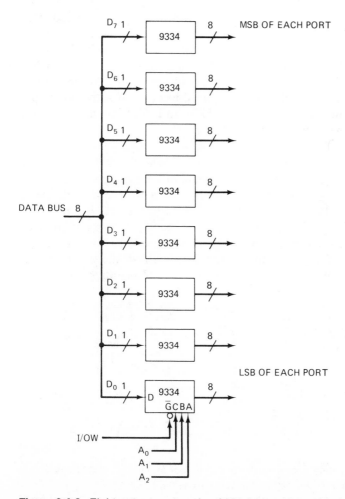

Figure 8.4-3. Eight output ports using 9334 8-bit addressable latches.

instance, to a single bit of the data bus. Each D latch is addressed by a different output instruction, changing 1 bit of an output port without affecting the other bits. Only two instructions are required to set or clear a bit: One loads the accumulator with 00H or 01H; the other is an output instruction for the selected port (bit). The following instruction sequence, for example, sets bit 7:

MVI A, 01H
OUT 7

Contrast this instruction sequence with that of Section 4.3, used to set or clear a single bit of an 8-bit port when all 8 bits are operated on simultaneously.

The latches and three-state outputs of the 74LS373 and 74LS374 allow these devices to be used as input ports. When an input device provides its own latch but does not have three-state outputs, separate three-state buffers are used. MSI circuits containing 4- and 8-bit inverting and non-inverting buffers are common. For example, the 74LS240 and 74LS244 are octal buffers with three-state outputs (see Fig. 8.4-4). The three-state buffers in each are divided into two groups of four, each group having a common active low enable. When used as an input port, the three-state buffer enables are driven by an active low input device select pulse. The buffers in the 74LS373 and 74LS374 have Schmitt trigger inputs for improved noise immunity.

MSI multiplexers with three-state outputs act as input port three-state buffers in systems requiring a large number of ports. With the address decoding logic as part of the multiplexer, limited additional decoding logic is necessary. As shown in Fig. 8.4-5, eight 16-to-1 multiplexers (8219s) provide 16 addressable 8-bit three-state buffers. Each multiplexer inputs 1 bit to the data bus from one of the 16 input ports. Four address bits, A_0–A_3, are decoded by the multiplexers. If there is call for additional decoding, it is done with decoders that control the enables for the group of eight multiplexers. When enabled, the output of the 8219 is the complement of the selected data input. Thus, to maintain the sense of

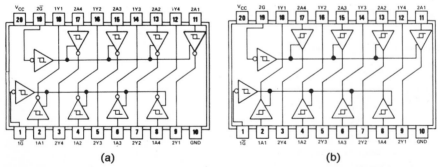

Figure 8.4-4. Octal buffers with three state outputs and Schmitt trigger inputs (a) 74LS240 inverting buffer; (b) 74LS244 noninverting buffer. (Courtesy of Texas Instruments, Inc.)

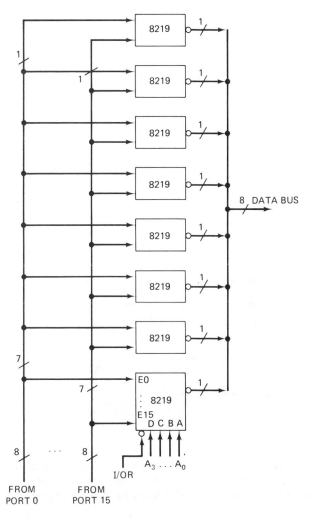

Figure 8.4-5. Eight 16-to-1 multiplexers with tri-state outputs (8219s) providing 16 addressable 8-bit input ports.

the data, the $\overline{Q}$ outputs of the input port latches must be used or the data must be complemented after it is input to the microprocessor.

A particularly useful and flexible device for implementing input and output ports is the 8212, 8-bit input/output port introduced in Section 2.1.2. This Schottky T^{2}L MSI device contains an 8-bit latch with three-state output buffers and device selection logic (see Fig. 2.1-7). Four control inputs—$\overline{DS1}$, DS2, MD, and STB—control device selection, data latching, the output buffer state, and a service request flip-flop.

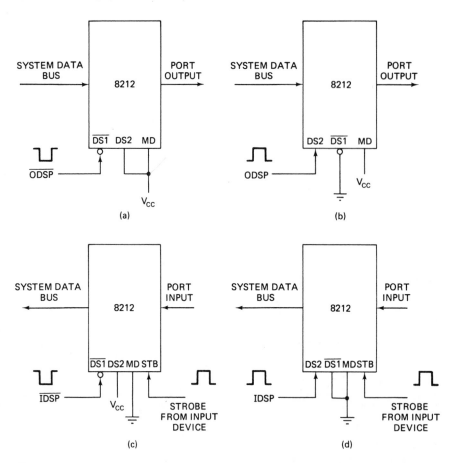

Figure 8.4-6. Connections for an Intel 8212 as (a) an output port clocked by an active low device select pulse; (b) an output port clocked by an active high device select pulse; and as (c) an input port clocked by an active low device select pulse; (d) an input port clocked by an active high device select pulse.

When used as an output port, the mode control of the 8212 is high, MD = 1, and the source of the clock, C, to the data latch is from the device selection logic ($\overline{DS1}$ and DS2). When $\overline{DS1}$ is logic 0 and DS2 is logic 1, the device is selected and the clock is logic 1. The data outputs follow the data inputs while C = 1. The input data is latched on the 1 to 0 transition of the clock. With the two device select inputs, $\overline{DS1}$ and DS2, an active low or high port select strobe controls the latching (see Fig. 8.4-6).

When used as an input port, the 8212 provides a three-state input buffer controlled by the microprocessor and a latch controlled by the input device. For input, the mode control is low, MD = 0, and the output buffer state is determined by $\overline{DS1}$ and DS2. The source of the clock input to the data latch is the strobe, STB (see Fig. 8.4-6).

8.5 PROGRAM CONTROLLED PARALLEL TRANSFER OF INFORMATION

Under program control, data transferred on the data bus between a microprocessor and an I/O device is transmitted in parallel, a word at a time. Two types of program controlled transfer are possible: unconditional and conditional.

An unconditional transfer is one in which an instruction conveys data to or from an I/O port without determining whether the port is ready to receive or transmit the data. Unconditional transfers handle command information, status information, or other data. Command information is transferred from the microprocessor to control the operation of an I/O device. Status information is transferred from an I/O device and is used by the microprocessor to monitor the state of the I/O device. Data is transferred in both directions and is distinguished from command or status information by the manner in which it is used by the microprocessor.

An example of an unconditional output data transfer is the transmission of BCD data from a microprocessor to a display. The microprocessor does not ascertain whether the display is ready to receive the data, it simply assumes the display is ready. Illustrative of an unconditional input data transfer is the input of data from a set of manual switches. Here again the microprocessor assumes the switches are set to their desired positions.

In conditional data transfers, execution of the I/O instruction transferring the data is conditioned on the I/O device being ready for the data transfer. Readiness is determined by an unconditional transfer of status information from the I/O device to the microprocessor which precedes the actual data transfer. Status information, in a bit pattern, indicates the present state of the I/O device hardware. Often fewer than 8 bits indicate the status of an I/O device; the software simply ignores the unused bits.

A single bit of status information indicates when a single input port has information available for input or when a single output port is ready to receive information. The software which tests the status flag increases the time associated with the I/O operation; the additional time is the *I/O overhead*.

Consider, for example, an input device which has data available at input port 1 (DATA) for transmission to a microprocessor (see Fig. 8.5-1). To indicate availability, the input device sets a flag, bit 7 of input port 0 (STATUS). The use of flags in controlling conditional transfers is referred to as **handshaking**. With programmed I/O, it is the only way of knowing when new data is available for input to the microprocessor.

To determine availability of data for input, the microprocessor periodically inputs the status word at input port 0 and tests bit 7; if bit 7 is 1, data is available, and an instruction inputs it from port 1. The input device select strobe which enables the data from port 1 also resets the data valid flag.

The frequency with which the status flag is checked determines the minimum length of time it takes to transfer the data. An input subroutine executes a

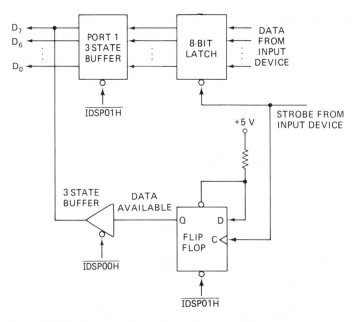

Figure 8.5-1. Handshaking using a data available flag.

tight loop to check the status flag. The subroutine of Fig. 8.5-2 for the system shown in Fig. 8.5-1 assumes that the number of bytes of data to be transferred is in B and that HL points to the starting address of the data buffer in memory before the subroutine is called.

Use of a tight loop to check the status bit creates a problem in systems where no method is provided for exiting the loop if the input device malfunctions and cannot set the status flag. A software solution programs the test loop as a controlled timeout. This ensures that if the status flag is not set within a

```
PIN:   IN STATUS   ;   INPUT STATUS BYTE
       ORA  A      ;   SET FLAGS
       JP PIN      ;   CHECK DATA AVAILABLE STATUS BIT (BIT 7), IF DATA IS NOT
                   ;   AVAILABLE, WAIT
       IN DATA     ;   DATA IS AVAILABLE, INPUT DATA, CLEAR DATA AVAILABLE FLAG
       MOV  M, A   ;   TRANSFER FLAG TO MEMORY BUFFER
       INX  H      ;   INCREMENT MEMORY POINTER
       DCR  B      ;   DECREMENT COUNTER
       JNZ  PIN    ;   BACK TO PIN IF MORE DATA IS TO BE INPUT
       RET
```

Figure 8.5-2. Subroutine to synchronize data transfer using the hardware of Figure 8.5-1.

given time, the loop is exited, and appropriate actions are taken for a no response condition from the I/O device.

When several input devices are used in a system with programmed I/O, a subroutine checks the ready flag of each device, in turn, to see which has data available for the microprocessor. This process is known as ***polling***. Figure 8.5-3 shows the flowchart of a polling subroutine for Fig. 8.5-4, which has eight input devices with their data available flags combined into one status byte.

The polling subroutine in Fig. 8.5-5 checks the status flag of each input device and branches to a service subroutine for the device if its flag is set. It also sets up a priority among the eight input devices by the order in which it tests the service request bits, with input device seven having the highest priority. The service subroutine for each input device saves the contents of the accumulator, A, then inputs the data byte and stores it in memory or processes it. Before returning from the service subroutine, A is restored. For output operations, a ready flag in the output device indicates when the device can accept the next

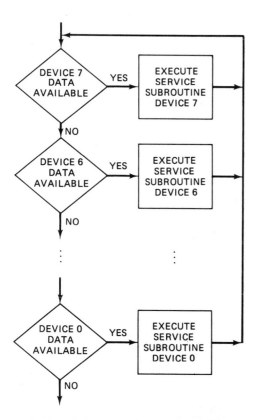

Figure 8.5-3. Polling subroutine flowchart.

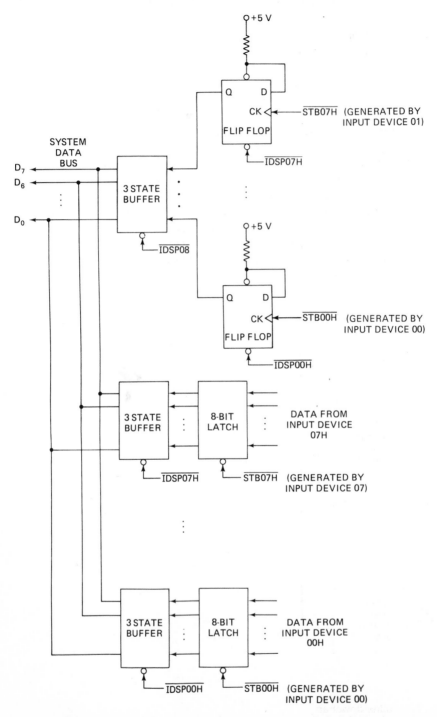

Figure 8.5-4. Combining data available flags of eight input devices into one status byte.

POLL:	IN STATUS	;	INPUT STATUS WORD
	RAL	;	ROTATE STATUS BIT 7 TO CARRY
	CC SRV7	;	CALL SUBROUTINE IF DATA IS AVAILABLE
	RAL	;	ROTATE STATUS BIT 6 TO CARRY
	CC SRV6	;	CALL SUBROUTINE IF DATA IS AVAILABLE
	RAL	;	ROTATE STATUS BIT 5 TO CARRY
	CC SRV5	;	CALL SUBROUTINE IF DATA IS AVAILABLE
	RAL	;	ROTATE STATUS BIT 4 TO CARRY
	CC SRV4	;	CALL SUBROUTINE IF DATA IS AVAILABLE
	RAL	;	ROTATE STATUS BIT 3 TO CARRY
	CC SRV3	;	CALL SUBROUTINE IF DATA IS AVAILABLE
	RAL	;	ROTATE STATUS BIT 2 TO CARRY
	CC SRV2	;	CALL SUBROUTINE IF DATA IS AVAILABLE
	RAL	;	ROTATE STATUS BIT 1 TO CARRY
	CC SRV1	;	CALL SUBROUTINE IF DATA IS AVAILABLE
	RAL	;	ROTATE STATUS BIT 0 TO CARRY
	CC SRV0	;	CALL SUBROUTINE IF DATA IS AVAILABLE
	RET		

Figure 8.5-5. Polling subroutine for the flowchart of Figure 8.5-3.

data word. This is necessary when an output device requires time to process the data previously transferred to it before it can accept new data.

8.6 PROGRAMMABLE LSI PORTS

Combinations of latches, buffers, and flags constituting I/O ports are available in LSI. Due to the number of pins available on larger LSI packages, a single package can contain several ports. And, for greater versatility in application, LSI devices are programmable; i.e., the mode of operation of each port is established under program control.

Programmable LSI ports are implemented in two ways: (1) as part of an LSI circuit which also serves other functions and (2) as a peripheral circuit whose exclusive function is providing I/O ports.

8.6.1 Multifunction Devices Containing Programmable I/O Ports

An example of the first case is the 8155, an LSI circuit containing a 256×8 R/W memory, three programmable I/O ports, and a 14-bit binary counter timer [2] (see Fig. 8.6-1). This circuit is directly compatible with the 8085A, as shown in Fig. 3.4-1. The 8155 contains a latch to demultiplex the low order address byte, A_0-A_7, from the address data bus, AD_0-AD_7. The logic value of the $IO/\overline{M}$ input determines whether the address refers to memory or I/O. The address and value of $IO/\overline{M}$ are latched by the 8155 on the falling edge of the

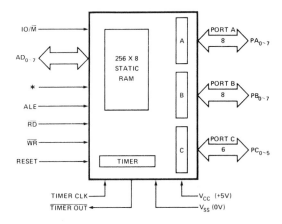

*: 8155/8155-2 = $\overline{CE}$, 8156/8156-2 = CE

Figure 8.6-1. Block diagram of an 8155. (Courtesy of Intel Corp.)

ALE signal. The chip enable signal is derived from the high order address byte. For a memory reference, $IO/\overline{M} = 0$, the latched low order address byte selects one of the 256 RWM locations.

The 8155 contains six registers which are addressed as I/O. These are the command status register, C/S; three ports, A, B, and C; and the high and low bytes of the timer.

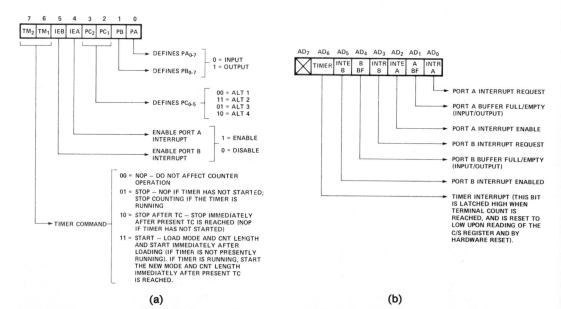

Figure 8.6-2. Command status register (a) bit assignment and (b) status word format. (Courtesy of Intel Corp.)

The ***Command/Status Register, C/S,*** (not shown in Fig. 8.6-1) serves two purposes: (1) It programs the function of the I/O ports when the command/status register is written by an I/O write operation, and (2) it provides information on the status of the ports and timer when the command/status register is read by an I/O read. Obviously, the command/status register is really two registers with the same I/O address, differentiated by the operation—write or read. The function of the various bits of the register for command and status are specified in Fig. 8.6-2.

Ports A and B (PA and PB) are 8-bit ports and can be input or output. Bits 0 and 1 of the command word specify the directions of these ports. When an 8155 I/O port is programmed for output, its contents can still be read by a read operation. This eliminates the need to keep an image of the port's contents in memory, as discussed in Chapter 4, when a simple latch is used as an output port to provide independent control signals. Port C, a 6-bit port, can also be input (ALT1) or output (ALT2), or it can supply handshaking signals for ports A and B (ALT3 and ALT4) (see Fig. 8.6-3). Port C's operation is defined by bits 2 and 3 of the command word. Bits 4 through 6 affect the interrupt signals and timer (see Chapter 9). When reset, the three ports, A, B, and C, of the 8155 are in the input mode.

The following addresses are assigned to the command/status register, ports, and timer:

Register	Address
C/S	XXXXX000
PA	XXXXX001
PB	XXXXX010
PC	XXXXX011
TIMER LOW	XXXXX100
TIMER HIGH	XXXXX101

The chip enable signal is derived from the high order address byte. However, the fact that the 8085A repeats the port address on AD_0–AD_7 and A_8–A_{15} during I/O references and the fact that in the 8155 memory and I/O share the same chip enable limits the number of bits in the high address byte which are decoded to select the 8155. In other words, the 8-bit port address is repeated as

Pin	ALT 1	ALT 2	ALT 3	ALT 4
PC0	Input Port	Output Port	A INTR (Port A Interrupt)	A INTR (Port A Interrupt)
PC1	Input Port	Output Port	A BF (Port A Buffer Full)	A BF (Port A Buffer Full)
PC2	Input Port	Output Port	A $\overline{STB}$ (Port A Strobe)	A $\overline{STB}$ (Port A Strobe)
PC3	Input Port	Output Port	Output Port	B INTR (Port B Interrupt)
PC4	Input Port	Output Port	Output Port	B BF (Port B Buffer Full)
PC5	Input Port	Output Port	Output Port	B $\overline{STB}$ (Port B Strobe)

Figure 8.6-3. Table of port control assignment. (Courtesy of Intel Corp.)

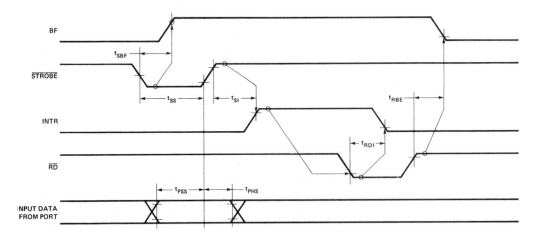

Figure 8.6-4. Timing diagram for strobe input mode of 8155. (Courtesy of Intel Corp.)

the low and high address byte, and the least significant 3 bits provide the I/O register address, leaving only the most significant 5 bits of the high address byte for chip enable decoding.

For example, if address decoding logic enables an 8155 when A_{15}–A_8 = 01000XXX, then the address of the C/S register on this 8155 is 40H. To program the 8155, the appropriate command word is written into the command status register.

Consider the following configuration for the 8155: Port A is input, port B is output, and alternative 4 is chosen for port C. (Port C provides handshaking signals for ports A and B; see Fig. 8.6-3.) Assume also that the interrupt capability and timer are not used. The required command word to program the ports of the 8155 is then:

$$00001010 = 0AH$$

And the following two instructions initialize the 8155:

```
MVI A, 0AH   ;   load A with command word
OUT 40H      ;   output to C/S register
```

When a port is in the input mode in ALT4 (for instance, port A) the input device places data on the 8155 inputs PA_0–PA_7, then provides an active low strobe to PC2 (see Fig. 8.6-4). This loads the data into input port A and sets the port A buffer full flag, (ABF), bit 1 of the status register. The buffer full condition is tested by reading the C/S register with an IN 40H instruction and testing bit 1. If the buffer is full, an IN instruction for port A, IN 41H, transfers the data from port A to the 8085A's accumulator. The read strobe generated by

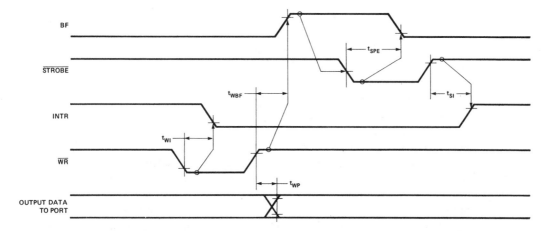

BF

STROBE

t_{SPE}

t_{WBF}

t_{SI}

INTR

t_{WI}

$\overline{WR}$

t_{WP}

OUTPUT DATA
TO PORT

Figure 8.6-5. Timing diagram for strobed out mode of 8155. (Courtesy of Intel Corp.)

IN 41H clears the BF signal for port A. Inclusion of handshaking logic in the same IC as the port saves constructing such logic with additional ICs.

When the input device generates a long strobe at pin PC2 of the 8155, there is a problem if the BF flag of the status register is tested by a program loop. When the strobe from the input device occurs, the BF flag is set. Assume that the strobe remains low for a period of time. The software being executed by the microprocessor tests the BF flag, finds it set, and executes an IN instruction to input the data from the port. The $\overline{RD}$ strobe during the input machine cycle of the IN instruction clears the BF flag; however, if the strobe from the input device is still low, the BF flag is set again, and the microprocessor again inputs the same data from the port. Thus, if the software is in a loop to read 10 bytes of data from the input port, it instead reads the same byte of data 10 times!

This problem can be prevented by designing logic to limit the duration of the strobe from the input device. An easier solution, however, is to test the INTR flag instead of BF, since INTR is set only when $\overline{STROBE}$ returns to logic 1.

The control signals also provide handshaking for an output port. In the previous example, where port B was an output port, bits PC3–PC5 provide the handshaking control signals. In the output mode, contents of the 8085A's accumulator are transferred to output port B of the 8155 by an OUT instruction which addresses this port. The $\overline{WR}$ strobe resulting from the OUT instruction makes B BF (PC4) logic 1 (see Fig. 8.6-5). The output device monitors B BF to determine when there is valid output data. When the output device is ready to take the data, it strobes PC5, and the strobe signal at PC5 clears B BF. The 8085A reads the status word and tests bit 4 to see whether the output device has accepted the data.

8.6.2 Peripheral Interface Devices

The 8255A Programmable Peripheral Interface[4] provides programmable I/O ports exclusively. [3][4] It can be used with the 8085A or any of a number of other microprocessors. The 8255A contains a control register, a status register, and three 8-bit I/O ports: A, B, and C, as shown in Fig. 8.6-6. Port C is actually two separately programmable ports: C-upper (C_4–C_7) and C-lower (C_0–C_3). An 8-bit data bus buffer transfers data between the external data bus and the control register, status register, or one of the I/O ports.

The 8255A is selected by a low signal at its chip select input, $\overline{CS}$. When not selected, the data bus buffers which connect the 8255A to the system data bus are floated. The source of the $\overline{CS}$ signal depends on whether isolated or memory mapped I/O is used. For isolated I/O, bits A_2 to A_7 are decoded to provide $\overline{CS}$, and bits A_1 and A_0 are used for selecting the control register, status register, or one of the ports. If the six address bits, A_2–A_7, are exhaustively decoded, as many as sixty-four 8255As can be used in a system. With isolated I/O, selection of the 8255A is further conditioned on $IO/\overline{M} = 1$.

Linear selection saves decoders and can select six 8255As, using isolated I/O with device and port selection as shown below.

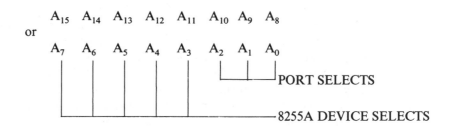

However, in order to condition the selection to isolated I/O, $\overline{I/OR}$ is connected to the $\overline{RD}$ input of the 8255A, and $\overline{I/OW}$ to the $\overline{WR}$ input of the 8255A.

With memory mapped I/O, $\overline{MEMR}$ is connected to the $\overline{RD}$ input of the 8255A and $\overline{MEMW}$ is connected to the $\overline{WR}$ input of the 8255A. And the address bits A_2–A_{15} are decoded to provide the $\overline{CS}$ signal.

In both the isolated I/O and memory mapped schemes, when the 8255A is selected, inputs A_0 and A_1, in turn, select the control register or one of the ports (A, B, or C) for the data transfer (see Table 8.6-1).

At system power up, a reset signal applied to the 8255A floats all 24 pins associated with the three I/O ports. The 8255A stays in this condition until the

---

[4]This overview of the 8255A provides an insight into the capability and flexibility of programmable LSI ports. Consult the manufacturer's literature for more details.

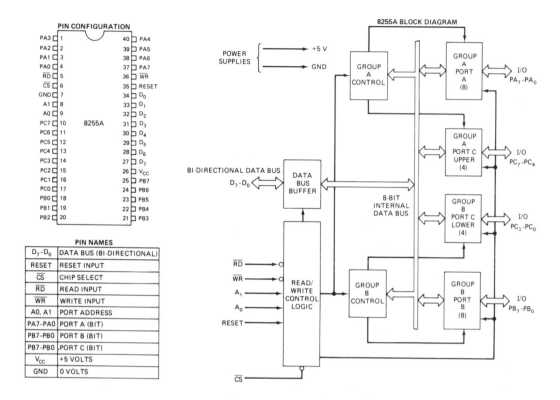

PIN CONFIGURATION

PA3	1	40	PA4
PA2	2	39	PA5
PA1	3	38	PA6
PA0	4	37	PA7
$\overline{RD}$	5	36	$\overline{WR}$
$\overline{CS}$	6	35	RESET
GND	7	34	D_0
A1	8	33	D_1
A0	9	32	D_2
PC7	10	31	D_3
PC6	11	30	D_4
PC5	12	29	D_5
PC4	13	28	D_6
PC3	14	27	D_7
PC2	15	26	V_{CC}
PC1	16	25	PB7
PC0	17	24	PB6
PB0	18	23	PB5
PB1	19	22	PB4
PB2	20	21	PB3

8255A

PIN NAMES

D_7-D_0	DATA BUS (BI-DIRECTIONAL)
RESET	RESET INPUT
$\overline{CS}$	CHIP SELECT
$\overline{RD}$	READ INPUT
$\overline{WR}$	WRITE INPUT
A0, A1	PORT ADDRESS
PA7-PA0	PORT A (BIT)
PB7-PB0	PORT B (BIT)
PB7-PB0	PORT C (BIT)
V_{CC}	+5 VOLTS
GND	0 VOLTS

Figure 8.6-6. Block diagram of 8255A Programmable Peripheral Inteface. (Courtesy of Intel Corp.)

application program writes a word into the control register which defines the 8255A's subsequent mode of operation. The three basic modes of operation are:

1. Mode 0: basic input-output.
2. Mode 1: strobed input-output.
3. Mode 2: bidirectional bus.

The mode definition format of the control word is shown in Fig. 8.6-7.

Mode 0 provides two 8-bit ports (A and B) and two 4-bit ports (C-upper and C-lower). Any port can be input or output; outputs are latched, inputs are not. There are 16 possible input-output configurations in this mode. For example, the control word 8AH sets port A for output, port C-upper for input, port C-lower for output, and port B for input. An 8255A used for isolated I/O and selected when A_2 to $A_7 = 0$, is initialized by the following instructions to the above configuration.

```
MVI A,8AH   ; load A with control word
OUT 03H     ; write control word into control   1000 1010
            ; register of 8255A
```

TABLE 8.6-1

8255A BASIC OPERATION [3]

A_1	A_0	$\overline{RD}$	$\overline{WR}$	$\overline{CS}$	INPUT OPERATION (READ)
0	0	0	1	0	PORT A $\Rightarrow$ DATA BUS
0	1	0	1	0	PORT B $\Rightarrow$ DATA BUS
1	0	0	1	0	PORT C $\Rightarrow$ DATA BUS
					OUTPUT OPERATION (WRITE)
0	0	1	0	0	DATA BUS $\Rightarrow$ PORT A
0	1	1	0	0	DATA BUS $\Rightarrow$ PORT B
1	0	1	0	0	DATA BUS $\Rightarrow$ PORT C
1	1	1	0	0	DATA BUS $\Rightarrow$ CONTROL
					DISABLE FUNCTION
X	X	X	X	1	DATA BUS $\Rightarrow$ 3-STATE
1	1	0	1	0	ILLEGAL CONDITION
X	X	1	1	0	DATA BUS $\Rightarrow$ 3-STATE

Mode 1 also provides two 8-bit ports, A and B, but here both inputs and outputs are latched. The two 4-bit ports (C) provide handshaking for ports A and B. Figure 8.6-8 shows the configuration of the 8255A for input and output in mode 1 operation along with the necessary control word.

For input in mode 1, port A is an input port, and bits C_3, C_4, and C_5 are used for associated handshaking. Port B is an input port with C_0, C_1, and C_2 used for handshaking. C_6 and C_7 can be used as input or output ports. The input device places 8 bits of data at A_0–A_7 (or B_0–B_7), then generates an active low strobe, $\overline{STB}$, which loads data into the input latch. This makes the input buffer full signal, IBF, logic 1. The microprocessor reads port C and checks the IBF signal to determine whether data is available for input to the microprocessor. The mode 1 status word format is shown in Fig. 8.6-9. If IBF is logic 1, the microprocessor reads port A (or B), which inputs the data and resets the IBF flag.

For output in mode 1, the microprocessor writes data to port A (or B), and the output buffer full flag, $\overline{OBF}$, goes low to indicate this. The output device monitors $\overline{OBF}$ to determine when output data is available. And, it acknowledges acceptance of the data by bringing the acknowledge input, $\overline{ACK}$, low, thus clearing the output buffer full flag.

Mode 2 provides a single 8-bit bidirectional bus: port A. Five bits of port C are used for status and control of port A, thus providing a handshaking

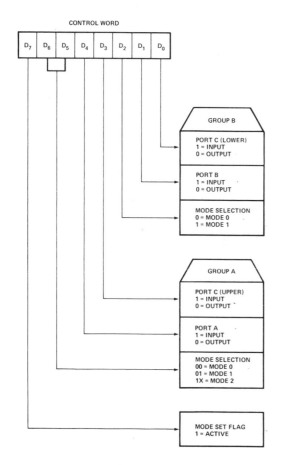

CONTROL WORD

| D_7 | D_6 | D_5 | D_4 | D_3 | D_2 | D_1 | D_0 |

GROUP B

PORT C (LOWER)
1 = INPUT
0 = OUTPUT

PORT B
1 = INPUT
0 = OUTPUT

MODE SELECTION
0 = MODE 0
1 = MODE 1

GROUP A

PORT C (UPPER)
1 = INPUT
0 = OUTPUT

PORT A
1 = INPUT
0 = OUTPUT

MODE SELECTION
00 = MODE 0
01 = MODE 1
1X = MODE 2

MODE SET FLAG
1 = ACTIVE

Figure 8.6-7. Mode definition format of control word for 8255A. (Courtesy of Intel Corp.)

capability similar to that of mode 1. Figure 8.6-10 illustrates the control word and the configuration of the 8255A in mode 2. The format of the status word when the 8255A is in mode 2 is shown in Fig. 8.6-11.

Various combinations of mode operation are possible. For example, while port A and C_5 to C_7 are used for bidirectional data transfer with handshaking in mode 2, port B can be used for input in mode 0.

The 8255A also has a bit set/reset capability for port C. When bit 7 of the control word is 0, the control word is interpreted by the 8255A as a port C bit set/reset command. Any bit of port C can be set or cleared. The bit set/reset format is shown in Fig. 8.6-12. The ability to directly set or reset a single bit is advantageous in applications where individual bits control separate external functions.

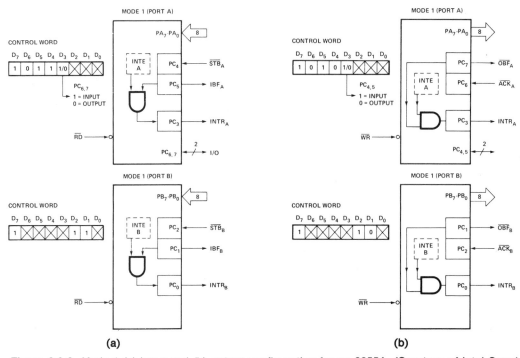

Figure 8.6-8. Mode 1 (a) input and (b) output configuration for an 8255A. (Courtesy of Intel Corp.)

Figure 8.6-9. Mode 1 status word for 8255A. (Courtesy of Intel Corp.)

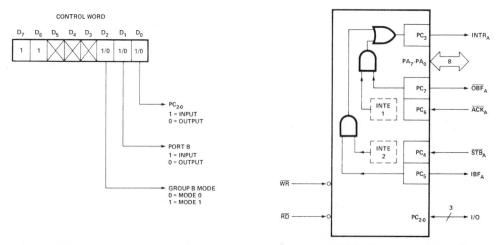

Figure 8.6-10. Mode 2 bidirectional port configuration for an 8255A. (Courtesy of Intel Corp.)

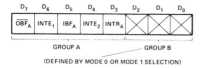

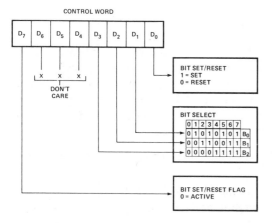

Figure 8.6-11. Mode 2 status word for 8255A. (Courtesy of Intel Corp.)

Figure 8.6-12. Bit set/reset format of 8255A. (Courtesy of Intel Corp.)

8.7 SERIAL TRANSFER OF INFORMATION

Although the data bus of a microprocessor is designed to transfer data to and from I/O devices in parallel—all bits of a data word being transferred simultaneously—there are cases when it is preferable to transfer data serially (1 bit at a time). Data transferred serially is often sent in groups of bits which constitute a character or word. Frequently, the characters are coded in ASCII. *Serial transfer* requires only one signal line or communications channel and is appropriate when:

1. The I/O device to/from which the data is transferred is inherently serial in operation.

2. The distance between the microprocessor and the I/O device is great.

Many I/O devices such as Teletypes and magnetic tape cartridges and cassettes are constrained by their design to receive or transmit data a bit at a time and thus operate in a serial fashion.

As the distance between a microprocessor and an I/O device increases, the cost differential between running a cable with a number of conductors equal to the data bus width and running a single cable becomes very significant. Not only is the multiple conductor cable more costly, but line drivers and receivers are necessary. A point is reached beyond which it becomes more economical to

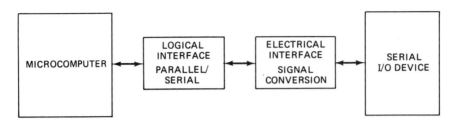

Figure 8.7-1. Interface between microprocessor and I/O device for serial transfer.

use serial data transfer, even though it requires additional hardware and/or software, than to use a multiple conductor cable. In other applications, the distance may be so great that common carrier facilities such as telephone lines are required, and thus the data must be transmitted in serial form. In general, an interface is required between the microprocessor and an I/O device for serial data transfer (see Fig. 8.7-1). The interface provides two functions:

1. The logical formatting of data, including serial-to-parallel/parallel-to-serial conversion.

2. Translation of logic signals to the electrical signals appropriate for transmitting data over the communications channel connecting the microprocessor and I/O device.

Voltage and current levels used for data communication are seldom T^2L compatible. Electrical signal translation is implemented by hardware. Logical formatting of data, however, may be implemented by software or hardware or by a combination of the two.

Serial data transfer systems are simplex, half duplex, or full duplex. In a *simplex* system, data is transferred only in one direction. In a *half duplex* system, it is transmitted in either direction, but in only one direction at a time. In a *full duplex* system, data is transferred in both directions simultaneously.

Consider the example of simplex serial data transfer shown in Fig. 8.7-2. A microprocessor transfers data to a shift register in an I/O device. The shift register is within several feet of the microprocessor, and the communications channel is a twisted pair of wires. The formatting of data is done by software. Data input to the shift register is connected to bit D_0 of the data bus, and the clock input of the shift register is driven by logic which generates an output device select pulse. Assuming that the data byte to be transferred is in A, the following subroutine formats the data and implements the transfer, least significant bit first:

```
SO8:    MVI C,8
LOOP:   OUT SR
        RAR
        DCR C
        JNZ LOOP
        RET
```

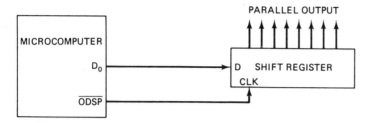

Figure 8.7-2. Serial data transmission to shift register receiver. The output device select pulse clocks the shift register.

This example illustrates an important aspect of serial data transfer: The receiver has to have some means of determining when its data input should be sampled, thus defining the occurrence of a new data bit. In this example a clock signal from the transmitter tells the receiving device when it should sample the data input line, thus synchronizing the data transfer. Use of the device select pulse for synchronization ensures that the data on the interconnecting line is sampled at the proper time. However, transferring a separate clock signal from the transmitter to the receiver for synchronization requires an additional connection between the devices.[5]

The ***baud rate*** is the rate at which data is transferred. It denotes the number of signal changes per second. When the signals being transmitted are binary, the baud rate is equivalent to the number of bits per second. Communications channels are rated by baud rate. If data is transmitted on a channel at a baud rate beyond the channel's capacity, the error rate of the transmission is unacceptably high.

Serial transfer of data is asynchronous or synchronous. In asynchronous transmission, a character is sent whenever it is available. Thus, the time interval between two characters is variable; however, the time interval between bits in a single character is fixed. When no character is available for transmission, the line is idle. With synchronous character transmission, one character is followed immediately by another. Whenever another data character is not immediately ready for transmission, the transmitter repeatedly sends a special SYNC character until it can transmit the next data character.

8.7.1 Asynchronous Serial Character Transfer

Asynchronous data transfer is used for low speed, low data rate transfers: Such transfers typically occur at 110, 300, 600, 1200, or 2400 baud, values commonly used by manufacturers of commercial communications equipment. The transfer of information between a teletypewriter and microprocessor is asynchronous. For instance Teletype's Models 33 and 35, transmit and receive data at 110 baud

---

[5]Techniques for the serial transfer of data which do not require a separate clock line from transmitter to receiver are considered in the following sections.

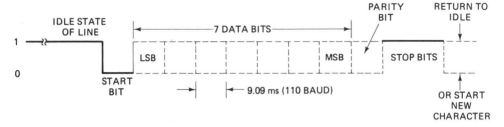

Figure 8.7-3. Seven bit asynchronous data character format, 110 baud.

or 110 bits per second. At this rate, each bit duration or ***bit time*** is 9.09 mS. Data is transferred as a group of serial bits constituting a character. The character is coded in ASCII as 7 bits, or ***seven level code***, and transmitted in the format shown in Fig. 8.7-3.

Even though the receiver and transmitter in an asynchronous data transfer are not synchronized with respect to the time at which a character is transmitted, once the transmitter starts to send a character, the receiver synchronizes itself with the bit times of the character in order to sample them at the correct time.

A ***start bit*** synchronizes the transmitter and receiver. It is the first bit of any character sent and is logic 0. When no character is being sent, the transmitter's output is logic 1, and the data line is ***idle*** or ***marking***. The receiver synchronizes its operation with the transmitter on the 1 to 0 transition of the data line. It waits one-half a bit time, checks the input to make sure it is still logic 0— and therefore a valid start bit—and begins sampling the data line at intervals equal to one bit time. The baud rates of the transmitter and receiver are set to the same value, and the data line is sampled at the center of each transmitted bit. This eliminates errors which might occur if sampling takes place at the beginning of each bit time since the leading or trailing edges of transitions on the data line are distorted in transmission. Following the start bit, the seven data bits of the ASCII character are transmitted—least significant bit first—followed by a parity bit, which is set or cleared to provide even or odd parity. For odd (even) parity, the parity bit is set to make the total number of bits (data bits and parity bit) in the ASCII character odd (even). Finally, two stop bits are transmitted. The start bit, logic 0, and two stop bits, both logic 1, ***frame*** the ASCII character.

On the microprocessor side, the logical formatting of data for serial transfer can be implemented in software, including the 9.09 mS delay and the other features required for transmitting or receiving. Hardware only provides electrical interfacing between the microprocessor and Teletype signals.

The disadvantage of software formatting and timing of a serial transfer is that the microprocessor is completely tied up during each character transfer. It takes 100 mS to transfer a single character at 110 baud; in this period of time, assuming an average instruction execution time of 2 μS, 50,000 instructions could be executed.

Parallel-to-serial conversion for transmitting and serial-to-parallel conversion for receiving and formatting with hardware use the microprocessor's time more effectively. The microprocessor transfers data in parallel to external hardware, which provides the necessary formatting and parallel-to-serial conversion. This hardware also receives serial data, removes the parity and framing information, and supplies the data in parallel to the microprocessor.

The Universal Asynchronous Receiver Transmitter, UAR/T [5], a full duplex device in a single 40-pin package, provides all the logic for asynchronous data transfer. It supplies logical formatting; its input and output signals are T^2L levels; and its receiver outputs are three-state. Additional circuitry may be necessary for the electrical interface, but no common clock signal is required between the UAR/T and the device with which it communicates. UAR/Ts which operate at rates up to 200 K baud are available (Intersil IM6402/6403). The UAR/T has become a de facto industry standard with several manufacturers providing pin compatible devices. Typically both the microprocessor and I/O device are connected in parallel to UAR/Ts which are interconnected to provide serial communication (see Fig. 8.7-4). A single UAR/T contains both a transmitter and a receiver. The transmitter and receiver portions of the UAR/T are independent except for the formatting of the words transmitted and received. The UAR/T inputs which program the device for number of data bits (5 to 8), parity (even, odd, none), and number of stop bits (1 or 2) apply to both transmitter and receiver portions of the system. The baud rate can be different for the receiver and transmitter and is set by external clocks which run at 16 times the desired baud rate and which are connected to the separate receiver and transmitter clock inputs.

Operation of the UAR/T in a microprocessor based system is simple. To transmit, data is output by the microprocessor in parallel to the UAR/T, and a device select pulse is sent to the data strobe input, $\overline{DS}$, which loads the data into the UAR/T and starts the serial transmission. The UAR/T is *double buffered* [see Fig. 8.7-4(a)], so a new character can be loaded as soon as the previous one starts transmission. An output from the UAR/T, transmitter buffer empty (TBMT), indicates that the UAR/T's data bits holding register is ready to accept the next character. This output can be tested by the microprocessor to provide handshaking. Or, the transfer from the microprocessor to the UAR/T can be unconditional, in which case, whenever the microprocessor has a character to send, it simply transfers it to the UAR/T. When an unconditional mode of operation is used, the average rate of data transfer to the UAR/T must be less than the word transmission rate of the UAR/T.

In the receiver portion of the UAR/T [Fig. 8.7-4(b)] a clock, running at 16 times the baud rate, operates logic which provides noise immunity. When a 1 to 0 transition is detected at the serial input, the input is tested half a bit time later to verify validity of the transition. The detection of a 1 to 0 transition following an idle period is used by the UAR/T to synchronize itself with the incoming character for the duration of the character. Continued sampling of the data input in the center of a bit time determines the remaining bit values.

An output from the receiver—data available, DAV—goes high, indicating that a character has been completely received. In addition to the parallel data

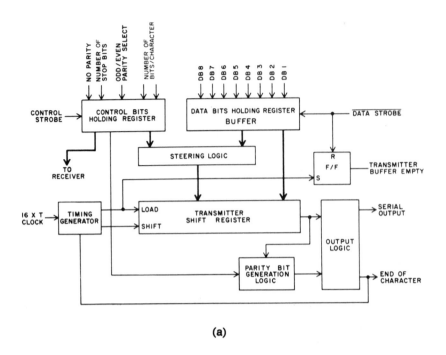

(a)

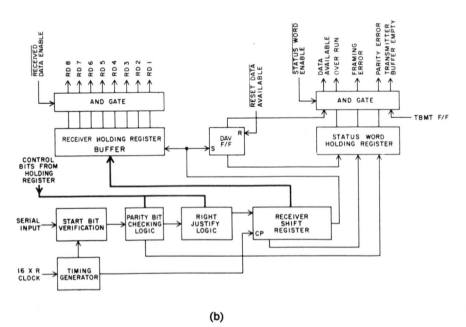

(b)

Figure 8.7-4. Block diagram of the internal structure of a UAR/T: (a) transmitter block diagram; (b) receiver block diagram. (Courtesy of General Instrument Corp.)

outputs which provide the received character, outputs are also available that indicate whether a parity, framing, or overrun error has occurred. When the receiver is operated in a handshaking mode, the microprocessor tests the data available flag, and, if a character is available, inputs it. If a second word is received before the previous word has been read, an *overrun error* occurs.

The microprocessor can also input error information. The parallel data outputs and error outputs are three-state and can be connected in parallel to the data bus and enabled separately. The received data enable, $\overline{RDE}$, and the status word enable, $\overline{SWE}$, inputs are controlled by device select pulses for this purpose. A strobe, reset data available, $\overline{RDAV}$, resets the UAR/T, indicating that the previous word loaded in the output buffer has been read before the next word is received. This strobe is provided by the microprocessor via the input device select pulse in the handshaking mode or by delaying the character received pulse by external hardware and using it to reset the UAR/T.

If the *control bits holding register* is connected to the data bus, it can be loaded under program control. The UAR/T is then operated as a programmable device. Further programmability is available if an LSI *baud rate generator* provides the receiver and transmitter clock frequencies. Baud rate generators provide a receiver and transmitter clock for UAR/Ts, and require only a crystal. Receiver and transmitter frequencies typically are externally selectable from 16 possible values by binary codes written into one of two 4-bit latches on the baud rate generator.

8.7.2 Synchronous Serial Character Transfer

Synchronous character transmission eliminates the noninformation-carrying start and stop bits associated with asynchronous transfers and allows faster data transmission. It usually occurs at rates of 3,800 and 9,600 baud. Synchronization between the receiver and transmitter is provided by one or two (bisync) synchronization characters. When transmitting in ASCII, for example, the SYN character is used.

In synchronous transmission, the data received is a continuous stream of bits with no indication of character boundaries. The receiver operates in a hunt mode—making a bit-by-bit comparison of the input stream with the stored values of the desired sync character—until it detects the sync character(s). Once the desired sync character(s) is detected, the receiver treats each subsequent group of *n* bits as a character. The transmitter continues to send characters to maintain the synchronization, even if the source of data characters does not have data ready for transmission. In this case, the transmitter sends the sync code or the code for a null character, and thus the time interval between two characters is fixed. The clocks in the transmitter and receiver operate at exactly the same frequency and must be very stable to maintain synchronization for a long period of time. Typically, thousands of blocks of characters can be sent without resynchronizing the receiver.

Single-chip LSI devices are available which provide the required logic for a bidirectional synchronous serial interface in a single package. The functional configurations of the device are programmed by writing information into the control registers. Devices, such as the Intel 8251 Programmable Communication Interface, provide both a synchronous and asynchronous interface in a single package.

8.8 DIRECT MICROPROCESSOR SERIAL I/O PINS

Some microprocessors have one or more pins for serial input and output of data. The 8085A, for instance, has a single serial input data, SID, pin and a single serial output data, SOD, pin. Data is input to the microprocessor at the SID pin by the RIM instruction and output from the SOD pin by the SIM instruction. The RIM instruction reads the data state of the SID input into bit 7 of the accumulator. The remaining six bits of the accumulator provide data on the status of the microprocessor's interrupt system (see Chapter 9).

The SIM instruction loads the contents of bit 7 of the accumulator into the SOD latch, if bit 6 of the accumulator is logic 1. If bit 6 is logic 0, the SOD latch is unaffected. When the 8085A is reset, the SOD latch is set to logic 0, and the other six bits of the accumulator set the interrupt masks of the 8085A (see Chapter 9). Appropriate program control of the SOD pin provides serial data directly to an output device. A subroutine for asynchronous serial data transfer using the SOD pin of the 8085A is given in Fig. 8.8-1. The subroutine is called with the 7-bit ASCII character and the parity bit in register B. The parity bit is bit 7 of register B.

```
SRLD0:    MVI  C, 10D     ;   INITIALIZE BIT COUNTER
          MVI  A, SOD0    ;   SET BIT 7 OF A TO 0 (SOD0 = 01XXXXXX)
          SIM  [RIM]      ;   OUTPUT START BIT
LOOP:     CALL DELAY      ;   DELAY ONE BIT TIME
          MOV  A, B       ;   LOAD A WITH DATA AND PARITY
          STC             ;   SET CARRY FOR STOP BITS
          RAR             ;   PUT BIT TO BE SENT IN CY
          MOV  B, A       ;   SAVE REMAINING BITS
          RAR             ;   PUT BIT TO BE SENT IN A7
          ANI  80H        ;   ZERO ALL BUT BIT 7 OF A
          ORI  SOD0       ;   OR REMAIN BITS REQUIRED FOR SIM
          SIM             ;   OUTPUT BIT 7
          DCR  C          ;   DECREMENT BIT COUNTER
          JNZ  LOOP
          RET
```

Handwritten annotations:
```
mvl C, 10D
RIM & datastat
          of SID input
LOOP: CALL DELAY into bit 7
DCR C
JNZ LOOP
RET
```

Figure 8.8-1. Subroutine for asynchronous serial data transmission using the SOD pin of the 8085A.

8.9 ELECTRICAL CHARACTERISTICS

As the physical distance between an I/O port and its associated I/O device increases, special consideration must be given to the electrical characteristics of the interconnection in order to minimize the error rate of the data received. As the propagation delay of the interconnection increases relative to the rise and fall time of the signal, interconnection lines cease to respond like simple interconnections and take on the aspects of transmission lines.

Three conditions produce a voltage at the receiving end significantly different from that at the transmitting end, causing received data to be invalid:

1. A noise voltage can be induced into the interconnection via capacitive and inductive coupling, or electrical noise sources, such as motors, in the environment.

2. The transmitting and receiving ends may have different ground connections between which a ground shift voltage exists.

3. The interconnection may act as a transmission line, and reflections of the transmitted voltage may occur on the line.

Typically, standard T^2L gates are restricted to driving lines of a maximum 2 feet in length. In electrically noisy environments, the small noise margin of T^2L voltage levels can result in seriously degraded performance.

8.9.1 Line Drivers and Receivers

Line driver ICs are available which convert T^2L levels into signals for driving transmission lines. Line receiver circuits convert these signals back to T^2L levels. There are three kinds of line driver and receiver interconnections: single-ended, balanced differential, or unbalanced differential (see Fig. 8.9-1).

A single-ended circuit uses one signal line and a common ground return to transmit the signal V_O. Although advantageous in that only one signal wire is required per data channel, the performance of the circuit can be degraded by a noise voltage, V_N, induced by inductive or capacitive coupling from adjacent signal lines or noise generators such as motors. There may be a voltage between the receiver and transmitter grounds due to a finite resistance between the driver and receiver ground points. The return signal current and possibly other system currents cause a voltage drop, V_G, across the resistance between the two ground points. The voltage at the receiver, V_R, equals $V_O \pm V_N \pm V_G$. The receiver cannot distinguish what portion of the signal is V_O and may assign it an incorrect logic value.

A balanced differential system uses a differential driver and a differential receiver. The driver produces the logic value of the data to be transmitted on one output and its complement on the other. The receiver converts the differential signal into a T^2L level at its output.

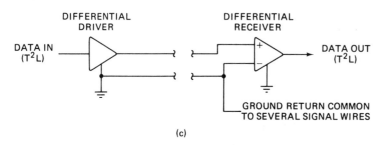

DRIVER   RECEIVER

DATA IN   SIGNAL LINE   DATA OUT
(T²L)   (T²L)

(a)

DIFFERENTIAL   DIFFERENTIAL
DRIVER   RECEIVER
                SIGNAL LINES

DATA IN   DATA OUT
(T²L)   (T²L)

(b)

DIFFERENTIAL   DIFFERENTIAL
DRIVER   RECEIVER

DATA IN   DATA OUT
(T²L)   (T²L)

GROUND RETURN COMMON
TO SEVERAL SIGNAL WIRES

(c)

Figure 8.9-1. Line driver and receiver interconnections: (a) single-ended; (b) balanced differential; and (c) unbalanced differential.

The driver and receiver are connected by a twisted pair of wires which cancel magnetically induced currents. Electrostatically coupled noise equally affects both lines of the twisted pair and thus appears at both inputs of the differential receiver. This noise voltage, common to both inputs, is referred to as a *common mode signal*. The ground potential voltage also appears to the receiver as a common mode signal. The voltage at the plus input of the differential receiver is $V_O \pm V_N \pm V_G$, and at the minus input terminal is $\pm V_N \pm V_G$. The differential receiver takes the difference of the signals at its plus and minus inputs, eliminates the noise and ground shift voltage, and leaves V_O, which it converts to a T²L logic level, at the output.

In the unbalanced differential method, the minus input of the differential amplifier is connected to the ground return, eliminating one wire. However, performance is diminished because inductive coupling is increased by the use of the common ground return.

8.9.2 Termination

Improperly terminated transmission lines are subject to errors from reflections of the transmitted signals. When data bit duration is long in comparison with the propagation delay of the line, the effects of the reflection die away in a relatively short period of time. However, when the data bit duration is short in comparison with the propagation time, the line must be properly terminated.

The characteristic impedance of a transmission line, R_O—which is a function of its geometry and dimension—typically falls between 50 and 200 ohms. To preclude reflections, a transmission line must be terminated by a resistance equal to its characteristic impedance. Line receivers have a high input impedance and thus require the addition of resistors for proper termination.

8.9.3 Standards

Commercial I/O devices, particularly data communications devices, are frequently designed to meet the requirements of one or more formal interface standards. Such standards specify the electrical characteristics and the protocol for transferring data between devices adhering to the standard. A commonly used standard is the RS 232C [6]. The electrical interface is simplex, single-ended, and unterminated. Line length and slew rate limit control reflections. The recommended maximum line length is 50 feet, and the maximum data rate is 20 K baud; logic 1 is -3 to -25 V, and logic 0 is $+3$ to $+25$ V. IC line drivers and receivers are available which meet the electrical requirements of this standard.

More recent standards allow longer line lengths and higher data rates. Standard RS422 [7] covers the electrical characteristics of a balanced differential interface. This standard allows line lengths of 1,200 meters (4,000 feet) and data rates of 10 M baud. Standard RS423 [8] pertains to unbalanced differential circuits and allows a line length of 1,200 meters (4,000 feet) and data rates of 100 K baud. IC drivers and receivers are also available which meet these standards.

ANSI/IEEE Std. 488 [9] is a standard for interconnecting electronic instrumentation. As many as 15 instruments can be connected with a total cable length of 20 meters. When fewer instruments are used, the maximum cable length is 2 meters of cable per instrument. An 8-bit data bus and a number of control signals provide handshaking, and data transfer occurs at 250 K bytes per second. The protocol of the standard allows a device connected to the bus to function as a listener, which only receives data; as a talker, which only transmits data; or as a controller, which manages the operation of the bus. Many instruments are designed with this interface; thus, automatic test systems are easily configured. The instrument is connected to the bus, and a microprocessor or even a programmable calculator can be the controller.

REFERENCES

1. *MCS-80 User's Manual*. Santa Clara, California: Intel Corporation, 1977.

2. *MCS-85 User's Manual*. Santa Clara, California: Intel Corporation, 1978.

3. *Peripheral Design Handbook*. Santa Clara, California: Intel Corporation, 1978.

4. EBRIGHT, A., *8255A Programmable Peripheral Interface Applications*, (Application Note AP-15). Santa Clara, California: Intel Corporation, 1976.

5. *UAR/T Universal Asynchronous Receiver Transmitter*, (AY-5-1013 Data Sheet). Hicksville, New York: General Instruments Corporation, 1974.

6. *Interface Between Data Terminal Equipment and Data Communication Equipment Employing Serial Binary Data Interchange*. Washington, D.C.: Electronic Industries Association, 1969.

7. *Electrical Characteristics of Balanced Voltage Digital Interface Circuits*. Washington, D.C.: Electronic Industries Association, 1978.

8. *Electrical Characteristics of Unbalanced Voltage Digital Interface Circuits*. Washington, D.C.: Electronic Industries Association, 1978.

9. *IEEE Standard Digital Interface for Programmable Instrumentation*. New York: The Institute of Electrical and Electronics Engineers, Inc., 1978.

BIBLIOGRAPHY

CLULEY, J.C.,, *Computer Interfacing and On-Line Operation*. New York: Crane, Russak & Co., Inc., 1975.

DONAGHEY, L.F., G.M. BOBBA, and X.K. RUBIN, "Decision-Making With Flags in Process Control," *Computer Design*, December 1976, pp. 77–83.

FALK, H., "Linking Microprocessors to the Real World," *IEEE Spectrum*, Vol. 11, No. 9, September 1974, pp. 59–67.

HOFFMAN, A.A.J., R.L. FRENCH, and G.M. LANG, "Minicomputer Interfaces: Know More, Save More," *IEEE Spectrum*, February 1974, pp. 64–68.

KNOBLOCK, D.E., D.C. LOUGHRY, and C.A. VISSERS, "Insight into Interfacing," *IEEE Spectrum*, May 1975, pp. 50–57.

LOUGHRY, D.C., "What Makes a Good Interface?" *IEEE Spectrum*, November 1974, pp. 52–57.

MOFFA, R., "Interfacing Peripherals in Mixed Systems," *Computer Design*, Vol. 14, No. 4, April 1974, pp. 77–84.

NADLER, W., "Data Transfer With ASCII Eliminates Computer Interface Problem," *Computer Design*, June 1975, pp. 74–78.

STEELE, J.M., R.C. MATTSON, "Architecture of a Universal Communications Processor," *Computer Design*, November 1973, pp. 63–68.

WHARTON, J., *Using the Intel 8085 Serial I/O Lines,* (Application Note AP-29). Santa Clara, California: Intel Corporation, 1977.

PROBLEMS

8-1.   List the eight unique hexadecimal port addresses possible using isolated I/O and linear selection. Assume that the address line associated with each port is logic 1 when the port is selected.

8-2. Repeat problem 8-1 assuming that the address line associated with each port is logic 0 when the port is selected.

8-3. List all the instructions which will create each of the following device select pulses with the hardware of Fig. 8.2-4. Specify the instructions' addresses in hexadecimal.
   a. $\overline{\text{IDSP00H}}$
   b. $\overline{\text{IDSP05H}}$
   c. $\overline{\text{ODSP03H}}$
   d. $\overline{\text{ODSP06H}}$

8-4. Using three 8205s, NAND gates, and inverters, draw the logic diagram of a circuit that generates 24 output device select pulses, $\overline{\text{ODSP00H}}$ to $\overline{\text{ODSP17H}}$.

8-5. Design an 8-bit extended address register, as in Fig. 8.2-6, using an 8212 and NAND gates. Make the address of the extended address register 00H. Show all the connections required to an 8085A system bus.

8-6. Using 8205s and common gates, design the logic required to generate 24 input device select pulses, $\overline{\text{IDSP08H}}$ to $\overline{\text{IDSP1FH}}$.

8-7. Design the logic necessary to generate eight device select pulses for input and eight device select pulses for output using memory mapped I/O. Make the port addresses FFF0H to FFF7H. Use 8205s, NAND gates, and inverters.

8-8. List the advantages and disadvantages of isolated and memory mapped I/O.

8-9. Draw the logic diagram of the interconnection as output ports of (a) a 74LS373 octal latch and (b) a 74LS374 octal flip-flop (see Fig. 8.4-1) to an 8085A system bus. Assume the existence of address decoding logic to generate the necessary output device select pulse. Show the connection of the output device select pulse to the output port.

8-10. Repeat problem 8-9 using the 74LS373 and 74LS374 to create input ports.

8-11. Draw the logic diagram to interface a 9334 addressable latch, Fig. 8.4-2, to an 8085A system data bus to provide eight single bit output ports.

8-12. Draw a logic diagram to show how a 4-bit extended address register is placed in an 8085A system and utilized. Compute the maximum number of output ports used for data transfer with this technique. Give the instruction sequence used to output data. Also, give the preferred order of addressing these ports to minimize software.

8-13. An input device is interfaced to an 8085A microprocessor. The device has one input, RUN, which, when high, operates the device. The device then outputs bytes of data asynchronously on its eight data lines. It has one data valid, DAV, status output, which indicates valid data each time it makes a 1 to 0 transition. The RUN, DAV, and eight data outputs are the only connections to the device. These inputs and outputs are T^2L. Design the hardware and draw the logic diagram for this interface with the following port assignments:

RUN	bit 7	output port 0
DAV	bit 7	input port 0
Data (8 bits)		input port 1

Write a subroutine that starts the device, inputs 64 bytes of data, stores them in a memory buffer, BUFF, and then turns the device off.

8-14. There are certain types of registers which are common to all programmable devices, including the 8155, 8255, and UAR/T. Describe, in general, these registers and their functions. For the 8155 describe the function and/or information provided by these registers in detail.

8-15. Design the interface between seven input devices and an 8085A microprocessor system which transfers data using programmed I/O. The devices are numbered 1 through 7; device number 1 has the highest priority. Use a 74148 priority encoder to speed up priority arbitration. The 74148 has eight active low inputs and three outputs. Input 7 of this encoder has the highest priority. The output of the priority encoder is the complement of the binary equivalent of the number of its highest priority active input.

    a. Draw a logic diagram of the interconnection of the data available flip-flops to the priority encoder and a single input port which provides the microprocessor with the status of all the input devices. Also show the logic necessary to clear the data available flip-flops.

    b. Write a program which checks the status and jumps to the appropriate service routine via a jump table.

8-16. Modify subroutine PIN, shown in Fig. 8.5-2, for conditional data transfer to provide a controlled timeout feature. If the input device does not respond in 100 mS with each byte of data, the subroutine, PIN, should be returned from, with the carry cleared. If all bytes of data are transferred successfully, the subroutine returns with the carry set.

8-17. An 8155 is used with port A as output, port B as input, and with port C used for handshaking for ports A and B. The 8155 is enabled when A_{15} to $A_8 = 00110XXX$. Write the instruction sequence to program the 8155 for this mode of operation.

8-18. For the 8155 of problem 8-17, write a subroutine which outputs 40 bytes of data from a memory buffer labeled LINE, to port A using handshaking. The subroutine should check the 8155's status word to determine when the output device has accepted the data.

8-19. Determine the control words necessary to put an 8255 in mode 0 with the following configuration:

    a. port A, input; ports B and C output

    b. ports A and C lower, output; ports B and C upper, inputs

    c. ports A and C upper, input; ports B and C lower, output

    d. ports A and B, input; port C, output

9

Interrupts and DMA

Interrupts increase processor system efficiency by letting an I/O device request CPU time only when that device needs immediate attention. Main-line programs can then perform routine tasks without continually checking I/O device status. Among routine duties, interrupts generally accomplish programmed I/O upon device demand; respond to time-critical events; establish a time base with a timer or clock; or count external events.

Ronald L. Baldridge*

*"Interrupts Add Power, Complexity to µC-System Design," EDN, Vol. 22, No. 14, August 5, 1977, pp. 67–73.

9.1 INTERRUPTS

Polling of I/O service request flags monopolizes a significant amount of a microprocessor's time. This reduces system *throughput*—the total, useful information processed or communicated during a specified time period. Therefore, it is advantageous, in terms of increasing throughput as well as reducing program complexity, if an I/O device demands service directly from the microprocessor.

Interrupts provide this capability. Essentially, an *interrupt* is a subroutine call initialized by external hardware. A simple structure that allows a single device to interrupt a microprocessor is shown in Fig. 9.1-1.

When an I/O device requires service, it sets its interrupt request flip-flop. This flip-flop is functionally the same as the service request flip-flop of Chapter 8, except that instead of its output being connected to an input port, it is connected to a special interrupt pin of the microprocessor. Thus, this flip-flop stores the I/O devices's interrupt request until it is acknowledged by the microprocessor.

Since the interrupt request is asynchronous, it may occur at any point in a program's execution. When a program is interrupted, the execution of the current instruction is completed, the interrupt is acknowledged by the microprocessor, and control is transferred to a subroutine which services the interrupt (see Fig. 9.1-2). When the microprocessor responds to the interrupt, the interrupt request flip-flop is cleared by a signal directly from the microprocessor (Fig. 9.1-1) or by a device select pulse generated by the service subroutine. To resume program execution at the proper point when the I/O service subroutine is finished, the program counter is automatically saved before control is transferred. The service subroutine saves the contents of any register it uses. The contents of the program counter, flag register, accumulator, and general purpose registers together represent the state or status of the microprocessor.

There are two types of interrupt inputs: nonmaskable and maskable (see Fig. 9.1-3). When a logic signal is applied to a nonmaskable interrupt input, the microprocessor is interrupted. When a logic signal is applied to a maskable

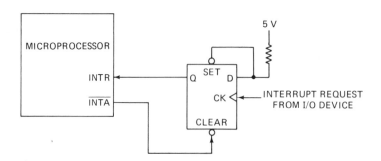

Figure 9.1-1. Generation of microprocessor interrupt for a single I/O device via an interrupt request flag.

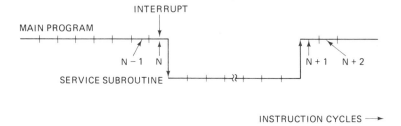

Figure 9.1-2. Transfer of program control in response to an interrupt.

interrupt input, the microprocessor is interrupted only if that particular input is enabled. Maskable interrupts are enabled or disabled under program control. If disabled, an interrupt signal is ignored by the microprocessor.

A nonmaskable interrupt input can be masked externally by an interrupt mask signal from an output port. The mask bit from an output port shown in Fig. 9.1-4 gates the interrupt signal. If an output instruction writes a 1 in the mask bit position, the interrupt is enabled; if it writes a 0, it is disabled.

In response to an interrupt, the following operations occur:

1. The processing of the current instruction is completed.

2. An interrupt machine cycle is executed during which the program counter is saved and control is transferred to an appropriate memory location.

3. The state of the microprocessor is saved.

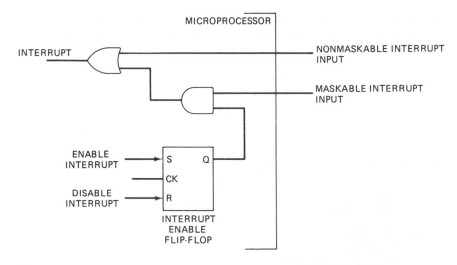

Figure 9.1-3. Representation of maskable and nonmaskable interrupts.

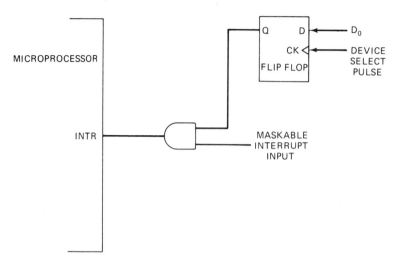

Figure 9.1-4. Creating a maskable interrupt from a nonmaskable interrupt.

4. If more than one I/O device is associated with the location transferred to, the highest priority device requesting an interrupt is identified.

5. A subroutine is executed which services the interrupting I/O device.

6. The saved state of the microprocessor is restored.

7. Control is returned to the instruction that follows the interrupted instruction.

Figure 9.1-5 illustrates the above sequence. Each step requires a certain amount of time. The combined times for a given microprocessor and external

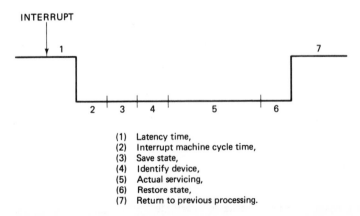

(1) Latency time,
(2) Interrupt machine cycle time,
(3) Save state,
(4) Identify device,
(5) Actual servicing,
(6) Restore state,
(7) Return to previous processing.

Figure 9.1-5. Sequence of actions associated with servicing an interrupt.

interrupt logic determine how quickly the microprocessor responds to an I/O device's request for service.

The time which elapses between the occurrence of the interrupt and the beginning of the execution of the interrupt-handling subroutine is the *response time*, the sum of the times of steps (1) through (4). The difference between the total time that the microprocessor is interrupted and the actual execution time of the service subroutine is referred to as *overhead*. Interrupt structures with low overhead allow greater throughput.

9.2 8085A INTERRUPT STRUCTURE

The 8085A has five interrupt inputs: TRAP, RST7.5, RST6.5, RST5.5, and INTR. TRAP is nonmaskable; the others are maskable. When the 8085A is reset, its internal interrupt enable flip-flop, INTE FF, is reset. This disables all the maskable interrupts, so the microprocessor only responds to TRAP. For maskable interrupts to be effective, they must be enabled under program control.

Two program steps are required to enable the RST7.5, RST6.5, and RST5.5 interrupts: (1) setting the interrupt masks, and (2) enabling the interrupts. Each interrupt can be masked independently by the *set interrupt mask*, SIM, instruction:

SIM (Set Interrupt Masks) [1]

During the execution of the SIM instruction, the contents of the accumulator will be used in programming the restart interrupt masks. Bits 0–2 will set/reset the mask bit for RST5.5, 6.5, 7.5 of the interrupt mask register, if bit 3 is 1 ("set"). Bit 3 is a "Mask Set Enable" control.

Setting the mask (i.e., mask bit = 1) **disables** the corresponding interrupt.

	Set	Reset
RST5.5 MASK	if bit 0 = 1	if bit 0 = 0
RST6.5 MASK	bit 1 = 1	bit 1 = 0
RST7.5 MASK	bit 2 = 1	bit 2 = 0

The RST7.5 (edge triggered) internal request flip flop will be reset if bit 4 of the accumulator = 1; regardless of whether RST7.5 is masked or not.

A hardware RESET of the 8085A will set all RST MASKs, and reset/disable all interrupts.

SIM can also load the SOD output latch. Accumulator bit 7 is loaded into the SOD latch if bit 6 is set. The latch is unaffected if bit 6 is a zero. $\overline{\text{RESET IN}}$ input sets the SOD latch to zero.

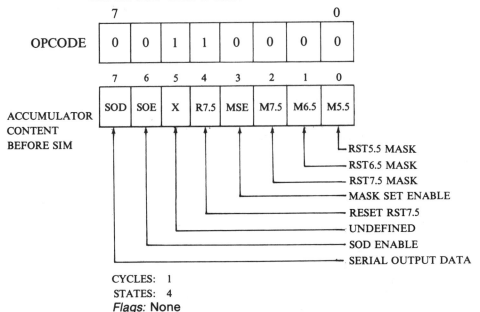

```
CYCLES:   1
STATES:   4
Flags: None
```

For example, the following instruction sequence enables RST7.5 and RST5.5 and disables RST6.5:

```
MVI A, 1AH    ;  load A with interrupt mask
SIM           ;  set interrupt mask
```

In step (2), the microprocessor's interrupt enable flip-flop, INTE FF, is set by the *enable interrupt* instruction, after execution of the instruction *following* EI:

Enable interrupts

EI

(INTE FF) ← 1

The *disable interrupts* instruction disables all maskable interrupts:

Disable interrupts

DI

(INTE FF) ← 0

Maskable interrupts are disabled immediately after the execution of the DI instruction. They are also automatically disabled when the microprocessor enters an interrupt machine cycle, which prevents it from responding to further interrupts until the EI instruction is executed.

The interrupt input, INTR, is not affected by SIM and requires only execution of the EI instruction to be completely enabled. Thus, in the 8085A the conditions for a valid interrupt are:

$$\text{VALID INT} = \text{TRAP} + \text{INTE} \cdot (\text{INTR} + \text{RST7.5} \cdot \overline{\text{M7.5}}$$
$$+ \text{RST6.5} \cdot \overline{\text{M6.5}} + \text{RST5.5} \cdot \overline{\text{M5.5}})$$

where M(n) refers to the mask bit for RST(n) controlled by the SIM instruction.

Most microprocessor interrupt inputs are level sensitive; however, some are edge sensitive, and others are both edge and level sensitive. Interrupt inputs to the 8085A encompass all three types. The TRAP input, for example, is both edge and level sensitive and must make a low-to-high transition and remain high to be acknowledged. After acknowledgement, it is not recognized again until it goes low, then high again and remains high—this avoids false triggering due to noise or logic glitches.

RST7.5 is rising edge sensitive: Only a pulse is required to set the interrupt request. This request is remembered until the 8085A responds to the interrupt or until the request is reset by the SIM instruction or a $\overline{\text{RESET IN}}$ signal. In effect, the interrupt request flip-flop for RST7.5 is internal to the microprocessor. RST6.5 and RST5.5 are high level sensitive. The signal at these pins must be maintained until the interrupt is acknowledged. Thus, external interrupt request flip-flops are required for RST6.5 and RST5.5.

The *read interrupt mask*, RIM, instruction loads the status of the interrupt masks, the pending interrupts, and the contents of the serial input data line, SID, into the accumulator. Thus, their respective statuses can be monitored under program control. When interrupts are disabled but pending, the program can selectively enable a particular interrupt to service it.

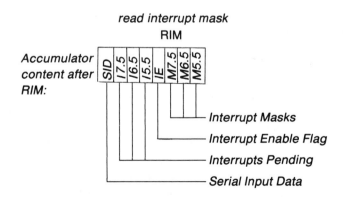

Flags: None

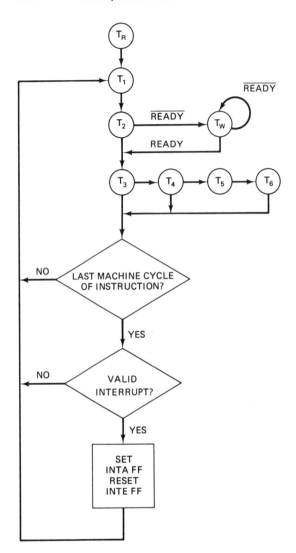

Figure 9.2-1. Simplified machine cycle of 8085A, including interrupt logic.

Using interrupts, the programmed polling of service request flags is, effectively, replaced by an automatic hardware polling. As shown in Fig. 9.2-1, the interrupt inputs are checked by the 8085A during the clock of the next to last state of each instruction cycle and during every clock pulse if the microprocessor is in the HALT state. Automatic polling of interrupt requests allows completion of the current instruction cycle before an interrupt. When there is a valid interrupt request, the INTE FF is cleared, and the interrupt acknowledge flip-flop (INTA FF) is set. The next machine cycle is a special one for handling the interrupt. For TRAP, RST7.5, RST6.5, and RST5.5, it is the BUS IDLE, BI, machine cycle. For INTR, it is the INTERRUPT ACKNOWLEDGE, INA.

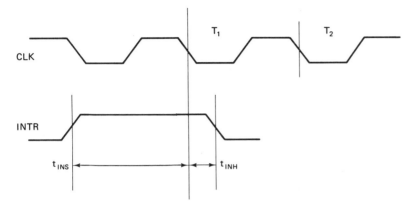

Figure 9.2-2. Setup and hold times, t_{INS} and t_{INH}, for an interrupt signal with respect to the microprocessors clock.

Latency time, t_{LAT}, is the time between the occurrence of an interrupt request and the beginning of the interrupt machine cycle (see Fig. 9.1-5). As shown in Fig. 9.2-2, the interrupt signal must be valid for a period equal to the interrupt setup time, t_{INS}, before the leading edge of CLK for the next instruction cycle. For the 8085A, the minimum value of t_{INS} is $(\frac{1}{2})T + 200$ nS, where T is the state time of the microprocessor.

If the interrupt becomes valid precisely t_{INS} seconds before the beginning of the next instruction cycle, then that cycle is an interrupt cycle with a minimum latency time, $t_{LAT\ MIN} = t_{INS}$. If, however, the interrupt signal becomes valid just after this setup time, then it is not responded to until after the next instruction is executed. This provides a worst case latency time of

$$t_{LAT\ MAX} = t_{INS} + t_{MAX\ INSTRUCTION\ CYCLE}$$
$$= \left(\tfrac{1}{2}\right)T + 200\ \text{nS} + 18T$$
$$= 18.5T + 200\ \text{nS}$$

Maximum, or worst case, latency time is an important factor in determining response time.

This relationship assumes there are no WAIT states or HOLD[1] states in the instruction cycle during which an interrupt request occurs. If, in fact, there are WAIT or HOLD states, then the maximum times for these conditions are included when determining $t_{LAT\ MAX}$. A further assumption is, of course, that the interrupt is enabled when the interrupt request occurs. If this is not the case, the $t_{LAT\ MAX}$ additionally includes the longest period of time that the interrupt(s) are disabled in the program.

The interrupt machine cycle has a fixed duration of $12T$ during which the value of the PC—the address of the instruction following the interrupted instruction—is saved on the stack, and control is then transferred to an address

---

[1]The HOLD state is discussed in Section 9.7.

associated with the specific interrupt. This implements a hardware initiated subroutine call. The method for transferring control to the address associated with the interrupt differs, depending on which interrupt is involved.

For TRAP, RST7.5, RST6.5, and RST5.5, the mechanism is the same: The microprocessor transfers control to a predetermined address associated with each of these inputs:

Interrupt	Restart address
TRAP	24H
RST5.5	2CH
RST6.5	34H
RST7.5	3CH

The interrupt machine cycle for these is a BUS IDLE, BI, during which the microprocessor internally generates the operation code for a restart instruction with the appropriate restart address. The PC is not incremented during BI and, thus, contains the address of the instruction following the one being executed when the interrupt occurs. The action of this internally generated instruction is as follows:

$$RST \text{ (internal)}$$
$$((SP) - 1) \leftarrow (PCH)$$
$$((SP) - 2) \leftarrow (PCL)$$
$$(SP) \leftarrow (SP) - 2$$
$$(PC) \leftarrow restart\ address$$

The BI machine cycle is like an OPCODE FETCH, OF, except the $\overline{RD}$ line remains high. The operation code, which is generally read in during OF, is instead generated internally during the BI machine cycle by the microprocessor hardware.

After an RST is executed, the PC contains the address of the starting location for the subroutine which handles the interrupt. This procedure for identifying the interrupting device and directly transferring control to the starting location is called a *vectored interrupt*. Since only a few memory locations separate the different vector addresses, there is usually a jump instruction at the vector address which transfers control to another memory location where the actual service subroutine begins.

In the case of an INTR interrupt, the interrupt machine cycle entered is an INTERRUPT ACKNOWLEDGE, INA. INA is similar to OF except that $IO/\overline{M} = 1$, instead of a $\overline{RD}$ the microprocessor generates an $\overline{INTA}$ strobe, and the value of the program counter is not incremented during INA. Thus, the PC contains the address of the instruction following the one being executed when the interrupt occurred.

In response to the $\overline{INTA}$ strobe, external logic places an instruction OP code on the data bus. In the case of a multibyte instruction, additional INA machine cycles are generated by the 8085A to transfer the additional bytes into the microprocessor. Theoretically, the external logic can place any instruction on the data bus in response to the $\overline{\text{INTA}}$. However, only CALL and RST, which save the PC contents before transferring control, allow a proper return from a service subroutine. The *restart* instruction, RST n, has $0 \le n \le 7$.

$$\text{RST n}$$
$$((SP) - 1) \leftarrow (PCH)$$
$$((SP) - 2) \leftarrow (PCL)$$
$$(SP) \ \ \leftarrow (SP) - 2$$
$$(PC) \ \ \leftarrow 8*n$$

This instruction is essentially the same as the previously mentioned internal restart, except for the restart address and the fact that it is generated by external hardware. *Restart* has the following bit pattern, frequently referred to as the *restart* or *interrupt vector*:

11NNN111

where n = NNN is a 3-bit binary number. When this instruction is executed, the program counter is saved on the stack, thus saving the return address. And control is transferred to a location with an address which is eight times NNN, thus facilitating a branch to any one of eight fixed addresses—00H, 08H, 10H, 18H, 20H, 28H, 30H, or 38H—depending on the value of NNN. These addresses are referred to as *restart locations*, 0, 1, 2, etc., to 7.

External logic controls a three-state buffer with the $\overline{\text{INTA}}$ signal in order to place a restart vector onto the data bus. In Fig. 9.2-3 a single I/O device is connected to the microprocessor's interrupt structure. The output of its interrupt request flip-flop is directly connected to the INTR interrupt pin of the micro-processor. When the interrupt request flip-flop of the I/O device is set, the microprocessor completes execution of the current instruction and then initiates an interrupt acknowledge machine cycle. During this cycle, the internal INTE FF is cleared, disabling further interrupts from affecting the microprocessor. The $\overline{\text{INTA}}$ signal that is generated enables the three-state buffer whose data inputs are hardwired to the value of the interrupt vector, RST 7, in this example. $\overline{\text{INTA}}$ also clears the interrupt request flip-flop. The microprocessor inputs the restart vector, saves the program counter, and branches to memory location 38H. The subroutine which starts at that location services the I/O device.

In the discussion of Fig. 9.2-3, two assumptions were made: (1) only one interrupt input was involved in creating the valid interrupt condition and (2) only one interrupting device was associated with each input. Given these conditions, once an interrupt occurs, control is transferred to the restart location for that interrupt. Execution of a restart during the interrupt machine cycle saves the value of the PC. The remainder of the information that comprises the state of the microprocessor is saved by pushing the program status word (registers A and F) and the other register pairs onto the stack.

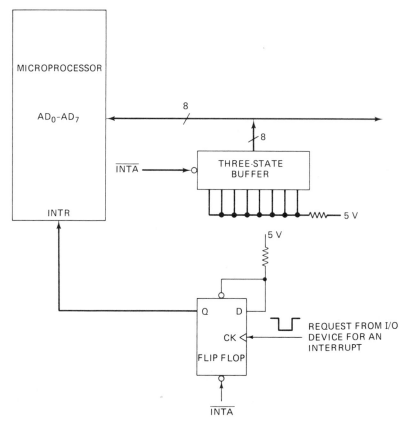

Figure 9.2-3. Vectored interrupt with RST 7 "jammed" on interrupt acknowledge.

The following four instructions save the entire state of the microprocessor.

PUSH PSW
PUSH B
PUSH D
PUSH H

The time required to execute these instructions constitutes the save state of step (3) of Section 9.1. Any registers not used by the service routine do not have to be saved, thus reducing this time period.

This sequence of instructions is executed at the beginning of the I/O service routine. Once the state of the microprocessor has been saved, the interrupt service subroutine is free to use any of the microprocessor's registers. With only one I/O device connected to each interrupt input, identification of the interrupting device is automatic, in that each restart location is associated with only a single device. Thus, step (4) of Section 9.1, requires no additional time. At the end of the I/O service subroutine, the state of the processor which has been stored on the stack is restored by executing the first four of the following sequence of instructions:

> POP H
> POP D
> POP B
> POP PSW
> EI
> RET

Note that the order of the POP sequence is the reverse of the PUSH since the stack is a last-in/first-out type. The *pop processor status word*, POP PSW, instruction restores the accumulator and flag registers from the stack.

The enable interrupt instruction in the previous instruction sequence allows the microprocessor to respond to interrupts again only after the execution of the return instruction. RET replaces the contents of the program counter with the saved value, which corresponds to the address of the instruction following the instruction being executed when the interrupt occurred, thus completing the last step of the sequence.

The 8080A has a single interrupt input, INT, which is functionally equivalent to INTR of the 8085A. Thus, the 8080A supports a vectored interrupt structure with eight vectors. This maskable interrupt is enabled and disabled by the EI and DI instructions, respectively.

9.3 PRIORITY INTERRUPT STRUCTURES

In reality, interrupts are asynchronous; they do not occur one at a time in an orderly fashion. Microprocessors have certain priorities established for their various interrupt inputs. A *priority interrupt* structure arbitrates among several devices simultaneously requesting service and assures that the device with the highest assigned priority is serviced first.

The five interrupt inputs of the 8085A have an internally established, fixed, multilevel priority structure. From highest to lowest they are TRAP, RST7.5, RST6.5, RST5.5, and INTR. TRAP, since it is not maskable, is usually reserved to handle catastrophies such as power failures. I/O devices are associated with the other four interrupt inputs in such a way that the highest priority device is connected to RST7.5, the next highest priority device to RST6.5, etc. Devices which require the fastest response time or which interrupt the microprocessor with the greatest frequency are usually given the highest priority.

Once an interrupt occurs, the internal interrupt enable flip-flop, INTE FF, is automatically cleared, allowing no more interrupts until an EI instruction is executed. However, if, for example, an RST7.5 interrupt occurs, and the service subroutine for that interrupt subsequently enables the microprocessor interrupt

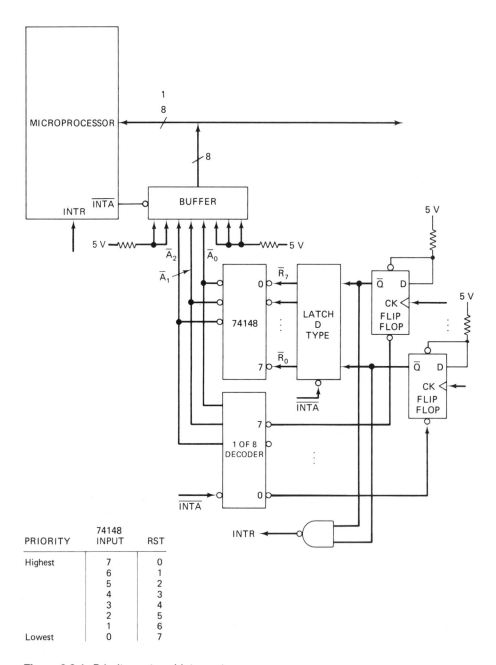

Figure 9.3-1. Priority vectored interrupt.

feature before its completion, the microprocessor can be interrupted by a lower priority interrupt, for instance, an RST5.5.

Several I/O devices can be connected to a single microprocessor interrupt input by ORing their interrupt service request flags. When an interrupt request occurs at such an input, the particular device requesting an interrupt must be identified. For INTR of the 8085A and INT of the 8080A, identification and transfer of control to the starting address of the service subroutine are done in a vectored manner for as many as eight devices. Each of the eight is assigned a different interrupt vector in the RST n instruction. The appropriate RST n instruction OP code is placed on the data bus in response to $\overline{\text{INTA}}$. The I/O devices' interrupt request flip-flop outputs are ORed together and connected to the microprocessor's interrupt input (see Fig. 9.3-1). In that figure, the *restart* instruction is generated with the aid of a priority encoder which supplies the three bits, NNN, of the interrupt vector. An 8-line-to-3-line priority encoder allows the highest priority device, with its interrupt request flag set, to generate NNN, and thus be identified immediately.

The truth table for an SN74148 priority encoder is shown in Fig. 9.3-2. There are eight active low inputs to the priority encoder. When an input is held low, the 3-bit code representing its complement appears at outputs $\overline{\text{A}}_2$, $\overline{\text{A}}_1$, and $\overline{\text{A}}_0$. When two or more inputs are active, the output is the complement of the input with the highest numerical value.

The D-type positive level triggered latch shown in Fig. 9.3-1 allows the inputs to the priority encoder to follow the $\overline{\text{Q}}$ outputs of the interrupt flags until an interrupt acknowledge, $\overline{\text{INTA}}$, occurs. The $\overline{\text{INTA}}$ signal allows the latch outputs to retain the values that existed at the occurrence of the $\overline{\text{INTA}}$, and enables the three-state buffer, placing an RST instruction on the data bus. The microprocessor inputs this instruction on the rising edge of $\overline{\text{INTA}}$, and control is transferred to the location associated with the RST n instruction.

The instruction RST 0 transfers control to the first memory location, the same location used when an external reset is applied to the system. Thus, RST 0 is usually not used for interrupts.

The priority encoder shown in Fig. 9.3-2 establishes priority among interrupts that occur simultaneously. That is, if one device sets its interrupt request flag, causing an interrupt, and another device also sets its flag before the interrupt acknowledge ($\overline{\text{INTA}}$) occurs, the device serviced is the one connected to the highest numbered input of the priority encoder.

The INA machine cycle automatically disables the interrupt so that no other interrupts can occur until the one being processed is completed. Since any one or more of eight devices can interrupt the microprocessor, only the interrupt request flip-flop of the device being serviced is cleared. $\overline{\text{INTA}}$ and additional logic to gate $\overline{\text{INTA}}$ clear the appropriate flip-flop. In Fig. 9.3-1 $\overline{\text{INTA}}$ is gated with a 1-out-of-8 decoder; however, a programmed pulse generated by each device service subroutine would have the same effect. The next to last instruction in the service subroutine enables the interrupt, and the last instruction

'148, 'LS148

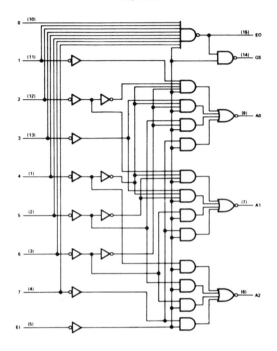

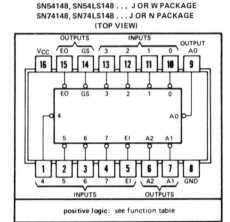

SN54148, SN54LS148 . . . J OR W PACKAGE
SN74148, SN74LS148 . . . J OR N PACKAGE
(TOP VIEW)

positive logic: see function table

'148, 'LS148
FUNCTION TABLE

INPUTS									OUTPUTS				
EI	0	1	2	3	4	5	6	7	A2	A1	A0	GS	EO
H	X	X	X	X	X	X	X	X	H	H	H	H	H
L	H	H	H	H	H	H	H	H	H	H	H	H	L
L	X	X	X	X	X	X	X	L	L	L	L	L	H
L	X	X	X	X	X	X	L	H	L	L	H	L	H
L	X	X	X	X	X	L	H	H	L	H	L	L	H
L	X	X	X	X	L	H	H	H	L	H	H	L	H
L	X	X	X	L	H	H	H	H	H	L	L	L	H
L	X	X	L	H	H	H	H	H	H	L	H	L	H
L	X	L	H	H	H	H	H	H	H	H	L	L	H
L	L	H	H	H	H	H	H	H	H	H	H	L	H

Figure 9.3-2. An 8-line-to-3-line priority encoder, 74148. (Courtesy of Texas Instruments, Inc.)

transfers control back to the instruction following the one which was interrupted. The lower priority of the two interrupt requests will then cause another INA machine cycle to occur. The low priority interrupt will then be serviced.

In some applications it is essential that a higher priority device interrupt the servicing of a lower priority device or any device with a priority above a certain value interrupt the processing of a current interrupt service subroutine. The value may be fixed or it may be a function of the previous interrupt's priority. An integrated circuit which facilitates this is the 8214 *Priority Interrupt Control Unit, PICU*, whose logic diagram is shown in Fig. 9.3-3. In addition to including

PIN CONFIGURATION

LOGIC DIAGRAM

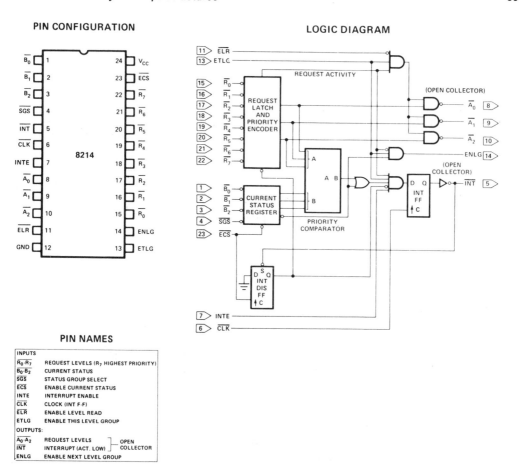

PIN NAMES

INPUTS	
$\overline{R_0}\text{-}\overline{R_7}$	REQUEST LEVELS (R$_7$ HIGHEST PRIORITY)
$\overline{B_0}\text{-}\overline{B_2}$	CURRENT STATUS
$\overline{SGS}$	STATUS GROUP SELECT
$\overline{ECS}$	ENABLE CURRENT STATUS
INTE	INTERRUPT ENABLE
$\overline{CLK}$	CLOCK (INT F-F)
$\overline{ELR}$	ENABLE LEVEL READ
ETLG	ENABLE THIS LEVEL GROUP
OUTPUTS:	
$\overline{A_0}\text{-}\overline{A_2}$	REQUEST LEVELS — OPEN
$\overline{INT}$	INTERRUPT (ACT. LOW) — COLLECTOR
ENLG	ENABLE NEXT LEVEL GROUP

Figure 9.3-3. 8214 priority interrupt control unit. (Courtesy of Intel Corp.)

the functions of the D-type latch and 74148 priority encoder of Fig. 9.3-1, the 8214 contains a current status register and a priority comparator. The current status register is treated as a 4-bit output port by the microprocessor. Its inputs, $\overline{B_2}$, $\overline{B_1}$, $\overline{B_0}$, and $\overline{SGS}$, are connected to bits D_0 through D_3 of the data bus. The latch's strobe input is $\overline{ECS}$. A 4-bit code is written into the current status register to control the priority arbitration logic. If bit $\overline{SGS}$ is 0, an interrupt is generated by the 8214 when any of the interrupt request inputs are logic 0. However, if $\overline{SGS}$ is 1, bits $\overline{B_2}$, $\overline{B_1}$, and $\overline{B_0}$ represent the complement of the minimum priority level of an interrupt request which the 8214 passes on to the microprocessor.

When the 8214 generates an interrupt request, the interrupt disable is set, and subsequent requests are ignored until the current status register is reloaded with the priority threshold code. This resets the interrupt disable flip-flop, allowing an interrupt request which exceeds the threshold to be transmitted to the microprocessor.

A more sophisticated programmable interrupt controller, the 8259A [2] provides eight levels of priority and a number of different arbitration modes. In response to the 8085A's $\overline{\text{INTA}}$ strobes, it furnishes a CALL instruction whose addresses are established under program control when the device is initialized. Thus, the locations branched to in response to an interrupt can be established anywhere in the microprocessor's address space.

When several I/O devices are associated with a single interrupt vector or interrupt input, their interrupt request flip-flops can be ORed together to create a single interrupt. The outputs of each of these interrupt flip-flops are connected to an input port. The service subroutine then inputs the status of the interrupt request flip-flops from this port to determine which of the I/O devices to service. In the case of simultaneous interrupts, priority is implemented in software, as was illustrated in Chapter 8 when polling devices for programmed I/O.

9.4 FIFO BUFFERS

Thus far, two handshaking methods have been discussed which synchronize the data transfer between an I/O device and a microprocessor: polling and interrupting. Each technique transfers a single word of data every time it is invoked, and each involves a certain amount of overhead. In some applications, however, it is more efficient to transfer data between an I/O device and a microprocessor in blocks. A hardware device, the *First-In/First-out, FIFO*, buffer or memory facilitates this.

A FIFO is a memory unit with separate data inputs and outputs but no address inputs. Data is read from the memory in the same order in which it is written into it; i.e., the first word written in is the first word read out. An important feature of the FIFO is that it can be written into and read from at two different data rates, simultaneously and independently.

When placed between an I/O device and a microprocessor, a FIFO accepts data at the I/O device's rate and is read from at the microprocessor's rate. One of two conditions exists: either the I/O device is slower than the microprocessor or it is faster. If the I/O device is slower, e.g., an electromechanical device, it loads data into the FIFO at a slow rate. When the FIFO is filled with a block of data, the FIFO interrupts the microprocessor, and the service subroutine inputs the entire block. This substantially reduces the overhead per data word transferred.

In a situation where the I/O device generates bursts of data at a high data rate, the FIFO accepts the data at the faster rate and the microprocessor reads it at a slower rate. Of course, the average data rate of the I/O device must be low enough to be handled by the microprocessor, and the capacity of the FIFO must be great enough to average out the data rate of the burst data appropriately.

The logic symbol for a 32 × 8 FIFO, Am2812, is shown in Fig. 9.4-1, [3]. Initially, the device is reset by pulsing the master reset input, $\overline{\text{MR}}$. After

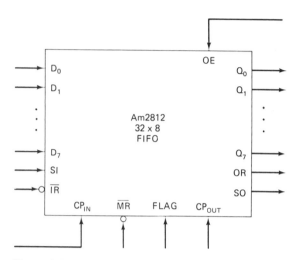

Figure 9.4-1. Logic symbol for a 32 × 8 FIFO Am2812.

resetting, the input ready output, $\overline{\text{IR}}$, is low—indicating that the FIFO is ready to receive new data. The output ready, OR, is also low—indicating that valid data is not available at the output. A low-to-high transition at the shift input, SI, loads data into the first register of the FIFO and sets $\overline{\text{IR}}$ high. When SI is brought low again, data in the first register is automatically shifted to the output register of the FIFO. Once the data word in the first register is shifted to the second register, $\overline{\text{IR}}$ goes low and new data can be entered. The amount of time required for the data at the input to be shifted to the output is the ***ripple through time*** and is proportional to the number of registers in the FIFO.

Internal logic associated with each register in the FIFO determines whether the next register is empty; if so, it shifts data into it, and the register's control logic enters its empty state. Thus, data entered into the FIFO ripples or falls from the first register to the last empty register. When the FIFO is full, $\overline{\text{IR}}$ remains high, and additional data cannot be input until a word is removed.

When the output read, OR, signal is high, valid data is available to be read from the FIFO. A pulse on the shift out input, SO, reads the data in the last register and shifts data from the next to last register into it. This starts a ripple process whereby the remaining data in the FIFO shifts one register closer to the output.

The Am2812 has three-state outputs controlled by an output enable input, OE. If the output is not enabled, data cannot be read out of the FIFO. A flag output on the Am2812 also indicates whether it is more or less than half full. The flag goes high when the 15th $\pm$ 1 word is loaded into the FIFO and remains high until there are fewer than 15 $\pm$ 1 words in the memory.

Am2812 FIFOs are cascaded by connecting the OR and SO outputs of one FIFO to the SI and IR inputs of the next FIFO. When an SI signal loads the last register in an Am2812, the $\overline{\text{IR}}$ output stays high, so no pulse is applied to the preceding FIFO. As a result, its output and the input of the filled FIFO contain

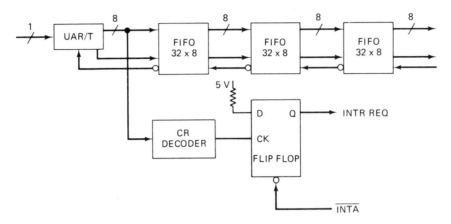

Figure 9.4-2. 94 × 8 FIFO constructed from three 32 × 8 FIFOs cascaded and used to buffer serial data received from a UAR/T.

the same word until a word is read from the FIFO. Thus, the total number of words that can be stored in n cascaded FIFOs is $31n + 1$, not $32n$. In Fig. 9.4-2, three Am2812s are cascaded, making a 94 × 8 FIFO. This FIFO receives data from a UAR/T connected to a terminal. Characters received from the terminal are stored in the FIFO until a carriage return, CR, indicates the end of a line of data. A combinational decoder detects the CR(0DH) and generates an interrupt request to the microprocessor. The service routine then inputs an entire line of data each time it is invoked.

The Am2812 is also capable of accepting serial data at its D_0 input and outputting that data at D_7. In this configuration, the device looks like a 256 × 1 FIFO. Inputs CP_{in} and CP_{out} strobe data into and read data from the FIFO.

9.5 REAL-TIME CLOCKS AND INTERVAL TIMERS

For microprocessor systems, time is generally measured for two reasons: to keep a record of the time of day and to chart the elapsed time between two events. Several approaches, with varying hardware/software tradeoffs, can be used in these measurements.

A *real-time clock* keeps track of the passage of time (e.g., the time of day) and can be implemented either in software or in hardware. One software implementation uses three RWM locations to store the decimal digits corresponding to seconds, minutes, and hours. The routine counts pulses from an external, 1-second pulse generator and updates the three memory locations. A pulse train with a 1-second period is obtained by converting a 60 Hz AC power line signal to a T^2L level pulse train or by counting down the output of a crystal oscillator. The pulse from the generator is counted via an interrupt; i.e., the pulse creates an interrupt, and the interrupt service routine then increments the stored time. An additional routine initially sets the clock. The interrupt service

```
TOD:      PUSH PSW       ;    SAVE REGISTERS THAT WILL BE MODIFIED
          PUSH B
          PUSH H
          MVI C, 2H      ;    SET UP SEC-MIN LOOP COUNTER
          LXI H, SEC     ;    SET POINTER TO SECONDS LOCATION
LOOP:     MOV A, M
          INR  A         ;    INCREMENT SECS (MIN)
          DAA            ;    CORRECT RESULT TO BCD REPRESENTATION
          MOV  M, A      ;    STORE SECS (MIN)
          CPI  60H       ;    IF NOT EQUAL TO 60, RETURN
          JNZ FIN
          MVI M, 0       ;    IF EQUAL TO 60, SET TO 0
          INX  H         ;    POINT TO NEXT MEMORY LOCATION
          DCR  C         ;    IF PREVIOUS PASS INCREMENTED SECONDS TO 60, THEN LOOP AND
                         ;    INCREMENT MIN
          JNZ LOOP
          MOV  A, M      ;    IF PREVIOUS PASS INCREMENTED MIN TO 60, THEN HRS MUST BE
                         ;    INCREMENTED
          INR  A
          DAA
          MOV M, A
          CPI  24H       ;    IF HOURS LESS THAN 24, THEN FINISH
          JNZ FIN
          MVI  M, 0 H    ;    IF HOURS EQUAL 24, THEN SET TO 0
FIN:      POP  H         ;    RESTORE PRE-INTERUPT STATE
          POP  B
          POP  PSW
          EI
          RET
          .
          .
          .
          ORG XXX        ;    RESERVED MEMORY FOR SEC, MIN, AND HRS MUST BE IN RWM
SEC :     DS  1
MIN :     DS  1
HRS:      DS  1
```

Figure 9.5-1. Service subroutine for time of day clock.

subroutine shown in Fig. 9.5-1 keeps time in response to interrupts from the 1-second oscillator. Other routines which need to know the time read it from the three memory locations; e.g., an indication of the time of day along with data being output to a printer. The clock reading routine disables the interrupt before reading the seconds, minutes, and hours. Typically, the highest priority interrupt is used for the clock. If it is nonmaskable, then the clock routine must provide a mechanism to prevent time read errors caused if another clock interrupt occurs during reading. For example, a simple mechanism requires two successive, identical clock readings.

A real-time clock can also be implemented in hardware. The hardware clock, an input device whose time is read through input ports, uses clock or calendar ICs. Hardware implementation is advantageous during a power failure because the clock or calendar IC can be powered from a battery backup system.

Elapsed time can also be measured with a software real-time clock, if a resolution of 1 second is adequate. The time at the start of the interval is simply saved in a block of memory. At the end of the interval, the start time is subtracted from the finish time, giving the elapsed time. For greater resolution a faster clock is used, and another memory location records fractions of a second.

As the required resolution for elapsed time measurements increases, use of an interrupt-driven, software, real-time clock becomes inefficient because the processor is continually servicing interrupts from a fast pulse generator used as a clock. An alternative approach uses external counters to count pulses either directly or stepped down from the microprocessor's clock or a pulse generator. A pulse at the start of the interval clears and enables the counter, and a pulse at the end of the interval disables the counter and interrupts the microprocessor. The counter contents are then input by the microprocessor.

9.5.1 The 8155's Timer

The 8155 discussed in Chapter 8 contains a 14-bit programmable counter/timer in addition to RWM and I/O ports (see Fig. 8.6-1). The timer counts pulses at the TIMER IN input and provides either a square wave or a pulse when the terminal count is reached at the TIMER OUT output. The 8155 timer is primarily a square wave generator, not an event counter. To facilitate the generation of square waves, the counter counts down by two for each pulse at the TIMER IN input. This procedure is repeated twice, for one complete cycle.

This 14-bit counter is part of the 16-bit count length register, CLR, which can be either written or read. The most significant two bits of the CLR determine the counter's mode of operation (see Fig. 9.5-2). The address for the low order byte of the CLR is XXXXX100, and for the high order byte, XXXXX101.

In operation, the 8155 is first loaded with a code which defines the timer mode and the desired count length. The possible modes are:

M_2	M_1	
0	0	Timer output low during second half of count.
0	1	Square wave output with period equal to the count length and automatic reload of count length at terminal count.
1	0	Single pulse when terminal count is reached.
1	1	Single pulse at terminal count with automatic reload.

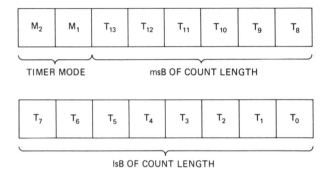

Figure 9.5-2. Bit designation of the 8155 timer's count length register.

The counter is started or stopped when a control word is written into the command status register of the 8155 (see Fig. 8.6-2). Bits 6 and 7 of the control word program the counter as follows:

C/S_7	C/S_6	
0	0	NOP: Does not affect counter's operation.
0	1	STOP: Stop counting if timer is running; NOP if timer has not been started.
1	0	STOP AFTER TC: Stop immediately after present terminal count is reached; NOP if timer has not started.
1	1	START: Load mode, count length, and start immediately after loading. If timer is already running, start new mode and count length immediately after present TC is reached.

When the counter has reached its terminal count—when operating in mode two, $M_2 = 1$, $M_1 = 0$—the single pulse generated at TIMER OUT can interrupt the microprocessor. Otherwise, the end of a count is determined by software polling of bit 6 of the command/status register (see Fig. 8.6-2). This bit is latched high when a terminal count is reached and reset when the C/S register is read or a new count is started.

In a microcomputer system, a programmable timer generates accurate time delays under software control without requiring software loops. Thus, the overhead is minimized, and the microprocessor can carry out other processing tasks during the delay. Once the delay is counted out, the timer interrupts the microprocessor and indicates the end of the delay period. The timer can be programmed so that its output implements several functions, such as a square wave generator or a divide by N counter.

To use the timer as an event counter, for example, to measure the period of a waveform, the pulses from a clock oscillator, the event, that occur during one period of the waveform are counted. The waveform is input to a toggle flip-flop (Fig. 9.5-3), which creates a square wave with a period twice that of the signal to be measured. (It is assumed that the original waveform is not necessarily a square wave; i.e., its duty cycle is not necessarily 50 percent.) Thus, the square

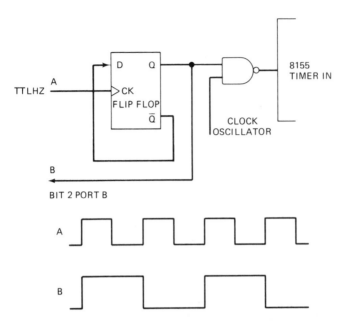

Figure 9.5-3. Circuit for measurement of the period of waveform TTLHZ.

wave is logic 1 for a length of time equal to the period of the original waveform. The output of the toggle flip-flop gates the signal from the clock oscillator to the TIMER IN input of the 8155. To count pulses during one period, the subroutine, HTOL, waits for a high-to-low transition of the flip-flop output and starts the counter. However, no clock pulses are gated to the counter until the flip-flop's output is logic 1 again. Since the flip-flop's output is logic 1 for one period of the original waveform, pulses are counted during this period (see Fig. 9.5-4).

At the same time the counter is counting pulses, the microprocessor monitors the output of the flip-flop for the next 1 to 0 transition. When this occurs, the microprocessor stops the counter, and clock pulses are accumulated for only one period of the original waveform. The count in the CLR is then input to the microprocessor, and the most significant two of the 16 bits are masked to 1s. Registers B and C, therefore, contain the two's complement of twice the number of clock pulses.[2]

This technique allows a very precise measurement of elapsed time. However, it requires polling the flip-flop output while the counter is running, and this adds software overhead to the measurement. An alternative technique, which reduces software overhead, uses the 1 to 0 transition of the flip-flop output to interrupt the microprocessor and a service subroutine to start the counter. At the next 1 to 0 transition, the flip-flop causes a second interrupt and the service subroutine

[2]The timer circuit of the 8155 is designed to be a square wave timer, not an event timer. To achieve this, it counts down by two twice in completing one cycle.

```
PERIOD:     XRA  A              LOAD COUNT LENGTH REGISTER WITH 0, SET MODE = 0
            OUT  CLRL
            OUT  CLRH
            CALL HTOL       ;   WAIT FOR 1-TO-0 TRANSITION
            MVI  A, START   ;   START COUNTER
            OUT  CSR
            CALL HTOL       ;   WAIT FOR 1-TO-0 TRANSITION
            MVI  A, STOP    ;   STOP COUNTER
            OUT  CSR
            IN   TIMEL      ;   INPUT LOW BYTE OF COUNT
            MOV  C, A       ;   LEAVE IN C
            IN   TIMEH      ;   INPUT HIGH BYTE OF COUNT
            ORA  MSKPD      ;   SET BITS 14 AND 15 (MODE) TO 1s
            MOV  B, A       ;   LEAVE IN B
            RET
            ;  HTOL—IMPLEMENTS A WAIT VIA LOOPING
            ;  UNTIL A 1-TO-0 TRANSITION OCCURS IN THE
            ;  BIT OF PORT A INDICATED BY THE MASK TTLHZ
            ;  NO PARAMETERS
            ;  REQ MODIFIED A
HTOL:       IN   PORTA
            ANI  TTLHZ
            JZ   HTOL       ;   IF LOW WAIT IN LOOP
TTLH:       IN   PORTA
            ANI  TTLHZ
            JNZ  TTLH       ;   IF HIGH WAIT IN LOOP
            RET
```

Figure 9.5-4. Subroutine to measure the period of a waveform using the hardware of Figure 9.5-3.

stops the counter. The service subroutine complements and tests one bit of a reserved memory location to determine whether it should start or stop the counter.

Programmable interval timers are also available as separate LSI devices. For example, the 8253 Programmable Interval Timer contains three, independent, 16-bit counters. These counters are software programmable and count in either binary or BCD. In addition, any one of several modes of output from each of the individual timers is software programmable.

9.6 CONSIDERATIONS FOR USING INTERRUPTS

Although the use of interrupts is advantageous for allowing concurrent processing while I/O is performed and/or external events are responded to, interrupts must be used with considerable care. For example, suppose a subroutine used by the main program is also used by an interrupt service subroutine, or by two or more interrupts at different priority levels. Assume that the subroutine is being executed as the result of a call by the main program, that an interrupt occurs, and that the interrupt service subroutine calls the subroutine. This process of calling a subroutine that is only partially through execution is referred to as *reentering* the subroutine. The result of reentering can be the loss of data and subsequent failure of the system.

9.6.1 Shared Subroutines

Three techniques preclude these problems. By the first method, the subroutine is duplicated rather than shared. Duplicated subroutines are totally independent of each other; not only must they have different names and instruction labels, but they cannot share reserved memory. The cost of duplication is the additional memory required.

Not all subroutnies which need to be shared can be duplicated. I/O driver subroutines, for instance, cannot be duplicated because the I/O device is a single resource and must be shared. In such cases, the second method, described next, is employed.

By the second method, reentry of shared subroutines is prevented by disabling the interrupts before the subroutine is called and enabling them after the return from the subroutine. This increases the interrupt response time to a value greater than the execution time of the shared subroutine. In a system where critical response times must be met, such a solution may not be acceptable.

By the third method, for situations other than those where a single physical device is being controlled by a subroutine, a reentrant subroutine can be written and shared. *Reentrant subroutines* can be reentered without loss of temporary results. They are written in pure code, with a separate temporary storage or work area for each entry into the subroutine. *Pure code* does not modify itself in any way. All but the simplest subroutines require temporary storage for parameters, data, and temporary results. This storage, or work area, is unique for each call of a reentrant subroutine. If the only temporary storage needed is provided by general purpose registers in the microprocessor, then this work area is effectively separate from the main program and interrupt service routines for different levels, since the contents of these registers are saved and restored at an interrupt. If the subroutine requires a larger work area, the address of the work area is provided in one of the register pairs in the microprocessor.

9.6.2 Disabling Interrupts

Often during the execution of time critical routines, interrupts must be disabled. If software delay routines and interrupts are used, the interrupts must be disabled before any delay is initiated; otherwise, the delay may be of unpredictable duration. Subroutines which act as drivers for certain I/O devices may also need to function uninterrupted.

Situations where interrupts are disabled must be taken into consideration when determining worst-case response time. And, as the number of interrupt sources increases, so does the complexity of the design and timing analysis.

9.6.3 Priority Assignments

Generally, it is advisable to avoid the use of interrupts in a design unless the need for concurrent processing, fast response time, or other restrictions make them necessary. If used, it is advantageous in limiting complexity to have all interrupts on a single level, if possible. If a multilevel or priority interrupt structure is essential, however, the assignment of interrupts is usually made as follows. The unmaskable interrupt, which is the highest level, is used for catastrophic events such as power failures. If a high resolution real-time clock is used, it is associated with the next highest interrupt so that clock ticks will not be lost. The remaining devices or events are associated with priority levels such that devices or events requiring the shortest response times are assigned the highest levels.

Another reason for avoiding interrupts is the difficulty of debugging a system. Since interrupts are asynchronous events and unpredictable in terms of time of occurrence, it is hard to simulate worst-case conditions to determine whether the system will respond properly to combinations of interrupts.

9.7 DIRECT MEMORY ACCESS (DMA)

Program controlled data transfers require a significant amount of a microprocessor's time to transmit a rather small amount of data per unit time, i.e., a low data rate. And the microprocessor cannot execute any other processing functions during program controlled I/O operations. Although interrupts increase the attainable data rate, require less software, and allow concurrent processing, applications exist where the required data rate is simply too high to be achieved by using interrupts or where the data rate is such that the time spent in interrupt service routines impacts the concurrent processing to an unacceptable degree.

However, *Direct Memory Access, DMA*, facilitates maximum I/O data rate and maximum concurrency. Unlike programmed I/O and interrupt I/O that route data through the microprocessor, DMA directly transfers data between an I/O device and memory. For DMA transfers, the microprocessor must have a DMA feature. Additional external logic is also necessary. This additional logic, the *DMA controller*, contains its own address register, word count register, and logic for reading or writing data to or from memory. Figure 9.7-1 illustrates the basic components of a DMA controller.

DMA is commonly used for three types of data transfer: burst, cycle stealing, and transparent. *Burst* DMA transfers a block of data at the highest rate possible. The steps in the execution of a data transfer using burst DMA are as follows:

1. The microprocessor loads the DMA controller with a starting address for the memory transfer and the number of words to be transferred.

2. When the input device has the data ready to be transferred to the memory or when the output device is ready for the transfer

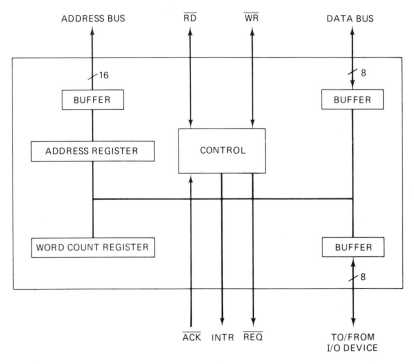

Figure 9.7-1. Basic DMA controller.

from the memory, the DMA controller sends a DMA request to the microprocessor.

3. The microprocessor acknowledges the DMA request, floats its address and data buses and appropriate control lines, and suspends any processing that requires use of the address and data bus.

4. The DMA controller provides an address to memory and control strobes to read or write memory. The I/O device provides or accepts the data on the data bus. After a data byte is transferred, the DMA controller increments its address register and decrements its word count register. If the required number of words has not been transferred, the DMA controller repeats this step when the I/O device is ready with the next data word.

5. When the required number of words has been transferred, the DMA controller terminates the DMA request and interrupts the microprocessor to indicate that the DMA transfer is complete.

The maximum data rate of a burst DMA transfer is limited only by the read or write cycle time of the memory and by the speed of the DMA controller. Below this maximum, the data rate is limited by the rate at which the I/O device can supply or receive data. Burst data transfers are commonly used in transferring data to or from a floppy-disk mass storage unit or for refreshing a CRT display (see Chapter 10).

In *cycle stealing* DMA, data is transferred concurrently with other processing being carried out by the microprocessor. The steps in execution are similar to those for burst DMA except that after one word of data is transferred in step 4, if the required number of data words have not been transferred, then steps 2, 3, and 4 are repeated for each data byte, until the requisite number of bytes has been transferred. Thus, the DMA controller steals cycles (state times) from the microprocessor, during which it transfers data. The processing carried out by the microprocesor is slowed accordingly.

For some microprocessors, external logic can be designed so that cycle stealing occurs during internal processing when the system address and data buses are not being used. Such DMA transfers are transparent to the microprocessor in that they do not interfere with or slow down its normal rate of instruction execution. *Transparent* DMA, in addition to the normal logic, requires logic to detect the occurrence of microprocessor states which involve only internal processing.

For the three types of DMA transfer, the only software required is that necessary for initializing the DMA controller's address and word count registers. In the 8085A, a DMA controller requests a DMA operation by bringing the HOLD input of the microprocessor high. The microprocessor then synchronizes the asynchronous hold request and, at the proper time in the machine cycle, provides a hold acknowledge (HLDA) signal to the DMA controller and floats its address and data buses and the $\overline{RD}$, $\overline{WR}$, and $IO/\overline{M}$ control lines. The microprocessor continues internal processing and then enters a hold state (see Fig. 9.7-2). By floating its address, data, and control buses, the microprocessor effectively disconnects itself from the memory. From this point on, it is up to the DMA controller to provide addresses, data, and control signals to the memory to implement the data transfer. The DMA controller then enables its three-state buffers, which connect it to the address, data, and control buses. When the DMA processor is through using memory, it floats its address, data, and control buses, and then brings the HOLD input of the microprocessor low. The microprocessor exits the hold state and continues its previous operation from the point at which it was suspended by the hold request. The DMA controller subsequently interrupts the microprocessor, indicating that the DMA transfer is complete.

DMA controllers range from random logic structures to special LSI devices and even to dedicated microprocessors. An LSI DMA controller such as the Intel 8257-5 is programmable and controls the DMA operations of several I/O devices [1].

The only additional hardware this 4-channel device requires is an 8212 latch to demultiplex the addresses it generates. The 8257-5 uses a clock input with a minimum clock period of 320 nS. Four clock cycles are required to transfer 1 byte of data. With a 3 MHz clock, a transfer rate of 750 K bytes per second is achieved.

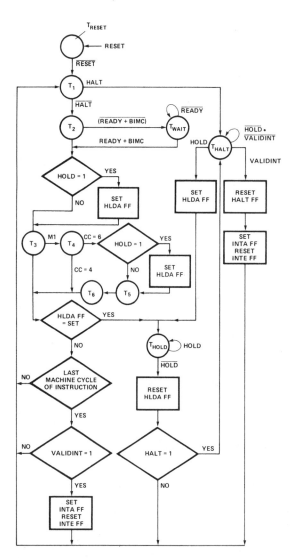

Figure 9.7-2. Complete state transtition diagram for 8085A. (Courtesy of Intel Corp.)

Figure 9.7-3 shows how the 8257-5 and the 8212 are interfaced to an 8085A to provide DMA capability for up to four I/O devices.[3] Consider the case of a DMA read operation, a transfer from memory to a peripheral. Assume that only a single DMA channel (channel 0) is used in the system. Prior to a DMA transfer, both the DMA controller and the controller of the output device are initialized.

The DMA controller contains two 16-bit registers, a DMA address register and a terminal count register, for each channel, that must be initialized. It also

---

[3]Throughout the remainder of this section, any reference to a DMA controller means the 8257-5 controller.

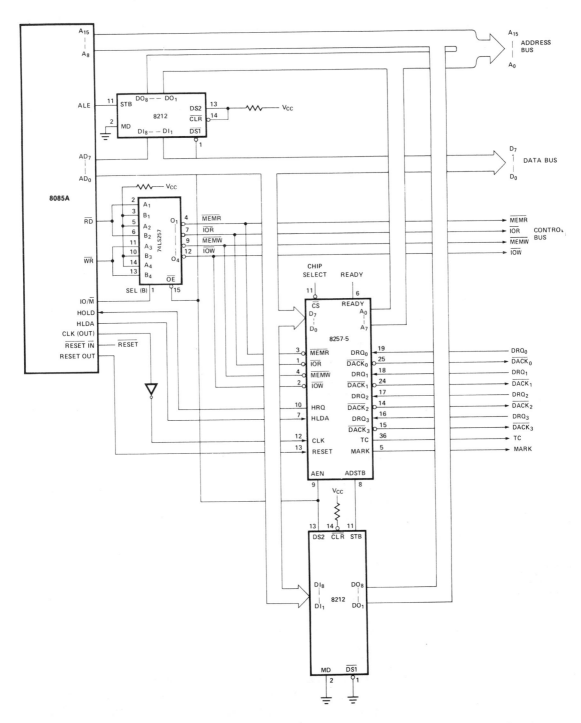

Figure 9.7-3. 8257-5 DMA controller interface to an 8085A microprocessor. (Courtesy of Intel Corp.)

contains an 8-bit mode register and an 8-bit status register which are shared by the four channels. The data required for initialization is written into the DMA controller by the microprocessor. The microprocessor treats the DMA controller as an I/O device and uses its address inputs A_0–A_3 to select the register to be written.

The address and terminal count registers for channel 0 are initialized by loading the DMA address register with the address of the first memory location to be accessed. The least significant 14 bits of the terminal count register are loaded with the number of DMA cycles[4] (words to be transferred) before the terminal count output is activated. The other two, and most significant, bits of this register are loaded with a code indicating that channel 0 is to operate in the DMA read mode. To load a 16-bit channel register, the low order byte is written first and then the high order byte.

Each 16-bit register has a single address because the DMA controller contains a first/last, F/L, flip-flop that is cleared when the controller is reset. Whenever a channel register (DMA address or terminal count register) is written, the F/L flip-flop is toggled. This flip-flop provides the additional address bit necessary to select the low or high byte of the 16-bit register. The mode register is loaded with an appropriate bit pattern to enable channel 0.

The microprocessor then initializes the output device's controller, the requirements for initalization varying with the nature of the output device. When the output device is ready to accept the first byte of data, its controller makes the request input of the DMA controller logic 1. The DMA controller then outputs a hold request, HRQ, to the 8085A, which returns a hold acknowledge, HLDA, indicating that it has relinquished control of the system bus. The DMA controller then takes control of the system bus, and addresses memory with the address in its DMA address register. The high address byte is output by the DMA controller onto the data bus and latched by its associated 8212. Pins A_0–A_7 provide the low address byte. The DMA controller then generates a $\overline{\text{MEMR}}$ strobe, and the memory drives the data bus with the data to be transferred (see Fig. 9.7-4).

Note that address lines A_0–A_3 of the DMA controller are bidirectional. These lines serve as address inputs when the registers of the DMA controller are loaded by the microprocessor. At such a time the DMA controller operates as a slave device. When it operates as a master (controlling the system bus), these address lines are outputs.

The DMA controller also generates a DMA acknowledge signal, $\overline{\text{DACK}_0}$, which selects the output device and, after the data is stable on the data bus, generates an $\overline{\text{I/OW}}$ strobe, which writes data into the output device. Channel 0's DMA address register is incremented and the terminal count register decremented.

For a burst DMA transfer, the controller of the output device keeps the DRQ_0 input logic 1 until the DMA controller indicates that the last byte of data has been transferred, TC = 1. On the other hand, for cycle stealing DMA, the

---

[4]For N DMA cycles, the actual value loaded into the terminal count register is N-1.

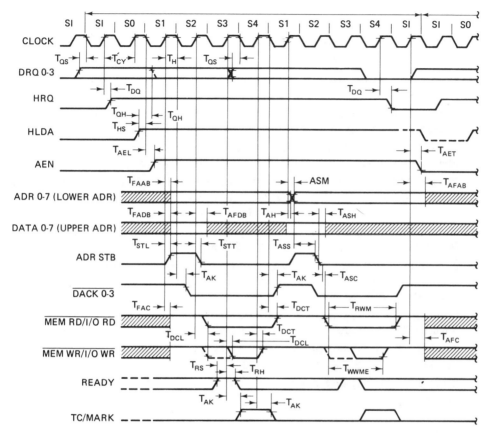

Figure 9.7-4. 8257-5 timing diagram for DMA cycles. (Courtesy of Intel Corp.)

output device's controller returns the DRQ_0 line to logic 0 when it receives $\overline{DACK_0}$, and only a single byte is transferred. The output device's controller subsequently requests a sufficient number of DMA cycles to transfer the remaining bytes.

The terminal count, TC, output of the DMA controller interrupts the microprocessor. A block of data is then transferred and the interrupt service subroutine takes whatever action is appropriate for the particular application. Note that if the microprocessor is not interrupted at the completion of a block transfer, it has no way of knowing when the transfer is complete.

REFERENCES

1. *MCS-85 User's Manual.* Santa Clara, California: Intel Corporation, 1978.

2. BEASTON, J., *Using the 8259 Programmable Interrupt Controller*, (Application Note 31). Santa Clara, California: Intel Corporation, 1977.

3. SPRINGER, J., *Application of First-In First-Out Memories*, (Application Note). Sunnyvale, California: Advanced Micro Devices, Inc., 1973.

BIBLIOGRAPHY

BALDRIDGE, R.L., "Interrupts Add Power Complexity to μC-System Design," *EDN*, Vol. 22, No. 14, August 1977, pp. 67-73.

BEASTON, J., "Interval Timer Serves as a Baud Rate Generator," *Computer Design*, Vol. 17, No. 8, August 1978, pp. 112-119.

CARLIN, F.H., and J.A. HOWARD, "Programmable Timer Provides Accurate Interval Measurements," *Computer Design*, Vol. 18, No. 5, May 1979, pp. 213-218.

COSLEY, J., and S. VASA, "Block Transfer with DMA Augments Microprocessor Efficiency," *Computer Design*, Vol. 14, No. 22, January 1977, pp. 81-85.

DEJONG, M.L., J.A. TITUS, C. TITUS, P.R. RONY, and D.G. LARSEN, "Microcomputer Interfacing: Characteristics of the 8253 Programmable Interval Timer," *Computer Design*, Vol. 17, No. 2, February 1978, pp. 136-140.

KARSTAD, K., "Software Control of Microprocessor Based Real Time Clock," *Computer Design*, Vol. 17, No. 10, October 1978, pp. 99-106.

LARSEN, D.G., P.R. RONY, M.L. DEJONG, C. TITUS, and J.A. TITUS, "Microcomputer Interfacing: A Demonstration Program for the 8253 Timer," *Computer Design*, Vol. 17, No. 3, March 1978, pp. 134-136.

NICHOLS, J.L., "Hardware Versus Software for Microprocessor I/O," *Computer Design*, August 1976, pp. 102-107.

RAJEN, J., "Designing Interrupt Structures for Multiprocesor Systems," *Computer Design*, Vol. 17, No. 9, September 1978, pp. 101-110.

TITUS, J.A., "Starting μP Software," *Electronic Design*, Vol. 24, No. 25, December 1976, pp. 74-77.

PROBLEMS

9-1. Describe how each step in the list of operations which occur in response to an interrupt is implemented by an 8085A system.

9-2. Interrupt request flip-flops should be cleared when a microprocessor is first powered up or reset. Why? In what ways can this be accomplished?

9-3. Design the external hardware necessary to make the TRAP interrupt of an 8085A maskable. Write two macros: ENAT to enable the TRAP interrupt, and DAT to disable the TRAP interrupt.

9-4. Write a sequence of instructions which enables the RST6.5 and RST7.5 interrupts and disables the RST5.5 interrupt of an 8085A.

9-5. To interrupt an 8085A microprocessor, an I/O device generates a 100 nS positive pulse. Design the logic to interface this device to each of the following interrupts of an 8085A:
   a. RST5.5
   b. RST6.5
   c. RST7.5

9-6. The BI and INA machine cycles are similar to the OF machine cycle in that they load the instruction register with an OP code. However, OF increments the PC, and BI and INA do not. Explain why the PC is handled differently by BI and INA.

9-7. Assume eight I/O devices are to share a single interrupt input, RST5.5. Design the logic to interface the interrupt request flip-flops to an 8085A. Implement priority arbitration by a 74148 priority encoder whose outputs are available through an input port. Write a subroutine which uses the priority encoder's output as an index into a jump table for the purpose of transferring control to the individual service subroutines.

9-8. Is it possible to devise a software method to establish a rotating priority among the interrupt inputs RST5.5, RST6.5, and RST7.5 so that lower priority interrupts can not be completely locked out by the continual occurrence of higher priority interrupts? If it is possible, write a program which establishes this rotating priority. If it is not possible, discuss why.

9-9. Assume that the UAR/T in Fig. 9.4-2 receives ASCII encoded characters at a rate of 10 characters per second. Assume that up to 80 characters can be received before a carriage return occurs and the microprocessor is interrupted. Write an interrupt service subroutine which transfers data from the FIFO buffer to the microprocessor system's RWM. Compare the software overhead required to transfer 80 characters using this structure with that required using a hardware structure without FIFOs, where the UAR/T interrupts the microprocessor to transfer each byte of data.

9-10. Two bytes of reserved memory are used to store a 16-bit count of the number of times an external event occurs. The least significant of the 2 bytes is stored in location CNT, and the most significant is stored in location CNT + 1. An interrupt service subroutine starting in location 38H increments the 16-bit events counter each time it is called. Write this interrupt service subroutine, and draw a complete logic diagram of the external hardware required to interrupt an 8085A and directly vector to the interrupt service subroutine. Use the 8085A interrupt input, INTR.

9-11. Using the real time clock of Fig. 9.5-1, write a pair of interrupt service subroutines which together compute the elapsed time between two events and store this elapsed time in three reserved memory locations: ELSEC, ELMIN, and ELHRS. The first event generates an RST5.5 interrupt and the second event generates an RST6.5 interrupt.

9-12. Repeat problem 9-11 with both events generating an RST6.5 interrupt.

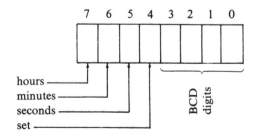

9-13. Write a subroutine to set the real time clock of Fig. 9.5-1. Assume that the time is input through a port, TSET, by inputting two digits for hours, two for minutes, and two for seconds. The format of the input data is as follows:
Write the subroutine in such a way that only one of the most significant 4 bits is set at a time and only the last two digits input for any particular parameter (hours, minutes, or seconds) are valid. The actual setting of the clock should take place when bit 4 is 1; this would be the last data byte entered.

9-14. In a microprocessor system using CMOS RWM with a battery backup, the contents of the RWM are not lost if the system's power is interrupted. Assume that a system of this type has external circuitry which detects the initial loss of power and interrupts the microprocessor. Write a service subroutine which saves the microprocessor's state before the power supply output drops below the operating level. Also design software and hardware which automatically restore the microprocessor's state when the supply of power is reestablished. Note that upon a power ON reset a determination must be made as to whether it is a normal power ON reset or whether it is a power ON reset following a power failure.

10

Digital Peripheral Devices

*The ubiquitous microprocessor has stimulated the growth
of increasingly complex peripherals. Some of these, such as the
floppy disk formatter/controller, rival the complexity
of the microprocessor itself. The proliferation of these monolithic
peripherals is due to the use of the processor in diverse
fields requiring minimum package count, reduced power,
increased reliability and lower cost.*

Smolin, Graves, Winter, and Schwartz*

*"Unified Buses Make the Peripheral IC/μC Connection," *Digital Design*, Vol. 8, No. 7, July 1978, pp. 86-97.

The term "peripheral device," as applied to microprocessor systems, covers a wide range—from single ICs, like UAR/Ts, multipliers, and arithmetic processing units, to complete systems such as floppy-disk storage systems. Any device attached to a microprocessor, exclusive of those such as a clock and memory required for fundamental operation, is considered a peripheral device. Typically, peripheral devices are connected to the microprocessor through I/O ports and provide the system with additional logic or computational capabilities or an interface to nonelectronic systems.

In some cases, functions which are implemented by peripheral devices can be effected either by software, eliminating the peripheral entirely, or by a combination of software and less costly peripheral devices. This is another example of the constantly recurring hardware/software tradeoff.

The hardware/software tradeoff with regard to peripheral devices is an important consideration in the design of microprocessor systems. Peripheral devices that provide manual data entry to a microprocessor system are one of the most common types of peripherals and are an ideal illustration of the hardware/software tradeoff.

10.1 MANUAL DATA ENTRY

Methods of digital data entry to a microprocessor are either manual or automatic. Manual entry is the direct input of data by an operator, whereas automatic entry involves input by another machine or process. In both methods, the provision of appropriate input data signals from a digital source requires one or more of the following operations:

1. Conversion: distinguishing between two states of the input and generating an electrical signal with the appropriate logic level for that state;
2. Sensing: detecting a change in an input signal or the occurrence of new data;
3. Debouncing: providing a single transition for each change of state in an electromechanical device that inherently creates multiple output changes during its transition from one state to another;
4. Encoding: converting a multivalued input state to a desired binary code.

10.1.1 Mechanical Switches

Mechanical switches are used for manual data entry in many microprocessor systems. Such systems require a provision for an operator to input data to the system. The amount of data input varies from very little at system initiation only, as in some controllers, to large amounts during the entire operation, as in interactive systems. Design and selection of devices for manual data entry,

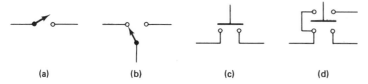

Figure 10.1-1. Simple mechanical switches: (a) single-pole/single-throw; (b) single-pole/double-throw; (c) single-pole/single throw momentary contact switch; (d) single-pole/double-throw momentary contact switch.

therefore, are based on the type and quantity of data to be entered and the times at which data entry is required.

A large number of mechanical switches are available, which vary significantly in design. Single-pole/single-throw (SPST) and single-pole/double-throw (SPDT), toggle, and momentary contact (pushbutton) switches are considered here (see Fig. 10.1-1).

When using mechanical switches for data entry, the position of the switch must be converted to an electrical signal compatible with the system's logic circuits. Figure 10.1-2 shows how a switch and pull up resistor to +5 V provide a signal compatible with T^2L circuits for the various switch configurations. When the switch is closed, it provides an output voltage of 0 V. When open, it provides a voltage $V_{OUT} = 5\ V - IR$, where I is the logic 1 current required by the load connected to the switch output. The value of R limits the power dissipated when the switch is closed and provides a voltage above 2.4 V at the required input current of the load when it is open.

When a mechanical switch opens or closes, the contacts bounce, actually opening and closing many times before coming to rest. A typical switch bounces for many milliseconds, 5–20 mS is common, resulting in a sequence of logic signal transitions at the switch output instead of a single, smooth transition (see Fig. 10.1-3). If a microprocessor repeatedly inputs the switch output during the bounce period, it appears to the microprocessor that the switch has been operated several times instead of once. To preclude this possibility, the switch

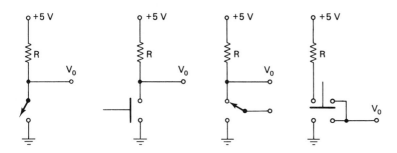

Figure 10.1-2. Generation of T^2L logic levels from mechanical switch positions.

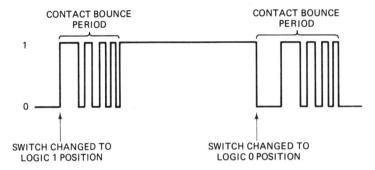

CONTACT BOUNCE
PERIOD

CONTACT BOUNCE
PERIOD

1

0

SWITCH CHANGED TO
LOGIC 1 POSITION

SWITCH CHANGED TO
LOGIC 0 POSITION

Figure 10.1-3. Multiple signal transitions caused by contact bounce of a mechanical switch.

must be debounced. Debouncing can be accomplished by using either hardware or software.

An RS latch, as shown in Fig. 10.1-4, can debounce a single-pole/double-throw switch. The output of the latch changes state only once when the switch position is changed. RS latches are available, four to a package, as quad debouncer ICs (74279).

Both SPST and SPDT switches can be debounced with software. For example, a microprocessor can repeatedly input the output of a switch and, if its value remains the same for a period of time in excess of the switch's bounce period, accept the input value as valid. The same technique provides noise immunity when inputting data from a bounce-free source: The microprocessor repeatedly samples the input line until it remains at the same logic value a fixed number of times in succession before interpreting the value as valid.

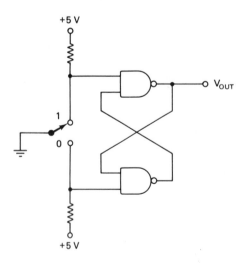

Figure 10.1-4. Use of an RS latch to debounce a single-pole/double-throw toggle switch.

Another method of software debouncing is carried out by the subroutine, PBCNT, which counts the number of times a pushbutton is pressed. The pushbutton output, wired as in Fig 10.1-2, is connected to bit 7 of input port 0. The operation of the subroutine is flowcharted in Fig. 10.1-5, and the actual subroutine appears in Fig. 10.1-6. The subroutine first checks that the pushbutton has been released; if not, it waits in a loop until it is released. The subroutine then waits a period of time in excess of the pushbutton's bounce by calling a delay subroutine, after which it waits in a second loop to detect the pressing of the button. When the button press is detected, a second delay is initiated, and the pushbutton's value is input and checked one more time to verify that the button was actually pressed—as opposed to a noise pulse having been detected.

Regardless of whether a switch is debounced by hardware or software, the microprocessor must sense the switch's output with sufficient regularity to detect its operation and release.

When several bits of data are provided to a microprocessor via mechanical switches, the data can be entered in parallel from a bank of single switches. A more convenient method, however, employs a rotary switch that mechanically generates a binary code representing the switch position. One type of rotary switch with this capability is the thumbwheel. As shown in Fig. 10.1-7, a thumbwheel switch indicates the switch setting by a symbol on the wheel. The output of the switch is a parallel set of contact closures that provides a binary code corresponding to the switch position. Thumbwheel switches which provide a number of different binary output codes are readily available; ten-position thumbwheel switches with BCD coded outputs are commonly used for the entry of decimal data. These switches can be stacked (thus using minimal panel space) to accommodate several decades of input. Other commonly available codes include octal, hexadecimal, excess-3, and ten's complement.

10.1.2 Keypads and Keyboards

When manual entry of a large number of data symbols is essential, keyboards containing up to 100 pushbutton switches, or keys, are commonly used. The term "keypad" is applied to keyboards containing a small number of keys. In keypads and keyboards each key is associated with a particular symbol or binary value. When a key is pressed it generates a corresponding binary code. When the number of keys is less than or equal to 16, key closures are efficiently encoded into parallel data by using combinational circuitry. For example, an IC encoder, which encodes eight inputs, has a special output which is active if any one of its inputs is low. This output can be used by circuitry or software which debounces the encoder's output or can be latched and used to generate an interrupt, allowing the microprocessor to read the encoder's output. The 74148 priority encoder presented in Chapter 9 encodes eight contact closures into a 3-bit code, as shown in Fig. 10.1-8. The keys in Fig. 10.1-8 have one contact connected in common.

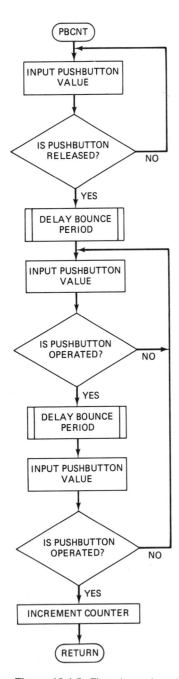

Figure 10.1-5. Flowchart of pushbutton debounce subroutine.

PBCNT:	IN PB	;	INPUT PUSHBUTTON OUTPUT
	ORA A	;	SET FLAGS
	JP PBCNT	;	IF BUTTON NOT RELEASED LOOP
	CALL DELAY	;	BUTTON RELEASED TIMEOUT BOUNCE
PBNP:	IN PB	;	INPUT PUSHBUTTON OUTPUT
	ORA A	;	CHECK FOR PUSHBUTTON PRESSED
	JM PBNP	;	IF PUSHBUTTON NOT PRESSED LOOP
	CALL DELAY	;	PUSHBUTTON PRESSED TIMEOUT BOUNCE
	IN PB	;	INPUT PUSHBUTTON OUTPUT
	ORA	;	SET FLAGS
	JM PBNP	;	CHECK FOR ERRONEOUS SIGNAL TRANSITION
	INX D	;	PUSHBUTTON PRESS VERIFIED, INCREMENT
	RET	;	COUNTER

Figure 10.1-6. Subroutine to debounce a mechanical switch.

As an alternative to the linear arrangement of keys in Fig. 10.1-8, keys can be arranged at the intersection of wires which form a matrix, as shown in Fig. 10.1-9(a). This arrangement is advantageous when a large number of keys are involved because it allows a reduction in the amount of hardware for encoding. To determine that a key has been pressed, and to identify that key, the matrix is **scanned**. Associating a digital code with each key is referred to as **encoding** the keyboard.

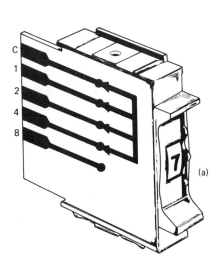

B02

DIAL	BCD, 1-POLE, 10-POSITION			
	COMMON C CONNECTED TO TERMINALS INDICATED			
	1	2	4	8
0				
1	●			
2		●		
3	●	●		
4			●	
5	●		●	
6		●	●	
7	●	●	●	
8				●
9	●			●

(a)

(b)

Figure 10.1-7. Thumbwheel switch: (a) pictorial; (b) truth table indicating which terminals are connected to common for each dial position.

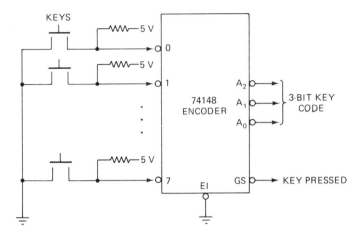

Figure 10.1-8. Use of a 74148 priority encoder to encode an eight-key keypad.

The key matrix is scanned, using either software or hardware, by making all the rows of the matrix logic 0 and sensing the logic values of the columns. If one or more columns is logic 0, then one or more keys has been pressed. To encode the key, each horizontal wire is, in turn, made logic 0 with all other horizontal wires logic 1. While a single horizontal wire is logic 0, each of the vertical wires is examined to see whether it is logic 0. When a vertical line is logic 0, the number of that line, together with the number of the logic 0 row, identifies the pressed key.

An example of the hardware used in key press detection and key scanning with software is shown in Fig. 10.1-10. The rows of the key matrix are controlled by an output port, and its columns are sensed through an input port.

To preclude a key being pressed and released without detection, the software scan subroutine is called repetitively. In addition, the routine which calls the scan algorithm must provide debouncing and must distinguish between a single key being operated several times or simply being pressed and held for a long period of time.

Problems arise when two or more keys are depressed simultaneously. This situation is called **rollover**. In the previous scan algorithm, if rollover occurs, the value of the key returned depends on the order of detection by that subroutine and not on the order in which the keys are depressed.

To prevent the problems inherent in rollover, two methods are used: two-key and N-key rollover—both of which describe the manner in which the keyboard is scanned and key closures are accepted. Two-key rollover handles cases where two keys are pressed simultaneously. In **two-key rollover**, a key closure is accepted, provided all other keys are released. When a key is pressed, that closure is processed, and the keyboard is ignored until it is released. If a

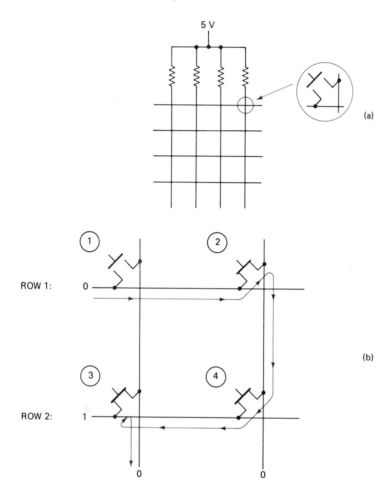

Figure 10.1-9. (a) Keyboard switch matrix; (b) sneak path in a switch matrix: key 1 appears pressed when keys 2, 3, and 4 are actually pressed.

second key is pressed before the first is released, it will be recognized only after the first is released.

N-key rollover processes each key closure in the order in which it is detected in the scan, regardless of the status of all other keys. This mode of operation is used when data entry is rapid, and the operator may press a second and possibly a third key before releasing the first.

Implementation of N-key rollover requires additional components in the key matrix. As shown in Fig. 10.1-9(a), each intersection of conductors in the matrix

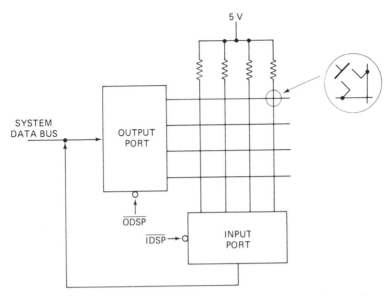

Figure 10.1-10. Hardware structure for software scanning of key matrix.

simply contains a switch between the row and column which electrically connects the two when closed. Consider the situation in Fig. 10.1-9(b), where row 1 has been selected in the scan, and switches 2, 3, and 4 are pressed. There is an electrical path, called a *sneak path*, through switches 2-4-3, which makes column 1's output logic 0. Since row 1 is selected and column 1 is 0, it appears that switch 1 has been pressed when, in reality, it has not. A diode connected in series with each switch prevents sneak paths in the matrix.

For hardware scanning of a key matrix, LSI keyboard encoders are available which scan small and large keyswitch arrays and produce an encoded output corresponding to the key pressed. Typical devices handle 16, 20, 64, 78, and 90 key matrices. A single IC keyboard encoder, the MM74C923, is shown in Fig. 10.1-11. This device handles 20 SPST keys. A 2-bit counter and a two-to-four decoder scan the columns of the switch matrix. Scan frequency is set by an external oscillator or by a capacitor for the internal oscillator. Encoding logic senses the rows and detects key closure. Additional circuitry provides contact bounce elimination and two-key rollover. The debounce period can be set by an external capacitor. When a key closure is accepted, three bits from the encoding logic are latched into a 5-bit register by a data available signal which provides a high output as long as the accepted key remains pressed. When the key is released, the data available signal goes low even if another key is depressed. The data available signal goes high again after a debounce period to indicate the availability of new data for the second key.

Use of hardware eliminates the requirement that the microprocessor scan the keyboard constantly within a prescribed time interval. The data available

BLOCK DIAGRAM

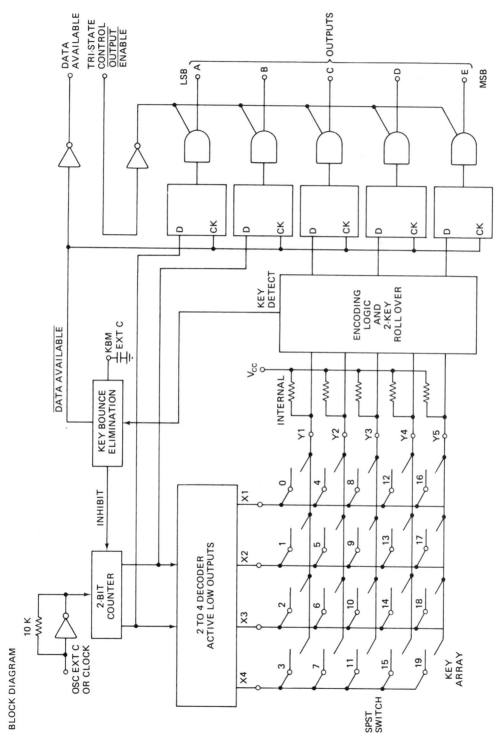

Figure 10.1-11. Integrated circuit 20-key keyboard scanner MM74C923. (Courtesy of National Semiconductor Corp.)

TRUTH TABLE

SWITCH POSITION	0 Y1,X1	1 Y1,X2	2 Y1,X3	3 Y1,X4	4 Y2,X1	5 Y2,X2	6 Y2,X3	7 Y2,X4	8 Y3,X1	9 Y3,X2	10 Y3,X3	11 Y3,X4	12 Y4,X1	13 Y4,X2	14 Y4,X3	15 Y4,X4	16 Y5*,X1	17 Y5*,X2	18 Y5*,X3	19 Y5*,X4
A	0	1	0	1	0	1	0	1	0	1	0	1	0	1	0	1	0	1	0	1
B	0	0	1	1	0	0	1	1	0	0	1	1	0	0	1	1	0	0	1	1
C	0	0	0	0	1	1	1	1	0	0	0	0	1	1	1	1	0	0	0	0
D	0	0	0	0	0	0	0	0	1	1	1	1	1	1	1	1	0	0	0	0
E*	0	0	0	0	0	0	0	0	0	0	0	0	0	0	0	0	1	1	1	1

(DATA OUTPUT)

*Omit for MM54C922/MM74C922

Figure 10.1-11. Continued.

signal interrupts the microprocessor, allowing keyboard scanning to take place concurrently with other microprocessor operations.

Larger keyboard scanners, such as the MM5740 keyboard encoder, can scan a 90-key array at a rate controlled by an external clock.[1] Internal ring counters select rows and columns of the array for scanning. These counters also address an internal ROM that provides the code corresponding to the key position being scanned. If the key is pressed, the code is placed in a single character register and a data available signal is generated. That signal can interrupt a microprocessor. The keyboard encoder has three-state outputs controlled by an output enable input. That input enables the three-state buffers and places the encoded character on the data bus.

The keyboard encoder debounces key closures and provides a number of other features useful in modern keyboard design. The encoder's inputs and outputs are all T^2L compatible. Versions of the MM5740 are available with the internal ROM programmed with the ASCII character set. Alternatively, the devices can be mask programmed with any desired character set.

10.2 DISPLAYS

Information displays for microprocessor systems range from simple annunciators (ON-OFF lights) to alphanumeric displays such as cathode ray tubes (CRTs). A wide range of technologies is used to implement these display devices, and, also, to control such devices. The two most common classes of displays use light emitting diodes (LEDs) and cathode ray tubes.

10.2.1 LED Displays

The most common and simplest display device used with IC logic is the ***Light Emitting Diode, LED***. LEDs are solid state devices, p-n junctions, which emit light energy when stimulated by a low voltage direct current. LEDs can be designed to emit light from ultraviolet, through the visible spectrum, to infrared. The most efficient LED is in the visible spectrum and emits red light; it is the most commonly used for LED displays. Amber and green LEDs are also available.

LEDs are popular display devices for many reasons. Because they can be operated from low voltages, they are compatible with systems that use integrated circuits. They are small, light weight, and mechanically rugged. As solid state devices, they are highly reliable and have a typical operating life of over 100,000 hours. LEDs are available as single devices or packaged together in various

---

[1]*Application Note AN-80 MOS Keyboard Encoding*, National Semiconductor Corp., Santa Clara, California.

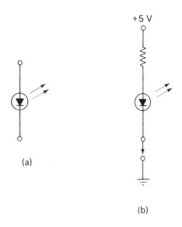

+5 V

(a)

(b)

Figure 10.2-1. Light emitting diode, LED: (a) circuit symbol; (b) drive circuit using a mechanical switch.

arrangements and are designed for displaying binary, numeric, and alphanumeric information.

The circuit symbol for an LED is shown in Fig. 10.2-1. The LED emits light when forward biased, and the intensity of the light is a function of the forward current through the LED. The voltage drop of a forward biased LED is fixed, typically 1.6 or 2.4 V. When driven as shown in Fig. 10.2-1, a resistor limits the current to the desired value. For DC operation, the nominal operating current is typically 20 mA for red LEDs and 25 mA for amber and green.

In general, the output of most logic circuits cannot drive an LED at rated current directly because they can't sink 20 to 25 mA. For example, a standard 74XXX series device can only sink 16 mA. However, some I/O ports, like the 8212, can handle the necessary current (see Fig. 10.2-2). Logic circuits with open collector outputs can drive an LED by using series or shunt switching, as shown in Fig. 10.2-3.

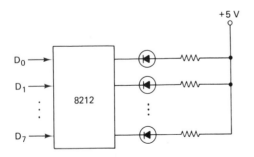

+5 V

D_0

D_1

8212

D_7

Figure 10.2-2. Using an 8212 latch to directly drive LEDs.

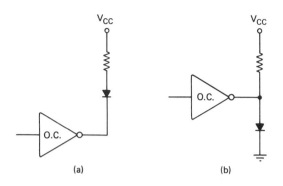

(a)   (b)

Figure 10.2-3. Driving a LED with an open collector inverter: (a) series switching: (b) shunt switching.

10.2.1.1 Seven Segment Displays

Decimal digits and some letters of the alphabet can be displayed by using seven segments in the font (arrangement) shown in Fig. 10.2-4. Seven segment LED displays use an LED (or sometimes two) for each segment and are represented in Fig.10.2-5. Here there are two variations of seven segment displays. In one all of the anodes are connected in common; in the other all of the cathodes are connected in common. These variations allow different drive arrangements. Each segment can be driven with 1 bit of an output port, as shown in Fig. 10.2-2, or decoder driver ICs can be used.

BCD-to-seven segment and hex-to-seven segment decoder drivers are available for driving seven segment displays. Figure 10.2-5 shows the connection of a common anode and common cathode seven segment display to appropriate drivers. In one the anode is connected to the 5 V supply, and a logic 0 decoder-driver output turns a segment ON. In the other, the cathodes are connected to ground. In this case, a logic 1 decoder-driver output turns a segment ON.

10.2.1.2 Multiplexed Displays

To display a small number of digits each segment can be directly driven from an output port or by a decoder driver connected to an output port. In this

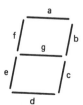

Figure 10.2-4. Seven segment display format.

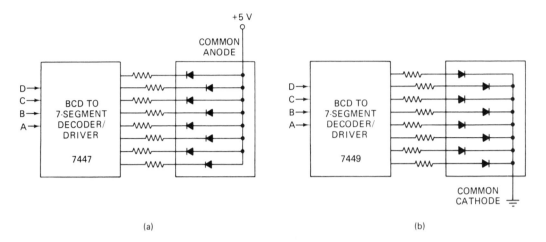

Figure 10.2-5. Driving seven segment LED displays from BCD inputs, using decoder drivers: (a) common anode circuit; (b) common cathode circuit.

arrangement, however, since each digit requires its own port and/or decoder driver, the number of ports and drivers increases in direct proportion to the number of display digits.

Multiplexing techniques allow one set of decoding and driving circuitry to be shared among the digits in a display. A six-digit multiplexed display is illustrated in Fig. 10.2-6. The microprocessor activates each digit, in turn. First, it loads the segment data for digit 1 into the segment output port. Then it loads the digit select output port with a value that makes the output connected to digit driver number 1 logic 0, turning on the first digit of the display. Loading the digit select port also fires the single shot, which is set to a time interval equal to the period of time each single digit in the display is turned ON. When the single shot times out, it sets the interrupt request flip-flop, interrupting the microprocessor. The interrupt service subroutine first turns OFF all digit drivers. Then it sets the segment data for the next display, outputs it to the segment port, and turns ON the digit driver by outputting the proper code to the digit select port. After the last digit in the display has been turned ON, the procedure is repeated, starting with the first digit. Each digit is turned ON, or *refreshed*, at a frequency called the *refresh rate*. If a digit is refreshed often enough, it appears to the human eye to be constantly ON. The minimum practical refresh rate is usually 100 Hz. Typically, multiplexed displays are refreshed at 1 kHz, or higher. [1] For N digits refreshed at f Hz, the maximum ON time, t_D, for each digit is:

$$t_D = \frac{1}{fN}$$

The *duty factor* for a single digit—the ratio of the time that the digit is ON with respect to the refresh period—is $1/N$. Therefore, not only is multiplexing efficient in terms of decoding and driving circuitry, it is also the most efficient

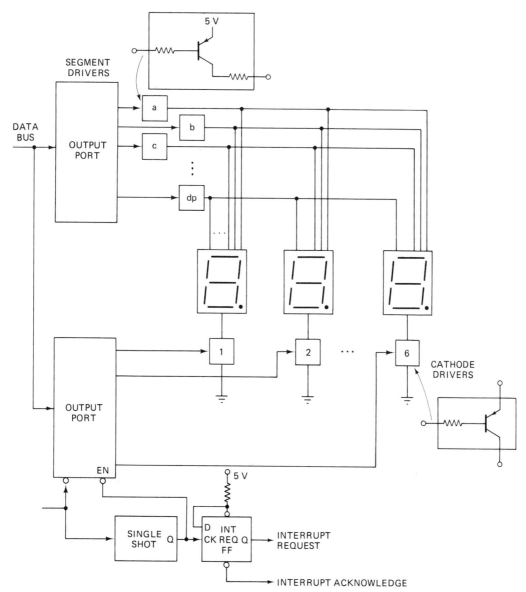

Figure 10.2-6. Six-digit multiplexed LED display.

way of operating an LED. Strobing an LED at a high peak current and low duty factor provides greater light output than DC drivers for a given average power dissipation. The service subroutine for the display of Fig. 10.2-6 is shown in Fig. 10.2-7.

The peak segment currents allowable when a display is multiplexed exceed the average allowable currents. Thus, if a digit is left ON for an extended period of time, it is damaged. To avoid damage, in the event that some system failure

```
MSDPY:    PUSH  B         ;    SAVE STATUS
          PUSH  D
          PUSH  H
          PUSH  PSW
          XRA  A          ;    TURN OFF DISPLAY
          CMA
          OUT  DSEL
          LDA  DIGIT      ;    GET NUMBER OF LAST DIGIT TURNED ON
          CPI  DMAX       ;    COMPUTE NEXT DIGIT TO BE TURNED ON
          JNZ  MDSP1
          XRA  A
MDSP1:    INR  A
          STA  DIGIT      ;    SAVE DIGIT NUMBER
          MOV  B, A
          LXI  H, STBLE   ;    COMPUTE TABLE ENTRY ADDRESS FOR DIGIT SEGMENT PATTERN
          ADD  L
          MOV  L, A
          MVI  A, 0
          ADC  H
          MOV  H, A
          MOV  A, M       ;    GET SEGMENT PATTERN
          OUT  SEG        ;    OUTPUT SEGMENT PATTERN
          MVI  A, 0FEH    ;    COMPUTE DIGIT SELECT PORT BIT PATTERN
MDSP2:    DCR  B
          JZ  MDSP3
          RLC
          JMP  MDSP2
MDSP3:    OUT  DSEL       ;    TURN ON SELECTED DIGIT
          POP  PSW        ;    RESTORE STATUS
          POP  H
          POP  D
          POP  B
          EI              ;    ENABLE INTERRUPT
          RET             ;    RETURN
```

Figure 10.2-7. Multiplexed display driver subroutines.

prevents the timely updating of the display, the digit select port 1 output from the single shot also enables the digit select port's output buffers. The outputs are pulled up to logic 1 values by the pull up resistors shown in Fig. 10.2-6. When the single shot times out, all digits turn OFF, providing the desired safeguard.

10.2.2 CRT Displays

A CRT display provides the lowest cost per character when a large number of characters is involved. It uses a cathode ray tube (CRT) to display alphanumeric or graphic information. The CRT generates an electron beam which, when it strikes the phosphor on the face of the CRT, creates a dot of light. Voltages applied to two sets of inputs control the X and Y coordinates of the position at which the beam strikes the CRT face. A third input to the CRT controls the intensity of the light emitted.

The CRT tube, combined with the electronics that control the position of the electron beam and its intensity, comprise a *monitor* (see Fig. 10.2-8). The monitor electronics include both horizontal and vertical oscillators that provide ramp outputs. These outputs are amplified by horizontal and vertical amplifiers, respectively. The output voltage from the horizontal amplifier sweeps the beam from left to right across the screen, and then back. The sweep from left to right is called the *horizontal sweep*. The return sweep from right to left is called the *horizontal retrace*. The vertical amplifier output sweeps the beam from the top to the bottom of the screen, and then back. The sweep from top to bottom is the *vertical sweep*, and the sweep from bottom to top is called the *vertical retrace*. The electron beam is turned OFF during the horizontal and vertical retraces. The combined action of these two oscillators controlling the CRT beam's position creates a pattern of lines called a *raster* (Fig. 10.2-9). Because the horizontal oscillator is run at a higher frequency (typically 15.75 kHz) than the vertical oscillator (typically 60 Hz), the raster consists of a number of horizontal lines if the beam is turned ON for the duration of each horizontal sweep. Each complete sweep of the raster scan from the upper lefthand corner to the lower righthand corner and back is called a *frame*.

The oscillators that provide the ramp outputs for sweeping the beam's position are usually free running, but they must be synchronized by external signals to provide the raster scan. Low cost CRT monitors have inputs for horizontal and vertical sync pulses. A third input to the monitor, the video input, is amplified by the monitor's video amplifier and controls the intensity of the dot produced by the electron beam. Other monitors accept a composite video

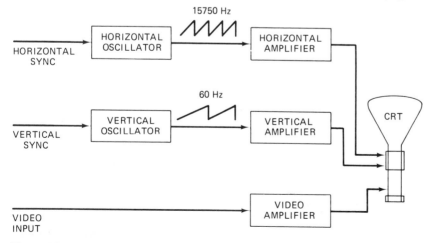

Figure 10.2-8. CRT monitor.

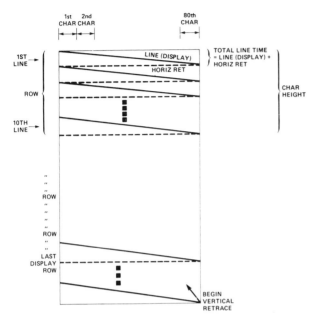

Figure 10.2-9. CRT raster scan. (Courtesy of Intel Corp.)

signal, which combines the horizontal sync, vertical sync, and video input into a single signal. Circuitry within these monitors separates the composite video signal into its components.

Patterns are made on the CRT screen by turning the beam ON and OFF during the horizontal sweep. Alphanumeric characters are created with dot matrix patterns. A basic 5×7 dot matrix character representation on a CRT includes an extra column on the left and right for spacing between characters, as shown in Fig. 10.2-10. An extra row beneath the character can also be reserved for an underline or cursor, and an additional row on the top and bottom for spacing between rows. The final matrix size, then, for this configuration is 7×10.

Each horizontal scan supplies the dots of one line of all the characters on a single character row of the display, as shown in Fig. 10.2-11. In addition to synchronizing the start of the horizontal and vertical traces, circuitry that controls the monitor also supplies the serial video signal which represents the sequence of dots for each horizontal sweep. This signal is the input to the video amplifier of the monitor.

In microprocessor systems, the characters to be displayed on the CRT are stored in 7-bit ASCII code in a reserved block of RWM called, appropriately, the *display memory*. The display memory must contain as many words as character positions in the display format.

A block diagram of the hardware interface between a video monitor and a microprocessor system is shown in Fig. 10.2-12. Primarily this interface refreshes the CRT screen by the periodic transfer of information from the display

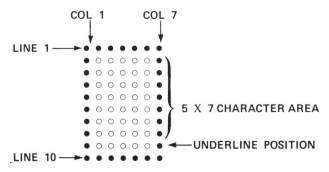

Figure 10.2-10. 5 × 7 dot matrix character representation.

memory to the screen. The displayed information must be written into the screen repetitively, and the process is known as refreshing the screen. The refresh rate is typically 60 Hz, in order to prevent flicker.

There are a number of programmable LSI CRT controllers on the market, including the Intel 8275. See Fig. 10.2-13. [2] This device sets screen and character formats by the parameters of commands sent to the controller at its initialization. These parameters specify the number of characters per row, the

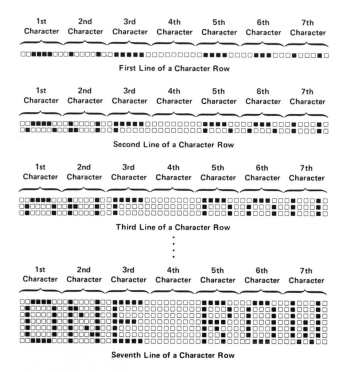

Figure 10.2-11. Single character row of a CRT display. (Courtesy of Intel Corp.)

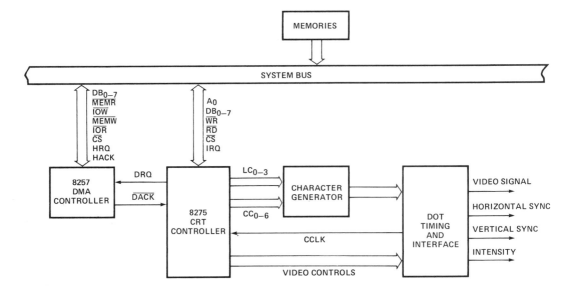

Figure 10.2-12. Block diagram of interface between microprocessor system memory and a CRT monitor. (Courtesy of Intel Corp.)

number of rows per frame, the character matrix size, and other attributes of the display.

To write a frame of information to the display, the 8275 requests a DMA operation to transfer one row of ASCII characters from the display memory to one of the 8275's row buffers, before the frame begins. When the first horizontal sweep is started, the character codes are output to the character generator in sequence. A character counter, driven by a character clock from the dot generation circuitry, keeps track of the character being displayed. The character code forms the most significant bits of the character generator ROM's address. The least significant bits of the address come from the line counter in the 8275. Each word in the character generator ROM contains the dot pattern for a single line of a single character. The 8275 holds the line count fixed while outputting the character codes during each horizontal sweep. During the horizontal retrace, the line counter is incremented, and the entire row of character codes is output again during the next sweep.

The character generator ROM outputs a 7-bit code corresponding to the line of the particular character being addressed. This code is the dot pattern for that line. The dot timing and interface circuitry converts the parallel dot pattern to a serial signal that controls the video signal. Thus, the video signal for a horizontal sweep corresponds to a serial version of the dot patterns for a single line of an entire character row.

At the initiation of the first horizontal sweep of a character row, a DMA operation is requested by the 8275 to fill the second of its two row buffers with the ASCII codes for the next row of characters to be displayed.

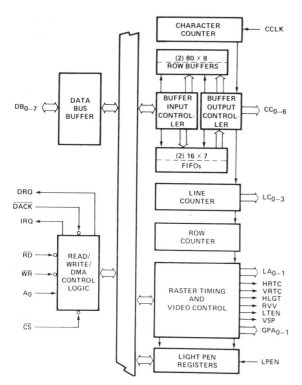

Figure 10.2-13. Block diagram of an Intel 8275 CRT controller. (Courtesy of Intel Corp.)

After all the lines of the character row being displayed have been scanned, the roles of the two row buffers are reversed. The most recently filled buffer now drives the display with the next character row. The recently displayed buffer is then filled with the next row of characters from the display memory via a DMA operation. With two buffers DMA operations obtain the data for the next character row from the display memory while concurrently outputting character data to the display for the present character row. Thus, the necessary speed requirements for refreshing the CRT are met.

This role reversal of the row buffers continues until all the character rows have been displayed. At the end of the frame, the 8275 interrupts the microprocessor and requests reinitialization of the DMA controller for the next frame.

For data entry, software maintains pointers to the display memory that define the location of a character on the screen and the cursor position. When a character is input from a device such as a keyboard, these pointers store it in the appropriate display memory location. Operations such as scrolling the display are carried out in software by changing the value of a pointer to the top of the display memory buffer. This value is used when the DMA controller is reinitialized at the completion of a frame.

The 8275 is also equipped with a light pen input and light pen registers. A light pen contains a light sensor which is activated by a microswitch when the pen is pressed against the face of the CRT. As the light beam strikes the sensor, the pen outputs a logic signal which can be input to the 8275. At this signal, the 8275 stores the row and character positions in the light pen register. These registers can be read under software control, thus identifying the position of the character pointed to by the operator.

10.3 PRINTERS

Printers produce hard copy output and vary widely in terms of product type and performance. They are classified either as serial or line. *Serial printers* print a single character at a time, while *line printers* print a group of characters simultaneously. Actually, printing only appears to be simultaneous because the groups of characters on a single line are printed so quickly. The method of character generation also categorizes printers either as impact or nonimpact. *Impact printers* strike the medium with the printing element to form a character. *Nonimpact printers* generally use thermal or electrostatic techniques that do not require impact. Character formation techniques provide yet another way to classify printers. *Character printers* use fully formed characters, whereas *matrix printers* use combinations of either dots or lines to form complete characters.

Serial dot matrix impact printers are particularly applicable for low cost microprocessor systems. These printers provide low to medium range printing rates of 30 to 330 characters per second. For example, the LRC 7040 is a dot matrix impact printer [3] (see Fig. 10.3-1). The print element consists of seven solenoids and print wires. The solenoids are arranged in a circle; however, the print wires driven by the solenoids are arranged in a column at the point where they impact the ribbon and paper. The printing element is driven across the paper via a spirally grooved plastic drum which is, in turn, driven by a synchronous AC motor. The design is such that the printing element travels across the paper at a constant speed of 10.75 inches per second. The timing diagram for the LRC 7040 is shown in Fig. 10.3-2.

In its simplest configuration, the LRC 7040 has eight inputs. Seven control the seven print solenoids, and the eighth turns the main drive motor ON or OFF. To print a line, the main drive motor is turned ON. To control the solenoids with T^2L logic levels, solenoid drivers are required that take T^2L logic inputs and drive the inductive load of the solenoid with the proper current levels. A motor driver is also required to allow a T^2L level to control the AC line power to the synchronous motor.

A microswitch (main drive switch or home switch) output from the printer indicates when the printhead has reached the lefthand margin of the print area. At that point, printing can begin. Characters are printed when external circuitry pulses the solenoids. The printable area is 3 1/3 inches wide, and thus the print element transverses the print area in 310 mS. The maximum rate at which the solenoids can be pulsed is once every 1.3 mS. If a 5 × 7 dot matrix is used for

Figure 10.3-1. LRC 7040 printer, shown with optional paper handling mechanism. (Courtesy of LRC, Inc.)

character formation with a one column space between characters, a maximum of 40 characters can be typed on a line. The main drive motor is kept ON until the main drive switch changes state again, indicating that the printing element has returned to its home position.

Thus, the 7040 provides a basic printer mechanism which is externally controlled by methods ranging from direct control by the microprocessor to the use of a dedicated hardware controller—another example of the hardware/software tradeoff.

With direct microprocessor control, printing a line is a nine-step process. The microprocessor:

1. Turns the main motor drive ON;
2. Samples the input from the home switch to detect when the printhead has reached the lefthand margin of the print area;
3. Outputs a byte of data specifying which solenoids are to be turned ON;
4. Turns on the selected solenoids for 400 μS;
5. Determines which solenoids are to be turned ON to print the next column;
6. Delays 900 μS;
7. Repeats steps 3 through 6 until all the characters in the line are printed;

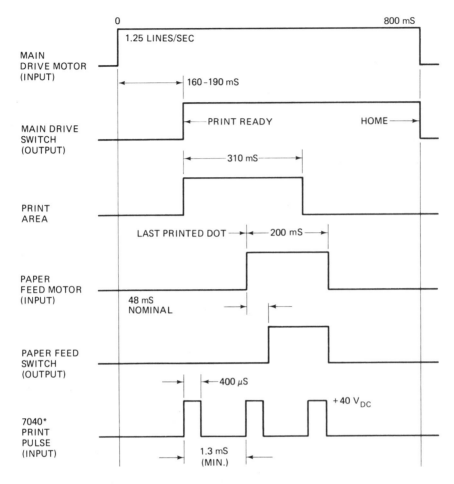

Figure 10.3-2. LRC 7040 printer timing diagram. (Courtesy of LRC, Inc.)

8. Samples the input from the home switch until it indicates that the printhead has returned to its home position; and

9. Turns OFF the main drive.

To carry out these steps using a minimum amount of hardware, the microprocessor polls the home switch and uses software delays to time out the 400 and 900 μS intervals. To print a character stored in a buffer in RWM as ASCII code, the microprocessor obtains the ASCII code for each character from the buffer, in turn, and obtains bit patterns for the columns of characters from a character generator table in ROM. These activities completely occupy the microprocessor while it prints a line.

If, however, the home switch interrupts the microprocessor and a programmable timer times out the necessary delays and interrupts the microprocessor, a much smaller percentage of the microprocessor's time is required to control the printer, and concurrent processing is possible. The smallest amount of processor time is taken up when a dedicated hardware controller is used. Several LSI single-chip controllers are available for the LRC 7040 printer: the Intel 8295, the Rockwell RC7000, and the Cybernetic Micro Systems CY480.

These controllers are similar in overall function to the Intel 8295. This dot matrix printer controller, a 40-pin IC, allows serial or parallel transfer of commands and data from the microprocessor to the printer controller. Commands set the format of characters to be printed and control other printer operations such as tab, line feed, and carriage return. The controller also contains a 40-character buffer. When the buffer is full or a carriage return is received, a line is printed. The controller also contains the character generator ROM and provides the solenoid drive outputs along with a properly timed strobe for the solenoids.

10.4 MASS STORAGE SYSTEMS

Mass storage systems store large quantities of information at a lower cost per bit than is possible with semiconductor memory. However, they have significantly longer access times for writing or reading data. The medium on which the data is stored provides nonvolatile storage. In most cases storage media can be easily removed from the system and transferred to another compatible storage system, facilitating low cost exchange or portability of large quantities of information. Three common types of mass storage are paper tape, cassettes and cartridges, and floppy disks.

10.4.1 Paper Tape

This method of mass storage involves the use of a tape of dry or oiled paper, Mylar, or polyester. Data is stored on the tape in frames, each *frame* corresponding to a column of holes punched into the tape (Fig. 10.4-1). Several code levels (the number of holes or channels per character) are used along with different widths of tape. These include 5 channel, 11/16 inch; 6 or 7 channel, 7/8 inch; and 8 channel, 1 inch.

In addition to the rows of data holes there is a single row of smaller sprocket holes having two purposes. The movement of the paper tape through a paper tape reader or punch is carried out by a sprocket wheel, which engages the sprocket holes. And, when reading the tape, the sensing element uses the sprocket hole to generate a pulse indicating that data is valid. The smaller size of the sprocket hole centers this pulse inside the data pulses.

As a storage medium, paper tape is inexpensive and rugged, and it can be read visually as well as by machine. Its disadvantages include low storage density, low speed, and bulkiness.

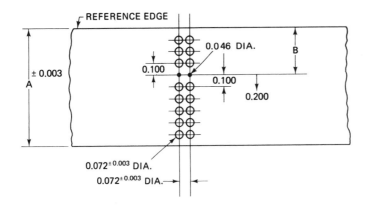

Figure 10.4-1. Paper tape storage medium.

NO. OF CHANNELS	A	B
5	0.676	0.392
7	0.875	0.392
8	1.000	0.392

Paper tapes are punched on electromechanical paper tape punches. Some Teletypes, the ASR models for example, are equipped with their own punches. When tape is punched manually, each key pressed punches its corresponding character into the paper tape as a single frame. The Teletype paper tape unit, for instance, can be used as an output device by a microprocessor, and each character sent to it in bit serial form is punched as a parallel code. Teletypes can punch paper tape at a rate of 10 characters per second, 10 cps. Higher speed, stand-alone punches with serial interfaces punch 30, 60, or 120 characters per second.

Paper tape readers sense the holes in the tape and produce a parallel output representing the character read. The most frequently employed sensing technique is photoelectric, having either LEDs or incandescent lamps for a light source. Phototransistors detect the passage of light through a punched hole in each channel. Recent devices incorporate fiber optic light emitters to simplify the optical systems.

Readers are either synchronous or asynchronous. Synchronous readers attain speeds of 1,000 cps, while asynchronous readers typically operate at speeds only as high as 300 cps. Stepping motors move the paper tape through the reader via a sprocket drive which engages feed holes that run the length of the tape.

Original Equipment Manufacturer, OEM, readers are available with all the required interface electronics on a single PC board. Such boards have T^{2}L compatible control inputs and control data outputs. The interface signals for a paper tape reader system are shown in Fig. 10.4-2. A subroutine which reads a single character from the paper tape reader is shown in Fig. 10.4-3. Some Teletypes contain paper tape readers that operate at 10 characters per second. Stand-alone paper tape readers typically operate at much higher speeds.

The data in each frame of the paper tape can be coded in a number of ways: straight binary and ASCII are common. OEM paper tape punches and readers can operate with any code, but those associated with Teletypes use ASCII. Data can also be formatted on the paper tape in several ways. Programs which punch or read such tapes are written to handle a particular format. Even tapes that are not formatted usually precede the data with a single code repeated several times, the *leader*, and follow it with another repeated code, the *trailer*. The ASCII NUL character is often used for this purpose.

BNPF, a simple, commonly used format, codes binary data in ASCII, each bit represented by a single ASCII character. The ASCII character for N represents logic 0, and the one for P represents logic 1. Each 8-bit word is preceded by the ASCII character for B, for beginning, and followed by the character for F, finish. Thus, the binary word 10101100 is BPNPNPPNNF. This code is frequently used to make paper tapes of memory contents representing the object code of a program. The tape is then read by a PROM programmer with a paper tape reader and used to program PROMs.

Another format, *hexadecimal*, is a record-oriented format. All characters are ASCII, and all numbers are ASCII hexadecimal. Intel's hexadecimal format is shown in Fig. 10.4-4. Each *record* starts with a *record mark*, an ASCII colon. The next two characters represent the number of data bytes in the record, a number between 0 and 255. A record length of zero indicates the end of a file. The address into which the data is to be loaded is given by the next four characters. A record type is then specified by a two-character code that is followed by the actual data. Each 8-bit data byte is coded with two characters.

Following the data is the *checksum*: two characters which represent the negative of the modulo-256 sum of all the bytes in the record following the record mark. The checksum provides a simple error detection scheme. The program which reads the tape and loads the data into memory simply adds up all the bytes between the record mark and the checksum, ignoring any carrys. If this sum is correct, the sum of this value and the checksum should be zero. The TRIN subroutine of Fig. 10.4-3 is used by a loader program to input each character. The loader program loads into memory the number of bytes indicated by the record length, starting at the load address given in the record. Using the checksum, the loader also confirms that there are no errors in reading the tape.

In a dedicated system, the loader program for reading data is contained in ROM. In some general purpose microcomputers, the data to be read is actually the object code of a program to be executed. If such a system does not contain any ROM, a simple loader program called a *bootstrap loader* is entered into RWM from the front panel. The bootstrap is a short binary program which can

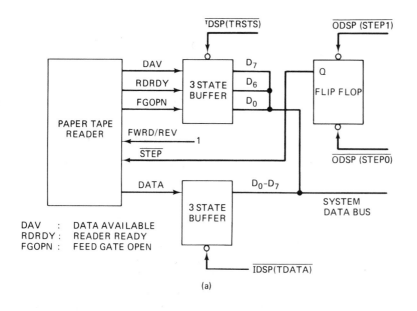

(a)

DAV : DATA AVAILABLE
RDRDY : READER READY
FGOPN : FEED GATE OPEN

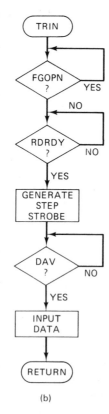

(b)

Figure 10.4-2. Paper tape reader (a) interface logic, (b) flowchart for driver routine.

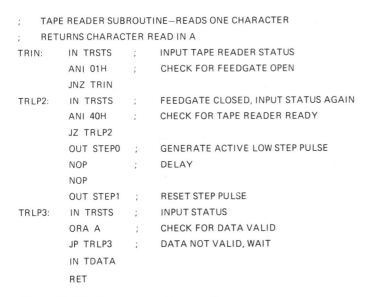

```
;     TAPE READER SUBROUTINE—READS ONE CHARACTER
;     RETURNS CHARACTER READ IN A
TRIN:    IN  TRSTS    ;    INPUT TAPE READER STATUS
         ANI 01H      ;    CHECK FOR FEEDGATE OPEN
         JNZ TRIN
TRLP2:   IN  TRSTS    ;    FEEDGATE CLOSED, INPUT STATUS AGAIN
         ANI 40H      ;    CHECK FOR TAPE READER READY
         JZ  TRLP2
         OUT STEP0    ;    GENERATE ACTIVE LOW STEP PULSE
         NOP          ;    DELAY
         NOP
         OUT STEP1    ;    RESET STEP PULSE
TRLP3:   IN  TRSTS    ;    INPUT STATUS
         ORA A        ;    CHECK FOR DATA VALID
         JP  TRLP3    ;    DATA NOT VALID, WAIT
         IN  TDATA
         RET
```

Figure 10.4-3. Tape reader driver routine.

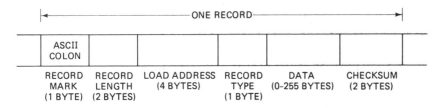

Figure 10.4-4. Intel hexadecimal paper tape format.

load another, more complex program, like the one described for handling ASCII coded hexadecimal files with record format. Once this more complex loader is input, it is then used to load subsequent programs on paper tape.

10.4.2 Cassettes and Cartridges

Magnetic tape stores fairly large quantities of digital data. A particularly convenient approach to the use of magnetic tape in microprocessor systems involves either digital cassettes or cartridges that permanently house the tape in a plastic container. These compact containers facilitate the handling and use of a magnetic tape.

Digital cassettes are very similar in appearance to the audio cassettes from which they descended and come in two sizes: the full size cassette and the minicassette. See Fig. 10.4-5(a). Full size cassettes contain 282 feet of 0.15 inch tape and store 720 kilobytes of unformatted data. Minicassettes contain 100 feet of 0.15 inch tape and store 200 kilobytes of data.

Data cartridges, which provide higher operating speeds and more storage than cassettes, also come in a full and minisize. See Fig. 10.4-5. A full size

Figure 10.4-5 Full and minisize data cartridges. (Courtesy of 3M Company.)

cartridge contains 300 feet of 0.25 inch wide tape and stores up to 2,870 kilobytes of unformatted data. Minicartridges contain 140 feet of 0.15 inch tape and store 772 kilobytes. Table 10.4-1 summarizes the storage capacities of cassettes and cartridges.

Cassette or cartridge tape drives or transports electromechanically control the direction and speed of the tape and contain the read/write heads which record and read data from the tape. Tape drives or transports range from a basic configuration without a read/write head or any electronics to systems with all the necessary electronics for interfacing through an RS 232 serial connection. OEM systems which use a parallel interface and contain all the electronics for microprocessor control are also commonly available.

A basic system is shown in Fig. 10.4-6. It includes a cassette or cartridge controller which interfaces to the microprocessor, providing parallel data transfer and a number of control and status signals. The controller encodes and decodes data to and from the read/write amplifiers. It also provides motion control commands to the servo electronics which control servo motors of the tape driver and, thus, its motion.

In digital tape systems data is recorded as changes in tape magnetization. Each change from one magnetic polarity to another is called a *flux change*, which is caused by switching the direction of the write head drive current. When the tape is read, the flux changes on the tape induce a voltage into the read head. The drive's read/write electronics amplify and shape the signals so that (1) digital logic levels representing flux transitions are obtained when reading, and (2) logic levels control the write head current when writing.

The coding scheme used by a particular digital tape system determines the way in which flux changes on the magnetic tape represent logic values. Coding schemes also prevent any loss of information due to the nonideal characteristics inherent in all systems. Many coding schemes have been devised with one or two flux changes representing each bit of digital data.

Encoding methods are either clocked or self-clocking. In *clocked encoding*, an extra recording track next to the data track provides synchronizing pulses which define the data cells on the tape. The clock track is either prerecorded or recorded concurrently with the data. With *self-clocking* techniques, on the other hand, a data encoding pattern changes state regularly and thus provides synchronization without the necessity of an extra clock track.

A popular self-clocking encoding technique is *phase encoding*, and the most widely used form of phase encoding is called *Bi-Phase-Level (B-Φ-L)*, split phase, or Manchester II + 180.[2] This technique represents each bit of data by a data cell. Flux changes may occur at the beginning (phase time) of a cell and always occur at the middle (data time) of the cell (Fig. 10.4-7).

The information stored in a data cell on the tape is specified by the direction of the flux change at data time. A south to north flux change represents a logic 1, and a north to south, logic 0. A flux change occurs at phase

[2]Bi-phase-level is the encoding technique used in ANSI recording standards for cassettes and cartridges [4, 5]. Many nonstandard cassette and cartridge systems use other recording techniques.

TABLE 10.4-1

Comparison Chart of Magnetic Storage Systems

	3M Cartridge	3M Mini Cartridge	Philips Cassette	Mini data Cassette	Floppy (single sided) (single density/ double density)	Single Density Mini Floppy (single sided)
Unformatted capacity (bytes)	2,870 K	772 K	720 K	200 K	400/800 K	110 K
Tracks	4	1	2	2	77	35
Heads	4	1	1	1	1	1
Transfer rate (BPS)	48 K	24 K	24 K	24 K	250/500 K	125 K
Relative head/media velocity (IPS)	30	30	30	30	120 (max)	80
Recording density (BPI)	1,600	600	800	800	3,200/6,400	2,600
Average access time (sec)	20	20	20	20	0.286	0.566
Media size (in.)	$4 \times 6 \times 0.67$	$2.4 \times 3.2 \times 0.4$	$4 \times 2.5 \times 0.4$	$2.125 \times 1.375 \times 0.313$	8.00×8.00	5.25×5.25
Error rate	1 bit in 10^8	1 bit in 10^8	1 bit in 10^7	1 bit in 10^8	1 bit in 10^9	1 bit in 10^9

BPS-Bits Per Second
IPS-Inches Per Second

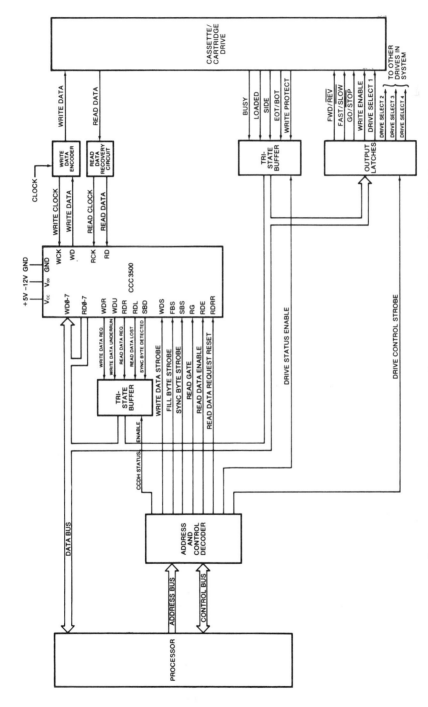

Figure 10.4-6. Cassette/cartridge drive interface to a microprocessor using a CCC3500 LSI cassette/cartridge data handler. (Courtesy of Standard Microsystems Corp.)

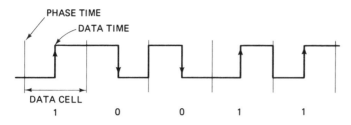

Figure 10.4-7. Phase encoding.

time to establish the right polarity for the following flux change at data time only if the preceding bit is the same as the next bit to be written.

Encoding electronics generate the proper flux changes for the tape as a function of the serial data received. Decoding circuitry reconstructs the clock from the flux changes on the tape and converts the flux changes occurring at data time into serial digital data.

Independent of the encoding scheme, data is placed on the tape according to some specified format. Usually it is recorded in blocks called *records*. These records are separated from each other by regions of erased tape called *inter-record gaps*. The lengths of the records and gaps depend on the standard or convention followed.

For example, in the proposed ANSI standard X3B144 for cartridges, the record starts with a 16-bit preamble consisting of 15 zeros followed by a single 1 (see Fig. 10.4-8). The preamble is followed by a minimum of 6 to a maximum of 2,048 data bytes. These bytes are, in turn, followed by a 16-bit cyclic redundancy character, CRC, used for error detection. Finally, a postamble consisting of a single 1 followed by 15 zeros completes the record. The inter-record gap which precedes the next record has a minimum length of 1.2 inches.

Cyclic redundancy is a common method of error detection for serial data. Cyclic encoding and decoding schemes are based on modulo-2 arithmetic operations on the data stream interpreted as a polynomial. The bits of an n-bit block of data are treated as coefficients of a polynomial of order $n - 1$ in the dummy variable X. During encoding, this data or message polynomial is divided, using modulo-2 arithmetic, by a generating polynomial. The remainder, after this division, is the cyclic redundancy check character. It is appended to the end of the data.

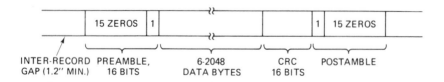

Figure 10.4-8. ANSI standard tape format for cartridges.

For error checking, the bit stream, containing the data and CRC bits, is divided by the polynomial used to generate the CRC bits. If this division results in a remainder of zero, then no detectable errors exist in the bit stream.

Various standards specify particular generating polynomials. For example, the polynomial $X^{16} + X^{15} + X^2 + 1$, referred to as CRC-16, is used in standards for cassettes and cartridges. It leaves a 16-bit remainder after dividing the data stream. This 16-bit remainder comprises the two 8-bit CRC characters that become part of the data block in the tape format.

In modulo-2 arithmetic, the division of the data stream can be carried out in hardware by using a feedback shift register which incorporates exclusive OR gates in the feedback paths. A circuit which implements CRC-16 is shown in Fig. 10.4-9. As the data stream is transmitted, it is simultaneously shifted into the shift register. When all the data bits are in the shift register, its contents—the CRC bits—are then shifted out and appended to the data bits.

Several CRC generator/checker integrated circuits carry out the above functions. For example, the Fairchild 9401 CRC Generator/Checker is contained in a 14-pin DIP. The 9401 has three select inputs through which it generates or checks serial data with any one of eight generator polynomials. The circuit in Fig. 10.4-9 is the equivalent circuit for the 9401 when its select inputs $S_2 S_1 S_0 = 000$. Figure 10.4-10 shows the additional logic required with the 9401 to generate and append the CRC bits to a data stream.

When used to check a message being received, the data and check bits are monitored. They are input to the 9401 while simultaneously being stored by the receiver. After the last check bit is entered, the error output, ER, is logic 1 if a detectable error has occurred.

A tape drive controller interfaces the microprocessor and the tape drive. Commands and data to be written on the tape are sent to the controller by the microprocessor, and status and data read from the tape are sent to the microprocessor by the controller. The controller also handles the timing considerations necessary to properly operate the tape drive. It formats for writing,

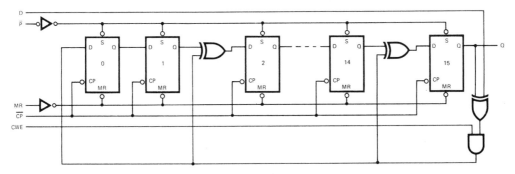

Figure 10.4-9. Circuit for implementing CRC-16. (Courtesy of Fairchild Camera and Instrument Corp.)

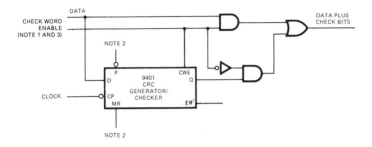

NOTES:
1. Check word Enable is HIGH while data is being clocked, LOW during transmission of check bits.
2. 9401 must be reset or preset before each computation.
3. CRC check bits are generated and appended to data bits.

Figure 10.4-10. Check word generation circuit using the 9401 CRC generator/checker. (Courtesy of Fairchild Camera and Instrument Corp.)

including generating CRC characters and encoding the data. It also decodes data, removing the preamble and postamble, and carries out the cyclic redundancy check on data read from the tape.

The design of cassette and cartridge controllers is simplified by using an LSI cassette/cartridge data handler like standard Microsystems CCC3500. See Fig. 10.4-6.

10.4.3 Floppy Disks

A floppy disk is another form of magnetic medium used for mass storage. Unlike paper and magnetic tape, however, it essentially provides random access to the data stored upon it. Floppy disks are made of a flexible, heavy, Mylar-based magnetic material. The disk is permanently housed in a thin, semistiff jacket or cartridge with a low friction liner. Floppy disks (see Fig. 10.4-11) come in two sizes: the full size floppy, which is housed in an 8×8 inch cartridge, and the minifloppy,[3] which is housed in a 5.25×5.25 inch cartridge. The floppy disks shown in Fig. 10.4-11 are single-sided, i.e., designed for recording on one side only.

Three holes cut in the cartridge allow access to the floppy disk. One is the spindle hole through which the floppy-disk drive spindle protrudes when the disk is loaded into the drive. The spindle turns the floppy disk inside its plastic jacket. Through the head access hole the floppy-disk drive read/write head comes into contact with the floppy disk.[4] The index hole in the jacket allows the index hole in the floppy disk to be optically sensed for the purpose of generating a synchronization signal.

---

[3]Minifloppy is a registered trademark of Shugart Associates.

[4]Double-sided floppy disks, those which can be recorded on both sides, have head access holes on both sides of the cartridge. The discussion in this text focuses on single-sided floppy disks.

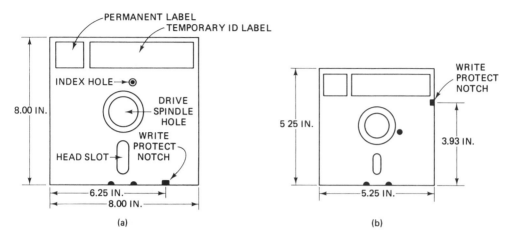

Figure 10.4-11. (a) Full and (b) mini size floppy disks.

Information is recorded on the floppy disk in concentric circles called *tracks*. The outermost track is track 00, and the innermost is track 76 for the full size floppy or, in the case of a minifloppy, track 34.

The floppy-disk drive has a door that covers a slot into which the floppy disk is placed (see Fig. 10.4-12). When the door is closed, the disk is clamped to the rotating spindle. Usually the read/write head is moved radially across the disk above the head access hole by a stepper motor and lead screw mechanism.

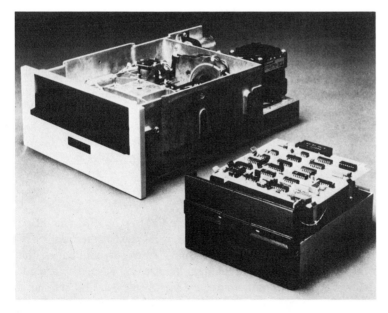

Figure 10.4-12. Full size and mini size floppy disk drives. (Courtesy of Shugart Associates.)

It is moved in increments equal to the distance between tracks on the floppy disk each time the stepper motor is stepped. In order to access a particular track, the head is brought to track 00 and its position detected by a limit switch. The head is then stepped *n* tracks to its destination by pulsing the stepper motor. Moving the head to the proper track is called a ***seek operation***. When the head is over the desired track, a control mechanism in the drive ***loads the head***, causing it to come into contact with the floppy disk. Data can then be written onto or read from the disk. After writing or reading data, the head is unloaded from the disk to minimize wear on both the disk and the read/write head.

A set of primary interface signals to a floppy-disk drive for the Shugart SA 400 minifloppy is shown in Fig. 10.4-13. The DRIVE SELECT lines allow any one of three drives to respond to the drive control signals. The MOTOR ON input turns the drive motor ON for reading or writing, and the DIRECTION SELECT line controls the direction of the read/write head motion when the STEP line is pulsed. When the TRACK 00 signal is logic 0, the read/write head of the drive is positioned at track 0. When the WRITE GATE is logic 0, data is written onto the disk; when it is logic 1, data is read from the disk.

The INDEX/SECTOR output from the drive provides a logic 0 pulse each time the sector hole in the floppy disk is sensed by the index/sector photodetector of the drive. The WRITE PROTECT output indicates whether a write-protected disk is in the drive—the drive prevents writing into a protected disk. The READ DATA line provides the data and clock together as read by the drive electronics. Data to be written on the disk is input on a WRITE DATA line. A flux reversal is written onto the disk during each transition from logic 1 to logic 0 on this line.

Data is recorded on a floppy disk in either single or double density. Single density, for a full size disk, is 3,200 bpi (bits per inch) and double density is 6,400 bpi. For a minifloppy, single density is 2,581 bpi. In both single and double density encoding, the data is divided into bit cells. The manner in which 0 or 1 is encoded in the bit cell depends on the encoding scheme. For single density recording, a frequency modulated, FM, encoding scheme is used whereby each bit cell begins with a flux transition or pulse. The bit cell representing logic 1 has an additional flux transition at its center; the bit cell representing logic 0, on the other hand, does not (see Fig. 10.4-14). This FM encoding scheme is called ***double frequency recording*** because a string of logic 1 data bits creates a frequency of pulses twice the frequency of a string of logic 0 data bits.

Double density recording uses MFM (modified FM) or M2FM (modified MFM), which doubles the density of data bits without increasing the number of flux reversals per inch. Both MFM and M2FM have rules for eliminating the need for some clock bits, as a function of the data bit stream, when they are not necessary for synchronization. [6] For example, by MFM rules, a 1-bit cell has a pulse at its center, and a 0-bit cell has one at the beginning of the bit cell except when preceded by a 1, in which case no pulse at all occurs during the bit cell.

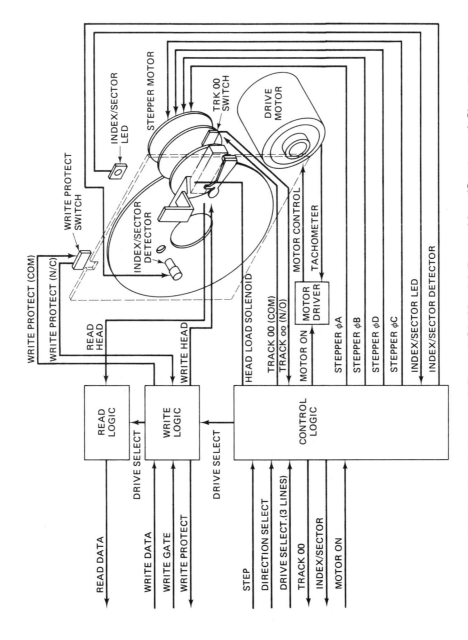

Figure 10.4-13. Functional diagram of Shugart SA400 mini floppy drive. (Courtesy of Shugart Associates.)

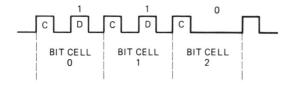

Figure 10.4-14. FM encoding.

Full size disk drives rotate the disk at 360 rpm. In single density recording, data is transferred to or from the disk at a nominal rate of 250 K bits per second; in double density, 500 K bits per second. Since each revolution of the disk takes 167 mS, the average time to access a particular record is 83 mS, assuming the read/write head is already located on the track. In general, the time required to access a randomly located record is dominated by the time it takes to move the read/write head to the appropriate track—a function of the track-to-track access time and the head loading time. Track-to-track access and head loading times vary with the electromechanical design of the specific disk drive. For the full size drive shown in Fig. 10.4-12, these times are 8 mS and 35 mS, respectively.

Minifloppy drives rotate the disk at 300 rpm and, for single density recording (2,581 bpi), data is transferred to or from the disk at 125 K bits per second. For the minifloppy drive shown in Fig. 10.4-12, the track-to-track access time is 40 mS, and the head loading time is 75 mS.

Data is written on a floppy disk in a particular format. The format divides each track into a number of smaller, fixed-length areas called *sectors*. Division is either soft sectored or hard sectored. Soft sectored disks have a single index hole, and sectors are identified by addresses which are permanently written onto the disk. Hard sectored disks contain a number of sector holes around the disk in addition to the index hole. These sector holes are sensed to identify the beginning of each sector.

The first floppy-disk system was developed by IBM. This system, the IBM 3740, has become a de facto standard for single density, full size, soft sectored systems. The IBM 3740 format is shown in Fig. 10.4-15. Each track contains the same sequence of control, address, and data fields. Data is written on the disk with frequency modulation, FM, encoding.

The preamble consists of 46 gap bytes. A gap byte is a sequence of 1s and 0s. Address marks indicate that the byte following the preamble is the beginning of an address or data field and are distinguished by missing clock bits. The last 3 bits in an address mark indicate whether the information that follows is deleted data, regular data, or an index, or ID, byte.

The index address mark indicates that 32 bytes follow before the first byte of the first sector. Each track contains 26 sectors of 188 bytes. The last sector is followed by the postamble.

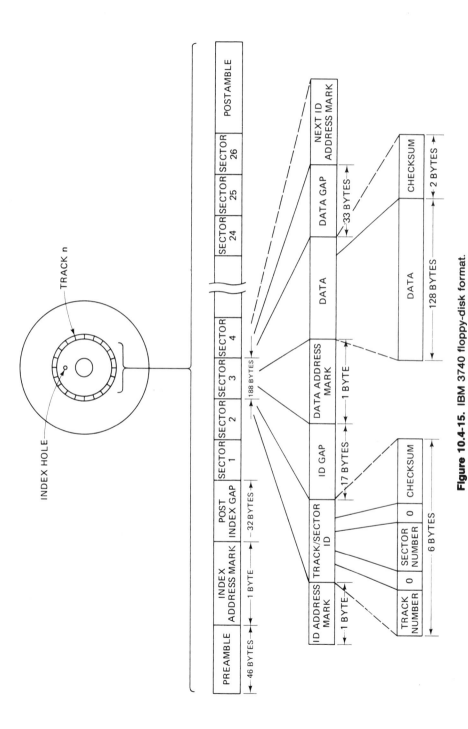

Figure 10.4-15. IBM 3740 floppy-disk format.

371

Each of the 26 sectors is, in turn, subdivided into a number of fields—the first byte of the sector is the ID address mark, which indicates that the track/sector ID field follows. This field consists of a 1-byte track number, then a byte of zeros followed by a 1-byte sector number, followed by another byte of zeros. The track/sector ID field is terminated by a 2-byte checksum. A 17-byte ID gap precedes the 1-byte data address mark, which itself indicates that the 130-byte data field follows. The sector is terminated by a 33-byte data gap. Out of a total of 188 bytes in a sector, only 128 bytes are actual data.

The Shugart minifloppy uses a modified IBM type format. The gap structure in this format differs somewhat from the 3740 format and there are only 18 sectors per track.

A floppy-disk controller interfaces the microprocessor and the floppy-disk drive. It receives commands and data from and provides status and data to the microprocessor. In response to the commands, the floppy-disk controller provides signals to the disk drive, which controls the reading and writing of data. The controller also carries out formatting of the disk and a CRC check for data errors.

The Shugart SA4400 is a typical minifloppy disk controller. See Fig. 10.4-16. It transfers data between one, two, or three disk drives and a microprocessor. It also formats disks according to the modified IBM format. An 8-bit bidirectional data bus transmits commands to the controller, transfers data between the microprocessor and controller, and provides floppy-disk status to the microprocessor. Additional control status lines initiate floppy-disk control operations and provide handshaking signals for transfers over the data bus.

The microprocessor controls the floppy disk with only eight commands. These commands are listed in Table 10.4-2. The controller itself contains a preprogrammed microprocessor which implements the commands.

It also contains a 128-byte sector buffer which allows the host microprocessor to transfer data to the buffer at its own rate and subsequently allows data to be transferred from the sector buffer to the disk, independent of the host. For read operations, the host microprocessor requests that data be transferred from the disk to the sector buffer and, subsequently, can read the buffer at its own rate.

Alternatively, data can be transferred directly between the host microprocessor and disk, byte by byte. Here the XRF and ACK lines are used for handshaking.

To store and read data as files, software interfaces the file commands of the user and the commands recognized by the floppy-disk controller. Such software constitutes a floppy-disk operating system. One portion of this system, called the *file manager*, keeps a directory of the location of all the files and remaining free space. When files longer than one sector are stored, the file manager breaks the block of data into single sectors. When the file is to be read, the file manager combines the data from various sectors into the original file.

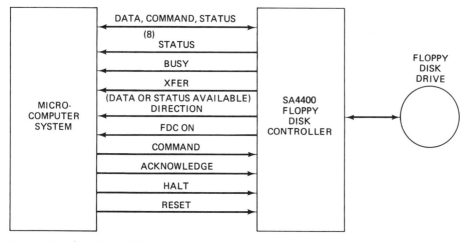

Figure 10.4-16. Shugart SA400 mini floppy controller interface.

TABLE 10.4-2
Commands for Shugart SA4400 Controller

Function Name	Function	Description
INIT	System reset	Resets controller and all floppy disks in system, and controls disk drive motor on/off.
SEEK	Position head on track	Steps head to specified track.
READ	Read disk sector	Reads a sector of data from specified sector.
READID	Read next ID	Reads the next sector ID information.
WRITE	Write disk sector	Writes a sector of data with normal data AM* to specified sector.
WRDEL	Write sector of deleted data	Writes a sector of data with deleted data AM to specified sector.
FORMAT	Format track	Writes address marks, gaps, and data on entire track per modified IBM-type format.
STATUS	Drive status	Returns status for addressed drive.

*Address Mark

10.5 HARDWARE IMPLEMENTATION OF MATHEMATICAL FUNCTIONS

Arithmetic functions implemented with hardware external to the microprocessor are advantageous in certain instances. For example, when the execution time of a software implementation exceeds that allowable in the particular application, a faster microprocessor or a hardware approach obviates the problem. Or, in the case of some complex arithmetic functions, special hardware eliminates the need for assembly language algorithms.

Hardware which implements arithmetic functions is interfaced to the microprocessor through I/O ports and is, in effect, a peripheral device. The microprocessor transfers operands and commands to the external arithmetic hardware and receives status information and computed results from it.

Four types of external hardware are commonly used to implement arithmetic in microprocessor systems:

1. Limited function high-speed arithmetic ICs.

2. Calculator ICs.

3. LSI Arithmetic Processing Units—APUs.

4. High-speed bit slice microprocessors.

10.5.1 Limited Function High-Speed Arithmetic ICs

Some real-time microprocessor applications require that only certain arithmetic functions—such as multiplication and/or division—be implemented at speeds exceeding those possible with the system's microprocessor. This is often the case even if the microprocessor contains instructions for multiplication and division. There are several bipolar ICs which implement one or a very limited number of mathematical operations at these high speeds. One example is an LSI multiplier.

An 8×8-bit parallel two's complement multiplier, the TRW MPY-8, is shown in Fig. 10.5-1. This multiplier is contained in a 40-pin package and executes multiplication in 130 nS, providing a 14-bit plus sign result. In operation X_{IN}, Y_{IN}, MSP_{OUT}, and LSP_{OUT} are connected in common to the data bus. If used with an isolated I/O structure, the X and Y registers are output ports, and CLKX and CLKY are controlled by their device select pulses. The registers MSP and LSP are input ports, and TRIM and TRIL—the enable lines for these ports—are controlled by their device select pulses. Assume that the multiplier is in register C and the multiplicand in register D; the subroutine in Fig. 10.5-2 implements the multiplication using the external hardware multiplier. The subroutine leaves the product in B and C. The format of the product duplicates the sign bit as the most significant bit of B and of C. This subroutine requires 84 states or 26.8 μS (8085A) for execution, including the subroutine call.

The actual hardware multiplication time, 130 nS, is overshadowed by the time required to load and read the registers of the hardware multiplier, which, in effect, becomes the multiplication time. This time can be minimized by reducing the load and read times by using memory mapped, instead of isolated, I/O;

374

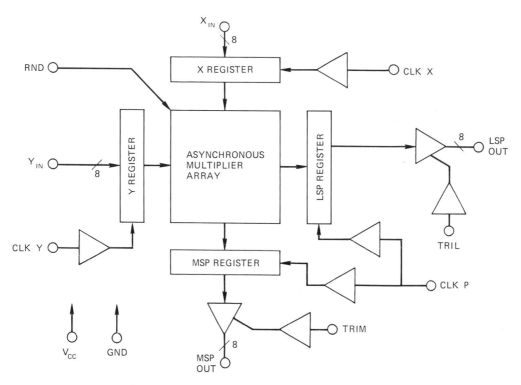

Figure 10.5-1. An LSI 8 × 8-bit parallel two's complement multiplier. (Courtesy of TRW)

using registers H and L for transferring the multiplicand, multiplier, and product; and writing a routine which transfers the operands and result as a macro.

In the memory mapped I/O scheme, registers X and Y are allocated to two consecutive memory locations, the first of which is labeled MPY. Registers LSP and MSP are also allocated to these two locations. Thus, a write operation to address MPY loads the multiplier into register X of the hardware multiplier, and

```
HTCM:    MOV  A, C    ;    LOAD MULTIPLIER
         OUT  X
         MOV  A, D    ;    LOAD MULTIPLICAND
         OUT  Y
         IN   LSP     ;    STORE LOW BYTE OF PRODUCT
         MOV  C, A
         IN   MSP     ;    STORE HIGH BYTE OF PRODUCT
         MOV  B, A
         RET
```

Figure 10.5-2. Subroutine to implement multiplication using the hardware multiplier of Figure 10.5-1.

a read operation from MPY reads the least significant byte of the product from register LSP of the multiplier. A write operation to address MPY +1 loads the multiplicand into register Y of the multiplier, and a read from MPY +1 reads the most significant byte of the product from register MSP of the multiplier.

To use a macro, the multiplicand and multiplier are placed in registers H and L, respectively, before the macro is referenced. The macro leaves the product in H and L. The memory mapped allocation of the hardware multiplier registers allows the loading and reading of the multiplier with only two instructions. The macro is:

```
MULT      MACRO
          SHLD MPY
          LHLD MPY
          ENDM
```

Memory mapping transfers the operands directly between an internal register pair and external registers without being routed through the accumulator. And use of a macro, instead of a subroutine, eliminates the time required for the subroutine call and return. The multiplication time is now only 10.2 μS.

10.5.2 Calculator ICs

The first hardware devices used with microprocessors to implement complex arithmetic were LSI calculator ICs, which predated the advent of general purpose microprocessors. A calculator IC is simply a microprocessor with a built-in microprogram for evaluating arithmetic functions and is designed for use in a hand calculator. These ICs are slow because the technology used in their manufacture is PMOS and because they incorporate features which are advantageous for interfacing to hand calculators but which are undesirable when used with microprocessors.

Most LSI calculator ICs accept data from a key matrix and are equipped with input logic for scanning and debouncing key closures. The debouncing logic introduces delays in the tens of milliseconds range for each digit of data entered.

The output of a typical calculator chip is a multiplexed 7-bit code for each digit of the result and a set of digit strobes which control display multiplexing. Because of this, additional logic is necessary to interface a calculator IC to a microprocessor. Hardware conversion of the seven segment output is facilitated by a MM74C915 seven-segment-to-BCD converter IC. A few calculator chips are designed for BCD input and output. In addition, most calculators have input and output signal levels which are not T^2L compatible and, therefore, require level shifting circuitry in order to interface with microprocessors which have T^2L compatible inputs and outputs. Even with their low speed and the necessity for additional interface logic, calculator chips are advantageous in applications where speed is not important and where reducing the cost of software development is.

If the interface is designed so that the calculator chip is loaded with the operands by the microprocessor, and, when the computation is complete, the calculator interface interrupts the microprocessor (see Chapter 9), the resulting concurrent processing capability minimizes the effect of the calculator IC's slowness on the system throughput. Several arithmetic subsystems are manufactured as printed circuit, PC, boards that use calculator ICs and provide the hardware and software for interfacing to a particular microprocessor. In most of these systems, the execution speed is only comparable to that achievable via software by the particular microprocessor; however, they do avoid additional software development.

Special calculator-type devices are designed for ease of interfacing to a microprocessor. National's 57109 Number Crunching Unit, NCU, is a PMOS device which is essentially an enhanced calculator chip. It implements arithmetic, trigonometric, logarithmic, and exponential functions. Its data format is floating point decimal with up to an 8-digit mantissa and a 2-digit exponent. Unlike most calculator chips, data is input to and output from the NCU in BCD. Instructions are input as a 6-bit code. Instruction execution times range from 1 to 500 mS, with 5 to 10 mS being typical.

10.5.3 Arithmetic Processing Units—APUs

LSI devices specifically designed as computational adjuncts to a microprocessor are also manufactured. The block diagram of one such device, the Am9511 Arithmetic Processing Unit, APU, is shown in Fig. 10.5-3. [7, 8] This is an NMOS device contained in a 24-pin DIP. It uses binary data formats and is capable of fixed and floating point calculations. Fixed point numbers are either 16 or 32 bits in two's complement form. Floating point numbers are 32 bits with the most significant byte containing the sign (1 bit) of the mantissa and the exponent (7 bits in two's complement form). The remaining 3 bytes contain the 24-bit mantissa.

Operands and commands are transferred to and results and status transferred from the APU through its 8-bit data bus buffer. The $C/\overline{D}$ input of the APU's bus control logic determines whether the data transferred is a command or status, $C/\overline{D} = 1$, or an operand or result, $C/\overline{D} = 0$. The $\overline{PAUSE}$ output of the APU synchronizes read and write operations between the microprocessor and APU. A simple interconnection between a microprocessor and APU to support programmed I/O transfers is shown in Fig. 10.5-4.

Reverse Polish Notation is used for the data and command input sequence to the APU. Data is written a byte at a time into the APU's 8×16 operand stack, least significant byte first. APU commands implement addition, subtraction, multiplication, division, trigonometric and inverse trigonometric functions, square roots, logarithms, exponentiation, and floating-to-fixed and fixed-to-floating point conversion. Some commands require two operands and use the top two on the stack; those which require a single operand use only the one on the top of the stack. Operation results are left on top of the stack. The command

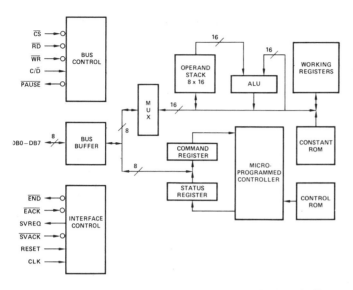

Figure 10.5-3. Block diagram of an Am9511 Arithmetic Processing Unit. (Copyright © 1979 Advanced Micro Devices, Inc. Reproduced with permission of copyright owner.)

format is shown in Fig. 10.5-5(a). Commands are also available which manipulate the contents of the stack, and a read operation can then retrieve the result from the stack. If an attempt is made to read the result before the computation has been completed, the $\overline{\text{PAUSE}}$ output forces the microprocessor to wait until the computation is complete.

Status of the APU is held in its status word register. See Fig. 10.5-5(b). A BUSY bit indicates whether the Am9511 is executing a command. When using

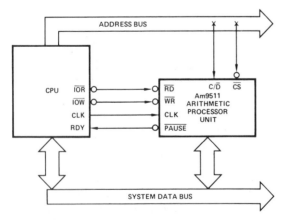

Figure 10.5-4. Programmed I/O interface to the Am9511 APU. (Copyright © 1979 Advanced Micro Devices, Inc. Reproduced with permission of copyright owner.)

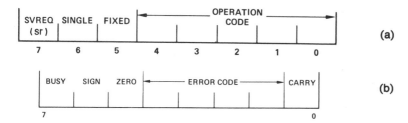

BUSY: Indicates that Am9511 is currently executing a command (1 = Busy).

SIGN: Indicates that the value on the top of stack is negative (1 = Negative).

ZERO: Indicates that the value on the top of stack is zero (1 = Value is zero).

ERROR CODE: This field contains an indication of the validity of the result of the last operation. The error codes are:

0000 – No error
1000 – Divide by zero
0100 – Square root or log of negative number
1100 – Argument of inverse sine, cosine, or e^x too large
XX10 – Underflow
XX01 – Overflow

CARRY: Previous operation resulted in carry or borrow from most significant bit. (1 = Carry/Borrow, 0 = No Carry/ No Borrow)

Figure 10.5-5. Command (a) and status (b) word format for the Am9511 APU. (Copyright © 1979 Advanced Micro Devices, Inc. Reproduced with permission of copyright owner.)

programmed I/O, this bit can be polled to determine when a computation is complete. If the BUSY bit is 1, the other status bits are not defined. If it is 0, the remaining bits of the status word provide information relating to the data on the top of the stack. The error code indicates whether an error occurred in the last operation and, if so, what type.

The APU has handshaking signals used when interrupts or DMA implement data transfers. The $\overline{\text{END}}$ signal indicates completed execution of a previously entered command and can be used as an interrupt request. $\overline{\text{EACK}}$ clears the $\overline{\text{END}}$ signal. The service request output, SVREQ, indicates the completion of a command execution only if the SVREQ bit, bit 7, of the command is set. For greater throughput, operand transfers can be handled by a DMA controller and CPU coordination handled by interrupts.

When operand transfer is included, execution time for the various operations is dependent on the method of transfer. Two versions of the Am9511 are available: a 2 MHz and a 4 MHz. Typical execution times for 32-bit floating point operands are listed as follows, in terms of the number of Am9511 clock cycles:

Operation	Clock Cycles
Multiplication	168
Square root	800
Cosine	4,118
Log	4,490
Power	9,292

REFERENCES

1. Applications Engineering Staff, Hewlett Packard Optoelectronics Division, *Optoelectronics Application Manual*. New York: McGraw-Hill Book Company, 1977.

2. *Peripheral Design Handbook*. Santa Clara, California: Intel Corporation, 1978.

3. *LRC Model 7040 Printer Manual*. Riverton, Wyoming: LRC, Inc., n.d.

4. *Magnetic Tape Cassettes for Information Interchange*. New York: American National Standards Institute, Inc., 1977.

5. *Unrecorded Magnetic Tape Cartridge for Information Interchange*. New York: American National Standards Institute, Inc. 1977.

6. KALSTROM, D.J., "Simple Encoding Schemes Double Capacity of a Flexible Disc," *Computer Design*, September 1976, pp. 98, 100, and 102.

7. *Am9511 Arithmetic Processor,* (Data Sheet). Sunnyvale, California: Advanced Micro Devices, Inc., 1978.

8. PARKER, R.O., and J.H. KROEGER, *Algorithm Details for the Am9511 Arithmetic Processing Unit*. Sunnyvale, California: Advanced Micro Devices, Inc., 1978.

BIBLIOGRAPHY

CARINALLI, C., "Slash CRT-Terminal Component Count," *Electronic Design*, Vol. 14, July 1978, pp. 88–95.

KEHL, T.H., and L. DUNKEL, "Simplified Floppy-Disc Controller for Microcomputers," *Computer Design*, June 1976, pp. 91–97.

MATIC, B., and L. TROTTIER, "Mate Microprocessors with CRT Displays," *Electronic Design*, Vol. 22, No. 14, September 1977, pp. 68–74.

µPD 371 Magnetic Tape Cassette/Cartridge Controller User's Manual. Lexington, Massachusetts: NEC Microcomputers, Inc., 1979.

µPD 372D LSI Floppy Disk Controller Chip User's Manual. Lexington, Massachusetts: NEC Microcomputers, Inc., 1977.

MOYERS, W.W., "Interfacing Calculator Chips as Microcomputer Preprocessors," *Computer Design*, Vol. 17, No. 5, May 1978, pp. 187–191.

MURRAY, J., and G. ALEXY, *CRT Terminal Design Using the Intel 8275 and 8279*, (Application Note AP-32). Santa Clara, California: Intel Corporation, 1977.

PARASURAMAN, B., "Hardware Multiplication Techniques for Microprocessor Systems," *Computer Design*, Vol. 16, No. 4, April 1977, pp. 75–82.

PETERSON, W.W., and E.J. WELDON, JR., *Error-Correcting Codes*. Cambridge, Massachusetts: M.I.T. Press, 1972.

RALLAPALLI, K., "CRC Error-Detection Schemes Ensure Data Accuracy," *EDN*, Vol. 23, No. 16, September 1978, pp. 119–123.

RAMPIL, I., "A Floppy Disk Tutorial," *Byte*, December 1977, pp. 24–45.

SA400 Minifloppy™ Diskette Storage Drive-OEM Manual, Shugart Associates, 1977.

SA4400 Ministreaker™ Floppy Disk Drive Controller-OEM Manual, Shugart Associates, 1977.

SKYETTE, K., "Incorporate a Calculator Chip, Instead of a Microprocessor, into Your Number-Processing Data System, and Avoid Software for Math Functions," *Electronic Design*, January 1976, pp. 96–99.

SMITH, L., *Printer Control with the UPI-41*, (Application Note AP-27). Santa Clara, California: Intel Corporation, 1977.

STAKEM, P.H., "Using a Calculator Chip to Extend a Microprocessor's Capabilities," *Computer Design*, September 1975, pp. 98–99.

SWANSON, R., "Understanding Cyclic Redundancy Codes," *Computer Design*, November 1975, pp. 93–99.

WASER, S. "State-of-the-Art in High Speed Arithmetic Integrated Circuits," *Computer Design*, Vol. 17, No. 7, July 1978, pp. 67–75.

WEISSBERGER, A.J., and T. TOAL, "Tough Mathematical Tasks are Child's Play for Number Cruncher," *Electronics*, Vol. 50, No. 4, February 1977, pp. 102–107.

WHITING, J.S., "An Efficient Software Method for Implementing Polynomial Error Detection Codes," *Computer Design*, March 1975, pp. 73–77.

WIESELMAN, I.L., "Trends in Computer Printer Technology," *Computer Design*, Vol. 18, No. 1, January 1979, pp. 107–115.

PROBLEMS

10-1. Design the hardware interface to and write a program for a microprocessor system that measures the contact bounce (in milliseconds) of single-pole/single-throw switches. Both the operate and release contact bounce times should be measured and each displayed on two two-digit seven segment displays.

10-2. Analyze the cross-coupled RS latch of Fig. 10.1-4 for any input waveform such as that shown in Fig. 10.1-3. Verify that it debounces a single-pole/double-throw mechanical switch.

10-3.   Two 74148 priority encoders and a quad two-input NAND gate can be used to encode the 16 keys of a keypad that has one terminal of each key connected in common. Determine the logic diagram that will accomplish this.

10-4.   A four-digit BCD thumbwheel switch is used to enter a control parameter into a microprocessor system while the system is running. Write a subroutine which, when called, checks the BCD switch outputs and updates, if necessary, the value of the control parameter in reserved memory. Assume that the subroutine is called approximately once every 30 seconds. Consider the time required for an operator to alter the value of all four thumbwheel switches before designing a solution.

10-5.   A 16-key keymatrix is interfaced to two 4-bit I/O ports whose directions are programmable. Develop an algorithm and flowchart that detects and identifies a key closure. Take advantage of the programmable nature of the I/O ports to make the algorithm as short as possible.

10-6.   Write a subroutine, SCAN, which when called scans a 16-key keypad similar to the keypad of Fig. 10.1-10. The subroutine should first detect whether any switch is closed, and, if not, return immediately. If one or more switches are closed, the subroutine should return with the code for the switch or switches in the accumulator.

10-7.   Draw the flowchart of a subroutine that scans the keyboard of Fig. 10.1-10 providing two-key rollover. Assume that the subroutine is called less often than the contact bounce period for the key switches used.

10-8.   Design the hardware to interface a 20-key keyboard to an 8085A system using the MM74C293 keyboard scanner of Fig. 10.1-11. The MM74C293 should interrupt the 8085A each time it has data available.

10-9.   A common anode seven-segment display is to be directly driven by an 8212 and used to display hexadecimal digits. Diagram the interconnection of the seven-segment display to the 8212. Segments a through g should be driven by bits D_6 to D_0 latched from the data bus. Determine the bit pattern required to display each of the hexadecimal digits.

10-10. Define rollover, and describe and distinguish between two-key and n-key rollover.

10-11. Draw the block diagram of a hardware interface between the LRC 7040 printer shown in Fig. 10.3-2 and an 8085A system showing the subsystems required. Data transfer is to be accomplished with program controlled I/O. The 8085A outputs ASCII characters using a 6-bit ASCII code. The 8085A uses 1 bit to start the printer's drive motor after which the interface must request data from the 8085A as needed. All timing is to be performed by the interface hardware.

10-12. Draw the block diagram of hardware interface between the LRC 7040 printer (Fig. 10.3-2) and an 8085A system where the hardware interface uses a FIFO buffer to accept ASCII characters from the 8085A. When a carriage return is received, the interface starts the printer and prints one line.

11

Analog Data Input and Output

A/D converters translate from analog measurements, which are characteristic of most phenomena in the "real world," to digital language, used in information processing, computing, data transmission, and control systems. D/A converters are used in transforming transmitted data or the results of computation back to "real-world" variables for control, information, display, or further analog processing.

D. H. Sheingold*

**Analog-Digital Conversion Notes*. Norwood, Massachusetts: Analog Devices, Inc., 1977.

11.1 ANALOG DATA

The data to be processed by a microprocessor system originates in either of two forms: digital or analog. And the data output from a microprocessor system may be either digital or analog. In electronic systems, digital data is represented by *digital signals*. Each signal is a voltage or current with one of two possible states: logic 1 or logic 0, both corresponding to discrete ranges of voltage or current. For example, for T^2L logic, the voltage range for logic 0 is 0 V to 0.8 V, and the voltage range for logic 1 is 2.0 V to 5.0 V. The precise voltage of the digital signal is not important, but it is critical that its value be within one of the two allowable ranges.

Many microprocessor applications involve the determination of the values of physical parameters such as temperature, position, pressure, etc. For example, whenever a microprocessor system is used in a closed loop system to control physical parameters, it must first measure the value of those parameters in order to make the decisions required for control. A transducer appropriate to each of the physical parameters generates an electrical signal which varies in a manner analogous to variations in the physical phenomenon. An electrical signal which is analogous to a physical parameter is an *analog signal*.

Analog data is data which has any one of a continuous set of values within a given range. Analog data is represented in electronic systems by analog signals which have any one of a continuous set of values in a fixed voltage or current range. The precise value of the voltage or current at a given time is important because it carries the information contained in the signal. For example, an analog voltage may have a range of 0 to 10 V and may be interpreted as representing temperatures from 0°C to 100°C. The analog voltage is expected to vary in proportion to the variable it represents; i.e., the variable to which it is electrically analogous.

There are many different types of transducers for various physical parameters. [1, 2, 3] But, in general, a *transducer* simply converts one form of energy to another. Transducers of interest here convert some form of energy to an electrical signal and are classified according to their transduction principle or according to the class of physical parameters that they transduce. *Transduction principles*, the physical principles upon which the operation of the transducer is based, include resistive, capacitive, inductive, piezoelectric, photoconductive, photovoltaic, and electromagnetic, and are used to transduce classes of physical parameters such as acceleration, displacement, flow, force, humidity, light, liquid level, pressure, sound, strain, temperature, and velocity.

Some transducers, those which are *self generating*, produce an electrical signal directly. A piezoelectric crystal, for example, directly converts a displacement into a voltage. *Non-self generating* transducers do not directly generate an electrical signal. Instead, they are used as components in an electrical circuit in such a manner that they control an electrical signal. A *thermistor* is a non-self generating temperature sensitive resistor. When it is used as one of the resistive components in a voltage divider, it controls an electrical signal which varies as the temperature varies.

For the analog signal from a transducer to be processed by a digital system, it must be converted to a digital code. Generally conversion is handled by several analog electronic subsystems which together comprise a data acquisition system, as shown in Fig. 11.1-1. Each analog input path to the data acquisition system is a *channel*. Data acquisition systems which handle several analog inputs are referred to as *multichannel*.

Many transducers output *low level signals*, those with less than 1 V amplitude. Frequently, such signals are in the millivolt or even microvolt range. Amplification is required to convert these to *high level signals* (1 to 10 V) so they can be further processed and converted. A filter may also be required to eliminate noise or undesired frequency components in a signal. *Analog signal conditioning*, which encompasses such operations as amplification, filtering, and linearization, transforms the transducer's output to a quantity suitable for conversion (see Fig. 11.1-1).

In a multichannel data acquisition system, an *analog multiplexer* selects the analog input for conversion to a digital code. The selected signal is input to a *sample and hold* circuit, which samples the analog input and provides a fixed output at the precise value of the sampled input signal. The sample and hold's output value is held fixed until it can be converted to a digital code. The actual conversion process itself is carried out by an *analog-to-digital converter*.

For applications where analog outputs are required, *digital-to-analog converters* generate a piecewise continuous analog output from digital codes. Several analog outputs may be generated using one D/A converter by following it with an analog demultiplexer and a sample and hold circuit for each channel (see Fig. 11.1-2). The analog demultiplexer transmits the output of the digital-to-analog converter to the selected sample and hold. Signal conditioning is often necessary at the output to amplify, buffer, or scale the analog output signals from the sample and hold circuits.

It is important that the designer of microprocessor systems be familiar with those analog devices that are necessary or useful in microprocessor applications involving analog signals. Such devices include analog-to-digital converters, digital-to-analog converters, operational amplifiers, sample and hold circuits, analog multiplexers, and analog demultiplexers.

11.2 OPERATIONAL AMPLIFIERS

Operational amplifiers (op-amps) are analog electronic devices that are used as components in many of the subsystems in an analog data acquisition system because of their low cost, high reliability, and ease of application. Operational amplifiers are the building blocks for current to voltage converters, voltage amplifiers, buffers, active filters, sample and holds, and a variety of other linear

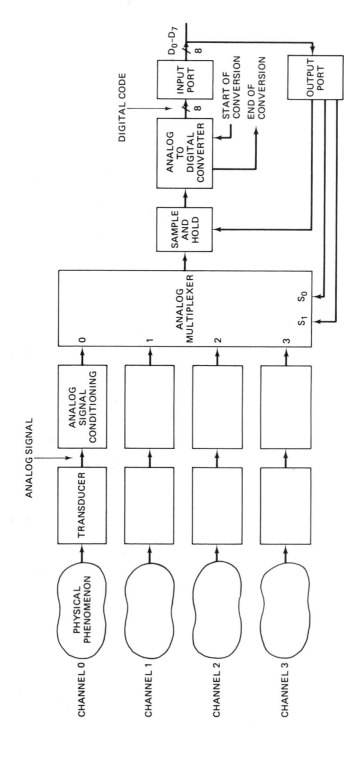

Figure 11.1-1. Multichannel data acquisition system.

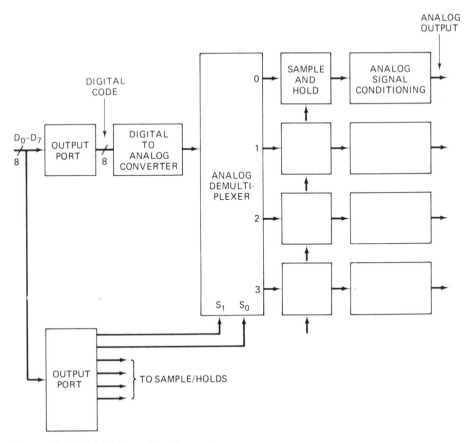

Figure 11.1-2. Multichannel analog output system.

and nonlinear analog signal processing circuits. They are available as separately packaged linear integrated circuits and are used as components in larger integrated circuits.

The characteristics of an operational amplifier are high gain, two analog signal inputs, and one or two analog signal outputs. In addition to the signal inputs and outputs, DC supply voltage(s), usually two of opposite polarity, are required for the op-amp's operation. The basic op-amp circuit symbol is shown in Fig. 11.2-1(a). All voltages applied to the op-amp are specified with respect to the circuit's ground terminal. The two signal inputs are the *inverting input* ($-$) and the *noninverting input* ($+$). The voltages at these inputs are labeled v_- and v_+, respectively. Input voltages can be positive or negative for those op-amps operating between two supply voltages of opposite polarity.

11.2.1 The Ideal Op-Amp

For purposes of analysis, the op-amp is assumed to be ideal. The output voltage of an ideal op-amp is a function of the difference between the two input

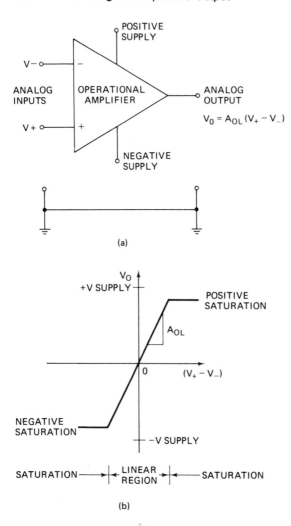

Figure 11.2-1. Operational amplifier: (a) symbol; (b) open loop transfer characteristic.

voltages, $v_+ - v_-$, the ***differential*** input voltage. There are three regions of operation of the op-amp. In the linear region, the output voltage, v_O, is the product of the open loop gain, A_{OL}, of the op-amp and the differential input voltage,

$$v_O = A_{OL}(v_+ - v_-)$$

This region is indicated by the diagonal line with slope A_{OL} in Fig. 11.2-1(b). The other two regions of operation are the saturation regions. In these, v_O is fixed at either the positive or negative saturation voltage and is no longer a linear function of $v_+ - v_-$. The value of the saturation voltage is usually 1 or 2 volts below that of the supply voltage.

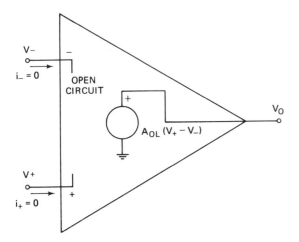

Figure 11.2-2. Equivalent circuit of ideal op-amp.

The input resistance at the inverting and noninverting terminals is assumed infinite in the ideal op-amp. Therefore, the currents into these terminals are zero: $i_- = i_+ = 0$. The output resistance of the ideal op-amp is assumed zero. A simple equivalent circuit for the ideal op-amp in its linear region of operation is indicated in Fig. 11.2-2. The dependent voltage generator, $A_{OL}(v_+ - v_-)$ models the output as a function of the input.

Open loop gains, A_{OL}, for practical IC op-amps range from 10^4 to 10^6. DC supply voltages are usually no greater than ± 15 V. Thus, a limit is placed on the range of the differential input voltage $(v_+ - v_-)$ that can be applied to the op-amp while maintaining linear operation. For a gain of 10^4 and a supply voltage of ± 15 V, the maximum differential input voltage is:

$$|v_+ - v_-| < \frac{V \text{ supply}}{A_{OL}}$$

$$< \frac{15 \text{ V}}{10^4}$$

$$< 1.5 \text{ mV}$$

Most applications involve input voltages of a much larger range, and the magnitude of the noise signals present in most environments in applications involving input voltages of very low magnitude cause the output to oscillate or saturate. For these reasons op-amps are not operated open loop in linear applications.

For closed loop operation of an op-amp, a portion of the output signal is fed back to one of the input terminals via an external connection. *Negative feedback*, used in implementing linear circuits, results if the feedback connection is made to the inverting terminal. *Positive feedback* results if the feedback connection is to the noninverting terminal and, under certain conditions, produces nonlinear circuits.

11.2.2 Common Op-Amp Circuits

When an op-amp with a high open loop gain is used with negative feedback to implement a linear circuit, the closed loop gain or transfer characteristic of the circuit and its input and output impedance is, to a first approximation, dictated entirely by the external feedback components. As a result, the analysis and design of linear signal processing circuits with op-amps is relatively straightforward.

There are a number of common op-amp circuits for implementing various functions, and their operations and characteristics, as a function of external components, have been thoroughly analyzed. [4, 5, 6, 7] See Fig. 11.2-3. The analysis of a circuit's transfer characteristics by using *virtual ground analysis* is presented in Appendix E. These characteristics are approximations determined from the circuit configuration, with the assumption that the op-amp in the circuit is ideal. However, for most applications, these approximations predict, with sufficient accuracy, the operation of a circuit containing an actual op-amp.

Figure 11.2-4 illustrates the use of op-amps in signal conditioning, where a thermistor, R_T, is used as a temperature sensor. The resistance of the thermistor decreases with an increase in temperature, as shown in Fig. 11.2-4(a). The intent is to generate an analog voltage representing temperatures from 0°C to 100°C, convert that voltage to an 8-bit binary code, and input that code to a microprocessor. The A/D converter used is designed to accept input voltages from 0 to 10 V and convert them to a binary code.

Ensuring the proper input to the A/D converter is a two-step process: (1) since the thermistor is not a self generating transducer, circuitry must be provided to convert the change in thermistor resistance to an analog voltage, and (2) the analog voltage from step (1) must be shifted and scaled so that it corresponds to a 0 to 10 V signal.

The first step is carried out by using the thermistor as part of a voltage divider circuit. The ratio of the output of the voltage divider, V_1, to its excitation voltage, V_S, is plotted in Fig. 11.2-4(b). The fact that this transfer characteristic is not linear poses no problem because linearization can be provided by a table lookup operation in the microprocessor. In the circuit of Fig. 11.2-4(c), $V_S = -15$ V. The voltage divider output thus increases negatively for increasing temperature. The output of the voltage divider ranges from -1.8 V at 0°C to -13.05 V at 100°C.

The next step converts the -1.8 V to -13.05 V range to a 0 V to $+10$ V range. Op-amp A_1 is a unity-gain buffer that prevents the following stage of circuitry from loading the voltage divider. Thus, $V_2 = V_1$. The next stage shifts and scales V_2. Voltage V_2 is shifted (biased) by 1.8 V so that a 0 V signal is obtained at 0°C instead of a -1.8 V signal, and its 11.25 V range, $|(-13.05) - (-1.8 \text{ V})|$, is scaled to a 10 V range. Op-amp A_2 and resistors R_1, R_2, and R_F form an inverting summing amplifier, as shown in Fig. 11.2-3(d). A value of 10 kΩ is assumed for R_1. At 0°C, $V_2 = -1.8$ V, and the current through R_1 and into the summing junction is $V_2/R_1 = -1.8 \text{ V}/10 \text{ k}\Omega = -0.18$ mA. One side

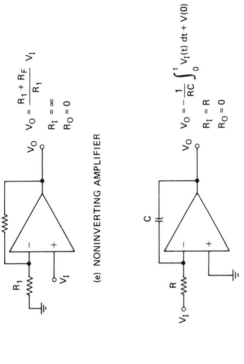
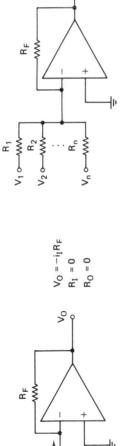
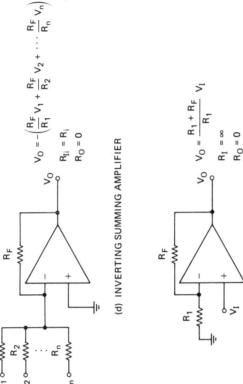

$$V_O = -i_I R_F$$
$$R_I = 0$$
$$R_O = 0$$

(a) CURRENT TO VOLTAGE CONVERTER

$$V_O = V_I$$
$$R_I = \infty$$
$$R_O = 0$$

(b) UNITY GAIN BUFFER

$$V_O = -\frac{R_F}{R_1} V_I$$
$$R_I = R_1$$
$$R_O = 0$$

(c) INVERTING VOLTAGE AMPLIFIER

$$V_O = -\left(\frac{R_F}{R_1} V_1 + \frac{R_F}{R_2} V_2 + \cdots \frac{R_F}{R_n} V_n\right)$$
$$R_{Ii} = R_i$$
$$R_O = 0$$

(d) INVERTING SUMMING AMPLIFIER

$$V_O = \frac{R_1 + R_F}{R_1} V_I$$
$$R_I = \infty$$
$$R_O = 0$$

(e) NONINVERTING AMPLIFIER

$$V_O = -\frac{1}{RC} \int_0^t V_I(t)\, dt + V(0)$$
$$R_I = R$$
$$R_O = 0$$

(f) INTEGRATOR

Figure 11.2-3. Common operational amplifier circuits.

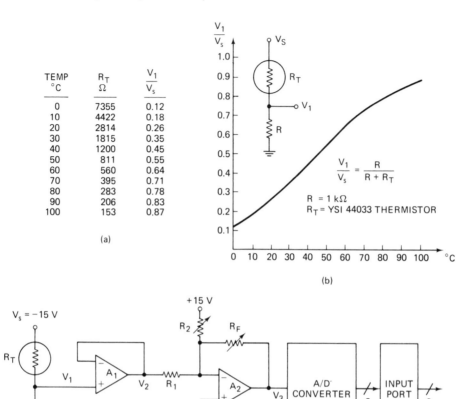

The table for part (a):

TEMP °C	R_T Ω	$\dfrac{V_1}{V_s}$
0	7355	0.12
10	4422	0.18
20	2814	0.26
30	1815	0.35
40	1200	0.45
50	811	0.55
60	560	0.64
70	395	0.71
80	283	0.78
90	206	0.83
100	153	0.87

(a)

$$\frac{V_1}{V_s} = \frac{R}{R + R_T}$$

$R = 1\ \text{k}\Omega$
$R_T = \text{YSI 44033 THERMISTOR}$

(b)

(c)

Figure 11.2-4. Temperature measurement circuit utilizing a thermistor as the temperature transducer: (a) thermistor characteristics; (b) transfer characteristic of voltage divider using thermistor; (c) diagram of complete circuit.

of R_2 is connected to $+15$ V. A value for R_2 is computed that causes a current through R_2, equal to that through R_1. This balances the current through R_1 and causes the current through R_F to be zero and, thus, the output voltage to be 0 V. Therefore,

$$\frac{V_2}{R_1} = \frac{15\ \text{V}}{R_2}$$

and

$$R_2 = \frac{15\ \text{V}}{V_2} R_1$$

$$= \frac{15\ \text{V}}{1.8\ \text{V}} 10\ \text{k}\Omega$$

$$= 83.3\ \text{k}\Omega$$

R_2 is an adjustable resistor (potentiometer) with a nominal value of 83.3 kΩ to compensate for slight errors in the actual resistor values and voltages.

The gain of the inverting amplifier circuit to V_2 is $-R_F/R_1$. The desired gain is:

$$-\frac{V_3}{V_2} = \frac{10 \text{ V}}{11.25 \text{ V}}$$

$$= -0.888$$

Therefore,

$$-\frac{R_F}{R_1} = -0.888$$

$$R_F = 0.888 R_1$$

$$= 8.88 \text{ k}\Omega$$

The output V_3 is an analog voltage with a range of 0 to 10 V corresponding to a temperature range of 0°C to 100°C. Note that in Fig. 11.2-4(c) the reference terminal (ground) with respect to which input and output voltages of the op-amp circuit are measured is omitted from the diagram, as is common practice.

Actual op-amps are not ideal. IC op-amps have such nonideal characteristics as offset voltage, bias and offset currents, drift, finite input and nonzero output impedance, finite response time, and nonzero response to common mode signals. Some op-amps provide terminals to which external components can be added, which partially compensate for some of these nonideal characteristics; others cannot be compensated for completely.

11.2.3 Differential and Instrumentation Amplifiers

Analog signals are divided into two categories: single-ended and differential. A *single-ended signal* appears on a single terminal and is measured with respect to the circuit ground, as shown in Fig. 11.2-5. Single-ended signals are usually high level signals. For short distances, the signal is transmitted over a single wire and referenced to circuit ground. For longer distances, a pair of twisted wires is used to minimize noise pickup. One of the wires in the twisted pair is grounded; the other carries the signal. Alternatively, shielded cable may be used to minimize the effects of noise in the circuit. The circuits shown in Figs. 11.2-3 and 11.2-4 are all designed to accept single-ended inputs and generate single-ended outputs.

Low level signals are usually handled as *differential signals* which require two signal wires. The information bearing signal is the difference between the voltages on the two wires, each measured with respect to ground. Most low level transducers generate differential signals. The environment of the transducer may induce electrical noise into the output signal, which may be comparable to or greater in magnitude than the signal itself. For our purposes, any signal other than the desired signal is considered noise.

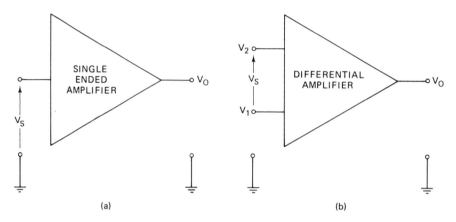

Figure 11.2-5. Generalized amplifier signal connections: (a) single-ended input—single-ended output; (b) differential input—single-ended output.

Differential and instrumentation amplifiers are designed to handle differential inputs. The output of these amplifiers is usually a high level, single-ended signal which can be processed by single-ended circuits, such as those of Fig. 11.2-3.

Figure 11.2-6 represents the type of application where a differential or instrumentation amplifier is required. The transducer generates a low level output represented by the voltage source, v_d, which is proportional to the physical parameter being measured. In addition, the model of the transducer contains a voltage source v_{CM}, a common mode voltage. It is possible for a portion of v_{CM} to result as a function of the design of the transducer, as in the case of a bridge circuit. And, v_{CM} includes noise induced in the conductors between the transducer and amplifier input and/or any difference in potential of the grounds at the transducer and amplifier. If a single-ended connection between the transducer and amplifier is used, V_2 only, the signal amplified is $v_d + v_{CM}$. If v_d is a low level signal, v_{CM} can be of comparable or greater magnitude, which results in a low signal to noise ratio, SNR, at the input of the amplifier, and the noise is amplified along with the signal. However, if a differential signal is obtained from the transducer, an amplifier designed to amplify the differential signal and reject the common mode signal can be used. Then the output is the product of the amplifier gain and the difference of its two input signals:

$$v_O = G(v_2 - v_1)$$

since $v_2 = v_d + v_{CM}$ and $v_1 = v_{CM}$.

$$v_O = G(v_d + v_{CM} - v_{CM})$$

$$= Gv_d$$

TRANSDUCER

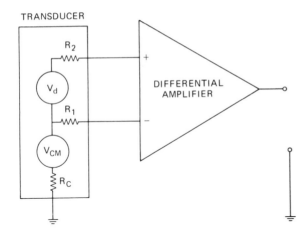

Figure 11.2-6. Simplified transducer model with differential outputs.

Figure 11.2-7 shows the circuit diagram of a differential amplifier constructed from a single op-amp. The output of this circuit is:

$$v_O = (v_2 - v_1)\frac{R_2}{R_1}$$

Thus, the output is the difference of $v_2 - v_1$, multiplied by a gain, $G = R_2/R_1$. A basic drawback of the circuit, however, is that the differential input impedance (i.e., from input to input) is only $2R_1$. This impedance loads the differential signal source and can attenuate it.

The amplifier of Fig. 11.2-7 has other limitations in addition to its low differential input impedance. If high input impedance and high gain are required, the input resistance has to be very large and the feedback resistance even larger, which entails the difficult matching of very high valued resistors. If the matching is not achieved, the common mode signal is also amplified. Also, changing the gain requires changing two matched resistors in the circuit.

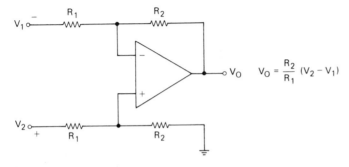

Figure 11.2-7. Differential amplifier constructed from a single op-amp.

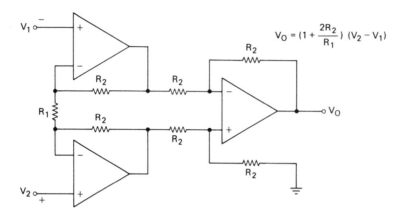

$$V_O = (1 + \frac{2R_2}{R_1})(V_2 - V_1)$$

Figure 11.2-8. Instrumentation amplifier constructed from three op-amps.

An instrumentation amplifier uses three operational amplifiers, Fig. 11.2-8, to solve these problems. The transfer function of the circuit is:

$$v_O = \left(1 + \frac{2R_2}{R_1}\right)(v_2 - v_1)$$

The two input op-amps provide very high input impedance, since the current into the noninverting terminals is very low, and the gain of the circuit can be adjusted by changing a single resistor, R_1. For high gain, the resistors R_2 that must be matched need not be excessively large. This type of instrumentation amplifier is available as a single IC with R_1 as an external resistor: for example, National Semiconductor's LH0036.

In practical differential and instrumentation amplifiers, the ideal characteristics obtainable, assuming perfectly matched resistors and ideal op-amps, are unachievable. The quality of practical circuits is measured by their common mode rejection ratio, CMRR (or CMR). This is the ratio of the circuit's gain for differential signals, A_d, divided by its gain for common mode signals, A_{CM}.

$$\text{CMRR} = \frac{A_d}{A_{CM}}$$

In the ideal circuit, $A_{CM} = 0$ and the CMRR $= \infty$. In practical IC circuits, CMRRs between 10^3 and 10^6 are common.

11.2.4 Delay and Settling Time

Settling time is a parameter that indicates the time response of analog circuits. It is defined as the time elapsing between the application of a full scale step input to the circuit and the output entering and remaining in a specified band of

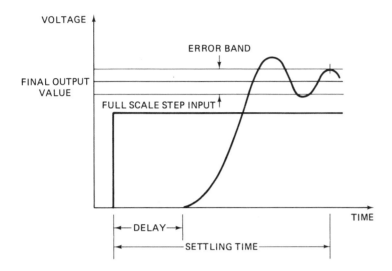

Figure 11.2-9. Settling time of an op-amp.

values near the final output value. For differential and instrumentation amplifier circuits, a step input is a full scale voltage or current input transition. For other devices, such as D/A converters, analog multiplexers, and sample and holds, the full scale transition involves a switching operation, and thus the settling time includes that switching time.

Settling time for an op-amp is illustrated in Fig. 11.2-9. After the application of a full scale step input, a period of time elapses before the op-amp output starts to change. This time period is known as the *delay time*. The op-amp output then changes at its maximum rate: the *slew rate*. The output eventually reaches the defined error band around the full scale value, and, if the circuit is underdamped, may overshoot and oscillate around the final value. Once the oscillations remain within the error band, the settling time is complete.

11.3 DIGITAL-TO-ANALOG CONVERTERS—DACS

A digital-to-analog converter (D/A converter or DAC) accepts an *n*-bit parallel digital code as input and provides an analog current or voltage as output. The DAC's output current or voltage is a function of the code at its input and changes in response to a change in the digital input. Among their many applications, digital-to-analog converters are used in digitally controlled CRT displays, in digitally controlled power supplies for automatic test equipment, for digital generation of analog waveforms, and for digital control of automatic process control systems. They are, as well, the basis for many analog-to-digital converter (A/D converter, ADC) designs.

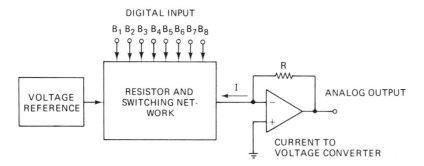

Figure 11.3-1. Digital-to-analog conversion system.

A DAC system typically consists of three basic subsystems: an accurate and stable voltage reference, the basic DAC itself, and an operational amplifier (see Fig. 11.3-1). For an n-bit straight binary[1] input code, the D/A output is:

$$V_O = V_{\text{REF}}\left(B_1 2^{-1} + B_2 2^{-2} + \ldots + B_n 2^{-n}\right)$$

where B_1 is the msb and B_n the lsb of the binary input.

A DAC consists of electronic analog switches controlled by the input code and a network of precision weighted resistors. The switches control currents or voltages derived from the reference voltage and provide an output current or voltage which is an analog representation of the applied code. An operational amplifier can be used at the output to provide current to voltage conversion and/or buffering. In some high-speed applications where a limited output voltage range is acceptable, a resistor, instead of an op-amp, provides current to voltage conversion, thus eliminating the delay associated with the operational amplifier.

The output from an ideal 3-bit DAC which accepts a straight binary code as input is shown in Fig. 11.3-2. As this figure illustrates, the analog output is not continuous but has one of eight possible values. Each value corresponds to one of the eight possible 3-bit codes at the input. These binary inputs are written as numbers ranging from 000 to 111. In actual fact, however, these numbers represent a discrete set of fractions that lie in the range of 0.000 to 0.111, that is, from 0 to the maximum, $1 - 2^{-n}$. The binary point is usually not written. For $n = 3$, as in the present case, the actual maximum output is seven-eights of the nominal full scale (FS) output. If the 3-bit DAC has a nominal output range of 0 to 10 V, the actual maximum output voltage is 8.75 V. The size of the step at the output, corresponding to a change in the input code of one least significant bit, is $FS/2^n$. For a 3-bit 0-to-10 V converter, the step size is $10/2^3$, or 1.25 V.

The requirements of a particular application dictate the number of bits required in a DAC. In DACs with a larger number of input bits, the number of

---

[1]The term straight binary is frequently used to refer to the usual (natural) binary code.

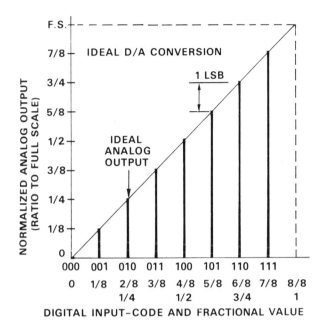

Figure 11.3-2. Conversion relationship for an ideal 3-bit straight binary D/A converter. (Courtesy of Analog Devices.)

steps is increased, and step size is reduced. A DAC with an 8-bit straight binary input code, for example, has 256 distinct output values corresponding to the number of distinct input codes possible. For a 10 V FS converter, the step size is 39.06 mV. Table 11.3-1 indicates the resolution of a DAC with straight binary input as a function of the number of input bits. **Resolution** is a measure of the size of the output step associated with a change of 1 lsb at the input. Thus, resolution is a measure of the precision of a DAC and is either expressed in bits or as a percentage. An 8-bit binary converter has a resolution of 1 part in 256 or 0.3906 percent, or 3,906 ppm (parts per million).

TABLE 11.3-1

Resolution as a Function of the Number of Bits for a Binary Converter

Number of Bits	Number of Quanta	Percentage	PPM
1	2	50	500,000
6	64	1.6	15,625
8	256	0.4	3,906
10	1,024	0.1	977
12	4,086	0.024	244
16	65,536	0.0015	15

11.3.1 Input Codes

Although straight binary is the most popular, a number of other input codes are used with DACs, including BCD and complementary binary. With binary coded decimal, since 4 bits are required to represent each decimal digit, resolution is lower for a BCD converter than for a binary converter using the same number of bits. This resolution is 1 part in 10^D, where D is the number of BCD digits, and the maximum output voltage is $FS(1 - 10^{-D})$. A 12-bit BCD converter has 1,000 output values in a range from 0 to 0.999 FS, with a step size of 0.001 FS and a resolution of 0.1 percent. A 12-bit straight binary converter has 4,096 output values in a range from 0 to 0.99976 FS, with a step size of 0.00024 FS and a resolution of 0.024 percent. Thus, the resolution of a 12-bit binary converter is better by a factor of 4 than the resolution of a 12-bit BCD converter.

Because of their method of construction, monolithic (integrated circuit) DACs frequently use complementary binary or complementary BCD codes (Table 11.3-2). In these codes, all bits are represented by their complements. Thus, in the previous case of a 3-bit binary DAC, 0 output is represented by 111, half scale by 011, and full scale (less 1 lsb) by 000.

TABLE 11.3-2

Binary Coding for 8-Bit Unipolar Converters.

Scale	+10 V FS	Straight Binary	Complementary Binary
+ FS − 1 lsb	+9.96	11111111	00000000
+3/4 FS	+7.50	11000000	00111111
+1/2 FS	+5.00	10000000	01111111
+1/4 FS	+2.50	01000000	10111111
+1/8 FS	+1.25	00100000	11011111
+1 lsb	+0.04	00000001	11111110
0	0.00	00000000	11111111

The D/A converters previously mentioned are unipolar; i.e., they provide a single polarity output. However, bipolar D/A converters which provide positive and negative output voltages are also available. The input codes of such converters correspond to those which represent positive and negative numbers in digital systems. These include sign-plus-magnitude, two's complement, and one's complement. Also used is a code called *offset binary*, which is identical to two's complement except that the msb is complemented. Table 11.3-3 illustrates the outputs for a bipolar converter with a nominal ±5 V range as a function of the offset binary and two's complement codes.

TABLE 11.3-3

Binary Coding for 8-Bit Bipolar Converters.

Scale	± 5 V FS	Offset Binary	2's Complement
+ FS − 1 lsb	+4.96	11111111	01111111
+3/4 FS	+3.75	11100000	01100000
+1/2 FS	+2.50	11000000	01000000
0	0.00	10000000	00000000
−1/2 FS	−2.50	01000000	11000000
−3/4 FS	−3.75	00100000	10100000
−FS + 1 lsb	−4.96	00000001	10000001
−FS	−5.00	00000000	10000000

11.3-2 Weighted Resistor D/A Converters

The *weighted resistor method* is a straightforward one for D/A converter implementation. This method creates an output current, I_T, which is the summation of several weighted currents. The selection of those currents to be summed is controlled by the bits of the digital code. An example of a weighted resistor circuit for straight binary codes is shown in Fig. 11.3-3. Its output is from an op-amp connected as an inverting summing amplifier. Thus,

$$V_{\text{OUT}} = -I_T R$$

The input to the circuit is a 3-bit digital word, $B_1 B_2 B_3$, which represents a straight binary fraction. B_1, the most significant bit, has a weight of 2^{-1}; B_2 has a weight of 2^{-2}; and B_3, the least significant bit, has a weight of 2^{-3}. Each bit controls an analog switch. When bit B_i is 1, its corresponding analog switch passes a current through a resistor of weight $2^i R$ and into the summing junction of the operational amplifier. The summing junction is held at ground by the action of the negative feedback through R. The value of the component of current into the summing junction for bit $B_i = 1$ is:

$$I_i = \frac{V_{\text{REF}}}{2^i R}$$

When bit B_i is 0, the analog switch directs the current through the associated resistor to the circuit ground instead of into the op-amp's summing junction.

Proper selection of the resistor ratios allows each bit of the digital word to control a properly weighted current. The resistors are weighted so that their resistances are inversely proportional to the numerical significance of the corre-

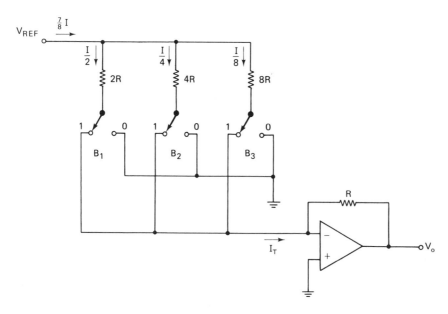

Figure 11.3-3. Three-bit weighted resistor D/A converter.

sponding bit. In terms of the digital word, the output of the weighted resistor D/A converter of Fig. 11.3-3 is:

$$V_{OUT} = -I_T R$$

$$= -\left(\frac{V_{REF}B_1}{2R} + \frac{V_{REF}B_2}{4R} + \frac{V_{REF}B_3}{8R}\right)R$$

$$= -V_{REF}\left(\frac{B_1}{2} + \frac{B_2}{4} + \frac{B_3}{8}\right)$$

$$= -V_{REF}\left(B_1 2^{-1} + B_2 2^{-2} + B_3 2^{-3}\right)$$

The output voltage is, therefore, directly proportional to the digital code. The factor of proportionality is equal to V_{REF}. If V_{REF} is -10 V, the D/A converter's output ranges from 0 V to $+8.75$ V (seven-eighths of full scale), corresponding to input codes from 000 to 111, respectively. This output is identical to that of Fig. 11.3-2, with FS = 10 V.

This circuit can be expanded to handle straight binary codes with a greater number of bits by the simple inclusion of additional analog switches and properly weighted resistors. Weighted codes other than straight binary can be converted by proper choice of the weighting resistor. As the number of bits increases, however, the range of the weighted resistors becomes prohibitively large for accurate implementation as an integrated circuit.

11.3.3 *R-2R* Ladder D/A Converters

A D/A converter which uses resistors of only two values, R and $2R$, is illustrated in Fig. 11.3-4. This type of converter is advantageous in that it does not require a large range of resistor values with precise ratios for a large number of input bits. But it does require twice as many resistors for the same number of bits as the weighted resistor network.

Like the weighted resistor D/A converter, this circuit creates an output current, I_T, proportional to the input code. An operational amplifier converts the current to an output voltage; therefore,

$$V_{OUT} = -I_T R$$

where I_T is the current into the summing junction of the operational amplifier. I_T, in turn, consists of the sum of the weighted currents through the analog switches in the logic 1 position.[2]

Due to the virtual ground effect, which is valid for the operational amplifier in its negative feedback configuration, the noninverting terminal is effectively at ground potential. Thus, each analog switch is connected to ground in either its 0 or 1 position, and the bottom of each $2R$ vertical resistor is grounded. If the Thevenin equivalent of the resistor ladder is computed by looking into the terminal connected to V_{REF}, the equivalent resistance of the ladder is found to be simply, R. Thus, the current into the ladder from the reference supply is always:

$$I = \frac{V_{REF}}{R}$$

When the equivalent resistance of the ladder network to the right of node A, i.e., to the right of the first vertical $2R$ resistor, is computed, it is $2R$. Thus, the current I into node A splits in half, resulting in a current $I/2$, through the vertical $2R$ resistor associated with bit B_1. The other half of the current is through R and into node B. The equivalent resistance to the right of node B is also $2R$. Thus, the current $I/2$ into node B splits, causing a current $I/4$ in the vertical resistor associated with bit B_2. A continuation of this analysis shows that the current splits at each node, resulting in currents through the vertical resistors that are weighted by powers of two. For each switch in the 1 position, the current through its associated resistor flows into the operational amplifier's summing junction. Thus, I_T is the sum of these weighted currents.

Both the weighted resistor and the R-$2R$ D/A converters discussed use an op-amp as a current to voltage converter to provide an output voltage. The output line from the D/A converter, which carries the binary weighted currents, is therefore terminated at virtual ground. Although some practical D/A converters require such a termination, others, those which use a simple external

---

[2]A method for determining the ratio of the currents through these switches is outlined here; a thorough analysis of the derivation is found in [7].

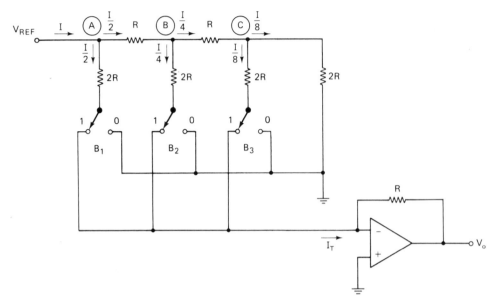

Figure 11.3-4. Three-bit R-2R ladder D/A converter.

resistor instead of an op-amp, provide current to voltage conversion without the delay inherent in an op-amp. The value of the resistor, and thus the value of the full scale output voltage, is limited by the compliance of the converter. The *compliance rating* is a limit of the maximum voltage of the output current terminal above ground. For many converters the compliance is as small as a few tenths of a volt.

11.3.4 $2^n R$ D/A Converters

A very simple and straightforward approach to D/A conversion is the $2^n R$ method. An n-bit $2^n R$ D/A converter requires 2^n resistors of equal value, R, and $2^{n+1} - 2$ analog switches. Although this approach necessitates a large number of components, they are economically manufactured in MOS LSI. As shown in Fig. 11.3-5, the 2^n resistors are connected in series to form a voltage divider which splits the reference voltage into 2^n analog levels. The analog switches are connected to form a tree structure and are controlled by the digital code in such a manner that each code word creates a single path from the voltage divider to the converter output. A unity gain buffer amplifier prevents loading of the voltage divider. The output of this converter is a voltage.

11.3.5 Reference Voltages

In most applications, a stable and accurate voltage reference is essential for the operation of a D/A converter. Some converters have an internal reference voltage derived from the supply voltage by a circuit that uses a temperature

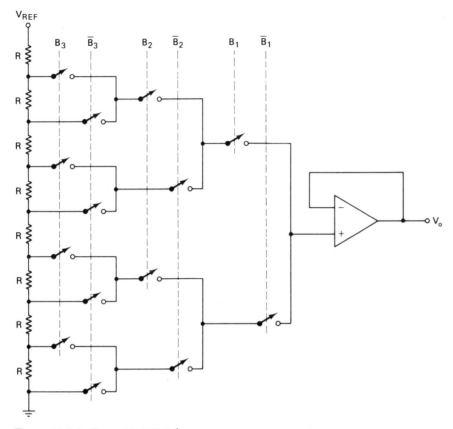

Figure 11.3-5. Three-bit 2^nR D/A converter.

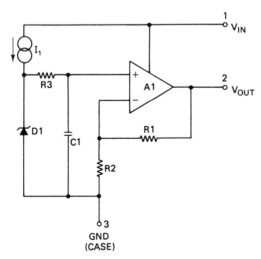

Figure 11.3-6. Equivalent schematic of LH0070 (10V) and LH0071 (10.24V) voltage references. These references are available in a 3-lead TO-5 package. (Courtesy of National Semiconductor Corp.)

compensated zener diode. In addition, these devices allow use of an external voltage reference for greater accuracy. Others have no internal voltage reference and require a separate one for operation.

Voltage references with temperature compensated zener diodes are available in IC form. In these devices, the diode is driven by a current regulator and buffer amplifier. Typically, their output voltages are accurate to ± 0.01 percent. For example, National's LH0070 and LH0071 voltage references (Fig. 11.3-6) provide output voltages of 10.0 and 10.24 V, respectively. With a 10.0 V reference for BCD converters and a 10.24 V reference for binary converters, step size is expressed as multiples or submultiples of 10 mV.

11.3.6 Multiplying D/A Converters

If an external reference voltage input to a D/A converter varies, the output voltage varies accordingly. For a fixed input code some D/A converters are designed so that the change in the output current, I_T, is linear with respect to the variation in the reference voltage. In such cases, the output of the D/A converter is the product of the digital input and the reference input. D/A converters designed for this type of operation are called *multiplying D/A converters*.

If a multiplying D/A converter is designed to accept a unipolar digital code and a positive reference voltage, it operates in a single quadrant. If it accepts a bipolar code, it operates in two quadrants. Two-quadrant multiplication also results when the multiplying D/A converter accepts only a unipolar digital code but operates with a reference voltage of either polarity. Four-quadrant multiplication results when a multiplying D/A converter operates with bipolar digital codes and a bipolar reference.

Multiplying D/A converters are used in microprocessor systems for digital gain control. A noninverting digitally controlled op-amp is shown in Fig. 11.3-7.

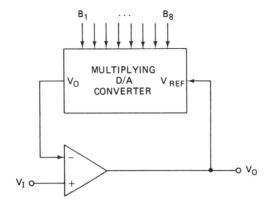

Figure 11.3-7. Multiplying D/A converter used to implement digitally programmed amplifier gain.

In this system, the multiplying D/A converter controls the fraction of the operational amplifier's output voltage which is fed back to the inverting input. Thus,

$$V_I = PV_O$$

where P is the fraction represented by the input code. Then:

$$V_O = \frac{1}{P} V_I$$

If an 8-bit multiplying D/A converter is used, V_O could range from

$$V_O = \frac{1}{\frac{255}{256}} V_I$$

$$= 1.004 V_I \text{ for a straight binary code, FFH}$$

to

$$V_O = \frac{1}{\frac{1}{256}} V_I$$

$$= 256 V_I \text{ for code 01H}$$

11.4 D/A CONVERTER SPECIFICATIONS[3]

The accuracy of a calibrated DAC is defined in several ways. In each definition, the value referred to as the device's **accuracy** is actually its *inaccuracy*, or error. For example, a device referred to as "having an accuracy of 1 percent" is, in fact, 99 percent accurate. Convention, however, dictates that the device be referred to as "having an accuracy of 1 percent"; "accurate to within 1 percent" would be a better statement.

One definition describes accuracy as the worst-case deviation of a DAC output from a straight line drawn between zero and full scale minus 1 lsb. The greatest attainable accuracy of a DAC is no better than $\pm 1/2$ lsb, due to its finite resolution. This definition encompasses all errors in a DAC, including its resolution, and is a measure of how closely its output approaches a desired voltage within the end points of its output voltage range.

Accuracy can also be defined as the difference between the actual output of the DAC and the output expected from calculation (see Fig. 11.3-2). This

---

[3]Resolution (Section 11.3) differs from D/A converter parameters discussed in this section in that it is a measure of the quality of a D/A converter which is strictly a function of the number of input bits and the code used. It is not a parameter which can be improved by improving the design of a D/A converter. Better resolution for a given type of code requires a converter with a greater number of bits.

definition does not include resolution error and theoretically, therefore, allows an accuracy of 0 (100 percent).

Most manufacturers' data sheets do not give accuracy specification for DACs. Instead, specifications are given for the component errors which contribute to the accuracy (or inaccuracy) of the device. These include offset, gain, linearity, and differential linearity, and are specified in terms of volts, a fraction of an lsb, or a fraction of full scale.

Two of the errors associated with a DAC, offset error and gain error, can be trimmed to zero at room temperature by using optional external adjustments. *Offset error* is the output of the DAC when the code for zero output is applied. For straight binary this is the code 00 . . . 0. Offset error is specified in millivolts, as a fraction of full scale, or as a fraction of an lsb (see Fig. 11.4-1). *Gain error* or *scale error* is the departure of the actual output from the design output for a given input code, usually full scale code.

A DAC is calibrated to reduce the offset error to zero by applying the zero digital input and adjusting an external offset trim potentiometer to produce zero analog output. To eliminate gain error, the full scale digital input is applied after zeroing the offset error, and an external gain trim potentiometer is adjusted to give full scale output minus 1 lsb. Calibration to eliminate offset and gain errors is only valid for the temperature at which the calibration is made. Changes in this temperature cause a nonzero offset and gain error, referred to as *offset drift* and *gain drift*, respectively. Offset and gain drift in parts per million per degree centigrade (ppm/°C) specify the sensitivity of a DAC to changes in temperature. Other sources of error in a DAC cannot be trimmed to zero.

Linearity (actually nonlinearity) specifies the deviation of the DAC output from a straight line drawn through the end points of its transfer function and is one of the major measures of a DAC's performance. A curve is monotonic if there is no change in the sign of its slope. For a DAC to be *monotonic*, each step must be greater than zero. The linearity of a DAC must be less than or equal to ±1/2 lsb for it to be monotonic. Thus a ±1/2 lsb linearity specification guarantees monotonicity.

Differential nonlinearity indicates the difference between the actual voltage step size and the ideal 1 lsb step size at any code change for the DAC. Differential linearity is a measure of the smoothness of the DAC's output curve.

Other specifications for a DAC relate to its dynamic performance. Settling time is the time required, after a code transition, for the output to settle to within a specified limit of the final value. This limit is frequently ±1/2 lsb or a percentage of FS (see Fig. 11.2-9). Settling time is primarily a function of the type of switches, resistors, and output amplifier (if any) used in the construction of the DAC. Often, it is defined as the time that elapses from the point at which the output begins to change to the point at which it reaches its final value, within a specified limit. This does not include the delay from the time of the input code changes to the time the output starts to change.

One of the major contributors to the settling time of a DAC, in addition to those normally associated with any electronic device, is the presence of glitches.

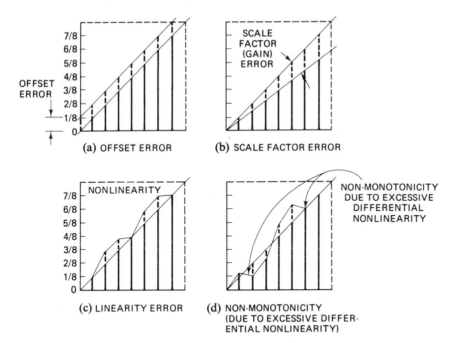

Figure 11.4-1. Typical sources of error for a 3-bit D/A converter. (Courtesy of Analog Devices.)

Glitches are spikes in the analog output that may result when, due to the occurrence of an intermediate input state, the output is driven toward a value opposite to its final value. An intermediate state is the result of one or more of the switches in the DAC being faster than the others. Consider the input of an 8-bit DAC being changed from 10000000 to 01111111. If the msb switches faster than the other bits, an intermediate state of 00000000 could occur, which would momentarily drive the output toward 0 V.

11.5 MICROPROCESSOR TO D/A CONVERTER INTERFACE

In principle, any D/A converter can be interfaced to any microprocessor. However, for some D/A converters a substantial amount of additional hardware and software is necessary. For others, the hardware for interfacing to the microprocessor is part of the D/A converter; these are *microprocessor compatible*.

Interfacing an 8-bit microprocessor to a D/A converter that is not directly microprocessor compatible is straightforward if the converter has 8 or fewer bits and accepts T^2L inputs. All that is necessary is a latch connected to the data bus to hold the inputs to the D/A converter and the generation of an appropriate device select pulse.

For D/A converters of 9 bits or more, special care is required. Assume that a 12-bit D/A converter is to be interfaced to an 8-bit microprocessor. Since only

8 bits of data can be transferred from the microprocessor at a time, two latches are needed just to hold the 12 bits of data. However, if the two latches which provide the input data to the D/A converter are loaded by two successive instructions or successive write machine cycles of a single instruction, a period of time exists where a portion of the data input to the D/A converter is from the previous word to be converted and a portion is from the new word to be converted. The output of the D/A converter during this period of time is erroneous and produces additional glitch problems.

Double buffering solves the problem, as is shown in Fig. 11.5-1. The 8 low order bits of the 12-bit word are output to latch 1 first. The 4 high order bits are then output to latch 3. The device select pulse, which clocks the 4 bits from the data bus into latch 3, also clocks the output of latch 1 into latch 2. Thus, all 12 bits, $B_1 \ldots B_{12}$, appear at the input of the D/A converter simultaneously.

If memory mapped I/O is used, a single instruction, SHLD, transfers all 12 bits. The first memory write cycle of the SHLD instruction transfers the contents of register L to latch 1. The second cycle transfers the low order 4 bits of register H to latch 3.

An example of a monolithic, microprocessor-compatible D/A converter is Analog Device's AD7522 (see Fig. 11.5-2). This device is a CMOS, 10-bit multiplying D/A converter packaged in a 28-pin DIP. The AD7522 requires a $+15$ V main supply and a logic supply of $+5$ V for a T^2L interface. It is double buffered, as shown in Fig. 11.5-2, allowing direct interface of the 10-bit converter to an 8-bit data bus. The 10-bit word to be converted is loaded as 2 bytes (Fig. 11.5-3). The least significant byte is loaded first on the positive edge of the Low Byte Strobe (LBS). The most significant 2 bits of the 10-bit word are

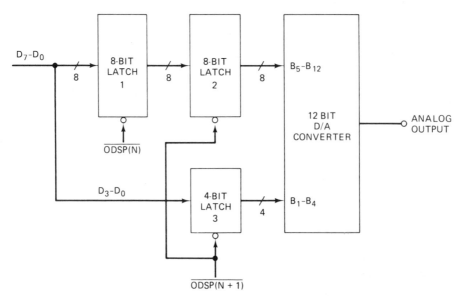

Figure 11.5-1. Double buffering inputs to a D/A converter.

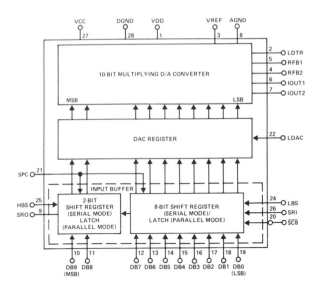

Figure 11.5-2. AD7522 10-bit, double buffered, multiplying D/A converter. (Courtesy of Analog Devices.)

obtained from D_1 and D_0 of the data bus and loaded by the positive edge of the High Byte Strobe (HBS). The DAC register is loaded by a positive level at LDAC. LDAC is connected in common with HBS in Fig. 11.5-3 to load the most significant 2 bits and the 10-bit DAC register simultaneously.

An external voltage reference and an op-amp for current to voltage conversion are necessary for AD7522 operation. Current to voltage conversion circuitry for unipolar binary operation is shown in Fig. 11.5-3. A fixed feedback resistor is also provided in the AD7522, and an adjustable resistor is added externally.

Fabrication methods other than monolithic are used in D/A converters: hybrid (multichip) circuit devices and discrete component converters—frequently packaged as potted modules—are common. Discrete component devices are noted for the highest performance, followed by hybrid, then monolithic devices. Binary converters with 6 to 16 bits and BCD converters with 2- to 4-digit resolution are common.

All commercial DACs are characterized by current or voltage output, or both. Voltage references and current to voltage output amplifiers, however, may or may not be included in the package. Frequently, monolithic D/A converters do not include either, as is the case with the AD7522. Those converters which do contain an internal voltage reference, however, often allow it to be bypassed by an external voltage reference when a voltage range other than that provided by the internal reference is desired or when higher accuracy and stability than those of the internal reference are required.

Hybrid and modular DACs specifically designed for use as microprocessor compatible peripherals contain, in addition to data latches, all the necessary

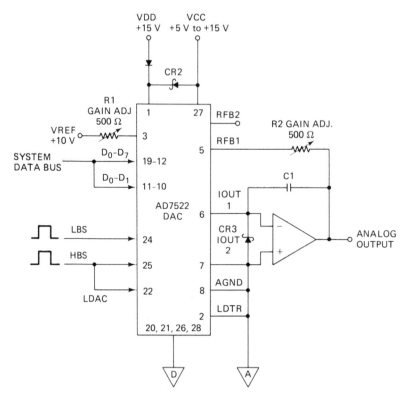

Figure 11.5-3. AD7522 10-bit D/A converter configured for unipolar binary operation and two-byte parallel loading.

interface timing and address decoding logic. For example, Burr-Brown's MP-10 hybrid DAC microperipheral contains two 8-bit DACs and the logic required for compatibility with the 8080/8085A microprocessor. The complete system is contained in a 32-pin, triple-width DIP. Address, data, and control pins facilitate connection to the microprocessor system buses.

During operation, the latches associated with the DACs are treated as two consecutive memory locations. The particular output channel is selected by address bit A_0, and a single SHLD instruction referenced to the lower of the two addresses loads both latches. The output voltage range is ± 10 V, and the input code is complementary offset binary. Output settling time is 25 μS.

11.6 ANALOG-TO-DIGITAL CONVERTERS

Analog-to-digital converters (A/D converters, ADCs) perform two basic operations: quantization and coding. *Quantization* is the mapping of a continuous signal into one of several possible discrete ranges, or quanta. *Coding* is the assignment of a binary code to each discrete range. The same codes used as inputs to D/A converters are used as outputs from A/D converters: binary, BCD, sign-plus magnitude, two's complement, one's complement, and offset binary.

Figure 11.6-1 illustrates the transfer characteristics of a 3-bit straight binary unipolar A/D converter. An n-bit binary A/D converter has 2^n distinct output codes. Thus, the 3-bit converter has eight distinct output codes represented on the vertical axis. The continuous analog input range on the horizontal axis is portioned into quanta by *transition points* or *decision levels*. The size of each quanta is its quantization size: $Q = FS/2^n$. The midpoint of each quanta is the analog voltage which is exactly represented by the output code assigned to that quanta. For example, transition points at $1/16$ FS and $3/16$ FS bracket the $1/8$ FS point. An analog input in the quanta from $1/16$ FS to $3/16$ FS is assigned the output code representing $1/8$ FS (001). Thus, quantization involves an inherent error of $\pm Q/2$. Ideally, the output, M, from an A/D converter indicates that the analog input has a value of $M \pm Q/2$ ($M \pm FS/2^{n+1}$). The only way that quantization error can be reduced is by using an A/D converter with a larger number of bits. In a practical converter, the placement of the transition points is not precise due to nonlinearity and offset and gain errors, and, therefore, additional error is introduced into the output along with the inherent quantization error.

Errors in A/D converters are defined and measured in terms of the location of the actual transition points in relation to their ideal locations (see Fig. 11.6-2).

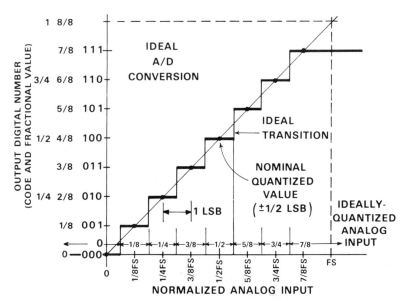

Figure 11.6-1. Conversion relationship for an ideal 3-bit straight binary A/D converter. (Courtesy of Analog Devices.)

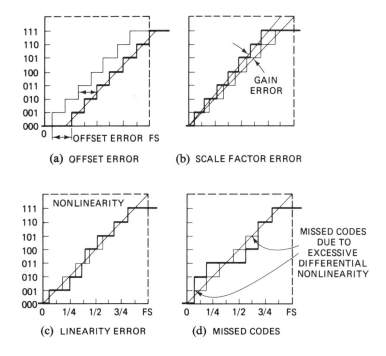

Figure 11.6-2. Typical sources of error for a 3-bit A/D converter. (Courtesy of Analog Devices.)

If the first transition does not occur at exactly $+1/2$ lsb, an offset error results. If the difference between the points at which the last transition and first transition occur is not equal to $FS - 2$ lsb, a gain error occurs. A linearity error occurs if the differences between transition points are not all equal, in which case the midpoints of some decision quanta do not lie on a straight line between 0 and $FS - 1$ lsb. Differential nonlinearity describes the variation in quanta size between adjacent pairs of codes. And, if the differential nonlinearity is greater than $\pm 1/2$ lsb, then the possibility of missing codes exists.

11.6.1 Comparators

The simplest ADC is a 1-bit converter constructed from a comparator. Even with its large quantization error, it is useful for determining whether an analog signal is above or below some threshold value. It is also used as a component in the construction of direct A/D converters with multibit outputs.

Comparators are available in integrated circuit form and are, essentially, open loop op-amps; i.e., their outputs saturate at the highest positive level if the noninverting input terminal is more positive than the inverting input terminal. If, on the other hand, the inverting terminal is more positive than the noninverting terminal, the output saturates at its most negative value. When providing logic level outputs, the output is clamped at the appropriate levels.

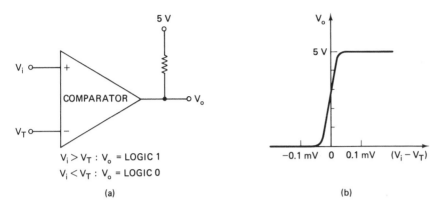

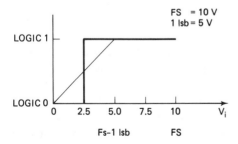

Figure 11.6-3. Comparator: (a) circuit; (b) voltage transfer characteristic.

The transfer characteristic of a comparator which has T^2L logic level outputs is shown in Fig. 11.6-3. When the comparator is used as a threshold detector, the inverting input is connected to a reference voltage equal to the threshold, and the analog signal is connected to the noninverting input. When the analog signal exceeds the threshold, the comparator outputs a logic 1. When it is below threshold, the output is logic 0.

The conversion relationship of a comparator implementing a 1-bit ADC with a nominal range of 0 to 10 V is shown in Fig. 11.6-4. The transition point is placed at $+1/2$ lsb, as is the convention for A/D converters with many bits. In the figure, 1 lsb is equal to 5 V. A reference voltage of 2.5 V is the single transition level at $+1/2$ lsb, dividing the 0 to 10 V FS range into two quanta. The end points of the transfer characteristic are 0 V and 5 V (FS − 1 lsb). The effect of actual full scale being nominal full scale minus 1 lsb is very clear and worthy of note in this example.

To construct A/D converters of n bits, two general techniques are used: direct and indirect conversion. In ***direct conversion***, the analog voltage is repeatedly compared to the output of a reference D/A converter. The D/A

Figure 11.6-4. Conversion relationship of a comparator connected to provide a 1-bit A/D converter with a nominal 0 to 10V input range.

converter's output is changed as a function of the comparison, until it eventually corresponds to the unknown analog voltage. The D/A converter's input is then the desired binary code.

With *indirect conversion*, the analog voltage is transformed to the frequency or time domain, and digital logic converts that time or frequency into a digital output code. Indirect conversion techniques are generally much slower than direct conversion techniques.

11.6.2 Counting A/D Converters

Direct conversion techniques use, as one input to a comparator, the analog voltage to be converted; the other input is the output of a D/A converter. These techniques differ, however, in the way in which the inputs to the DAC are changed to obtain the code that represents the analog input value.

The simplest implementation of these direct conversion techniques is the *counting converter*. A hardware approach (see Fig. 11.6-5) uses a counter which counts in the desired output code and provides inputs to the D/A converter. To initiate this conversion, the microprocessor generates a start of conversion, SOC, device select pulse. This pulse clears the counter and sets the flip-flop, and the Q output of the flip-flop enables the counter. The comparator's output is used as the clock input to the flip-flop. When the D/A converter's output exceeds the analog input, the comparator changes state, clocking a zero into the flip-flop and stopping the counter. The output of the flip-flop sets an end of conversion flag. When this flag is 1, the A/D converter is in operation; when it is 0, the conversion is complete.

The content of the counter is the digital code for the analog input. Conversion time for a counting converter is a function of the analog input value and the clock rate; worst-case n-bit conversion time is 2^n clock times.

A software approach to a counting converter replaces the 8-bit input port, counter, flip-flop, and clock with an 8-bit output port (see Fig. 11.6-6). A register in the microprocessor replaces the counter function. The tradeoff for hardware savings is that the microprocessor is dedicated to controlling the entire conversion and is, therefore, prevented from doing any other processing.

In operation, software first clears the counter, then outputs its contents to the port. The counter is then repeatedly incremented and output, and the comparator is checked for a change of state. When the comparator changes state, the contents of the counter and output port are equivalent to the code representing the analog voltage. The settling times of the D/A converter, of its output amplifier, if any, and of the comparator must be accomodated by the software to ensure that the comparator output is stable before it is checked by the microprocessor. The subroutine CNTCV returns the straight binary code for the analog input in register C. The subroutine is written to drive an 8-bit D/A converter that uses complementary binary input.

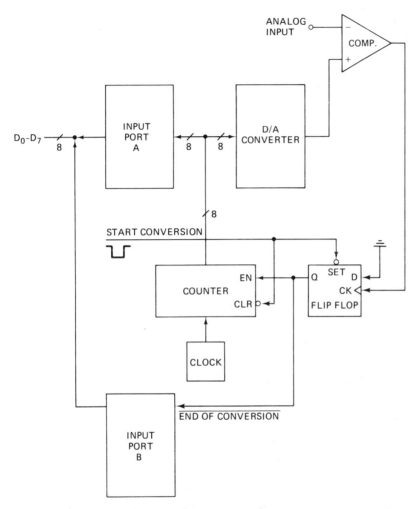

Figure 11.6-5. Hardware approach to a counting-type A/D converter.

```
CNTCV:   MVI C, 0FFH   ;  set counter to −1
STEP:    INR C
         MOV A, C      ;  complement for output
         CMA
         OUT DAC       ;  output code
         NOP           ;  as required
         IN EOC        ;  check comparator output
         ORA A
         JP STEP
         RET
```

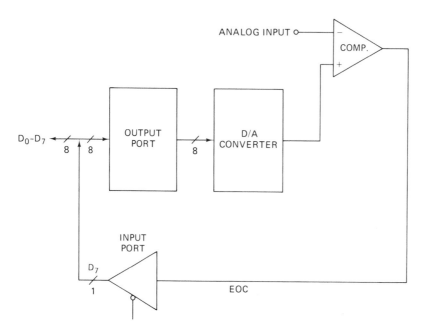

Figure 11.6-6. Basic hardware structure for software A/D conversion routines.

11.6.3 Successive Approximation A/D Converters

The most popular direct A/D conversion method, known as *successive approximation*, has the advantage of a fixed conversion time proportional to the number of bits, n, in the code. The successive approximation technique generates each bit of the code sequentially, starting with the msb. A hardware approach is similar to that for the counting A/D converter, except that the counter and flip-flop are replaced by a successive approximation register (Fig. 11.6-7). The *successive approximation register*, SAR, is a sequential control that generates inputs to the D/A converter to carry out the following successive approximation conversion algorithm:

1. The msb of the SAR output is set to 1.
2. If the comparator output is 1, this bit is reset; if not, it remains set.
3. If all bits have not been tested, the next most significant bit is set to 1, and then step (2) is repeated; if all bits have been tested, the conversion process is complete.

This algorithm first tests to see whether the analog voltage is greater or less than 1/2 FS. If it is greater, setting the most significant bit does not make the comparator output logic 1. The most significant bit output from the SAR is left logic 1, the next most significant bit is set to 1, and the analog input is tested to see whether it is greater than 3/4 FS. If the previous test of the most significant

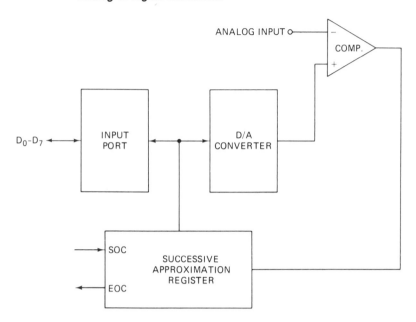

Figure 11.6-7. Hardware approach to successive approximation conversion.

bit made the comparator output logic 1, then the analog voltage is less than $1/2$ FS, and the most significant bit is cleared. The next most significant bit is then set to 1 and tested to determine whether the unknown voltage is less than $1/4$ FS. This process is repeated in succession, for each bit until the last bit is tested.

Integrated circuit successive approximation registers are available and contain all the storage and digital control required for implementing high-speed successive approximation A/D converters. [8] Codes other than straight binary are implemented by offsetting the comparator, by changing the weight of the most significant bit, and/or by manipulating the results of the conversion.

Successive approximation A/D conversion can also be implemented in software with the same hardware structure used for the counting A/D converter (see Fig. 11.6-6). The subroutine of Fig. 11.6-8 implements the successive approximation algorithm for an 8-bit conversion, using isolated I/O with an 8-bit output port and a 1-bit input port.

An interesting variation of this approach uses memory mapped I/O and no input or output ports. The inputs of the D/A converter are connected to the address bus, and the comparator's output is connected through a three-state buffer to the data bus. Thus the converter, comparator, and three-state buffer are treated as a 256×1 ROM. The code to be tested is created in the H and L registers and output to the D/A converter by executing a MOV M, A instruction. During instruction execution, the address bus supplies the input to the D/A converter. One bit of the data obtained in response to the address is the output of the comparator, which is input to the accumulator. The combined

```
SAAD:   LXI  B, 8000H   ;   SET MSB OF B, CLEAR C
TEST:   MOV  A, C       ;   CREATE CODE TO BE TESTED
        ORA  B
        MOV  D, A       ;   SAVE NEW TEST CODE
        CMA             ;   COMPLEMENT TEST CODE IF DAC REQUIRES
        OUT  DAC        ;   OUTPUT TO D/A CONVERTER
        IN   COMP       ;   INPUT COMPARATOR OUTPUT
        ORA  A          ;   SET FLAGS
        JM HIGH
        MOV  C, D       ;   REPLACE LAST APPROXIMATION WITH NEW
HIGH:   MOV  A, B       ;   ROTATE TEST BIT AND CHECK FOR END OF
        RRC             ;   CONVERSION
        RC              ;   RETURN WHEN ALL EIGHT BITS TESTED
        MOV  B, A       ;   ESTABLISH NEW TEST BIT
        JMP  TEST
```

Figure 11.6-8. Subroutine for successive approximation A/D conversion using the hardware shown in Figure 11.6-6.

settling time of the D/A converter and comparator must be less than 575 nS when used with an 8085A running at 3MHz, or a wait state is required. This technique provides a faster conversion time at the expense of a loss in available memory space.

11.6.4 Voltage to Frequency Converters

One method of indirect conversion transforms the unknown analog voltage to a frequency which is then converted to a digital word. See Fig. 11.6-9. Transformation of the analog voltage is handled by a *Voltage Controlled Oscillator, VCO*. The output frequency of a VCO is proportional to its input voltage. Low cost VCOs can be configured from a single IC together with a few discrete components. For example, the interconnection of a National LM 131 VCO, seven resistors, and three capacitors constitutes a circuit which accepts an input voltage in the range of 0 to 10 V and outputs a corresponding frequency between 10 Hz and 10 kHz, respectively. This circuit provides a linearity of ±0.03 percent.

The output from the VCO in Fig. 11.6-9 is gated by a fixed duration sample gate. This sampling gate can be 1 bit of an output port toggled under program control, in which case its duration is controlled by a software delay. The sampling gate could also be the output from a programmable timer. When the sampling gate is logic 1, pulses from the VCO are counted by the counter. At the end of the sample period, the counter contains a value corresponding to the unknown analog voltage.

The resolution of a voltage to frequency converter is partially determined by the number of counter bits. For maximum resolution, the designer must de-

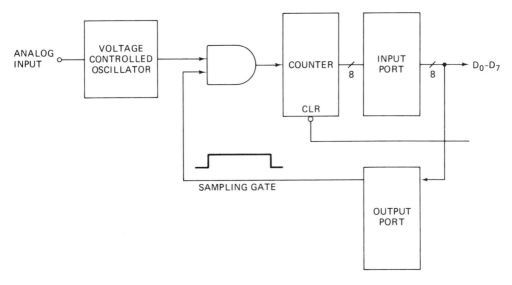

Figure 11.6-9. Voltage to frequency A/D converter.

termine the duration of the sample gate corresponding to the largest possible count, without overflow, for the frequency equivalent to full scale VCO output.

11.6.5 Pulse Width Converters

Another approach to indirect conversion transforms the unknown analog signal to the time domain by using the measurand to modulate the duration of a pulse. The width of the pulse changes in proportion to the changes in the measurand. This approach can be implemented with a monostable multivibrator, or single shot, if a transducer is available to transform changes in the measurand to a change in the resistance or capacitance. (See Fig. 11.6-10). The duration of the output pulse, T, from the single shot is a function of the external timing components R and C. For example, with a 74121 single shot, $T = RC\ln2$. Either R is a resistive or C is a capacitive transducer.

To carry out a conversion, the counter is cleared, and the single shot is triggered by device select pulses. The output of the single shot gates pulses from a stable, fixed frequency clock to the counter. After the single shot times out, the contents of the counter are used by the microprocessor to determine the desired digital code.

11.6.6 Dual Slope Integrating A/D Converters

Integrating A/D converters use an indirect method of A/D conversion, whereby the analog voltage is converted to a time period that is measured by a counter. There are several variations of the integrating A/D converter: single

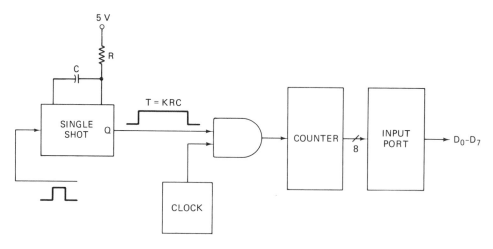

Figure 11.6-10. Pulse width A/D converter.

ramp, dual ramp, and triple ramp. The dual ramp or dual slope-type is employed in many monolithic A/D converters and digital voltmeters.

A dual slope A/D converter circuit is shown in Fig. 11.6-11. An electronic switch selects either an unknown analog voltage or a reference voltage as the circuit's input. At the start of the conversion, the counter is cleared, and the unknown analog voltage is selected as input to the integrator. When the output ramp of the integrator crosses the comparator's threshold, $v_O = 0$ V, the counter is enabled and counts clock pulses. It counts for a fixed time interval, T, until it overflows. For a constant value analog input, the slope of the integrator's ramp output is proportional to the unknown input, and thus the output voltage of the integrator at the end of the fixed time interval, T, is proportional to the analog output. If the analog input varies during the fixed time interval, the integrator's output at the end of this interval is proportional to the average value (integral) of the input, v_I, over the fixed time inteval.

$$v_O(T) = -\frac{1}{RC}\int_0^T v_I \, dt$$

At the end of T, the input of the integrator is switched from the analog input to the reference voltage, making the integrator output a ramp with a fixed positive slope. The counter counts the time required for the integrator's output to reach the comparator's threshold; when it is reached, the counter is stopped. The value left in the counter is the code for the analog voltage. This can be verified by examining the relationship for $v_O(T + \tau)$

$$v_O(T + \tau) = -\frac{1}{RC}\int_T^{T+\tau}(-V_{\text{REF}}) \, dt + v_O(T)$$

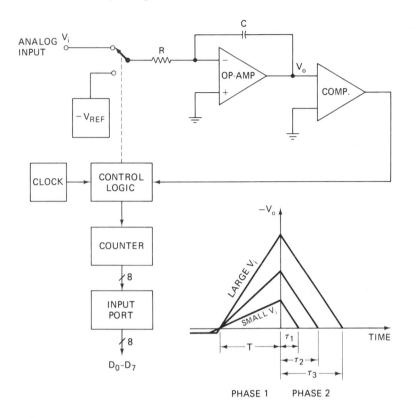

Figure 11.6-11. Dual slope integrating A/D converter.

$v_O(T)$ is the initial condition at time T, thus:

$$v_O(T + \tau) = -\frac{1}{RC}\int_T^{T+\tau}(-V_{\mathbf{REF}})\,dt - \frac{1}{RC}\int_0^T v_I\,dt$$

Since $v_O(T + \tau) = 0$,

$$\frac{1}{RC}\int_T^{T+\tau}V_{\mathbf{REF}}\,dt = \frac{1}{RC}\int_0^T v_I\,dt$$

$$v_{\mathbf{REF}}\tau = \hat{v}_I T$$

$$\hat{v}_I = \frac{\tau}{T}V_{\mathbf{REF}}$$

Thus, the average value of v_I, $\hat{v}_I$, is equal to the ratio of the counts multiplied by $V_{\mathbf{REF}}$, the value remaining in the counter.

Hardware integrating A/D converters are, typically, low-speed devices. However, they are capable of high accuracy at low cost. Commercial integrating

A/D converters generally include an additional phase which precedes the first phase of Fig. 11.6-11, during which the device carries out a self-calibrating auto zero operation.

11.7 SAMPLE AND HOLD CIRCUITS

A *sample and hold* circuit does for analog signals what a D-type flip-flop does for digital signals. At the command of a digital control signal, a sample and hold circuit stores the value of the input analog signal. The stored analog value is available to the circuit's output until the circuit is subsequently commanded to store a new value.

When used at the input to an A/D converter, a sample and hold acquires an analog signal at the precise time dictated by a digital control signal. The A/D converter can then convert the voltage held at the output of the sample and hold. This minimizes inaccuracies in the converted value of an analog signal due to changes in the signal's value during the conversion process. Without a sample and hold, an A/D converter must complete its conversion before the analog input changes $\pm 1/2$ lsb, or the result is inaccurate. Sample and hold circuits are also used at the output of D/A converters to minimize glitches that appear as the output changes from one level to another. Here the circuit samples the output after the settling time of the converter has elapsed.

In its simplest form a sample and hold circuit can be implemented by a switch and capacitor, as shown in Fig. 11.7-1. When the switch is closed, the circuit is in the sample mode and the output signal, v_O, follows the input signal, v_I. Since the circuit in this figure is ideal, the output voltage exactly follows the input voltage. When the switch is open, the circuit is in the hold mode, and the capacitor indefinitely maintains the output voltage at the value that existed at the instant the switch was opened.

Although the switch position in Fig. 11.7-1 is controlled by a logic level signal, a logic gate cannot implement the switch because the precise value of the voltage at the input and output of the switch is important. Instead, an analog switch or analog gate must be used. Analog switches can be constructed from diodes, bipolar transistors, or field effect transistors, and circuits can be constructed by using any one of the devices as the switch—as long as the resistance of the switch, when closed, is very small and, when open, is very large.

A practical sample and hold circuit buffers the switch and capacitor from the source and load. See Fig. 11.7-2. In this example, two operational amplifiers configured as unity gain buffers are used. Op-amp A_1 presents a high input impedance to the analog input voltage source and a low output impedance to the switch and capacitor. This allows the capacitor to be charged as rapidly as possible when the switch is closed. The time that elapses from the occurrence of the sample command to the point at which the output has a value within a specified error band around the input value is known as the *acquisition time* or *hold settling time*. After the output achieves this specified error band, it tracks

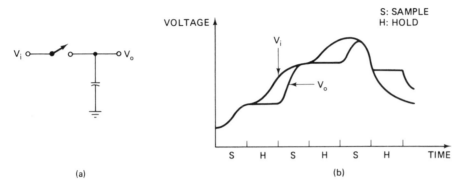

(a)   (b)

Figure 11.7-1. Idealized representation of a simple sample and hold circuit: (a) circuit; (b) input-output characteristic.

the input. The switch shown in Fig. 11.7-2 is closed when the control voltage, $V_C = 0$ V and is open when $V_C = 5$ V. When the control signal switches to 5 V, the switch opens, and the sample and hold is in the hold mode. The finite amount of time required between the transition of the control signal to the hold state and the actual opening of the switch is known as the *aperture time*.

Op-amp A_2 provides a buffer between the storage capacitor and the output. Without A_2, the capacitor could discharge very quickly through the load resistance. With the switch open in the hold mode, the charge on the capacitor, which stores the analog voltage, decays over a period of time because the resistance of the open analog switch and the resistance of the noninverting input terminal of A_2, although large, are not infinite. Thus, a practical sample and hold circuit cannot indefinitely maintain its output voltage in the hold mode. The rate at which the output voltage decays for a particular sample and hold circuit in the hold mode is its *decay* or *droop rate*. A number of variations exist in the circuit of Fig. 11.7-2 that provide improved operational characteristics.

Numerous integrated circuit sample and hold devices are available which contain buffer amplifiers, an analog switch, and a switch driver in a single package. An external hold capacitor completes the circuit. Such a sample and hold device is represented by the symbol shown in Fig. 11.7-3.

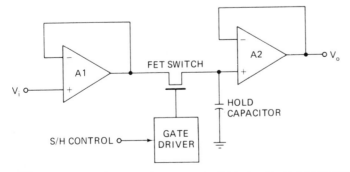

Figure 11.7-2. Implementation of a practical sample and hold circuit.

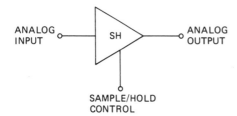

Figure 11.7-3. Symbol for a complete sample and hold circuit.

11.8 ANALOG MULTIPLEXERS AND DEMULTIPLEXERS

Although its data inputs and outputs are analog voltages, an analog multiplexer is similar in operation to a digital multiplexer in that a binary code at its address inputs selects one of several possible analog data inputs for transmission to the output. A multiplexer facilitates the handling by an ADC of several analog inputs on a time multiplexed basis. In Fig. 11.8-1, an analog multiplexer controlled by the microprocessor selects the channel to be input to the A/D converter.

Analog switches similar to the type used in sample and hold circuits (Fig. 11.7-2) can also be used to fabricate analog multiplexers. However, off-the-shelf integrated circuit analog multiplexers are available which include the necessary decoding logic for channel selection, level translators, switch drivers, and the analog switches themselves.

Connecting a voltage reference source, V_R, to one input channel of an analog multiplexer and connecting 0 V to another input of the analog multiplexer provides the capability to correct for offset and gain error in an A/D

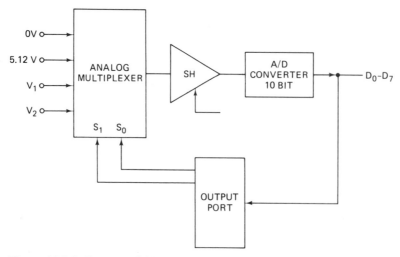

Figure 11.8-1. Data acquisition system with four-channel analog multiplexer.

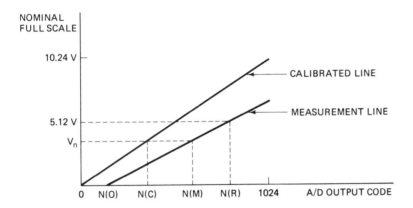

Figure 11.8-2. Graphical representation of calibration relationship for A/D conversion system of Figure 11.8-1.

output, when signals from the multiplexer channels carrying analog information are converted to digital. Ideally, the signal paths from the reference voltage and ground are identical to the signal paths from the analog information sources.

Prior to the conversion of an analog signal, the 0 V and V_R voltages are each converted, and these numbers—$N(0)$ and $N(R)$, respectively—are stored in memory. The analog signal, V_M, is then converted, giving $N(M)$, and this result is used by the microprocessor to compute the corrected measurand voltage.

$$V_M = \frac{N(M) - N(0)}{N(R) - N(0)} V_R$$

Figure 11.8-2 shows this relationship for a system that provides a 10-bit conversion of analog voltages of a nominal 10.24 V FS. The reference input voltage, V_R, is 5.12 V.

Analog demultiplexers are similar in operation to digital demultiplexers, with the exception that the data inputs and outputs are analog voltages. A binary code at the address inputs of the analog demultiplexer selects the channel on which the analog input voltage is output (see Fig. 11.1-2). If the output voltage at a particular channel must be maintained for a period of time, a sample and hold is used at the output.

11.9 MULTICHANNEL DATA ACQUISITION SYSTEMS

There are a multitude of structures for the acquisition and conversion of a number of channels of analog data. These multichannel *Data Acquisition Systems, DAS,* differ in the degree to which their various components are time shared.

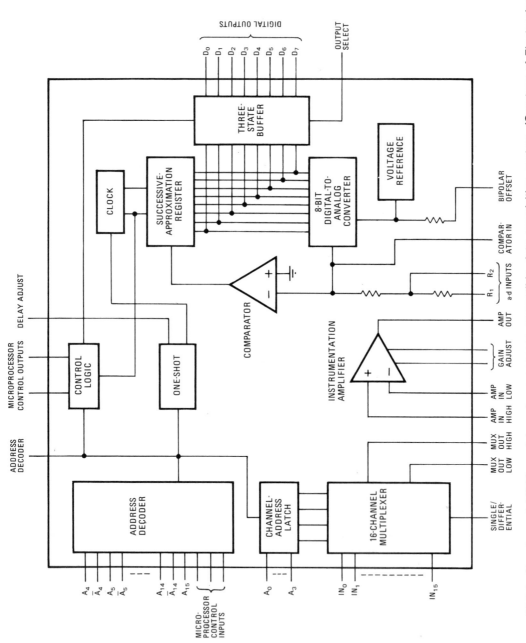

Figure 11.9-1. Structure of MP20 modular microprocessor compatible data acquisition system. (Courtesy of *Electronics*.)

Several modular and single board DASs are directly microprocessor compatible. Most of these are similar to the system shown in Fig. 11.1-1 and involve the greatest degree of component sharing. The structure of a typical modular unit, MP20, is shown in Fig. 11.9-1. This structure is implemented as a hybrid circuit contained in a single package. The unit contains an analog multiplexer, which accepts 16 single-ended or eight differential analog signals; an instrumentation amplifier; an 8-bit successive approximation A/D converter; three-state output buffers; and decoding and control logic. Sixteen-channel, single-ended or 8-channel differential operation is determined by external hardwired connections between the multiplexer output and instrumentation amplifier input. The gain of the instrumentation amplifier is programmed by a single external resistor, allowing input signal ranges as low as ± 10 mV.

This module is designed to be interfaced to a microprocessor using memory mapped I/O. Eleven address select lines are externally hardwired to establish the address to which the module will respond. The address decoder uses bits A_4–A_{15} to select the DAS. The remaining four address bits, A_0–A_3, select the channel to be converted. Each analog input channel occupies one memory location. An LDA or MOV instruction inputs the results of a conversion from one channel, or the LHLD instruction can input data from two channels. A READY signal places the microprocessor in the WAIT state until the conversion is complete. Conversion time is 35 μS per channel on the ± 5 V or 0 to 5 V input range to achieve an absolute accuracy of ± 0.4 percent.

Single board DASs provide additional capabilities such as software selectable gains for an instrumentation amplifier, allowing the selection of different gains for different channels or different gains for varying input levels on the same channel. Thus, the dynamic range of a 12-bit converter can be expanded to 15 bits if gains of 1, 2, 4, and 8 are selectable. Real-time clocks called *pacer clocks* are available on some systems to generate precisely timed pulses that trigger the accurately spaced A/D conversions.

Certain single board systems are designed to treat each analog channel as a memory location. Conversion is triggered by a memory read instruction, and the microprocessor is placed in a WAIT state until the conversion is complete. In systems which operate under program control, commands control those registers on the DAS which select the channel and gain and initiate the conversion. An end-of-conversion bit in a status word is checked to determine completion of the conversion. Alternatively, a pacer clock may initiate the conversion and generate an interrupt when the conversion is complete. Other multichannel data acquisition structures are implemented with integrated and modular components.

In contrast to the structure of multichannel DASs which utilize maximum sharing of components, in parallel structures each channel has its own signal conditioning, sample and hold, and A/D converter. Signals are multiplexed into the microprocessor by using a digital multiplexer. With the low cost of IC analog components, such a structure is economically feasible in many applications and provides a very high throughput.

REFERENCES

1. NORTON, H.N., *Handbook of Transducers for Electronic Measuring Systems*. Englewood Cliffs, New Jersey: Prentice-Hall, Inc., 1969.

2. OLIVER, F.J., *Practical Instrumentation Transducers*. Rochelle Park, New Jersey: Hayden Book Co., 1971.

3. HARVEY, G.F. (Ed.), *ISA Transducer Compendium*. New York: Instrument Society of America, IFI Plenum, Part 1, 1969; Part 2, 1970; Part 3, 1972.

4. WAIT, J.V., L.P. HUELSMAN, and G.A. KORN, *Introduction to Operational Amplifier Theory and Applications*. New York: McGraw-Hill Book Company, 1975.

5. STOUT, D.F., and M. KAUFMAN, *Handbook of Operational Amplifier Circuit Design*. New York: McGraw-Hill Book Company, 1976.

6. ROBERGE, J.K. *Operational Amplifiers: Theory and Practice*. New York: John Wiley & Sons, Inc., 1975.

7. HOESCHELE, D.F., Jr., *Analog-to-Digital and Digital-to-Analog Conversion Techniques*. New York: John Wiley and Sons, Inc., 1968.

8. GHEST, R.C., *A Successive Approximation Register*, (Application Note). Sunnyvale, California: Advanced Micro Devices, Inc.

9. FREEMAN, W., and W. RITMANICH, "Cut A/D Conversion Cost by Using Software and D/A Converters," *Electronic Design*, No. 9, April 26, 1977, pp. 86–89.

10. *Analog Switches and Their Applications*. Santa Clara, California: Siliconix, Inc., 1976.

BIBLIOGRAPHY

GARRETT, P.H., *Analog Systems for Microprocessors and Minicomputers*, Reston, Virginia: Reston Publishing Company, Inc., 1978.

MORRISON, R., *DC Amplifier in Instrumentation*. New York: John Wiley & Sons, Inc., 1970.

———*Grounding and Shielding Techniques in Instrumentation*. New York: John Wiley & Sons, Inc., 1967.

SCHMID, H., *Electronic Analog/Digital Conversions*. New York: Van Nostrand Reinhold Company, 1970.

SHEINGOLD, D.H. (Ed.), *Analog-Digital Conversion Notes*. Norwood, Massachusetts: Analog Devices Inc., 1977.

WOOLVET, G.A., *Transducers in Digital Systems*. Forest Grove, Oregon: International Scholarly Book Services, 1977.

PROBLEMS

11-1. Write the equation for the output voltage of a two-digit BCD D/A converter as a function of the reference voltage, V_{REF}, and the input bits d_1 to d_8, where d_1 is the most significant bit. Assume that the D/A converter uses a 10 V reference:
   a. what is the maximum output voltage?
   b. what is the step size?
   c. what is the percent resolution?

11-2. Using a single chip 8-bit binary D/A converter with a 10 V output and op-amp(s), design an 8-bit two's complement D/A converter with a -5 V to $+5$ V output. Also design an appropriate interface for the D/A converter to an 8085A system.

11-3. An 8-bit binary multiplying D/A converter is used in the feedback loop of a buffer amplifier circuit as shown to implement a programmable gain amplifier. The A/D converter has a 0 to 10 V input range.
   a. What is the equation for V_0 of the programmable gain amplifier as a function of its analog and digital inputs?
   b. What code should be applied to the programmable gain amplifier, for each channel in the diagram below, in order to provide maximum resolution?

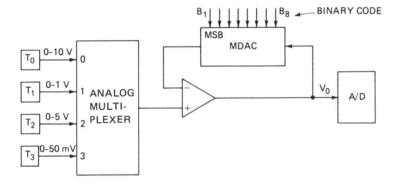

11-4. Draw the circuit diagram of a two-digit weighted resistor D/A converter which uses a single op-amp. Indicate the values of all resistors used in the circuit. Each of the input digits is coded in the 2421 code below. The smallest input resistor to be used is 1 kΩ. The output of the D/A converter is to be 0 to 10 V, nominal. What is the resolution and step size of the converter?

Decimal digit	Code 2421		Decimal digit	Code 2421
0	0000		5	1011
1	0001		6	1100
2	0010		7	1101
3	0011		8	1110
4	0100		9	1111

11.5.   A 10-bit binary analog-to-digital (A/D) converter is to be interfaced to an 8085A microprocessor using linear selection. The A/D converter has a control input, SOC, which, when triggered by the leading edge of a positive pulse, begins a conversion of the analog input. The signal, EOC, from the A/D converter goes low when a conversion is in progress, and becomes logic 1 at the end of the conversion. Using isolated I/O, draw a logic diagram of the hardware, and write a subroutine which causes a conversion, inputs the converted data, and stores it in two bytes of reserved memory labelled DATA.

11-6.   An A/D converter similar to the one in problem 11-5 but with an 8-bit output is to be interfaced to an 8085A. In this case synchronization is to be accomplished using the microprocessor's READY line. Draw the logic required for interfacing, and write the necessary driver subroutine.

11-7.   Draw the logic diagram of a hardware structure to support software driven A/D conversion. A 10-bit D/A converter, comparator, three-state buffer, and logic for device selection is all the hardware to be used. The D/A converter is to be treated as if it were a $1,024 \times 1$ block of memory. The data inputs of the D/A converter are to be connected to the address bus. Describe the timing constraints on the circuit for it to operate properly. Write a subroutine that implements a counting type A/D converter with this hardware.

11-8.   Draw a flowchart of a successive approximation A/D conversion which uses the hardware of Fig. 11.6-6.

11-9.   Draw the logic diagram of the hardware required to interface an AD7522 10-bit D/A (Fig. 11.5-3) to an 8085A system to implement a 10-bit software controlled successive approximation A/D converter. Write the conversion subroutine, and determine the time required to complete the conversion as a function of the microprocessor's state time.

11-10.   A voltage to frequency A/D converter is to be designed using a voltage to frequency converter with a 0 to 10 V input range and a corresponding output range of 10 Hz to 10 kHz. The A/D converter is to provide a 10-bit binary output to an 8-bit microprocessor. The gate strobe is to be provided as one bit of an output port controlled by the microprocessor.
a.   Draw a block diagram of the A/D converter and the circuitry required to interface it to an 8-bit microprocessor. It is not necessary to show address decoding.
b.   What is the duration of the gate strobe for maximum resolution? For this value of gate strobe duration, what is the A/D output count for the following input voltages: 0 V, 2.5 V, and 5 V?

11-11. Using as little additional hardware as possible, design using an op-amp, analog multiplexer, and comparator a 10-bit dual slope integrating A/D converter.

11-12. Write a subroutine which uses the circuit of Fig. 11.8-1 and the relationship of Fig. 11.8-2 to correct the binary result of the conversion of unknown voltages.

12

Microprocessor System Design

. . . we suggested that implementation, maintenance, and modification would be minimized if the system could be designed in such a way that its pieces were small, easily related to the application, and relatively independent of one another. This means, then, that good design is an exercise in partitioning and organizing the pieces of a system.

By partitioning we mean the division of the problem into smaller subproblems, so that each subproblem will eventually correspond to a piece of the system. The questions are: Where and how should we divide the problem? Which aspects of the problem belong in the same part of the system, and which aspects belong in different parts? Structured design answers these questions with two basic principles:

● Highly interrelated parts of the problem should be in the same piece of the system, i.e., things that belong together should go together.

● Unrelated parts of the problem should reside in unrelated pieces of the system. That is, things that have nothing to do with one another don't belong together.

Yourdon, E., and L. L. Constantine*

*Structured Design: Fundamentals of a Discipline of Computer Program and Systems Design. Englewood Cliffs, New Jersey: Prentice-Hall, Inc., 1979.

Previous chapters primarily concern the design of systems that implement functions of limited complexity, systems whose operation can be specified in at most a few pages of natural language description, flowcharts, timing diagrams, or some combination of these. In most cases, however, these systems are actually subsystems of a larger system.

Although a few of these, such as memory subsystems, are strictly hardware, the majority can be implemented through various combinations of hardware and software. Where several designs meet the systems' requirements, the rule of thumb is: Use the most economical.

The hardware portion of a subsystem consists of an interconnection of small, medium, and large scale ICs and, usually, a few discrete components. Each IC or discrete component can, in itself, be considered a subsystem. Each implements a well-defined function and interacts with other subsystems which connect to it via an interface of electrical signals. When these smaller subsystems are SSI circuits, formal digital system synthesis techniques are used to determine the most economical interconnection to implement the function. When the subsystems are MSI or LSI devices, few formal procedures are available to specify their interconnection, making the synthesis techniques heuristic.

The software portion of a subsystem consists of an interconnection of assembly language instructions, macros, and subroutines. Like the hardware, each of these software structures can be considered a subsystem which implements a well-defined function and interacts in a predetermined manner with the other subsystems to which it is connected. This interaction is carried out through registers, flags, and calling sequences. Software interaction not only takes place with other software but also with the hardware that supports it and with the hardware it controls.

The technique of viewing a system as a subsystem or component in a larger system and the converse–viewing a system as a collection of smaller subsystems —provides a basis for the specification, design, implementation, testing, and documentation of complex systems.

A systematic, five-stage methodology implements system synthesis:

> Stage 1: Requirements Definition
> Stage 2: Systematic Design
> Stage 3: System Implementation
> Stage 4: Testing and Debugging
> Stage 5: Documentation and Maintenance

12.1 REQUIREMENTS DEFINITION

The requirements definition involves a statement of the problem, the system features required to solve that problem, the boundary conditions or environment in which those features must operate, and a justification for using the proposed system as opposed to any other.

The importance of a complete requirements definition cannot be over emphasized. It is easy at this stage to put off finding answers to difficult questions in the hope that they will somehow answer themselves as later stages progress. However, it is far more likely that serious problems will arise to confront the designer who has postponed thorough analysis.

A requirements definition, the first stage of the five-stage methodology, is itself divided into three functions: context analysis, functional specification, and design constraints.[1]

12.1.1 Context Analysis

The purpose of a context analysis is to develop a clear statement of the problem which the system is intended to solve and to thoroughly understand the technical, operational, and economic environment in which the system will be used.

Although not necessarily involved in the original context analysis, it is important that the designer be completely familiar with both the results of the analysis and the reasoning which lead to those results.

12.1.2 Functional Specification

The system functional specification designates the overall purpose of the system —what it is to accomplish—*not* how it will be accomplished or what will be used to accomplish it.

A functional specification includes the following:

1. A complete description of what the system should do.
2. The performance requirements it must meet.
3. Specific details of the operator/system interaction.
4. A specification of the system's interface with the external environment.
5. Procedures for handling errors and diagnosing malfunctions.

The operational description is drawn up in terms of required and, often, desirable features. Its purpose is to facilitate implementation decisions in later stages of development. Performance requirements of the system must also be specified completely and in detail.

Operator/system interaction may be as simple as pressing a run button or as complex as having the system monitor the commands provided by the operator and indicate errors in these commands. Or, the system may prompt the operator by requesting commands or parameter values. A functional specification of the hardware interface of a system to its operating environment includes

[1]These specific three terms were used by Ross and Schuman in [1]. The operations thus named, however, are applied universally by system designers.

designating the characteristics of all input and output signals. Some of these characteristics are listed in Table 12.1-1. The software interface primarily involves parameter passing conventions, data transmission protocols, data formats, and data structures.

TABLE 12.1-1

Characteristics of System Input and Output Signals

 1. Number and function
 2. Number of bits per input/output
 3. Code/format
 4. Data rate
 5. Duration
 6. Data transfer method—program I/O, interrupt, or DMA
 7. Handshaking/control signals
 8. Service priorities
 9. Voltage levels
10. Buffering
11. Multiplexed signals

The functional specification must determine the types of errors likely to occur in the operation of the system, and designate a method of system recovery: i.e., the system's response to these error conditions. Errors may be caused by the operator, by communication or transmission difficulties, or by mechanical or electrical failures.

The aim of error diagnosis and recovery is a system which is easy both to service and to maintain.

12.1.3 Design Constraints

The specification of design constraints sets forth the way in which the system is to be constructed and implemented. It does not specify the components which will be in the system; rather it identifies the boundary conditions by which the components will be selected.

The designer must also consider the effect of the operating environment on the system. This manifests itself in terms of physical size constraints, temperature range of operation, and hostile environmental conditions such as electrical noise, corrosive atmosphere, etc.

12.2 SYSTEMATIC DESIGN

The aim of a formulated design approach, in applications of increased system complexity, is a conceptually integrated system consisting of appropriate subsystems. These subsystems or subfunctions should be modular in nature. A system composed of interconnected modular subsystems is easier to design, document, debug, and modify.

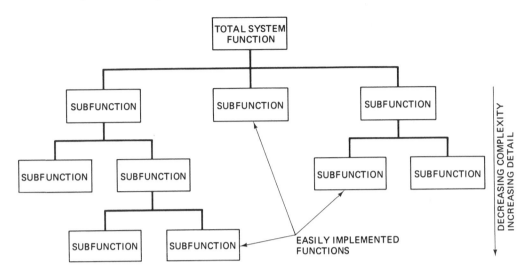

Figure 12.2-1. Partitioning of system function into less complex subfunctions.

One method, which for years has been used by engineers for designing all types of systems, has lately been given the name "top down design." Essentially, top down design identifies the total system function, then partitions it into less complex subfunctions, each of which performs a specific task. These subfunctions are, in turn, subdivided or partitioned into subfunctions of even less complexity (see Fig. 12.2-1). The partitioning process continues until relatively low complexity subfunctions amenable to easy implementation are reached.

12.2.1 Partitioning

Each level of partitioning involves increased detail. Partitioning decisions made at any particular level are constrained by decisions made at higher levels and, in turn, constrain partitioning decisions made at lower levels.

The first level partition determines the basic system structure. At its simplest, this level consists of three basic subfunctions: input, processing, and output. These are specified according to function and according to the method of interfacing with other subfunctions at the same level. Subfunctions of a modular nature, those which require minimal interfacing, are advantageous because they can be individually optimized, in terms of hardware/software tradeoffs, without seriously affecting the rest of the design. Also, at lower levels, partitioning is generally influenced by readily available software and hardware subfunctions: e.g., standard LSI.

12.2.2 Selection of an Overall Implementation Method

As partitioning continues, a sufficient amount of information is generated to reach a decision about implementation methods. At a given level, one subfunction might be implemented by one method and another by a different method.

Possible choices include nonprogrammed logic approaches, such as random logic design, or implementation with MSI or LSI. These are appropriate in low complexity systems or if standard MSI or LSI circuits easily implement the functions. They are also appropriate when very high-speed operation must be achieved, possibly by parallel execution of subfunctions. Programmed logic approaches include programmable logic arrays (PLAs) and ROM-based sequential machines. In other applications, custom LSI may be appropriate. These two methods are frequently used when the system is not of sufficient complexity to justify use of a microprocessor.

Microprocessor systems are, however, appropriate for an extremely wide range of applications. Devices used in such systems range from single-chip microcomputers to complex, high-speed microprogrammable bit slice devices. As system requirements increase, several microprocessors may be utilized within a single system. Implementation of multiple microprocessor systems requires special design considerations; see Section 12.6.[2]

12.2.3 Types of Microprocessors

In theory, any microprocessor can be used in any application as long as it is fast enough to meet the system performance requirements. In fact, however, because the choice of a microprocessor to a great extent determines the final cost of the system, microprocessor selection is of paramount importance. Although the microprocessor itself is usually an insignificant fraction of the final system cost, it does affect the selection of memory, interface circuits, power supply, and other hardware and, therefore, greatly affects the total system cost. In addition, the software development cost, the major portion of the total system cost in some designs, is also affected by the choice of microprocessor.

Microprocessors fall into three major categories:

1. Single-chip microcomputers.
2. General purpose microprocessors.
3. Bit slice microprocessors.

12.2.3.1 Single-Chip Microcomputers

Single-chip microcomputers are available in 4-, 8-, or 16-bit word lengths and typically contain the microprocessor, ROM, RWM, I/O ports, and a clock oscillator and timer. Some devices allow off-chip memory and/or I/O expansion; others don't. Many are organized for a specific class of applications; others are basically general purpose in nature. For applications which fit within the available ROM, RWM, and I/O lines, single-chip microcomputers are very cost effective.

---

[2]The presentation prior to Section 12.6 concentrates on designs where a single microprocessor is utilized.

To facilitate system development, some single-chip microcomputers are available in several versions. These microcomputers have identical architectures but differ in terms of the ROM they provide. One version, used in the final system, contains mask-programmed ROM. Another version, used in prototype development, contains EPROM, and still another version, used in the early stages of development, contains no ROM at all but allows the use of external RWM in place of it.

Single-chip microcomputer I/O lines may be fixed as input or output, or their direction may be programmable, either on a bit or word basis. Single-chip microcomputers with individually programmable I/O lines provide the greatest flexibility.

Table 12.2-1 lists a wide range of single-chip microcomputers and their features, including Intel's 8048 and 8748. The architecture of this 8-bit microcomputer is shown in Fig. 12.2-2.

The architecture of these two microcomputers is identical except the 8748 contains a 1K × 8 EPROM and the 8048 contains a 1K × 8 mask-programmable ROM. The 8748 is used for prototyping and low volume production; the 8048, for high volume production after the program code has been fully tested.

Also included in this family of devices is the 8035. This device is similar to the 8048/8748 except that it is used with external memory in place of the 1K × 8 ROM. Thus, the 8035 is not a single-chip microcomputer.

In addition to its 8-bit CPU and 1K × 8 ROM the 8048/8748 has a 64 × 8 RWM, three 8-bit I/O ports, an 8-bit timer/event counter, and three test/interrupt inputs.

The 8-bit CPU has 96 basic instructions, including many for bit, nibble, and byte manipulation. These instructions require one or two machine cycles, each consisting of five states. With a 6 MHz clock, instruction execution times are either 2.5 or 5 μs.

As shown in Table 12.2-1 Intel also provides an enlarged memory version of the 8048, the 8049. This device provides 2K × 8 of ROM and 128 × 8 of RWM. In lieu of using the 8049, however, memory expansion is possible with the 8048/8748. By using one of the ports of the 8048/8748 as a multiplexed address/data bus, devices such as the 8755 and 8155 can expand memory and I/O. An 8212 latch can demultiplex this address/data bus when standard ROM and RWM is used.

The 8048/8748 is a MOS device requiring a single 5 V supply and typically dissipating 325mW. For low power applications, Intersil provides a CMOS equivalent of the 8048/8748. This device, the 80C48/87C48 operates with a single supply voltage in the range of 5 to 10 V and dissipates only 50mW.

12.2.3.2 General Purpose Microprocessors

The category of general purpose microprocessors encompasses single and multichip devices which use external ROM, RWM, and I/O ports. External ROM and RWM are either standard semiconductor memories or multifunction devices containing a combination of ROM or RWM, I/O ports, and other

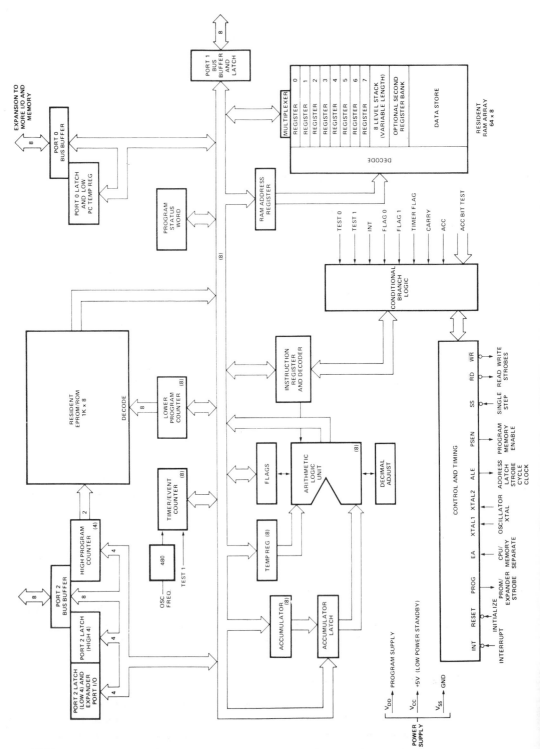

442

TABLE 12.2-1

Reprinted with permission from *Electronic Design*, Vol. 27, No. 24, November 22, 1979, copyright Hayden Publishing Co., Inc. 1979.

Original Source Manufacturer	Device	Process technology	Word size in bits (data/inst.)	On-chip RAM size	On-chip ROM/PROM size (words)	Off-chip memory expansion	Number of basic instructions	Maximum clock frequency (kHz)	On-chip clock	Instruction time (shortest/longest), μs	TTL compatible	BCD arithmetic	On-chip interrupts/levels	Subroutine nesting levels	General-purpose internal registers	Number of I/O lines	Additional special support circuits	Package size (DIP pins)	Voltages required (V)	Prototyping system avail	Assembly language programming system	High-level language programming system	Time-sharing cross software	Comments
AMI	S2000	NMOS	4/8	64×4	1024×8	No	51	1000	Yes	4.5/9	Yes	Yes	Yes/1	RAM	RAM	29	No	40	9	No	Yes	No	No	Includes display drivers and switch interface
	S2150	NMOS	4/8	64×4	1536×8	No	51	1000	Yes	4.5/9	Yes	Yes	Yes/1	RAM	RAM	29	No	40	9	No	Yes	No	No	Expanded ROM version
	S2200	NMOS	4/8	128×4	2048×10	Yes	59	1000	Yes	4.5/9	Yes	Yes	Yes/3	5	RAM	29	No	40	9	Yes	Yes	Yes	Yes	Both the 2200 and 2400 include an 8-bit a/d converter and an 8-bit d/a converter. All S2000 processors also come in an "A" version that can directly drive vacuum fluorescent displays
	S2400	NMOS	4/8	128×4	4096×10	Yes	59	1000	Yes	4.5/9	Yes	Yes	Yes/3	5	RAM	29	No	40	9	Yes	Yes	Yes	Yes	Has touch switch interface
Essex International	SX-200	PMOS	4/8	64×4	1024×8	Yes	41	400	Yes	20/20	No	Yes	Yes/1	1	RAM	16	No	28	10 to 20	No	Yes	No	Yes	Minimal I/O interface
Hitachi	HMCS42	PMOS/	4/10	32×4	512×10	No	74	780/500	Yes	10	No/Yes	Yes	Yes/2	RAM	RAM	22	No	28	-10/+5	No	Yes	No	Yes	Available in CMOS and PMOS versions
	HMCS43/43C	CMOS	4/10	80×4	1024×10	No	69	780	Yes	10	No	Yes	Yes/2	RAM	RAM	32	Yes	42	-10	Yes	Yes	No	Yes	Easily handles display driving
	HMCS44	PMOS	4/10	160×4	2048×10	No	69	780	Yes	20	No	Yes	Yes/3	RAM	RAM	31	Yes	54	-10	No	Yes	No	Yes	Comes in 54 pin flat package
	HMCS45	PMOS	4/10	160×4	2048×10	?	?	25	Yes	20	Yes	Yes	Yes/1	5	RAM	14	Yes	14/18/24	-15	No	Yes	No	No	Designed for washing machines
ITT Semiconductor	7150	PMOS	4/8	?	N/A¹	?	?	400	No	1220/1 S	Yes	Yes	Yes/1	?	1	11	Yes	28	9	Yes	Yes	No	Yes	Has scientific calculation ability
National Semiconductor	MM57109	NMOS	4/8	5×32	N/A¹	Yes	70	400	No	16/32	Yes	Yes	Yes/1	4	RAM	16	Yes	24	4.5 to 9.5	No	Yes	No	Yes	All COPs processors include serial I/O and event counting capability. Major differences between models include the I/O arrangements —input only, bidirectional, output only, etc. I/O options include LED direct segment drive, LED direct digit drive, three-state push-pull, push pull, open drain, and standard (active device to ground and a pull-up to VCC).
	COP410L	NMOS	4/8	32×4	512×8	No	40	250	Yes	16/32	Yes	Yes	No	2	RAM	16	No	20	4.5 to 9.5	No	Yes	No	Yes	
	COP411L	NMOS	4/8	32×4	512×8	No	40	250	Yes	16/32	Yes	Yes	Yes/1	2	RAM	15	No	28	4.5 to 9.5	Yes	Yes	No	Yes	
	COP420	NMOS	4/8	64×4	1024×8	No	49	1000	Yes	4/8	Yes	Yes	Yes/1	3	RAM	20	No	28	4.5 to 6.3	Yes	Yes	No	Yes	
	COP420L	NMOS	4/8	64×4	1024×8	No	49	250	Yes	16/32	Yes	Yes	Yes/1	3	RAM	20	No	28	4.5 to 9.5	Yes	Yes	No	Yes	
	COP420C	CMOS	4/8	64×4	1024×8	No	49	250	Yes	16/32	Yes	Yes	Yes/1	3	RAM	20	No	28	2.4 to 6.3	Yes	Yes	No	Yes	
	COP421	NMOS	4/8	64×4	1024×8	No	49	250	Yes	16/32	Yes	Yes	No	3	RAM	16	No	24	4.5 to 6.3	Yes	Yes	No	Yes	
	COP421L	NMOS	4/8	64×4	1024×8	No	49	250	Yes	4/8	Yes	Yes	Yes/1	3	RAM	16	No	28	4.5 to 9.5	Yes	Yes	No	Yes	
	COP421C	CMOS	4/8	64×4	1024×8	No	49	250	Yes	16/32	Yes	Yes	No	3	RAM	16	No	24	2.4 to 6.3	Yes	Yes	No	Yes	
	COP440	NMOS	4/8	128×4	2048×8	No	49	1000	Yes	4/8	Yes	Yes	Yes/1	3	RAM	32	No	40	4.5 to 6.3	Yes	Yes	No	Yes	
	COP444L	NMOS	4/8	128×4	2048×8	No	49	250	Yes	16/32	Yes	Yes	Yes/1	4	RAM	20	Yes	28	4.5 to 9.5	Yes	Yes	No	Yes	
NEC Microcomputers	μPD548	NMOS	4/10	96×4	1920×10	No	72	200	No	10/20	Yes	Yes	Yes/2	4	RAM	35	No	42	-10	Yes	Yes	No	Yes	Well suited for POS and ECR applications
	μPD546	PMOS	4/8	96×4	2000×8	No	80	440	Yes	4.5/9	Yes	Yes	Yes/1	3	RAM	35	No	42	-10	Yes	Yes	No	Yes	TTL-compatible I/O lines
	μPD553	PMOS	4/8	96×4	2000×8	No	80	440	Yes	4.5/9	Yes	Yes	Yes/1	3	RAM	35	No	42	-10	Yes	Yes	No	Yes	I/O handles —35-V vacuum fluorescent drive
	μPD650	CMOS	4/8	96×4	2000×8	No	80	440	Yes	4.5/9	Yes	Yes	Yes/1	3	RAM	35	No	42	+5	Yes	Yes	No	Yes	CMOS version of 546 (4% of the power)
	μPD547	PMOS	4/8	64×4	1000×8	No	58	440	Yes	4.5/9	Yes	Yes	Yes/1	3	RAM	35	No	42	-10	Yes	Yes	No	Yes	TTL-compatible I/O lines
	μPD547L	PMOS	4/8	64×4	1000×8	No	58	180	Yes	11/22	Yes	Yes	Yes/1	3	RAM	35	No	42	-8	Yes	Yes	No	Yes	Low power version of 547 (half the current)
	μPD552	PMOS	4/8	64×4	1000×8	No	58	440	Yes	4.5/9	Yes	Yes	Yes/1	1	RAM	35	No	42	-10	Yes	Yes	No	Yes	I/O handles —35-V vacuum fluorescent drive
	μPD651	CMOS	4/8	64×4	1000×8	No	58	440	Yes	4.5/9	Yes	Yes	Yes/1	1	RAM	21	No	42	+5	Yes	Yes	No	Yes	CMOS version of 547 (4% of the power)
	μPD550	PMOS	4/8	32×4	640×8	No	58	440	Yes	4.5/9	Yes	Yes	Yes/1	1	RAM	21	No	28	-10	Yes	Yes	No	Yes	I/O handles —35-V vacuum fluorescent drive
	μPD554	PMOS	4/8	32×4	1000×8	No	58	440	Yes	4.5/9	Yes	Yes	Yes/1	1	RAM	21	No	42	-10	Yes	Yes	No	Yes	I/O handles —35-V vacuum fluorescent drive
	μPD652	PMOS	4/8	64×4	1000×8	No	58	440	Yes	4.5/9	Yes	Yes	Yes/1	1	RAM	28	No	28	-10	Yes	Yes	No	Yes	I/O handles —35-V vacuum fluorescent drive
	μPD551	CMOS	4/8	64×4	1000×8	No	58	440	Yes	4.5/9	Yes	Yes	Yes/1	1	RAM	28	No	42	+5	Yes	Yes	No	Yes	CMOS version of 550 (5% of the power)
Panasonic	MN1400	NMOS	4/8	64×4	1024×8	No	75	300	Yes	10/20	Yes	Yes	Yes/1	2	2+RAM	30	No	40	5	No	Yes	Yes	Yes	Complete all-in-one controller
	MN1402	NMOS	4/8	32×4	768×8	No	57	300	Yes	10/20	Yes	Yes	Yes/1	2	RAM	19	No	28	5	No	Yes	No	Yes	Smaller I/O version of 1400
	MN1403	NMOS	4/8	16×4	512×8	No	50	300	Yes	10/20	No	No	Yes/1	2	RAM	13	No	18	5	Yes	Yes	No	Yes	
	MN1404	NMOS	4/8	16×4	512×8	No	48	300	Yes	10/20	No	No	Yes/1	2	RAM	13	No	16	5	Yes	Yes	No	Yes	
	MN1405	PMOS	4/8	128×4	2048×8	No	75	200	Yes	15/30	Yes	Yes	Yes/1	2	RAM	34	No	40	-15	Yes	Yes	No	Yes	All the processors in the MN1400 family are available in at least one other technology. The 18 and 16-pin versions are about the smallest μCs available, although most versions still retain at least 2/3 of the instructions available on the 1405. The CMOS versions can also be with operating voltages of up to 10 V.
	MN1430	PMOS	4/8	64×4	1024×8	No	75	200	Yes	15/30	Yes	Yes	Yes/2	2	RAM	30	No	40	-15	Yes	Yes	No	Yes	
	MN1432	PMOS	4/8	32×4	768×8	No	57	200	Yes	15/30	Yes	Yes	Yes/2	2	RAM	19	No	28	-15	Yes	Yes	No	Yes	
	MN1435	NMOS	4/8	128×4	2048×8	No	75	200	Yes	15/30	Yes	Yes	Yes/1	2	2+RAM	34	No	40	-15	Yes	Yes	No	Yes	
	MN1450	CMOS	4/8	64×4	1024×8	No	75	500	Yes	6/12	Yes	No	Yes/1	2	2+RAM	35	Yes	40	4.25 to 6	Yes	Yes	No	Yes	Includes a/d converter with 2% resolution, 4% accuracy
	MN1453	CMOS	4/8	16×4	512×8	No	50	500	Yes	6/12	Yes	No	Yes/1	2	RAM	13	No	18	4.25 to 6	No	Yes	No	Yes	
	MN1454	CMOS	4/8	16×4	512×8	No	48	500	Yes	6/12	Yes	No	Yes/1	2	RAM	10	No	16	4.25 to 6	Yes	Yes	No	Yes	

443

TABLE 12.2-1, continued

Original Source Manufacturer	Device	Process technology	Word size in bits (data/inst.)	On-chip RAM size	On-chip ROM/PROM size (words)	Off-chip memory expansion	Number of basic instructions	Maximum clock frequency (kHz)	On-chip clock	Instruction time (shortest/longest) μs	TTL compatible	BCD arithmetic	On-chip interrupts/levels	Subroutine nesting levels	General-purpose internal registers	Number of I/O lines	Additional special support circuits	Package size (DIP pins)	Voltages required (V)	Prototyping system avail.	Assembly language programming system	High-level language programming system	Time-sharing cross software	Comments
Rockwell	MN1455	CMOS	4/8	128×4	2048×8	No	75	500	Yes	6/12	Yes	No	Yes/4	2	2+RAM	34	Yes	40	4.25 to 6	Yes	Yes	No	No	All MN1500 family processors include an 8-bit counter/timer and an 8-bit serial shift register. All I/O lines are bidirectional and the chips also have a power-down made to minimize power dissipation
	MN1542	NMOS	4/8	152×4	2046×8	Yes	124	1000	Yes	2/4	Yes	Yes	Yes/4	16	4+RAM	24	Yes	40	5	Yes	Yes	No	Yes	
	MN1544	NMOS	4/8	256×4	4096×8	Yes	124	1000	Yes	2/4	Yes	Yes	Yes/4	16	4+RAM	24	Yes	40	5	Yes	Yes	No	Yes	
	MN1562	NMOS	4/8	152×4	2048×8	Yes	124	1000	Yes	2/4	Yes	Yes	Yes/4	16	4+RAM	48	Yes	64	5	Yes	Yes	No	Yes	
	MN1564	NMOS	4/8	256×4	4096×8	Yes	124	1000	Yes	2/4	Yes	Yes	Yes/4	16	4+RAM	48	Yes	64	5	Yes	Yes	No	Yes	
PPS-4	PPS-4	PMOS	4/8	0	0	Yes	50	200/400	No	5/15	No	Yes	Yes/1	2	1	12+	Yes	42	-17/+5,-12	Yes	Yes	No	Yes	Combination ROM/RAM/I/O available
PPS-4/1	PPS 4/2	PMOS	4/8	0	0	Yes	50	Two clocks	Yes	5/15	No	Yes	No	2	1	12+	Yes	42	-17/+5,-12	Yes	Yes	No	Yes	Same as PPS 4 but has internal clk I/O includes serial channel
	MN77/MM77L	PMOS	4/8	96×4	1344×8	RAM only	50	100/4	Yes	5/15	Yes	Yes	Yes/1	2	2+RAM	31	Yes	42	-15/+5,-10	Yes	Yes	No	Yes	Software compatible with 77
	MM78/MM78L	PMOS	4/8	128×4	2048×8	RAM only	50	100/4	Yes	10/40	Yes	Yes	Yes/1	2	2+RAM	31	Yes	42	-15/+5,-10	Yes	Yes	No	Yes	Primarily used for keyboard display
	MM76	PMOS	4/8	48×4	640×8	RAM only	50	100/4	Yes	10/40	Yes	Yes	Yes/1	1	1+RAM	31	Yes	42	-15/+5,-10	Yes	Yes	No	Yes	Has high-speed counter
	MM76/C	PMOS	4/8	48×4	640×8	RAM only	50	100/4	Yes	10/30	Yes	Yes	Yes/1	1	1+RAM	39	Yes	52	-15/+5,-10	Yes	Yes	No	Yes	Larger ROM than MM76
	MM76/E	PMOS	4/8	48×4	1024×8	RAM only	50	100/4	Yes	10/30	Yes	Yes	Yes/1	1	1+RAM	31	Yes	42	-15/+5,-10	Yes	Yes	No	Yes	Low power version of 76
	MM76/L	PMOS	4/8	48×4	640×8	RAM only	50	100/4	Yes	10/30	Yes	Yes	Yes/1	1	1+RAM	31	Yes	40	6 to 11	Yes	Yes	No	Yes	Expanded ROM version
	MM76/EL	PMOS	4/8	48×4	640×8	RAM only	50	100/4	Yes	10/30	Yes	Yes	Yes/1	1	1+RAM	31	Yes	42	-15/+5,-10	Yes	Yes	No	Yes	Reduced I/O version of 76
	MM75	PMOS	4/8	48×4	670×8	RAM only	50	100/4	Yes	10/40	Yes	Yes	No	1	1+RAM	22	Yes	28	9 or 15	Yes	Yes	No	Yes	Reduced I/O version of 76
Texas Instruments	TMS-1000	PMOS	4/8	64×4	1024×8	No	43	400	Yes	15/15	Yes	Yes	No	1	2+RAM	23/25	Yes	28/40	9 or 15	Yes	Yes	No	Yes	Aside from two supply versions, a 35 V vacuum fluorescent drive version is available (TMS 1070/1270)
	TMS-1000C	CMOS	4/8	64×4	1024×8	No	43	1000	Yes	6/6	Yes	Yes	No	3	2+RAM	22/32	N/A[1]	28/40	3 to 6	N/A[1]	N/A[1]	N/A[1]	Yes	CMOS version of TMS-1000
	TMS-1100	PMOS	4/8	128×4	2048×8	No	40	400	Yes	15/15	Yes	Yes	No	1	2+RAM	23/28	N/A[1]	28/40	9 or 15	N/A[1]	N/A[1]	N/A[1]	Yes	Also has VF drive versions (TMS 1170/1370) and is pin compatible with TMS-1000
	TMS-1018	PMOS	4/8	64×4	1024×8	No	43	400	Yes	15/15	Yes	Yes	N/A[1]	N/A[1]	N/A[1]	N/A[1]	N/A[1]	28	15	N/A[1]	N/A[1]	N/A[1]	N/A[1]	Dedicated number cruncher
	TMS1022	PMOS	4/8	64×4	2048×8	No	43	400	Yes	15/15	Yes	Yes	N/A[1]	N/A[1]	N/A[1]	N/A[1]	N/A[1]	28	15	N/A[1]	N/A[1]	N/A[1]	N/A[1]	Dedicated C8 PLL controller
	TMS1117	PMOS	4/8	128×4	2048×8	No	43	400	Yes	15/15	Yes	Yes	N/A[1]	N/A[1]	N/A[1]	N/A[1]	N/A[1]	28	15	N/A[1]	N/A[1]	N/A[1]	N/A[1]	Dedicated microwave oven controller
	TMS1121	PMOS	4/8	128×4	2048×8	No	42	400	Yes	15/15	Yes	Yes	N/A[1]	N/A[1]	N/A[1]	N/A[1]	N/A[1]	28	15	N/A[1]	N/A[1]	N/A[1]	N/A[1]	Dedicated appliance timer/controller
	TMS1400	PMOS	4/8	64×4	4096×8	No	41	550	Yes	11/11	Yes	Yes	No	3	2+RAM	19	Yes	28	9	Yes	Yes	No	Yes	VF drive version available (1470) and 15 V supply model coming
	TMS1600	PMOS	4/8	64×4	512×8	No	41	550	Yes	11/11	Yes	Yes	No	3	2+RAM	32	Yes	40	9	Yes	Yes	No	Yes	VF drive version available (1670) and 15 V supply model coming
Toshiba	TMS1700	PMOS	4/8	64×4	512×8	No	43	400	Yes	15/15	Yes	Yes	No	1	2+RAM	21	Yes	28	9 or 15	Yes	Yes	No	Yes	Reduced ROM and I/O version of TMS-1000
	T3444	NMOS	4/8	16×4	256×24	No	3	800	Yes	3	Yes	Yes	Yes/1	8	RAM	16	No	40	5	Yes	Yes	No	No	Intended for dedicated controllers
	T3472	NMOS	4/8	16×4	256×24	Yes	67	1000	Yes	33 360	Yes	Yes	Yes/2	1	RAM	27	No	42	5	Yes	Yes	No	No	Designed for keyboard/display interfacing
Western Digital	1872	NMOS	4/10	32×4	512×10	No	37	150	Yes	6.25 12.5	Yes	Yes	Yes/1	8	RAM	32	Yes	40	12	Yes	Yes	No	No	RAM holds BCD numbers
Fairchild	F38E70	NMOS	8/8	64×8	2048×8	Yes	70+	4000	Yes	1 65	Yes	Yes	Yes/4	8	RAM	32	Yes	40	5	Yes	Yes	Yes	Yes	On-chip UV EPROM instead of mask ROM version of 3870
	F3878	NMOS	8/8	64×8	4096×8	Yes	70+	4000	Yes	1 65	Yes	Yes	Yes/4	8	RAM	32	Yes	40	5	Yes	Yes	Yes	Yes	Similar to Mostek 3872 but has no standby RAM
General Instrument	PIC1645	PMOS	8/12	24×8	256×12	No	30	1000	Yes	4 8	Yes	No	Yes/1	2	RAM	16	Yes	24	5	Yes	Yes	Yes	No	Minimal I/O family members
	1650	NMOS	8/12	32×8	512×12	No	30	1000	Yes	4 8	Yes	No	Yes/1	2	RAM	32	Yes	40	5	Yes	Yes	Yes	No	32 programmable I/O lines
	1655	NMOS	8/12	32×8	512×12	No	30	1000	Yes	4 8	Yes	No	Yes/1	2	RAM	21	Yes	28	5	Yes	Yes	Yes	No	Reduced I/O version of 1650
	1670	NMOS	8/12	48×8	1024×12	Yes	30	3000	Yes	10 20	Yes	No	Yes/1	2	RAM	32	Yes	40	5	Yes	Yes	Yes	Yes	Increased memory version
Intel	8021	NMOS	8/8	64×8	1024×8	No	70	3000	Yes	10 20	Yes	Yes	No	RAM	RAM	21	No	28	5	Yes	Yes	Yes	No	Minimal I/O CPU version
	8022	NMOS	8/8	64×8	2048×8	No	70	3000	Yes	2.5 5	Yes	Yes	Yes/1	RAM	RAM	27	Yes	40	5	Yes	Yes	Yes	Yes	Contains two a/d converter channels
	8041/8741	NMOS	8/8	64×8	1024×8	Yes	90	6000	Yes	2.5 5	Yes	Yes	Yes/1	8	RAM	18	Yes	40	5	Yes	Yes	Yes	Yes	8041 has a ROM and 8741 a UV EPROM
	8048/8748	NMOS	8/8	64×8	1024×8	Yes	90	6000	Yes	1.4 2.8	Yes	Yes	Yes/1	8	RAM	27	Yes	40	5	Yes	Yes	Yes	Yes	8748 has UV EPROM
	8049	NMOS	8/8	128×8	2048×8	Yes	96	11000	Yes	2.5 5	Yes	Yes	Yes/1	8	16+RAM	27	No	40	5	Yes	Yes	Yes	Yes	Enlarged memory version of 8048
Intersil	87C41	CMOS	8/8	64×8	1024×8	Yes	96	6000 (5V)	Yes	2.5 5	Yes	Yes	Yes/1	8	RAM	18	Yes	40	5 to 10	Yes	Yes	Yes	Yes	CMOS equivalent to Intel 8041 dissipates 50 mW
	80C48/87C48	CMOS	8/8	64×8	1024×8	Yes	96	6000 (5V)	Yes	2.5 5	Yes	Yes	Yes/1	8	RAM	27	Yes	40	5 to 10	Yes	Yes	Yes	Yes	CMOS equivalent to Intel 8048/8748; dissipates 50 mW
Mostek	3870	NMOS	8/8	64×8	2048×8	Yes	70+	4000	Yes	1 65	Yes	Yes	Yes/4	RAM	RAM	32	Yes	40	5	Yes	Yes	Yes	Yes	Has 16 bit prog timer
	3872	NMOS	8/8	128×8	4096×8	Yes	70+	4000	Yes	1 65	Yes	Yes	Yes/4	RAM	RAM	32	Yes	40	5	Yes	Yes	Yes	Yes	Double the memory capacity of 3870, with a standby capability on the additional 64 bytes of RAM

TABLE 12.2-1, continued

Motorola	3873	NMOS	8/8	64×8	2048×8	Yes	70+	4000	Yes	1/6.5	Yes	Yes	Yes/4	RAM	RAM	32	Yes	40	5	Yes	Yes	Yes	Yes	Some I/O lines dedicated as serial port
	3876	NMOS	8/8	128×8	2048×8	Yes	70+	4000	Yes	1/6.5	Yes	Yes	Yes/4	RAM	RAM	32	Yes	40	5	Yes	Yes	Yes	Yes	Same as 3870 but double the RAM
	6801/68701	NMOS	8/8	128×8	2048×8	Yes	82	3580	Yes	2/12	Yes	Yes	Yes/1	RAM	RAM	31	Yes	40	5	Yes	Yes	Yes	Yes	6801 has masked ROM, 701 has UV EPROM
	6805/705	NMOS	8/8	64×8	1100×8	Yes	61	3580	Yes	2/4	Yes	Yes	Yes/1	0	RAM	20	Yes	28	5	Yes	Yes	Yes	Yes	Low cost 8 bit μC has 8-bit timer and prescaler, 705 version has UV EPROM
	6805R2	NMOS	8/8	64×8	2048×8	Yes	61	3580	Yes	2/4	Yes	Yes	Yes/1	0	RAM	20	Yes	28	5	Yes	Yes	Yes	Yes	CPU includes 8-bit a/d converter (available in mid-1980)
	146805	CMOS	8/8	64×8	1100×8	Yes	61	3580	Yes	2/4	Yes	Yes	Yes/1	0	RAM	20	Yes	28	5	Yes	Yes	Yes	Yes	CMOS version of the 6805
National Semiconductor	INS8050	NMOS	8/8	256×8	4096×8	Yes	96	11000	Yes	1.4/2.8	Yes	Yes	Yes/1	8	RAM	27	Yes	40	5	Yes	Yes	Yes	Yes	Enlarged proprietary version of Intel 8049 processor with transparent improvements
	INS8072	NMOS	8/8	64×8	2560×8	Yes	74	4k	Yes	3/1000	Yes	Yes	Yes/2	RAM	RAM	0	Yes	40	5	Yes	Yes	Yes	Yes	Three-state data/address bus for user selectable I/O
RCA	CDP1804	CMOS/SOS	8/8	64×8	2048×8	Yes	113	8000	Yes	2/3	Yes	Yes	Yes/1	RAM	RAM	13	Yes	40	5 to 10	Yes	Yes	Yes	Yes	Compatible with 1802 software
Rockwell	PPS-8	PMOS	8/8	0	0	Yes	100	256/4	No	4/12	No	Yes	Yes/3	16	2	15	Yes	42	−17/+5,−12	Yes	Yes	No	Yes	Combination RAM/ROM/I/O support
	PPS-8/2	PMOS	8/8	0	0	Yes	100	200/4	No	5/15	No	Yes	Yes/3	16	2	15	Yes	42	−17/+5,−12	Yes	Yes	No	Yes	I/O chip includes clock
	R6500/1	NMOS	8/8	64×8	2048×8	Yes	56	2000	Yes	1/3.5	Yes	Yes	Yes/1	RAM	RAM	32	Yes	40	5	Yes	Yes	Yes	Yes	Single chip version 6502
Zilog	Z8	NMOS	8/8	144×8	2048×8	Yes	47	8000	Yes	1.5/3.75	Yes	Yes	Yes/6	RAM	RAM	32	Yes	40	5	Yes	Yes	Yes	Yes	Has two counter/timers and UART
Texas Instruments	TMS 9940E/9940M	NMOS	②	128×8	2048×8	No	68	5000	Yes	2/452	Yes	Yes	Yes/4	64	RAM	16	No	40	5	Yes	Yes	Yes	Yes	Two versions available, one has a 2 k EPROM, the other 2 k ROM
Intel	2920	NMOS	25/25	40×25	192×24	No	21	2500	Yes	0.4/0.4	Yes	N/A¹	N/A¹	0	RAM	12	No	28	5,−5	Yes	Yes	No	Yes	Analog processor accepts four analog inputs and delivers up to eight digitally processed analog outputs

1. Not applicable   2. External 8 bits, internally 16 bits   3. User defined   ? Not available

features. The 8080A microprocessor, for example, uses standard memory; the 8085A, on the other hand, uses either standard memory or special memory and I/O devices such as the 8155 RWM with I/O ports and a timer or the 8355 ROM with I/O ports.

In either case, systems developed around general purpose microprocessors are easily expandable because memory and I/O ports are external. For large systems, separate memory and I/O are usually preferred over devices with a combination of the two, since in most applications the number of I/O ports does not increase in proportion to memory.

General purpose microprocessors are available in word lengths of 1, 4, 8, 12, or 16 bits and typically consist of one to three integrated circuits (see Table 12.2-2). Although a wide variety of architectures and instruction sets is available, all general purpose microprocessors contain an ALU with one or more registers which function as accumulators, a control unit, an instruction decoder which handles a fixed instruction set, and general and special purpose registers. The number and universality of general purpose registers varies significantly among devices. A microprocessor may have an internal stack of fixed length or use external memory for the stack, for the latter case one of its internal registers is used as a stack pointer.

12.2.3.3 Bit Slice Microprocessors

Unlike a typical single-chip microprocessor that contains on a single chip all the elements of a central processing unit—ALU, general purpose and special purpose registers, and control—bit slice microprocessors divide these functions among several ICs. For this approach, the registers and ALU are packaged separately from the control; each register and ALU (RALU) package is essentially equivalent to a small—2- or 4-bit wide—slice of the register and ALU portion of the complete microprocessor. Bit slice microprocessors can be cascaded to produce longer word lengths of 8, 12, 16, 32, or more bits. The control portion of a bit slice microprocessor is constructed from a microprogram sequencer IC and other logic. The *microprogram sequencer* contains an instruction register and additional logic to decode and execute instructions.

When the microprogram sequencer decodes an instruction from the main program memory, it generates a starting address to a special ROM, called a microinstruction ROM or control ROM, CROM. Each instruction in the main program ROM is like a machine language instruction on a single-chip microprocessor. For each such instruction, the microprogram sequencer creates a different starting address in the CROM—beginning at this address is a sequence of memory words, microinstructions, which implements the more complex machine language instruction. Microinstructions directly control the registers and logic of the RALU, causing the execution of the instruction.

Because the control ROM is a separate package or packages, the machine language instruction set can be customized for an application. The designer creates machine language instructions from sequences of primitive operations

TABLE 12.2-2

General Purpose Microprocessors. Reprinted with permission from *Electronic Design*, Vol. 27, No. 24, November 22, 1979, copyright Hayden Publishing Co., Inc. 1979.

Original source manufacturer	Processor	Process technology	Word size (data/instruction)	Direct addressing range (words)	Number of basic instructions	Maximum clock frequency (MHz)/phases	Instruction time shortest/longest² (μs)	TTL compatible	BCD arithmetic	On-chip interrupts/levels	Number of internal general-purpose registers	Number of stack registers	On-chip clock	DMA capability	Specialized memory & I/O circuits avail.	Prototyping system avail.	Package size (pins)	Voltages required (V)	Assembly language development system	High-level languages	Time-sharing cross software	Comments
Motorola	MC14500	CMOS	1/4	0	16	1/1	1/1	Yes	No	No	1	0	Yes	No	No⁴	No	16	3 to 18	No	No	No	Needs external program counter
Intel	4004	PMOS	4/8	4k	46	0.74/2	10.8/21.6	Yes	Yes	Yes/1	16	3x12	No	No	Yes	Yes	16	15	Yes	No	No	Superseded by 4040
Intel	4040	PMOS	4/8	8k	60	0.74/2	10.8/21.6	No	Yes	Yes/1	24	7x12	No	No	Yes	Yes	24	15	Yes	No	Yes	General-purpose 4-bit μP
NEC Microcomputers	μPD555	PMOS	4/10	1920 X10	72	0.2/1	10/20	Yes	Yes	Yes/2	96x4	7x12	Yes	No	No	Yes	64	-10	Yes	No	No	ROM-less version of μPD548
National Semiconductor	COP402	NMOS	4/8	1k	49	1/1	4	Yes	Yes	Yes/3	64x4	RAM	Yes	No	Yes	Yes	40	4.5 to 6.3	Yes	No	Yes	The 402, 402M and 404L are ROM-less versions of COP420 and 440
National Semiconductor	COP402M	NMOS	4/8	1k	49	1/1	4	Yes	Yes	No	64x4	RAM	Yes	No	Yes	Yes	40	4.5 to 6.3	Yes	No	Yes	Single chip μC. All three have serial I/O and event counting capability, as well
National Semiconductor	COP404L	NMOS	4/8	2k	49	0.25/1	16	Yes	Yes	Yes/3	128x4	RAM	Yes	No	No	Yes	40	4.5 to 9.5	Yes	No	Yes	As 20 I/O lines.
NEC Microcomputers	μPD556	PMOS	4/8	2k	80	0.44/1	4.5/9	Yes	Yes	Yes/2	96x4	3	Yes	No	No	Yes	64	-10	No	No	Yes	ROM-less version of μPD546
Panasonic	MN1498	NMOS	4/8	1k	66	0.3/1	10/20	Yes	Yes	Yes/1	64x4	RAM	Yes	No	Yes	Yes	40	5	Yes	No	Yes	ROM-less version of MN1402, but 66 instructions and come in a 40-pin package
Panasonic	MN1499	NMOS	4/8	2k	75	0.3/1	10/20	Yes	Yes	Yes/1	64x4	RAM	Yes	No	Yes	Yes	64	5	Yes	No	Yes	ROM-less version of MN1400
Panasonic	MN1499A	NMOS	4/8	2k	80	0.3/1	10/20	Yes	Yes	Yes/1	128x4	RAM	Yes	No	Yes	Yes	64	5	Yes	No	Yes	ROM-less version of MN1400, but 128 nibbles of on-chip RAM
Panasonic	MN1599	NMOS	4/8	4k	125	1/1	2/4	Yes	Yes	Yes/4	256x4	RAM	Yes	Yes	Yes	Yes	64	5	Yes	No	Yes	ROM-less version of MN1564, chip has 12 4-bit I/O ports
Fairchild	2 chip F8 (3850)	NMOS	8/8	64k	69	2/1	2/13	Yes	Yes	Yes/1	64	RAM	Yes	Yes	Yes	Yes	40	5,12	Yes	Yes	Yes	Usually used with program storage unit
General Instrument	8000	PMOS	8/8	1k	48	0.8/2	1.25/3.75	No	Yes	Yes/3	48	0	No	No	Yes	Yes	40	5,-12	No	Yes	Yes	Predecessor of F8
Intel	8008	PMOS	8/8	16k	48	0.8/2	12.5/37.5	No	Yes	Yes/1	6	7x14	No	No	Yes	Yes	18	5,-9	Yes	Yes	Yes	Predecessor of 8080, still in wide use
Intel	8035/8039	NMOS	8/8	64k	96	6/1	2.5/5	Yes	Yes	Yes/1	64	RAM	Yes	No	Yes	Yes	40	5	Yes	Yes	Yes	ROM-less versions of 8048/8049
Intel	8080A	NMOS	8/8	64k	78	2.6/2	1.5/3.75	Yes³	Yes	Yes/1	8	RAM	No	No	Yes	Yes	40	5,12,-5	Yes	Yes	Yes	By and large, still the most popular
Intel	8085	NMOS	8/8	64k	80	5.5/1	0.8/5.2	Yes	Yes	Yes/4	8	RAM	Yes	No	Yes	Yes	40	5	Yes	Yes	Yes	8080 code compatible, has built-in clock
MOS Technology	MCS 650X	NMOS	8/8	64k	56	4/1	0.5/3.5	Yes	Yes	Yes/1	0	RAM	Yes	No	Yes	Yes	40	5	Yes	Yes	Yes	Provides 13 addressing modes
MOS Technology	MCS 651X	NMOS	8/8	64k	56	4/2	0.5/3.5	Yes	Yes	Yes/1	0	RAM	No	No	Yes	Yes	40	5	Yes	Yes	Yes	Similar to 650X but needs 2φ clock
Mostek	3874	NMOS	8/8	64k	70+	4/1	1/6.5	Yes	Yes	Yes/4	64	RAM	Yes	Yes	Yes	Yes	40	5	Yes	No	Yes	ROM-less piggy-back version of 3870, accepts UV EPROMS on top
Motorola	6800	NMOS	8/8	64k	72	2/2	1/2.5	Yes	Yes	Yes/1	64	RAM	No	No	Yes	Yes	40	5	Yes	Yes	Yes	Available in depletion-load version
Motorola	6802/6808	NMOS	8/8	64k	72	2/1	2/5	Yes	Yes	Yes/1	128/0	RAM	No	No	Yes	Yes	40	5	Yes	Yes	Yes	6802 has 128x8 on chip RAM; 6808 has no RAM
Motorola	6803	NMOS	8/8	64k	82	3.58/1	2/12	Yes	Yes	Yes/1	128	RAM	Yes	No	Yes	Yes	40	5	Yes	Yes	Yes	ROM-less version of 6801 single-chip μC
Motorola	6809	NMOS	8/8	64k	59	2/1	2/5	Yes	Yes	Yes/1	8	RAM	Yes	No	Yes	Yes	40	5	Yes	Yes	Yes	Enhanced 6800 command set
National Semiconductor	INS8060	NMOS	8/8	4k	46	4/1	5/22	Yes	Yes	Yes/4	8	RAM	Yes	No	No⁴	Yes	40	5	Yes	Yes	Yes	Has handy daisy-chain capability
National Semiconductor	NSC800	CMOS	8/8	64k	150+	8/1	0.5/2.88	Yes	Yes	Yes/5	14	RAM	Yes	Yes	Yes	Yes	40	3 to 12	Yes	Yes	Yes	Executes 280 instructions and has 8085 bus structure
National Semiconductor	INS8040	NMOS	8/8	64k	96	11/1	1.4/2.8	Yes	Yes	Yes/1	256	RAM	No	No	Yes⁴	Yes	40	5	Yes	Yes	Yes	ROM-less version of INS8050 single chip μC
National Semiconductor	INS8070	NMOS	8/8⁷	64k	74	4/1	3/1000⁸	Yes	No	Yes/2	9	RAM	Yes	No	Yes	Yes	40	5	Yes	Yes	Yes	ROM-less version of INS8072; 64 bytes of on-chip RAM
NEC Microcomputers	μPD 8080A	NMOS	8/8	64k	78	2/2	1.92/8.16	Yes³	Yes	Yes/1	8	RAM	No	No	Yes	Yes	40	5,12,-5	Yes	Yes	Yes	Pin compatible but does BCD subtraction
RCA	1802	CMOS	8/8	64k	91	6.4/1	2.5/3.75	Yes	Yes	Yes/1	16	RAM	Yes	Yes	Yes	Yes	40	3 to 12	Yes	Yes	Yes	Superseded two-chip version
RCA	8085AC	CMOS	8/8	64k	80	0.8/2	0.8/5.2	Yes	Yes	Yes/4	8	RAM	Yes	Yes	Yes	Yes	40	5	Yes	Yes	Yes	CMOS equivalent to 8085A and pin-compatible
Signetics	2650	NMOS	8/8	32k	75	2/1	1.5/6	Yes	Yes	Yes/1	7	8x15	Yes	Yes	Yes	Yes	40	5	Yes	Yes	Yes	There are 1.25 and 2-MHz versions

TABLE 12.2-2, continued

Original source manufacturer	Processor	Process technology	Word size (data/instruction)	Direct addressing range (words)	Number of basic instructions	Maximum clock frequency (MHz)/phases	Instruction time shortest/longest[2] (µs)	TTL compatible	BCD arithmetic	On-chip interrupts/levels	Number of internal general-purpose registers	Number of stack registers	On-chip clock	DMA capability	Specialized memory & I/O circuits avail.	Prototyping system avail.	Package size (pins)	Voltages required (V)	Assembly language development system	High-level languages	Time-sharing cross software	Comments
Signetics	8X300	Bipolar	8/16	8k	NA[10]	4/1	0.25	Yes	No	No	8	0	No	No	No[4]	Yes	50	5	Yes	No	Yes	Intended for high-speed controllers
Zilog	Z80	NMOS	8/8	64k	150+	4/1	2.5/5.75	Yes	Yes	Yes/1	14	RAM	No	No	Yes	Yes	40	5	Yes	Yes	Yes	8080 instructions are a subset
Intersil	6100	CMOS	12/12	4k	81	4/1	2.5/5.5	Yes	No	Yes/1	0	RAM	No	No	Yes	Yes	40	4 to 11	Yes	No	Yes	Emulates PDP-8 instruction set
Toshiba	T3190	NMOS	12/12	4k	108	2.5/1	10/30	Yes	No	Yes/8	8	RAM	No	No	Yes	Yes	36	5,−5	Yes	Yes	Yes	Has multiply and divide inst.
Advanced Micro Devices	Am29116	ECL	16/16	64k	30+	10/1	0.1/0.2	Yes	No	No	32	32	No	No	Yes	No	48	5	Yes	No	Yes	Control-oriented microprogrammable CPU, can generate CRC bits
Data General	mN601	NMOS	16/16	32k	42	8.33/2	1.2/29.5	Yes	Yes	Yes/1	4	RAM	Yes	Yes	Yes	Yes	40	5,10,14,−4.25	Yes	Yes	Yes	Emulates NOVA instruction set
Data General	mN602	NMOS	16/16	32k	82	8.3/2	2.4/53	Yes	Yes	Yes/16	4[6]	RAM	Yes	Yes	Yes	Yes	40	3,12,±5	Yes	Yes	Yes	Executes NOVA instruction set and addresses double the memory of the mN601
Fairchild	9440	I³L	16/16	64k[5]	42	12/19	1.25/3.5	Yes	No	Yes/16	4	RAM	Yes	No	Yes	Yes	40	5	No	No	No	Executes NOVA 3 and 4 instruction sets
Fairchild	9445	I³L	16/16	64k	100	20/19	0.3/5.7	Yes	No	Yes/16	4	RAM	Yes	Yes	Yes	Yes	40	5	Yes	Yes	Yes	Executes NOVA 3 and 4 instruction sets
Ferranti	F100L	Bipolar	16/16	32k	153	14/1	1.19/14	Yes	No	Yes/1	RAM	RAM	No	No	Yes	Yes	40	5.1.2	Yes	Yes	Yes	Can do double word operations
General Instrument	CP1600/1610	NMOS	16/16	64k	87	4/2	1.6/4.8	Yes	No	Yes/1	8	RAM	No	Yes	Yes	Yes	40	5,12,−3	Yes	Yes	Yes	All internal registers can be accumulators
Intel	8086	NMOS	16/16	1M[5]	97	5/1	0.4/37.8	Yes	Yes	Yes/1	8	RAM	No	Yes	Yes	Yes	40	5	Yes	Yes	Yes	Has 24 addressing modes
Intel	8088	NMOS	16/16	16M[5]	97	5/1	0.4/37.8	Yes	Yes	Yes/1	8	RAM	No	Yes	Yes	Yes	40	5	Yes	Yes	Yes	8-bit bus version of 8086 microprocessor
Motorola	MC68000	NMOS	16/16	16M[5]	61	8/1	0.5/NA[10]	Yes	No	Yes/8	16	RAM	No	Yes	Yes	Yes	64	5	Yes	Yes	Yes	Has 32-bit-wide internal structure
National Semiconductor	INS8900	NMOS	16/16	64k	45	2/1	2.5/5	Yes	Yes	Yes/6	4	10x16	No	Yes	Yes	Yes	40	5	Yes	Yes	Yes	Architecture intended for data handling
National Semiconductor	NS16008	NMOS	16/16	64k[5]	78/100+	NA[10]	NA[10]	Yes	Yes	Yes/16	8	RAM	Yes	Yes	Yes	Yes	40	5	Yes	Yes	Yes	8-bit bus version of dual language (8080/native) CPU, has internal 16-bit bus
National Semiconductor	NS16016	NMOS	16/16	64k	78/100+	NA[10]	NA[10]	Yes	Yes	Yes	8	RAM	Yes	Yes	Yes	Yes	40	5	Yes	Yes	Yes	Full 16-bit version, offers 8080A and native instruction sets
National Semiconductor	NS16032	NMOS	16/16	16M[5]	100+	NA[10]	NA[10]	Yes	Yes	Yes	8	RAM	Yes	Yes	Yes	Yes	48	5	Yes	.	Yes	Expanded 16-bit version with eight 32-bit registers, six 24-bit registers and two 16-bit registers; can address 16 Mbytes
Panafacom	MN1610	NMOS	16/16	64k	33	2/2	2/6	Yes[3]	No	Yes/3	5	RAM	Yes	Yes	Yes	Yes	40	5,12,−3	Yes	No	Yes	The 9981 requires external clock
Texas Instruments	TMS9980/9981	NMOS	16/16[7]	8k	69	4/4	3.2/49.6	Yes[3]	Yes	Yes/4	16	RAM	Yes	Yes	Yes	Yes	40	5,12,−5[11]	Yes	Yes	Yes	ROM-less version of 9940
Texas Instruments	TMS9985	NMOS	16/16	32k	68	5/1	2.4/50	Yes	No	Yes/4	RAM	RAM	Yes	Yes	Yes	Yes	40	5	Yes	Yes	Yes	Emulates 990 mini instructions
Texas Instruments	TMS/SBP9900	NMOS/I²L	16/16	32k	69	4/4	2/31	Yes[3]	No	Yes/16	16	RAM	No	Yes	Yes	Yes	64	5,12,−5	Yes	Yes	Yes	Emulates 990 mini instructions
Western Digital	WD-16	NMOS	16/16	64k	116	3.3/4	2.1/780	Yes	Yes	Yes/16	6	RAM	No	Yes	Yes	Yes	40	5,12,−5	No	Yes	No	Very similar to DEC LSI-11
Western Digital	Pascal Microengine	NMOS	16/16	64k	150+	3/4	2.4/300[8]	Yes	Yes	Yes/4	RAM	RAM	No	Yes	Yes	Yes	40	+12,±5	No	Yes	No	Five-chip set directly executes Pascal p-code
Zilog	Z8000	NMOS	16/16	48M[5]	110+	8/1	0.75/90	Yes	Yes	Yes/1	16	RAM	No	Yes	Yes	Yes	40/48	5	Yes	Yes	Yes	40-pin version is the Z8002; 48-pin, the Z8001

1 Has 8-bit external buses and 16-bit internal buses. 2 With maximum clock. 3 Except clock lines.

4 Standard TTL or MOS circuits will suffice. 5 Range in bytes. 6 Frame Pointer too.

7 Double-precision 16-bit operations available. 8 String search.

9 Clock internally divided by 4 or 6 depending on instruction. 10 Not applicable. 11 9980 only.

which are implemented by microinstructions. Creating an instruction set in such a manner or writing an entire application program by using microinstructions is referred to as *microprogramming*. Note that microprogramming is not equivalent to programming a microprocessor. It is a way of implementing the control portion of a CPU and was used on mainframe computers long before microprocessors came into existence.

Designing with a bit slice microprocessor is much more difficult than using a fixed instruction set microprocessor because the designer must configure the CPU and the system hardware as well and microprogram the instruction set. This has already been done by the IC manufacturer in a fixed instruction set microprocessor. In addition, because bit slice microprocessors have both unique architectures and unique instruction sets, few software development aids are available.

However, bit slice microprocessors do have certain advantages. First, most are bipolar, and because of the inherent speed advantages of bipolar technology, they are faster than single-chip MOS processors. Second, spreading the bipolar logic over several packages eliminates power dissipation problems. A third advantage is the flexibility they provide for designing a microprocessor. The designer can build a system of any desired word length and create an optimal instruction set for a particular application. Bit slice devices are also used to emulate other microprocessors or minicomputers with microprograms which execute the target computer's instruction set. Table 12.2-3 lists a number of bit slice microprocessors and their features.

12.2.4 Microprocessor Selection

A general list of considerations in the selection of a microprocessor or microcomputer is presented in Table 12.2-4. The relative importance of each item in this list varies, depending on the application.

For low complexity systems which can be implemented with a single-chip microcomputer, selection criteria primarily center around the capabilities and limitations of available microcomputers and their software development aids. The largest application of single-chip microcomputers is in small dedicated controllers. The rationale for their use is a system with a minimal package count. To this end, a device is sought which provides the required capability without requiring additional packages.

Before selecting a single-chip microcomputer, a designer's major consideration should be whether the device provides a sufficient number of I/O lines for the application. Although some microcomputers provide I/O expansion capability, the requisite additional devices detract from the minimal package count goal. For those devices with sufficient I/O lines, the flexibility of the I/O lines and the instructions which control them are compared.

Another consideration is program size, since single-chip microcomputers have a fixed amount of ROM within which an application program must fit. Execution speed must also be taken into account in real-time applications.

TABLE 12.2-3

Bit Slice Microprocessors. Reprinted with permission from *Electronic Design*, Vol. 27, No. 24, November 22, 1979, copyright Hayden Publishing Co., Inc. 1979.

Original source company	Series	Process technology	ALU part number	ALU word size (bits)	Number of ALU instructions	Can ALU do BCD arithmetic?	Maximum ALU clock rate (MHz)	General-purpose registers in ALU	ALU package size (DIP pins)	Microprogram sequencer number	Number of address bits	Maximum sequencer clock rate (MHz)	Number of sequencer commands	Sequencer stack size	Sequence package size (DIP pins)	Are parts TTL-compatible?	Voltages required (V)	Prototyping system available	Development software available	Specialized support circuits available	Comments
Advanced Micro Devices	2900	STTL	2901A	4	16	No	16.67	16	40	2909/11	4	10	12	4×4	28/20	Yes	5	Yes	Yes	Yes	Has widest number of second sources
		STTL	2903	4	25	No	10	16	48	2910	12	10	16	5×12	40	Yes	5	Yes	Yes	Yes	ALU has nine more instructions than 2901, including multiply and divide
Fairchild	Macrologic	STTL/CMOS	9405/34705	4	64	No	10	8	24	9406	4	10	4	16×16	24	Yes	5	Yes	Yes	Yes	CMOS version (34705) operates at 2 MHz.
	F100220	ECL	F100220	8	27	Yes	50	1	68[1]	F100224	N/A[2]	N/A[2]	N/A[2]	N/A[2]	N/A[2]	N/A[2]	-4.2 to -5.7	1979	1979	1980	Only 8 bit slice, sub-ns instructions
Motorola	10800	ECL	10800	4	100+	Yes	20	0	48	10801	4	20	16	4×4	48	No	-2, -5.2	Yes	Yes	Yes	Fastest 4-bit slice available
Signetics	3000	STTL	3002	2	40	No	10	11	28	3001	9	10+	11	0	40	Yes	5	Yes	Yes	Yes	Only 2-bit ALU available
Texas Instruments	SBP-0400A	I²L	SBP-0400	4	512	No	5	10	40	74S482	4	20	64	4×4	20	Yes	Current	Yes	No	No	Has pipeline register
	SBP-0401A	I²L	SBP-0401	4	512	No	5	10	40	74S482	4	20	64	4×4	20	Yes	Current	Yes	No	No	Does not have pipeline register
	54/74S481	STTL or LSTTL	S481 / LS481	4	24,780	No	10	0	48	74S482	4	20	64	4×4	20	Yes	5	Yes	No	Yes	Very flexible instruction set

1. Leadless carrier   2. Not available

TABLE 12.2-4

General Considerations for Microprocessor Selection

Software

word size	: data and instructions
register complement	: number and flexibility
instruction set	: type and number of instructions—suitability for application
instruction cycle time	: instruction execution speed
address capacity	: number of directly addressable memory and I/O ports
addressing modes	: direct, indirect, indexed, relative, etc.
stack	: location and length

Hardware

package size	: number of package pins
minimal system parts count	: number of packages required for minimal system
parts family completeness	: compatable ROM, RWM, and peripheral ICs
power requirement	: number of power supply voltages and power dissipation
logic compatability	: input and output logic levels
drive capability	: number of unit loads drivable by output pins
interrupt structure	: number and type of interrupt inputs
DMA provisions	: provision for DMA, additional hardware required
second sources	: independent manufacturers of microprocessor and support ICs
availability	: actual availability of microprocessor and required support ICs in small and large quantities

Support

documentation	: completeness of hardware and software manuals, data sheets
development system	: range, performance, and flexibility of development system
development software	: assemblers, compilers, editors, debuggers, and subroutine library
application notes	: hardware and software device interface and system design examples
prototype hardware	: single and multicard prototype hardware
diagnostic hardware	: device specific system analyzers
application support	: field application engineering support available from vendor

Systems of medium to high complexity typically use general purpose microprocessors. Here selection criteria encompass total system solutions: the microprocessor, support devices, hardware packaging, and software. The use of powerful programmable I/O interface devices, including interfaces which are themselves special or general purpose microprocessors, contributes substantially to the complexity of selection. These devices, although generally usable with most microprocessors, are frequently designed for direct compatibility with a particular microprocessor or series of microprocessors.

Response and data rates must also be considered, in terms of interrupt and DMA capability. In some applications, the speed requirements of certain subfunctions may be greater than the capability of any microprocessor. In such instances, external hardware is necessary to preprocess data prior to its input.

Programmability is another important consideration. The architecture of each microprocessor determines its instruction set. Generally speaking, the more instructions available, the easier the programming and the less memory required for storage. But, more important than a large number of instructions is the number which are useful in the particular application under consideration. Programming ease is also facilitated by the number and power of on-chip registers because they allow intermediate data to be stored internally during calculations rather than requiring external references to memory for temporary storage. Internal reference also provides faster execution time.

Most microprocessors are part of a family of LSI components, and completeness of this family is an important hardware consideration. These components, sometimes referred to as *support circuits*—clock drivers, system controllers, peripheral interface adapters, communication interface circuits, DMA controllers, etc.—are designed for intrafamily interfacing. And, while it is usually possible to use a device from one family with those of another, the electrical interface between the circuits may require additional logic. Since package count minimization is a design goal, the smallest number of ICs required for a complete system with a specified number of I/O lines is also a selection consideration.

12.2.4.1 Benchmarking

Benchmarking is a technique for evaluating microprocessor performance. As originated in the computer industry, benchmarking involves comparing the performance of several computers in executing a set of programs or benchmarks. The performances are compared in terms of speed and memory requirements. This technique has been adapted for comparing microprocessors for selection.

The designer must first identify tasks critical to the specific application and then write a benchmark program which implements these tasks for each microprocessor under consideration. If the benchmark programs are written in assembly language, their execution speeds are determined by ascertaining the number of states required for the execution of each individual instruction. This number is multiplied by the number of instructions in the benchmark. That product is, in turn, multiplied by the processor state time. This product is the total execution time for the benchmark. Computation of both worst-case and typical execution times is helpful for comparison. The amount of memory used by a benchmark program is determined from the number of bytes of memory required for each instruction. Paper and pencil calculations are usually sufficient for estimating both execution times and memory requirements.

As adapted for use with microprocessors, benchmarking also evaluates performance in terms of a microprocessor's ability to execute critical subfunctions in the time allotted by the performance requirements and in terms of its ability to meet the performance requirements of a particular subfunction in the overall system. If a microprocessor fails to meet these requirements, either the main program must be optimized, or hardware must be added to speed up the processing. If a more efficient routine cannot be written, or if the additional hardware is not economically acceptable, either a faster microprocessor or a change in the functional partitioning of the system is necessary. Benchmarking is also beneficial in that it familiarizes the designer with the ease or difficulty of programming a particular microprocessor.

12.2.4.2 Hardware/Software Tradeoffs

The purpose of a hardware/software tradeoff is to optimize performance and minimize cost. It involves determining the amount of hardware versus the amount of software to be used in implementing a particular function. Typically, software is traded off for hardware to increase the speed of execution at a concomitantly higher cost. Hardware is traded off for software to decrease cost, with a concomitantly slower execution time.

There are, basically, two types of speed problems: (a) data transfer rate problems and (b) data manipulation rate problems. And there are several tradeoffs possible as solutions to these problems.

For example, the hardware/hardware tradeoff involves the selection of hardware having a higher speed than that originally considered. This either means using a different, faster processor than the original selection or a graded, high-speed version of the same microprocessor. For example, the nominal clock frequency for an 8085A is 3 MHz; however, a faster version of this microprocessor, the 8085A-2, operates at a clock frequency of 5 MHz. If a microprocessor is being used with memory which has a slow access time, such that the microprocessor must wait on the memory, an increase in execution speed is possible by using the same microprocessor with faster memory. Keep in mind, however, that faster hardware costs more.

Data transfer rate problems are the result of a disparity in the rates at which the microprocessor and I/O devices transfer data. In some cases, the transfer rate of the I/O device is much slower than the microprocessor can handle. This is true, for example, where a microprocessor transfers data to or from a Teletype or other low-speed electromechanical device.

In this case, the microprocessor could completely control the transfer, both formatting and timing, with software. However, if many transfers are involved, the system can become I/O bound. When a system is *I/O bound*, or *I/O limited*, it must wait for data transfers from external devices to continue its operation. If the microprocessor still has adequate time to carry out the required data manipulations, then there is really no problem. If, however, additional computation time is needed, the software controlling the serial-to-parallel conversion and formatting can be traded off for a UAR/T. Data can be transferred to the UAR/T under program control, and computation can be carried on concurrently with the UAR/T receiving or transmitting data. Even less processor time can be devoted to the transfer by having the UAR/T interrupt the processor when it has received data or is free to transmit another word of data. This involves trading off that portion of the software that polls the status flags of the UAR/T for any additional hardware required to generate an interrupt to the microprocessor.

Transferring blocks of data at high speed to or from an I/O device is an example of a case where the I/O device data rate is in excess of that of the microprocessor. This necessitates using a DMA transfer, which, of course, requires a DMA controller.

FIFO buffers are another hardware approach to eliminating data transfer rate disparities. FIFOs are useful when the average data rate is low but occasional high-speed bursts of data occur. When the I/O data rate is much higher than the microprocessor's, the I/O device transfers data to the FIFO at its transfer rate, and the microprocessor removes it at a lower transfer rate. In the other direction, the microprocessor fills a FIFO at one transfer rate, and the I/O device inputs data from the FIFO at its higher transfer rate.

Data computation rate problems arise when data must be processed within a prescribed time interval. There are two possible solutions: a hardware/software tradeoff or a software/software tradeoff. The software/software tradeoff is essentially the design of a faster algorithm.

The hardware/software tradeoff is one of two types. In the first, software is modified to reduce the execution time of the algorithm. This is accomplished by replacing subroutine calls with the instructions which comprise the subroutine's function. This saves the time required to call and return from the subroutine and the time needed for subroutine passing. It also adds more instructions to the program. This hardware/software tradeoff requires additional memory only in cases where the additional instructions cross a memory package boundary.

In the second case, software is traded off for hardware which either executes the function faster or preprocesses data. The APU exemplifies the use of hardware to implement functions providing both an increase in execution speed and the possibility of concurrency.

12.3 SYSTEM IMPLEMENTATION

After the system has been functionally partitioned and a microprocessor selected, the actual media with which to implement the hardware and software are selected.

12.3.1 Hardware Implementation

A number of alternatives are available to the designer for developing a hardware prototype and for implementing the final system hardware in production. In any case, the designer can develop the system from the ground up, starting with ICs, or can use either prefabricated printed circuit boards or completely packaged microcomputer systems containing all the hardware (power supplies, front panel, etc.), in a cabinet.

As the complexity and availability of functions implemented in LSI has increased, the difficulty of designing a microprocessor system from ICs has been minimized. This is particularly true when a compatible family of LSI devices is used.

The advantage of designing a system from the chip level is cost-effectiveness. No hardware beyond that absolutely required in the design is utilized. This minimization of package count results in substantial hardware savings where large production numbers are expected. Another advantage in designing a system from the chip level is flexibility in packaging. For small systems, all the hardware can be placed on a single printed circuit board, and an expansion capability can be built in by laying out the PC board to allow for additional RWM, ROM, and I/O. Where the designer foresees a series of models of the same basic system or foresees functionally different systems with essentially the same hardware requirements, a single, sufficiently flexible PC board can be designed to handle the different requirements. Such systems would differ significantly only in their application programs. Note, however, that flexibility via software changes is only possible if provision for the supportive hardware has been made.

In larger systems, hardware is partitioned by function over several PC boards or PC cards. A common bus with address, data, and control signals interconnects the PC cards. The bus can be physically implemented by a **motherboard** which is an additional PC card on which the bus connections are laid out and into which other system PC cards plug via card connectors. Or, the bus signals can be brought out to edge connectors on each card and connected by flat cable, eliminating the need for a motherboard.

Bus signals can be limited to those necessary to support a particular system, or a complete set of bus signals can be provided for generality. Use of one of the de facto industry standard bus structures popularized by various manufacturers allows use of a number of commercially available prefabricated support cards designed to be compatible with various buses.

Prefabricated boards, which include single board and multicard systems, eliminate the need for much of the hardware design. Single board computers, for instance, contain a complete microcomputer system on a single printed circuit card, including the microprocessor, ROM and RWM, and parallel and serial I/O lines. The most flexible single board computers use programmable peripheral interface and communication devices. Some have connector provision that only bring out the I/O lines; others bring out both the I/O lines and system bus connections.

Multicard prefabricated systems typically contain one card for the CPU, one for ROM, one for RWM, and another for I/O. In some cases, the CPU card is itself a single board computer with a limited amount of ROM, RWM, and I/O, and with a complete bus structure brought to connectors at the card's edge. Other bus compatible cards include memory cards with extensive amounts of ROM or RWM, and I/O cards with serial and parallel I/O lines having logic level conversion for standard I/O interfaces such as a 20 mA current loop and RS 232. Other special purpose PC cards are available for high-speed arithmetic and for controlling floppy disks and CRTs. Various analog data acquisition and control boards are also available, including A/D and D/A converters, optoisolators, and solid state relay boards.

The range of functional cards is so extensive that in many applications the designer can simply select an appropriate set of PC cards, plug them onto a motherboard or into a card cage, and thus have configured the majority of the system hardware. Any special functions not available can be designed and implemented on PC cards compatible with the system's bus structure and mechanical hardware.

Prefabricated boards are economical for low to medium volume production runs, in cases where design time is of primary concern, and where the microcomputer portion of a system represents only a very small fraction of the system cost. Completely packaged microcomputer systems are appropriate for implementing general purpose systems, for instance, low cost data processing or word processing systems. Here the microcomputer is used in the same manner in which minicomputers have traditionally been used. These systems usually have an operating system and use one or more higher level languages.

12.3.2 Software Implementation

Designers can write applications programs in assembly language or in a high level language, since translators—which generate object code for specific microprocessors—are available for a number of high level languages. Both approaches have advantages and disadvantages which must be weighed.

High level languages make it possible to program in a natural algorithmic language that is closer to English than assembly language. Many high level languages are structured or block oriented.

PLM, a language similar to PL-1, appeared in 1973 and was the first high level language available for use with microprocessors. It was originally developed by Intel for use with the 8008 and 8080 microprocessors. The high level languages now available for use with microprocessors, include BASIC, FORTH, PASCAL, and FORTRAN.

An objective of high level languages is machine (microprocessor) independence: their statements should not depend upon the architecture of a specific microprocessor. When machine independence is achieved, high level language programs are portable; i.e., they can be run on any microprocessor for which there exists a translator for converting them to the microprocessor's machine language. The question of whether a particular high level language is available for a specific microprocessor is actually a question of whether there is a compiler to translate the particular high level language to machine code for a specific microprocessor. Like assemblers, compilers can be written to run on the microprocessor for which they generate machine code or written to run on a different microprocessor. These are referred to as *self-compilers* and *cross-compilers*, respectively.

The objective of a compiler is to translate a high level source program into *efficient* machine code. Since the statements of the high level language bear no relationship to the microprocessor architecture, the compiler must determine what sequence of machine language instructions best implements those statements. In addition, the compiler must decide how memory is to be allocated, in what memory locations data will be stored, which registers of the microprocessor are to be used for each task, whether the previous contents of these registers must be saved, and what optimizations can be performed.

The output of a compiler can either be machine code or assembly language. If the output is assembly, the statements are then assembled to provide the machine code. Some compilers provide as output a listing of the high level language statements followed by their equivalent assembly language statements and corresponding machine code equivalents.

When a high level language is suitable for a specific application, it has advantages over assembly language. Software development time and cost are significantly reduced because fewer program statements are necessary. Also, programs written in a high level language are generally more reliable than those written in assembly language. This is true for several reasons. Since fewer program statements are required by a high level language, there are fewer chances for error when writing the source program. In fact, errors resulting from the incorrect usage of registers or from the incorrect allocation of registers or memory are entirely eliminated. In addition, if the high level language is of the structured variety, the structure inherently leads to fewer program errors.

However, high level languages do have their drawbacks. For many applications, none of the available high level languages is appropriate. This is particularly true when direct control over the microprocessor's architectural features is required by the designer. One approach to resolving the problem of inapplicability is the use of software development systems that allow software written in high level languages and assembly language to be combined. Another approach is to provide special instructions in the high level language that carry out machine dependent operations. However, use of either of these approaches precludes program portability, as does a third approach: use of a *system implementation language*. This class of machine dependent programming languages contains a mixture of assembly and high level instructions.

Another drawback to using a high level language is that the amount of machine code produced by the compiler is greater than that produced when an equivalent assembly language program is converted to machine code. Thus, high level languages are generally less efficient than assembly language in terms of the memory required for the resultant object code in the microprocessor system.

The tradeoff in memory inefficiency versus reduced development costs using a high level language, as opposed to assembly language, is illustrated in Fig. 12.3-1. The figure shows that programming costs are independent of the number of systems produced; however, memory costs are not. Therefore, since an assembly language system typically requires less memory than an equivalent high level language system, the rate of cost increase is less for the assembly language system. This is true, however, only in cases where the additional words of memory required by the high level language program necessitate one or more additional memory packages. If no memory package boundary is crossed, no additional cost is incurred. A crossover point exists such that when the number of systems required is less than n, high level language is the most cost effective, and when the number is greater than n, assembly language is the choice.

Use of a systems implementation language produces an intermediate situation, with a software development cost between that of a high level language and assembly language and memory requirements in some cases no greater than those of assembly language.

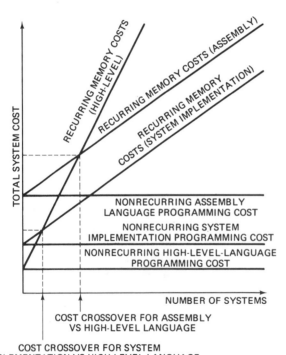

Figure 12.3-1. Effect of programming language choice on system cost.

12.4 TESTING AND DEBUGGING

Testing a system is the process of determining the existence of errors in the operation of the system;[3] *debugging* is the process of locating the source of those errors and correcting them.

For most applications, the only viable strategy is bottom up testing. A top down approach requires an inordinate amount of extra programming and equipment. Bottom up testing is appropriate for finding and correcting hardware, software, and total system errors. With this strategy, the modules comprising the lowest levels of a partitioned system are tested and debugged first. But prior to this, appropriate sets of test data and expected results are determined from the original functional specification for each module. A test is useless if the expected results are not completely known before it is begun.

The testing and debugging of hardware, software, and the total system, in that order, are consistent with the use of low cost tools which range from simple to sophisticated. The primary focus here is on simple tools because they are readily available, although more costly sophisticated tools allow a great deal of parallelism when checking for and eliminating software and hardware errors.

When a microprocessor system is implemented from the bottom up, each module can be tested and debugged immediately following its completion. Indeed, it is advantageous to determine whether critical modules at the lower levels of a functional partition meet their performance requirements before proceeding with the detailed design and implementation of higher level modules. If they do not, the design can be modified accordingly at an early stage.

12.4.1 Hardware Testing and Debugging

A number of tools are used for testing and debugging a system's hardware: logic probes, multitrace oscilloscopes, logic analyzers, and microprocessor development systems. The simplest of these is, of course, the *logic probe*. A logic probe contains two LEDs that indicate the logic state of any point within a circuit touched by the probe. One LED signals a logic 0 state; the other, a logic 1. Pulse trains, or periodic waveforms, light both LEDs. A pulse stretching feature in the probe allows the observation of nonrepetitive pulses by using a single shot in the probe that, when triggered by the pulse, turns on the LED for sufficient duration to be observed. Probes are commonly available for T[2]L and MOS logic levels.

An *oscilloscope* displays DC and AC electrical signals in a system. It is the only tool which facilitates observation of the precise characteristics of time varying signals such as rise and fall time and duration of pulses. Multitrace

---

[3]Software testing by using a simulator was introduced in Chapter 5 and expanded on in Chapter 6. This section considers the testing and debugging of an entire system, including hardware and software and their interaction.

oscilloscopes display the timing relationships among several waveforms, and oscilloscopes with storage features display a single event, such as a pulse, for an extended period of time. Thus, a multitrace storage oscilloscope provides considerably more information than a logic probe—at a considerably increased cost.

The *logic analyzer* is a relatively new instrument, specifically designed for testing digital systems. It does in the digital domain what the multitrace scope does in the analog domain; i.e., it provides a display of multiple channels of sequential digital data. Multichannel probes enable the logic analyzer to acquire 4 to 32 channels of digital data simultaneously. The data acquired on a single pass is stored in the memory of the analyzer for indefinite display.

A simplified block diagram of a logic analyzer is shown in Fig. 12.4-1. A multiple channel probe connects to the signals which are to be monitored simultaneously. An external clock or a clock internal to the analyzer continuously inputs the multichannel data into the analyzer's memory until a trigger signal occurs. Word recognition logic can create a trigger signal when a specified bit pattern occurs at the multiple input data channel. Or a delay counter can cause the trigger at some desired time interval following recognition of the trigger word. When the last memory location in the logic analyzer fills with data, writing continues in the first memory location.

The logic analyzer's display generator shows the acquired data on a CRT screen in one of several formats: a binary or hexadecimal state table, a timing

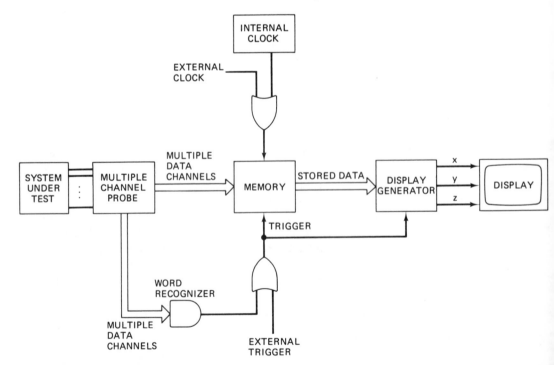

Figure 12.4-1. Simplified block diagram of a logic analyzer.

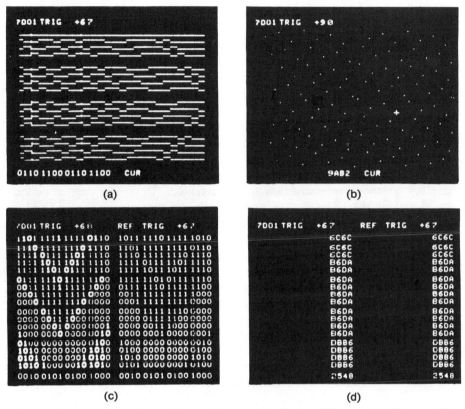

Figure 12.4-2. Logic analyzer display formats: (a) timing, (b) map, (c) binary, (d) hexadecimal. (Courtesy of Tektronix, Inc.)

diagram, or a map (see Fig. 12.4-2). A map display portrays each stored logic word as a dot. The vertical position of each dot is proportional to the most significant half of the word, and the horizontal position is proportional to the least significant half. The pattern of dots for a given sequence of data words forms a unique signature for that block of data.

The key to successful testing of both hardware and software is to check one thing at a time in a modular fashion. When making corrections, make one at a time, then retest. When a system is being prototyped from LSI devices, it is generally brought up in the following order:

1. Wire the microprocessor, its immediate support circuitry, and a minimal amount of RWM and ROM memory into the system.

2. With the integrated circuits removed from their sockets, check for proper power supply voltages at the appropriate socket pins. Also check for a good ground connection at the sockets and an absence of voltage at nonsupply connections.

3. Insert the IC circuits and again check for proper power supply levels and ground.

4. If the microprocessor uses an external clock generator, check the clock waveforms with an oscilloscope to determine that they meet the manufacturer's specifications. If the microprocessor provides an external clock out, check for the existence and validity of that signal.

Additional testing of the basic system hardware requires the execution of short diagnostic routines. For the simplest approach, three routines are written and programmed into EPROMs and executed.

The first routine is an instruction which jumps back to itself. It is placed in memory as the first instruction to be executed. This loop creates periodic waveforms on the address, data, and control lines that can be checked with an oscilloscope to verify proper operation. The second routine verifies the operation of the system RWM. A simple program which writes then reads back patterns of all 0s, all 1s, and checker board patterns is usually adequate. And third, a routine which checks the proper operation of input and output ports is executed with a set of switches providing inputs in place of the actual input devices and a set of LEDs and their drivers replacing the output devices. At this stage, it is sufficient to determine that the output ports can actually be written and that data can be input through the input ports.

Once the basic system is operational, it can be used to check the operation of I/O devices under software control. Eventually, the entire system hardware is interconnected and its basic functionality tested.

12.4.2 Software Testing and Debugging

Thorough testing of a microprocessor system's software is imperative to ensure that the system operates as required by its functional specification. While it may be impossible to find all the bugs in a complex system during the testing and debugging stages, the motivation to do so is great. If systems are produced in large quantities, using masked ROMs, the detection of a software error after the ROMs have been produced leaves the designer with a large collection of useless ROMs. PROMs which have been programmed with unreliable software are also useless. And although EPROMs, if used, can be reprogrammed to correct the errors, even with EPROMs software changes are costly when carried out after the systems have been constructed. These are merely economic considerations; the consequences of unreliable software may be even more drastic, depending on the system's application. A strategy for software testing and debugging should, therefore, be well established early in the design process.

Software designed in a modular fashion can be tested and debugged from the bottom up. In bottom up software testing, independent modules (subroutines[4]) are tested first; then groups of related subroutines are tested until the entire system's software is tested as a unit.

---

[4]See Chapters 5 and 6 for the testing of individual subroutines.

Partitioning provides functional specifications for each subroutine. From these a set of test cases or input data is established which is sufficiently exhaustive to test every decision statement in the subroutine and to verify that the subroutine operates reliably. Initial subroutine testing begins as soon as the subroutine is written. Syntax errors can be identified and corrected as the subroutine is translated. Test cases can then be run.

Tested and confirmed subroutines are combined into subsystems which, in turn, are tested. At this second stage, testing detects both logic and interface errors. Finally, all the modules are combined, and the complete software system is tested.

As the complexity of the subsystems increases, exhaustive testing becomes an impossibility. One of the problems all designers face is determining how much testing to do, as well as determining an appropriate set of test cases.

12.4.3 System Testing and Debugging

Software is tested initially with a simulator or by execution on a development system. But final testing requires a prototype of the actual system. For most dedicated systems this means transferring the machine code version of the application program to EPROM or PROM. And, depending on the environment in which the system is ultimately expected to operate, simulation of some of the system's inputs and outputs may be necessary. For example, in most process control applications, final testing cannot be carried out while a system is on line, i.e., actually controlling the process.

The objective of the system test is to determine whether the system operates as required by the functional specification and to determine whether it meets its specified performance requirements. There are several different types of bugs, including logical errors as well as timing, throughput, and capacity errors.

12.5 DOCUMENTATION AND MAINTENANCE

If the requirements definition for a microprocessor system remains unchanged over the useful life of the system, maintenance becomes a continuation of the testing and debugging stage for both the system hardware and software. Hardware maintenance involves two types of system faults: design errors and component failures. The correction of design errors may require engineering changes in the systems already in the field as well as in those to be produced. Component failures can occur which are the result of neither poor design nor of the component being operated outside of its electrical limits. This type of maintenance properly belongs in the category of system repair.

During the initial stage of hardware maintenance, the source of the fault is determined and analyzed. It is at this point, therefore, that the proper documentation of the hardware and its operation has the greatest impact—this is particularly true when maintenance is provided by someone other than the original system designer.

There are also two types of software maintenance: correction of software design errors and system improvement. If the software is complex, in all probability subtle errors will remain even after testing and debugging. Again, if an error is serious enough, it requires correction in existing units as well as in units to be produced. Since such corrections often require field changes of ROMs, they can be very costly.

Modifications in software to implement minor improvements or performance enhancement are easier if the software has been developed in a modular fashion. It is also easier if the software has been well and thoroughly documented. It is difficult and time consuming for a designer to go back, several months later, and understand poorly documented software; and even more difficult, if not impossible, for someone else to understand it. High level languages are advantageous in this respect because, to a limited extent, they are self-documenting.

12.6 MULTIPLE MICROPROCESSOR SYSTEMS

The low cost of microprocessors makes it possible to use more than one in a system. Then the total system function is partitioned into tasks and each task allocated to a different microprocessor. A multiple microprocessor system has many advantages over single microprocessor systems, including higher throughput, faster real-time response, greater modularity, and improved reliability.

Concomitant with these advantages, however, are a number of design problems, including the most effective partitioning of a process into parallel tasks, allocation of these tasks, sequencing and control of the microprocessor's interprocessor connections, and control of shared resources. As a solution, a number of sophisticated schemes for interconnecting multiple processors (micros, minis, or mainframes) have been proposed, and a few have been implemented. Much of the research in this area has been aimed at achieving super computer performance via a number of low cost processors.

Two practical multiple microprocessor architectures—distributed systems and multiprocessor systems—are achievable with off-the-shelf products. These are both in a class called *Multiple Instruction Multiple Data, MIMD*, systems. MIMD architectures achieve parallelism by concurrently performing independent tasks on separate data and combining the results when appropriate.

Distributed systems differ from multiprocessor systems in the way that tasks are handled. The tasks assigned to each microprocessor in a distributed system are permanently fixed when the system is designed. In a *multiprocessing system* a complex operating system runs on one of the microprocessors and allocates tasks to microprocessors in a dynamic fashion in order to implement the overall system function in the most efficient manner. Multiprocessing systems are beyond the scope of this text. However, the more commonly used distributed systems are considered briefly.

12.6.1 Distributed Systems

In a distributed system, each microprocessor performs a dedicated function defined during the system partitioning. Software for each processor is developed in a modular fashion with the goal of minimizing the interaction between programs on separate microprocessors.

Each processor in a distributed system has two sets of interfaces: one to the external system and one to the other microprocessors. The external system activity usually involves either controlling an external process or preprocessing or postprocessing data to or from another microprocessor. Microprocessors usually communicate by passing messages or blocks of data through I/O ports or shared memory.

Distributed systems are divided into master/slave and multiple master systems.

12.6.1.1 Master/Slave Distributed Systems

Master/slave distributed systems are the simplest of the multiple processor systems because of the fixed hierarchy of their system microprocessors. A single master microprocessor controls the system. And although each microprocessor has its own I/O interface to any external activities associated with its individual tasks, an additional I/O interface connects each processor to the common system bus, which is controlled by the master. The slave processors communicate with the master, and via the master with other slave microprocessors, through the common system bus. The requests for transferring data over the common bus are arbitrated by the master. Common bus systems are designed to minimize data transfer, and parallelism is achieved by each slave processor handling its processing tasks asynchronously. A master/slave system utilizing a common bus for intercommunication is shown in Fig. 12.6-1.

Any microprocessor can be used as either a master or slave. A slave processor is chosen for its ability to optimally perform certain tasks, and several

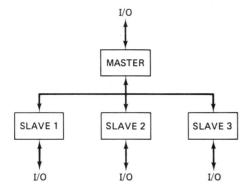

Figure 12.6-1. Generalized master/slave system with a common bus.

different types of microprocessors can be used as slaves in a single system. The hardware interfacing between the master and each slave must be bidirectional and must provide the handshaking logic necessary to allow synchronization of data transfers between the asynchronous master and slaves. Devices such as the 8255 programmable peripheral interface are used for master/slave interfacing. Many of the sophisticated peripheral control chips mentioned in Chapter 10 are, in effect, microprocessors which implement fixed, internally microcoded programs to carry out their functions.

Particularly appropriate as slave processors are microcomputer *Universal Peripheral Interface, UPI*, devices. Because these are specifically designed to be used as slave processors, they contain all the logic necessary for interfacing between master and slave. These devices can be programmed to implement the entire control algorithm for a function or peripheral device. For example, the Intel 8041 and 8741 are versions of a single-chip microcomputer optimized to function as a universal peripheral interface in a multiprocessor environment [2]. Each contains an 8-bit CPU, 64 bytes of RAM, 1,024 bytes of ROM, an 8-bit timer/counter, and 18 I/O lines. Whereas the 8041 contains a mask programmable ROM, the 8741 contains an EPROM and has a hardware single step capability for system development. The instruction sets of both contain over 90 instructions and are designed to efficiently handle single bit manipulations in computation and I/O. A master/slave distributed system using an 8085A as the master and UPIs as slaves is shown in Fig. 12.6-2.

Of principal interest here is the interface between the UPI and the master processor (system interface) and between the UPI and its external activity (peripheral interface). The master processor and UPI communicate through an asynchronous *Data Bus Buffer, DBB*, register in the UPI (see Fig. 12.6-3). Data and commands are received by the UPI, and status and data are transferred to the master through the DBB register. The master uses four control lines, $\overline{WR}$, $\overline{RD}$, $\overline{CS}$, and A_0, to read or write the UPI's DBB register. Control signal A_0 specifies whether a command or data word is being sent.

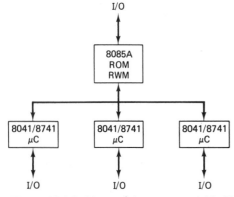

Figure 12.6-2. Master/slave system with 8085A as master and 8041/8741 as slaves.

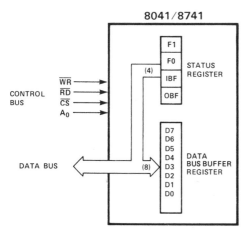

Figure 12.6-3. Communication structure between 8085A and the UPI. (Courtesy of Intel Corp.)

Execution of the program within the UPI is asynchronous to transfers through the DBB register. Thus, the UPI continues to execute its application program while transfers to and from the master are being made through the DBB register.

The flags in the 8041/8741 used to synchronize transfers to and from the master are defined as follows:

OBF: The OBF (Output Buffer Full) flag is automatically set when the UPI outputs data to the DBB register and is cleared when the master processor reads the register.

IBF: The IBF (Input Buffer Full) flag is set when the master processor writes data into the DBB register and is cleared when the UPI inputs the data into its accumulator.

F_0: This is a general purpose flag which can be cleared or toggled by UPI software. It can be used as a lockout signal to the master processor to indicate when the UPI is about to load data into the DBB register.

F_1: This flag is automatically set to the condition of the A_0 input line when the master processor writes to the DBB register. The status of the F_1 flag indicates whether the transfer is command ($F_1 = 1$) or data ($F_1 = 0$). F_1 can be cleared or toggled by UPI software.

In applications requiring two-way data transfer between the master and a UPI, simultaneous writing of the DBB must be precluded. And although the UPI does not provide a hardware lockout to prevent such, a software protocol which utilizes the status flags guarantees that each processor can read or write the DBB without interference. The key to this software protocol is the UPI's subservience to the master processor in all DBB operations; i.e., the UPI writes into the DBB register only when commanded to do so by the master. In response to a transfer to the DBB by the master, the UPI sets F_0 to lock out the master until it either loads the DBB with the data or status requested by the master or determines that no response is required.

The master protocol sequence is shown in Fig. 12.6-4. The master reads the UPI status: If the previous character written into the DBB by the master has not been input by the UPI (IBF = 1) or if the UPI has set $F_0 = 1$ to lockout the master, then the master must wait. If both IBF and $F_0 = 0$ and the master is expecting a transfer from the slave, then OBF is 1, and the master reads the DBB, automatically setting OBF to 0. The master then processes this data. Note that the UPI does not set $F_0 = 0$ until after it has loaded requested data or peripheral status into DBB, making OBF equal to 1. If the master is not expecting a transfer from the slave, OBF is 0, and the master can write a

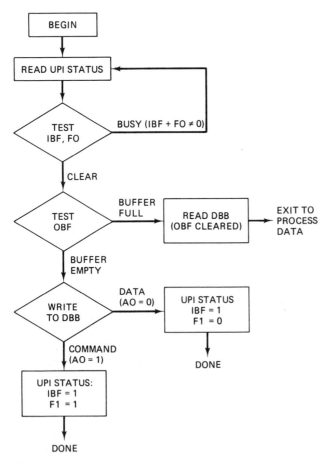

Figure 12.6-4. Master protocol sequence. (Courtesy of Intel Corp.)

command ($A_0 = 1$, causing $F_1 = 1$) or data ($A_0 = 0$, causing $F_1 = 0$) into the DBB. The IBF flag is set when the master writes data into the DBB.

The UPI protocol is shown in Fig. 12.6-5. When the DBB is written by the master, concomitant setting of the IBF flag causes an internal interrupt if the UPI interrupt feature is enabled. Or the UPI can periodically poll its IBF flag. If IBF is set, the UPI sets F_0 to lock out the master. It then transfers the content of the DBB to its accumulator with an IN A, DBB instruction. The UPI checks F_1 for data, $F_1 = 0$, or a command, $F_1 = 1$. If the content is data, the UPI clears F_0 and exits to process it. If the content is a command, the UPI executes it. If the command requires that the UPI return data or peripheral status to the master, it

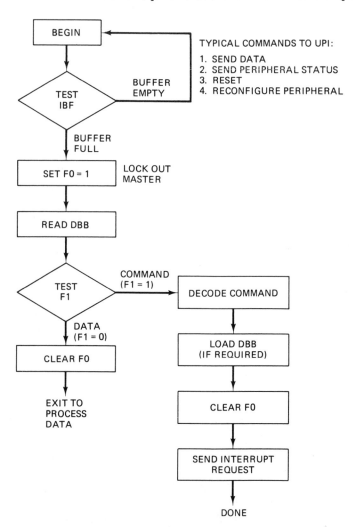

TYPICAL COMMANDS TO UPI:

1. SEND DATA
2. SEND PERIPHERAL STATUS
3. RESET
4. RECONFIGURE PERIPHERAL

Figure 12.6-5. UPI protocol sequence. (Courtesy of Intel Corp.)

loads the DBB with these before clearing F_0. The UPI can interrupt the master, using a bit from one of its output ports to indicate that the requested data is in DBB. Or the master can poll the UPI by reading the UPI's OBF flag to determine that the requested data is available.

12.6.1.2 Multiple Master Distributed Systems

In a multiple master distributed system, each microprocessor is essentially independent and is able to control the system. In addition, they share the system resources, including common RWM, disk storage, high-speed arithmetic processors, etc. Master processors generally communicate via buffers in common RWM, and access to shared resources is through the common bus. Masters gain control of the common bus on a priority basis; therefore, two primary considerations for the design of a multiple master distributed system are arbitration of bus control requests and mutual exclusion of the simultaneous use of shared resources.

These problems and some approaches to their solution are illustrated by a brief examination of the Intel MULTIBUS structure—a bus structure and bus arbitration logic which allow several microcomputers to share a common bus [3]. The MULTIBUS is implemented on Intel single board computers which can, together with shared resources, be plugged into a common bus structure. Each single board computer has its own microprocessor, memory, and external I/O interconnected by an internal bus on the single board computer (see Fig. 12.6-6). Bus arbitration and control logic facilitate data flow between the single board computer's internal bus and the common bus.

Access to MULTIBUS is requested by a master only when a global (resident on the MULTIBUS and accessible by multiple masters) memory location or I/O device is referenced during an instruction execution cycle. Local/global (onboard/offboard) distinction is defined through the value of the physical address referenced. If no other master is currently using the common bus, the new master is granted access immediately; however, if another master is currently using the bus, then the new master must wait. Simultaneous requests by masters for bus control are arbitrated by either of two techniques: serial (daisy chain) or parallel (encoded). Four control lines and a bus clock (all active low) control serial or parallel arbitration:

Bus Clock (BCLK/): The negative edge of BCLK/ synchronizes arbitration (minimum bus clock period, 100 nS).

Bus Priority In (BPRN/): This indicates to a master that no higher priority master is requesting the use of the bus.

Bus Priority Out (BPRO/): BPRO/ is passed to the BPRN/ input of the master with next lower bus priority.

Bus Busy Signal (BUSY/): This signal, driven by the bus master currently in control of multibus, indicates current bus usage. BUSY/ prevents other masters from gaining control of the bus.

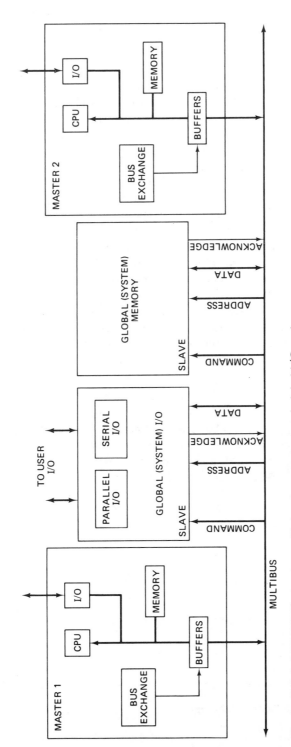

Figure 12.6-6. MULTIBUS structure with two bus masters and global I/O and memory.

471

Bus Request Signal (BREQ/): This is used with a parallel bus priority network to indicate that a particular master requires use of the bus for one or more transfers.

The hardware interconnection for serial arbitration is shown in Fig. 12.6-7. When a master requires the common bus, its BPRO/ line inhibits lower priority masters. BUSY/, by the same token, ensures that in-process operations of lower priority masters are not destroyed by asynchronous requests of higher priority masters. In addition, a bus lock function, which asserts the BUSY/, enables a master to retain control of the bus until it issues an unlock command. The bus lock function is used in high-speed memory or I/O transfers and in critical read-modify-write operations. Bus transfers normally take place on an interleaved basis (bus arbitration being performed for each cycle). For example, if master$_i$ requires the common bus, it first examines its BPRN/ input; if it is low, it then examines BUSY/. If inactive, master$_i$ asserts it and takes control of the bus. If BUSY/ is active, master$_i$ examines BUSY/ on the falling edge of each BCLK/ until BUSY/ is inactive. Master$_i$ then asserts BUSY/ and takes control of the common bus.

Additional masters can be added as long as the cumulative BPRN/ to BPRO/ propagation delay is such that BPRN/ of the lowest priority master is driven inactive before the next BCLK/ falling edge after the highest priority master requests the bus:

$$\sum_{i=1}^{N-1} (t_{\mathrm{BPRN-BPRO}})_i < t_{\mathrm{BCLK}} - t_{\mathrm{sh}}$$

where $(t_{\mathrm{BPRN-BPRO}})_i$ is the propagation delay for master$_i$, t_{BCLK} is the bus clock period, and t_{sh} is the bus set up and hold time.

Parallel arbitration uses the hardware structure shown in Fig. 12.6-8. In the Intel MULTIBUS structure, each master asserts BREQ/ when it requires access

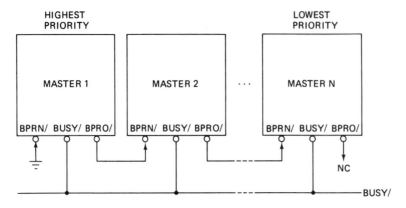

Figure 12.6-7. Serial MULTIBUS arbitration.

to the system bus. The 74148 (an 8-line-to-3-line priority encoder) encodes the requests of the highest priority master, and the 8205 (a 3-to-8-decoder) asserts its BPRN/ line. The use of two 74148s and two 8205s provides a 16-level priority network.

The second consideration for designing a multiple master distributed system is the mutual exclusion of the simultaneous use of shared resources. Certain segments of a master's program which access shared resources constitute *critical sections*; i.e., to preclude errors in system operation, once entered these sections must be completed before another critical section accessing the same shared resource can begin.

Thus, it is necessary to have a mechanism which allows only one related critical section at a time to be entered and fully executed. Critical sections are related if they utilize the same shared resource.

One method, by which simultaneous access of critical sections to shared resources is prohibited, utilizes a semaphore. A *semaphore*, as used here, is a binary variable. One semaphore is associated with each shared resource and is

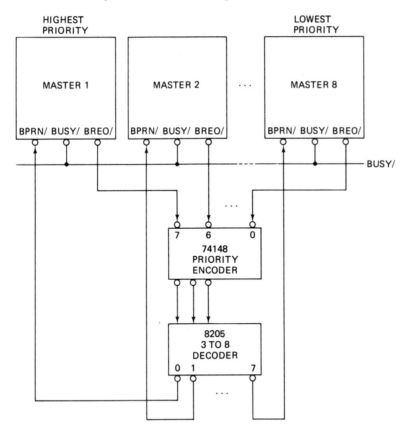

Figure 12.6-8. Parallel MULITIBUS arbitration.

implemented as a reserved memory location. The use of a semaphore, S, requires two primitive or indivisible operations on the memory location used for that semaphore. An indivisible operation enables the completion of reading, modifying, and writing a memory location prior to access by any other process. The two operations are defined as:

1. P(S): If S = 1, S is decremented by 1. Testing and decrementing S is a single indivisible operation. If S = 0, the process which invoked the P operation must wait until it finds S = 1.
2. V(S): S is incremented by 1 as a single indivisible operation.

A semaphore provides mutual exclusion for a shared resource in the following manner:

1. Initially the semaphore is set to 1, S = 1.
2. The related critical sections of each program are preceded by a P operation on S, P(S). If several masters attempt a P operation on S simultaneously, the operations occur sequentially in an arbitrary manner. The first master which finds S = 1 completes the P operation, leaving S = 0, and enters its critical section of code. The remaining master's P operations will be unsuccessful, and they will continually wait in a loop doing P operations on S.
3. The critical section of each program is followed by a V operation on S, V(S). When a master executing in its critical section leaves that section, its V operation sets S = 1. Another master, waiting to use the shared resource, then completes its P operation and enters its critical section.

The remaining problem is how to implement the indivisible P and V operations. The semaphore S is assumed to be a global memory location in common memory. For the V operation, the machine cycles which read S, increment its value, and write it back must be indivisible to prevent other masters gaining control of the common bus. This is accomplished in the MULTIBUS structure by the BUSLOCK operation. For a V operation, once the master controls the MULTIBUS, it locks the bus, increments the semaphore memory location, and then unlocks the bus. For the P operation, when the master gains control of the common bus, it tests the semaphore. If it is 0, the master continues in a wait loop; if 1, the master locks the bus and retests the semaphore. If the semaphore is still equal to 1, it is decremented, the bus is unlocked, and the master enters its critical section of code. If, at the second test, the semaphore is 0, the master unlocks the bus and waits in a loop. The first test for S = 1 prevents a master from continually locking and unlocking the bus while S = 0.

Semaphores also protect the writing and reading of buffers in common memory which provide communication between masters. In addition, semaphores synchronize masters cooperating in a computation.

REFERENCES

1. Ross, D.T., and K.E. Schoman, Jr., "Structured Analysis for Requirements Definition," *IEEE Transactions on Software Engineering*, Vol. SE-3, No. 1, January 1977, pp. 6–15.

2. *UPI-41 User's Manual.* Santa Clara, California: Intel Corporation, 1979.

3. *Intel Multibus Specification.* Santa Clara, California: Intel Corporation, 1978.

BIBLIOGRAPHY

Adams, G., "Reduce Your μC-Based System Design Time by Using Single-Board Microcomputers," *Electronic Design*, February 1978, pp. 56–64.

Adams, G., and T. Rolander, "Design Motivations for Multiple Processor Microcomputer Systems," *Computer Design*, Vol. 17, No. 3, March 1978, pp. 81–89.

Ballard, D.R., "Designing Fail-Safe Microprocessor Systems," *Electronics*, Vol. 52, No. 1, January 1979, pp. 139–143.

Benson, T., "Microcomputers: Single-Chip or Single-Board?" *Electronic Design*, June 1978, pp. 2–6.

Caplener, H.D., and J.A. Janku, "Top-Down Approach to LSI System Design," *Computer Design*, August 1974, pp. 143–148.

Caudill, P., "Using Assembly Coding to Optimize High-Level Language Programs," *Electronics*, Vol. 52, No. 3, February 1979, pp. 121–124.

Conway, J.C., "Hardware Approaches to Microprogramming with Bipolar Microprocessors," *Computer Design*, Vol. 17, No. 8, August 1978, pp. 83–91.

Cushman, R.H., "Microprocessor Benchmarks: How Well Does the μP Move Data?" *EDN*.

———"Exposing the Black Art of Microprocessor Benchmarking," *EDN*.

Down, R.L., "Understanding Logic Analyzers," *Computer Design*, Vol. 16, No. 6, June 1977, pp. 188–191.

Force, G, "Microprocessor Bus Standard Could Cure Designers' Woes," *Electronics*, Vol. 51, No. 15, July 1978, pp. 113–118.

Gray, L., "What Type of Programming Language Best Suits OEM Designs?" *EDN*, Vol. 23, No. 12, June 1978, pp. 78–84.

Hicks, S.M., "Forth's Forte is Tighter Programming," *Electronics*, Vol. 52, No. 6, March 1979, pp. 114–118.

HIRSCHMAN, A.D., G. ALI, and R. SWAN, "Standard Modules Offer Flexible Multiprocessor System Design," *Computer Design*, Vol. 18, No. 5, May 1979, pp. 181–189.

HUGHES, P., "Factoring in Software Costs Avoids Red Ink in Microprocessor Projects," *Electronics*, Vol. 51, No. 13, June 1978, pp. 126–130.

JONES, T., and P. THOMAS, "Challenges in Microprocessor System Design," *Computer Design*, Vol. 15, No. 11, November 1976, pp. 109–118.

LIPPMAN, M.D., and E.S. DONN, "Design Forethought Promotes Easier Testing of Microcomputer Boards," *Electronics*, Vol. 52, No. 2, January 1979, pp. 113–120.

LORENTZEN, R., "Troubleshooting Microprocessors With a Logic Analyzer System," *Computer Design*, Vol. 18, No. 3, March 1979, pp. 160–164.

Microbus, National Semiconductor Standard for Microprocessor Interfaces. Santa Clara, California: National Semiconductor Corp., 1977.

ROLANDER, T., "Intel Multibus Interfacing," (Application Note AP-28), Santa Clara, California: Intel Corporation, 1977.

ROSENFELD, P., "Is There a High Level Language in Your Microcomputer's Future?" *EDN*, Vol. 21, No. 10, May 1976, pp. 62–67.

WEISSBERGER, A.J., "Analysis of Multiple-Microprocessor System Architectures," *Computer Design*, Vol. 16, No. 6, June 1977, pp. 151–163.

PROBLEM

12-1. Design a microprocessor system! More specifically, select an application that you are familiar with and that you feel might be appropriately handled by a low to medium complexity microprocessor system. You may wish to select a very simple application for your first microprocessor system design and after its completion repeat this problem attempting a different more complex design or a substantial enhancement (second generation) of your first design. Some possible applications are listed below if you need suggestions.

For your design carry out each of the five stages in the five-stage methodology as thoroughly as possible within the limits of time, information, and facilities available to you.

a. Requirements Definition: Develop a complete written requirements definition. In doing so consider the capabilities and limitations of any existing systems designed for the same applications. Ideally you should be developing a system which is competitive with existing systems in terms of cost and performance.

b. Systematic Design: Functionally partition your system. Your partition should take full consideration of existing common LSI subsystems. Select an appropriate microprocessor or microcomputer for your application. Since a low to medium complexity system is being designed, it should be implementable with a single-chip microcomputer or a low end or mid-range general purpose microprocessor.

c. System Implementation: Determine the method of hardware implementation: individual ICs, prefabricated single board computers, or prefabricated card sets. If individual ICs are the chosen approach, select and identify the actual devices, and also reconsider the system partition, and hardware/software tradeoffs in light of the available IC devices. Also consider how your ICs will be physically placed among the PC boards. If a prefabricated single board microcomputer or PC card set is the chosen approach, identify the actual parts, and determine what special circuitry must be designed and how it will interface with the prefabricated hardware. Draw the logic diagram of any circuitry to be designed.

Determine what language you will program the system in: assembly language or one of the high level languages available for the microprocessor or microcomputer of your choice. For your choice of language, determine what software development aids are available. Flowchart the overall application program logic. Design and code any critical subroutines whose implementation is not readily apparent. If time and facilities permit, write the entire application program.

d. Flowchart routines for testing and debugging the various hardware subsystems.

e. Translate and debug the application program to whatever extent is possible with the facilities available to you.

f. Compile and write the documentation for the system hardware and software.

Possible microprocessor system applications:
1. EPROM programmer
2. Home security system (smoke, fire, and intrusion)
3. Integrated circuit tester
4. Commercial paint mixing system
5. Piece counting by weight system
6. Printed circuit board drilling system
7. Taxi meter
8. Swimming (or running) competition timing and display system
9. Automobile trip computer

Appendices

A

Open Collector and Three-State Outputs

Regardless of the technology used or the function implemented by an IC logic device, its output can be one of three types: standard totem pole, open collector, or three-state.

The circuit diagram of a simple T^2L inverter with a standard totem pole output is shown in Fig. A.1(a). The totem pole output stage consists of transistors Q_1 and Q_2. Transistor Q_1 is ON and transistor Q_2 is OFF to provide a logic 1 output. Because of the way it is used, Q_1 is called an active pull-up transistor. When ON, it pulls the output voltage up to its logic 1 level. The output impedance in the logic 1 state is very low. A logic 0 output results when transistor Q_1 is OFF and Q_2 is ON. The output impedance in the logic 0 state is also very low. The design of the circuit is such that one of these transistors is always ON and the other OFF. An advantage of the totem pole output stage is its fast switching speed even when driving highly capacitive loads.

When a logic circuit is constructed from devices with standard totem pole outputs, these outputs are only connected to the inputs of other logic devices. *Outputs of devices with standard totem pole output stages are never connected.* For example, if T^2L standard totem pole outputs are connected and one of the outputs is driven low while the other is driven high (as shown in Fig. A.1(b)), the devices will be damaged. This is due to the fact that one transistor is always ON and the other is always OFF in the standard totem pole output stage. When output A is high, the top transistor is ON, and the bottom transistor is OFF; if output B is low, the top transistor is OFF, and the bottom transistor is ON. With outputs A and B connected, there is only a very small resistance (typically 130 Ω) between V_{cc} and ground, and the resultant current can destroy the devices. Figure A.1(c) shows, in logic diagram form, the unacceptable connection of the outputs of two T^2L inverters with standard totem pole output stages.

The output stages of open collector devices are not totem pole configurations nor is a pull-up transistor used. Instead, the output circuit of an open

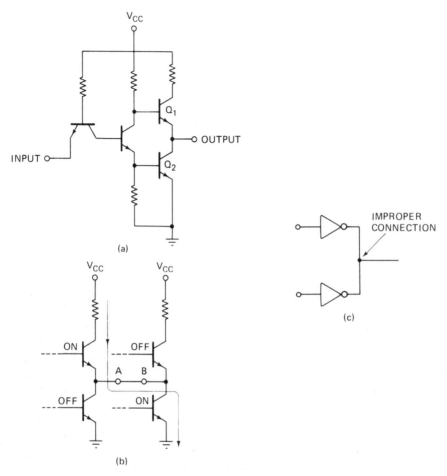

Figure A.1. (a) Standard T²L inverter with totem pole output, (b) short circuit of two inverters with outputs connected. (c) logic diagram of improper connection.

collector device is completed by the addition of an external ***pull-up resistor***. (See Fig. A.2(a)). The use of a passive pull-up resistor with open collector outputs results in a device which switches more slowly when changing from logic 0 to logic 1 than does a device having an output stage with an active pull up. If the outputs of two or more open collector devices are connected, only a single pull-up resistor is required. (See Fig. A.2(b)). The value of the pull-up resistor is selected so that there is no danger of damage to devices when the outputs are connected. (See Fig. A.3). If either device is driven low, their common output, F, is low; if both are high, their common output is high. Thus, $F = A \cdot B$ or $\overline{F} = \overline{A} + \overline{B}$. This connection is frequently referred to as a ***wired AND*** or ***wired OR*** connection. To be more exact, the wired OR reference is actually to a negative logic wired OR.

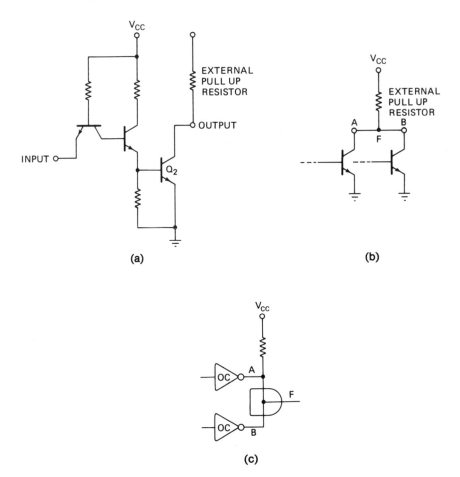

FigureA.2. (a) Open collector T²L output; (b) valid common connection of open collector outputs using a pull up resistor; (c) logic schematic showing "dot AND" effect of connecting open collector outputs together.

This connection is sometimes represented on a logic diagram by a gate symbol with a dot in its center. The gate does not exist physically in the system, only the wire connections and the logical effect of the gate exist.

The ability to directly connect the outputs of open collector devices without damage and the logic functions that derive from that interconnection allow the outputs of these devices to be multiplexed without separate multiplexer ICs. This is particularly important when connecting several devices to the same bus. Figure A.4 shows two devices, each with two data outputs. The outputs are provided from output stages consisting of open collector NAND gates. One input to each NAND gate is the complement of the data, and the other is an enable signal. Outputs on a single device have a common enable signal. When

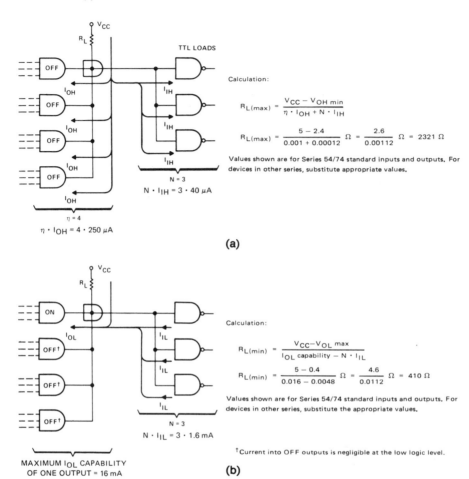

Calculation:

$$R_{L(max)} = \frac{V_{CC} - V_{OH\ min}}{\eta \cdot I_{OH} + N \cdot I_{IH}}$$

$$R_{L(max)} = \frac{5 - 2.4}{0.001 + 0.00012}\ \Omega = \frac{2.6}{0.00112}\ \Omega = 2321\ \Omega$$

Values shown are for Series 54/74 standard inputs and outputs. For devices in other series, substitute appropriate values.

(a)

Calculation:

$$R_{L(min)} = \frac{V_{CC} - V_{OL\ max}}{I_{OL}\ \text{capability} - N \cdot I_{IL}}$$

$$R_{L(min)} = \frac{5 - 0.4}{0.016 - 0.0048}\ \Omega = \frac{4.6}{0.0112}\ \Omega = 410\ \Omega$$

Values shown are for Series 54/74 standard inputs and outputs. For devices in other series, substitute the appropriate values.

†Current into OFF outputs is negligible at the low logic level.

(b)

Figure A.3. (a) Relationships for determining the value of the pull-up resistor in open collector circuits: high level circuit conditions; (b) low level circuit conditions. (Courtesy of Texas Instruments, Inc.)

the enable signal of one device is logic 0, its outputs are logic 1; if the enable signal of the other device is logic 1, its outputs are the complement of the data inputs to its open collector NAND gates, and drive the common bus. For example, if ENX = 1 and ENY = 0, then $Z_0 = X_0$ and $Z_1 = X_1$.

The output stages of devices with three-state outputs provide three possible output conditions. Two are identical to those of standard T^2L, and one of these two conditions exists whenever the device is enabled: a low impedance output with a high voltage level (logic 1), or a low impedance output with a low voltage level (logic 0). The third state, a high impedance output, exists when the device is not enabled. The output stage of a three-state device is similar to that of a

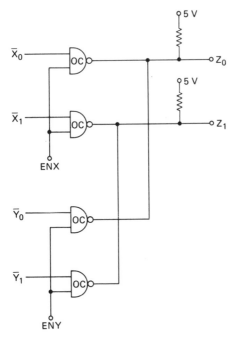

Figure A.4. Multiplexing signals to a common bus using NAND gates with open collector outputs.

standard totem pole T^2L output stage except it includes circuitry which allows an enable signal to turn both output transistors OFF simultaneously, providing a high impedance output state (Fig. A.5(a) and (b)). The high impedance state makes the output function as if it is not electrically connected to any other device to which it is actually physically connected. If several three-state outputs are connected, all but one must be disabled; only the enabled output determines the logic level of the connection. If the outputs of two three-state devices are enabled simultaneously, a situation similar to that in Fig. A.1(b) is possible, and the devices are subject to damage. Three-state outputs allow the multiplexing of several outputs without the use of multiplexer ICs or pull-up resistors. The symbol for a three-state output buffer is shown in Fig. A.5(c). This device is enabled with a logic 1 at the enable input. The output of this device is the complement of its input. This is one of four possible variations of enable levels and output levels. The logic symbols for all four variations of three-state buffers are shown in Fig. A.6.

Many logic devices are designed with three-state outputs so they can be multiplexed to a bus easily. For devices which do not have three-state outputs, separate three-state buffer ICs between the output of the device and the bus carry out the same function at the cost of an additional package.

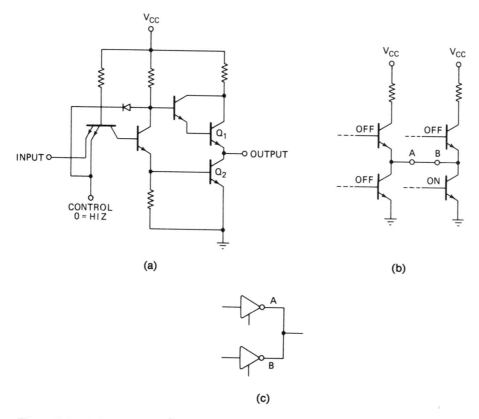

Figure A.5. (a) Three state T²L circuit; (b) common connection of three state outputs—only one gate enabled; (c) logic schematic showing connection of three state outputs.

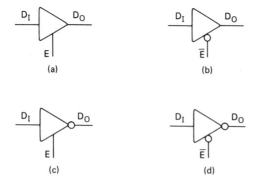

Figure A.6. Three state buffers: (a) noninverting buffer with active high enable; (b) noninverting buffer with active low enable; (c) inverting buffer with active high enable; (d) inverting buffer with active low enable.

B

Octal and Hexadecimal Numbers

The octal (base 8) and hexadecimal (base 16) numbers and their binary (base 2) and decimal (base 10) counterparts from 0 to 15 are as follows

Decimal (base 10)	Binary (base 2)	Octal (base 8)	Hexadecimal (base 16)
00	0000	00	0
01	0001	01	1
02	0010	02	2
03	0011	03	3
04	0100	04	4
05	0101	05	5
06	0110	06	6
07	0111	07	7
08	1000	10	8
09	1001	11	9
10	1010	12	A
11	1011	13	B
12	1100	14	C
13	1101	15	D
14	1110	16	E
15	1111	17	F

The octal number system has eight digits (0–7), and the hexadecimal system contains 16 digits (0–9 and A–F). Because 8 and 16 are both powers of 2, conversion between binary and octal (2^3) or binary and hexadecimal (2^4) numbers is very simple. To convert a binary number to octal, the bits of the binary number are grouped in threes starting at the binary point and moving left for integers and right for fractions. Each group of three is then converted to the proper octal digit. For example

binary	11	011	101	000	.	010	11
octal	3	3	5	0	.	2	6

Note that zeros are assumed to the extreme left and right of the binary number to make the leftmost and rightmost groupings consist of the necessary three digits.

Octal numbers are written with a subscript 8 or a suffix O or Q to indicate that they are octal numbers.

$$3350.26_8 = 3350.26Q$$

Binary numbers are converted to hexadecimal numbers by separating the binary number into groups of 4 bits and converting each group to a hexadecimal digit. For example

binary	110	1110	1000	.	0101	1
hexadecimal	6	E	8	.	5	8

Hexadecimal numbers are written with a subscript 16 or a suffix H to indicate that they are hexadecimal numbers.

$$6E8.58_{16} = 6E8.58H$$

To convert an octal or hexadecimal number to its binary equivalent, each octal or hexadecimal digit is replaced by its binary equivalent. An example of converting an octal number 743.16Q to binary is

octal	7	4	3	.	1	6
binary	111	100	011	.	001	110

Similarly for the hexadecimal number A29.C4H

hexadecimal	A	2	9	.	C	4
binary	1010	0010	1001	.	1100	0100

Octal and hexadecimal numbers are commonly used to represent bit patterns in a concise manner in microprocessor systems. Hexadecimal is preferred over octal because it is the most concise, and register sizes in microprocessor systems are multiples of 4 bits (4, 8, 12, or 16 bits). For example, if register A contains 10110011 it is simply written as B3H. Furthermore, a 16-bit address 0000 0100 0001 1101 is written 041DH.

C

The Intel 8085A Instruction Set

INSTRUCTION SET ENCYCLOPEDIA

In the ensuing dozen pages, the complete 8085A instruction set is described, grouped in order under five different functional headings, as follows:

1. **Data Transfer Group** — Moves data between registers or between memory locations and registers. Includes moves, loads, stores, and exchanges. (See below.)
2. **Arithmetic Group** — Adds, subtracts, increments, or decrements data in registers or memory. (See page 4-13.)
3. **Logic Group** — ANDs, ORs, XORs, compares, rotates, or complements data in registers or between memory and a register. (See page 4-16.)
4. **Branch Group** — Initiates conditional or unconditional jumps, calls, returns, and restarts. (See page 4-20.)
5. **Stack, I/O, and Machine Control Group** — Includes instructions for maintaining the stack, reading from input ports, writing to output ports, setting and reading interrupt masks, and setting and clearing flags. (See page 4-22.)

The formats described in the encyclopedia reflect the assembly language processed by Intel-supplied assembler, used with the Intellec® development systems.

Data Transfer Group

This group of instructions transfers data to and from registers and memory. **Condition flags are not affected by any instruction in this group.**

MOV r1, r2   (Move Register)
(r1) ← (r2)
The content of register r2 is moved to register r1.

| 0 | 1 | D | D | D | S | S | S |

Cycles: 1
States: 4
Addressing: register
Flags: none

MOV r, M   (Move from memory)
(r) ← ((H) (L))
The content of the memory location, whose address is in registers H and L, is moved to register r.

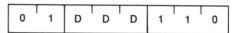

| 0 | 1 | D | D | D | 1 | 1 | 0 |

Cycles: 2
States: 7
Addressing: reg. indirect
Flags: none

MOV M, r   (Move to memory)
((H)) (L)) ← (r)
The content of register r is moved to the memory location whose address is in registers H and L.

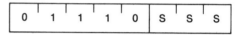

| 0 | 1 | 1 | 1 | 0 | S | S | S |

Cycles: 2
States: 7
Addressing: reg. indirect
Flags: none

MVI r, data   (Move Immediate)
(r) ← (byte 2)
The content of byte 2 of the instruction is moved to register r.

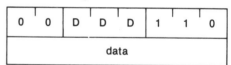

| 0 | 0 | D | D | D | 1 | 1 | 0 |
| data |

Cycles: 2
States: 7
Addressing: immediate
Flags: none

MVI M, data   (Move to memory immediate)
((H) (L)) ← (byte 2)
The content of byte 2 of the instruction is moved to the memory location whose address is in registers H and L.

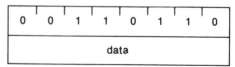

| 0 | 0 | 1 | 1 | 0 | 1 | 1 | 0 |
| data |

Cycles: 3
States: 10
Addressing: immed./reg. indirect
Flags: none

(All mnemonics copyright Intel Corporation 1976.)

LXI rp, data 16 (Load register pair immediate)
(rh) ← (byte 3),
(rl) ← (byte 2)
Byte 3 of the instruction is moved into the high-order register (rh) of the register pair rp. Byte 2 of the instruction is moved into the low-order register (rl) of the register pair rp.

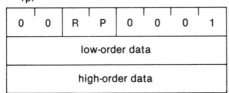

0	0	R	P	0	0	0	1
low-order data							
high-order data							

Cycles: 3
States: 10
Addressing: immediate
Flags: none

LDA addr   (Load Accumulator direct)
(A) ← ((byte 3)(byte 2))
The content of the memory location, whose address is specified in byte 2 and byte 3 of the instruction, is moved to register A.

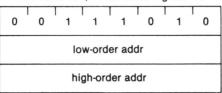

0	0	1	1	1	0	1	0
low-order addr							
high-order addr							

Cycles: 4
States: 13
Addressing: direct
Flags: none

STA addr   (Store Accumulator direct)
((byte 3)(byte 2)) ← (A)
The content of the accumulator is moved to the memory location whose address is specified in byte 2 and byte 3 of the instruction.

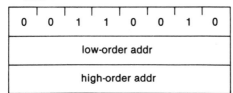

0	0	1	1	0	0	1	0
low-order addr							
high-order addr							

Cycles: 4
States: 13
Addressing: direct
Flags: none

LHLD addr   (Load H and L direct)
(L) ← ((byte 3)(byte 2))
(H) ← ((byte 3)(byte 2) + 1)
The content of the memory location, whose address is specified in byte 2 and byte 3 of the instruction, is moved to register L. The content of the memory location at the succeeding address is moved to register H.

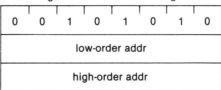

0	0	1	0	1	0	1	0
low-order addr							
high-order addr							

Cycles: 5
States: 16
Addressing: direct
Flags: none

SHLD addr   (Store H and L direct)
((byte 3)(byte 2)) ← (L)
((byte 3)(byte 2) + 1) ← (H)
The content of register L is moved to the memory location whose address is specified in byte 2 and byte 3. The content of register H is moved to the succeeding memory location.

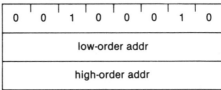

0	0	1	0	0	0	1	0
low-order addr							
high-order addr							

Cycles: 5
States: 16
Addressing: direct
Flags: none

LDAX rp   (Load accumulator indirect)
(A) ← ((rp))
The content of the memory location, whose address is in the register pair rp, is moved to register A. Note: only register pairs rp = B (registers B and C) or rp = D (registers D and E) may be specified.

0	0	R	P	1	0	1	0

Cycles: 2
States: 7
Addressing: reg. indirect
Flags: none

(All mnemonics copyright Intel Corporation 1976.)

STAX rp   (Store accumulator indirect)
((rp)) ← (A)
The content of register A is moved to the memory location whose address is in the register pair rp. Note: only register pairs rp = B (registers B and C) or rp = D (registers D and E) may be specified.

0	0	R	P	0	0	1	0

Cycles: 2
States: 7
Addressing: reg. indirect
Flags: none

XCHG   (Exchange H and L with D and E)
(H) ↔ (D)
(L) ↔ (E)
The contents of registers H and L are exchanged with the contents of registers D and E.

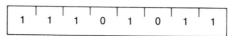

1	1	1	0	1	0	1	1

Cycles: 1
States: 4
Addressing: register
Flags: none

Arithmetic Group

This group of instructions performs arithmetic operations on data in registers and memory.

Unless indicated otherwise, all instructions in this group affect the Zero, Sign, Parity, Carry, and Auxiliary Carry flags according to the standard rules.

All subtraction operations are performed via two's complement arithmetic and set the carry flag to one to indicate a borrow and clear it to indicate no borrow.

ADD r   (Add Register)
(A) ← (A) + (r)
The content of register r is added to the content of the accumulator. The result is placed in the accumulator.

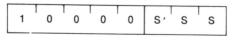

1	0	0	0	0	S′	S	S

Cycles: 1
States: 4
Addressing: register
Flags: Z,S,P,CY,AC

ADD M   (Add memory)
(A) ← (A) + ((H) (L))
The content of the memory location whose address is contained in the H and L registers is added to the content of the accumulator. The result is placed in the accumulator.

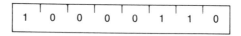

1	0	0	0	0	1	1	0

Cycles: 2
States: 7
Addressing: reg. indirect
Flags: Z,S,P,CY,AC

ADI data   (Add immediate)
(A) ← (A) + (byte 2)
The content of the second byte of the instruction is added to the content of the accumulator. The result is placed in the accumulator.

1	1	0	0	0	1	1	0

Cycles: 2
States: 7
Addressing: immediate
Flags: Z,S,P,CY,AC

ADC r   (Add Register with carry)
(A) ← (A) + (r) + (CY)
The content of register r and the content of the carry bit are added to the content of the accumulator. The result is placed in the accumulator.

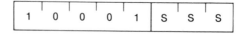

1	0	0	0	1	S	S	S

Cycles: 1
States: 4
Addressing: register
Flags: Z,S,P,CY,AC

(All mnemonics copyright Intel Corporation 1976.)

ADC M (Add memory with carry)
$(A) \leftarrow (A) + ((H)(L)) + (CY)$

The content of the memory location whose address is contained in the H and L registers and the content of the CY flag are added to the accumulator. The result is placed in the accumulator.

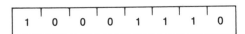

1	0	0	0	1	1	1	0

Cycles: 2
States: 7
Addressing: reg. indirect
Flags: Z,S,P,CY,AC

SUB M (Subtract memory)
$(A) \leftarrow (A) - ((H)(L))$

The content of the memory location whose address is contained in the H and L registers is subtracted from the content of the accumulator. The result is placed in the accumulator.

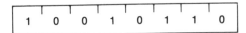

1	0	0	1	0	1	1	0

Cycles: 2
States: 7
Addressing: reg. indirect
Flags: Z,S,P,CY,AC

ACI data (Add immediate with carry)
$(A) \leftarrow (A) + (byte\ 2) + (CY)$

The content of the second byte of the instruction and the content of the CY flag are added to the contents of the accumulator. The result is placed in the accumulator.

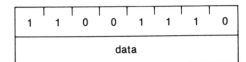

1	1	0	0	1	1	1	0

data

Cycles: 2
States: 7
Addressing: immediate
Flags: Z,S,P,CY,AC

SUI data (Subtract immediate)
$(A) \leftarrow (A) - (byte\ 2)$

The content of the second byte of the instruction is subtracted from the content of the accumulator. The result is placed in the accumulator.

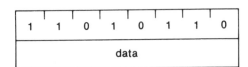

1	1	0	1	0	1	1	0

data

Cycles: 2
States: 7
Addressing: immediate
Flags: Z,S,P,CY,AC

SUB r (Subtract Register)
$(A) \leftarrow (A) - (r)$

The content of register r is subtracted from the content of the accumulator. The result is placed in the accumulator.

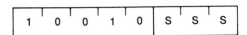

1	0	0	1	0	S	S	S

Cycles: 1
States: 4
Addressing: register
Flags: Z,S,P,CY,AC

SBB r (Subtract Register with borrow)
$(A) \leftarrow (A) - (r) - (CY)$

The content of register r and the content of the CY flag are both subtracted from the accumulator. The result is placed in the accumulator.

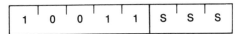

1	0	0	1	1	S	S	S

Cycles: 1
States: 4
Addressing: register
Flags: Z,S,P,CY,AC

SBB M   (Subtract memory with borrow)
(A) ← (A) − ((H) (L)) − (CY)
The content of the memory location whose address is contained in the H and L registers and the content of the CY flag are both subtracted from the accumulator. The result is placed in the accumulator.

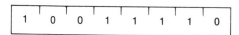

1	0	0	1	1	1	1	0

Cycles: 2
States: 7
Addressing: reg. indirect
Flags: Z,S,P,CY,AC

SBI data   (Subtract immediate with borrow)
(A) ← (A) − (byte 2) − (CY)
The contents of the second byte of the instruction and the contents of the CY flag are both subtracted from the accumulator. The result is placed in the accumulator.

1	1	0	1	1	1	1	0

data

Cycles: 2
States: 7
Addressing: immediate
Flags: Z,S,P,CY,AC

INR r   (Increment Register)
(r) ← (r) + 1
The content of register r is incremented by one. Note: All condition flags **except CY** are affected.

0	0	D	D	D	1	0	0

Cycles: 1
States: 4
Addressing: register
Flags: Z,S,P,AC

INR M   (Increment memory)
((H) (L) ← ((H) (L)) + 1
The content of the memory location whose address is contained in the H and L registers is incremented by one. Note: All condition flags **except CY** are affected.

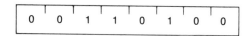

0	0	1	1	0	1	0	0

Cycles: 3
States: 10
Addressing: reg. indirect
Flags: Z,S,P,AC

DCR r   (Decrement Register)
(r) ← (r) − 1
The content of register r is decremented by one. Note: All condition flags **except CY** are affected.

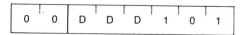

0	0	D	D	D	1	0	1

Cycles: 1
States: 4
Addressing: register
Flags: Z,S,P,AC

DCR M   (Decrement memory)
((H) (L)) ← ((H) (L)) − 1
The content of the memory location whose address is contained in the H and L registers is decremented by one. Note: All condition flags **except CY** are affected.

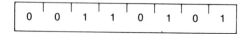

0	0	1	1	0	1	0	1

Cycles: 3
States: 10
Addressing: reg. indirect
Flags: Z,S,P,AC

INX rp　　　(Increment register pair)

(rh) (rl) ← (rh) (rl) + 1

The content of the register pair rp is incremented by one. Note: **No condition flags are affected.**

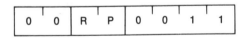

| 0 | 0 | R | P | 0 | 0 | 1 | 1 |

```
Cycles:      1
States:      6
Addressing:  register
Flags:       none
```

DCX rp　　　(Decrement register pair)

(rh) (rl) ← (rh) (rl) − 1

The content of the register pair rp is decremented by one. Note: **No condition flags are affected.**

| 0 | 0 | R | P | 1 | 0 | 1 | 1 |

```
Cycles:      1
States:      6
Addressing:  register
Flags:       none
```

DAD rp　　　(Add register pair to H and L)

(H) (L) ← (H) (L) + (rh) (rl)

The content of the register pair rp is added to the content of the register pair H and L. The result is placed in the register pair H and L. Note: **Only the CY flag is affected.** It is set if there is a carry out of the double precision add; otherwise it is reset.

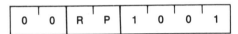

| 0 | 0 | R | P | 1 | 0 | 0 | 1 |

```
Cycles:      3
States:      10
Addressing:  register
Flags:       CY
```

DAA　　　(Decimal Adjust Accumulator)

The eight-bit number in the accumulator is adjusted to form two four-bit Binary-Coded-Decimal digits by the following process:

1. If the value of the lease significant 4 bits of the accumulator is greater than 9 **or** if the AC flag is set, 6 is added to the accumulator.

2. If the value of the most significant 4 bits of the accumulator is now greater than 9, **or** if the CY flag is set, 6 is added to the most significant 4 bits of the accumulator.

NOTE: All flags are affected.

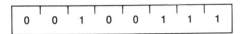

| 0 | 0 | 1 | 0 | 0 | 1 | 1 | 1 |

```
Cycles:      1
States:      4
Flags:       Z,S,P,CY,AC
```

4.6.3 Logic Group

This group of instructions performs logical (Boolean) operations on data in registers and memory and on condition flags.

Unless indicated otherwise, all instructions in this group affect the Zero, Sign, Parity, Auxiliary Carry, and Carry flags according to the standard rules.

ANA r　　　(AND Register)

(A) ← (A) ∧ (r)

The content of register r is logically ANDed with the content of the accumulator. The result is placed in the accumulator. **The CY flag is cleared and AC is set.**

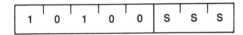

| 1 | 0 | 1 | 0 | 0 | S | S | S |

```
Cycles:      1
States:      4
Addressing:  register
Flags:       Z,S,P,CY,AC
```

(All mnemonics copyright Intel Corporation 1976.)

ANA M   (AND memory)

(A) ← (A) ∧ ((H) (L))

The contents of the memory location whose address is contained in the H and L registers is logically ANDed with the content of the accumulator. The result is placed in the accumulator. **The CY flag is cleared and AC is set.**

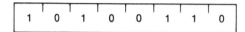

1	0	1	0	0	1	1	0

Cycles:	2
States:	7
Addressing:	reg. indirect
Flags:	Z,S,P,CY,AC

ANI data   (AND immediate)

(A) ← (A) ∧ (byte 2)

The content of the second byte of the instruction is logically ANDed with the contents of the accumulator. The result is placed in the accumulator. **The CY flag is cleared and AC is set.**

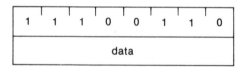

1	1	1	0	0	1	1	0
data							

Cycles:	2
States:	7
Addressing:	immediate
Flags:	Z,S,P,CY,AC

XRA r   (Exclusive OR Register)

(A) ← (A) ∀ (r)

The content of register r is exclusive-OR'd with the content of the accumulator. The result is placed in the accumulator. **The CY and AC flags are cleared.**

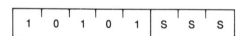

1	0	1	0	1	S	S	S

Cycles:	1
States:	4
Addressing:	register
Flags:	Z,S,P,CY,AC

XRA M   (Exclusive OR Memory)

(A) ← (A) ∀ ((H) (L))

The content of the memory location whose address is contained in the H and L registers is exclusive-OR'd with the content of the accumulator. The result is placed in the accumulator. **The CY and AC flags are cleared.**

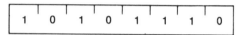

1	0	1	0	1	1	1	0

Cycles:	2
States:	7
Addressing:	reg. indirect
Flags:	Z,S,P,CY,AC

XRI data   (Exclusive OR immediate)

(A) ← (A) ∀ (byte 2)

The content of the second byte of the instruction is exclusive-OR'd with the content of the accumulator. The result is placed in the accumulator. **The CY and AC flags are cleared.**

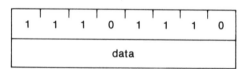

1	1	1	0	1	1	1	0
data							

Cycles:	2
States:	7
Addressing:	immediate
Flags:	Z,S,P,CY,AC

ORA r   (OR Register)

(A) ← (A) V (r)

The content of register r is inclusive-OR'd with the content of the accumulator. The result is placed in the accumulator. **The CY and AC flags are cleared.**

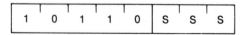

1	0	1	1	0	S	S	S

Cycles:	1
States:	4
Addressing:	register
Flags:	Z,S,P,CY,AC

(All mnemonics copyright Intel Corporation 1976.)

ORA M   (OR memory)
(A) ← (A) V ((H) (L))
The content of the memory location whose address is contained in the H and L registers is inclusive-OR'd with the content of the accumulator. The result is placed in the accumulator. **The CY and AC flags are cleared.**

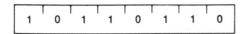

1	0	1	1	0	1	1	0

Cycles: 2
States: 7
Addressing: reg. indirect
Flags: Z,S,P,CY,AC

ORI data   (OR Immediate)
(A) ← (A) V (byte 2)
The content of the second byte of the instruction is inclusive-OR'd with the content of the accumulator. The result is placed in the accumulator. **The CY and AC flags are cleared..**

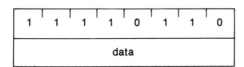

1	1	1	1	0	1	1	0
data							

Cycles: 2
States: 7
Addressing: immediate
Flags: Z,S,P,CY,AC

CMP r   (Compare Register)
(A) − (r)
The content of register r is subtracted from the accumulator. The accumulator remains unchanged. The condition flags are set as a result of the subtraction. **The Z flag is set to 1 if (A) = (r). The CY flag is set to 1 if (A) < (r).**

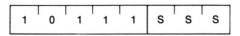

1	0	1	1	1	S	S	S

Cycles: 1
States: 4
Addressing: register
Flags: Z,S,P,CY,AC

CMP M   (Compare memory)
(A) − ((H) (L))
The content of the memory location whose address is contained in the H and L registers is subtracted from the accumulator. The accumulator remains unchanged. The condition flags are set as a result of the subtraction. **The Z flag is set to 1 if (A) = ((H) (L)). The CY flag is set to 1 if (A) < ((H) (L)).**

1	0	1	1	1	1	1	0

Cycles: 2
States: 7
Addressing: reg. indirect
Flags: Z,S,P,CY,AC

CPI data   (Compare immediate)
(A) − (byte 2)
The content of the second byte of the instruction is subtracted from the accumulator. The condition flags are set by the result of the subtraction. **The Z flag is set to 1 if (A) = (byte 2). The CY flag is set to 1 if (A) < (byte 2).**

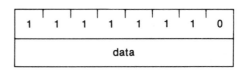

1	1	1	1	1	1	1	0
data							

Cycles: 2
States: 7
Addressing: immediate
Flags: Z,S,P,CY,AC

RLC   (Rotate left)
$(A_{n+1}) ← (A_n) ;(A_0) ← (A_7)$
$(CY) ← (A_7)$
The content of the accumulator is rotated left one position. The low order bit and the CY flag are both set to the value shifted out of the high order bit position. **Only the CY flag is affected.**

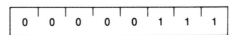

0	0	0	0	0	1	1	1

Cycles: 1
States: 4
Flags: CY

(All mnemonics copyright Intel Corporation 1976.)

497

RRC (Rotate right)
$(A_n) \leftarrow (A_{n+1}); (A_7) \leftarrow (A_0)$
$(CY) \leftarrow (A_0)$
The content of the accumulator is rotated right one position. The high order bit and the CY flag are both set to the value shifted out of the low order bit position. **Only the CY flag is affected.**

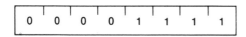

0	0	0	0	1	1	1	1

Cycles: 1
States: 4
Flags: CY

RAL (Rotate left through carry)
$(A_{n+1}) \leftarrow (A_n); (CY) \leftarrow (A_7)$
$(A_0) \leftarrow (CY)$
The content of the accumulator is rotated left one position through the CY flag. The low order bit is set equal to the CY flag and the CY flag is set to the value shifted out of the high order bit. **Only the CY flag is affected.**

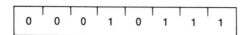

0	0	0	1	0	1	1	1

Cycles: 1
States: 4
Flags: CY

RAR (Rotate right through carry)
$(A_n) \leftarrow (A_{n+1}); (CY) \leftarrow (A_0)$
$(A_7) \leftarrow (CY)$
The content of the accumulator is rotated right one position through the CY flag. The high order bit is set to the CY flag and the CY flag is set to the value shifted out of the low order bit. **Only the CY flag is affected.**

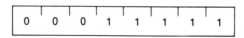

0	0	0	1	1	1	1	1

Cycles: 1
States: 4
Flags: CY

CMA (Complement accumulator)
$(A) \leftarrow (\overline{A})$
The contents of the accumulator are complemented (zero bits become 1, one bits become 0). **No flags are affected.**

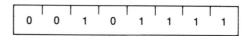

0	0	1	0	1	1	1	1

Cycles: 1
States: 4
Flags: none

CMC (Complement carry)
$(CY) \leftarrow (\overline{CY})$
The CY flag is complemented. **No other flags are affected.**

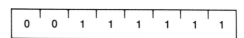

0	0	1	1	1	1	1	1

Cycles: 1
States: 4
Flags: CY

STC (Set carry)
$(CY) \leftarrow 1$
The CY flag is set to 1. **No other flags are affected.**

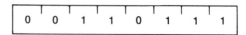

0	0	1	1	0	1	1	1

Cycles: 1
States: 4
Flags: CY

THE INSTRUCTION SET

Branch Group

This group of instructions alter normal sequential program flow.

Condition flags are not affected by any instruction in this group.

The two types of branch instructions are unconditional and conditional. Unconditional transfers simply perform the specified operation on register PC (the program counter). Conditional transfers examine the status of one of the four processor flags to determine if the specified branch is to be executed. The conditions that may be specified are as follows:

CONDITION		CCC
NZ —	not zero (Z = 0)	000
Z —	zero (Z = 1)	001
NC —	no carry (CY = 0)	010
C —	carry (CY = 1)	011
PO —	parity odd (P = 0)	100
PE —	parity even (P = 1)	101
P —	plus (S = 0)	110
M —	minus (S = 1)	111

JMP addr   (Jump)
    (PC) ← (byte 3) (byte 2)
    Control is transferred to the instruction whose address is specified in byte 3 and byte 2 of the current instruction.

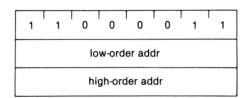

        Cycles: 3
        States: 10
    Addressing: immediate
        Flags: none

Jcondition addr (Conditional jump)
    If (CCC),
        (PC) ← (byte 3) (byte 2)
    If the specified condition is true, control is transferred to the instruction whose address is specified in byte 3 and byte 2 of the current instruciton; otherwise, control continues sequentially.

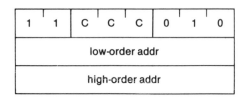

        Cycles: 2/3
        States: 7/10
    Addressing: immediate
        Flags: none

CALL addr   (Call)
    ((SP) − 1) ← (PCH)
    ((SP) − 2) ← (PCL)
    (SP) ← (SP) − 2
    (PC) ← (byte 3) (byte 2)
    The high-order eight bits of the next instruction address are moved to the memory location whose address is one less than the content of register SP. The low-order eight bits of the next instruction address are moved to the memory location whose address is two less than the content of register SP. The content of register SP is decremented by 2. Control is transferred to the instruction whose address is specified in byte 3 and byte 2 of the current instruction.

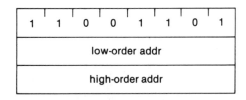

        Cycles: 5
        States: 18
    Addressing: immediate/
                     reg. indirect
        Flags: none

(All mnemonics copyright Intel Corporation 1976.)

Ccondition addr (Condition call)
If (CCC),
((SP) − 1) ← (PCH)
((SP) − 2) ← (PCL)
(SP) ← (SP) − 2
(PC) ← (byte 3) (byte 2)
If the specified condition is true, the actions specified in the CALL instruction (see above) are performed; otherwise, control continues sequentially.

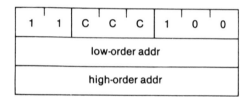

1	1	C	C	C	1	0	0
low-order addr							
high-order addr							

Cycles: 2/5
States: 9/18
Addressing: immediate/
              reg. indirect
Flags: none

RET   (Return)
(PCL) ← ((SP));
(PCH) ← ((SP) + 1);
(SP) ← (SP) + 2;
The content of the memory location whose address is specified in register SP is moved to the low-order eight bits of register PC. The content of the memory location whose address is one more than the content of register SP is moved to the high-order eight bits of register PC. The content of register SP is incremented by 2.

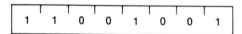

1	1	0	0	1	0	0	1

Cycles: 3
States: 10
Addressing: reg. indirect
Flags: none

Rcondition   (Conditional return)
If (CCC),
(PCL) ← ((SP))
(PCH) ← ((SP) + 1)
(SP) ← (SP) + 2
If the specified condition is true, the actions specified in the RET instruction (see above) are performed; otherwise, control continues sequentially.

1	1	C	C	C	0	0	0

Cycles: 1/3
States: 6/12
Addressing: reg. indirect
Flags: none

RST n   (Restart)
((SP) − 1) ← (PCH)
((SP) − 2) ← (PCL)
(SP) ← (SP) − 2
(PC) ← 8 * (NNN)
The high-order eight bits of the next instruction address are moved to the memory location whose address is one less than the content of register SP. The low-order eight bits of the next instruction address are moved to the memory location whose address is two less than the content of register SP. The content of register SP is decremented by two. Control is transferred to the instruction whose address is eight times the content of NNN.

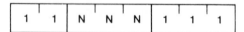

1	1	N	N	N	1	1	1

Cycles: 3
States: 12
Addressing: reg. indirect
Flags: none

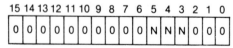

15	14	13	12	11	10	9	8	7	6	5	4	3	2	1	0
0	0	0	0	0	0	0	0	0	0	N	N	N	0	0	0

Program Counter After Restart

(All mnemonics copyright Intel Corporation 1976.)

THE INSTRUCTION SET

PCHL   (Jump H and L indirect —
                  move H and L to PC)
(PCH) ← (H)
(PCL) ← (L)
The content of register H is moved to the
high-order eight bits of register PC. The
content of register L is moved to the low-
order eight bits of register PC.

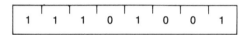

1	1	1	0	1	0	0	1

Cycles: 1
States: 6
Addressing: register
Flags: none

Stack, I/O, and Machine Control Group

This group of instructions performs I/O, manipu-
lates the Stack, and alters internal control
flags.

Unless otherwise specified, **condition flags are
not affected by any instructions in this group.**

PUSH rp   (Push)

$((SP) - 1) \leftarrow (rh)$
$((SP) - 2) \leftarrow (rl)$
$((SP) \leftarrow (SP) - 2$

The content of the high-order register of
register pair rp is moved to the memory
location whose address is one less than
the content of register SP. The content of
the low-order register of register pair rp is
moved to the memory location whose address is two less than the content of
register SP. The content of register SP is
decremented by 2. **Note: Register pair rp =
SP may not be specified.**

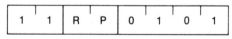

1	1	R	P	0	1	0	1

Cycles: 3
States: 12
Addressing: reg. indirect
Flags: none

PUSH PSW   (Push processor status word)
$((SP) - 1) \leftarrow (A)$
$((SP) - 2)_0 \leftarrow (CY) , ((SP) - 2)_1 \leftarrow X$
$((SP) - 2)_2 \leftarrow (P) , ((SP) - 2)_3 \leftarrow X$
$((SP) - 2)_4 \leftarrow (AC) , ((SP) - 2)_5 \leftarrow X$
$((SP) - 2)_6 \leftarrow (Z) , ((SP) - 2)_7 \leftarrow (S)$
$(SP) \leftarrow (SP) - 2$ X: Undefined.

(All mnemonics copyright Intel Corporation 1976.)

The content of register A is moved to the
memory location whose address is one
less than register SP. The contents of the
condition flags are assembled into a processor status word and the word is moved
to the memory location whose address is
two less than the content of register SP.
The content of register SP is decremented
by two.

1	1	1	1	0	1	0	1

Cycles: 3
States: 12
Addressing: reg. indirect
Flags: none

FLAG WORD

D_7	D_6	D_5	D_4	D_3	D_2	D_1	D_0
S	Z	X	AC	X	P	X	CY

X: undefined

POP rp   (POP)

$(rl) \leftarrow ((SP))$
$(rh) \leftarrow ((SP) + 1)$
$(SP) \leftarrow (SP) + 2$

The content of the memory location, whose
address is specified by the content of
register SP, is moved to the low-order
register of register pair rp. The content of
the memory location, whose address is one
more than the content of register SP, is
moved to the high-order register of register
rp. The content of register SP is incremented by 2. **Note: Register pair rp =
SP may not be specified.**

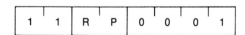

1	1	R	P	0	0	0	1

Cycles: 3
States: 10
Addressing: reg.indirect
Flags: none

POP PSW   (Pop processor status word)

$(CY) \leftarrow ((SP))_0$
$(P) \leftarrow ((SP))_2$
$(AC) \leftarrow ((SP))_4$
$(Z) \leftarrow ((SP))_6$
$(S) \leftarrow ((SP))_7$
$(A) \leftarrow ((SP) + 1)$
$(SP) \leftarrow (SP) + 2$

The content of the memory location whose address is specified by the content of register SP is used to restore the condition flags. The content of the memory location whose address is one more than the content of register SP is moved to register A. The content of register SP is incremented by 2.

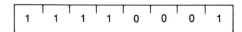

1	1	1	1	0	0	0	1

Cycles: 3
States: 10
Addressing: reg. indirect
Flags: Z,S,P,CY,AC

XTHL   (Exchange stack top with H and L)

$(L) \leftrightarrow ((SP))$
$(H) \leftrightarrow ((SP) + 1)$

The content of the L register is exchanged with the content of the memory location whose address is specified by the content of register SP. The content of the H register is exchanged with the content of the memory location whose address is one more than the content of register SP.

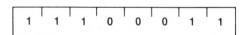

1	1	1	0	0	0	1	1

Cycles: 5
States: 16
Addressing: reg. indirect
Flags: none

SPHL   (Move HL to SP)

$(SP) \leftarrow (H) (L)$

The contents of registers H and L (16 bits) are moved to register SP.

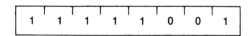

1	1	1	1	1	0	0	1

Cycles: 1
States: 6
Addressing: register
Flags: none

IN port   (Input)

$(A) \leftarrow (data)$

The data placed on the eight bit bi-directional data bus by the specified port is moved to register A.

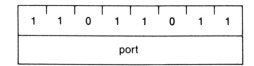

1	1	0	1	1	0	1	1
port							

Cycles: 3
States: 10
Addressing: direct
Flags: none

OUT port   (Output)

$(data) \leftarrow (A)$

The content of register A is placed on the eight bit bi-directional data bus for transmission to the specified port.

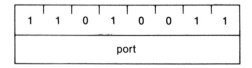

1	1	0	1	0	0	1	1
port							

Cycles: 3
States: 10
Addressing: direct
Flags: none

(All mnemonics copyright Intel Corporation 1976.)

EI   (Enable interrupts)
The interrupt system is enabled **following the execution of the next instruction.**

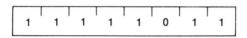

| 1 | 1 | 1 | 1 | 1 | 0 | 1 | 1 |

Cycles: 1
States: 4
Flags: none

NOTE: Interrupts are not recognized during the EI instruction. Placing an EI instruction on the bus in response to INTA during an INA cycle is prohibited.

DI   (Disable interrupts)
The interupt system is disabled **immediately following the execution of the DI instruction.**

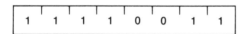

| 1 | 1 | 1 | 1 | 0 | 0 | 1 | 1 |

Cycles: 1
States: 4
Flags: none

NOTE: Interrupts are not recognized during the DI instruction. Placing a DI instruction on the bus in response to INTA during an INA cycle is prohibited.

HLT   (Halt)
The processor is stopped. The registers and flags are unaffected. A second ALE is generated during the execution of HLT to strobe out the Halt cycle status information.

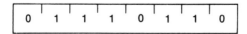

| 0 | 1 | 1 | 1 | 0 | 1 | 1 | 0 |

Cycles: 1+
States: 5
Flags: none

NOP   (No op)
No operation is performed. The registers and flags are unaffected.

(All mnemonics copyright Intel Corporation 1976.)

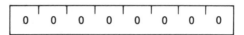

| 0 | 0 | 0 | 0 | 0 | 0 | 0 | 0 |

Cycles: 1
States: 4
Flags: none

RIM   (Read Interrupt Masks)
The RIM instruction loads data into the accumulator relating to interrupts and the serial input. This data contains the following information:

- Current interrupt mask status for the RST 5.5, 6.5, and 7.5 hardware interrupts (1 = mask disabled)
- Current interrupt enable flag status (1 = interrupts enabled) except immediately following a TRAP interrupt. (See below.)
- Hardware interrupts pending (i.e., signal received but not yet serviced), on the RST 5.5, 6.5, and 7.5 lines.
- Serial input data.

Immediately following a TRAP interrupt, the RIM instruction must be executed as a part of the service routine if you need to retrieve current interrupt status later. Bit 3 of the accumulator is (in this special case only) loaded with the interrupt enable (IE) flag status that existed prior to the TRAP interrupt. Following an RST 5.5, 6.5, 7.5, or INTR interrupt, the interrupt flag flip-flop reflects the current interrupt enable status. Bit 6 of the accumulator (I7.5) is loaded with the status of the RST 7.5 flip-flop, which is always set (edge-triggered) by an input on the RST 7.5 input line, even when that interrupt has been previously masked. (See SIM Instruction.)

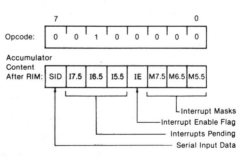

Cycles: 1
States: 4
Flags: none

SIM   (Set Interrupt Masks)

The execution of the SIM instruction uses the contents of the accumulator (which must be previously loaded) to perform the following functions:

- Program the interrupt mask for the RST 5.5, 6.5, and 7.5 hardware interrupts.
- Reset the edge-triggered RST 7.5 input latch.
- Load the SOD output latch.

To program the interrupt masks, first set accumulator bit 3 to 1 and set to 1 any bits 0, 1, and 2, which disable interrupts RST 5.5, 6.5, and 7.5, respectively. Then do a SIM instruction. If accumulator bit 3 is 0 when the SIM instruction is executed, the interrupt mask register will not change. If accumulator bit 4 is 1 when the SIM instruction is executed, the RST 7.5 latch is then reset. RST 7.5 is distinguished by the fact that its latch is always set by a rising edge on the RST 7.5 input pin, even if the jump to service routine is inhibited by masking. This latch remains high until cleared by a RESET IN, by a SIM Instruction with accumulator bit 4 high, or by an internal processor acknowledge to an RST 7.5 interrupt subsequent to the removal of the mask (by a SIM instruction). The RESET IN signal always sets all three RST mask bits.

If accumulator bit 6 is at the 1 level when the SIM instruction is executed, the state of accumulator bit 7 is loaded into the SOD latch and thus becomes available for interface to an external device. The SOD latch is unaffected by the SIM instruction if bit 6 is 0. SOD is always reset by the RESET IN signal.

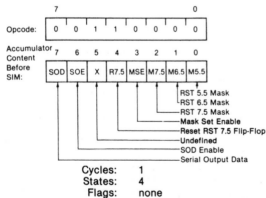

7							0

Opcode:

0	0	1	1	0	0	0	0

Accumulator Content Before SIM:

7	6	5	4	3	2	1	0
SOD	SOE	X	R7.5	MSE	M7.5	M6.5	M5.5

- RST 5.5 Mask
- RST 6.5 Mask
- RST 7.5 Mask
- Mask Set Enable
- Reset RST 7.5 Flip-Flop
- Undefined
- SOD Enable
- Serial Output Data

Cycles: 1
States: 4
Flags: none

504

D

ASCII Character Set

Seven-bit ASCII code, with the high-order eighth bit (parity bit) always reset.

GRAPHIC OR CONTROL	ASCII (HEXADECIMAL)	GRAPHIC OR CONTROL	ASCII (HEXADECIMAL)	GRAPHIC OR CONTROL	ASCII (HEXADECIMAL)
NUL	00	+	2B	V	56
SOH	01	,	2C	W	57
STX	02	–	2D	X	58
ETX	03	.	2E	Y	59
EOT	04	/	2F	Z	5A
ENQ	05	0	30	[	5B
ACK	06	1	31	\	5C
BEL	07	2	32	]	5D
BS	08	3	33	∧(↑)	5E
HT	09	4	34	–(←)	5F
LF	0A	5	35	'	60
VT	0B	6	36	a	61
FF	0C	7	37	b	62
CR	0D	8	38	c	63
SO	0E	9	39	d	64
SI	0F	:	3A	e	65
DLE	10	;	3B	f	66
DC1 (X-ON)	11	<	3C	g	67
DC2 (TAPE)	12	=	3D	h	68
DC3 (X-OFF)	13	>	3E	i	69
DC4 (TAPE)	14	?	3F	j	6A
NAK	15	@	40	k	6B
SYN	16	A	41	l	6C
ETB	17	B	42	m	6D
CAN	18	C	43	n	6E
EM	19	D	44	o	6F
SUB	1A	E	45	p	70
ESC	1B	F	46	q	71
FS	1C	G	47	r	72
GS	1D	H	48	s	73
RS	1E	I	49	t	74
US	1F	J	4A	u	75
SP	20	K	4B	v	76
!	21	L	4C	w	77
"	22	M	4D	x	78
#	23	N	4E	y	79
$	24	O	4F	z	7A
%	25	P	50	{	7B
&	26	Q	51			7C
'	27	R	52	}(ALT MODE)	7D
(	28	S	53	~	7E
)	29	T	54	DEL (RUB OUT)	7F
*	2A	U	55		

E

Virtual Ground Analysis

When an op-amp with a high open loop gain is used with negative feedback to implement a linear circuit, the closed loop gain or transfer characteristic of the circuit is to a first approximation dictated entirely by the external feedback connections. As a result, the design of linear signal processing circuits with op-amps is relatively straightforward.

Op-amp circuits with negative feedback can be analyzed and designed through a technique called virtual ground analysis. One of the bases of *virtual ground analysis* lies in the fact that with negative feedback if the output of the operational amplifier is linearly related to its input, and the open loop gain of the op-amp is large, then the voltage $v_+ - v_-$ must be very small. (See Fig. E.1.) Let $v_+ - v_- = \epsilon$; thus, as a first approximation, $v_+ = v_-$. Then ϵ is approximately zero. This approximation, along with the assumption that the input currents to the op-amp i_- and i_+ are also zero, is the basis of virtual ground analysis. With virtual ground analysis and other elementary circuit laws, such as *Kirchhoff's Current Law, KCL,* (the sum of the currents into and out of a node equals zero) and *Kirchhoff's Voltage Law, KVL,* (the sum of the voltages around a closed loop is zero), the operation of any operational amplifier circuit using negative feedback can be analyzed. As a case in point, the characteristics of several op-amp circuits commonly used in data acquisition systems are determined below by using virtual ground analysis.

Consider the current to voltage converter circuit in Fig. E.2. Negative feedback is provided between the output and inverting terminals by the feedback resistor, R_F. Because the current into the circuit's input, i_I, cannot flow into the inverting terminal of the operational amplifier, it must flow through the feedback resistor, R_F. The output voltage, v_0, equals the sum of the voltage drop across R_F, v_{R_F}, and the differential input voltage ϵ. Thus, since $v_{R_F} = -i_I R_F$

$$v_0 = v_{R_F} + \epsilon$$
$$v_0 = -i_I R_F + \epsilon$$

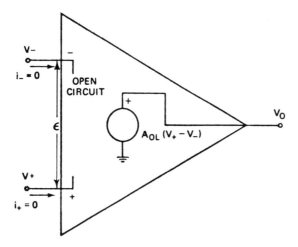

Figure E.1. Equivalent circuit of an ideal op-amp.

By the virtual ground assumption, $\epsilon = 0$. Thus

$$v_0 = -i_I R_F$$

An important point about one of the virtual ground approximations is illustrated by this example: Even though the voltage drop ϵ between the inverting $(-)$ and noninverting $(+)$ terminals is assumed zero, no current flows between these terminals. The voltage ϵ is approximately zero because of the effects of negative feedback, not because there is a low impedance path between these two terminals. The input impedance for the circuit is also approximately zero. This is because input impedance for the circuit is by definition $R_I = v_I/i_I$, and v_I, in this circuit, is equal to ϵ which is approximately zero. The output resistance, R_0, of the circuit is essentially equal to or less than the output resistance of the op-amp, and this in the ideal case, is zero.

The unity gain buffer circuit in Fig. E.3 is used as an isolator between other circuits to prevent a circuit with a low input impedance from loading (drawing excessive current from) the output of either a transducer or another circuit. The input impedance of the buffer amplifier is, for all intents and purposes, infinite

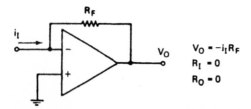

Figure E.2. Op-amp current to voltage converter circuit.

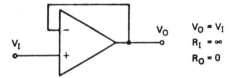

Figure E.3. Op-amp unity gain buffer circuit.

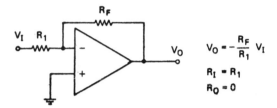

Figure E.4. Op-amp inverting voltage amplifier circuit.

due to the assumption that the current into the noninverting terminal is zero. $R_I = v_I/i_I \simeq \infty$, for i_I approaching zero. The output voltage is

$$v_0 = \epsilon + v_I$$
$$v_0 = v_I$$

Figure E.4 shows an inverting voltage amplifier. The current, i_I, through R_1 is equal to v_I/R_1. This same current flows through R_F, since there is no current into the input terminal of the op-amp. Applying KVL, then $v_0 = -v_{R_F} - \epsilon$. Since $\epsilon = 0$,

$$v_0 = -v_{R_F}$$

Substituting $v_{R_F} = i_I R_F$ gives

$$v_0 = i_I R_F$$

and further substituting $i_I = v_I/R_1$ gives

$$v_0 = -\frac{V_I}{R_1} R_F$$

The input impedance of this circuit is $v_I/i_I = R_I$.

A variation of this circuit, Fig. E.5, uses two or more input resistors and is used to sum several input voltages. The current into the junction at the inverting terminal is the sum of the currents through the input resistances. For this reason, the junction at the inverting input is frequently referred to as the **summing junction** in various op-amp circuits. This current flows through the feedback resistor, R_F.

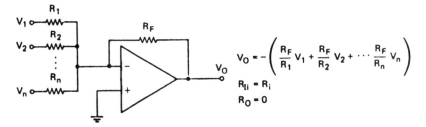

Figure E.5. Op-amp inverting summing amplifier.

A noninverting voltage amplifier is shown in Fig. E.6. The voltage at the inverting terminal is $v_- = v_0 R_1/(R_1 + R_F)$ as a result of the fact that R_F and R_1 form a voltage divider which splits the output voltage. The voltage at the inverting terminal, v_-, is the same as that at the noninverting terminal, v_I, since $\epsilon = 0$. Thus,

$$v_I = \frac{v_0 R_1}{R_1 + R_F}$$

$$v_0 = \frac{(R_1 + R_F)}{R_1} v_I$$

Since the input current for this circuit configuration is assumed to be zero, the input impedance is infinite.

Operational amplifiers derive their name from their use in constructing circuits used in analog computers for carrying out mathematical operations. One of these circuits, an integrator, is shown in Fig. E.7. The feedback element in this circuit is a capacitor. Using virtual ground analysis, the output voltage is the negative of the voltage drop across the capacitor.

$$v_0 = -v_C$$

And, the voltage drop across the capacitor is the integral of the current through it divided by the capacitance:

$$v_0 = -\frac{1}{RC} \int_0^t v_I \, dt + v_i(0)$$

where $v_i(0)$ is the initial voltage across the capacitor at time $t = 0$, and the output of the circuit is the integral of the input voltage.

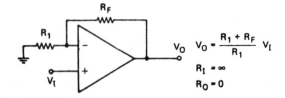

Figure E.6. Op-amp noninverting amplifier.

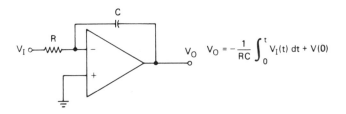

Figure E.7 Op-amp integrator.

While virtual ground analysis is an approximation technique, it very accurately predicts the operation of an op-amp circuit with negative feedback under certain conditions. First, the op-amp must have a high open loop gain. Secondly, the output of the op-amp must be in the linear range. This places a restriction on the allowable closed loop gain and on the input signal range.

The actual effect of negative feedback can be qualitatively illustrated by considering the operation of the inverting amplifier of Fig. E.4. Assume that the circuit is in a stable condition, with input voltage v_I and output voltage v_0, and with $\epsilon \simeq 0$. If the input voltage is increased by a value, Δ, this tends to increase ϵ by Δ from zero. The change in ϵ toward $\epsilon + \Delta$ causes the output to change in the negative direction by a much larger amount—$A_{0L}\Delta$. And this causes an increase in the current through R_F and R_1, which in turn increases the voltage drop across R_1, forcing ϵ back toward zero and increasing the voltage drop across R_F. Of course, all these actions occur instantaneously. The net effect is that a change in the input voltage causes the output voltage to change by a factor determined by the external resistances and leaves ϵ near 0 V.

Index

V

Vectored interrupt, 302
Vertical retrace, 347
Vertical sweep, 347
Virtual ground analysis, 507–11
Volatile memory, 39
Voltage controlled oscillator, 420–21
Voltage reference, 398, 404, 406

W

Wait state, 95–97
Weiss, D. C., 109
Wired OR, 482–83
Word, 34

Word length, 34
Write, 34

X

XS-64, 236

Y

Yourdon, E., and L. L. Constantine,
435

Z

Z80, 84
ZERO flag, 122–23